RELIGION AND AMERICAN EDUCATION

RELIGION &

RETHINKING

AMERICAN

A NATIONAL

EDUCATION

DILEMMA

WARREN A. NORD

The University of North Carolina Press   Chapel Hill and London

© 1995 The University of North Carolina Press

Manufactured in the United States of America

The paper in this book meets the guidelines for permanence and durability of the Committee on Production Guidelines for Book Longevity of the Council on Library Resources.

This book was published with the assistance of the H. Eugene and Lillian Youngs Lehman Fund of the University of North Carolina Press. A complete list of books published with the assistance of the Lehman Fund appears at the end of the book.

Library of Congress Cataloging-in-Publication Data

Nord, Warren A. Religion and American education : rethinking a national dilemma / by Warren A. Nord. p. cm. Includes bibliographical references (p.   ) and index. ISBN 0-8078-2165-9 (cloth : alk. paper). — ISBN 0-8078-4478-0 (pbk. : alk. paper) 1. Religion in the public schools—United States. 2. Moral education—United States. 3. Christian education—United States. 4. Church and state—United States. I. Title. LC111.N67 1994   377′.1′0973—dc20   94-4589   CIP

Portions of this work have appeared previously, in somewhat different form, in "The Place of Religion in the World of Public School Textbooks," *Educational Forum* 54 (Spring 1990): 247–79, © 1990 by Kappa Delta Pi International Honor Society in Education; "Religious Literacy, Textbooks, and Religious Neutrality," *Religion and Public Education* 16 (Winter 1989): 111–21; "Taking Religion Seriously," *Social Education* 54 (October 1990): 287–90, © 1990 by the National Council for the Social Sciences; and "Teaching and Morality: The Knowledge Most Worth Having," in *What Teachers Need to Know*, ed. David D. Dill (San Francisco: Jossey-Bass, 1990), © 1990 by Jossey-Bass, and are used here with permission.

00 99 98 97 96   6 5 4 3 2

For Nancy and Jeremy

CONTENTS

PREFACE

From the beginning, many of the most violent battles in our ongoing culture wars have been fought over the proper place of religion in public education. Unhappily, in the heat of battle—in court fights, direct mail campaigns, school board elections, and the dispatches of journalists from the front—public opinion has been all too easily polarized. As a result, we are apt to find ourselves uncomfortably (and uncritically) caught in a dilemma defined by the most militant of the combatants for their own ideological or even tactical purposes.

As the story is usually told, on the one side of our culture wars are those religious conservatives (the "Religious Right," or the "Radical Right," as their opponents would have it) who believe that American education has been captured by the forces of secular humanism and thus has become godless and hostile to religion. It is their goal to *restore* religious purposes, practices, and teaching to public education. On the other side are those liberals (or "secular humanists") for whom the "Religious Right" is a dangerous intruder into the secular space of modern public institutions. For them, religion is properly a private matter, irrelevant to the purposes and content of education, and it is their goal to *remove* any vestiges of religious purpose, practice, and teaching from public schools and universities.

The battle lines of our culture wars run through every community in America, but our dilemma is very much a national dilemma in a more profound way, for it is bound up with the way in which we have constituted ourselves as a nation. The proper place of religion in our public life generally, and in public education in particular, is governed by the Constitution of the United States. For most religious conservatives, America is a Christian (or Judeo-Christian) nation, and to further their ends they would dismantle the wall of separation between religion and government. Most liberals, by contrast, believe that America is a secular, religiously neutral nation, and they would keep the wall of separation high and impregnable.

In logic a dilemma is a specific kind of problem—one that presents us with two equally unacceptable alternatives. Happily, the dilemma I have outlined is a false dilemma; our alternatives need not be drawn in such stark terms. We need not make schools Christian or eliminate all religion from public education; there are alternatives. We need not dismantle the wall of separation or build it higher; there are alternatives. Indeed, we need not be religious conservatives or secular liberals; there are alternatives.

Nonetheless, truths can be found in each of the positions I have sketched. I will agree with those religious conservatives who claim that public education is hostile to religion; indeed, I will argue that students are all but indoctrinated against religion in public schools and universities. But I will also agree with those liberals who claim that it cannot be the purpose of public education to promote religion or allow its practice in public schools and universities. I believe that educators must take religion seriously for a variety of philosophical, political, moral, and constitutional reasons that I will take some care to spell out, but taking religion seriously cannot be a matter of governmental endorsement or practice; we must continue to separate church and state—though not so strictly as some would advocate.

This third alternative, located in what I take to be the "Reasonable Center" of our cultural politics, is, happily, an increasingly common position—although the voice of reason is often hard to hear above the noise of battle. I should mention, however, that many of my allies in the center fail to appreciate what is involved in taking religion seriously. If justice is to be done, significant changes must come about in the ways we conceive and practice education. Indeed, our problem cuts to the heart—might I say the soul?—of public education and is not easily solved.

As I write, we are caught up yet again in a heated national debate about school prayer. I trust that I do not underestimate the religious significance of prayer in suggesting that whether or not children pray in schools is a matter of considerably less importance than the issue that I will address in this book: the proper role of religious ideas and values in the curriculum of American schools and universities. (Of course I will say something about prayer as well.)

One reason our situation is so difficult is that most educators are not very well educated about religion. The temper of modern intellectual life and the conventional wisdom of professional education are, after all, deeply and pervasively secular. Indeed, here we encounter the most fundamental of our problems: What claim, if any, does religion make on the modern mind? Why, if at all, should religion be taken seriously? What place, if any, should it have in textbooks and the curriculum?

Of course we disagree about all of this profoundly—and *this* is a fact of no small significance for our discussion. How should public education deal with matters about which the public is so deeply divided? How are we to live with our deepest differences?

I write not as a specialist in religion or education or constitutional law, but as a philosopher and generalist. It has been my intention to expose the deep assumptions that shape our thinking about religion and education and to provide an interdisciplinary overview—a kind of conceptual map—of those ideas and ideals, traditions and worldviews, that clash in our culture wars. No doubt some points of detail and nuance have been lost in trying to cover so much ground, but only by acquiring some perspective on the complex web of historical, philosophical, political, and constitutional relationships that define our cultural location will we acquire the sense of direction that will enable us to make our way through the policy minefields of our culture wars.

My debts are considerable. Maynard Adams's influence on my thinking and on this book is pervasive and far exceeds the number of notes citing his work. Charles Haynes has been an unfailing source of insight into the relationship between religion and education. In addition, each of the following individuals has read parts or, in a few cases, all of the manuscript, and I have benefited greatly from their advice: David Dill, Martha Dill, John Dixon, David Halperin, Peter Kaufman, David Larson, Robert Michaelsen, Sidney Rittenberg, Benjamin Sendor, Gilbert Sewall, Jonathan Sher, Grant Wacker, and James Wilde. Needless to say, the willingness of friends and colleagues to undertake this task implies nothing about whether they agree with (or find outrageous) the claims I make. David Perry, my editor at the University of North Carolina Press, has provided much-needed encouragement and advice at virtually every step along the way. By her close and careful reading of the manuscript, Trudie Calvert has improved this book in many ways.

My wife Nancy has worked hard to convince me that there is virtue in timeliness as well as in perfection and that it is more important to be read and understood by all concerned than by scholars only. It is due to her that I have finally finished this book and that is as readable as it is. Our son Jeremy was born shortly after I began writing, and all too often he has had to share his father's time with the computer. His presence has deepened my concern about education and enriched in wonderful, often unexpected, ways my sense of how we find meaning in the world. It is to Nancy and Jeremy that I dedicate this book.

RELIGION AND AMERICAN EDUCATION

INTRODUCTION

Once, when St. Petersburg was still Leningrad, the economist E. F. Schumacher was lost there. Although he was standing near several enormous churches, they didn't appear on his tourist map. When his interpreter showed him where he was, Schumacher asked why the churches were not on the map. He was told: "We don't show churches on our maps." Schumacher protested that one nearby church was on the map. But that is not a church, he was told. "That is a museum. . . . It is only the 'living churches' we don't show." "It then occurred to me," Schumacher wrote, "that this was not the first time I had been given a map which failed to show many things I could see right in front of my eyes. All through school and university I had been given maps of life and knowledge on which there was hardly a trace of many of the things that I most cared about and that seemed to me to be of the greatest possible importance to the conduct of my life."[1] Just as churches did not appear on his tourist map, so religions had been left off the conceptual maps his education had provided him. Or if they did show up, they did so in ancient times and faraway places, more or less as a museum pieces.

In the last few years, the maps of St. Petersburg have changed. The conceptual maps we provide students in our public schools and universities continue to chart a world without religion.

Perspective

It is a striking fact that in American public schools and universities students can—and most do—earn high school diplomas, college degrees, M.B.A.'s, J.D.'s, M.D.'s and Ph.D.'s without ever confronting a live religious idea. We take it for granted that students can know everything they need to know about whatever they study without knowing anything about religion. Although students may receive a smattering of facts about it here and there, religion is almost always encountered in a historical setting, as a "museum piece." They are not likely to confront it as a live option for understanding the here and now. The conventional wisdom among educators is that religion is irrelevant to virtually everything that is taken to be true and important.

This situation is so striking because for all of history—at least until fairly recently in the West—people have oriented themselves in the world by way of religious maps. The idea that the sacred and the secular could be separated and that one could know everything true and important about virtually all aspects of the world without knowing anything about God would have struck most people as nonsense.

No doubt the world has become much more secular, but religion is far from dead, even in the modern West. Garry Wills has suggested that the "learned have their superstitions, prominent among them a belief that superstition is evaporating. Since science has explained the world in secular terms, there is no more need for religion, which will wither away. . . . [Yet] nothing has been more stable in our history, nothing less unbudgeable, than religious belief and practice. Religion does not shift or waver; the attention of its observers does."[2] Polls consistently show that nine out of ten Americans believe in the existence of God. More than seven out of ten believe in life after death.[3] Some 55 percent of Americans say that religion is "very important" in their lives.[4] Forty percent "value their relationship with God above all else" (while only 2 percent say that a well-paying job is the most important thing in their lives).[5] Based on decades of polling data, George Gallup, Jr., and Jim Castelli claim that America "cannot by any stretch of the imagination be described as secular in its core beliefs."[6] The Swiss theologian Hans Küng asks: "Why don't people openly admit the fact . . . [that the] death of religion expected in late modernity has not taken place."[7] For the American theologian Richard John Neuhaus, the "proposition that America is a secular society is contrary to sociological fact. The American people are more incorrigibly religious than ever before."[8] And *Time* magazine began a 1991 cover story on religion in American public life: "To say that God is everywhere in American life is as much a statement of fact as of faith. His name appears on every coin, on every dollar bill and in the vast majority of state constitutions. Schoolchildren pledge allegiance to one nation, under him. The President of the United States ends his speeches with a benediction. God bless America."[9]

Here we have something of a paradox. If we are so religious, why does our educational system ignore religion? If seven out of ten of us believe in the immortality of the soul, why does the subject *never* come up in any course or textbook? Where in the curriculum are religious conceptions of social justice or religious assessments of abortion discussed? If almost everyone believes that God exists—and, presumably, that our hopes for salvation and the meaningfulness of our lives depend on knowing God—how can education ignore this? What could possibly be more important? How are we to account for the absence of *living* religion from education?

We can quickly dispense with two commonly given answers—though I shall have a good deal to say about them in chapters to come. First, the Constitution forbids the study of religion in public schools and universities. This, of course, is simply false. It is true that the courts have removed the *practice* of religion from public education, but any number of times the Supreme Court has affirmed the constitutional legitimacy of the *study* of religion.

Second, religion is too controversial. There is more to this argument. Precisely because religion continues to be a powerful force in our culture, and because we are a pluralistic nation in which people do not agree about religion, the treatment of religion in education is controversial. Still, the fear of controversy is not the primary reason that religion has been exiled from education. The simple proof lies in our universities. Research universities are well insulated from controversy, yet religion is almost as much ignored in universities as in public schools. True, many public universities have departments of religious studies, but most discussion of religion is segregated into those departments so that every other discipline is free to ignore religion. (One will have to look long and hard to find a discussion of the soul in a psychology textbook or of self-sacrificing love in an economics text.) And, because courses in religious studies are always electives, if they are offered at all, students also are free to ignore religion. Indeed, what historian George Marsden claims for Christianity is true of all religion: it has "become not only entirely peripheral to higher education but has also often come to be considered absolutely alien to whatever is important to that enterprise." [10]

There are two much better reasons for the absence of religion from public schools and universities. First, all of the survey data and American religiosity notwithstanding, Western civilization has become *very* secular. Religion, in response, has become increasingly, though not entirely, a private matter, disengaged from the dominant institutions, ideas, and values of modern civilization. Religion simply does not play the role in our political and economic life, in our art or our culture, that it once did. We no longer live our lives in the shadow of the village church steeple. For a century, steeples have been overshadowed by skyscrapers, monuments to our secular modernity. Most people have learned to compartmentalize religion so that it has few implications for how we live our lives or how we think about the world in academic disciplines. In fact, we have become so secular that most of us do not find the absence of religion from education particularly striking.

Ernest Gellner has discussed the emergence of "ironic cultures" in the modern world. In dealing with the "frills of life," he argues, in choosing our menus and our rituals, we adopt the colorful and cozy beliefs of religion; but when "serious issues are at stake—such as the production of wealth, or the maintenance of health—we want and expect *real* knowledge"—that is, the hard, cold knowledge of medical and management science. [11]

There is a good deal to this. Most of us place our hopes for well-being in the hands of research scientists and economists, engineers and physicians, politicians and psychologists. According to the theologian Don Cupitt, since Darwin, religion has played "no part in any major branch of knowledge." Like a coat of arms, he suggests, religious belief "may anchor us reassuringly in the past; but it is of little use in the present."[12]

Of course, religion is less relevant for some than for others. Here we come to the second reason for religion-free education. The truth is that intellectuals (and highly educated folk generally) are much less religious than most people (survey data show this as well), and it is intellectuals who write textbooks, shape curricula, and teach teachers. The great majority of scholars view religion as irrelevant to their subjects, and a few regard it as superstition to be combated. The intellectual orthodoxy of our time—of the past hundred years or so—is fully secular. It need no longer be militantly secular because of the widespread assumption that the intellectual and cultural wars of religion have been won. Religion is an anachronism, a museum piece, for most intellectuals.

Mammoth segments of modern life and culture have been secularized. Our intellectual and educational worlds are almost completely secular. And yet most Americans continue to hold on to their religion. True, many are only nominally religious. Still, when all is said and done, religion shows considerable vitality in our culture. Americans not only continue to believe, but almost half of us worship in a church or synagogue or mosque in any given week. Religious voices are still to be heard in the public debate of such issues as abortion, euthanasia, pornography, social justice, civil rights, and war and peace. Our cultural terrain continues to have religious contours though the conceptual maps that modern education provides its students usually fail to show them.

The Problem

What passes for the truth on one side of the Pyrenees, Blaise Pascal once wrote, is taken for falsehood on the other side. For many Americans nothing is so obviously true and important as God and salvation. For other Americans, nothing is so obviously false, so assuredly a matter of blind faith and superstition, as religion. (Of course, America is land of many mountain ranges: there are not just two competing views of what is true, but many.)

We disagree profoundly about the truth, and our disagreements cut to the bone, to what we believe about human nature, history, morality, society, the universe—and reason. How, then, are we to live with our deepest differences?[13] What do we teach in public schools and universities when our disagreements about the truth cut so deep? More to the point, what obligation, if any, do educators have to take religion seriously, particularly when it is no longer a part of their worldview?

No doubt everyone agrees that there is some place for religion in education, for we cannot understand history and historical literature without understanding a good deal about religion. I agree, but I am more concerned with the place of religion in the here and now.

What hearing should *live* religious voices receive in public schools and universities? Should religion be taken seriously as a candidate for the truth? Should scholars and the educational establishment have the right to take some views seriously and ignore others, to define the truth for students when that truth is deeply contested in our culture? Does academic freedom give teachers the right to ignore religion, to teach that it is false—or perhaps to teach that some version of it is true? What right do elected officials have to resolve these problems by determining the shape and substance of the curriculum? What constraints do courts legitimately impose on public schools and universities by way of the religion clauses of the First Amendment? What right do parents have to educate their children religiously, in private schools, in accord with their consciences—and should the state subsidize such a right? What is academically respectable? What is politically acceptable? What is constitutionally required? What is pedagogically sound? What would constitute indoctrination? What are the ethics of education when religion is at issue? These are my questions.

I am not concerned (here) about whether any religion or any secular way of understanding the world is *true*. I will be obstinately agnostic about that. My problem is this: what should be taught about religion when we disagree profoundly about the truth?

This is a problem in the philosophy of education to which there are analogues. What should students be taught about politics, about the economy, about human psychology, or about morality, when we disagree deeply about them? In many ways the question about religion is more difficult, however. Religion is intensely personal and is of overriding importance to many people. Because it has been ignored in education, and because it has become so much a private matter, most of us have had little practice talking about it in public places. Unlike any of these other matters, the treatment of religion in public education is regulated by the Constitution by way of the religion clauses of the First Amendment. Perhaps most important, religion is sufficiently problematic given the reigning orthodoxies of our intellectual culture that it is very hard for most educators to take it seriously—at least in their own fields.

The Conventional Wisdom

Three fundamental assumptions about religion and modern culture together constitute a kind of conventional wisdom which is deeply embedded in the beliefs and attitudes of modern American educators. Each assumption is controversial within our larger culture, however.

Assumption 1: The secular and the sacred can be separated, and the greater part of our world can be understood in purely secular terms. So, for example, it is possible to understand the mind (and the brain) without reference to the soul; it is possible to understand the economic world without reference to divine justice; it is possible to understand history and nature without reference to God's purposes. As we shall see, a major theme of modern Western history, perhaps *the* major theme, is the secularization of the world: what had been understood in religious terms can now be understood in secular terms. God is irrelevant to education.

Response: Needless to say, the divorce of the sacred from the secular continues to be contested. Historically, most all religions have held that the sacred and the secular are wed in virtually all domains of life. Some religious liberals have worked hard to find amicable terms of separation, but their separation remains deeply controversial in our culture.

Assumption 2: Secular ways of understanding the world are religiously neutral; hence secular education is religiously neutral. Most educators, judges, and a good deal of public opinion assume that purely secular accounts of the world have no implications for the truth or falsity of religion. Teaching secular ways of thinking about the world neither promotes nor is hostile to religion. Not to mention the soul in a psychology class is to take no position on the soul; not to mention God in a history class has no implications for whether there is divine purpose in history. Justice Robert Jackson summarized this view nicely when he wrote in *Everson* v. *Board of Education* (1947) that public education "is organized on the premise that secular education can be isolated from all religious teaching so that the school can inculcate all needed temporal knowledge and also maintain a strict and lofty neutrality as to religion."[14] This claim is crucial, for the Supreme Court has interpreted the First Amendment to require that public schools *must* be neutral between religion and nonreligion.

Response: Even the most cursory look at modern Western intellectual history reveals a different picture. The cultural and intellectual wars of religion of the last few centuries were not fought over nothing; they were about who was right and who was wrong. It is simply not plausible to argue that religion and its secular opposition were (and are) neutrals who, for several centuries, mistakenly took each other for belligerents.

Arguably, the governing methods, assumptions, and conclusions of much modern secular scholarship are not neutral to religion, but hostile. Of course, some religion is much more compatible with modernity and accommodating to modern scholarship than is other religion: distinctions need to be drawn (and I will draw some). Nonetheless, there are fundamental tensions between most all religion (conservative and liberal) on the one hand and most all secular, scientific scholarship on the other. They claim contested ground. Yet the religious claims to that ground are virtually never heard in public schools and universities, and secular, scientific ways of understanding the world pervade the curriculum.

Assumption 3: Critical reason is the ally of modern secular thought, whereas religion lives and dies by irrational faith. As education must be objective and rational, education must be secular. Religion can be studied, but only in objective—secular—ways. To promote religious belief is to indoctrinate—and indoctrination is not education.

Response. It is true that religion has often gloried in irrationality; but it has just as often claimed the mantle of reason and scholarship. Moreover, in the last few decades many secular scholars have argued that modern science is anything but the epitome of disinterested reason and objectivity; rather, it reflects ideology, power relationships, even faith-commitments. Such "postmodern" thought typically denies science any special standing as the arbiter of truth. That is, both the equation of reason with science and secular thought and the equation of religion with indoctrination and irrationality are open to question. We need to be very careful in defining reason and faith.

Now, if the sacred and the secular cannot be disentangled, and if (much) modern, secular thought is in fact hostile to religion (rather than neutral), and if religion can be rational or if secular thought is a matter of ideological commitments or faith, then the conventional wisdom of modern American education is profoundly mistaken.

Conclusions, Qualifications, Pious Intentions

It goes without saying that students at all levels should study the secular and scientific ways of understanding the world that define modernity. I do not need to argue this point for American education already does so with great vigor. Instead, I will be concerned to restore the tension between religious and secular ways of making sense of our world. The conventional wisdom of modern American education is deeply controversial if not profoundly mistaken; in either case there are a variety of reasons for taking religion seriously as a part of public school and university education.

There are conservative religious reasons for incorporating religion into public education. Many people believe that America is a Christian nation and that it should be the task of schools to nurture and promote Christian (or Judeo-Christian) beliefs and values. Hence it is almost always assumed that anyone who argues for taking religion seriously must have a religious (and probably a fundamentalist) agenda. I have already said that I will remain agnostic about the truth of religion. In fact, my arguments will be secular and liberal. I will argue that all students should receive a liberal education that takes seriously a variety of ways of making sense of the world, religious ways included, if they are to be informed, reasonable, and responsible individuals. Current American education is profoundly illiberal in its refusal to take religion seriously. Public education should be politically liberal (or multicultural) in the sense that it should give voice to various subcultures—religious subcultures included—which currently have little say in the world of intellectual and educational elites. In effect, the educational establishment has disfranchised large segments of the American people.

And I will argue that on a liberal reading of the First Amendment public education is obligated to take religion seriously. Judicial conservatives typically argue that the Establishment Clause allows the state to promote nonsectarian religion so long as it does so noncoercively; this is a mistaken reading of the First Amendment. Liberals argue, rightly, that the state and public education must be neutral both among religions and between religion and nonreligion. What liberals seldom acknowledge is that by ignoring religion, and by promoting secular views hostile to religion, public education in effect takes sides against religion. Therefore, if neutrality is to be restored as the First Amendment requires, religion must be given its voice. It is not the task of public education to promote any particular religion, or religion generally, but it should not ignore or denigrate religion either.

Historically, political liberalism has underwritten a constitutional framework that allows people to live together peacefully in spite of their deep differences. Properly understood, it should provide a point of agreement between secular and religious folk who disagree about what is ultimately important and how to make sense of the world. Because our culture is so deeply divided, public education should not take sides in our culture wars but should maintain neutrality, treating the contending alternatives fairly. Indeed, *only by taking each other seriously* can we resolve our national dilemma about religion and education.

It is my hope that I can find enough common moral and political ground with my readers so that we can agree about how religion should fit into education even if we do not agree about the truth of religion (or science). I am not so naive as to believe that everyone can be brought into the fold: no doubt there will be some religious conservatives, some secular liberals, and some members of minority religious traditions who will find the broad middle ground I hope to stake out uninviting. Still, my intention is to make a case that is compelling for people who hold a wide variety of views on religion.

In making a case for religion in public education I do not want to be interpreted as being hostile to science or modernity. Modern science is without a doubt the greatest of all human intellectual achievements, and while much that is new in the world hardly counts as progress, the modern world is, all things considered, a great improvement on the ancient world. Although I wish to raise questions about the truth and adequacy of scientific ways of understanding the world and secular ways of living in the world, it is not my goal to settle them or even to stake out a position on them. My question, as I have said, is different: how should education be structured when we, in our culture, disagree so profoundly about where the truth lies?

I should acknowledge that I have paid far more attention to some aspects of American education than to others. First, I will have much more to say about public education than about private education—though the question of vouchers and parental rights will inevitably bring private schools into the discussion. Second, I am primarily concerned with high school and undergraduate education, for it is after students acquire general skills and before they specialize that they pursue what passes for a liberal education, and it is then that they should be exposed to a wide variety of voices, religious voices included. Third, I will have much more to say about the study of religion than about the practice of religion in the schools. There has probably been more heated controversy over school prayer and religious holidays than over textbooks and curricula. I do not suggest that these matters are unimportant, but I do believe that curricular issues relating to the study of religion are much more important.

Henry Fielding's Parson Thwackum once announced: "When I mention religion, I mean the Christian religion; and not only the Christian religion, but the Protestant religion; and not only the Protestant religion, but the Church of England."[15] I will not be so particular. I will have more to say about Christianity than about other religions because Christianity has been America's dominant religion, but it is very important to keep in mind that there has never been only a single religious tradition in America. We are a multicultural, multireligious nation, and the educational implications of this fact are considerable.

Finally, a pious intention. I have intended to write a book as free of technical language as possible. Every discipline is entitled to its specialized vocabulary—disciplines in the humanities as well as in the sciences—but too often these semiprivate languages keep us from understanding each other. Indeed, uncritical specialization is one of the villains in my story. Of course, the vernacular can remain very ambiguous. Words such as "religion" and "humanism" and "morality" have different meanings for different people. We make what sense we can of language given our cultural backgrounds, our worldviews. Such ambiguity can be pointed out—and I will do so at crucial points in the argument—but it cannot be avoided. In this context I might note that throughout the book I will use "public education" as an umbrella term covering both public schools (K–12 education) and public higher education.

One final item is on the agenda before we leap into the mainstream of the argument. "Worldview" is one of those quasi-technical, almost-vernacular terms that could stand some clarification, especially as I will be using it a good deal. Hence I close this introduction with . . .

A Note on Worldviews

When I was a small boy I believed that God's name was Harold. Did we not, after all, pray: "Our Father Who art in Heaven, Harold be thy name"? I did not yet know the word "hallowed," but I did have an Uncle Harold. I made sense of my experience in terms that were familiar to me; I used my all too meager conceptual resources to render the world meaningful as best I could.

Do two people hear the same thing if one is familiar with symphonic music and the other is hearing classical Western music for the first time? Can the novice hear the bassoon part or the recapitulation or the minor seventh chords or the leitmotif? A musician can pick them out from the background, can discern structure, harmony, and purpose where the novice hears, as William James might have put it, a "booming, buzzing confusion." To make sense of and appreciate various kinds of experience, we must have a fairly sophisticated conceptual vocabulary. If we have that vocabulary then we can discern aspects of the world—dimensions of reality, we might say—to which we had been deaf before: we hear music, not just noise.

Consider another example. According to Jonathan Swift, the Lilliputians who investigated Gulliver's belongings reported back to their King that out of his pocket

> hung a great silver chain, with a wonderful kind of engine at the bottom. We directed him to draw out whatever was fastened to that chain; which appeared to be a globe, half silver, and half of some transparent metal: on the transparent side we saw certain strange figures circularly drawn, and

thought we could touch them, till we found our fingers stopped by that lucid substance. He put this engine to our ears, which made an incessant noise like that of a water-mill: and we conjecture it is either some unknown animal, or the god that he assures us (if we understood him right, for he expressed himself very imperfectly) that he seldom did any thing without consulting it: he called it his oracle, and said it pointed out the time for every action of his life.[16]

Here the problem is not just that the Lilliputians lack the concept of a clock, it is that their conceptual resources are not sufficiently rich to allow them to see Gulliver's watch for what it is: because Gulliver does nothing without consulting his watch, it must be oracular; because it makes a noise, it must be alive. Because of their lack of mechanical sophistication, they take a machine to be a divinity.

It is one kind of mistake to confuse a pocket watch with a calculator, a symphony with a sonata, the world "hallowed" with the word "Harold." It is a mistake of a different kind to confuse a machine with a divinity, music with noise, the profane with the sacred. In these latter cases, we are confusing orders of reality, rather than two comparable things within the same order.

I will use the term "worldview" to name the most fundamental interpretive frameworks we use to understand reality. A worldview marks out various orders of reality and illusion, it gives some sense of what is reasonable and irrational, it orients action by defining the concepts in terms of which we discern what is good and bad, it provides the framework within which we have some sense of what might be hoped for and what it is unrealistic to expect. Philosophers, theologians, and scientists who do highly theoretical work often transform aspects of a worldview into formal philosophical systems, theologies, or scientific theories by organizing, clarifying, systematizing, or reforming the fundamental commitments embedded with the more vague and informal worldview of a culture. But as I will use the term, a worldview may be largely unarticulated; indeed, what distinguishes a worldview philosophically is often what goes without saying, what is so basic that it is simply assumed and never questioned. For example, the philosopher John Hick has suggested that the

idea that we have lived many times before and must live many times again in this world seems as self-evident to most people in the hindu and buddhist east as the contrary idea that we came into existence at conception or birth, and shall see the last of this world at death, seems self-evident to almost everyone in the christian and post-christian west. . . . Western religious thinkers have seen . . . little reason to provide arguments for their own assumption that a new human soul is created, or emerges, for every new baby born. That this must be what happened has usually seemed so evident to orthodox christian theologians that they have not stopped to examine or defend its plausibility.

But from the perspective of Indian religion, our Western assumptions seem "utterly unreasonable, implausible and unattractive."[17] Our sense of personal identity and the afterlife are basic constituents of our worldview.

It is important to recognize that what makes the respective Indian or Western views of the afterlife so plausible to their adherents is that they are integrated into a way of life; they are not simply abstract propositions to be believed or not. They figure into moral traditions that define what is expected of us, they serve to explain our lot in life, they are assumed in our rituals, they are a part of our emotional sense of what is to be feared or hoped for. That is, worldviews hang together emotionally, behaviorally, and institutionally; they are more than just a set of beliefs.

It has become a commonplace over the last two centuries, since Immanuel Kant, to hold that we do not all experience the same "objective" world. Instead, we interpret the world, bringing to our confrontation with it a framework for making sense of it. So, for example, the world acquires its color, tone, and texture because we have the sense organs we have (and the worlds of bats and bees must appear quite different to them). Of course, in some sense we all experience the same world; it is not entirely the creation of our sense organs. As Ian Barbour puts it, our "experience isn't entirely *subjective*, since we cannot make of it what we will. It is at least in part a 'given' which we are powerless to alter, a demand upon us to which we must conform." But, he continues, experience "is not purely *objective*" either, "for it is qualified by the memories, feelings and concepts of the experiencing subject. . . . We don't simply see; we 'see as.' In the act of perception, the irreducible 'data' are not isolated patches of colour or fragmentary sensations, but total patterns in which interpretation has already entered. Our experience is organized in the light of particular interests. Language itself also structures our experience in specific ways." Indeed, he concludes, "what we count as 'given' depends on our conceptual framework and the interests which it serves."[18] There is no such thing as uninterpreted experience. We live, as Ernst Cassirer has put it, in a symbolic universe: "No longer can man confront reality immediately; he cannot see it, as it were, face to face."[19]

As we grow into a language and culture, the interpretation they provide seems natural and inevitable. If we are brought up—as most children initially are—knowing only one tradition, we will come to believe that our language, our distinctions, and our conceptual resources mirror reality; we take ourselves to experience reality *as it is*. Peter Berger and Thomas Luckmann have called this "the most important confidence trick that society plays on the individual."[20] Different languages and cultures (indeed, different academic disciplines and professions) teach people to conceptualize their experiences differently. Knowing what we now know about other languages and cultures, other ways of thinking about the world than our own, our natural tendency to believe we know reality for what it is has become problematic. We are constantly interpreting reality rather than encountering it directly.[21]

A further point of great importance—one to which I shall come back again and again—is that worldviews cannot in any straightforward way be verified or falsified. Any worldview that has come of age will have developed conceptual resources to handle most any contingency; it will possess resilience in the face of potentially falsifying experiences. In fact, for most adherents, their own worldview will define common sense and reality with such self-evident force that it is hard to imagine what could shake their confidence. Claims made within rival worldviews, dimly understood, will seem implausible if not sheer nonsense.

Of course, within a worldview it will often be clear how to go about verifying and falsifying claims. A Hindu can appeal to age-old spiritual traditions to justify belief in reincarnation, a fundamentalist Christian can appeal to scriptural proof-texts to falsify claims about reincarnation, and a scientist may appeal to neurological evidence regarding the dependency of consciousness on the brain and the dissolution of the brain at death to falsify all claims about the existence of consciousness after death.

The problem comes when we attempt to assess contending worldviews and their claims in ways that are not question-begging, for different worldviews have different conceptions of what counts as evidence, as good arguments, and as reasonable. Should moral or religious experience count in verifying the claims of a worldview? The answer is typically no if one works within science but yes if one works within a religious worldview. Why adopt the vantage point of one worldview rather than another in the first place?

There are relativists who say we cannot raise the question of the truth or reasonableness of contending worldviews, for what counts as rational is so systematically ambiguous that any argument will inevitably be question-begging. The whole idea of verifying or falsifying worldviews makes no sense. I am not inclined to agree, and I will have more to say about this.

In summary, a worldview provides people with their most general concepts for making sense of their experience; it defines reality for them. Worldviews may remain relatively implicit or they may become explicit and formally articulated within philosophy, theology, and science. When someone lives within a worldview and is largely unfamiliar with others, that worldview seems natural, a direct encounter with reality rather than one interpretation among others. Worldviews have a coherence that reinforces their plausibility; they are not simply grab bags of abstract beliefs. Their survival requires that they hang together emotionally, institutionally, and intellectually. Although most claims can be tested within a worldview, it is much less clear how one tests the truth of a worldview itself, or how one adjudicates the conflicting claims of competing worldviews.

The historian Alan Gilbert has argued that "the crisis of contemporary Christianity lies not in challenges to the truth of its dogmas, but in the fact that . . . people in a secular culture have become increasingly 'tone-deaf' to any orchestration of those dogmas. A secular culture, in short, is an environment in which the very *a priori* plausibility of a religious worldview is at stake."[22] From within what has become the characteristically modern worldview, it is all but impossible to discern religious harmonies in the world. For many folk, securely ensconced within modernity, religion has come to seem implausible, a museum piece, a relic of olden times; they have become tone-deaf to its charms.

RELIGION AND MODERNITY

We cannot explain the absence of religion from modern American education by appealing to Supreme Court decisions, the liberalism of the 1960s, or cabals of secular humanists. Modern education, like the culture in which it is embedded, is the product of profound secularizing forces at work in Western civilization over the last several hundred years. Unless we appreciate this history, our analysis will be hopelessly superficial.

In this chapter I will sketch the main plot line of one of the great dramas of modern history: the secularization of modern Western civilization. I will also describe two quite different religious responses to modernity—"liberal" responses, which draw heavily on modern ideas and values to reinterpret religious traditions, and "conservative" responses, which reject the religious relevance of modern ideas and values (at least on theological essentials). It is tremendously important to recognize that religion takes many forms, some more at home in the modern world than others. Finally, I will say something about postmodern ways in which intellectuals have made war on modernity for fully secular reasons.

Religion in the Premodern World

Until the beginnings of modernity—in, let us say, the seventeenth century—Western civilization had been, like all others, religious through and through. But as the historian of religion Wilfred Cantwell Smith has shown, the word "religion" is a peculiarly modern, Western word with no synonyms in most languages at most times. Most cultures have not divided the world up as we now do. "Religion" is a word *we* have come to use to categorize culture for our purposes.[1]

For us, "religion" names one aspect of life among many. We take religions to be discrete institutions and systems of belief which stand alongside scientific and political and economic institutions and ideas. We have built intellectual walls of separation between religion and the other institutions of culture. In traditional cultures religion was not so distinguishable but was integrated into the total life of the people. What we now call "religious" ideas and values pervaded science and politics and economics. Indeed, for the millennium before modernity, the West was called Christendom.[2]

How religion came to be wrenched out of its traditional cultural context to be remade into a discrete and largely private institution is a large part of the story I have to tell in this chapter. The whole structure of our academic and intellectual life depends on this being an acceptable story, for only if religion can be separated from our academic disciplines is it justifiable to teach them as we do without reference to religion.

All premodern civilizations had some notion of God (or the gods, or the spirit world, or transcendence) such that reality was experienced as richer than modern science now takes to be the case. Much Eastern religion rejected the idea that the transcendent (Brahman, Nirvana, the Tao) was a *personal* God, but in the West, God was understood by analogy with a person: He, to use the traditional language, created the world, and through His plan nature and history were given purpose. The existence of God rendered the events of this life meaningful (and the events of this life could not, consequently, be understood without reference to God). Although much inevitably remained a mystery, and God was taken to be largely beyond our knowing, we could have confidence that the world is not the result of random events or blind causal laws; it is a place in which all things work ultimately for His ends, toward that which is good.

The concern of the oldest religions was to secure the goods of life—rain, harvest, children, and health; their goal, as John Hick put it, was "to keep fragile human life on an even keel."[3] But in the first millennium B.C.E. an extraordinary revolution took place across the world as people began to reject life in this world for life in a radically different order of reality—in Heaven, in the Kingdom of God, in Nirvana.[4] We must live in this fallen world for the time being, but our salvation is to be had in the world to come.

In the old view, the fundamental truths of life are remembered, not discovered. According to the Indian *Brahmanas*, "We must do what the Gods did in the beginning."[5] Lao Tzu would have us "Hold fast to the way of antiquity / In order to keep in control the realms of today. / The ability to know the beginning of antiquity / Is called the thread running through the way."[6] Veneration of ancestors dominated Confucian thought. In Greek myth, the Golden Age gave way to the Silver and the Bronze. In Jewish and Christian thought, the story of the Garden of Eden and the Fall makes perfection a thing of the past and the present a fallen time. Reformers appear and change takes place, but the goal of the reformers is typically to revive the blessings and wisdom of the past: the Messiah would restore the Kingdom of David; Jesus was the second Adam; and the Protestant Reformers were not creating a new Christianity but returning to the true Christianity of the Church Fathers. Premodern civilizations revered tradition: they idealized the past, the time when God established the world. *In the beginning was the truth.* The truth is not waiting to be discovered; it has been given.[7]

All of the great world religions have taught the importance of overcoming self-interest and living a life of love, of justice, of reconciliation—indeed, sometimes of renunciation. Our fallen state, they told us, is one of selfishness and self-sufficiency. We are invariably sinful. But we have the ability—with religious discipline, or perhaps with the grace of God—to overcome our sinful selves. Indeed, with salvation we are transformed.

Finally, traditional religion was largely a community affair. No doubt individuals could be saved, but premodern civilization sustained the idea that God's relationship was with a community of people, not just with individuals. According to the Bible, God often punished—and protected—whole peoples. We were born into a religion; we did not choose it for we were not, as individuals, competent to make these decisions. For a thousand years—until the modern period—almost everyone in the West was *born* Christian.

On the eve of modernity, religion pervaded the Western world. As James Turner put it, "birth meant baptism; adulthood brought marriage by the priest; and life's journey ended in the churchyard." Indeed, the church was "as inevitable as death and taxes, one of which it presided over and the other of which it collected."[8] In the mass the priest performed the miracle of transubstantiation, changing bread and wine into the body and blood of Christ.

Prayer was powerful; churches were built on the belief that prayers offered there could help save the souls of their founders languishing in purgatory. Monasteries and convents dotted the landscape. The world was filled with holy relics, holy shrines, holy places, and holy ground. People made pilgrimages. The liturgical calendar dictated the activities of life, and holidays were holy days, religious festivals.

The world was populated with supernatural beings. Martin Luther threw his ink bottle at Satan, and thousands of women were burned as witches. Everyone believed in providence: there was no chance or accident in the world. Outbreaks of plague were understood as God's punishment for the sinfulness of people. Dreams were prophetic. Everyone believed that the world was only a few thousand years old, and most everyone believed that the end could not be far off. Even into the seventeenth century, according to Margaret Jacob, virtually every "English scientist or promoter of science from Robert Boyle to Isaac Newton believed in the approaching millennium, however cautious they may have been in assigning a date to its advent."[9]

On some accounts kings ruled by divine right—and popes occasionally excommunicated them to bring them to their knees. Bishops helped elect the Holy Roman Emperor and cardinals conducted foreign policy. Keith Thomas reminds us that during this time,

> Clerics played a dominant part in the censorship of the press, the licensing of school-masters and doctors, and the government of the universities. In an age without radio, television or (until the mid-seventeenth century) newspapers, the pulpit was the most important means of direct communication with the people. Contemporary sermons discussed not just theology, but morals, politics, economics and current affairs generally. The Church's tentacles stretched out through the ecclesiastical courts, which exercised a wide jurisdiction over marriage and divorce, defamation, the probate of wills and every conceivable aspect of private morality.[10]

Justice was discerned through oaths and ordeals in which God guaranteed the soundness of the verdict. The church regulated the economy through canon law and interfered with supply and demand by setting "just prices." Strangest of all, it was widely believed that the pursuit of self-interest was a sin and that poverty was holy.

The greatest theme of the artist was the life and death of Christ; the greatest task for the architect was to build a cathedral; the greatest work of literature in the thousand years before modernity was Dante's account of Hell, Purgatory, and Paradise.

In such a world, James Turner tells us, the answers to all questions of any importance, "elaborated in a thousand tales, sermons, treatises, and summas, led back ultimately to God. Without some sort of God, the world disintegrated into incomprehensibility."[11] In such a world unbelief was all but unthinkable.

For most of us this is a foreign world.

The Reformation

No man had a greater influence on the shape of the modern world than Martin Luther. Leszek Kolakowski has written that whatever happened "in European history after Luther is, as we see it retrospectively, hardly conceivable without him: wars and philosophy, national movements and literature, religious conflicts and the reform of the Roman Church, economic development and education."[12] Of course, things did not always turn out as Luther intended; Kolakowski calls Luther the "accidental father" of modernity.

The theological origin of the Reformation is to be found in Luther's overpowering sense of sin and his redeeming experience of grace. We are saved, Luther declared, not through our works or the works of the church, but by the mysterious and unmerited grace of God.

In medieval Catholicism the church was the intermediary between humankind and God, proclaiming the authoritative reading of Scripture, channeling God's grace through its sacraments, and regulating the lives of the people. Luther and the Reformers would have none of this. For them the church separated us from God; we confront God and Scripture directly and receive His grace (or damnation) as individuals, not as children nestled in the arms of the church.

If salvation is a matter of grace, if there is nothing we can do to *earn* it (sinful creatures that we are), then the Catholic emphasis on penance, monasticism, and the heroic life of virtue made little sense. What is important is not how we live but what we believe by the grace of God. The Reformation, Charles Taylor tells us, brought the affirmation of ordinary life: "The fullness of Christian existence was to found within the activities of this life, in one's calling and in marriage and the family."[13] (Luther left the monastery and married a nun.) With this new emphasis on grace, faith, and belief (rather than works, law, and tradition), religion began to withdraw to private places, leaving the public world free to be secular.

The Reformation secularized much of daily life. In the first half of the sixteenth century, according to Steven Ozment,

> cities and territories passed laws and ordinances that progressively ended or severely limited a host of traditional beliefs, practices, and institutions that touched directly the daily life of large numbers of people: mandatory fasting; auricular confession; the veneration of saints, relics, and images; the buying and selling of indulgences; pilgrimages and shrines; wakes and processions for the dead and dying; endowed masses in memory of the dead; the doctrine of purgatory; Latin Mass and liturgy; traditional ceremonies, festivals, and holidays; monasteries, nunneries, and mendicant orders; the sacramental status of marriage, extreme unction, confirmations, holy orders, and penance; clerical celibacy; clerical immunity from civil taxation and criminal jurisdiction; nonresident benefices; papal excommunication and interdict; canon law; papal and episcopal territorial government; and the traditional scholastic education of clergy.[14]

The Reformation displaced, Ozment argues, "the beliefs, practices, and institutions that had organized daily life and given it security and meaning for the greater part of a millennium."[15]

The Reformers did not seek religious liberty and the secularization of the state. The Protestant states maintained established religions: the Lutheran church in the Scandinavian and many of the German states; Calvinism in Geneva and Scotland and New England; Anglicanism in England. Each of the confessions, Roland Bainton reminds us, was concerned only with its own liberty, and "the possibility never so much as glimmered for most that divergent views might contain each a measure of truth, and that variance in practice even to the point of error might better be suffered than suppressed."[16] Nonetheless, the Reformation helped spawn the modern secular state in two—albeit unintended—ways.

The alternative Christianities created by the Reformation found it impossible to coexist with Catholicism or with each other; about all they agreed on was the importance of converting (or if need be, obliterating) their opposition. The result was the great religious wars of the sixteenth and seventeenth centuries. The willingness of Christians to persecute and slaughter each other was not a point in their favor for the enlightened eighteenth century; the wars and continuing persecution did a good deal to discredit religion and, more particularly, the role of religion in state policy. No doubt the most powerful argument for religious toleration was based in self-interest: if peace—which most everyone desired—was to be possible, societies must tolerate religious differences. Indeed, following the peace of Westphalia ending the Thirty Year's War in 1648 and the restoration of Charles II in England in 1660, Europe, exhausted by its religious wars and persecution, began, albeit grudgingly, to accept the practice of rough religious toleration; established religions began to lose their authority.

But Reformation Protestantism also contained a theological argument for religious liberty. Luther had claimed that because "belief or unbelief is a matter of everyone's conscience" the state "should be content and attend to its own affairs and permit men to believe one thing or another, as they are able and willing, and constrain no one by force. For faith is a free work, to which no one can be forced."[17] Working against the idea of religious liberty was the Reformers' conviction that people are profoundly sinful—that, after all, was why God had instituted governments among men. Wickedness requires constraint, and ignorance demands guidance. Hence established religions remained the rule. Still, in time, the individual Protestant conscience would begin to assert itself against established religion—be it Catholic or Protestant—in defense of liberty and the religiously neutral state. Insofar as this was the case, Owen Chadwick notes, "Christian conscience was the force which began to make Europe 'secular.'"[18] So it would be in America, as we shall see in chapter 3.

Finally, just as Luther separated faith from works, so he separated faith from reason. From the time the author of the Gospel of John wrote the prologue to his gospel, Christian theologians sought to make sense of the Christian revelation in terms of Greek philosophy. Almost from the beginning it was their goal to harmonize faith and reason—Augustine employed neoplatonic philosophy and Aquinas the newly discovered writings of Aristotle to this end. Like many of the reformers, Luther was a scholar; for him, as for them, reason was no mean thing—at least when it knew its place. But reason could not know the sovereign God and His mysterious ways. We must give unto God his glory, Luther wrote, "notwithstanding that he speaketh those things which seem both foolish, absurd, and impossible to reason." What is important is that we *believe*, not that we *understand*. So Luther railed against reason, that "fountain and headspring of all mischiefs," the "enemy to God," the "pestilent beast."[19] As a result, reason began to be secularized, judged competent to deal with the mundane matters of this world but judged incompetent to deal with the religious realm. Reason and faith began to go their separate ways.

In many ways the Protestant Reformation was the last great flowering of religion in the Middle Ages; it was an attempt to recover the "uncorrupted"

Christianity of Augustine, Paul, and the Gospels. Nonetheless, it played a powerful role in secularizing civilization. Luther and the Reformers secularized huge segments of public life, cutting the theological cord that bound good works and the religious governance of society to salvation. They legitimized secular culture and secular rulers, and in their emphasis on conscience they provided theological support for the idea of religious liberty and the secular state. By glorifying the irrationality of grace and faith they began to secularize reason. And they encouraged individualism—making individuals responsible for working out their own salvations, undermining, in the process, the corporate religious culture of medieval Catholicism. Protestantism was something radically new on the world stage.

Pluralism

Even before the Reformation, Europe knew religious divisions. There were Muslims in Spain and eastern Europe, and pockets of Jews lived here and there. Christianity was split between the Orthodox East and the Catholic West. Indeed, the meaning of Christianity varied from place to place as it was overlaid on local folk traditions and as reformers and heretics attempted to reform the church. Still, compared with what was to follow, Christendom possessed an impressive unity in the year 1500. But beginning in the fifteenth century, and then much more obviously in the sixteenth century, this unity suffered attacks from several directions. Most obviously, the Reformation established a plethora of warring Christianities. But there were four other attacks on the unified religious culture of Europe.

First, Renaissance scholarship began to take the past seriously. Christian theologians had used Greek philosophy for their own purposes almost from the beginning, but they had never taken classical thought seriously on its own terms. The humanists of the Renaissance, virtually all of whom would have considered themselves good Christians, were much taken with the beauty and wisdom of classical literature and did not automatically incorporate it within a Christian worldview. A "new sense of historical distance" was acquired, as Quentin Skinner puts it; as a result, classical civilization "began to appear as a wholly separate culture, one which deserved—and indeed required—to be reconstructed and appreciated as far as possible on its own distinctive terms."[20] So, for a small group of intellectuals, scholarship began to institutionalize alternative ways of thinking and living to those found in traditional Christianity.

Second, the fifteenth and sixteenth centuries were the great Age of Discovery. What the Renaissance scholars did for culture historically, the explorers did geographically. They introduced Europe to a variety of foreign cultures and religions; the myth of the noble savage was born and Christians learned that they had no monopoly on goodness or civilization. In his *Characters*, Jean de La Bruyère observed "Some men complete their demoralization by long voyages, and lose whatever shreds of religion remained to them: every day they see a new religion, different customs, different ceremonies."[21]

Third, foreign cultures became accessible to all literate people with the spate of travel books that became popular in the seventeenth and eighteenth centuries, and, of course, the printing press made the historical past and alternative Christianities available to a wider reading public. So long as people had their only understanding of other times and cultures from the parish priest and occasional wanderers, there was little threat to tradition. But books gave immobile people access to other traditions in imaginatively powerful forms.

The literate public also acquired access to the Bible, and with the Reformation the Bible could be read in the vernacular. (Catholicism had insisted on a Latin Bible and a Latin mass.) Scripture was demystified. People who could read the Bible on their own often concluded that they could understand it better than the authorities (and the Protestant idea of the priesthood of all believers encouraged them in this view). Theological controversies mushroomed.

Fourth, spurred by the Industrial Revolution, urbanization began to play a major role in secularizing the life of city dwellers. Supplying churches and clergy for rapidly growing cities created financial and bureaucratic problems. The city supplied sources of sin that were not available in the country. Government began to replace the church as a source of social services. But most important, cities brought together people with different ideas and values. Jean Jacques Rousseau, in his novel *The New Eloise*, described the move of his young hero from the (traditional) country to the (modern) city: "I'm beginning to feel the drunkenness that this agitated, tumultuous life plunges you into. With such a multitude of objects passing before my eyes, I'm getting dizzy. Of all the things that strike me, there is none that holds my heart, yet all of them together disturb my feelings, so that I forget what I am and who I belong to." He went on to cite the "continual flux and reflux of prejudices and conflicting opinions" and concluded that "everything is absurd, but nothing is shocking, because everyone is accustomed to everything."[22] In many European cities, church attendance dropped under 5 percent by the second half of the nineteenth century.

Modern civilization has institutionalized pluralism, openness, autonomy, self-transformation—and skepticism. Marshall Berman puts it more strongly: to live in modernity "is to experience personal and social life as a maelstrom, to find one's world and oneself in perpetual disintegration and renewal, trouble and anguish, ambiguity and contradiction."[23]

Since the beginning of history people had been at least tacitly aware that other peoples thought differently from them, but this did not pose a problem when those people were "barbarians" who lived on the other side of the mountains. But in the modern period this isolation broke down; through scholarship, through foreign travel and trade, through reading, through the growth of cities, and through political liberty and religious pluralism, people come to know "the other" and discover that they are not barbarians but have to be taken seriously.

Peter Berger has argued that traditional religious belief is endangered by institutionalized religious pluralism, for a religion,

> just like any other body of interpretations of reality, is dependent upon social support. The more unified and reliable this support is, the more these interpretations of reality will be firmly established in consciousness. The typical premodern society creates conditions under which religion has, for the individual, the quality of objective certainty; modern society, by contrast, undermines this certainty. . . . The premodern individual was linked to his gods in the same inexorable destiny that dominated most of the rest of his existence; modern man is faced with the necessity of choosing between gods, a plurality of which are socially available to him. If the typical condition of premodern man is one of religious certainty, it follows that that of modern man is one of religious doubt.[24]

Berger points out that our word "heresy" comes from the Greek word "hairein," which means "to choose." Traditionally, the heretic was someone who picked and chose which parts of the tradition to accept. Now, picking and choosing have become necessities, for "heresy no longer stands out against a clear background of authoritative tradition."[25] Our choices no longer receive massive social confirmation. Religion is no longer supported by *common* sense; instead it becomes a matter of *private* faith—or doubt.

Given this natural tendency to take as reasonable that which we have in common, rather than that which divides us, there has been, historically, a regression to the lowest common cultural denominator such that the more general moral values that cut across religious traditions came gradually to be taken as the bedrock upon which institutions are founded and social and political decisions are made. A desacralized morality became the common coin of the public realm and religion because it divided us, was relegated to our private lives.

It is also, in part, pluralism and the failure to agree upon religious truth in early modern Europe, that opened the door to modern science.[26]

Modern Science and Technology

The great seventeenth-century scientists who made the scientific revolution were not enemies of religion; most of them were deeply religious. Nonetheless, their methods, their conclusions, and their technology all served, implicitly and eventually, to undermine traditional religion.

In science we learn by way of experience and experiments, by trial and testing: no conclusion is sacred; knowledge claims are tentative. The truth was not given by God some time in the past; it is for us to discover. Michael Barnes has written that religion, by contrast, "has not often been the friend of pluralism, tentativeness, and changeability. It serves to provide security in the face of life's threats; it is a haven from insecurity and confusion."[27] Or, as Martin Luther once wrote, "uncertainty is the most miserable thing in the world."[28] Yet modern science has made questioning, critical thinking, tentativity—and a measure of uncertainty—into virtues; in the process, tradition, authority, and the wisdom of the past were discredited.

The new astronomy quickly discredited a good deal more. For traditional religion our world was at the center of things with the heavens above and the underworld below. This was not an old world—a few thousand years, perhaps. Judaism, Christianity and Islam would all have had us believe that God made the world for us; that it was designed for our good. This was our *home*.

Yet when Blaise Pascal surveyed the brave, new world of modern science in the seventeenth century he was shaken to the depths: "When I consider the brief span of my life absorbed into the eternity which comes before and after . . . the small space I occupy and which I see swallowed up in the infinite immensity of spaces of which I know nothing and which know nothing of me, I take fright. . . . When I see the blind and wretched state of man, when I survey the whole universe in its dumbness and man left to himself with no light, as though lost in the corner of the universe . . . I am moved to terror."[29] In our time Carl Sagan rather matter-of-factly tells us that

there are cataclysms and catastrophes occurring regularly in the universe and on the most awesome scale. There are, for example, quasar explosions which probably decimate the nuclei of galaxies. It seems likely that every time a quasar explodes, more than a million worlds are obliterated and countless forms of life, some of them intelligent, are utterly destroyed. This is not the traditional benign universe of conventional religiosity in the West, constructed for the benefit of living and especially of human beings. Indeed, the very scale of the universe—more than a hundred billion galaxies, each containing more than a hundred billion stars—speaks to us of the inconsequentiality of human events in the cosmic context.[30]

Many have found it hard to find God in this immense and violent universe.

More important, if more subtle, is that by virtue of the categories it uses to make sense of reality modern science has "disenchanted" the world, to use Max Weber's term. For medieval Catholicism our world was enchanted: God became incarnate in the person of Jesus of Nazareth; in the person of the Holy Spirit God infuses the lives of the godly; the sacraments are physical channels of divine grace; the world is filled with a panoply of sacred beings and is governed by natural (that is, divine) law.[31] Medieval Christianity and medieval science shared a worldview: nature is the arena of God's actions; we understand natural events when we discern their purpose in God's scheme of things. Why does water fall and why does fire rise? Because the "natural place" of water is down and fire is up; this is where they *should* be. Why do acorns grow? To become oaks, to realize their *purpose*. Why are lambs born in the spring? Because that is when the grass is most nourishing. In Ian Barbour's words, this search for purpose was "the result of conceiving every object as having a place in a cosmic hierarchy, the creation of *a purposeful God*."[32] Because God has structured this world in accord with his purposes, the processes of nature are value-laden: what comes to be is (in the end) what ought to be. What is fully real, is good.

With the scientific revolution nature came to be understood as matter in motion. The ultimate constituents of the world were atoms, and change was understood as their rearrangement in space and time. Nature could be described as quantitative rather than qualitative or normative change. So, for example, qualitative colors became purely "subjective" as reality came to be understood quantitatively in terms of the frequency of light waves. In E. A. Burtt's words, the "world that people had thought themselves living in—a world rich with color and sound, redolent with fragrance, filled with gladness, love, and beauty, speaking everywhere of purposive harmony and creative ideals—was crowded now into minute corners in the brains of scattered organic beings. The really important world outside was a world hard, cold, colorless, silent, and dead: a world of quantity, a world of mathematically computable motions in mechanical regularity."[33]

This revolution—from purposes to causes, from myth to math—was, according to the philosopher W. T. Stace, "the greatest revolution in human history, far outweighing in importance any of the political revolutions whose thunder has reverberated through the world. For it came about in this way that for the past three hundred years there has been growing up in men's minds, dominated as they are by science, a new imaginative picture of the world. The world, according to this new picture, is purposeless, senseless, meaningless. Nature is nothing but matter in motion. The motions of matter are governed, not by any purpose, but by blind forces and laws."[34] The story has been told that Napoleon once said to the physicist Pierre-Simon de Laplace: "I understand, M. Laplace, that you have written a great book on the system of the universe, and have never even mentioned its Creator," to which Laplace replied: "I have no need of that hypothesis."[35]

Biological evolution is religiously problematic for two different reasons. Perhaps most obviously, the idea of evolution over vast periods of time seems to contradict a literalist reading of the Genesis account of creation. This is the problem fundamentalists have with it. Many liberals have simply accepted evolution as "God's way of doing things." Modern biology does not take evolution to be purposeful, however; instead, it is the result of random mutations and recombinations of genes and natural selection; it is intrinsically *purposeless*. The great biologist Jacques Monod once described evolution as "the product of an enormous lottery presided over by natural selection, blindly picking the rare winners from among numbers drawn at utter random."[36] It makes no scientific sense to say that evolution is the transition from morally or spiritually lower to higher forms of life; it is not the realization of what ought to be. A completely naturalistic explanation is sufficient; again, there is no need of the God hypothesis.

Scientists are free, of course, to believe that God is the "first cause" of the universe, that "in the beginning" God created nature and set things in motion before the Big Bang. Modern science is, perhaps, agnostic about that, and often distinctions are drawn between science (which knows its limitations) and "scientism" or "naturalism," which purport to be adequate to explain everything. The God behind the Big Bang is not the God of traditional religion, however, but a dim and distant being with whom it is hard to have a personal relationship. The God of traditional religion is actively involved in the world, shaping it, intervening in it, relating to people. There is no room for this God in the modern scientific worldview.

Over time more and more of reality was brought under the jurisdiction of science. Already in the eighteenth century the great historians Voltaire, David Hume, and Edward Gibbon were excising God's purposes from history, and in the nineteenth century fully secular interpretations of society became a major theme of the new social sciences. Auguste Comte, usually credited as being the father of sociology, argued that civilization had passed through two stages—the religious and metaphysical (or philosophical)—and was, in his day, entering the third and final stage of social evolution, the positive, or scientific. We can now safely dispense with religious dogma, Comte argued, for we have science and social scientists to guide us into the future. The new discipline of cultural anthropology worked hard to undermine traditional religion by developing an evolutionary view of culture. As James Turner put it, the "rites and doctrines central to Christianity began to look like savage survivals. Baptism appeared remarkably like one more purification ritual, the Eucharist like the widely diffused ceremonial eating of a god, even the Incarnation like many another myth of a God-man."[37] Religion was a superstitious survival from primitive times, bound to disappear with the advance of enlightenment and modernity.

I have suggested that the great scientists of nature were not, for the most part, avowed opponents of religion, but many of the great social scientists were. One important reason is that the social sciences were, in the beginning, morally and politically motivated: early social scientists were social critics who saw organized religion propping up reactionary regimes, inhibiting free inquiry and social progress. Of course, social science also inherited the tension all scientific method had with religion. As a result, many of the great social scientists of the nineteenth and early twentieth centuries took it as a special responsibility to discredit religion by arguing that it could be "reduced" to a more basic social reality, that it had naturalistic causes.[38] Indeed, we acquire maturity as individuals and as a society when we can see religion for what it is. Sigmund Freud wrote: "The scientific spirit brings about a particular attitude towards worldly matters; before religious matters it pauses for a little, hesitates, and finally there too crosses the threshold. In this process there is no stopping."[39] Religion is but a form of neurosis. Robert Bellah has noted that by early in our century the "best minds" in social science were "deeply alienated from the Western religious tradition,"[40] and surveys continue to show social scientists to be even less religious than their notably skeptical academic colleagues.[41]

Much social science holds that to explain human behavior we must set it in the context of its causes and develop social (or psychological) laws that allow us to predict (and control) future behavior.[42] Persons and societies are not, in principle, different from physical objects or systems. We know, from Boyle's law, that if we change the temperature of a gas in an enclosed container, we will affect the pressure; so if we change the climate, or the reinforcement contingencies, or the brain chemistry, or the genes, or the level of material deprivation, then we will change the resulting behavior, and the changes can (again, in principle) be calculated to conform to law. Persons are no longer free and responsible subjects but objects acted upon by an enveloping environment, understood scientifically. There is no room in such a picture for freedom, soul, conscience—or the hand of God. Religious experience provides no evidence for God; rather, it is symptomatic of weak egos and the inability to cope. Hearing voices suggests schizophrenia, not saintliness. Charles Dickens captured the thesis nicely when he had the skeptical Scrooge say that there was more of gravy than the grave about Marley's ghost.[43] The world of spirits is caused by our indigestion (or brain chemistry or the power of suggestion), not by the supernatural. Indeed, Dickens's utilitarian schoolmaster Thomas Gradgrind was only a slight caricature of the spirit of the age: "With a rule and a pair of scales, and the multiplication table always in his pocket," he was "ready to weigh and measure any parcel of human nature, and tell you exactly what it comes to. It is a mere question of figures, a case of simple arithmetic."[44]

I do not want to overstate my case. Modern social science is badly divided—almost as much as modern theology. Indeed, many social scientists employ the methods of the humanities more than they pretend to the methods of natural science. Nonetheless, Dorothy Ross is surely right in suggesting that mainstream social science invites us "to look through history to a presumably natural process beneath. Here the social world is composed of individual behaviors responding to natural stimuli, and the capitalist market and modern urban society are understood, in effect, as part of nature. We are led toward quantitative and technocratic manipulation of nature."[45] The world of science and much social science is "value-free," a world of pure "factuality."

Science has secularized the world in another very different way. No doubt the emotional significance of religion for many people has been that it is a help in time of trouble and, after all, life has been, for most people, a matter of almost constant suffering. And yet things have gotten better, considerably better, in modern civilization. We have conquered diseases, ended famines, invented creature comforts, and prolonged life. How? Not through religion but through science and technology. One nineteenth-century French peasant is reported to have said: "'I've tried everything. I've had masses said and got no profit from them. I've bought chemicals and they worked. I'll stick to the better merchandise."[46] It is, no doubt, the technological payoff, as much as the intellectual insight, that has given science its prestige in our culture.[47]

Franklin Baumer has described the "faith of the engineer" as the "working faith" of the modern world.[48] American opinion surveys have shown that the public places much more faith in science and technology to improve human life than in religion.[49] To whom do we turn in times of trouble, after all? Economists and physicians and psychotherapists. Ian Barbour suggests that faith in science is characteristic of modern "technological man," who "is impressed by the trustworthiness and reliability of science, which becomes his ultimate loyalty. Technology is . . . the source of salvation, the agent of secularized redemption; technological advance is his secularized eschatology."[50]

The major issue here is not truth but relevance: in a world over which we have so much technical control, religion has become much less important.[51]

Once, not too long ago, it took an extraordinarily imaginative and daring individual to deny the truth of religion, for there seemed no other way of explaining the world. But we now have science, and it works—at least most of the time. It possesses the massive credibility that religion once possessed. And its credibility cuts across all cultures and ideologies. As A. R. Hall put it in his study of the scientific revolution, science "is the one product of the West that has had a decisive, probably permanent, impact upon other contemporary civilizations. Compared with modern science, capitalism, the nation-state, art and literature, Christianity and democracy, seem regional idiosyncrasies, whose past is full of vicissitudes and whose future is full of dark uncertainty."[52]

In the process of adopting the scientific worldview, Western civilization changed what Maynard Adams has called its "culture-generating stance in the world." From within the framework of traditional civilization humankind faced the world asking, What is demanded of me? How do I set myself right with the world? Within the modern world we ask, How do I impose my will on the world? How can I control it? Why did this shift take place? Adams argues that it was because people "became more concerned with the acquisition of power and wealth than with the higher values and the perfection of their souls; they became more concerned with living by their own wills and satisfying their own wants and desires than with fulfilling the requirements imposed on them by traditional society, nature, or God."[53] Science and technology are important not least because they give us the power to carry out the agenda of economic liberalism. It is to that agenda I now turn.

Economics

Within medieval culture economic interests were largely subordinated to salvation. Indeed, the very idea of economic gain was viewed with deep suspicion. As one fourteenth-century theologian put it: "He who has enough to satisfy his wants and nevertheless ceaselessly labors to acquire riches" is "incited by a damnable avarice, sensuality, or pride."[54] This is not to say that people did not seek wealth. Robert Heilbroner explains:

> Wealth, of course, there has always been, and covetousness is at least as old as the Biblical tales. But there is a vast deal of difference between the envy inspired by the wealth of a few mighty personages and a general struggle for wealth diffused throughout society. . . . As long as the paramount idea was that life on earth was only a trying preamble to Life Eternal, the business spirit was neither encouraged not did it find spontaneous nourishment. Kings wanted treasure and for that they fought wars. . . . But most people—serfs, village craftsmen, even the masters of the manufacturing guilds—wanted to be left alone to live as their fathers had and as their sons would in turn.[55]

The desire for wealth was taken to be unnatural, and at every turn the church regulated and restricted the economy.[56] Economics and religion were inextricably meshed. Medieval Catholicism had an elaborate system of religious principles regulating just prices, usury, charity, labor, and guilds.

By the eighteenth century the world had changed. The free market had become the key to economics: usury, which had once been a sin, was rehabilitated as interest and took its inevitable place in the process of capital formation; the concept of a just price gave way to supply and demand; guilds collapsed before the need for free labor; charity and begging, once cardinal virtues and signs of saintliness, became vices; self-interest and acquisitiveness, once vices, became the governing virtues of the economic world; economic guidance was no longer sought in theology but in the value-free calculus of economists and hardheaded businessmen. "Man" became "rational, economic man," a utility maximizer, moved by self-interest and unlimited wants to compete for scarce resources in a market freed of any religious constraints or values. Economics drove religion out of the marketplace: "free enterprise" requires freedom from religious as well as from governmental regulation. The world of economics has been secularized.

Although a nascent capitalism already existed in the city-states of late medieval and Renaissance Italy, the Protestant Reformation played a powerful role in legitimizing the development of market economies. The Reformers radically devalued the church's role in regulating social life at the same time they affirmed "ordinary life" and secular vocations. Moreover, in the aftermath of the religious wars of the sixteenth and seventeenth centuries moneymaking and the economic interests seemed to be particularly safe and predictable forms of activity. Dr. Johnson claimed: "There are few ways in which a man can be more innocently employed than in getting money," and Montesquieu wrote: "Wherever there is commerce, there the ways of men are gentle."[57] Business interests became respectable.

Of course, the influence of science and technology on economics was evident everywhere. Technological developments—the printing press, roads, shipping, mechanical clocks, and then the technology that fueled the Industrial Revolution—played vital roles in creating wealth. As important was the new secular, scientific understanding of persons and society. Modern thinkers no longer conceived of society as an organic whole in which people are bound together by moral and religious obligations; it is nothing more than a collection of individuals, each acting on the basis of self-interest. Society is much like nature, and individuals are much like atoms, propelled by their interests, bouncing off one another in competition for scarce resources according to predictable scientific laws. The impact of Darwinism on economics was profound, and if the most extreme versions of Social Darwinism have been discredited, lingering echoes of Charles Darwin are still to be heard in the marketplace (and we should remember that Darwin's original insight into natural selection came from the economist Thomas Malthus).

So, for a variety of reasons, a new and radically secularized economic world came into existence. The market was no longer subjected to religious regulation, and persons were redefined in narrowly economic and fully secular terms. Modern capitalism, John Maynard Keynes once wrote, is "absolutely irreligious," often, if not always, "a mere congeries of possessors and pursuers." Unhappily, Keynes adds, "the moral problem of our age" is "the love of money, with the habitual appeal to the money motive in nine-tenths of the activities of life." And, he notes, the "decaying religions around us . . . have lost their moral significance just because—unlike some of their earlier versions—they do not touch in the least degree on these essential matters."[58]

But the most direct way in which the market revolution secularized the world was by undermining traditional communities. In Joseph Schumpeter's classic formulation, *creative destruction* is the "essential fact" about capitalism.[59] The market required free and mobile labor, able to move with the availability of work; as a result, families were uprooted, kin networks were wrenched apart, and communities were transformed. People were separated from the rhythms of nature, crowded into the traditionless cities, often living in inhumane conditions. Karl Polanyi comments: "A blind faith in spontaneous progress had taken hold of people's minds, and with the fanaticism of sectarians the most enlightened pressed forward for boundless and unregulated change in society. The effects on the lives of the people were awful beyond description."[60] So much for Dr. Johnson's innocence and gentility.

There is, of course, an irony here: the industrialists, the new ruling class, proclaimed themselves the party of order at the same time they were destroying the traditional order. At the midpoint of the nineteenth century, Karl Marx and Friedrich Engels noted the "constant revolutionizing of production, uninterrupted disturbance of all social relations, everlasting uncertainty and agitation" that had come to characterize the market-driven societies of the West and concluded that all "ancient and venerable prejudices and opinions, are swept away, all new-formed ones become antiquated before they can ossify. All that is solid melts into air, all that is holy is profaned."[61] Marx and Engels were not alone in this assessment of the situation: many nineteenth-century conservatives were horrified by what they saw around them, for it was their world—the world of tradition—which market economies were destroying.

Americans often use the term "conservative" to describe both traditionalists and advocates of market economies, but in the nineteenth century the advocates of capitalism were called "liberals" (we would now say *classical* liberals) or "radicals" for they advocated unfettered liberty in the marketplace—even if that meant the disruption of people's lives and the loss of tradition. Ironically, nineteenth-century socialists and conservatives often found themselves united in opposition to the radical individualism and moral indifference of the new market economies.[62] Peter Berger, no leftist, acknowledges that one may view the dynamism of capitalism "as finally good, bad, or a mixed bag, but there can be little doubt about its *anti-traditional* thrust. Before its dynamism *all* traditions—social, political, and cultural—shake, wilt, often disappear, invariably change. . . . Those with a stake in traditional hierarchies and beliefs, therefore, cannot be faulted if they look upon capitalism as an adversary force."[63]

But if the market revolution was extraordinarily disruptive, it was also highly successful—at least in the long run—and that very success has lured people away from religion. The Calvinist ethics that Max Weber believed made capitalism successful was ascetic, emphasizing hard work, minimal consumption, and maximum savings and investment. But the very success of market economies created a new world of material satisfactions, leisure, and wealth. In the eighteenth century John Wesley was fretting: "I fear, wherever riches have increased, the essence of religion has decreased in the same proportion. Therefore I do not see how it is possible, in the nature of things, for any revival of true religion to continue long. For religion must necessarily produce both industry and frugality, and these cannot but produce riches. But as riches increase, so will pride, anger, and love of the world in all its branches."[64] "Who hinders the prosperity of religion?" the great German theologian Friedrich Schleiermacher asked at the height of the Industrial Revolution: "the discreet and practical men of to-day."[65] Here we have an effect parallel to that created by technology. As we achieve control over our world and as our wealth increases, happiness is to be had in this world and we become mindless of the world to come. Increasingly our hearts are not in our religion but in the comforts and consumer goods of the market.

There is another way in which business and science have conspired together to secularize the world. In the first chapter of *The Wealth of Nations*, Adam Smith described a pin factory in which the division of labor allowed for much greater productivity than if each worker were responsible for making whole pins. The complexity of modern life, the need for economic efficiency and technological progress, requires *specialization*—not just in the manufacture of products but intellectually, in how we think about the world. As a result, our vocational, intellectual, and spiritual worlds have fragmented. Our view of the world has become increasingly narrow as we have been caught up in the technical problem-solving of science and the economic imperatives of the marketplace. To be a specialist about something all too often means that we are ignorant about many other things—religion included. In particular, we have lost the old religious sense of calling, the notion that our work must be grounded in a moral or religious understanding of the world. In fact, religion has itself become just another specialty. Smith noted the dehumanization of work in a pin factory; it is sometimes argued that the problem may be more general as the world of work has been reconceptualized—and secularized—in terms of manageable, technical specialties.

Defenders of a market economy typically assume that its potential vices— its emphasis on self-interest, competition, ceaseless change, specialization, consumerism, and its determined this-worldliness—will be compensated for by other social institutions—the family, the church, education, and the virtues of good citizenship. The problem, as Christopher Lasch has noted, is that the market "notoriously tends to universalize itself. It does not easily coexist with institutions that operate according to principles antithetical to itself. . . . Sooner or later the market tends to absorb them all. It puts an almost irresistible pressure on every activity to justify itself in the only terms it recognizes—to become a business proposition."[66] Like science, the market is imperialistic. The virtues of a market economy are considerable, but they are bought at a cost—at least for religious folk—for tradition and traditional religion are not economically expedient. Modern life has become, for the most part, a business proposition; nowadays we seek wealth and happiness, not salvation.

Politics

As Peter Kaufman has noted, "From the time of Constantine's conversion to that of Oliver Cromwell's civil war, Christianity and politics were often so closely joined that it is difficult now to tell whether we are looking back at religious or political convictions."[67] What counted in medieval days, according to Walter Ullmann, "was the undifferentiated Christian: religion was not separated from politics, politics not separated from morals. . . . [One's] actions were not thought, at least in the public sphere, capable of being judged by any other norm than by the Christian."[68]

Three principles cut across medieval and Reformation thinking about politics. First, the powers that be are ordained by God: so said Paul in his letter to the Romans; so said Augustine, the greatest of Christian theologians; and so said Luther. Second, there was never any question but that the state must be a Christian one governed by laws that reflect God's law. The state was in no sense neutral among religions but practiced what Kaufman has felicitously called "redeeming politics."[69] Third, society was understood communally. With birth in a particular family, estate, and fiefdom, people acquired an identity defined by a set of binding obligations they were not free to reject.

The roots of political liberalism grow deep in the religious soil of early modern Europe. (By "liberalism" I mean not the left wing of the Democratic party but the framework of ideas and institutions that gives priority to liberty in social and political matters—what is sometimes called "classical" liberalism.) Constitutional scholar Michael McConnell argues that liberalism "came about when and where it did because the Protestant Reformation made the individual believer the judge of religious truth ('God Alone is Lord of the Conscience') and thus made freedom of thought a pressing question for all thinking individuals. Religion and religious freedom were therefore at the very heart of the liberal project."[70] As we have seen, religion played another, rather less happy role in bringing liberalism onto the world stage, for the religious wars that followed the Reformation made religion a divisive rather than a unifying force in many nations, and a measure of toleration and liberty was required for peace. For several reasons, then, the religious ideas and conflicts of early modern culture required the kind of state in which individuals could privately pursue the dictates of their consciences while the state remained at least relatively neutral. At least in northern Europe and America, states began the slow process of religious disestablishment.

Like the philosopher John Rawls, we might distinguish this merely "political" liberalism from the more "comprehensive" or ideological liberalism that
followed in the wake of modernity.[71] Comprehensive liberalism is a richly developed philosophical position that stands in some tension with traditional religion rather than simply a neutral political framework within which various
religious and secular ideas and values may coexist.

For a variety of reasons, ideological liberals have argued not just for liberty
of conscience but for individualism over the more communal forms of society
that had dominated traditional religious cultures. Writing in the nineteenth
century, Alexis de Tocqueville claimed that the word "individualism" was "unknown to our ancestors, for the good reason that in their days every individual
necessarily belonged to a group and no one could regard himself as an isolated
unit."[72] With modernity, individuals acquired identities apart from traditional
communities: we are not born into a station and its duties; we are born free, as
Rousseau put it in his *Social Contract*. And because we are born free, we
must consent to be governed. So, in the seventeenth and eighteenth centuries,
the idea of the social contract came to ground our obligations to obey political
institutions and rulers.

Talk of rights and utility, liberty and moral autonomy, began to crowd talk
of natural law and community, obligation and God, off the cultural stage precisely when, as Jeffrey Stout puts it, "appeals to a wide range of assumptions
and categories in the traditional ethos . . . became more likely to generate
conflict than agreement. Recoiling from Reformation polemics and the religious wars, modern ideologues and ethical theorists increasingly had good
reason to favor a vocabulary whose sense did not depend on prior agreement
about the nature of God and the structures of cosmos and society ordained by
him."[73] As important, this shift in vocabulary took place as science was
achieving dominance as the arbiter of truth: moral and political talk had to be
scientifically respectable. Hence, morality could no longer be grounded in
theology but must instead find its source in utility and the market, in self-
actualization and psychology, in the autonomous choices of free individuals
rather than religious authority.

Finally, the dynamism of science, technology, and market economies generated a powerful belief in progress and the possibility of happiness in this
world. It became the purpose of the state to provide the political infra-
structure that would nourish human happiness. Indeed, the centrality of
happiness to liberalism represents, in Anthony Arblaster's words, "the culmination of the secularization of moral and political thought."[74] "There is only
one duty," Diderot wrote at the height of the Enlightenment: "it is to be
happy."[75] The American Declaration of Independence guaranteed the inalien-

able right to pursue happiness—not salvation. Gone were the days of redeeming politics.

Michael McConnell concludes that with the shift from a merely political liberalism to an ideological or comprehensive liberalism, "freedom *of* religion came to be seen as less important than freedom *from* religion."[76] The vocabulary, the governing purposes, and the normative assumptions that grounded the liberal understanding of morality, politics, and the state became at least implicitly secular. And, in fact, religion is often perceived by liberals to be an intruder in the public square.

By the nineteenth century it was clear that the West would be liberal and that religion would be relegated to the private sphere of life for almost everything other than broadly ceremonial purposes.

The established religions did not help their cause by stubbornly siding with the old order in Europe. The Catholic church vacillated between conservative and reactionary policies over the centuries of the modern period, breaking this pattern decisively only with the Second Vatican Council in the 1960s, and the established Protestant churches did but little better, opposing virtually all liberal reform movements.[77] The churches had no program of their own for dealing with the problems of the new industrial society (other than justice in the afterlife), which demonstrated to many on the Left the irrelevance, indeed the evil, of religion.[78] In France, where the church sided with the ancien régime, the middle class became strongly anticlerical at the time of the French Revolution, and almost everywhere in Europe the working classes rejected religion. In nineteenth-century England, working-class church attendance was often no more than one-tenth of what it was in the middle classes, and in 1876 in Saxony, church attendance sometimes dropped to 1 percent in small industrial towns.[79] Indeed, Hugh McLeod suggests that the "central theme" of European religious history after the French Revolution was the "widespread revolt against the various official churches that had emerged triumphant from the turmoil of the Reformation and Counter-Reformation."[80]

Religion had been politicized. Tocqueville claimed that "in Europe, Christianity has been intimately united to the powers of the earth. Those powers are now in decay, and it is, as it were, buried under their ruins."[81] When religion is enmeshed with politics, rejecting the latter typically means rejecting the former. It was to avoid this fate that the Founders separated religion from government in America—with considerably happier results all around.

In a famous essay published in 1989, Francis Fukuyama announced the "end of history." The death of communism had ended the ideological battles that moved history. We have witnessed, Fukuyama claimed, "an unabashed victory of economic and political liberalism," the "triumph of the West."[82] Maybe. But the resurgence of nationalism in the former Soviet Union and the countries of eastern Europe, where communism had repressed it for forty-five years, provides powerful support for Arthur Schlesinger's claim that nationalism "remains, after two centuries, the most vital political emotion in the world," far more vital even than democracy.[83]

Modern nationalism has carried on its own war on traditional religion. When the French revolutionaries jettisoned the Christian calendar, replacing it with one dating events from the Revolution, the symbolism was apt: the birth of the French Republic, not Christ, was the central focus of history for them. In fact, nationalism often functions much as does a religion. National history often assumes mythic proportions and, as Ninian Smart describes it,

> The myth includes heroes and other holy figures.... Every nation has its rituals—the use of the flag, singing the national anthem, sporting victories, parades, memorial days for the war dead. . . . Every nation inculcates and focuses experience—feelings of pride as evoked by the rituals, a sense of identity with one's people, and so forth. Every nation inculcates the ethics of citizenship. . . . Every nation becomes incarnated, hopefully, in a State, which then employs a kind of priesthood—the teachers, especially—and creates a symbolic centre in the capital. . . . Above all, it has sacred territory.[84]

The heavy "sacrificial" demands of the nation, Smart argues, create great pressure to make it the source of one's "ultimate concern."[85]

Throughout the nineteenth century there was a growth in nationalist feeling: Holy Mother Russia, the German Fatherland, American Manifest Destiny. The weaknesses of liberalism, of traditional religion, and of socialism became clear at the beginning of World War I as national loyalties proved stronger than political ideology, class consciousness, or Christianity.[86] Perhaps even sadder was the utter inability of traditional religion to mount any challenge to nationalist socialism in the 1930s. Paul Johnson notes that both Lutherans and Catholics in Nazi Germany "gave massive support to the regime," and he concludes that "the Second World War inflicted even more grievous blows on the moral standing of the Christian faith than the First. It exposed the emptiness of the churches in Germany, the cradle of the Reformation, and the cowardice and selfishness of the Holy See."[87]

Of course, nationalism can strengthen religion—as Polish and Irish nationalism have strengthened Catholicism—at least in the short run. But in the long run, nationalism wars against both liberalism and traditional religion, for it focuses people's strongest sense of meaning, identity, and value in a different location. For the liberal, one's primary identity is as a free individual; for the traditional Christian one's ultimate identity is as a follower of a religious tradition that cuts across lines of race and nationality and can stand in prophetic judgment on them. Nationalism reshapes our identities. If asked to identify themselves while traveling in an alien culture, how many Christians would think to say, "I am a Christian" or "I am a free individual"? How many would say, "I am an American"?

In sum, political liberalism disestablished religion, contributing to the ongoing privatization of religion; the entanglement of traditional religion with conservative politics discredited it in the eyes of many liberals and especially the working class; over the last two centuries nationalism has come to be a powerful rival to religion for the ultimate concern and allegiance of humankind. Modern politics have not been kind to religion—though as we shall see in chapter 3, the situation is not so bleak in America.

The Secularization of the Modern World

Scholars often distinguish between secularism and secularization. Secular*ism* is an ideology advocated by secular*ists*, who are opposed to religion and believe that secularization is good. *The secularization of the modern world is not the work of secularists.* Most people have never read a word of Hume or Nietzsche or Ingersoll or Freud or Russell. It was not secularism that secularized the world—it was Protestantism and pluralism, science and technology, economic and political liberalism. Indeed, the secularization of modern civilization was largely unintended.

Of course, there are other actors in the drama. As we shall see in the next chapter, public education has played an important role in secularizing American culture (again in unintended ways). No doubt television and twentieth-century mass culture have been particularly potent carriers of secular modernity. But the root causes of twentieth-century culture were already entrenched by the end of the nineteenth century. In that crucial century Darwin removed the last vestiges of divine purpose from nature, the social sciences made God irrelevant to our understanding of psychology and society, industrialization and market economies gave new luster to mammon while continuing to uproot traditional religious communities, politics and pluralism undermined established religions—and religion lost its cultural authority. By the end of the century Friedrich Nietzsche had proclaimed the death of God.

And yet, 90 percent of Americans profess belief in God.

At the beginning of this chapter I outlined six characteristics of religious culture in the premodern West: belief in God; the meshing of sacred and secular ways of thinking; the centrality of salvation to people's lives and an orientation toward the world to come; a sense of time in which truth had been given in the past; an ethics of love and self-denial; and a corporate (and cooperative) rather than individualistic (and competitive) understanding of society. In the modern world, these are all, now, minority views, with the possible exception of the first.

Most of us do believe in God, but our understanding of God is increasingly nontraditional. Only 65 percent of Americans believe in the traditional, personal God of Western religion as opposed to "some sort of spirit or life force," and the correlative figures for European countries are considerably lower: Norway, 40 percent; the Netherlands, 34 percent; Great Britain, 31 percent; Italy and France, 26 percent; Germany, 24 percent; Denmark and Sweden, 19 percent.[88] Perhaps more important, the percentage of Americans who say that religion is "very important" in their lives—54 percent—is rather less impressive than the percentage of Americans who claim to believe in God.[89] An even smaller percentage of Europeans—27 percent—say this.[90] The younger generation is considerably less committed to religion. While in America 41 percent of "youths" agree that "religion should be very important in my life," elsewhere the numbers are much lower: Japan, 9.9 percent; Great Britain, 9.4 percent; West Germany, 7.4 percent; and France, 6.9 percent.[91] Although church attendance in America has held fairly steady over the last fifty years (at about 40 percent), a greater percentage of people (45 percent) never attend or attend only several times a year, and the rate of weekly church attendance in most European countries is about half that: West Germany, 21 percent; Great Britain, 14 percent; and France, 12 percent.[92] After reviewing surveys of religious belief and practices in many countries, Ronald Inglehardt finds long-term shifts away from traditional religion throughout Western industrial societies.[93] Indeed, two-thirds of Americans believe that religion is losing its influence.[94]

There is, of course, a vitally important difference between belief and behavior. People can profess religious beliefs, attend church or synagogue, and live almost totally secular lives. The effect of secularization is not so much a lack of belief as it is secular life-styles in a secular culture. Harvey Cox has written:

The forces of secularization have no serious interest in persecuting religion. Secularization simply bypasses and undercuts religion and goes on to other things. It has relativized religious world views and thus rendered them innocuous. Religion has been privatized. It has been accepted as the peculiar prerogative and point of view of a particular person or group. Secularization has . . . persuaded the devotee that there are more important things than dying for the faith. The gods of traditional religions live on as private fetishes or the patrons of congenial groups, but they play no significant role in the public life of the secular metropolis.[95]

Our reluctance to see just how secular we are is, in part, a legacy of the Reformation, for Protestantism made doctrine and belief, rather than good works and religious practices, central to religion (unlike Catholicism, Islam, and Judaism). Many Americans believe that believing is enough.

Most important for our purposes, *we have separated the sacred and the secular*. Most of us no longer believe that religious ideas and values are integral to our understanding of history and nature, psychology and society, the economy, and politics. As Wilfred Cantwell Smith put it, religious traditions that were once "coterminous with human life in all its comprehensiveness, have actually found themselves supplemented more and more by considerations from other or newer sources, so that the religious seems to be one fact of a person's life alongside others."[96]

Religion is one thing, science another. Modern science has taught us to think of nature as purposeless and without inherent meaning. We no longer discern the "thou" in nature or the God behind nature. "Once upon a time the wood was bewitched," Owen Chadwick writes; "But now the wood is administered by the Forestry Commission."[97] Leo Tolstoy once compared scientists to "plasterers set to plaster one side of a church wall, who . . . in the excess of their zeal plaster over the windows and the holy images, and the woodwork . . . and rejoice that from their plasterers' point of view everything was now so smooth and even."[98] Nor is there room for miracles or divine purpose in history, and no talk of souls or Scripture muddies the waters of modern psychology and social science. The theories we use to explain physical and human nature are devoid of religious reference. "God used to function as the central explanatory concept" in Western intellectual life, James Turner tells us, but now "the linchpin is missing; our culture, in this sense, now lacks a center."[99]

No longer do we look for truth in the past. Since the Enlightenment the characteristic experience of time in the West has been an openness to the future, a self-conscious desire to escape the shackles of time-worn institutions and the dead hand of tradition—and traditional religion. We need not stand uncomprehending before the mysteries of nature; we need not have the poor and infirm with us always. The world is ours to know and change for the better. Much like the scientists who, in C. P. Snow's apt phrase, "have the future in their bones," we have come to a (perhaps measured) optimism about the world.[100] Truth is to be discovered. We must experiment, we must explore. With time comes progress.

And happiness. Indeed, happiness, not salvation, is the goal of most of us, and we seek happiness in this world, not in a world to come. Technology and economic growth have convinced us we are not fated to live in a vale of suffering. No longer need we turn to religion for solace.

Indeed, our whole moral and political vocabulary has changed. We talk of rights more than duties, autonomy more than authority, utility more than stewardship, self-interest more than charity, self-actualization more than love, individualism more than community. In the old view, society was seen as a "natural" association, governed by a common (higher) purpose in which individuals found the meaning of their lives and made sacrifices in pursuit of the common good and God's will. No longer. We are free to make what commitments we will, to define ourselves, to obligate ourselves as we see fit. We are to be the judges of our own good. The characteristic institutions of our time are the liberal state and the market, and to a considerable extent it is not the business of either to define the good by which people should live their lives. The defining value of modernity is liberty.

There is a measure of coherence to be found in the ideas and institutions of modernity: science and technology, political and economic liberalism, pluralism and individualism, reinforce each other. Modern civilization has worked toward consistency in its philosophical and cultural foundations. There is something like a modern worldview.

I make no claims about the measure of truth to be found in modernity. Nor am I arguing that secularization is good or bad, only that it has happened (and I suspect most religious fundamentalists and most secular social scientists would agree). I do suspect that everyone, including the most religious among us, finds some aspects of secularization and modernity congenial.

Finally, I suggest that these are the trends of our times, not the last word. Religion is not without its resources, and secular postmodern intellectuals take issue with much of the modern worldview. It is to these responses to modernity that I now turn.

Liberal Religious Responses to Modernity

During the early heady days of the Enlightenment there was a good deal of optimism that modern science could underwrite "natural theology" and a religion of reason. Scientists saw design in the intricate workings of nature revealed by modern physics, and philosophers claimed to discern universal moral laws on which all reasonable people would agree. The resulting God of Deism was the "clockmaker" God, the First Cause who designed and created the universe, established moral law, and then withdrew, knowing that humankind would eventually be able to rule itself by natural reason. Deism was, for a while, a powerful movement among intellectuals (including the American Founding Fathers), but it never converted the common folk. It did not have the emotional appeal or the ballast of tradition to give it cultural weight; Deism lacked "the personal touch." [101] More important, as the eighteenth century wore on, it became increasingly clear that modern science was problematic for religion, not supportive.

In 1799, Friedrich Schleiermacher—the most important Christian theologian since Calvin—published a powerful book, *On Religion: Speeches to Its Cultured Despisers.* It is important both for what it says about religion and for what it says about the people to whom it is addressed. I start with the latter claim. Schleiermacher wrote: "Now especially the life of cultivated people is far from anything that might have even a resemblance to religion. . . . Suavity and sociability, art and science have so fully taken possession of your minds, that no room remains for the eternal and holy Being that lies beyond the world. I know how well you have succeeded in making your earthly life so rich and varied, that you no longer stand in need of an eternity. Having made a universe for yourselves, you are above the need of thinking of the Universe that made you." [102] Schleiermacher's book marks a cultural watershed: by the end of the eighteenth century a religious worldview could no longer be assumed among the cultured—at least in Europe; indeed, they were apt to be, as he put it, "despisers" of religion. Schleiermacher's purpose, in Rudolf Otto's words, was "to lead an age weary with and alien to religion back to its very mainsprings; and to reweave religion, threatened with oblivion, into the incomparably rich fabric of the burgeoning intellectual life of modern times." [103]

There were, Schleiermacher acknowledged, good reasons for modern folk to reject *traditional* religion; but *true* religion could be defended. And what is true religion? It is the "immediate consciousness" of the eternal in the temporal; it is "a revelation of the Infinite in the finite, God being seen in it and it in God." [104] That is, Schleiermacher grounded religion not in Scripture or tradition or authority or natural reason but in feeling, in immediate experience. Schleiermacher's God is not unlike William Wordsworth's

. . . presence that disturbs me with the joy
Of elevated thoughts; a sense sublime
Of something far more deeply interfused . . .

A motion and a spirit, that impels
All thinking things, all objects of all thought,
And rolls through all things."[105]

Like his fellow romantics, Schleiermacher emphasized God's immanence rather than His transcendence. God is not what the Deists would have Him be: a creator-God, the intellectual conclusion of an argument based on evidence of design in the world. Such "cold argufying," as Schleiermacher called it, misses the whole point of religion.[106] God is an immediate presence in nature and in our lives. Nor are we to understand God as the anthropomorphized being of traditional religion whom we have created, modeled on ourselves: "The usual conception of God as some single being outside of the world and behind the world is not the beginning and the end of religion. It is only one manner of expressing God, seldom entirely pure, and always inadequate."[107] The true nature of God, Schleiermacher held, is to be found in "neither this idea nor any other." Religions provide only inadequate human ways of giving shape to the ineffable God of experience. To believe on the basis of doctrine is no more than accepting "what another has said," and such faith is no more than "an echo" proving "that a man is incapable of [true] religion."[108]

James Livingston has called this a "Copernican Revolution" in theology.[109] Schleiermacher's historical significance is, Livingston suggests, that he "reversed the traditional method of proceeding theologically."[110] Religion does not acquire its authority from Scripture or doctrine or tradition. Rather, they acquire their authority from our religious experience. Schleiermacher freed religion from the authority of the past, leaving us free to reconstruct religion symbolically based on *our* developing experience of God.

Two of Schleiermacher's (almost equally) influential contemporaries deserve more space than I can give them here. In his *Critique of Pure Reason*, Immanuel Kant sought to show the incoherence of philosophical arguments for the existence of God, but his broader strategy was to save religion from science and philosophy by locating it in another realm of experience; he held that it is through our efforts to make sense of a moral world order that we are led to God. Indeed, for Kant and for many liberals who have followed him, religion is primarily a matter of morality.

The third member of our liberal trinity, Georg W. F. Hegel, argued that reality must be understood historically. The idea of timeless truths, whether scientific or theological, is problematic, for reality is not static but is always in process, evolving. All ideas of God have been historically conditioned and reveal as much about their time and place as they do about reality.

Indeed, by the middle of the century, biblical scholars were using their knowledge of history, languages, and philology to read Scripture historically as any ancient text might be read. The Pentateuch, they argued, was not the work of Moses but of an editor drawing on at least four quite different sources, and far from revealing the historical Jesus, the Gospels screened him from our view by presenting the conflicting accounts of his life found in different faith communities. Historical criticism was perhaps the most important development in nineteenth-century religion for, as John Dillenberger and Claude Welch have suggested, it was now "all up with the dogma of the inerrancy of Scripture."[111]

For liberals, scripture is not the timeless, propositional revelation of God but a record of the historically developing, culture-bound experiences of fallible people, inspired though they may be. God did not speak to the Biblical authors in language, in propositions; rather, revelation is to be understood nonpropositionally, as religious experience clothed in the mythological garb made available by traditional communities. But that garb is symbolic; it is not to be taken literally. We must, in Paul Tillich's terms, "break the myth" and recognize it for what it is: language that points us toward religious truth but never captures it fully. This being the case, there is a sense in which revelation can be progressive. There is no sharp distinction to be drawn between the experiences of biblical writers and peoples in later times and other cultures. The truth was not just "given"; it is progressively discerned through critical reflection on our own experiences.

Liberal theologians were convinced by modern science and historical scholarship that the Bible is largely mythological. The biblical authors worked within worldviews that are false if taken literally. For example, the biblical three-story universe—the earth with Heaven above and Hell beneath—is, as the great German theologian Rudolf Bultmann claimed, "incredible" to men and women in the light of modern science.[112] We cannot, he wrote, "use electric light and radio, call upon modern medicine in case of illness, and at the same time believe in the world of spirits and miracles of the New Testament."[113] Nonetheless, Bultmann held that there is a truth to be had in Scripture, but we must demythologize Scripture to find it. Liberals want to distinguish a (literally false) mythological husk, known to be false in terms of modern, critical thought, from the religious truth buried in it.

The idea of God as a supernatural person who spoke in Hebrew or Greek is part of the mythological baggage which must be seen for what it is. Of course, we understand God not just as a person but as a particular kind of person: as a warrior, as a king, as a judge, as a shepherd, as a father.

Perhaps most significant, God has almost always been understood to be a "He." Liberals are wary of such imagery; many take it to be morally problematic. So, for example, the Catholic theologian Rosemary Radford Ruether writes that theologically speaking, "whatever diminishes or denies the full humanity of women must be presumed not to reflect the divine."[114] For Ruether, as for Schleiermacher, traditional theology makes our inherited symbols dictate what we experience, but if our reflection must and should be shaped by Scripture, we must reinterpret those symbols in terms of our ongoing moral and religious experience. Just as we now reject biblical texts that sanction slavery in light of the moral progress of the last two centuries, so must we reject male images of God, even though they are biblical.[115] Liberal theology does not depend for its vindication on biblical texts, for it is open to revelatory experience that is postbiblical. Indeed, Ruether argues that we may be engaged in idolatry if we take images we have inherited of God as literally true: "When the word *Father* is taken literally to mean that God is male and not female, represented by males and not females, then this word becomes idolatrous."[116]

Liberals accuse conservatives of committing the sin of idolatry—of confusing the symbols and myths we use to point to God *with* God. As Bishop John A. T. Robinson put it, conservatives have simply substituted mental for metal idols.[117] There is no factual or literal language in which God can be captured. Tillich would prefer to use images of depth (God as the ground of our being) rather than height (God's in His heaven) to point to God—and this tells us something important about a common liberal way of understanding God. God is not a transcendent or supernatural person but is *immanent* in the working of the world. Liberals are not so likely to see God in miracles performed by a supernatural being as in the love that permeates reality.

For a liberal, then, there is always a back-and-forth movement between inherited historical revelation and contemporary moral and religious experience. Scripture is always the starting point; it *is* revelatory. But it is never the ending point; it is never to be accepted uncritically. It must be reinterpreted and sometimes reformed in accord with the developing insights of critical scholarship and the experiences of the Christian and perhaps even other religious communities.

Historically, of course, Christianity insisted that it possessed the *exclusive* truth, that salvation came only through orthodoxy, but liberals are not likely to believe in a God who gave the truth to one people or one tradition only and then damned those who did not hear the truth. We do not honor God, John Bennett once said, "by insisting upon . . . the 'parsimony' of his revealing or re-

demptive activity, assuming that God cannot be known apart from one chan-
nel of revelation."[118] Liberalism is open to the possibility of religious truth in
other religious traditions.

Religious liberals, like political liberals, are, relatively speaking, optimists.
They place a fair amount of confidence in human reason to sort out good and
evil, truth and falsehood; hence their openness to traditions other than their
own. Hence, also, the value they place on liberty and liberal social institutions;
in this too, they have kept in harmony with the spirit of the age. They have
nurtured religious individualism, holding that people should be free to pursue
God as their own lights lead them; they have supported the separation of
church and state.

At the same time, liberals have aimed to transform society—in part, at
least, because (like Kant) they take morality to be the heart of religion rather
than the mythological framework conservatives believe to be essential. Too
often, liberals argue, the conservative response to injustice has been an appeal for personal salvation and a turn of the head. Shailer Mathews once proclaimed: "The world needs new control of nature and society and is told that
the Bible is verbally inerrant. It needs a means of composing class strife, and
is told to believe in the substitutionary atonement. It needs a spirit of love and
justice and is told that love without orthodoxy will not save from hell. . . . It
needs faith in the divine presence in human affairs and is told it must accept
the virgin birth of Jesus Christ."[119] We have seen that liberals have not understood God in supernaturalistic, otherworldly ways; instead, they see God
at work in this world, in the actions of men and women, transforming it
through love and the search for justice. It is in large part through political and
economic activism that oppression is ended, salvation becomes possible,
and—to use mythological terms—the Kingdom of God is realized. The Kingdom is not a supernatural creation of a transcendent God; it is, as Walter
Rauschenbusch put it, "the energy of God realizing itself in human life."[120]
Rauschenbusch and most of the early liberals were ardent advocates of the
Social Gospel; today, the dominant moral expression of liberal Christianity is
often called "liberationism"—ending the oppression of the poor, of minorities,
of women.[121]

By its very nature there can be no single liberal tradition, only variations on
liberal themes, but I suggest two broad generalizations.

First, liberals are open to the insights of modern science and other religious traditions; they are committed to modern critical scholarship and a

progressive understanding of the religious dimension of reality. The modern
situation does not allow us to grant automatic validity to any reading of Scripture or any traditional image of God. As Dillenberger and Welch put it, the
central characteristic of liberalism is its "spirit of openmindedness, of tolerance and humility, of devotion to truth wherever it might be found."[122] Liberals have been willing to revise their traditions where they no longer capture
or enlighten our experience of the world.

Second, William Hutchison has suggested that the effort to break down the
distinction between the "religious" and the "secular" is the most important
claim of religious liberalism.[123] Liberalism is very much a religion of *this*
world. Liberals are inclined to emphasize God's immanence; salvation is more
a matter of love and justice in this world than immortality in the world to
come. Our task is to liberate the oppressed and build the Kingdom of God in
this life. Religion is less a matter of private faith than of public action.

Liberals have adopted much of the modern agenda: they are committed to
democracy and liberal social institutions, science and critical scholarship. It is
also true that most liberals find that secular modernity provides us with an inadequate map of reality at best. Conservatives often paint liberals as thinly
disguised secularists (and some no doubt are), but most liberals would describe themselves as committed to a worldview with God—albeit a demythologized God—very much at its center.

Protestant theologians were the first, among the world's religious thinkers,
to take on the challenge of modernity. Why? Protestantism was the religion
of the most highly modernized countries of the world in the nineteenth century. Indeed, I have suggested that Protestants helped spawn modernity by
their emphasis on individualism and liberty of conscience—characteristics
of considerable value in developing heterodox theologies. Also, there was no
Protestant Pope to keep the troops in line. Therefore, for more than a hundred years, liberalism has dominated mainline Protestant theology in Europe
and America.[124]

Much like liberal Protestantism, Reform Judaism began in Germany in the
early nineteenth century, shaped by the Enlightenment and romanticism.
Abraham Geiger, the most influential of the early Reform rabbis, argued that
Judaism was a historically developing religion; he believed in progressive revelation, in the creative adaptation of Jewish law to changing historical circumstances through the insights of scientists and poets and philosophers. The
essence of Judaism, he argued, was its growing insight into God understood as

moral will. In 1885, American Reform rabbis adopted the "Pittsburgh Platform" asserting that Judaism is "a progressive religion, ever striving to be in accord with the postulates of reason." As such, it would choose from the Mosaic Law as binding only such moral laws and ceremonies "as elevate and sanctify our lives, but reject all such as are not adapted to the views and habits of modern civilization." The platform acknowledged "in every religion an attempt to grasp the Infinite One" and extended "the hand of fellowship to all who cooperate with us in the establishment of the reign of truth and righteousness." It committed Reform Judaism to a special obligation to regulate "the relation between rich and poor" and promote justice and end the "evils of the present organization of society."[125] In the last several decades Reform Jews have continued to demonstrate a commitment to modern ideas and ideals in ordaining women rabbis, in welcoming gay congregations, in openness to mixed marriages, and, perhaps most important, in emphasizing the importance of personal choice and downplaying tradition and biology in determining what it means to be a Jew.[126]

Catholicism, by contrast, was much slower to warm to modernity. The Council of Trent, which sat intermittently from 1545 to 1563, clarified, occasionally modified, but largely reaffirmed traditional Catholicism in response to the challenge of the Protestant Reformation, and that reaffirmation largely defined Catholicism until the Second Vatican Council.[127] But in his opening speech to that council in 1962, Pope John XXIII criticized those who "see nothing but ruin and calamity" in the modern world and behave as though history "has nothing to teach them." On the contrary, he asserted, "Divine Providence is leading us towards a new order in human relationships which . . . are tending towards the fulfillment of higher and, as yet, mysterious and unforeseen designs."[128] The church must be open to change. In addition to various liturgical and ecclesiastical reforms, the council endorsed religious freedom, the principle that God speaks through religions other than Christianity, ecumenism, and a progressive understanding of revelation. Catholicism moved into the modern world with a sudden lurch. The Catholic historian Jay Dolan has written that "for the first time Catholic church leaders came to grips with the issues of modernity in a constructive manner. . . . The classicist or neo-Scholastic worldview, which focused on the static, unchanging nature of theology, was giving way to the modern, historical perspective, which emphasized development in theology."[129] The church now embraces a broad spectrum of views among its theologians—although Pope John Paul II has recently reasserted the authority of the church over its most wayward liberal theologians.[130]

Conservative Religious Responses to Modernity

As liberals began to modify theology to accommodate modern science, historical criticism, and liberal social values, more traditional Protestant theologians reacted by initiating heresy trials, establishing new seminaries, and for-
mulating a tighter account of what they took Christian orthodoxy to be. By
the end of the nineteenth century almost every American Protestant denomination was experiencing warfare between its conservatives and liberals.

The strongest reaction came from Protestant fundamentalism—so named
because of a series of booklets called *The Fundamentals* published between
1910 and 1915. (Lists differ, but it is often claimed there are five fundamentals: the inerrancy of Scripture; the deity of Christ; the virgin birth; the aton-
ing death of Christ; and His bodily return to this world.) Fundamentalist fire
was directed at liberal Christianity as much as at secularism, for by adopting
historical criticism it had turned traitor.[131] Indeed, fundamentalism was more
than a reassertion of traditional American Protestantism; it was a lurch to the
theological Right in reaction to liberalism. As the battle lines hardened, fundamentalism turned anti-intellectual, and with the much publicized debacle
over evolution in the Scopes Trial in 1925 it was largely discredited in the
wider culture. American civilization was on the move; the mainline Protestant
denominations were moving steadily to the Left.

Following World War II there was a resurgence of conservative religion,
spearheaded by Billy Graham's crusades, but the new "evangelicals" were distinguishable in some respects from the old fundamentalists. According to the
evangelical theologian Carl Henry, evangelicals were wary of the fundamentalists' "suspicion of advanced education, disdain for biblical criticism per se,
polemical orientation of theological discussion, judgmental attitudes toward
those in ecumenically related denominations, and uncritical political conservatism."[132] Evangelicals and fundamentalists shared, however, a fundamental
commitment to the authority of Scripture.

Conservative Protestants take the Bible to be true in a nonmythological
sense; indeed, they typically take it to be inerrant. As the "Chicago Statement
on Biblical Inerrancy" puts it: "Holy Scripture, being God's own Word, written by men prepared and superintended by His Spirit, is of infallible divine
authority in all matters upon which it touches. . . . Being wholly and verbally
God-given, Scripture is without error or fault in all its teaching."[133] Revelation is *propositional*. Francis Schaeffer understands the Bible to be "God's
communication of propositional truth . . . not some kind of contentless, existential experience."[134] For J. I. Packer, "the biblical position is that the mighty
acts of God are not revelation to man at all, except in so far as they are accom-

panied by words of God to explain them. Leave man to guess God's mind and purpose, and he will guess wrong; he can know it only by being told it." [135] Who would have guessed God's purpose in the death and resurrection of Christ had He not told us? And it is the final truth: revelation is not progressive but was given fully in biblical times.

For Protestant conservatives, the great problem is that of authority, and Scripture provides the bedrock. The liberals' commitment to reasoned reflection on Scripture and religious experience seems hopelessly subjective to them, for there is no agreement to be had. With Luther they respond: *sola scriptura*, back to the Bible. Conservatives reject the Enlightenment emphasis on the goodness and rationality of humankind. Instead, they emphasize the sinfulness of humankind and the impotence of critical reason. No doubt many conservatives believe in "general revelation" or "common grace," which God has given to all persons: whatever our religious traditions we can know *something* of the truth on our own. But they are likely to believe that we are so limited in what we can know that without the "special revelation" of the Christian Bible we cannot know what we must do to be saved. Of course, not all conservatives read the Bible the same way, but ultimately recourse is to inspiration, not to critical reason and modern historical scholarship: as Packer puts it: "God's book does not yield up its secrets to those who will not be taught of the Spirit." [136]

For conservative Christians, the Christ event is the central fact of history. Jesus said: "I am the way, the truth and the life. No one comes to the Father except through me." [137] Because salvation is possible only in Christ, there is a powerful obligation on Christians to convert those who are not Christian. The approach of conservative Protestantism to the world religions is one of conversion, not dialogue. [138] Religions other than Christianity represent, as William Demarest puts it, "a perverted response to God's universal general revelation" and "are essentially false." [139]

Because they do not share the liberals' relative optimism about human reason, conservatives have not expected the Kingdom of God to arrive via human action and social change. God, not social activists, will usher in the millennium. Therapy and politics cannot transform human lives. Fundamental change must come first in the heart, as the result of God's grace. In the words of J. Gresham Machen, "Human goodness will avail nothing for lost souls; ye must be born again." [140] Because of their emphasis on human sinfulness, conservatives are skeptical about personal freedom. They see in modern life a falling away from God's law, a chaos that requires more than ever the moral regulation of society. (Ironically, conservatives also tend to be strong supporters of unregulated free enterprise.)

Conservatives are concerned about social ills: their activist opposition to alcohol and abortion, their support of hospitals, orphanages, inner-city missions and schools suggest a powerful social conscience. Still, relative to liberals they are otherworldly. Salvation is a matter of standing in a right relationship to God, not to humankind, and the hope of salvation lies in the afterlife, not in bringing about justice in this world. Their concern is not to transform society but to hold it together in anticipation of Christ's return. What is important for most conservatives is that we are caught up in a cosmic war between God and the forces of evil; the battlefield is creation itself. To those who are aligned with God, victory means eternal life. The triumphs and defeats, the justice and injustice of this life are important, but they are not nearly so momentous as the larger battle in which we are engaged. In that battle, our power is feeble, and salvation becomes possible only in giving ourselves over to God. Conservatives resist the liberal translation of religion into morality.[141]

Conservative religion enjoyed a resurgence in the 1950s and again in the 1970s; indeed, with the help of televangelism, fundamentalism again acquired a measure of cultural influence. Although church membership has held fairly constant over the last several decades, there has been a major ideological shift within that membership as conservative churches (Southern Baptists, Assemblies of God, Seventh-Day Adventists, Church of the Nazarene) have experienced significant increases in membership while the more liberal churches (Methodist, Presbyterian, Lutheran Church of America, Episcopal, Disciples of Christ, United Church of Christ) have lost members steadily.[142]

How do we account for the survival, indeed for the growth of conservative religion? In America, Nathan Hatch has observed, "the principal mediator of God's voice has not been state, church, council, confession, ethnic group, university, college, or seminary; it has been, quite simply, the people."[143] Religion acquired its authority by appealing to the "common sense" of ordinary folk, not the wisdom and scholarship of intellectuals. In Protestant Europe, by contrast, religious elites acquired their authority from the intellectual and cultural establishments and hence came to reflect much more than in America the developing intellectual ethos of modernity so that liberalism became the norm. Historically, American evangelicals and fundamentalists educated their ministers and followers in Bible colleges and denominational seminaries, not in major universities. Until very recently, Hatch suggests, they have "sustained the conviction that religious knowledge is not an arcane science to be mediated by an educated elite."[144] They have survived because the pluralism of American society has allowed them to carve their own religious niches out of the dominant secular culture and because they have evaded the liberalizing and secularizing influences of secular education.[145]

It is also true that conservative religion provides something wanting in modern culture. According to Carl Henry, the strength of evangelical religion stems from "its offer of religious realities that human unregeneracy desperately needs and cannot otherwise provide. In a time of spiritual rootlessness Christianity proclaims God the self-revealed heavenly Redeemer. In a time of intellectual skepticism, it adduces fixed truths about God's holy purpose for man and the world. In a time of ethical permissiveness, it offers moral absolutes and specific divine imperatives. In a time of frightful fear of the future, it presents a sure and final hope."[146] All is not well in the modern world, and conservative religion offers a solution other than therapy and government programs. There are fixed truths and moral absolutes; we have assurance of a better world to come.

Correlatively, it has often been argued, it is because of its willingness to accommodate modernity that liberal religion is faltering. The success of conservative churches must be seen, Leonard Sweet argues, against the "backdrop of a dispirited and ailing conventional Protestantism that had little to declare theologically."[147] Liberalism capitulated to secular ideas and values that in the end rob religion of its meaning. (Sweet calls it "Burger King" theology: have it your way.) As a result, evangelical religion "came to function as a primary carrier of affirmations for an American culture otherwise in disarray."[148] In many ways President Ronald Reagan's victories marked a parallel political affirmation of American values over a political liberalism in disarray.

But it may also be true, as James Davison Hunter has recently argued, that in subtle but significant ways conservative religion has begun to accommodate itself to modernity. Its list of sins has become shorter (as dancing, smoking, and drinking have become more acceptable), and it now allows "a widening diversity of life-style behaviors."[149] The powerful value of tolerance in modern culture has led evangelicals to downplay absolutism, Hell, and heresy. Modern science and scholarship make belief in the inerrancy of Scripture increasingly difficult. Hunter claims that 40 percent of evangelical theologians have abandoned belief in the inerrancy of Scripture and 48 percent of them have made their peace with evolution.[150] It would be superficial to say, Hunter suggests, "that Evangelical theology . . . is becoming more liberal. Yet the evidence is suggestive of a common trend, one in which the theological tradition is conforming in its own unique way to the cognitive and normative assumptions of modern culture."[151] At least some conservative theology is running the gauntlet of modernity.

In some ways, "conservative" is not the most apt term for the theology I have described. Martin Marty has noted, for example, that fundamentalism "did not 'conserve' much of what Roman Catholic, Eastern Orthodox, and mainline Protestant churches—which must make up nine-tenths of Christendom—would have regarded as the tradition worth preserving."[152] In making the Bible the measure of everything, conservative Protestants dispensed with the theological traditions that have developed since biblical times, and in asserting the inerrancy of Scripture and the importance of a literal reading of it, they have departed from what was, for most of Christian history, a somewhat more liberal orthodoxy that accepted a variety of ways of reading the Bible. Indeed, the great historian of Christian doctrine, Jaroslav Pelikan, claims that none of the five "fundamentals" were a part of traditional Christian orthodoxy.[153]

There is, in this respect, a significant difference between the conservatism of Catholicism and that of Protestant fundamentalism and evangelicalism. In a 1993 report, the Pontifical Biblical Commission asserted that "fundamentalism actually invites people to a kind of intellectual suicide. It injects into life a false certitude, for it unwittingly confuses the divine substance of the biblical message with what are in fact its human limitations."[154] While Protestant conservatives hold fast to *sola scriptura*—Scripture only—Catholics accept as authoritative *tradition* as shaped by the Church. As Pelikan puts it, for Catholics the "authority of Scripture is not the authority of a naked book, but the authority of a book in the process of being interpreted. Tradition is that by which Scripture is continually being interpreted."[155] The Profession of Faith issued by the Council of Trent in the sixteenth century affirmed "Holy Scripture according to that sense which our holy Mother Church has held and does hold, whose [office] it is to judge of the true meaning and interpretation of the Sacred Scriptures."[156] If the truth was given in Scripture, it was not given clearly or totally; it is for the church to interpret Scripture and develop religious doctrine. In his 1993 encyclical, *Veritatis Splendor*, Pope John Paul II reaffirmed for our time that "within Tradition, the authentic interpretation of the Lord's law develops, with the help of the Holy spirit." His conservatism is evident, however, when he adds that tradition "can only confirm the permanent validity of revelation."[157]

If Catholicism was open, in principle, to a developing theological tradition, the church turned its face unambiguously against the ideas that shaped Protestant liberalism in the nineteenth century. In 1864, Pope Pius IX condemned the forces of modernity in his *Syllabus of Errors*, denying that the pontiff should "reconcile himself, and come to terms with progress, liberalism and modern civilization." He also rejected the idea that "Divine revelation is imperfect, and therefore subject to a continual and indefinite progress, corresponding with the advancement of human reason."[158] His successor, Leo XIII, was a moderate by comparison; nevertheless, he reasserted the importance of St. Thomas and medieval scholastic theology and stated that the conclusions of modern thought were not to be allowed to challenge the faith.[159] And in his first encyclical, Leo's successor, Pius X, promised to "safeguard our clergy from being caught up in the snares of modern scientific thought—a science which does not breathe the truths of Christ, but by its cunning and subtle arguments defiles the mind of the people with the errors of Rationalism and semi-Rationalism"; in 1907 he required all Catholic bishops, priests, and teachers to take an antimodernist oath.[160] The result was what Catholic scholar John A. Coleman has called a "veritable reign of terror against the world of scholarship."[161]

For about a hundred years now there has been something of a Catholic equivalent to Protestant fundamentalism. Like their Protestant counterparts, Catholic "integralists" and "traditionalists" have rejected modernity and liberal theology in favor of a premodern, ahistorical orthodoxy. Unlike Protestant fundamentalists, they do not find certainty in inerrant Scripture (read literally) but in the pronouncements of the pope and the church (particularly as formulated by St. Thomas and in the Council of Trent). Like the Bible for Protestants, the pope and the church are viewed, as Coleman puts it, "as above history, free from every hermeneutic of suspicion," and "uncritical acceptance of this authority . . . becomes the litmus test of orthodoxy."[162]

Catholic conservatives and traditionalists have strongly opposed the separation of church and state, resisted the development of democratic institutions, been wary of capitalism, and, much more than Protestant conservatives, rejected modern individualism in an attempt to sustain the remnants of medieval corporate culture. If the theological liberalism of Vatican II contributed to a traditionalist reaction within the church, it also ensured that this reaction would be a minority position.

The conservatism of traditional Judaism resembles Catholicism much more than Protestant fundamentalism for, as Leon Wieseltier puts it, Judaism is "based on the authority of *commentary*."[163] Judaism exhibits "no hostility whatsoever to the idea or the reality of development. . . . Indeed, the Jewish commitment to development is so great that Rabbinic Judaism actually came to fear a restoration in the end of days, because it seemed to abrogate and make obsolete much of the massive corpus of philosophy and law that was sustaining Jewish thought through the centuries."[164] And yet, as for traditional Catholicism, the importance of developing commentary and tradition must not obscure the fact that for traditional Jews, the truth (the Law) had been given in the past. The object of Rabbinic learning, as Joseph Blau put it, is "the maintenance of the old, the traditional, the time-hallowed."[165]

In discussing the "conservative" Jewish response to modernity we have to be careful, for in America "Conservative" Judaism (with a capital "C") is more or less a denomination of Judaism, a middle way between liberal Reform Judaism and the varieties of Orthodox Judaism.[166] The Orthodox provide the clearest parallel with conservative Christianity.

Just as liberal Christianity spawned a fundamentalist reaction, so nineteenth-century Reform Judaism was quickly confronted by an orthodox or "neo-orthodox," response first in Germany, then in the United States. Neo-orthodox Judaism was not just the reassertion of traditional Judaism, however. Like Reform, it was a product of Jewish emancipation; neo-orthodoxy accepted secular learning and the participation of Jews in secular life, thereby acknowledging a more limited role for Judaism as a religion, rather than a complete way of life. But, as Jacob Neusner puts it, while "the Reformers held that Judaism could change and was a product of history, their Orthodox opponents denied that Judaism could change and insisted that it derived from God's will at Sinai and was eternal and supernatural, not historical and man-made."[167] It asserted the authority of the "dual Torah" (the biblical Torah plus the rabbinic commentary) as supernatural revelation, reaffirming the traditional God of Judaism.

But by accepting the role of Jews in modern, secular life neo-orthodoxy compromised itself irretrievably for those traditional Jews from cultures in eastern Europe largely untouched by the Enlightenment and emancipation—many of whom came to America in the two decades following World War II.[168] For the "ultra-orthodox," as Jack Wertheimer puts it, "any compromise with modern culture is to be rejected as un-Jewish and inferior."[169] Hence they segregate themselves as much as possible from the corrosive effects of Western civilization, rejecting modern dress, secular education, and participation in the larger culture. They place great emphasis on religious schooling; more than 80 percent of Orthodox children are educated in Jewish day schools. In effect, as Alan Unterman puts it, "they prefer to live within a self-imposed cultural ghetto."[170] Indeed, they are highly critical of the great majority of American Jews—to the point of launching missions to convert them back to true Judaism.

In 1990, 38 percent of American Jews identified themselves with Reform, 35 percent with Conservative, and 6 percent with Orthodox Judaism, though of Jews who join a synagogue, 43 percent join Conservative, 35 percent join Reform, and 16 percent join Orthodox synagogues.[171] It would appear that the more liberal one is, the less likely he or she is to take (institutional) religion seriously.

Probably the great majority of Americans hold to some amalgam, some moderating mix of liberal and conservative ideas, such that most American churches and synagogues fall somewhere nearer the theological center than either end of my liberal-conservative spectrum. In 1989, 33 percent of Americans identified their religion as fundamentalist, 41 percent as moderate, and 26 percent as liberal.[172] If respondents are given the choice between calling themselves liberals or conservatives (and "moderate" is not one of the choices), the percentages change: according to a 1984 study, 43 percent of Americans called themselves religious liberals (and 19 percent called themselves "very liberal") while 41 percent called themselves religious conservatives (and 18 percent "very conservative"). Sixteen percent claimed neither label.[173] In 1991, on the key question of scriptural inerrancy, 32 percent of Americans agreed that "the Bible is the actual word of God and is to be taken literally, word for word," while 49 percent agreed with the somewhat more liberal position that "the Bible is the inspired word of God but not everything in it should be taken literally, word for word." Sixteen percent held that "the Bible is an ancient book of fables, legends, history, and moral perceptions recorded by men," and 3 percent had no opinion.[174]

I have already noted that of Americans who believe in God, almost two-thirds (65 percent) translate this to mean that there is a personal God, while only 26 percent hold the more liberal position that there is "some sort of spirit or life force" (though this is hardly an inspiring description of the God of liberals).[175] But other polls suggest that we are more liberal than conservative. For example, 75 percent of Americans in 1985 held to the liberal position that faith "is strengthened by questioning early beliefs" (only 19 percent disagreed); 65 percent said a person's faith "should change throughout life just as one's body and mind change"; and 62 percent agreed that "God reveals himself through a variety of religious beliefs and traditions" (only 22 percent disagreed). A striking 81 percent of Americans agreed that "an individual should arrive at his or her own religious beliefs independent of any churches or synagogues," and some 78 percent believed that one can be a good Christian or Jew without attending church or synagogue.[176]

Europeans are decidedly more liberal than Americans. On one count, only about 10 percent of western Europeans could be called evangelical or conservative Christians.[177] In England the number is closer to 2 percent.[178] In the

Scandinavian countries and West Germany about 25 percent hold to a traditional notion of a personal God, while about 40 percent take a more liberal
view ("There is some sort of spirit or life force") and 35 percent claim some
form of agnosticism or skepticism.[179] About 40 percent of the people in these
countries believe in an afterlife; only 10 percent believe in the existence
of Hell.[180]

James Davison Hunter has argued that as recently as three decades ago,
American Catholics, Protestants, and Jews "retained a very clear theological
and ideological distinctiveness."[181] This distinctiveness has virtually disappeared. What has become increasingly important is one's inclination toward
what Hunter calls orthodoxy or progressivism—what I have called conservatism or liberalism. According to Hunter, "Progressive circles within Protestantism, Catholicism, and Judaism, on the one hand, express virtually identi-
cal ideological concerns and programmatic interests. So too the orthodox
within each of these traditions also display virtually indistinguishable anxi-
eties and agendas."[182] For example, the orthodox within each religion and
denomination are opposed to abortion, gay rights, feminism, and euthanasia
and are pro-choice on education, while progressives are pro-choice on abortion and for gay rights, women's rights, the right to euthanasia, and public
education. At least among the leadership, progressives are considerably more
supportive of welfare and foreign aid, and more critical of capitalism, than the
orthodox. In the last several decades hundreds of special interest groups have
been created, cutting across denominations, uniting progressives on the one
hand and the orthodox on the other.
    What accounts for these basic differences, according to Hunter, is our
conflicting views of authority. Upon what do we ground our knowledge of the
world, our understanding of truth, and our conception of moral and ethical behavior? The orthodox, according to Hunter, ground their moral judgments in
the "commitment to transcendence," in a supernatural God who has revealed
the truth, propositionally, in the past, providing us with "an authority that is
universally valid."[183] Protestants, Catholics, and Jews read this authority in
somewhat different ways, but they agree that such authority exists. Progressive Protestants, Catholics, and Jews hold that "moral and spiritual truth is
not a static and unchanging collection of scriptural facts and theological
propositions but a growing and incremental reality.... There is, therefore, no
objective and final revelation directly from God, and Scripture (of whatever
form) is not revelation but only, and at best, a *witness* to revelation."[184]

What is striking is the extent to which religious liberals/progressives are aligned with secular liberals against religious conservatives/orthodox with whom they share a belief in God. In some things, at least, our moral stance is less determined by our belief in God than our acceptance (or rejection) of modernity. Pollsters and social scientists have looked for correlations between one's religious and denominational affiliation and political and cultural beliefs, failed to find any, and concluded that religion plays little role in shaping people's actions.[185] Hunter claims that they have missed the determining factor in religion and morality: one's identification with orthodox or progressive, conservative or liberal, views of religious authority. It is here, in the confrontation of tradition and modernity, that the shape of our culture wars is determined.[186]

Postmodern Responses to Modernity

Many secular intellectuals now hold that modernity has spent itself and that we live in an increasingly *postmodern* world. What this means is anything but clear, however. "Modernism" and "Postmodernism" are notoriously ambiguous terms whose meanings vary in different disciplines and in different cultures. Much of what is called postmodernism is a reaction to modernism as a movement (or set of overlapping movements) in twentieth-century architecture, art, and literature. This is not my concern; I am interested instead in postmodernism as a response to modernity, to the governing ideas and institutions of the modern period of Western history.

The origins of postmodernism can be dated back to the seminal ideas of Nietzsche at the end of the nineteenth century, or to turn-of-the-century American pragmatism, or to the horrors of World War I and the Holocaust, or to the philosophy of the later Ludwig Wittgenstein, or to the countercultural 1960s, or to the ideas of Jacques Derrida, Michel Foucault, and Jean-François Lyotard and French intellectuals in the 1960s and 1970s. Wherever we begin, however, postmodernism swims, in David Harvey's words, "in the fragmentary and chaotic currents of change as if that is all there is." Like Nietzsche, it "emphasizes the deep chaos of modern life and its intractability before rational thought."[187] The quest for coherence is quixotic at best and repressive, even terroristic, at worst.

In *The Postmodern Condition*, Jean-François Lyotard defined postmodernism as an "incredulity toward metanarratives"—toward overarching accounts of reality. Postmodernism "refines our sensitivity to differences and reinforces our ability to tolerate the incommensurable."[188] Richard Rorty argues that "it is impossible to step outside our skins—the traditions, linguistic and other, within which we do our thinking and self-criticism—and compare ourselves with something absolute."[189] We never encounter reality directly but approach it only through conventions of our own making.[190] For Stanley Fish, the key is the "interpretive turn" to language; indeed, "in recent years language has been promoted to a constitutive role and declared by theorists of various stripes . . . to bring facts into being rather than simply report on them."[191] All knowledge is "local knowledge" rooted in interpretive communities, and all "norms and standards are specific, contingent, historically produced, and potentially revisable."[192] There are no foundations; as Fish puts it, "it is difference all the way down."[193] Finally, for Michel Foucault, "Truth isn't outside power. . . . Truth is a thing of this world: it is produced only by virtue of multiple forms of constraint. And it induces regular effects of power. Each society has its regime of truth, its 'general politics' of truth."[194] Objectivity is a myth; truth-claims are, in the end, mere assertions of interest-group politics.

For postmodernism, the scientific metanarrative must be "deconstructed." According to Terry Eagleton, "Science and philosophy must jettison their grandiose metaphysical claims and view themselves more modestly as *just another* set of narratives."[195] As Richard Tarnas puts it, postmodernism sees individuals who subscribe to the scientific worldview of modernity as having "failed to engage the larger intellectual challenge of the age—thereby receiving the same judgment in the postmodern era that the ingenuous religious person received from science in the modern era."[196] Times have changed; the old foundations have crumbled.

Postmodernists are also suspicious of the autonomous, "rational" individual. We are the products of our gender, the languages we speak, the cultures we are part of, the history we inherit; we are shaped by social class and by the workings of our unconscious minds. There is no escaping our contexts, our subjectivity. Postmodernism has Marx, Freud, and above all Nietzsche, as its intellectual heroes. It sees its task as deconstructing "great" literature, demythologizing religious and political traditions, exploding appearances, and unmasking power relationships. Its approach is aptly characterized as a "hermeneutics of suspicion," and much of the ire of postmodernist thinkers has been directed at liberal "pieties" which mask the repression of women and minorities, of the poor and the Third World.

Not surprisingly, the idea of progress is problematic. Postmodernists often argue that totalitarianism, the death camps, the nuclear arms race, and the environmental crisis are the logical culmination of modernity—of technology and technical reason. There is, of course, a deeper problem: if there is no coherent account of reality to be had, then there can be no progress toward Truth or the Good.

In our postmodern world, according to David Ray Griffin, the modern worldview is but one among many, "useful for some purposes, inadequate for others." Indeed, modernity is, he suggests, more and more seen as an aberration.[197] Maybe. No doubt there is a good deal of disquiet among intellectuals, though outside the halls of academe postmodernism appears to be a curiosity at most. And as Tarnas notes, "In the absence of any viable, embracing cultural vision, old assumptions remain blunderingly in force."[198] By its very nature, postmodernism can offer no embracing cultural vision. Science and liberalism remain potent forces in our still modern world.[199]

Conclusions

For several hundred years, the driving forces of our civilization—science and technology, economic and political liberalism, pluralism and individualism—have contributed to the secularization of the modern world. No doubt the great majority of Americans continue to believe in God. But the great majority of Americans also lead largely secular lives and think about the world in largely secular terms. An intellectual wall of separation divides religion from our public culture; it is no longer obvious to most of us what difference our religious beliefs and traditions should make. We have privatized our religion as we have secularized our culture.

These are, I have suggested, the trends of the times, not the last word. Religion maintains a striking measure of vitality in America despite everything—though it has become largely reactive before the shaping forces of modernity. We need to recognize two different religious reactions, however: within Christian and Jewish thought of the last two hundred years we find distinctly liberal and conservative tendencies. For liberals theology is a critical discipline that, if it takes as its starting point a particular religious tradition, ventures outside that tradition to explore, and sometimes employ, other ways of understanding the world. Liberal religion is progressive as traditions are rethought and reformed in light of modern critical scholarship and reflection on moral and religious experience. Conservative theology, by contrast, holds that the truth has been given us; hence to open ourselves up to other traditions and critical reflection is to forsake the firm foundation we need for judging truth and falsity. No doubt most conservatives, indeed most fundamentalists, have come to terms with large segments of secular modernity in their everyday lives, but they hold fast to the premodern truths of Scripture and tradition—at least concerning what they take to be the theological essentials.

The situation is made more complicated (and interesting) because many postmodern intellectuals now reject much of the modern worldview from the cultural Left. There is no such thing as truth; all knowledge claims are local and culturally relative. For many secular intellectuals science and liberalism have lost their status as rational arbiters of truth and goodness.

No doubt there is much that can't easily be located on my conceptual map, but I trust these four ways of orienting ourselves in the world—secular modernity, liberal and conservative religion, and postmodernism—will provide us with a measure of perspective on the problems of religion and public education as we proceed.

THE SECULARIZATION OF AMERICAN EDUCATION

If there was an overriding purpose to American colonial education it was to nurture and sustain a Christian civilization, but between the time of the American Revolution and the end of the nineteenth century an educational revolution took place: religion dropped by the wayside as America marched into the modern world. The mantle of high purpose in the schools was passed on to democracy and Americanism, the new faiths of the new nation. At the same time, education became more and more utilitarian, serving whatever purposes individuals might happen to have: in an increasingly commercial society, those purposes were largely vocational; in an increasingly modern society, they were almost invariably secular.

As a result, by the year 1900, forty years before the Supreme Court began to apply the First Amendment to public education, there was little religion left in schools or universities. True, some prayer and Bible reading took place in many public schools, and chapel was required in a few state colleges. Religion continued to inform the ceremony and rhetoric of education. But it was no longer to be found in the heart of education, in the curriculum or in textbooks. The governing purposes of education had changed.

Education in Colonial America

Bernard Bailyn has noted that "seventeenth century records abound with efforts to rescue the children from an incipient savagery."[1] In a frontier society education had to be worked at. As a result, both Massachusetts and Virginia passed laws in the 1640s requiring that children receive some education. Unfortunately, schools were not easily established in the rural and sparsely populated southern states and Virginia's efforts were not notably successful. The towns of New England proved more hospitable. The Puritans placed a powerful emphasis on learning; their church services emphasized not emotion or ritual but reasoned theological discourse. Of the Puritans who immigrated to New England between 1630 and 1646, 130 were graduates of either Cambridge or Oxford, 98 of whom served in the ministry.[2] Until the Revolution, only 5 percent of Congregationalist (Puritan) ministers lacked college degrees.[3]

In 1647 Massachusetts passed the "Old Deluder Satan" Act. Its preamble began: "It being one of the chief projects of that old deluder Satan to keep men from the knowledge of the Scriptures" by way of the "false glosses of saint-seeming deceivers," compulsory education is necessary.[4] That is, learning is necessary to distinguish true from false religion. Towns of fifty families or more were required to appoint schoolmasters to teach children how to read and write and something of religion, and larger towns were ordered to establish grammar schools to prepare children for advanced education so "that learning may not be buried in the graves of our fathers in the church."[5]

John Winthrop had written of Old England: "The fountains of learning and religion are so corrupted" that "most children, even the best wits and of fairest hopes, are perverted."[6] In New England it would be different. So, as Lawrence Cremin put it, "Seeking to execute their special commission from God, the Puritans sought to establish a wilderness Zion, a community of 'visible saints' committed to Christian brotherhood and conduct. And within such a society education would assume utmost importance, not merely as an instrument for systematically transmitting an intellectual heritage, but as an agency for deliberately pursuing a cultural ideal."[7] Variations on this theme might be found from colony to colony, but the general purpose of education would not change. "Almost everywhere, and in almost every case," Will Herberg writes, "the avowed purpose of founding schools was religious: the schools were there to make Christians."[8]

For more than a hundred years, beginning about 1690, the most commonly used schoolbook in the colonies was the *New England Primer*; perhaps 3 million copies were circulated. The *Primer*, according to one scholar, was "in prose as bare of beauty as the whitewash of [Puritan] churches, in poetry as rough and stern as their storm-torn coast."[9] Its great theme was God and our relationship to Him. The *Primer* taught the alphabet as follows:

A wise son makes a glad Father, but a foolish son is the heaviness of his mother.
B etter is little with the fear of the Lord, than great treasure and trouble therewith.
C ome unto CHRIST all ye that labour and are heavy laden, and He will give you rest.

After the alphabet came "The Dutiful Child's Promises" ("I Will fear GOD, and honour the KING"), the Lord's Prayer, the Apostle's Creed, the Ten Commandments, the "Duty of Children Towards Their Parents," and a list of the books of the Bible. A list of numbers is prefaced by the claim that they will "serve for the ready finding of any Chapter, Psalm, and Verse in the Bible." The *Primer* concludes with the Westminster Assembly's Shorter Catechism (which, at forty pages, is not so short): "What is the chief end of Man?" Answer: "Man's chief end is to glorify God, and to enjoy him forever." Question: "What rule hath God given to direct us how we may glorify and enjoy him?" Answer: "The Word of God which is contained in the Scriptures of the Old and New Testament, is the only rule to direct us how we may glorify and enjoy him."[10]

Many New England towns had tax-supported "town schools," but nowhere was there any organized educational system; throughout the colonies formal schooling was typically a mix of private academies and local denominational religious schools. With the Great Awakening in the eighteenth century schooling expanded as the contending denominations used schools more and more for their missionary purposes.

Higher education was similarly dominated by religious purposes. *New England's First Fruits* (1643) states that after "God had carried us safe to New England, and we had built our houses, provided necessities for our livelihood, reared convenient places for God's worship, and settled the civil government: one of the next things we longed for, and looked after was to advance learning and perpetuate it to posterity; dreading to leave an illiterate ministry to the churches, when our present ministers shall lie in the dust.[11] Harvard College opened its doors in 1638, primarily to educate students for the ministry. One of two admission requirements was that "Every one shall consider the main End of his life and studies, to know God and Jesus Christ which is Eternal life."[12] Between 1642 and 1689 about half of the graduates of Harvard entered the ministry.[13] In 1661 the Virginia Assembly declared the "want of able and faithful ministers" as the reason for creating the college of William and Mary.[14] In 1701 Yale became the third American college. Its laws declared: "Every student shall consider the main end of his study to wit to know God in Jesus Christ and answerably to lead a Godly sober life."[15]

By the time of the Revolution there were nine colleges in America. Eight had denominational origins: Harvard, Yale, and Dartmouth were Congregationalist; William and Mary and King's College (later Columbia) were Anglican; the College of New Jersey (later Princeton) was Presbyterian; the College of Rhode Island (later Brown) was Baptist; and Queen's College (later Rutgers) was Dutch Reformed. Only the College of Philadelphia (later the University of Pennsylvania) was nonsectarian. According to Richard Hofstadter, the desire to educate clergy was "the most urgent and immediate reason" for founding seven of the nine colleges, but he adds that "it is equally true and equally important that their curricula were not those of divinity schools but of liberal arts schools."[16]

The Puritans were heirs to the classical tradition of Renaissance Europe. Because many of them were Cambridge men, it should not be surprising that "Harvard's curriculum included all the principal subjects of the arts course at contemporary Cambridge, with the notable exception of music. The traditional trivium—grammar, rhetoric, and logic—stood at the heart of the program, and was supplemented by mathematics and astronomy, the three philosophies (natural, moral, and mental), the ancient languages (Biblical as well as classical), belles-lettres, and divinity."[17] As Frederick Rudolph put it, the curriculum bore the burden of accommodating the "not always compatible urgencies of scholastic philosophers, Renaissance gentlemen, and Westminster Calvinists."[18] But the center of the curriculum, not just at Harvard but at all of the colonial colleges, was ancient languages and the classics. Indeed, Harvard, Yale, and William and Mary all required that applicants demonstrate an ability to read and write Greek and Latin and possess a knowledge of the standard classical authors.[19]

As part of the "Old Deluder Satan" Act, the Puritans had established not just elementary-level "town schools," where students learned reading, writing, arithmetic, and religion, but secondary-level grammar schools to prepare bright students for college. The grammar schools typically provided a seven-year program concentrating on Latin grammar, conversation, and composition, Latin literature, Greek grammar and literature (including the Greek New Testament), and Hebrew grammar.[20] The Bible was, of course, more than just one of the classics, but it existed at least relatively comfortably in a course of study that found wisdom and beauty in the past.

Religion and Nineteenth-Century Schoolbooks

The McGuffey Readers were to nineteenth-century America what the *New England Primer* had been to colonial America. Over 120 million copies were printed, and they stayed in use well into the twentieth century. Henry Steele Commager characterized the message of the Readers as follows:

> God was omnipresent. He had His eye on every child every moment of the day and night, watched its every action, knew its every thought. He was a just God, but a stern one, and would not hesitate to punish even the smallest children who broke His commandments. The world of the McGuffeys was a world where no one questioned the truths of the Bible, or their relevance to everyday conduct, and where the notion that the separation of church and state required the exclusion of religion from the schoolroom or from schoolbooks seemed preposterous. The Readers, therefore, are filled with stories from the Bible, and tributes to its truth and beauty.[21]

In his study of the McGuffey Readers, John Westerhoff suggests that they read more like a theology text than a schoolbook. Life was understood as "God-conscious and God-centered." The natural world could be understood only as the expression of God's order. Every person must live in harmony with God and be a steward of His creation. The Readers directed students to "live for salvation." This world "is not ultimate, for we are children of eternity. While we are born in sin and destined to damnation, God, in Christ, reconciles those who repent to himself and rewards them with eternal life."[22] The index to *The Annotated McGuffey* contains more references to God than any other subject. The second greatest number of references is to death.[23]

Ruth Miller Elson surveyed more than a thousand of the most popular nineteenth-century texts used for the first eight years of schooling, and her study is fascinating for what it reveals about religion. Nature, in these books, cannot be understand apart from God and His purposes. Before the Civil War, schoolbooks accepted without question the biblical account of the world, Adam and Eve included. When evolution appeared in the second half of the century, it was not (purposeless) Darwinian evolution, but was teleological—the working out of God's purposes. "All the works of God are founded in wisdom and intended for some benevolent purpose," a McGuffey Reader tells students. Lessons on nature were lessons in religion. "Throughout the century," Elson writes, "nature is studied to reveal the glory of God by understanding the perfection of his creation." As one geography text puts it, the "study of geography may lead your mind to pious reflections by bringing to your view the power, wisdom, and goodness of God," for when we consider His creatures, "the power which He has displayed in their creation, the wisdom which He has fitted them to their variousness, and the goodness with which He has adapted them to the wants of His living creatures, while we contemplate *them*, we shall learn to adore Him."[24]

Toward the end of the century descriptions of nature devoid of moral or religious meaning started to appear, a more straightforward science began to be taught, and the practical application of scientific knowledge—useful knowledge—was much praised. Creation was pushed farther and farther back in time to accommodate fossils and the "new geography;" still, "evolution is always teleological and God's creation."[25]

Just as God orders nature, so does God guide history. God led Columbus to America, not a matter of inspiration but of miracles. The analogy with the ancient Hebrews was used over and over: God led the first settlers to America as God led Israel out of Egypt to the Promised Land. In some histories and readers, God sent plagues on the Indians to create room for the Pilgrims much as God routed the enemies of Joshua. New England was the New Israel. George Washington was divinely ordained to deliver us. A political catechism asked: "Who was in command in the revolution?—George Washington, Esq., whom God raised up and fitted for these times of travail and made him instrumental of delivering our country from foreign domination." Washington was compared to Moses and Christ. The writing of the Constitution showed "the finger of that Almighty Hand, which has been so frequently and signally extended to our religion in the critical stages of the revolution." The deaths of both John Adams and Thomas Jefferson on the fiftieth anniversary of the Declaration of Independence was another sure sign of divine approval. Abraham Lincoln, like Washington, was divinely appointed to his task: one reader declared that "God raised him up for a great and glorious mission," and a history text recorded: "That such a man as Abraham Lincoln represented the Union, and stood ready to live or die for it, was one of the greatest blessings which God has bestowed upon the nation." Innumerable times, Elson writes, "instances of God's direct interposition in favor of the American people are given to support the idea that Americans are the people chosen by God in the modern world for a special destiny."[26]

Not only did God intervene in the great events of history; God commanded the rewards and punishments that shaped the daily lives of all people. Elson writes that "the schoolbooks bombard the child with the idea, elaborately and richly illustrated, that virtue is rewarded and vice punished in an immediate and material sense. God does not wait for the after-life to distribute rewards and punishments." Often the message was less than subtle: children were warned that plagues would come upon them, or they would be orphaned, if they disobeyed their parents. One speller told the story of a group of children who were teasing another child when "raging bears . . . tore them limb from limb to death, with blood and groans and tears." And how do we know what virtue is? A Webster Speller contained the following catechism:

Q. What is moral virtue?

A. It is an honest upright conduct in all our dealings with men. . . .

Q. What rules have we to direct us?

A. God's word contained in the Bible has furnished all necessary rules to direct our conduct.

Q. In what part of the Bible are these rules to be found?

A. In almost every part; but the most important duties between men are summed up in the beginning of Matthew, in Christ's Sermon on the Mount.[27]

By the second half of the century the virtues most often praised in the texts were the economic virtues of industry and frugality, and the Bible, Calvin, and Benjamin Franklin were all quoted liberally in their support. Affluence and success in life were a sure sign of virtue and divine favor. Religion sanctioned the making of money, and "every book contains many tales of the rewards God bestows on [a virtuous] man." "Riches are the baggage of virtue," according to one Speller. The idle rich, those who inherited their money, conspicuous consumption, and luxury were criticized (though it was usually noted that such wealth was more characteristic of corrupt Europe than America). The self-made man was idolized. Wealth was to be used for charity; it was "a gift of God and should be used for 'God's glory and other men's good.'" Of course the great prosperity of America was a sure sign of our virtue as God's chosen nation.[28]

The fundamental assumption in nineteenth-century schoolbooks, according to Elson, was "the moral character of the universe." If nineteenth-century intellectuals were coming to question—and reject—this claim, it was still a part of the popular culture and it was reflected in the textbooks. The values taught in the books were "absolute, unchanging, and they come from God." Elson characterizes the books as "guardians of tradition"; they were the defenders of virtue, patriotism, religion, and what was becoming the "traditional" American social order. Indeed, Elson notes that "*only* the social ideals of the more conservative members of the society were offered the nineteenth-century child."[29]

Priorities and content did change over the course of the nineteenth century. Later editions of the books became more secular. After the 1830s the readers for the first time contained more nonbiblical than biblical stories. Gradually more purely scientific accounts of nature made their way into the textbooks. The God of the first part of the century was the Calvinist Jehovah, a "benevolent despot," but as the century went on, "He is increasingly a deity who tempers His justice with loving kindness."[30] Theology virtually disappeared from the later books—though religion remained as the guarantor of virtue. In fact, religion became primarily a matter of ethics.[31]

Anti-Catholicism was, according to Elson, the most common theme in schoolbooks before 1870, denounced not only as a false religion but as a danger to the state. The condemnation was softened somewhat toward the end of the century, as theology became less important and Catholics became more middle class. Generally, religious institutions played a less prominent role in the books as industrialization and the westward movement "absorbed energies that had once centered on sectarian controversy."[32] Correlatively, questions of race and nationalism became more important.

Dan Fleming's study of nineteenth-century American history textbooks used in secondary schools shows that they did not place nearly so much emphasis on religion as did the readers and elementary school books. All of the texts were authored by Christians who were clearly interested in religious freedom, tolerance, and virtue; indeed, they were "laced with Christian, Protestant beliefs." But their treatment of religion was limited largely to the colonial period. Roger Williams and the struggle for religious freedom was their "single most consistent theme." Puritans, Quakers, and Mormons received "considerable attention," but religion received "very limited coverage," and that coverage diminished significantly in the second half of the century. Fleming notes that the most widely used history text of the century—Charles Goodrich's *History of the United States*—incorporated the author's Christian views, but it "never went into any depth concerning religion" and, like all the histories of the century, it focused on political and military history.[33]

In her study of twentieth-century American history textbooks, Frances Fitzgerald claims that religion virtually disappeared from the textbooks by the 1890s. Before this time, most of the authors were ministers or teachers in religious schools, "and for them American civilization was . . . an arm of Christian civilization extending into the new continent." By the 1890s public high schools became more common than church-related private schools, and for "the new generation of teachers, who were the servants of various bits of the state, the proper subject of American history was politics and the activities of government. The texts of the eighteen-nineties are silent on religious matters . . . and highly articulate on the subject of the nation-state."[34] By the turn of the century, social scientists, not clergymen, were writing the texts.

As important as religion was in the nineteenth-century—and in nineteenth century textbooks—it would be impossible to argue that the primary purpose of the schools or colleges in the nineteenth century was to make students good (Protestant) Christians, though that claim might very well be made regarding many of the town schools and private academies in colonial America.

The Common School

Control over education remained in local hands in the early years of the new republic, and schooling remained religious. Some states retained religious establishments into the nineteenth century and as the idea of a truly nonreligious education was unimaginable, considerable tax support was provided for religious schools. Horace Mann wrote of the Massachusetts schools of the 1830s: "I found books in the schools as strictly and exclusively *doctrinal* as any on the shelves of a theological library. I hear teachers giving oral instructions as strictly and purely *doctrinal* as any ever heard from the pulpit or from the professor's chair."[35]

The movement for tax-supported state systems of "common schools" began in the 1830s. There is a great deal of scholarly controversy regarding the motivation of those who fought for common schools. Some scholars see the movement as a natural extension of democracy and liberalism, making education available to all children, others as a conservative effort to shore up the status quo and defend economic privilege by providing trained workers, socialized to accept the values of order and discipline. It has also been argued that the common schools were designed to preserve religious privilege, that is, Protestant culture and values, in the face of growing religious pluralism.[36]

The common schools were officially nonsectarian. Horace Mann, their most influential spokesman, argued in the spirit of James Madison and Thomas Jefferson that establishments of religion have always led to persecution and tyranny. In America a different principle had been embraced, "that government should do all that it can to facilitate the acquisition of religious truth, but shall leave the decision of the question, what religious truth is, to the arbitrament, without human appeal, of each man's reason and conscience." The terms "public school" and "common school," Mann argued, "bear upon their face that they are schools which the children of the entire community may attend. Every man not on the pauper-list is taxed for their support; but he is not taxed to support them as special religious institutions; if he were, it would satisfy at once the largest definition of a religious establishment."[37]

Nonetheless, Mann declared that "religious instruction in our schools, to the extent which the constitution and laws of the State allowed and prescribed, was indispensable to [the students'] highest welfare, and essential to the vitality of moral education." Sectarian no; religious, yes. "Our system," he wrote, "earnestly inculcates all Christian morals; it founds its morals on the basis of religion; it welcomes the religion of the Bible; and, in receiving the Bible, it allows it to do what it is allowed to do in no other system,—*to speak for itself*. But here it stops." That is, Bible reading was to be allowed—the Bible could "speak for itself"—but no doctrinal gloss was to be given; no denominational interpretation of religion was to be permitted. Religious education was not for the purpose of converting students to any denomination but was to underwrite moral values and enable a student "to judge for himself, according to the dictates of his own reason and conscience, what his religious obligations are."[38]

By the middle of the nineteenth century William Ruffner (sometimes called the "Horace Mann of the South") had established in Virginia common schools that taught a "common" or nonsectarian Christianity, largely through the use of the Bible. In 1869 the National Teachers Association passed resolutions declaring that the Bible should be "devotionally read, and its precepts inculcated in all the common schools of the land." But it also held that the teaching of "partisan or sectarian principles in our public schools is a violation of the fundamental principles of our American system of education." In his study of the history of religion in American education Robert Michaelsen writes that "by 1870 Protestants generally had arrived at the conclusion that the public school system was best for America, that sectarianism—as they understood it—had no place in that system, but that religion—'nonsectarian,' 'common' religion—was essential to the school."[39]

Of course, the claim that public schools were nonsectarian was disingenuous. Horace Mann and most of his fellow reformers in Massachusetts were Unitarians, committed to a liberal religion of moral duty and enlightenment. The foe was traditional, revealed religion, which they took to be divisive and socially dangerous. Hence, Charles Glenn has argued, the common schools were "profoundly subversive of the beliefs of most Protestants," at least most conservative Protestants.[40] Indeed, most of the early opposition to common schools came from conservative Protestants.[41]

Eventually, Protestants united behind common schools because of the growing flood of immigration—particularly, in the case of Massachusetts, from Catholic Ireland. The Protestant hope was that nonsectarian schools would be acceptable to Catholics, who would be socialized into becoming good Americans. To this end, Protestants were willing to dispense with much doctrinal content. The Congregationalist journal *New Englander* editorialized: "It is better that Roman Catholic children should be educated in public schools in which the Bible is not read, than that they should not be educated at all, or educated in schools under the absolute control of their priesthood."[42] Of course, the Bible continued to be read—and this was a major reason Catholics would not attend public schools. But even if there was no denominational catechism, schools used the Protestant rather than the Catholic Bible. Indeed, to read the Bible without comment itself was not neutral but was a Protestant notion; for Catholics, the Bible required the gloss of the church to be understood. In response, Catholics developed a massive parochial school system.

In some places Catholics pressed for tax support of parochial schools—after all, Protestant common schools were tax supported. Not only was no such aid forthcoming but several states adopted constitutional amendments prohibiting the use of tax funds for "sectarian" schools. In 1875 Congress fell a few votes short of passing a constitutional amendment that would have prohibited the use of public funds (at all levels of government) for the support of sectarian education. Nonetheless, Congress did pass a law requiring that states admitted to the Union after 1876 include provisions for establishing public schools "free from sectarian control," and many states adopted constitutional amendments prohibiting the use of state funds for sectarian schools. By 1900 most states prohibited the use of public funds for sectarian purposes, and many prohibited religious instruction in the public schools.[43] So by the end of the century there were legal impediments to religious education in many states, though unadorned Bible reading was often taken to be nonsectarian and hence permissible.

The motivation for outlawing sectarian schools, according to constitutional scholar Douglas Laycock, was "not pretty. It traces not to any careful deliberation about constitutional principles of the proper relations of church and state. Rather it traces to vigorous nineteenth century anti-Catholicism and the nativist reaction to Catholic immigration. The fact is that no one in America worried about religious instruction in schools before Catholic immigration threatened the Protestant hegemony."[44] The common school movement began, after all, at a time Sydney Ahlstrom describes as "the most violent period of religious discord in [America's] history."[45] There were anti-Catholic riots in Boston and New York, and in 1843, when the Philadelphia school board ruled that Catholic students could use the Douay (Catholic) Bible, riots erupted again; by the time they ended, two Catholic churches and dozens of homes had been burned down, the militia had fired point-blank on crowds, mobs ruled the city for three days, and thirteen people had been killed. In 1854 the anti-Catholic Know-Nothing party elected seventy-five men to Congress, dominated state politics in Massachusetts, and did very well in several other states.[46] Only the politics of race and the Civil War put the politics of anti-Catholicism to rest, though it resurfaced with a vengeance again at the end of the century.

There is much more to the story than this, but a part of the motivation for common schools was to assure the hegemony of Protestantism in American culture. Robert Michaelsen concludes: "Thus the deep-seated emotions of the sixteenth and seventeenth centuries lingered on and the public school became a major arena for the continuation of the Protestant-Catholic conflict."[47]

Even if nineteenth-century common schools were rather less nonsectarian than they claimed to be, the logic of secularization was clearly at work. In a religiously pluralistic culture, peace is achieved by eliminating what is divisive—that is, religion—from public institutions. In the twentieth century Bible reading and prayer became increasingly uncommon as the schools attempted to become truly common schools, acceptable to all religious and secular communities. Of course, in eliminating all religion from schools it may be that a new sectarianism—a secular sectarianism—has been established in the place of the old Protestant hegemony.

Americanism and Democracy

The early years of the nineteenth century were, Lawrence Cremin has written, an age of "exuberant faith in the power and possibility of education. . . . The goal was nothing less than a new republican individual, of virtuous character, abiding patriotism, and prudent wisdom, fashioned by education into an independent yet loyal citizen. Without such individuals, the experiment in liberty would be short-lived at best." Indeed, by the 1820s, "the need of a self-governing people for universal education had become a familiar part of the litany of American politics."[48]

From the beginning it was the purpose of common schools and their advocates to make children virtuous—and good Americans. Horace Mann worried that the Revolution had substituted liberty and the forces of passion for the traditional constraints under which people lived. But unless passions were controlled by morality, "the fruits of liberty would be worse than the ills of tyranny." Hence it became, for him, "a momentous question, whether the children in our schools are educated in reference to themselves and their private interest only, or with a regard to the great social duties and prerogatives . . . for, however loftily the intellect of man may have been gifted, however skillfully it may have been trained, if it be not guided by a sense of justice, a love of mankind and a devotion to duty, its possessor is only a more splendid, as he is a more dangerous barbarian."[49] It was the task of the schools, Noah Webster argued, to "implant in the minds of the American youth the principle of virtue and of liberty and inspire them . . . with an inviolable attachment to their country." "Good republicans," he wrote, "are formed by a singular machinery in the body politic, which takes the child as soon as he can speak, checks his natural independence and passions, makes him subordinate to superior age [and] to the laws of the state."[50] The common school movement was to a considerable extent the creation of Whigs (like Horace Mann) who were social conservatives (if religious liberals).[51] The dominant values of the new common schools were to be, unsurprisingly, the dominant values of the American culture and the growing middle class: Protestantism, capitalism, and Americanism.

Nineteenth-century textbooks assigned America a special place in the divine scheme of things: Americans are the most prosperous, the most happy, and the most virtuous people in the world. One geography text declared: "The good and wise of every land look to [America] to move, before the nations, as did the pillar of fire before the Israelites, to lead the way to liberty and happiness." According to Elson, in the nineteenth century "clearly the first duty of schoolbook authors in their own eyes was to attach the child's loyalty to the state and nation. The sentiment of patriotism, love of country, vie with the love of God as the cornerstone of virtue. . . . Every book contains many pieces sustaining the doctrine that one's loyalty to country must be paramount to all other loyalties." Initiating children into a love of their country and its heroes could not begin too soon. The title page of a Webster Reader set an ambitious goal for parents: "Begin with the infant in his cradle. Let the first word he lisps be Washington."[52]

Americanism took on new educational importance with the growing waves of immigrants during the twenty years on either side of the year 1900. In 1909, 57.8 percent of the children in public schools in the thirty-seven largest American cities had foreign-born parents.[53] Public schools became the cultural factories of Americanization, transforming the raw material of foreign cultures into good American citizens.

Democracy and Americanism acquired almost sacred status. The public school created a community that, in Robert Michaelsen's words, had redemptive qualities, for "the common school brings common experience which precipitates a common faith which is essential to the common welfare."[54] Even so secular a thinker as John Dewey could talk about Americanizing and democratizing students as "an infinitely significant religious work."[55] Dewey's disciple Sidney Hook argued that public schools provided the common institutional ground for those "shared human values which must underlie all differences within a democratic culture if it is to survive. Where churches and sects and nations divide . . . the schools can unite by becoming the temples and laboratories of a common democratic faith."[56] By the end of the nineteenth century, according to Will Herberg, the effective religion of the public schools "was no longer Christianity, but the 'religion of democracy,' the religion of the American Way. It was a religion that enjoyed the favor of the modern-minded educators, that appealed to the American people (though very few ever thought of it as a religion), and that therefore soon acquired the status of the unofficially established spiritual foundation of American education."[57]

Through a subtle and gradual process, Americanism—or nationalism—came to replace traditional religion in the institutions, and eventually in the hearts and minds, of people.

Utility

In the eighteenth century the utilitarian values of the growing merchant and middle classes began to shape the development of schooling. The goal was a more useful education. In his *Proposals Relating to the Education of Youth in Pennsylvania*, Benjamin Franklin argued for a curriculum in which students would "be taught 'to write a fair hand' and 'something of drawing'; arithmetic, accounts, geometry, and astronomy; English grammar out of Tillotson, Addison, Pope, Sidney, Trenchard, and Gordon; the writing of essays and letters; rhetoric, history, geography, and ethics; natural history and gardening; and the history of commerce and principles of mechanics; Instruction would include visits to neighboring farms, opportunities for natural observations, experiments with scientific apparatus, and physical exercise." Franklin's goal was to produce men qualified "to pass through and execute the several offices of civil life, with advantage and reputation to themselves and country."[58] The Boston English High School—in 1821 the first American high school—offered a curriculum that included English, geography, arithmetic, algebra, geometry, trigonometry, history, navigation, and surveying. Other schools followed suit in nurturing the new spirit of science, technology, and industrial and economic development.[59]

According to Elson, nineteenth-century textbooks impressed upon students the importance of "useful" knowledge—indeed, the word "knowledge" was almost inevitably preceded by the word "useful." Virtue was considered useful, in part because it was believed that virtuous people would prosper, but "practical" knowledge, knowledge that leads to a comfortable material life, was also clearly useful. While other countries hoped to develop high culture, Americans prided themselves on their concern with private and public utility. Indeed, an anti-intellectualism ran through schoolbooks. Elson notes that "the fact that we have not produced scholars is mentioned with pride as a sign that knowledge is democratically diffused instead of being concentrated in the hands of an upper class." Some books counseled against reading too much, for the "brain must have a rest." The American hero was manly, and life experience was much to be preferred over book experience. One reader told students: "Manhood is better than Greek. Self-reliance is worth more to a man than Latin." Elson concludes: "The frontier did not need scholarship, whereas 'useful knowledge' was essential to survival." And, she adds, the needs of the frontier were "reinforced by the needs of expanding business. Thus an 1875 Speller records current attitudes in saying: 'We do not blame a man who is proud of his success, so much as one who is vain of his learning.'"[60]

A major reason for the proliferation of high schools at the end of the nineteenth century was that business required a better-trained work force. There was growing concern about American competitiveness in world markets. A 1905 report from the National Association of Manufacturers argued that "technical and trade education for youth is a national necessity, and the . . . nation must train its youth in the arts of production and distribution." In 1912, a report of the Committee on Industrial Education expressed concern about America's failure to develop its human capital; the result was industrial disadvantage: "We should act at once because of the stress of foreign competition. We are twenty-five years behind most of the nations that we recognize as competitors. We must come nearer to the level of international competition."[61] In 1917 Congress responded with the Smith-Hughes Act, the first of a series of acts that encouraged and funded vocational education.

It was not only business which demanded a more practical curriculum. According to Lawrence Cremin, "Proponents of virtually every progressive cause from the 1890's through World War I had their program for the school." As Cremin tells it, for example, the advocates of agricultural education in Wisconsin argued that

> school gardens, field trips, and practical courses in the work of farm and kitchen were the answers to an overly bookish program which overemphasized the accumulation of useless knowledge. "Grammar, history, geography are bundles of abstractions, while the child is interested in the world of realities," one speaker inveighed. "Rotation of crops is as inspiring as the position of the preposition; the fertilization of apples and corn as interesting as the location of cities and the course of rivers; the economy of the horse and cow and sheep as close to life as the duties of the President and the cause of the Revolutionary War.

Hence, by the early years of this century, "literally thousands of boys and girls the country over were tending gardens, raising chickens, collecting insects and wild flowers, and cooking, canning, and baking, all under the sponsorship of local school authorities."[62]

This emphasis on utility, on the benefits of modern science, on individual and social betterment, was part of the broad movement of Progressivism, both in politics and in education. In contrast to traditional religious and classical education, Progressivism placed a powerful emphasis on personal experience, on openness, on nonauthoritarian teaching, and on the uniqueness of the individual child. Modern social science would underwrite this new agenda, and early in the twentieth century scientific testing, educational psychology, classroom management, and scientific administration became integral parts of education. As David Tyack and Elizabeth Hansot note, "Whereas the educational evangelists of the mid-nineteenth century aroused the citizenry against *evils*, the administrative progressives talked increasingly of *problems* to be solved by experts. . . . Professional management would replace politics; science would replace religion and custom as sources of authority; and experts would adapt education to the transformed conditions of modern corporate life."[63] No longer would ministers, amateur politicians, voters, or the marketplace make decisions. Education was professionalized.

The results of these various movements can be seen in a series of reports issued by the National Education Association (NEA). In 1893 its Committee of Ten had argued for a rigorous intellectual curriculum for high schools, but by 1911 (when high school teachers had replaced college professors on NEA committees) the Committee of Nine argued that the purpose of high schools was "to lay the foundations of good citizenship and to help in the wise choice of a vocation." It warned against a "bookish curricula" responsible for "leading tens of thousands of boys and girls away from the pursuits for which they are adapted" and giving them "false ideals of culture." Then, in 1918, the Commission on the Reorganization of Secondary Education proposed seven objectives of secondary education: "health, command of fundamental processes [the three R's], worthy home-membership, vocation, citizenship, worthy use of leisure, and ethical character." The report called for the creation of "comprehensive high schools" that would provide both a common experience for students (through studying English and social studies, through the mingling of the social classes, and through common activities such as athletics and student government) and sufficient specialization to enable students to pursue their own interests and fill the needs of society.[64]

Hence, in the early years of the twentieth century, academic high schools with core curricula gave way to comprehensive schools with largely elective curricula—typically offering academic, general, and vocational tracks—to prepare students for their different social roles and vocational niches in society. The goal, in the language of the time, was "social efficiency." Frances Fitzgerald argues that

> administrators and teachers put increasing faith in the notion that vocational training was the democratic alternative to the academic elitism of the European secondary schools. The idea that academic education might be made universal and therefore democratic had very little appeal—and not unnaturally since the high-school teachers would have been incapable of putting it into practice. The ideology of the teachers, however, merely reflected the fact that the community at large had no interest in providing intellectual training for the mass of high-school students; its concern was to train skilled workers for industry.[65]

This has been the pattern of high school education ever since.

America's colleges underwent a similar transformation of purpose. The sciences had appeared in Harvard's curriculum early on, though they clearly were less important than the classics and divinity. By 1776 six of the colonial colleges had professorships of mathematics and "natural philosophy"—the sciences. In 1779 Thomas Jefferson, as a member of the Board of Visitors of William and Mary, reorganized that college, abolishing the divinity and Oriental languages professorships—the two professorships having to do with religion—and adding professorships in public administration, modern languages, and medical sciences.[66]

By the end of the eighteenth century, the Enlightenment had taken hold of American higher education. Newton and Locke had arrived; mathematics and the natural sciences were moving toward the center of the curriculum. The important texts were no longer the classics but those written in modern languages—often English. Increasingly it was believed that the truth was not to be had by rediscovering the past but in experimenting and observing the world. More and more students attended college with vocational goals other than the ministry. Richard Hofstadter has suggested that the "most significant trend in collegiate education during the eighteenth century was the secularization of the colleges."[67]

Secularization had not won a complete victory, however. At the beginning of the nineteenth century "The Great Retrogression," as Hofstadter called it, set in. The Second Great Awakening and conservative reaction to the Enlightenment prompted religious denominations to create a welter of small religious colleges and exert what control they still could over the larger, well-established colleges. The importance of religion and the classics was reaffirmed—but only for a while. The long-term trend toward secularization continued. Throughout the nineteenth century the college curriculum was, in Frederick Rudolph's words, shifting "from explaining the ways of God to exploring the ways of man."[68] In the second half of the century the process shifted into high gear.

In 1862 Congress passed the Morrill Act, making federal aid available to states that supported colleges in which agricultural and mechanical instruction was given. Such aid provided a significant motivation for legislators who wished to influence the direction of higher education toward more practical concerns and occupations—extending even to carpentry and blacksmithing on occasion. Similar carrots were dangled in front of private institutions by major donors. Ezra Cornell established Cornell University declaring: "I would found an institution where any person can find instruction in any study."[69] Everything from classical studies to theoretical research to practical vocational studies had its place at Cornell, and theoretically everything was of equal value. Andrew D. White, the first president of Cornell, declared: "Four years of good study in one direction are held equal to four years of good study in another."[70] The professor of Greek had nothing up on the professor of agriculture. Midwestern universities, much influenced by Cornell, lined up behind the battle flag of utility.

"Social efficiency" appeared in the rhetoric of college presidents as often as it did in the rhetoric of public school reformers. Increasingly, the utilitarian values of the middle class—but especially of pragmatic legislators, wealthy donors, businessmen, and industrialists on boards of trustees—dictated college policy. According to Rudolph, "The evidence would suggest that when a generation of self-made manufacturers, engineers, and merchants were ready to attach their names and their fortunes to the development of schools of applied science, the classical colleges were standing in line with their hands out."[71]

Technology and the practical sciences had long been valued for utilitarian reasons, but beginning in the 1870s, influenced by the great German universities, a growing number of scientists begin to pursue research in American colleges. The growing interest in "pure research" and the development of "research universities" must not be understood as simply another aspect of the overriding value of utility, for the research scientist was often contemptuous of social utility and skeptical of democratic control of education.[72] No doubt many scientists came to see practical reasons (often financial) to link their research with utility in the public mind; still, their primary concern was often with knowledge for its own sake. Research scientists were less interested in changing society than in changing the minds of their colleagues; they were less interested in undergraduate education than in graduate students and the education of other specialists.

Laurence Veysey suggests that two basic changes in American higher education were brought about by the new emphasis on research. The first, "a tendency toward ever increasing specialization of knowledge, it shared with the movement toward practicality. The second, the liberation of intellect for its own sake, resulted more exclusively from the climate of abstract investigation."[73] Both changes created tensions with religion and traditional education. The traditional curriculum emphasized general education, general principles, and classical literature, which all students should master. As important, traditionalists were skeptical of pure research that started from doubt and questioning, was tentative (at least in principle), and placed great value in unaided reason—and took no overt notice of religion.

Perhaps no educational reform had greater significance than the move toward electives. From the beginning, Cornell gave its students great freedom in designing their own curricula. In 1850 the Massachusetts General Court proposed that Harvard adopt "a wholly elective curriculum and that the professors be paid by the size of their classes." By 1897, Harvard had eliminated all requirements but composition. In 1899, David Starr Jordan, president of Stanford, said: "It is not for the University to decide on the relative values of knowledge. Each man makes his own market, controlled by his own standards."[74] By 1901, many of the most prestigious colleges had followed Harvard in giving up virtually all course requirements. Neither the totally prescribed curriculum nor abolishing all requirements was to be the rule in the twentieth century, however. By 1910, most colleges had some set of distribution requirements (three humanities courses, three natural sciences courses, and so on) as well as departmental majors. More often than not, however, such curricula were determined more by administrative convenience and departmental politics than by any intellectual consensus about what constituted a good education. Still, what is remarkable is the extent to which colleges relinquished their prerogative to define what an "educated" person would be to the interests and vocational goals of their students.

By the end of the nineteenth century those quintessentially modern values of individualism and democracy, science and technology, profession and prosperity, had come to dominate higher education. The traditional curriculum rooted in religion and the classics, uniform for everyone, was no more.

The Liberal Arts

I have mentioned that the traditional classical curriculum gained strength for a while in the early nineteenth century and survived the century here and there.[75] But classical education was clearly living on borrowed time, and its decline was swift in the second half of the century. It was, after all, largely incompatible with the spirit of the country: egalitarian, individualistic, experimental, practical, committed to liberty and progress. High schools began to proliferate at the end of the nineteenth century under the pressures of vocationalism and utility. If the classical curriculum maintained a toehold in colleges that could keep some distance from public pressures, by the end of the century it was clear that science, vocationalism, utility, pure research, pragmatism, specialization, and the elective system had united to dethrone the classical curriculum. There was an heir apparent, however: liberal education.

Bruce Kimball has shown that there are two different notions of liberal education in the Western tradition. The first—what he calls the *artes liberales* or liberal arts tradition—is grounded in the classical canon. It assumes that moral truths and ideals of civic virtue are to be found in classical literature, and it is largely a literary education. It forms character and is meant to be the ideal education for public leaders—and gentlemen. It is typically elitist and disclaims any crass commercial value. A liberal arts education binds one to the past, to a tradition. Cicero is its patron saint. It was the educational ideal of late Greece and Rome, the early Middle Ages, the Renaissance, and early America.[76]

The second tradition—what Kimball calls the *liberal-free* ideal—takes as its patron saint Socrates, and it is moved by the continuing search for truth. It values free, reasoned inquiry and tolerance; it is skeptical. It inclines toward egalitarianism and individualism. It is little interested in civic virtue or public leadership but finds its full justification in itself. The liberal-free ideal pays scant attention to the classics but is concerned with philosophical inquiry and scientific experiment; it assumes no truth in the past but is critical, constantly looking for new truths. It *liberates* individuals, rather than binding them to a tradition. The liberal-free ideal was foreshadowed in Greek philosophy and the philosophy of the high Middle Ages but came into its own with the Enlightenment, the scientific revolution, and nineteenth-century German research universities—and it became the dominant face of liberal education in American universities at the end of the nineteenth century.[77]

A famous exchange between Thomas H. Huxley and Matthew Arnold captured the differences nicely. In 1880 Huxley, the great promoter of Darwin and modern science, argued that education should be founded on "an unhesitating faith that the free employment of reason, in accordance with scientific method, is the sole method of reaching truth."[78] Arnold responded by claiming that education involved teaching "the best which has been thought and uttered in the world" for it speaks to "our need for conduct, our need for beauty."[79] Huxley argued for the liberal-free ideal, Arnold for the *artes liberales*.

The liberal-free ideal had captured higher education by the end of the century, at least in the major universities. But in the ebb and flow of cultural politics there was something of a resurgence of the *artes liberales* ideal—what was then commonly called "liberal culture" or "neohumanism"—in reaction to the reigning values of utility, specialization, and the liberal-free ideal in education. The new advocates of the liberal arts drew on philosophy—particularly on the idealism of Josiah Royce at Harvard—but their heart was in literature and the arts.[80] Their goal was to inspire students with the profound truths of great literature and, as Gerald Graff puts it, they "channeled into literature emotions that, a half-century earlier, would have likely been expressed in evangelical Christianity." They cultivated the appreciation of beauty and sought to nurture a more spiritual sense of the world through the study of the best that has been thought and said. They rejected the fragmentation and specialization of graduate education in favor of a unified, largely literary undergraduate curriculum, and they "saw themselves as the upholders of spiritual values against the crass materialism of American business life."[81] They could be elitist. George Santayana, who taught philosophy at Harvard, put the matter frankly: "There are always a few men whose main interest is to note the aspects of things in an artistic or philosophical way. They are rather useless individuals, but as I happen to belong to the class, I think them much superior to the rest of mankind."[82] In the end "liberal culture" was unsuccessful at stemming the tide. It was too elitist, too far out of the mainstream of American culture.

By the first years of the twentieth century, the liberal arts were, to a considerable extent, alienated from religion. Irving Babbitt wrote that the "humanities need to be defended to-day against the encroachments of physical science, as they once needed to be against the encroachments of theology."[83] He assumed that the battle against religion had been won. Scholars in literature and philosophy were, like their colleagues in the sciences and social sciences, an increasingly secularized lot. If they had a religion, it was likely to be civilization itself. Their concern lay, in Veysey's words, with "a chain of artists and thinkers inhabiting a small part of the globe"—not with the Kingdom of God.[84]

Higher Education in the Nineteenth Century

In the early years of the century, Yale stipulated that "if any student shall profess or endeavor to propagate a disbelief in the divine authority of the Holy

Scriptures, and shall persist therein after admonition, he shall no longer be a member of the College." James McCosh, president of Princeton at midcentury, declared: "Religion should burn in the hearts, and shine . . . from the faces of the teachers. . . . And in regard to religious truth, there will be no uncertain sound uttered within these walls."[85] In 1877, William B. Angell, president of the University of Michigan, wrote that "Michigan is a Christian State, and her University can be true to her only by cherishing a broad unsectarian but earnest Christian spirit. I think that her sister universities in the Northwest are pervaded by the same spirit, and that they are contributing their full share to the dissemination of a Christian culture."[86] Religious qualifications for faculty positions were a well-known fact of life in many state as well as private colleges.[87] In 1860, 262 of 288 college presidents were members of the clergy and more than a third of the faculty were ministers.[88] In 1890 President Angell reported that "twenty-two of twenty-four *state* universities he surveyed conducted chapel services; at twelve of those schools attendance was compulsory, and four of them required church attendance as well."[89] Much like their common-school counterparts, state universities were, in some significant ways, nonsectarian, more or less Protestant institutions in the nineteenth century.

Nonetheless, higher education was essentially secular by the end of the century. Religion had always stood in some tension with the classical curriculum and, as D. G. Hart puts it, whereas "colonial colleges had combined the study of classics with Protestant divinity, the classical curriculum at antebellum colleges lost its pious hue as educators identified the liberal arts with good breeding and the training of gentlemen."[90] In part because theology was disappearing from the curriculum, the training of ministers was moved to separate (doctrinally safe) divinity schools.[91] This, in turn, exacerbated the tendency already in place to ignore religion in the undergraduate curriculum. Increasingly religion became a specialized topic for professionals rather than a necessary dimension of liberal education for all undergraduates. In 1830, one out of three graduates of Harvard, Yale, and Princeton entered the ministry; by 1876 the number was one out of thirteen.[92]

Economics also played a role in undermining the denominational identification of colleges for, as George Marsden has pointed out, in a free enterprise system "a strong emphasis on theological distinctions could limit a college's constituency and be a competitive disadvantage." Perhaps most important, money from business and government was used to transform many of the small classical colleges of the nineteenth century into the research universities of the twentieth century. After all, America needed specialized knowledge, science, and technology to compete in the marketplace. The old religious and classical education was hopelessly backward-looking and saddled with the heavy weight of amateurism. College education had to be freed from clerical control; the vocation of teacher and scholar had to be separated from the vocation of minister. Convinced of this, the Carnegie Pension Fund was established in 1906 to wean universities from the church by establishing generous pensions for teachers at colleges and universities free from sectarian control and teaching. Many private religious colleges and universities severed their denominational ties as a result.[93]

The trends of the times can be seen in the rise and fall of the required senior year capstone course in moral philosophy, typically taught by the college president, usually a minister. The moral philosophy course grew out of the older divinity courses; it was an effort to bring together systematically the diversity of undergraduate studies, drawing out the moral (and usually the Christian) implications for society. By the mid-eighteenth century, according to Rudolph, the course in moral philosophy had achieved a dominance over theology in the curriculum and for a century it was the culminating undergraduate course—a way station between the older, overtly theological curriculum and secular modernity. But by the second half of the nineteenth century, it could no longer hold in check the forces of specialization and intellectual fragmentation: psychology, sociology, and economics were becoming separate disciplines; philosophy was becoming increasingly academic; theology was increasingly discredited. In the colleges of the early nineteenth century, Rudolph writes, the study of society still belonged "to the benign amateurs who were not intimidated by cosmic questions or their own ignorance." But the "narrow competence and specialization of the economists, historians, political scientists, and others who took their place deflected the classroom from advocacy and conspicuous moral judgment to a style that bore the approved description—'scientific,' a style that was objective, cautious, and wary of judgment. . . . [Scholars] were developing an academic style that was . . . removed from moral judgment, and . . . unrelated to the traditional social purposes of higher education."[94] So much for the capstone course in moral philosophy.

There is some irony in the extent to which the secularization of higher education was aided by religious liberals. In their efforts to demythologize traditional religion and bring about social progress, liberals often gave their unqualified blessing to the forces of secularization. In an address to the alumni of Harvard in 1866, Professor Fredric Henry Hedge said: "The secularization of the College is no violation of its motto, '*Christo et Ecclesiae*.' For, as I interpret those sacred ideas, the cause of Christ and the Church is advanced by whatever liberalizes and enriches and enlarges the mind."[95]

In the naive optimism of nineteenth-century America, science could still be seen as the ally of religion, liberating humankind from the dead hand of tradition and injustice. Daniel Coit Gilman, the founder of Johns Hopkins, America's first research university, told the Evangelical Alliance in 1887, "Science is the handmaid of Religion."[96] Richard T. Ely, a Social Gospeler and prominent economist, believed that economics could help usher in the Kingdom of God; hence he sought "to bring science to the aid of Christianity."[97] The relationship between Christianity and social science, according to Washington Gladden, the great minister of liberal Christianity, is "the relation of an offspring to its parent. Social science is the child of Christianity. The national and international associations that are so diligently studying the things that make for human welfare in society are as distinctly the products of Christianity as is the American Board of Missions."[98]

Of course, the child quickly overthrew the parent: religion was soon exiled to the private realm of subjectivity and superstition by quantitative, specialized, value-free social science. The celebrated sociologist (and onetime Episcopal minister) William Graham Sumner remarked once that in doing sociology he had put his religious beliefs in his desk drawer, only to discover, when he checked twenty years later, that they were gone.[99]

James Burtchaell has argued that if nineteenth-century colleges were Christian, it was not because of their curriculum but "their immersion in the conventional piety of the surrounding church. The church was not so much *in* as it was *round about* a college." It was in chapel, in student associations, and in rhetoric, that the college was religious, not in its ideas. As Burtchaell says, its religion "was nothing very reflective."[100]

Moreover, the openness and universalism of liberal Protestantism made it difficult to maintain Protestant hegemony in the face of cultural pluralism and the new ideas of science and social science. When in the twentieth century, Catholics, Jews, and secularists pressed the argument for truly nonsectarian universities, liberal Protestants found it "awkward," as George Marsden put it, "to take any decisive stand against the secularizing trends." Liberals believed that religion should be voluntary in any case, not imposed. Hence it was doctrinally easy to end compulsory chapel and other aspects of their control over the life of students and the curriculum.[101] As Burtchaell tells the story, liberals "unwittingly deprived their institutions of any capacity to retain their Christian identity when exposed to a secularist faculty" in succeeding generations.[102]

The Purposes of Contemporary American Education

There is no neat or uncontroversial way to classify the various voices arguing about the purposes of contemporary education. I will try to give coherence to the discussion by defining four more or less distinct positions around which advocates rally. Alliances between these various parties are sometimes formed, and there are advocates of midway positions; still, there is some integrity in each of the four.

Liberal Arts Education. There continues to be considerable support for liberal education in both its *artes liberales* and liberal-free forms. If the older classical versions of the "liberal arts" are long forgotten and little missed, newer variations continue to play an important role in the contemporary discussion of the purposes of education.

There are six major emphases. (1) Advocates reject the idea that education should be specialized or vocational. A liberal arts education should liberalize—or broaden—a student's understanding of the world; it is at odds with parochialism. Students should be required to take a core curriculum, and electives should be limited. (2) Most advocates agree that a liberal arts education is for everyone, not just for some elite group of students. Mortimer Adler and E. D. Hirsch argue that only if we all share a "cultural literacy" can we thrive as individuals and our society work as a democracy.[103] (Here there is a significant departure from the classical tradition, according to which a liberal education was for the leisured or ruling classes.) (3) A liberal arts curriculum is intellectually rigorous; indeed, it is, in a sense, philosophical. It is concerned with the fundamental ideas, with the "big" questions of life. Its goal is a kind of reflective wisdom. (4) It emphasizes ideals as much as ideas; it is concerned with moral and political and, in principle, at least, spiritual questions. (5) If a liberal arts education broadens students' understanding of the world, it is also likely to provide a kind of conservative ballast. It is rooted in history and historical literature. It typically draws on Matthew Arnold's notion that education should initiate students into understanding the best that has been said and thought. (6) Finally, advocates of the liberal arts often share a historical pessimism: modern civilization is problematic; things are getting worse, not better. Allan Bloom captured the spirit of this last emphasis when he complained that in our time "the delicate fabric of the civilization into which the successive generations are woven has unraveled, and [nowadays] children are raised, not educated." Parents (and teachers) no longer have anything to give children "in the way of a vision of the world, of high models of action or profound sense of connection with others." Bloom's solution to the problem caught up several of the emphases of a liberal arts education: it is through the Great Books that students gain "an acquaintance with what big questions were when there were still big questions; models, at the very least, of how to go about answering them; and, perhaps most important of all, a fund of shared experiences and thoughts."[104]

Leftist critics argue that such an education is oppressive in that it limits the voices to which students are introduced to white, male, Western voices; it simply reproduces the value judgments of traditional elites. For example, Henry Giroux argues that in the liberal arts tradition Western civilization is presented "as a storehouse of treasured goods constituted as a canon and ready to be passed 'down' to deserving students. Not surprisingly, teaching in this instance is often reduced to the process of transmitting a given body of hallowed knowledge with student learning squarely situated in 'mastering' the 'basics' and appropriate standards of behavior."[105] Of course, defenders of the Great Books can point out that any canon that contains Marx and Darwin and Freud and Dostoyevsky (as most versions of the canon, at least at the college level, do) cannot be safely conservative, and they have a point. Their more liberal or radical critics respond that any canon that does not include women or black or Third World authors is not as liberal as it might be—and they have a point.

My point would be that the canon can be defined more or less conservatively. There is no good reason why the canon cannot be broadened—indeed, the logic of a "liberal" arts education, its opposition to specialization and its commitment to philosophical thinking, would seem to be inherently expansive, broadening the exposure of (all) students to a variety of literature. Indeed, a liberal arts education has considerable liberating potential, even when the canon is relatively conservative, for it should not allow uncritical acceptance of tradition; it understands education as a "great conversation" (to use Robert Hutchins's phrase), and even within the most conservative canons, the discussants do not agree. It forces critical thinking about major issues that often call tradition and the status quo into question. In fact, of course, this liberating potential often remains largely unrealized, perhaps because the historical pessimism of its advocates works against adding new voices to the conversation.

In principle, religion should be a topic of some importance in a liberal arts education. Religious writers and themes are a powerful part of our cultural conversation. It is perhaps another sign of the times that some of the strongest advocates of the liberal arts say so little about religion. For all of Allan Bloom's talk about the big questions, religion is conspicuous by absence from *The Closing of the American Mind*. Mortimer Adler provides a syllabus of 237 books for high school students as part of his Paideia Program, but only one—Augustine's *Confessions*—is by a theologian and, amazingly, Adler recommends that students read only through Book VII, stopping one book short of Augustine's conversion to Christianity in Book VIII.[106]

Expressive Education. In *Habits of the Heart*, Robert Bellah and his colleagues characterize the development of modern American culture in terms of "expressive" and "utilitarian" individualism. I will use their language (and much of their analysis) in describing expressive and utilitarian education as the characteristically modern forms of American education.

What I will call "expressive" education has it roots in Rousseau and romanticism, in the individualism and social liberalism of American culture, in the openness and skeptical inquiry of the liberal-free tradition, and in the optimism and child-centered emphasis of educational Progressivism. Many of the revolutionary educational movements of the 1960s and 1970s—open education, free schools, alternative schools, and deschooling society (aptly described as the New Progressivism[107] and the New Romanticism[108])—were particularly clear developments of expressivist themes; other variations can be found in the values clarification movement and in the influence of Abraham Maslow, Carl Rogers, and the human potentials movement in educational psychology. The purpose of expressive education is to nurture the development of the child's individual interests and potential.

Beyond the basic skills that all students must acquire, advocates of expressive education trust students to chart their own way. They note the differences among children and favor diversity; they are wary of forcing children to fit one mold. Liberty is the great virtue; bureaucracy and conformity the great vices; electives are encouraged and core curricula are suspect. Expressivists are more likely to use the language of self-actualization and modern psychology than the language of morality or religion. They believe teachers should be nonjudgmental, and they are suspicious of authority. They often downplay exams and grades and at the college level have (largely) done away with in loco parentis. They are much more likely than advocates of liberal arts education to talk about autonomy and the rights of students. Teachers should not be instructors so much as facilitators, providing students with the freedom to learn for themselves. They would have teachers start where the student is and favor flexibility over programmed learning, process over conclusions. They tend to favor learning how to learn, rather than learning anything in particular. They are not much interested in history or tradition but are very much interested in spontaneity, creativity, and the here and now.

Answers are provisional. Expressive education is often less concerned with intellect than with feelings or affect, though advocates typically argue that education should speak to the whole child. Expressivists favor doing as much as thinking; education should be self-initiated, experimental, and experiential. They are optimists.

Expressive education can be understood much as classical political liberals understand the state: as a morally neutral institution that might provide a modicum of support but essentially lets individuals pursue their own interests and ideals as they see fit. It is not the business of government or schools to impose some official understanding of the good on everyone. Theodore Sizer, for example, argues that although it is legitimate for schools to require students to acquire literacy, numeracy, decency, and some understanding of their role as citizens, beyond that there is no consensus to be had: "American values vary too richly for that." What should schools do? "The only sensible answer," according to Sizer, "is for them to make choices available, to give students, teachers, and their families the opportunity to follow their preferences. . . . The alternative—a course of study mandated as the result of decisions reached through special interest politics and unrelieved majority rule—is both insensitive educationally (no one of us, including an adolescent, learns much from things that, forced on us, we resent) and un-American (the tradition of minority rights is an important aspect in American liberty)." Educational decision making should be decentralized. Centralization leads to bureaucracies and standardization; it invariably depends on measurement and, as Sizer notes, the "endless and exclusive talk of attendance rates, dropout rates, test scores, suspension rates, teachers' rank in class in their colleges, reminds one of Vietnam War body counts."[109]

Expressive education reflects much of the mood of modernity. It is democratic and egalitarian. Who is to say what is good for you or me? As for Ezra Cornell, each subject is as good as any other. It finds the meaning of education in the subjectivity of individuals, in their search for self-fulfillment. This need not imply selfishness or narcissism—indeed, advocates of expressive education typically have great confidence in the innate goodness of individuals. But because of that trust, and because of a suspicion of elites and bureaucrats, they are not particularly concerned about traditional values or the wisdom of the past. In defining what counts as a good education, Carl Rogers offers a capsule summary of modernity: education is "to free curiosity; to permit individuals to go charging off into new directions dictated by their own interest, to unleash the sense of inquiry; to open everything to questioning and exploration, to recognize that everything is in a process of change."[110]

If the liberal arts are grounded in history and the humanities, expressive education has its roots in modern psychology. It has been almost entirely a secular movement. Religion is usually identified with the dead hand of tradition, with constraints on spontaneity, and with the closed past rather than the open and elective future.

Arguably much of what goes under the name of liberal education nowadays is an uneasy synthesis of "liberal arts" and expressive education. We do not have the confidence in human nature that Charles W. Eliot did in eliminating all electives at Harvard—or that Carl Rogers does in proposing open schooling, or that Ivan Illych does in arguing that we abolish formal schooling altogether. We compromise by requiring a few things—a modicum of English and math and American history—in high schools while allowing a good number of electives, and then in college we typically find distribution requirements and an undergraduate major a happy middle ground between a core curriculum and an entirely elective curriculum.

Utilitarian Education. Depending on what our goals are, various forms of education can have utility value. A religious education has utility value in a traditional culture. In a largely secular society governed by technology and economic development, utility value is to be found elsewhere.

In the 1950s, galvanized by *Sputnik*, America turned away from many of the excesses of the progressive education of the first half of the century. A much greater emphasis was placed on math and science, testing, intellectual standards—and federal funding of education. In the 1970s, reacting against the excesses of the counterculture, declining SAT scores, and the New Progressivism, there was a move "back to the basics" and career education. Then in the 1980s, a series of national reform reports fretted about the economic challenges to America, and the search for *excellence* was on.

The most famous of the reform reports of the 1980s—that of the National Commission on Excellence in Education—began:

Our nation is at risk. Our once unchallenged preeminence in commerce, industry, science, and technological innovation is being overtaken by competitors throughout the world. This report is concerned with only one of the many causes and dimensions of the problem, but it is the one that undergirds American prosperity, security, and civility. We report to the American people that while we can take justifiable pride in what our schools and colleges have historically accomplished and contributed to the United States and the well-being of its people the educational foundations of our society are presently being eroded by a rising tide of mediocrity that threatens our future as a Nation.[111]

Or consider the first substantive paragraph of *Action for Excellence*, the report of the Education Commission of the States:

> Technological change and global competition make it imperative to equip students in public schools with skills that go beyond the "basics." For productive participation in a society that depends ever more heavily on technology, students will need more than minimum competence in reading, writing, mathematics, science, reasoning, the use of computers, and other areas. Mobilizing the education system to teach new skills, so that new generations reach the high general level of education on which sustained economic growth depends, will require new partnerships among all those who have a stake in education and economic growth. . . .[112]

The drive for excellence requires standards; standards require accountability; accountability requires testing; testing means competition. Merit pay should go to teachers who produce, and voucher schemes are advocated to allow discerning parents to reward successful schools. Government and business should invest in "quality" programs. "Behavioral objectives" and "time on task" become educational slogans. Teachers become technicians, and principals become business managers, manipulating human and financial resources to produce the best product. The knowledge that moves markets and machines becomes the knowledge most worth having. The goal is no longer an old-fashioned vocationalism that prepares students for a particular niche in the economy but basic skills—reading, writing, math, computer literacy, "critical thinking"—which give workers a vital flexibility in responding to the changing needs of a high-tech economy.

For utilitarians, education is reconceived on the model of a business, and the big questions are whether it can turn out a better product, whether it can be made more cost-effective.

Utilitarian and expressive education share the same cultural heritage of modernity; their governing values are those of liberal individualism. The differences between them are significant, however. Expressive education is much more concerned with feelings and creativity, with personal exploration and freedom; it is grounded in psychology and political theory. Utilitarian education is more concerned with expertise and hard facts, with technology and markets; it is grounded in economics and business. Expressivists are concerned with process, utilitarians with products.

Like market economies, utilitarian education is indifferent to religion. The subject does not come up in the reform reports or in the rhetoric of utilitarian reformers. For their purposes, it simply is not important.

The Cultural Left and Postmodern Education. Henry Louis Gates, Jr., has defined the Cultural Left as a loose and uneasy alliance "formed by feminist critics, critics of so-called 'minority' discourse, and Marxist and post-structuralist critics." A little tongue-in-cheek, he refers to it as "the Rainbow Coalition of contemporary critical theory."[113]

The Cultural Left would have us approach the world from within a "hermeneutics of suspicion," to use the usual phrase. Marxists see economic causes and class conflict below the surface of everyday politics; feminists find sexual oppression; and black critics see racism shaping our basic institutions and values. A great deal of the passion of the Left comes from the conviction that the moral pieties of conservatives and liberals need to be unmasked, for they use the language of morality (sometimes unconsciously) to rationalize their own self-interest. Schools and universities have a "hidden curriculum"— one that transforms children into compliant citizens, into "good" workers who uncritically accept an unjust status quo, into sexists and racists. A major theme of the Left, according to David Purpel, is

> the school's role in 'reproducing the culture,' in sorting out the candidates for class and caste system through its various testing and classification systems. The school's hidden curriculum also includes ways in which students learn to be obedient and passive, to work at meaningless tasks without complaining, to defer their pleasure, to value achievement and competition, and to please and respect authority figures. . . . It is, in this analysis, in the culture's interest to have schools that do *not*, structurally and purposely, promote excitement, a critical capacity, or creative potential.[114]

In its "preoccupation with accountability schemes, testing, accreditation, and credentializing," Henry Giroux suggests, "educational reform has become synonymous with turning schools into 'company stores.'"[115] For Michael Apple, in modern education "technique wins out over substance. . . . Rationality is redefined to signify not thoughtfulness but meeting bureaucratic needs and conforming to the requirements of 'our' economy."[116]

For many on the Cultural Left, truth is the outcome of a power struggle, knowledge is a social construct that groups use to oppress each other, and morality signals, as Giroux puts it, a retreat "into an unproblematic past in order to bolster unquestionable support of existing dominant social institutions and values." The canon must be exploded—or at least greatly expanded. Hence the need for multicultural education, for women's studies, for gay studies, for black and minority studies, and for courses that expose the relationship of power, oppression, and ideology. People within various traditions and communities must be able to speak for themselves. Teachers must be what Giroux has called "transformative intellectuals," emancipating students from an oppressive social order, empowering them to think critically about their world, recognizing it for what it is—a scene of struggle and exploitation, and teaching them to act politically so as to change it.[117] Education is inevitably political, and politics inevitably shapes education.

If liberal arts education is the modern standard-bearer of traditional classical education, and expressive and utilitarian education embody the dominant ideas and ideals of modernity, the Cultural Left speaks for postmodernism. It not only rejects the premodern world of religion and traditional moral values, it is highly suspicious of the modern values of science and technology, capitalism and political liberalism; it finds oppression, hypocrisy and rationalization in virtually all existing arrangements.

For the Cultural Left, a major purpose of education is the "deconstruction" of the dominant (or "hegemonic") systems of meaning in our culture, and many would agree with Lynda Stone, who argues for a postmodern "valorization of difference" in which "there is no move toward consonance, no 'minority,' or merely 'marginalized' view." Instead, "all opinions, ideas, and even 'facts of the matter' remain marginal, partial, ambiguous and tentative. And," she adds, "they remain all that there is."[118]

The Fragmentation of Education. In the end, of course, education is driven less by (overt) philosophy than by politics, special interest groups, the market, technology, cultural traditions—and inertia. In the recent Carnegie study of American high schools Ernest Boyer notes that "high schools have accumulated purposes like barnacles on a weathered ship. As school population expanded from a tiny urban minority to almost all youth, a coherent purpose was hard to find. The nation piled social policy upon educational policy and all of them on top of the delusion that a single institution can do it all. . . . What do Americans want high schools to accomplish? Quite simply, we want it all."[119]

Perhaps the most common perception of the purpose of education is captured nicely by Theodore Sizer. Press most adults about what it is all about and you hear: "High School? That's where you learn English and math and that sort of thing. Ask students, and you get the same answer. . . . 'Taking subjects' in a systematized, conveyer-belt way is what one does in high school."[120] John Goodlad comments: "Teachers are oriented to teaching particular things—the particular things they were taught in school. Relating these particular things to some larger purpose is not something they think about very much or have been prepared to do."[121]

And what about higher education? Boyer notes that at most colleges there is great difficulty,

> sometimes to the point of paralysis, in defining essential purposes and goals. Colleges, searching for students, are adding programs that they think will sell. The curriculum is controlled by academic departments. Teaching is organized around single courses that are only loosely related, if at all. . . . Faculty agree on the number of credits for a baccalaureate degree, but not on the meaning of a college education. Students, geared toward job training, complete courses, but general education is something to 'get out of the way,' not an opportunity to gain perspective."[122]

Since the 1980s there has been some movement to add coherence to the curriculum, but it is probably fair to characterize it as tinkering rather than anything significant.

And what about students? The annual surveys of incoming college freshmen conducted by the American Council on Education consistently show that when they are asked to choose from among twenty possible objectives in life they consider to be essential or very important, they consistently choose "being very well off financially" more than any other—73.0 percent in 1992. (Of course, religious objectives are not listed among the possibilities.) Hence it should not be surprising that the most important reason students give for going to college is to get a better job (chosen by 78.5 percent) and to make more money (73.3 percent).[123]

There is certainly nothing wrong with wanting a better job, though the desire to be "very well off" financially may be more troublesome. Still, the statistics show a lack of balance, at least, in the overall interests and educational goals of students. This should not be surprising. Today's graduates are, as Ernest Boyer reminds us, "the products of a society in which the call for individual gratification booms forth on every side while the claims of community are weak." Getting a good job and sustaining America's economic competitiveness provide the context in which almost everyone thinks about education. Arguably, high schools and universities exacerbate these tendencies by failing to provide an education that is coherent in any significant moral, social, or spiritual way. We provide students with (endless) information; we teach them technical skills; we teach them how to solve discrete problems but, Boyer notes, all of this leaves open the essential questions: "Education for what purpose? Competence to what end? At a time in life when values should be shaped and personal priorities sharply probed, what a tragedy it would be if the most deeply felt issues, the most haunting questions, the most creative movements were pushed to the fringes of our institutional life."[124]

Conclusions

The Supreme Court is often blamed for taking religion out of public education, and it is true that beginning in the 1940s the Court began to remove the practice of religion from public schools. But the Supreme Court had nothing to do with removing the religious purposes or content of American education, for they had virtually disappeared by the end of the nineteenth century. The lower courts played a role in the process of secularization only by enforcing anti-Catholic legislation prohibiting state support for sectarian schools.

It is true that prayers, devotional Bible reading, and chapel (at some public universities) survived into the twentieth century. Indeed, in the first several decades of the century, eleven states passed laws requiring devotional Bible reading (and an additional seven made Bible reading a matter of local option).[125] No doubt it is also true that individual teachers continued, on occasion, to express their personal religious views in the classroom, and schools continued to celebrate religious holidays. All of this is far from unimportant. Nonetheless, textbooks, the official curriculum, and the governing purposes of education had become almost completely secular by the end of the nineteenth century. Indeed, the fact that a ceremonial religious shell continued to envelop public education into the twentieth century only helped obscure the fact that its substance was now almost entirely secular.

It had been the central purpose of both the early Massachusetts schools and colonial colleges to nurture Christian belief and action: a fixed curriculum, employing religious texts (from the *New England Primer* to the Greek New Testament) conveyed to students the unquestioned truths of this world and the world to come. Education was secularized not as the result of direct attacks by militant secularists. Instead, as with modern civilization generally, secular values and ways of thinking gradually (and for the most part unobtrusively) acquired power in the hearts and minds of people.

The need for American values and a common culture in a religiously pluralistic society made sectarian education impossible in the nineteenth century. The result was the common school, where a vaguely "nonsectarian" Protestantism was influential for a while, but eventually Protestantism became too heavy a burden for common schools, and Americanism emerged as the dominant ideology—some would say the secular "religion"—of public education. In higher education the classics overshadowed theology almost from the start, and by the end of the eighteenth century the influence of the Enlightenment started science on its rise to prominence. By the end of the nineteenth century, an individualistic, pragmatic, business culture demanded electives, vocationalism, and research—particularly in science and technology. Surveying was valued more than Cicero, agriculture more than culture. What science can tell us is a matter of experiment and discovery: education must liberate students from the superstitions of the past. And because science and technology are complex, education must be specialized.

By the end of the nineteenth century not just theology but the capstone course in moral philosophy and the classics had fallen by the wayside. With this history it should not be surprising that contemporary education takes virtually no note of religion. Its overriding values are Americanism, pluralism and liberty, science and technology, economics and vocationalism.

This is the main plot line of American education. Public education (and much private education) has long since given up the ghost of religion. True, school prayer and religious symbols and holidays continue to be matters of controversy, and there are occasional battles over textbooks, but it is remarkable how little concern there is for incorporating religion into public education.

If the Supreme Court and the First Amendment had nothing to do with the secularization of American education historically, they have a great deal to do with how religion must be treated in public education now, for since the 1940s the Court has applied the First Amendment to public education. As we shall see, the proper role of religion in public schools and universities should depend on much more than what the courts will and will not allow. Nonetheless, an understanding of the law is important, not just so lawsuits can be avoided but because what is at issue is constitutional law—part of the very framework of America. To understand how religion should fit into education we must understand something about how America is constituted.

Hence, one more historical tour is necessary before we settle ourselves in the present for the remainder of the book. I begin this chapter by saying something about the movement for religious liberty in colonial America that culminated in the adoption of the religion clauses of the First Amendment to the Constitution in 1791. Next we will look at how the Supreme Court has interpreted those clauses, particularly at how they have been applied to public education. Finally, I'll offer my own assessment of how we (and the courts) should interpret the "separation of church and state" in America with an eye toward the controversies we will discuss in later chapters.

Religious Liberty in Colonial America

People came to America for a variety of reasons, religious reasons prominent among them. Sydney Ahlstrom, perhaps the greatest of American historians of religion, has stressed "the remarkable degree to which religious and missionary motives functioned in the thought of the entire age. . . . The seventeenth century was an age of faith, a time when few Englishmen would take lightly any precept clearly set forth in Scripture, and when God's providence was seen behind every occurrence. Scoffers and skeptics were the exception." Christian concerns, Ahlstrom suggests, were a "shaping force of such strength as to be almost unfathomable to the modern mind," thus it is "as dangerous to attribute purely secular motives to anyone as it is to regard pious phraseology as proof of any exceptional degree of religious concern."[1] The secular and the sacred had not yet been disentangled.

The City on a Hill.Most Americans think of Puritan New England as the birthplace of America, forgetting that Catholic Spain was here long before the Puritan English, that a somewhat less godly lot had left England to populate Virginia a few years before the Puritans embarked for Massachusetts, and that Native Americans, with their own religious traditions, were here long before anyone else. The Puritans do have a special place in the American story, however, precisely because they *did* come to America for religious reasons and because their pilgrimage has become so much a part of the "established" American story.

In his sermon upon their arrival in Massachusetts Bay, John Winthrop, their governor, beseeched them "to love mercy, to walke humbly with our God." To this end, he said, "wee must be knitt together in this worke as one man . . . allwayes havieing before our eyes our Commission and Community . . . soe shall wee keepe the unitie of the spirit in the bond of peace, the Lord will be our God and delight to dwell among us, as his owne people and will commaund a blessing upon us in all our wayes." The Puritans understood themselves to have entered into a covenant with God; their "errand into the wilderness" was to establish a holy commonwealth, a "citty on a hill" for "the eies of all people are uppon us."[2]

The Puritans came to America for religious liberty—their own, not anyone else's. Moved by a sense of divine mission and confident of the truth, they, like most believers of that day, were decidedly intolerant. In this, Ralph Barton Perry has noted, Puritanism resembled "its God, who might be merciful, but was not tolerant. . . . [Puritanism] enjoyed an invincible sense of truth and felt no compunction in saving unwilling men from the effects of their own blindness."[3] "Toleration," the Puritan John Cotton wrote, "made the world anti-Christian."[4] As a result, the New England Puritans saw fit, on occasion, to brand, bore the tongues, or cut the ears off heretics, and between 1649 and 1651 they hanged four Quakers. A few years later, Puritans in Maryland outlawed Roman Catholicism, plundered Catholic estates, banished priests, and executed four Catholics.[5]

Depending on what we mean by the word, Puritan New England may or may not have been a *theocracy*. The clergy did not rule; the responsibilities of minister and magistrate were separate. Still, the state had religious functions and the Puritan religion was *established*. All were taxed for its support; all were required to attend church services; only church members could vote or hold public office; dissenters were banished. It was the duty of the magistrates, not just the ministers, to enforce a religious conception of the public good. As John Cotton saw it, the ecclesiastical and civil orders should not be set "in opposition as contraries" but should work together "for the welfare of both according to God." Hence, civil magistrates should "subject themselves spiritually to the power of Christ in church-ordinances," for "'a good magistrate is within the church, not above it.'"[6]

Puritanism—which became, eventually, Congregationalism—was the established religion in all of New England except Rhode Island. Anglicanism— the Church of England—was the established church in most of the southern colonies. The Puritans who emigrated to New England brought their religion with them; it was established by the people. The English government established the Church of England in Virginia and the southern colonies; it was imposed by the crown.

Religious Pluralism. "For over a thousand years," Winthrop Hudson has written, "it had been generally assumed that every member of society was automatically a member of the church." But only "in Virginia and in New England did a parish system, designed to embrace a total community, function with any real degree of success." Most other colonies had established religions and practiced varying degrees of intolerance, but "the religious diversity which was present from the beginning compromised any attempt to establish a system which presupposed that the whole community would belong to a single church."[7]

Most colonists were Calvinists, but there were also Catholics and Quakers and Moravians and Mennonites and Methodists and Lutherans and freethinkers and the religiously indifferent and a few Jews and, on the colonial margins, Native Americans with their own religions. Even within the Calvinist tradition there were Congregationalists, Presbyterians, Baptists, and the Dutch and French Reformed, and there was constant warfare between the

"Separationist" and "Non-Separationist" Puritans as there would be between New Light and Old Light Congregationalists.

And there were Anglicans. Most colonists were English, but they were atypical in not being Anglican. America was settled much more by dissenters than by members of England's established church (who had no religious reason for emigrating). Nonetheless, at one time or another the Anglican church was established in Maryland, North Carolina, South Carolina, Georgia, New York, and, of course, Virginia. These establishments tended to be weak, though as the Anglican Society for the Propagation of the Gospel became more aggressive in its missionary efforts in the 1760s fears of Anglican establishments increased. After the Revolution John Adams claimed that "apprehensions of episcopacy" contributed a great deal to "close thinking on the constitutional authority of parliament over the colonies."[8] In 1776 the Presbytery of Hanover petitioned the General Assembly of Virginia for relief from paying taxes to support the Anglican church. They said: "But now when the many and grievous oppressions of our mother country have laid this continent under the necessity of casting off the yoke of tyranny and of forming independent governments upon equitable and liberal foundations, we flatter ourselves that we shall be free from all the encumbrances which a spirit of domination, prejudice, or bigotry has interwoven with most other political systems. . . . Certain it is that every argument for civil liberty gains additional strength when applied to liberty in the concerns of religion." The authors added: "We ask no ecclesiastical establishments for ourselves; neither can we approve of them when granted to others."[9]

Not just Anglican establishments were resented. As every denomination was in a minority somewhere (in that different states established different religions), there was reason to be opposed to establishments quite apart from feelings about England and the Church of England. Voltaire once said "If there had been in England only one religion, its despotism would have been fearful. If there had been two religions, they would have cut each other's throat. But as there are thirty they live peacefully and happily."[10] (Of course they *did* cut each other's throats for a while.) In America, there were, almost from the start, twenty or thirty sects, and with the Great Awakening nonestablished religions flourished. If there was not too much throat-cutting, there was constant turmoil when ministers of different sects were imprisoned by local establishments and people were required to pay taxes to support some religion other than their own or be married by a clergyman of another religion. There was tax resistance and constant political maneuvering as dominations sought exclusions from discriminatory laws.

In *Federalist 10*, James Madison argued that the existence of factions enables liberty to thrive, for factions will mutually ensure each other's relative powerlessness: "The influence of factious leaders may kindle a flame within their particular States, but will be unable to spread a general conflagration through the other States: a religious sect, may degenerate into a political faction in a part of the Confederacy; but the variety of sects dispersed over the entire fact of it, must secure the national Councils against any danger from that source."[11] Religious pluralism makes religious liberty necessary; it also makes it possible.

The Transformation of American Religion. Dissenting churches had powerful practical reasons for favoring religious liberty, but theological arguments for separating church and state began to be heard in the seventeenth century.

The Puritan notion of establishing a New Israel, a theocracy grounded in a special covenant with God, was, for Roger Williams, an Old Testament notion. Williams argued that the church should be purely spiritual and not be identified with the things of this world: "Can the sword of steel or arm of flesh make man faithful or loyal to God? Or careth God for the outward loyalty or faithfulness, when the inward man is false and treacherous? Or is there not more danger from a hypocrite, a dissembler, a turncoat in his religion (from the fear or favor of men) than from a resolved Jew, Turk, or papist, who holds firm unto his principles?"[12] "The civil sword," Williams wrote, "may make a nation of hypocrites and anti-Christians, but not one true Christian."[13] Faith is a gift of God; it is not something the state can require. His modest conclusion was that to link church and state is to make the church a "filthy dunghill and whorehouse of rotten and stinking whores and hypocrites."[14] For its own health the church must be separated from the state. Correlatively, statecraft required no great religious faith: "A pagan or anti-Christian pilot may be as skillful to carry the ship to its desired port as any Christian mariner or pilot in the world."[15] Williams's Rhode Island never had a religious establishment. No wonder the Puritans kicked him out of Massachusetts.

William Penn founded Pennsylvania as a "holy experiment" in religious freedom. As a Quaker, Penn could not accept a state that required religious conformity, for people must be free to follow their own inner lights. Neither a fallible church nor a fallible state can stand between a person and God. One must be king over one's own conscience, he wrote, for if men "shall be subject to their fellow-creatures, what follows, but that Caesar, however he got it, has all, God's share, and his own too, and, being Lord of both, both are Caesar's and nothing God's." This defeats God's work of Grace and "the invisible operation of his eternal spirit, which can alone beget faith, and is only to be obeyed." Hence no man should be "accountable to his fellow-creatures, as to be imposed upon, restrained, or persecuted for any matter of conscience whatever."[16]

The logic of separating church from state was implicit in the Protestant Reformation in its removal of mediating institutions between people and God, in its emphasis on personal religious experience and conscience, and in its idea of the priesthood of all believers. But these elements in Reformation theology continued to be subordinated to the idea of an established church in Europe, and so it was in America for some time. The influence of Williams and Penn was limited to their own colonies.

In the late 1720s and 1730s scattered revivals of highly emotional religion began to appear here and there. This "awakening" from the increasingly intellectual religion of the time became *great*—that is, a part of life in all of the colonies—when George Whitefield came to America in 1739. Whitefield was an astounding orator: it was said that people could be brought to tears when he uttered the word "Mesopotamia," and even Ben Franklin emptied his pockets into the collection plate when he heard Whitefield preach. In a series of missionary journeys he preached to huge crowds of people up and down the coast.

Whitefield was the friend and colleague of John and Charles Wesley, and like them he preached a religion of the heart. (The Puritans and Anglicans were, on the whole, highly educated and gave relatively more attention to the head than the heart.) Whitefield and the other preachers of the Great Awakening called for a sudden and emotional conversion, a new birth. Whitefield did not limit himself to working within a specific church; like modern evangelists, he preached to all who would hear him. His message, and the experience to which he called people, was more important than any institutional or theological trappings it might take on. Preaching in Philadelphia, he turned his eyes upward and thundered: "Father Abraham, whom have you in heaven? Any Episcopalians? No! Any Presbyterians? No! Any Independents or Methodists? No, no no! Whom have you there? We don't know those names here. All who are here are Christians. . . . Oh, is this the case? Then God help us to forget party names and to become Christians in deed and truth."[17] This was controversial stuff. It made salvation possible outside the doors of established churches and orthodox theologies. Many of the American clergy were sympathetic and supportive, though many were not, recognizing the threat to doctrinal orthodoxy—and their authority.

New churches proliferated. As Martin Marty puts it, "free enterprise had come to the world of religion." No longer was a person born into a church; one chose a particular church. No longer was it possible to think about a unified relationship between a single church and community as the Puritans had done: "Where once a single steeple towered above the town, there soon would be a steeple and a chapel, Old First Church and competitive separatist Second Church or Third Baptist Chapel—all vying for souls."[18]

No church benefited more from the new understanding of religion than did the Baptists, who were united in their loathing of established religion. In part this was because they were subjected to persecution by the established churches. But the pursuit of religious liberty was also a matter of Baptist theology as it had been for Roger Williams. Isaac Backus, the great eighteenth-century Baptist minister, wrote: "As God is the only worthy object of all religious worship, and nothing can be true religion but a voluntary obedience unto his revealed will, of which each rational soul has an equal right to judge for itself, every person has an inalienable right to act in all religious affairs according to the full persuasion of his own mind, where others are not injured thereby." John Leland, the Virginia Baptist leader, asked whether Christ or his apostles "ever gave orders to, or intimated, that the civil powers on earth, ought to force people to observe the rules and doctrine of the gospel." Muhammad, Leland suggested, "called in the use of the law and sword, to convert people to his religion; but Jesus did not." And in 1785, in response to the Virginia Assessment Bill (which would have taxed people to support the religion of their choice) the Virginia Baptists resolved "That it is believed to be repugnant to the spirit of the gospel for the legislature thus to proceed in matters of religion; that the holy author of our religion needs no such compulsive measures for the promotion of his cause; that the gospel wants not the feeble arm of man for its support; that it has made and will again through divine power make its way against all opposition; and that should the legislature assume the right of taxing the people for the support of the gospel it will be destructive to religious liberty."[19] William R. Estep concludes that at "every point in the struggle for religious freedom in the colonies, the Baptists led the way. Indeed, Estep notes, "From the beginning of the Baptist movement, all major Baptist confessions have contained articles on religious liberty and the separation of church and state."[20] Only in the 1980s did Southern Baptists break with this tradition.

Indifference and Economics. In spite of the Great Awakening, the late eighteenth century was a time of great indifference to religion. Arguably, the Awakening was but a short-term, if significant, reversal of the ongoing secularization of America. According to Richard Hofstadter, by 1750 fewer than one in seven was a church member in New England, and further south the number was less than one in fifteen.[21] Sydney Ahlstrom puts church membership somewhere between 5 and 10 percent of the population in the last two decades of the century, and adds that "in many churches membership itself became increasingly nominal."[22] In part this was the result of the inaccessibility of churches in a frontier society. But in 1782, after a tour of the middle colonies, Hector St. John de Crèvecoeur wrote that "religious indifference is imperceptibly disseminated from one end of the continent to the other. . . . Persecution, religious pride, the love of contradiction, are the food of what the world commonly calls religion. These motives have ceased here; zeal in Europe is confined; here it evaporates in the great distance it has to travel; there it is a grain of powder inclosed, here it burns away in the open air, and consumes without effect."[23] Hofstadter notes that "Christian theorists of persecution have always held that toleration was bred by indifference. The presence of large numbers of those who did not care to join the churches was a constant deadweight upon those who did care enough not only to join but to compel others to do so."[24]

Bernard Bailyn has shown in fascinating detail the secularization of Puritan New England over the course of the seventeenth century. The orthodox Puritan view, Bailyn reminds us, was that

toleration was an unmitigated evil, a sinful welcome to Satan's clamorous hordes. But it had become clear that this precept, made effective in law, was as harmful to trade as it was beneficial to the perpetuation to orthodoxy. Persecution, a growing number of merchants discovered, was simply bad for trade; it "makes us stinke every wheare," as the business-minded George Downing wrote to Winthrop, Jr. Not only did it lessen the appeal of New England to immigrants, but it also blackened the reputation of New Englanders in English trading circles. At each point of controversy merchants appeared in defense of a softer, more latitudinarian policy.

To be a city on a hill requires isolation, whereas trade requires mobility, immigration, growth, material possessions, and the enjoyment of life. As the seventeenth century moved toward its close, the Puritan ministers saw everywhere "the evidence of a decay of piety" and "the calamitous failure to perpetuate the ideals and standards of the Founders. Instead of devotion to the life of the spirit they saw only a mad pursuit of gain. . . . At trade and its propagators they hurled their bitterest invective, for in them lay one of the deep roots of malignancy."[25] At midcentury Captain Edward Johnson wrote: "An overeager desire after the world hath so seized on the spirits of many that the end of our coming hither is forgotten; and notwithstanding all of the powerful means used, we stand at a stay, as if the Lord had no farther work for his people to do but every bird to feather his own nest." And at the end of the century, Cotton Mather wrote: "Religion brought forth prosperity and the daughter destroyed the mother."[26]

Often English authorities adopted an explicit policy of religious toleration for economic reasons. So, for example, the Lords of Trade in London wrote to their colleagues in Virginia: "A free exercise of religion . . . is essential to enriching and improving a trading nation; it should be ever held sacred in His Majesty's colonies." Hofstadter concludes that "in an age of commercial expansion the profit motive quietly undermined the desire to impose a creed. . . . It was the English proprietors, hungry for revenue and hence for settlers, who opened the colonial gates to members of all faiths."[27] Religious freedom would motivate people to emigrate from England to the New World and do England's business.

Not all of America's religious leaders were hostile to such reasoning. William Penn, himself a proprietor, argued for toleration in part because it would increase tax revenues and, as a result, Quaker Pennsylvania suffered the same decline in religiosity as Puritan New England when its citizens transferred their treasures from the meetinghouse to the countinghouse.[28] In their petition to the General Assembly of Virginia in 1776, the Presbytery of Hanover argued that an established church retards economic growth:

Witness the rapid growth and improvements of the northern provinces compared with this. No one can deny that the more early settlement and the many superior advantages of our country would have invited multitudes of artificers, mechanics, and other useful members of society to fix their habitation among us, who have either remained in their place of activity, or preferred worse civil governments and a more barren soil where they might enjoy the rights of conscience more fully than they had a prospect of doing it in this. From which we infer that Virginia might have now been the capital of America . . . had it not been prevented by her religious establishment.[29]

America had mixed motives for religious toleration, some less noble perhaps, but no less important, than others.

The Enlightenment. For the enlightened thinkers of the eighteenth century, deeply influenced by the scientific revolution and liberal political philosophy, truth was to be discovered through the use of reason, not accepted uncritically as a matter of tradition or Scripture. "Have the courage to use your own reason!," wrote Immanuel Kant, was the motto of the Enlightenment.[30] No doubt most Americans were somewhat more traditional and less "enlightened" than the spirit of the age demanded. Still, many of the Americans who played the most important roles in the founding of the country were solidly grounded in Enlightenment thought and the virtues of reason.

For Thomas Jefferson, truth is discovered through natural reason operating freely, and it needs no special favors from government. "It is error alone which needs the support of government," Jefferson claimed. Indeed, "difference of opinion is advantageous in religion." After all, the effects of religious establishments have been the torture and imprisonment of millions of innocent people. Indeed, coercion serves only "to make one half the world fools, and the other half hypocrites." "Reason and persuasion," Jefferson argued, "are the only practicable instruments," and "to make way for these, free inquiry must be indulged. . . . But every State, says an inquisitor, has established some religion. No two, say I, have established the same. Is this a proof of the infallibility of establishments?"[31] James Madison saw similar dangers in religious establishments. During "almost fifteen centuries has the legal establishment of Christianity been on trial. What have been its fruits? More or less, in all places, pride and indolence in the clergy; ignorance and servility in the laity; in both, superstition, bigotry, and persecution. Enquire of the teachers of Christianity for the ages in which it appeared in the greatest lustre; those of every sect point to the ages prior to its incorporation with civil policy."[32]

Here we find many of the great themes of the Enlightenment: disgust with traditional religious establishments and the moral and political corruption that follows in their wake and a good deal of optimism about human nature and the power of reason. Reason and free inquiry will support *true* religion by, in Jefferson's words, "bringing every false one to their tribunal, to the test of investigation."[33] Government is no better able to legislate in matters of religion than in physics: the justification for Galileo's arguments lay in the reasoned evidence he could bring to bear in their support, not in their agreement with established belief. So it must be with religion.

Not only are the consequences happier if religious liberty is secure; it is also the right of all people to follow their individual consciences. We are individuals, possessing natural rights, in the state of nature. We contract away some rights to make society and government possible, but some rights—those to life, liberty, and the pursuit of happiness, for example—are so basic that we call them inalienable; they are part of our being. Because we are rational beings, the right to liberty of conscience cannot be taken from us. As Jefferson says in the first line of the Virginia Statute of Religious Liberty, "Whereas Almighty God hath created the mind free" we are unjustly constrained should our leaders force our compliance with religious beliefs or practices; any such act shall be "an infringement of natural right."[34]

In his "Memorial and Remonstrance on the Religious Rights of Man" Madison argued that it is a fundamental truth that "religion, or the duty which we owe to our creator, and the manner of discharging it, can be directed only by reason and conviction, not by force and violence." Hence religion "must be left to the conviction and conscience of every man; and it is the right of every man to exercise it as these may dictate. This right is, in its nature, an unalienable right." For before "any man can be considered as a member of civil society, he must be considered as a subject of the governor of the universe." Therefore, "in matters of religion no man's right is abridged by the institution of civil society."[35]

In America the Enlightenment was not hostile to religion per se; it was hostile only to traditional, established religion.

Religious liberty was not created by the Founding Fathers in one generation. Instead, there was a considerable movement toward religious liberty over the course of the seventeenth and eighteenth centuries. Much of the movement came from dissenting religious denominations, from new ways of thinking about conscience and conversion, as well as from political battles fought to overcome the oppression of established churches. And much of the pressure for religious liberty came from Enlightenment thinkers who believed that natural reason, operating in a free culture, was the way to the truth. Evangelicals and Enlightenment rationalists made strange bedfellows but an effective coalition. And, of course, these battles were fought against the backdrop of an increasingly secular society in which many were indifferent to religion, individualism was a frontier virtue, and pluralism required a policy of toleration (if not full-fledged liberty) for the sake of community peace.

Religion and the Constitution

By the time the Constitution was drafted, freedom of conscience was protected in all the colonies. According to Walter Berns, "no one, ratifier or non-ratifier . . . expressed an opinion opposed to freedom of conscience. There was simply no debate on the subject, nor even a recorded difference of opinion."[36] This did not mean that all religious establishments had been abolished, however, for freedom of conscience and the right to the "free exercise" of one's religion were taken to be compatible with the "establishment" of religion. (In many European countries today, there continue to be established churches *and* "free exercise," the right to practice nonestablished religions.) Four colonies (Rhode Island, New Jersey, Delaware, and Pennsylvania) never had

established religions, and another three colonies had abolished their establishments by the time the Constitution was written. In none of the six remaining states was a single denomination established, however; instead, the
remaining six states had multiple establishments, such that voters in each
community could choose which church to support with tax revenues. The
money would typically go for ministers' salaries or to pay for new churches. In
most New England communities Congregationalism continued to be the de
facto "established" religion because it was the religion of the majority of the
people; but it was not the de jure established religion. By 1833 all states had
abolished their establishments, with Massachusetts the last to do so.

Even after disestablishment many states retained religious tests for officeholders; some required the officeholder to be a Protestant and some a Christian, though by 1868 all states had abolished such oaths or modified them to
require only a belief in God.[37] States passed Sunday closing laws, and citizens
could be convicted of blasphemy. Some states discriminated *against* religion
in forbidding clergymen to serve in legislatures or hold some public offices.

The picture, then, is complicated. A majority of the states had abolished
their own religious establishments by the time the Constitution was written,
and all had done so by 1833. Although many states retained laws restricting or
promoting religion well into the nineteenth and occasionally the twentieth
centuries, the movement for religious liberty and against religious establishment progressed rapidly in the colonies and states in the eighteenth and nineteenth centuries, quite apart from the Constitution.

What, then, does the American Constitution say about religion? The answer is very little. Only once does religion come up: Article VI, clause 3, stipu-
lates that "no religious test shall ever be required as a qualification to any
office or public trust under the United States." In light of the number of states
requiring such tests, this was not an insignificant restriction to put on the federal government. Still, the Constitution did not speak to the question of religious liberty.

Indeed, there was no discussion of religious liberty at the Constitutional
Convention and little discussion of a Bill of Rights. This was not because
the Framers were hostile to rights. Rather, it was because they believed
that the new federal government would have only those powers delegated to
it by the Constitution; the Constitution delegated no power to the federal
government regarding religion so it had no power to infringe on religious liberty. Hence, the Framers believed, there was no need for a Bill of Rights to
protect religious liberty.

Not everyone was convinced by this logic (Jefferson being one), and the
ratification debates within the states showed considerable desire for a Bill of

Rights. Indeed, the ratifying conventions in six states recommended an amendment that would secure religious liberty. The First Congress took up the matter of a Bill of Rights and discussed a number of amendments dealing with religion. In the end, the House amendment read: "Congress shall make no law establishing religion, or prohibiting the free exercise thereof, nor shall the rights of conscience be infringed." The Senate adopted a somewhat narrower version: "Congress shall make no law establishing articles of faith or a mode of worship, or prohibiting the free exercise of religion." The Senate did not insist on its version, however, and in Conference Committee the House members (led by James Madison) prevailed. The final version was, "Congress shall make no laws respecting an establishment of religion, or prohibiting the free exercise thereof."[38]

The First Congress approved twelve amendments to the Constitution; the religion clauses were part of the third amendment on the list. The states refused to ratify the first two, so the third became our First Amendment.

The Fourteenth Amendment. As enacted by the Framers, the First Amendment was a prohibition on Congress only, and states could maintain religious establishments and laws restricting the rights of religious believers. It was not until 1940 that the religion clauses of the First Amendment were first held to be binding on the states as well as on the federal government. How did this come about?

Following the Civil War, the Fourteenth Amendment was passed to restrict the power of the states. It said: "No State shall make or enforce any law which shall abridge the privileges or immunities of citizens of the United States; nor shall any State deprive any person of life, liberty, or property without due process of law, nor deny to any person within its jurisdiction the equal protection of the laws." What liberties could the states not abridge? Beginning in the 1920s the Supreme Court answered that First Amendment rights were to be protected from state governments as well as the federal government, and in 1940, in *Cantwell* v. *Connecticut*, the Court applied for the first time one of the religion clauses to the states when it overturned the conviction of a Jehovah's Witness who failed to comply with a Connecticut law requiring him to secure a license to engage in religious solicitation. This, the Court said, was an unconstitutional restriction of his religious liberty.[39]

It is doubtful that the framers of the Fourteenth Amendment intended for the religion clauses to be applied to the states by way of their amendment. In 1876 Congress considered and rejected a constitutional amendment that would have directly applied the religion clauses to the states; no one then suggested that the Fourteenth Amendment had already done the job. In 1884 the Supreme Court rejected a direct claim that the Fourteenth Amendment made the Bill of Rights binding on the states.[40] Nonetheless, since the 1940s the Supreme Court has applied the religion clauses to the states; this has become an established part of American law.

The Free Exercise Clause

There are two religion clauses: the Establishment Clause ("Congress shall make no law respecting an establishment of religion") and the Free Exercise Clause ("or prohibiting the free exercise thereof"). I begin with the Free Exercise Clause, though it is the second of the clauses and the one least at issue in cases having to do with religion and public education, because it is the simpler of the two.

The Free Exercise Clause says that Congress (and after 1940, government at any level) shall not restrict religious liberty by law. The first important free exercise case demonstrated that there were limits on the protection of religious liberty, however. In *Reynolds* v. *United States* (1879) the Supreme Court upheld an 1862 federal law prohibiting polygamy in territories under the jurisdiction of the federal government over the free exercise objections of Mormons. In his reading of the First Amendment, Chief Justice Morrison Waite declared: "Congress was deprived of all legislative power over mere *opinion*, but was left free to reach *actions* which were in violation of social duties or subversive of good order."[41] Polygamy, Waite wrote, is "odious" to the nations of Western civilization in that it undermines the institution of marriage, upon which society is built, and is no more defensible on free exercise grounds than child sacrifice or suttee would be. That is, maintaining public morality (as defined by the great majority of Americans) is sufficiently important to override the free exercise of religion.

In recent years the Court has made little of the distinction between opinion and action, recognizing that unless the Free Exercise Clause protects action as well as opinion it has little force. The question is rather one of which actions should be protected, for it is probably fair to say that no one believes that people should have the right to practice their religion *whatever* it requires. At some point, free exercise rights must give way before the rights of others and before the public good. How, then, are free exercise rights to be adjudicated?

A law might violate the Free Exercise Clause and be declared unconstitutional because it picks out a particular religious group for discriminatory treatment, but the much more common situation is one in which individuals seek exemptions from general laws that do not overtly discriminate against them but nonetheless restrict their religious liberty. For example, are

Seventh-Day Adventists entitled to unemployment compensation when they refuse to take a job that requires them to work on Saturday, their Sabbath? In *Sherbert* v. *Verner* (1963) the Supreme Court held that they are; to condition their receipt of government benefits on their willingness to violate their Sabbath unjustifiably burdens their religious liberty.[42] The "Sherbert Test," first used in this case, came to be used by the Court for adjudicating free exercise cases until 1990. In Justice Sandra Day O'Connor's summary: "First, when the government attempts to deny a Free Exercise claim, it must show that an unusually important interest is at stake, whether that interest is denominated 'compelling,' 'of the highest order,' or 'overriding.' Second, the government must show that granting the requested exemption will do substantial harm to that interest, whether by showing that the means adopted is the 'least restrictive' or 'essential,' or that the interest will not 'otherwise be served.'"[43] That is, the courts must apply a balancing test, weighing the free exercise rights of individuals against the interests of the state. If the state's interests are "compelling" and if there is no less burdensome way of accomplishing its interests, then free exercise rights must give way. Needless to say, the test does not provide a neat formula for resolving any claim, only a rough procedure by which to do so. It does not define what counts as a compelling claim, or the least restrictive means. That is left for the court to decide on a case-by-case basis.

Almost all commentators view *Wisconsin* v. *Yoder* (1972) as remarkable for the extent to which the Court went to protect free exercise rights. The issue was whether the Amish should be exempted from obeying a Wisconsin law requiring children to attend school until the age of sixteen. The Amish were willing to send their children through the age of fourteen, but they objected to high school education because they believed it would expose their children to "worldly" influences that conflicted with their beliefs. Chief Justice Warren Burger acknowledged the compelling state interest in education, but he argued that the "inherently simple and uncomplicated" way of life of the Amish is "difficult to preserve against the pressure to conform." The compulsory attendance law "carries with it a very real threat of undermining the Amish community and religious practice as they exist today; they must either abandon belief and be assimilated into society at large, or be forced to migrate to some other and more tolerant region."[44] This, the Court held, would unduly burden their free exercise rights. The Amish were exempted from obeying the law.[45]

Yoder was the only case other than a series of unemployment compensation cases in which the Court used the Sherbert Test to protect free exercise. Almost always the Court decided that whatever the governmental interest, it was sufficiently compelling to override the right of free exercise. Nonetheless, the test did seem to capture something of what a broad consensus of jurists believed to be the proper way to adjudicate free exercise cases. Hence there was considerable distress when the Court threw the test out in *Employment Division* v. *Smith* (1990).

In *Smith* the Court denied that the First Amendment protected members of the Native American Church who use peyote as part of their religious ritual from an Oregon law prohibiting its use. Peyote has been used in Native American religion for centuries; it is not a "recreational" drug, and many states have exempted it from their drug laws when used in religious services. In the majority opinion, Justice Antonin Scalia distinguished between laws whose direct object is to regulate religion—and are unconstitutional—and laws that have, as an *incidental* effect, the abridgment of free exercise. For example, states cannot make laws prohibiting the use of wine in the mass; that would be to burden the religious freedom of Catholics. But they can prohibit the use of alcohol generally; the fact that an incidental effect of the law would be to make the use of wine in the mass illegal would not, on the majority's reading, unconstitutionally burden the free exercise of religion. The Oregon law prohibiting the use of peyote was not designed to regulate the Native American Church; its effect on that church was incidental. Hence there is no free exercise case to be made. No balancing between the interests of the state and free exercise is necessary any longer; if there is a valid general law, that is all there is to it. Scalia argued that the Sherbert Test opened the door to religious exemptions "from civic obligations of almost every conceivable kind" and that its rigorous application would be "courting anarchy" for it would replace general law with private conscience.[46] Religious minorities should use the political process to change laws with which they disagree. He acknowledged "that leaving accommodation to the political process will place at a relative disadvantage those religious practices that are not widely engaged in; but that unavoidable consequence of democratic government must be preferred to a system in which each conscience is a law unto itself or in which judges weigh the social importance of all laws against the centrality of all religious beliefs."[47]

Four justices dissented vehemently from Scalia's opinion. Justice O'Connor argued that the majority opinion "dramatically departs from well-settled First Amendment jurisprudence . . . and is incompatible with our Nation's fundamental commitment to individual religious liberty." The First Amendment, she claimed, "does not distinguish between laws that are generally applicable and laws that target particular religious practices." General laws that are seemingly "neutral" toward religion "can coerce a person to violate his religious conscience or intrude upon his religious duties just as effectively as laws aimed at religion." Indeed, states are not so naive as to burden religious practice as such; hence, "If the First Amendment is to have any vitality, it ought not to be construed to cover only extreme and hypothetical situations in which a State directly targets a religious practice." For O'Connor, the Sherbert Test "effectuates the First Amendment's command that religious liberty is an independent liberty, that it occupies a preferred position, and that the Court will not permit encroachments upon this liberty, whether direct or indirect, unless required by clear compelling governmental interests 'of the highest order.'" O'Connor noted that the use of the Sherbert Test over the last several decades had not led to a state of anarchy. Indeed, it had worked well to "strike sensible balances between religious liberty and competing state interests."[48]

Virtually everyone—from fundamentalists to the ACLU—thought *Smith* was an appallingly bad decision. In fact, legal scholar Douglas Laycock has claimed that *Smith* created the legal framework for religious persecution. "What prevents Oregon," he asks, "from creating a special task force to hunt down peyote worshipers, break up their services, prosecute all those in attendance, and send them all to prison for long terms? The answer is the lack of stomach for persecution. . . . The Constitution of the United States does *not* stand in the way. The Supreme Court does *not* stand in the way." Laycock cites a dozen cases in the two years after *Smith* in which lower courts have failed to take free exercise rights seriously. "In effect," Laycock concludes, "*Smith* repealed the substantive component of the Free Exercise Clause."[49]

In the fall of 1993, in response to the overwhelming opposition to the Court's ruling in *Smith*, Congress passed, and President Bill Clinton signed, the Religious Freedom Restoration Act, which requires the courts to return to using the Sherbert Test for adjudicating free exercise cases.

How the courts read the Free Exercise Clause is crucial for dealing with a number of important religious matters in public education, for parents are increasingly seeking legal exemptions from school policies they claim burden their religious liberty—mandatory AIDs education, condom distribution, use of textbooks hostile to their religion, immodest gym-class dress, and values clarification exercises, for example.[50]

The Establishment Clause

In the first case applying the Establishment Clause to the states, *Everson* v. *Board of Education* (1947), Justice Hugo Black set the terms that continue to govern the Court's interpretation of the clause:

The "establishment of religion" clause of the First Amendment means at least this: Neither a state nor the Federal Government can set up a church. Neither can pass laws which aid one religion, aid all religions, or prefer one religion over another. Neither can force nor influence a person to go to or to remain away from church against his will or force him to profess a belief or disbelief in any religion. . . . No tax in any amount, large or small, can be levied to support any religious activities or institutions, whatever they may be called, or whatever form they may adopt to teach or practice religion. . . . In the words of Jefferson, the clause against establishment of religion by law was intended to erect "a wall of separation between church and state."

Black went on claim that the First Amendment requires the state "*to be neutral* in its relations with groups of religious believers and non-believers." The First Amendment declares not just that a state church shall be unconstitutional, not just that the state must be neutral among religions, but that the state must be *neutral between religion and nonreligion*. Of course, neutrality is a double-edged sword. If the state cannot promote religion, it cannot be hostile to religion either: "State power is no more to be used so as to handicap religions than it is to favor them."[51]

The two most important Establishment Clause rulings relating to public education were handed down in 1962 and 1963. In the first of these, *Engel* v. *Vitale*, the issue was a prayer written by the State Board of Regents in New York: "Almighty God, we acknowledge our dependence upon Thee, and we beg Thy blessings upon us, our parents, our teachers and our Country." The prayer was to be said at the beginning of each school day. Justice Black, writing for the majority, said that there can be no doubt but that

the Regents' prayer is a religious activity. It is a solemn avowal of divine faith and supplication for the blessings of the Almighty. . . . We think that the constitutional prohibition against laws respecting an establishment of religion must at least mean that in this country it is no part of the business of government to compose official prayers for any group of the American people to recite as a part of a religious program carried on by government. It is a matter of history that this very practice of establishing governmentally composed prayers for religious services was one of the reasons which caused many of our early colonists to leave England and seek religious freedom in America.

That the prayer was nonsectarian made no difference, for it promoted religion generally. That schools had an excusal policy ensuring that students prayed voluntarily made no difference, for the Establishment Clause "is violated by the enactment of laws which establish an official religion whether those laws operate directly to coerce nonobserving individuals or not."[52] What is forbidden is that the government take sides, not that the government force anyone else to take sides.

Black argued that the ruling should not be taken as an indication of hostility to religion. The First Amendment was the creation of people concerned to protect religious liberty; for them, government should not be used "to control, support or influence the kinds of prayer the American people can say." History shows, he argued, that whenever religion and the state became allied, religion "incurred the hatred, disrespect and even contempt of those who held contrary beliefs." And if the prayer seemed brief and innocuous James Madison's warning must be remembered that it "is proper to take alarm at the first experiment with our liberties. . . . Who does not see that . . . the same authority which can force a citizen to contribute three pence only of his property for the support of any one establishment, may force him to conform to any other establishment in all cases whatsoever."[53]

Then, in *Abington Township School District* v. *Schempp* (1963), the Court ruled that devotional Bible reading was no more permissible than prayer. The Commonwealth of Pennsylvania required that at least "ten verses from the Holy Bible shall be read, without comment, at the opening of each public school on each school day." Children could be excused at the written request of their parents. Writing for the majority, Justice Tom Clark proposed a two-part test for resolving establishment questions: "What are the purpose and the primary effect of the enactment? If either is the advancement or inhibition of religion then the enactment exceeds the scope of legislative power as circumscribed by the Constitution. That is to say that to withstand the strictures of the Establishment Clause there must be a secular legislative purpose and a primary effect that neither advances nor inhibits religion."[54] Government—and public schools—must be religiously neutral. Clearly devotional Bible reading is a religious activity whose purpose and effect are to advance religion.

The sole dissent came from Justice Potter Stewart, who worried that a substantial free exercise claim was at issue. Shouldn't students have the right to read the Bible as an exercise of their religious liberty? Indeed, shouldn't they have a free exercise right to pray? Shouldn't the Free Exercise Clause take precedence if it conflicts with the Establishment Clause? Stewart argued that the ruling threatened state neutrality for "a compulsory state education system so structures a child's life that if religious exercises are held to be an impermissible activity in schools, religion is placed at an artificial and state created disadvantage. Viewed in this light, permission of such exercises for those who want them is necessary if the schools are truly to be neutral in the matter of religion. And a refusal to permit religious exercises thus is seen, not as the realization of state neutrality, but rather as the establishment of a religion of secularism."[55]

Justice William Brennan, agreeing with the majority, responded to Stewart's concern by acknowledging that a free exercise claim can take precedence over the Establishment Clause in some situations. In the military or in penal institutions, for example, the state often deprives people of the opportunity to worship as they please; hence it is legitimate for the state to provide them with chaplains. But a student's "compelled presence in school for five days a week in no way renders the regular religious facilities of the community less accessible to him than they are to others."[56] There is no free exercise or neutrality issue here, for a student's religious beliefs are not burdened because religious activities are excluded from a part of the day. (Brennan went on to note that peer pressure would likely keep many children from taking advantage of their right not to participate in religious activities.)

The *Schempp* decision is particularly important for our purposes, for in the majority opinion Justice Clark added, in much quoted words, that although devotional Bible reading is unconstitutional, "it might well be said that one's education is not complete without a study of comparative religion or the history of religion and its relationship to the advancement of civilization. It certainly may be said that the Bible is worthy of study for its literary and historic qualities. Nothing we have said here indicates that such study of the Bible or of religion, when presented objectively as part of a secular program of education, may not be effected consistently with the First Amendment."[57] That is, the Court has prohibited the *practice* of religion in public education; it has not prohibited the *study* of religion. The Bible may be read in public schools, but the purpose of reading it cannot be to promote religion; it cannot be read devotionally. Or, as Justice Arthur Goldberg put it in his concurring opinion, the public schools may teach students *about* the Bible, neutrally as it were.[58]

The two tests by which Justice Clark evaluated devotional Bible reading in *Schempp* became the first two prongs of a three-prong test which the Court has often used (sometimes with variations) in adjudicating Establishment Clause cases. The "Lemon Test," as Chief Justice Burger defined it in *Lemon* v. *Kurtzman* (1971), is, "First, the statute must have a secular legislative purpose; second, its principal or primary effect must be one that neither advances nor inhibits religion; finally, the statute must not foster 'an excessive government entanglement with religion.'" The purpose of the third prong is "to prevent, as far as possible, the intrusion of either [government or religion] into the precincts of the other;" the term "excessive" acknowledges that the separation of church and state can never be complete.[59]

The Court has found that a number of state laws had the unconstitutional purpose of promoting religion in public schools. In *Epperson* v. *Arkansas* (1968) the Court ruled that Arkansas could not prohibit the teaching of evolution in its public schools, for, according to Justice Abe Fortas, it was "clear that fundamentalist sectarian conviction was and is the law's reason for existence."[60] The law served no secular purpose; rather, its purpose was to promote religion. Because the Court would not allow states to ban the teaching of evolution, several states passed "balanced-treatment" laws, requiring that creation-science be taught along with evolution. In *Edwards* v. *Aguillard* (1987) the Court rejected Louisiana's version. Citing the legislative debates that preceded passage of the law, Justice Brennan held that the "preeminent purpose of the Louisiana legislature was clearly to advance the religious viewpoint that a supernatural being created mankind."[61] In *Stone* v. *Graham* (1980) the Court ruled that the state of Kentucky could not require that the Ten Commandments be posted on classroom walls. In spite of the state's claim that it had a secular purpose—to make evident to students the role of the Ten Commandments in our legal tradition—the Court ruled that the state's real purpose was religious: "to induce the school children to read, meditate upon, perhaps to venerate and obey, the Commandments."[62] In 1985, in *Wallace* v. *Jaffre*, the Court returned to the question of prayer, ruling unconstitutional an Alabama law authorizing a one-minute period of silence in public schools "for meditation *or voluntary prayer.*" Justice John Paul Stevens concluded from the history of the statute that the legislators had no secular purpose and that the clear purpose of the law was to promote prayer and religion.[63]

The Court also struck down a variety of ways in which states attempted to provide funding for religious schools. It ruled unconstitutional state funding for instruction in secular subjects in religious schools (*Lemon* v. *Kurtzman*, 1971); remedial or therapeutic services or counseling done in religious schools (*Meek* v. *Pittenger*, 1974); instructional supplies or field trips for students in religious schools (*Wolman* v. *Walter*, 1977); public school teachers who teach secular subjects on a part-time basis in religious schools (*Grand Rapids School District* v. *Ball* and *Aguilar* v. *Felton*, 1985); the maintenance and repair of facilities at parochial schools; and tuition reimbursement for children attending religious schools (*Committee for Public Education and Religious Liberty (PEARL)* v. *Nyquist*, 1973). In some of these cases the problem was that the aid had the (primary) effect of promoting religion in violation of the second prong of the Lemon Test. So, for example, in *Nyquist* the Court held that tuition reimbursement was unconstitutional because it provided indiscriminate financial support for the religious as well as the secular mission of parochial schools.[64] In other cases, where the aid might (but need not) have the effect of promoting religion, the supervision necessary to ensure that the aid was properly used would involve the excessive entanglement forbidden by the third prong of the Lemon Test. For example, public school teachers paid to teach secular subjects in parochial schools would need "detailed monitoring" to ensure that they did not promote religion.[65] (This has sometimes been characterized as a Catch-22 requirement: the supervision necessary to ensure that the aid is constitutionally used is itself unconstitutional.[66])

But the Court has also *allowed* certain forms of aid to parochial schools. It has approved state funding for secular textbooks used in religious schools (*Cochran* v. *Louisiana State Board of Education*, 1930); bus transportation for children to parochial schools (*Everson* v. *Board of Education*, 1947); speech, hearing, and psychological diagnostic services (*Wolman* v. *Walter*, 1977); standardized texts in secular subjects (*Committee for Public Education and Religious Freedom* v. *Regan*, 1980); and translators for deaf students attending religious schools (*Zobrest* v. *Catalina Hills School District*, 1993). Sometimes such funding was justified on the grounds that the benefit went to students and their families rather than the parochial schools, but in every case it was important that the funding went to students attending public as well as religious schools—so that it was awarded neutrally—and that it served secular purposes, albeit in the context of religious schooling.

No doubt the most significant accommodation of religious schooling was made possible by *Mueller* v. *Allen* (1983), in which, in spite of its earlier ruling in *Nyquist*, the Court upheld a Minnesota law allowing parents to take tax deductions for the tuition, textbook, and transportation expenses of children attending public, private, or sectarian schools.[67] Writing for the Court, Chief Justice William Rehnquist argued that such aid was constitutional because it was neutrally available to all parents (not just parents of children in parochial schools). Moreover, because private schools relieve the burden that added children would place on public schools, and because they provide a "wholesome competition" with public schools, the law had a clear secular purpose and did not fall victim to the first prong of the Lemon Test. This was an extremely important decision, and I will return to it in discussing vouchers in Chapter 12.

There are several other cases in which the Court has allowed the state to accommodate religion in public schools. Although the Court prohibited in-school religious release time as a "utilization of the tax-established and tax-supported public school system to aid religious groups to spread their faith,"[68] it held in *Zorach* v. *Clauson* (1952) that out-of-school religious release time was constitutional so long as it was truly voluntary and not tax-supported. Writing for the majority Justice William O. Douglas declared that the separation of church and state does not mean that there can be no relationship at all between them; that would rule out fire and police protection. Douglas recommended what Chief Justice Burger would later call a "benevolent neutrality" which accommodates religion but stops short of actively promoting it. To forbid release time, Douglas argued, would be "to find in the Constitution a requirement that the government show a callous indifference to religious groups. That would be preferring those who believe in no religion over those who do believe."[69]

In *Board of Education of the Westside Community Schools* v. *Mergens* (1990), the Court upheld the congressional Equal Access Act. According to that act, if a public secondary school has a "limited open forum" allowing *some* noncurricular student group to use school facilities, it must allow *all* student groups, including religious groups, to use those facilities. (The forum is limited in that only students, not adults, can form groups.) Allowing religious groups to use state facilities does not violate the Establishment Clause, Justice O'Connor wrote, because the message of the act "is one of neutrality rather than endorsement; if a State refused to let religious groups use facilities open to others, then it would demonstrate not neutrality but hostility toward religion."[70]

Finally, in its most recent ruling on religion and public education—*Lee* v. *Weisman* (1992)—the Court struck down graduation prayers. Writing for the majority Justice Anthony Kennedy ignored the Lemon Test, arguing that "government may not coerce anyone to support or participate in religion or its exercise." Even though students were not legally required to attend their own (middle school) graduation, there was considerable social pressure to attend; after all, "graduation is one of life's most significant occasions."[71] For Kennedy the problem was not that the state promoted religion, but that it coerced others into participating in a religious ceremony. Justices Harry Blackmun and David Souter wrote concurring opinions (signed by Justices O'Connor and Stevens) making clear their view that the Establishment Clause is violated if the state takes sides on a religious matter whether or not anyone is coerced.

The Separation of Church and State

To the uninitiated (that is, to most of us), these rulings are likely to appear as a hodgepodge of unprincipled decisions—indeed, not a few constitutional scholars have come to the same conclusion. In reading the majority and dissenting opinions, we can discern, however, the outlines of an ongoing argument about the proper role of religion in American life.

Since the Court began to apply the religion clauses to the states in the 1940s it has usually taken a liberal or "separationist" position. For a time in the early 1990s it appeared that a five-justice conservative or "accommodationist" majority was about to begin dismantling the wall of separation, and most observers thought the Court would begin the process by approving graduation prayers in the *Weisman* case, but Justice Kennedy broke ranks with his conservative colleagues, and with the (presumably liberal) Justice Ginsburg replacing (the clearly conservative) Justice White, it appears the liberal majority will hold for a while longer. What then are the liberal and conservative, the separationist and accommodationist, positions on the religion clauses?

Conservative justices favor a weak reading of both the Free Exercise and Establishment clauses, while the (relatively) more liberal justices favor a strong reading of both. That is, conservatives have been less concerned about the dangers of establishment, and less concerned to protect the free exercise rights of religious minorities, than liberals. Liberals have been opposed to any possibility of establishment, and they have been especially concerned about the free exercise rights of religious minorities.

There are at least two reasons for this. First, judicial liberals, like political liberals generally, have been relatively more concerned with individual rights, including the rights of unpopular groups, than conservatives, who find virtue to lie with political majorities and conserving the status quo. Hence Justice Scalia recommended to Native Americans who wished to use peyote in their religious rituals that if they felt their rights had been abridged, they should go out and collect the votes to change the law. On Establishment Clause issues conservatives have been much more willing than liberals to accommodate the interests of the majority—to allow governmental prayer in at least some circumstances, for example.

The second reason is related. Judicial conservatives are opposed to "judge-made law" or "judicial activism." They believe that law and policy are best made by legislatures responding to democratic majorities and, as Chief Justice Rehnquist put it in a 1976 speech, the Court does not have "a roving commission to second-guess Congress, state legislatures and state and federal administrative officers concerning what is best for the country."[72] Judicial liberals have been much more concerned to defend the rights of individuals (as they understand them) against legislatures and democratic majorities.

There is a nice historical continuity—and perhaps something of an irony as well—in this division of perspectives. At the time of the Framers, a coalition

of religious evangelicals and Enlightenment liberals provided the force behind the drive for religious liberty. Today, liberals and religious minorities
still line up on the same side of First Amendment politics against conservative
defenders of accommodation and a nonpreferential establishment. The irony
is that many (though far from all) evangelical Protestants have switched
sides: when they were persecuted minorities they wanted strong free exercise rights and no establishment. As they have become the religious majority,
they have sought accommodation—quasi-establishment—and have become
considerably less sympathetic to the free exercise rights of minorities (whom
they often referred to as "cults"). As Richard John Neuhaus once put it: "A religious community that no longer understands itself as an embattled minority
begins to think more about influence than about tolerance."[73]

The Court's interpretation of the Free Exercise Clause has never turned on
the intentions of the Framers.[74] It is otherwise with regard to the Establishment Clause—as Justice Black's crucial appeal to Jefferson's wall makes clear.
Indeed, disagreement about the meaning of the Establishment Clause is
bound up with quite different understandings of American history and the intentions of the Framers.

There have been two broad traditions governing the relationship of religion
and government that have stood in marked tension with each other. Grant
Wacker has aptly called them the "custodial" and the "plural" traditions, but
they might also be called the "conservative" and "liberal" or the "accommodationist" and "separationist" traditions. Within the first of these pairs, the
state is understood to have, in Wacker's words, a "custodial responsibility for
the spiritual as well as the physical well-being" of the people, while in the
plural tradition the state refuses this responsibility; citizens are responsible
for their own spiritual welfare, and no religious tradition is entitled to special
standing.[75] The custodial tradition embodies the remnants of the traditional
fusion of the sacred and the secular; the pluralist ideal resonates with modern
liberalism.

I suggest that we add nuance to this picture by distinguishing two versions
of both the custodial and pluralist traditions.

For many religious conservatives America is a Christian nation, and it
properly nurtures and legislates Christian values. Jerry Falwell has written:

I believe America has reached the pinnacle of greatness unlike any nation
in human history because our Founding Fathers established America's
laws and precepts on the principles recorded in the laws of God, including

the Ten Commandments. God has blessed this nation because in its early days she sought to honor God and the Bible, the inerrant Word of the living God. Any diligent student of American history finds that our great nation was founded by godly men upon godly principles to be a Christian nation. . . .

It is God Almighty who has made and preserved us as a nation, and the day that we forget that is the day that the United States will become a byword among the nations of the world. . . . I do not believe that God is finished with America yet. America has more God-fearing citizens per capita than any other nation on earth.[76]

In a demographic sense we are a Christian nation. Indeed, it may be true that America has more "God-fearing citizens"—and Christians—per capita, than any other country. In 1988, 84 percent of Americans told Gallup pollsters that they believed that Jesus was the Son of God.[77]

Moreover, many of our laws are based on the laws of God as understood in the Christian tradition. Indeed, the influence of Christianity on American culture has been immense; there is no way of making sense of American history apart from Christian tradition. (Of course, the influence of the Enlightenment has also been immense.)

But was our country founded "by godly men upon godly principles to be a Christian nation"? In one of the most careful studies of the origins of religious liberty in America Thomas Curry has claimed that at the time the First Amendment was passed the "vast majority of Americans assumed that theirs was a Christian, i.e. Protestant, country, and they automatically expected that government would uphold the commonly agreed on Protestant ethos and morality." Not only was tax money devoted to supporting Christian churches, chaplains, and proclamations, but at the time of the Constitution, eleven of the thirteen original states had laws limiting officeholding to either Protestants or Christians.[78] In the nineteenth century several state supreme courts made claims to the effect that this is a Christian country,[79] and Justice Joseph Story, who sat on the United States Supreme Court from 1811 to 1845 and who authored the much used *Commentaries on the Constitution*, wrote that at the time the First Amendment was adopted "the general if not the universal sentiment in America was, that Christianity ought to receive encouragement from the State so far as was not incompatible with the private rights of conscience and the freedom of religious worship. An attempt to level all religions, and to make it a matter of state policy to hold all in utter indifference, would have created universal disapprobation, if not universal indignation."[80] Indeed, in 1892, in *The Church of the Holy Trinity* v. *United States*, Justice Brewer wrote for the U.S. Supreme Court that our cultural and legal traditions make it clear that "this is a Christian nation."[81]

If this was the general sentiment of Americans, it was not obviously the sentiment of the Founders, however. Although any generalization will have exceptions, Martin Marty's characterization of them is a fair one: they "respected the Bible but they began to speak of the deity as an abstraction, not an impersonal Person, and they played down miracles. Jesus was respected as possibly the greatest human, but he was not the supernatural divine Son of God. [They] tore the old drama of heaven and hell from the sky and the netherworld and instead anchored religion in earthly behavior. Reason for them counted more than faith, and morals more than grace."[82] Fifty-two of the fifty-six signers of the Declaration of Independence and a majority of members of the Continental Congress were Masons.[83] (Freemasonry was a secret society whose members accepted a more or less Deist view of God.)

Our founding documents are not in any explicit sense Christian. The Declaration of Independence appeals not to the Christian God but to "nature's God" and "Divine Providence" and mentions neither the Bible nor Jesus. The truths to which the signers appealed are not revealed but self-evident. It is true that the Constitution is dated "In the year of our Lord," but this was more convention than anything, and not only is there no substantive reference to Jesus, the Bible, or Christianity in the Constitution, there is no reference to God. The only mention of religion comes in excluding religious tests for holding office. The Preamble to the Constitution is written in the form of a social contract of the people, not a covenant between the people and God. (And though every president has mentioned God in his inaugural address, not one has mentioned Jesus.[84])

In their book *The Search for Christian America* the evangelical Christian historians Mark Noll, Nathan Hatch, and George Marsden argue that "no matter how favorable toward Christianity some of the founders may have been, their goal was pluralism, rather than the preferment of one religion to all others. Certainly they did not design the American government so as to ensure that the nation would be Christian in the sense that today Iran is Moslem or Russia is Marxist. Rather the system was intended to guarantee that Christianity and other religions, including various versions of secularized beliefs, *all* should be permitted influence in public discourse." The symbolism of the new government was as secular as its Constitution: the "United states was the first Western nation to omit explicitly Christian symbolism, such as the cross, from its flag and other early national symbols." And they cite a 1797 treaty with the Islamic nation of Tripoli that was "negotiated under Washington, ratified by the Senate, and signed by President John Adams," according to which, as "the government of the United States of America is not in any sense founded on the Christian Religion,—as it has in itself no character of enmity against the laws, religion or tranquility of Musselmen [Muslims] . . . it is declared by the parties that no pretext arising from religious opinions shall ever produce an interruption of the harmony existing between the two countries."[85]

But perhaps we need to go back farther in our history. What of the Puritan founding of America? Did not John Winthrop say: "Thus stands the cause between God and us, we are entered into Covenant with him for this work, we have taken out a Commission"? The problem is that in the days before the Declaration of Independence and the Constitution we were not America but a hodgepodge of colonies, and why should we take the Puritan experience in New England as normative for America rather than the Anglican experience in Virginia, the Quaker experience in Pennsylvania, or the separation of church and state in Rhode Island? Indeed, as Thomas Curry remarks, "No other major religious group in the colonies proved so wrong in anticipating the future of Church and State as the Puritans who settled Massachusetts and Connecticut in the 1630s."[86]

Of course, the idea of a Christian America is controversial even among conservative Christians, many of whom take their cue not from Winthrop and the Puritans but from Roger Williams; for them it is the church, not the state, that is the vehicle of God's work in the world. This is the position of Noll, Hatch, and Marsden: the "New Testament teaches unmistakably that Christ set aside national and ethnic barriers and that he has chosen to fulfill his central purposes in history through the church, which transcends all such boundaries."[87]

According to *accommodationism* (the other custodial position) the Establishment Clause was intended to prohibit the establishment of a state church; Christianity is not the established religion of the United States. But the state may legitimately promote religion nonpreferentially and noncoercively. So, to cite the most prominent accommodationist, Chief Justice Rehnquist, the Establishment Clause "forbade establishment of a national religion, and forbade preference among religious sects or denominations. . . . The Establishment Clause did not require government neutrality between religion and irreligion nor did it prohibit the federal government from providing non-discriminatory aid to religion."[88]

The accommodationist case is based primarily on the actions of the First Congress—the Congress that wrote and passed the First Amendment—and the first presidents. The First Congress approved paid chaplains for the House and Senate as well as for the armed services. It reenacted the

Northwest Ordinance of 1787, which provided that "religion, morality, and knowledge, being necessary to good government and the happiness of mankind, schools and the means of education shall forever be encouraged." It requested President Washington to issue a Thanksgiving Proclamation recommending to the people "a day of public thanksgiving and prayer, to be observed by acknowledging with grateful hearts the many and signal favors of Almighty God."[89] President Washington complied, and this became a tradition followed by his successors—Jefferson excluded. Even Jefferson approved a treaty with the Kaskaskia Indians which provided tax support for a Roman Catholic priest and church. Surely Congress could not have "accommodated" religion so clearly if its members believed they had just passed a constitutional amendment which required them to be neutral between religion and nonreligion. "What is beyond question," Walter Berns has written, "is that both the states and the federal government have traditionally acted as if the language [of the First Amendment] permitted assistance to religion."[90]

But such arguments can prove too much. I've already cited Justice Story's claim that it was the general sentiment of the founding generation of Americans that Christianity ought to receive support from the state. This being the case, he argued, "the real object of the [First] amendment was, not to countenance, much less to advance Mahometanism, or Judaism, or infidelity, by prostrating Christianity; but to exclude all rivalry among Christian sects."[91] No doubt some of the Framers were willing to countenance a good deal of (nonpreferential) state support for Protestantism or Christianity. Many of the Framers, I have noted, were Deists, some of whom might well have allowed a measure of public acknowledgment of their rather austere God. What is much less likely is that there was any significant support among the Framers for a nonpreferential accommodation of *all* religions—of Judaism or Islam, for example—yet that is the position of contemporary accommodationists. Most likely it was the intention of the great majority of Founders either to allow public support of Protestantism or Christianity or to require neutrality between religion and nonreligion.

It might also be argued that in promoting religion on occasion the First Congress was inconsistent, naive, or played politics with religion. Madison claimed that he issued his Thanksgiving proclamations only in wartime to build morale, and in his "Detached Memoranda," written after he was president, he said that he regretted this and indicated that he then viewed such proclamations as unconstitutional.[92] More important, the very fact that America was so thoroughly Christian made it difficult to appreciate the logic of separationism. Few politicians and statesmen were philosophers even among the generation of the Founding Fathers. Because they were enmeshed in the nets of a pervasively Protestant culture, concerned with the practical matters of running a new government, and with no tradition of the separation of church and state to draw on for guidance, it is not surprising if their practice did not measure up to their principles. Garry Wills has written that no "other government in history had launched itself without the help of officially recognized gods and their state-connected ministers. It is no wonder that, in so novel an undertaking, it should have taken a while to sift the dangers and the blessings of the new arrangement, to learn how best to live with it, to complete the logic of its workings."[93]

Separationists have proposed a number of arguments to advance Justice Black's claim in *Everson* that the Establishment Clause was meant to keep government neutral between religion and nonreligion by way of constructing a wall of separation between them.

First, at the time the First Amendment was passed, only six states still had established religions, and each of these had multiple establishments. Hence, when the Framers wrote that Congress shall make no law respecting an establishment of religion, they surely meant not just to rule out a national church but to rule out multiple establishments and the support of *all* religion.[94]

Second, I have mentioned that a Bill of Rights was not given serious attention at the Constitutional Convention because the delegates held that the new federal government would have only those powers delegated to it, and the Constitution delegated no powers to the federal government to make laws respecting religion. Therefore, as Leonard Levy puts it, "Congress was powerless, *even in the absence of the First Amendment*, to enact laws that benefited one religion or church in particular or all of them equally and impartially." In the debates over the ratification of the Constitution, "Edmund Randolph of Virginia declared that 'no power is given expressly to Congress over religion,' and added that only powers 'constitutionally given' could be exercised. Madison said, 'There is not a shadow of right in the general government to intermeddle with religion.' Richard Dobbs Spaight of North Carolina maintained: 'As to the subject of religion . . . no power is given to the general government to interfere with it at all. Any act of Congress on this subject would be a usurpation.'" Surely the First Amendment, which was designed to *limit* the powers of the federal government, cannot be taken to *add* to the power of government to establish religion, even religion generally. The Bill of Rights, Madison said, was not framed "to imply powers not meant to be included in the enumeration."[95]

Third, the Senate's version of the First Amendment—which declared that "Congress shall make no law establishing articles of faith or a mode of worship"—would have sufficed to rule out a national church; but the

Conference Committee instead adopted the broader wording of the House version—that "Congress shall make no laws respecting an establishment of religion." The committee, Levy argues, "flatly refused to accept the Senate's version . . . indicating that the House would not be satisfied with merely a ban on preference of one sect or religion over others."[96] The Senate acquiesced.

Fourth, Justice Souter has recently noted that the absence of the article "a" is significant: the Establishment Clause does not forbid laws respecting the establishment of *a* religion; it forbids law "respecting the establishment of religion"—that is, religion generally.[97]

Whether or not one finds these arguments convincing it can be argued that the Court should not be bound by the Framers' intentions. According to Justice Brennan, "Our religious composition makes us a vastly more diverse people than were our forefathers. They knew differences chiefly among Protestant sects. Today the Nation is far more heterogeneous religiously, including as it does substantial minorities not only of Catholics and Jews but as well of those who worship according to no version of the Bible and those who worship no God at all. In the face of such profound changes, practices which may have been objectionable to no one in the time of Jefferson and Madison may today be highly offensive to many persons, the deeply devout and the nonbelievers alike."[98] Consider an analogy. In ruling "separate but equal" schools unconstitutional in 1954, the Supreme Court concluded that "we cannot turn the clock back to 1868" in deciding the meaning of the Fourteenth Amendment but "must consider public education in the light of its full development and its present place in American life throughout the nation."[99] In requiring equal protection of the laws, the authors of the Fourteenth Amendment surely did not intend to eliminate segregation. But as Christopher Mooney has argued, "to formulate intent by restricting it to the contemporary outlook of the legislators is clearly not the right way to formulate it. . . . Some larger conviction of principle must be attributed to them, such as the overall intention to outlaw discrimination on the basis of race."[100] So it should be with the Establishment Clause: in determining its meaning we must consider the pluralism of contemporary American life.

In any case, the Framers' original intent can hardly be binding when the Court has applied the First Amendment to the states by way of the Fourteenth Amendment, for certainly it was not the intent of the Framers of the First or the Fourteenth Amendments that the First Amendment should constrain the states, yet this has become a central dogma of recent jurisprudence. Constitutional scholar Harold Berman argues that "it would be a sign not of respect but of disrespect to constitutional history for the courts to overrule the precedents of the past 45 years in favor of the precedents of a more distant past. Our constitutional history is an ongoing history. It is a living tradition."[101] In *Federalist 14* Madison wrote: "Is it not the glory of the people of America, that whilst they have paid a decent regard to the opinions of former times and other nations, they have not suffered a blind veneration for antiquity, for custom, or for names, to overrule the suggestions of their own good sense, the knowledge of their own situation, and the lessons of their own experience?"[102] In our highly pluralistic times there is surely some merit in reading the Establishment Clause to require neutrality between religion and nonreligion, not just between various Protestant or Christian sects.

If it is fairly clear that Madison and Jefferson were separationists, the historical record remains scanty and ambiguous. No doubt the Framers and the legislators who approved the First Amendment had different and conflicting notions of what they were doing and, as John Semonche has noted, "the majority of votes cast in support of the religion clauses, both in Congress and the state legislatures were recorded without explanation."[103] Still, I am inclined to think the argument for separationism to be stronger than the argument for accommodationism. The Framers established a liberal, religiously neutral federal government. The Constitution is neither a religious nor a Christian document. One purpose of the religion clauses was to protect religious liberty. Another was to make clear that the federal government was not to legislate *for or against* religion—that was a power reserved for the states. Of course, the federal government *did* promote religion in some ways; this shows the temptations of politics and the limitations of fallible men who do not fully appreciate the meaning of the principles they have articulated. In any case, the Supreme Court has, for the time being at least, accepted the separationist position so that must be our starting point—regardless of what we think the ending point should be.

But there are two ways of parsing separationism. As I use these terms, "strict" separationists take their guidance from Justice Black's appeal to Jefferson's "wall of separation," while "neutral" separationism derives from Black's contention that the Establishment Clause requires neutrality between religion and nonreligion. Strict separationists would have government provide *no* support for religion, keeping the two as separate as possible; neutral separationists would allow support if that is necessary to maintain the state's neutrality between religion and nonreligion. In this debate it seems to me that the strict separationists seek to build too high and impenetrable a wall.

The purpose of the Framers of the First Amendment was to protect religious liberty (at the federal level), and to this end the federal government was to stay out of religious matters, neither taking sides with religion nor against it. The Framers' purpose clearly was *not* to transform America into a secular culture. Of course, in early America government was limited in what it did. And, as Michael McConnell puts it,

> a small government could be entirely secular, and would have little impact on culture. But when the government owns the street and parks, which are the principal sites for public communication and community celebrations, the schools, which are a principal means for transmitting ideas and values to future generations, and many of the principal institutions of culture, exclusion of religious ideas, symbols, and voices marginalizes religion in much the same way that the neglect of the contributions of African American and other minority citizens, or of the viewpoints and contributions of women, once marginalized those segments of the society.

Suppose, McConnell says, that a socialist government owned all land and property. In such a society a truly neutral government would be required to fund and sponsor religious activities; if it did not there would be no religious liberty. Indeed, "a 'neutral' state would attempt to replicate the mix of religious elements that one would expect to find if the institutions of culture were decentralized and private. . . . No one would contend, in a socialist context, that a policy of total secularization would be neutral."[104] Although benign neglect of religion sufficed for the purposes of neutrality in early America, McConnell argues, the expansive welfare-regulatory state now needs a policy that actively includes religion, for to exclude it is to marginalize it, and this defeats the purpose of the religion clauses.

A part of the problem is that strict separationists tend uncritically to conflate neutrality with secularity, but we saw in chapter 1, and as we shall see over and over through the rest of this book, what is secular is often hostile to religion. And, as McConnell argues, a pervasively secular public realm would certainly not be neutral.

Strict separationists are likely to hold that any funding or sponsorship of religion is ipso facto a violation of religious neutrality. Again, this is not true. Justice Brennan, the Court's strictest separationist, argued on free exercise grounds that it may be incumbent on government to fund chaplains and places of worship (in prisons or in the military) when government so structures the environment that people have no access to them. But it is important to recognize that this is no violation of neutrality; in fact, to deny prisoners or people in the military access to religion would be to demonstrate hostility to religion rather than neutrality. Or, to take another example, to grant tax exemptions to religious organizations is not to promote religion but to treat religion neutrally with other private, nonprofit institutions.[105]

In fact, the Supreme Court has noted any number of times that government justifiably provides police and fire protection for religious organizations; it allows public schools to release children during school time for off-campus religious instruction; student religious clubs may meet to pray in school rooms before and after school hours; and, of course, students may study the Bible—albeit not devotionally—in public school classes. As Justice Burger wrote in *Lemon*, the "line of separation, far from being a 'wall,' is a blurred, indistinct, and variable barrier."[106] Well, sometimes. At other times, particularly in funding cases, the Court has tended to adopt a much stricter separationism.

The purpose of the Establishment Clause should be to promote what Douglas Laycock has called "substantive neutrality." Such neutrality requires government "to minimize the extent to which it either encourages or discourages religious belief or disbelief, practice or nonpractice, observance or nonobservance." Religion "should proceed as unaffected by government as possible."[107] Substantive neutrality is more complicated than a purely "formal" neutrality. So, for example, a law prohibiting the use of alcoholic beverages that does not pick out Catholics for discrimination is formally neutral; but it would actively discourage Catholic religious practice. A legal exemption for Catholics to use wine in the mass would not be formally neutral because it would give them special standing, but it would be substantively neutral for it would avoid hostility to religion while providing "only an infinitesimal tendency" to encourage religious activity.[108] Judgments about what is substantively neutral may require a measure of subtlety.

As we shall see, for public education to be substantively neutral, for it to minimize the extent to which it actively discourages religion, it must take religion seriously as part of the curriculum.

First Principles

The motto on our dollar bill declares the United States to be *novus ordo seclorum*—the "new order of the ages." Yet, as Garry Wills has recently pointed out, virtually everything in our Constitution "had been anticipated both in theory and practice." Everything, that is, but religious disestablishment. That, "more than anything else, made the United States a new thing on the earth."[109] Religious liberty and freedom of conscience do not have the sanction of history. Traditionally, both church and state have seen fit to regulate and censor the life of the mind and of the spirit. The "first principles" articulated in the religion clauses of the First Amendment mark a radical departure from the wisdom of the past.

As we have seen, Jefferson and Madison, like many of their time, believed that as individuals we possess rights to liberty and freedom of conscience. These rights are not the gift of the state or of the church but are inalienable. We are individuals before we are members of communities. The old view— that one was born into a religion inherited with the territory—violated these rights. We are to live, Madison said, by reason and conviction, not by force. Indeed, for many of that Enlightenment generation, if truth is to be discovered, "free inquiry must be indulged"—as Jefferson put it.[110] Freedom is the precondition of sorting out truth from error; only in a free society is progress possible.

There was another, equally powerful, argument for religious liberty and freedom of conscience for the Founders. Because America was from the beginning religiously pluralistic, and because religion was divisive (as the great religious wars demonstrated beyond any doubt), civil peace required that the state be built on a foundation that was not sectarian. Because we are all concerned to live in peace, we must constitute ourselves in terms of principles that unite rather than divide us.

These continue to be potent arguments. In 1988, a group of prominent Americans—including Presidents Ford and Carter and Chief Justices Burger and Rehnquist—signed the Williamsburg Charter, reaffirming the importance of religious liberty in our national life. The charter grew out of a widespread conviction that religious liberties are threatened, here and abroad, and that there is too little appreciation and understanding of the religion clauses of the First Amendment. The charter claims that the "right to religious liberty based upon freedom of conscience remains fundamental and inalienable. While particular beliefs may be true or false, better or worse, the right to reach, hold, exercise them freely, or change them, is basic and non-negotiable." Religious liberty must depend, the charter claims, "on neither the favors of the state and its officials nor the vagaries of tyrants or majorities. Religious liberty in a democracy is a right that may not be submitted to vote and depends on the outcome of no election. A society is only as just and free as it is respectful of this right, especially toward the beliefs of its smallest minorities and least popular communities."[111]

The object of the religion clauses—and of the Williamsburg Charter—is to affirm that we shall be free from established religions and from state regulation of religion. Neither the church nor the state shall have the authority to restrict religious liberty or freedom of conscience. The result, according to the charter, "is neither a naked public square where all religion is excluded, nor a sacred public square with any religion established or semi-established. The result, rather, is a civil public square in which citizens of all religious faiths, or none, engage one another in the continuing democratic discourse."[112]

This right to religious liberty, the charter claims, "is premised upon the inviolable dignity of the human person." No doubt many of the signers, like the Founders, believed that such dignity, with its attendant rights, comes from God. But, as the charter makes clear, "signing this Charter implies no pretense that we believe the same things or that our differences over policy proposals, legal interpretations and philosophical groundings do not ultimately matter. The truth is not even that what unites us is deeper than what divides us, for differences over belief are the deepest and least easily negotiated of all." Using the language of the theologian John Courtney Murray, the charter claims that the religion clauses are not "articles of faith" but are "'articles of peace' concerned with the constitutional constraints and the shared prior understanding within which the American people can engage their differences in a civil manner and thus provide for both religious liberty and stable public government." The Williamsburg Charter, like the religion clauses of the First Amendment, affirms a way in which Americans can "live with their deepest differences."[113]

Our most fundamental commitments—be they secular or religious—will often separate us. Nonetheless, we are likely to share in what the philosopher John Rawls has called an "overlapping consensus" of moral commitments, for there *are* some values we hold in common—even if we disagree about how to justify them—including the obligation to seek peace and live civilly with those with whom we disagree in an inescapably pluralistic culture. Rawls argues that in a modern democracy it is inevitable that there will be a variety of conflicting (but reasonable and comprehensive) doctrines of the good, such that no agreement about the *truth* of any one of them is possible. Hence it is necessary to construct a *purely political* conception of justice (embodied in the modern liberal state) that can be endorsed, and given moral and religious force, from within each of the respective comprehensive doctrines.[114] Os Guinness has recently argued along similar lines: "The present state of intellectual division in modern pluralistic societies does not permit agreement at the level of the *origin* of beliefs (where justifications of behavior are theoretical, ultimate, and irreconcilable), but a significant, though limited, agreement is still possible at the level of the *outworking* of beliefs (where the expression of beliefs in behavior is more practical, less ultimate and often overlapping with the practical beliefs and behavior of other people)."[115] We can agree to disagree; indeed, in our pluralistic culture we *must* agree to disagree, and this agreement, embodied in the First Amendment, is given moral force from the respective moral and religious perspectives we bring to it.

Religious Arguments for Separating Church and State

John Courtney Murray has rightly noted that if we are prohibited by the First Amendment from establishing religion in America, we can hardly justify (in any official way) our constitutional arrangements on religious grounds.[116] Nonetheless, there are religious arguments to be made for religious liberty and the modern liberal state.

Of course, the practical politics of separation are particularly compelling to those religious minorities that can never hope to be established. For example, there is nothing to be said for separating religion and government in the Jewish tradition—except for the practical political reality of being a small minority within an overwhelming Christian country.[117] As Nicholas Wolfson has put it, should any breach appear in the wall of separation the "dominant religious forces will flood the schools and public life with the majoritarian religious beliefs of the day. There will soon be no breathing space for minority voices."[118] A strong commitment to religious liberty and a strict separationism has always been—and still is—the majority view among American Jews, albeit on practical rather than theological grounds.

Similarly, there is nothing in the traditions of many Christian denominations that calls for the separation of church and state. But in colonial America, where all denominations were somewhere in the minority, it became evident to all alike that no religion should be established and that religious liberty should be everywhere protected by government.

Indeed, it is not implausible to believe that religion has thrived in America in large part because of religious liberty. When the state provides no support for the church, it must support itself and here (as in the world of business, many would say) free enterprise brings about prosperity. Benjamin Franklin once said: "When a religion is good, I conceive it will support itself; and when it does not support itself so that its professors are obliged to call for the help of the civil power, it is a sign, I apprehend, of its being a bad one."[119] Lyman Beecher fretted about the disestablishment of religion in his native Connecticut in 1818, but he later wrote that it was "the best thing that ever happened to the State of Connecticut. It cut the churches loose from dependence on state support. It threw them wholly on their own resources and on God."[120] A few years later Tocqueville wrote: "On my arrival in the United States [in 1831] the religious aspect of the country was the first thing that struck my attention. . . . All attributed the peaceful dominion of religion in their country mainly to the separation of church and state. I do not hesitate to affirm that during my stay in America I did not meet a single individual, of the clergy or the laity, who was not of the same opinion on this point."[121]

Certainly there is a great deal of evidence that religions have thrived in America as they have not in European countries with established churches. In Europe religious establishments were inevitably saddled with the politics of the reigning party to their disadvantage sooner or later. As Tocqueville put it: "The church cannot share the temporal power of the state without being the object of a portion of that animosity which the latter excites."[122] In the fall of 1991, when the Bush administration argued the case for prayer in public schools before the Supreme Court, some 230 religious leaders sent the president a letter stating, in part, that "history teaches us that religious freedom and diversity have flourished where government remains neutral towards religion, as in our society today. Where government establishes or promotes religion, as with the state-endorsed churches of Europe, pews have emptied and the free exercise of religion has withered."[123] There are many reasons why religion thrives in America more than in Europe, but a case can be made that separation of church and state is a part of the explanation.

There is, then, a practical argument for favoring religious liberty, but there are also theological arguments to be made for it from some religious vantage points.

When Justice Black introduced the metaphor of a "wall of separation" in the *Everson* decision, he took it from President Jefferson's letter to the Danbury Baptists in 1802. "Believing with you that religion is a matter which lies solely between man and his God," Jefferson wrote, ". . . I contemplate with sovereign reverence that act of the whole American people which declared that their legislature should 'make no law respecting an establishment of religion, or prohibiting the free exercise thereof,' thus building a wall of separation between church and state."[124]

But the metaphor of a wall of separation is older than Jefferson. It was first used by Roger Williams in the seventeenth century. Williams viewed the Puritan ideal of a New Israel fusing church and state as an Old Testament ideal which is incompatible with the New Testament requirement that God's kingdom be a spiritual kingdom. When men "opened a gap in the hedge or *wall of separation* between the garden of the church and the wilderness of the world," Williams wrote, "God hath ever broke down the wall itself, removed the candlestick, and made His garden a wilderness, as at this day." To fulfill its mission, the church "must of necessity be walled in peculiarly unto Himself from the world."[125] If Jefferson was primarily concerned that mixing religion and politics would corrupt politics, Williams believed that the wall of separation is necessary to protect religion from the spiritual wilderness of politics.[126]

Like Roger Williams, many Christians believe on theological grounds that religion is no business of the state. One is not born into a religion which one acquires with the political territory, but chooses it, and our consciences are not to be forced. This "theology" of religious liberty has been held primarily by Protestants, at least until recently. With Vatican II, however, Catholicism came to place increasing emphasis on religious liberty. In all our actions, that council declared, "a man is bound to follow his conscience faithfully, in order that he may come to God, for whom he was created. It follows that he is not to be forced to act in a manner contrary to his conscience." All people have a right to religious freedom, grounded in their dignity as persons, and this right "should be recognized in the constitutional law whereby society is governed."[127]

Conclusions

Constitutionally, America is not a Christian (or even a Judeo-Christian) nation but is best understood as a religiously neutral, liberal state. Justice Frankfurter once commented that in matters of church and state, "good fences make good neighbors."[128] I agree, and I favor a "separationist" reading of the First Amendment. But I hasten to add that I favor a neutral, rather than a strict, separationism. Fences are for talking over. The "wall of separation" was not meant to isolate religion from our public life.

Some liberals have become concerned about the secularizing effects of a *strict* separationism. Stephen Carter's recent, much discussed, book *The Culture of Disbelief: How American Law and Politics Trivialize Religious Devotion*, is a kind of liberal manifesto on this point. Carter writes: "The potential transformation of the Establishment Clause from a guardian of religious liberty into a guarantor of public secularism raises prospects at once dismal and dreadful."[129]

Some measure of this concern can be found in the fact that over the course of the last decade or two a significant (if still minority) position of dissent from strict separationism has developed among American Jews.[130] For example, Matthew Berke argues that although "Jews are understandably wary about the potential for discrimination by the Christian majority in a theologized public square," the dangers of secularism created by a strict separationism pose the greater threat to Judaism.[131] Rabbi Walter Wurzburger claims that the secularization of American culture brought on, in part, by the clamor for an impenetrable wall of separation has been "a disaster" for Jews who have become increasingly "alienated from their religious tradition."[132] Richard Rubenstein argues that because religion has been "humanity's shield against anomie," the "ideal of a 'wall of separation' between church and state" must not be used "to foster an ever greater secularization of American life."[133]

In fact, because religion has traditionally provided the foundation for morality, it is often claimed that by undermining religion a too strict separationism may endanger the moral virtues citizens must possess to live together civilly. In *Habits of the Heart*, Robert Bellah and his colleagues argue that because our dominant culture is so powerfully utilitarian, fragmented, individualistic, and concerned above all else with satisfying self-interest, the public virtue necessary to maintain our society has been undermined. In response, they call for reinvigorating our biblical and republican traditions of civic virtue. Unfortunately, we have privatized religion, relegating it to a "compartmentalized sphere" where it can provide "loving support" but can "no longer challenge the dominance of utilitarian values in the society at large. Indeed, to the extent that privatization succeeded, religion [is] in danger of becoming, like the family, 'a haven in a heartless world,'" which does "more to reinforce that world, by caring for its casualties, than to challenge its assumptions."[134] Richard John Neuhaus sees still greater dangers in the "naked, public square." Where there is a religious vacuum in society, when religious transcendence is excluded from public life, that space is open to new and dangerous aspirants to authority—and he cites the "great social and political devastations of our century" that have been perpetrated by secular replacements for religion in the regimes of Hitler, Stalin, and Mao.[135]

I have argued that the Founders did not intend for the religion clauses to secularize American life; nor should that be their purpose now. A neutral separationism has very different implications from a strict separationism that forbids government and religion to have anything to do with one another. Too often strict separationism has excluded religion from the public square generally, and from education in particular, in ways that are not religiously neutral but hostile to religion and contribute to the secularization of our culture. True, it is not permissible for government (and public education) to *promote* religion; official prayers and devotional Bible reading put government on the side of religion and violate neutrality. But it is equally impermissible for government (and public education) to discriminate against religion. That is also a violation of neutrality. As Justice Black put it in *Everson*: "State power is no more to be used so as to handicap religions than it is to favor them."[136]

As we shall see, if we take neutrality seriously there are significant implications for public education.

It has been claimed that (conscientious) students are likely to have read more than thirty thousand pages of textbook prose by the time they have finished high school; perhaps 75 percent of school classwork and 90 percent of homework focus on textbooks.[1] Needless to say, we are not likely to remember many of the dates and battles, the facts and formulas, the ideas and theories, that fill those pages. This does not mean we have not been deeply influenced by textbooks, however. Frances Fitzgerald suggests that what "sticks to the memory" is "not any particular series of facts but an atmosphere, an impression, a tone. And this impression may be all the more influential just because one cannot remember the facts and arguments that created it." What we believe about the world is typically not the result of carefully constructed arguments based on hard evidence and careful reasoning but impressions gained more or less unconsciously from a meshing of schooling and life experiences, and our understanding of some aspects of life—of history, for example—is likely to be gained almost entirely from a few courses in school, from a few textbooks. The responsibility of textbook authors and publishers, Fitzgerald suggests, is "awesome, for, as is not true of trade publishers, the audiences for their products are huge, impressionable, and captive."[2]

As we saw in chapter 2 religion had all but disappeared from textbooks by the end of the nineteenth century. To locate it in contemporary textbooks we must consult texts that chart old traditions and, for the most part, distant lands. I will demonstrate this in graphic detail by way of a review of high school textbooks in a variety of subjects. (I will have a little to say about college and elementary school texts as well.) And why is religion absent from the texts? A part of the reason is, no doubt, that religion is controversial; textbook publishers, eager to maximize profits, exile it to safe and distant places. But I trust that it will come as no surprise at this point in the book that there is a more fundamental reason: textbook authors and publishers are sufficiently secular that religion is no longer considered relevant enough, or sufficiently likely to be true, to have anything other than a historical role to play in the stories textbooks tell.

History Texts

In 1989 and 1992 I reviewed forty-two high school textbooks in American and world history, economics, home economics, biology, physics, and physical science, which are approved for use in North Carolina schools. (North Carolina uses the standard textbooks of the major publishers, so there is no reason to believe that they are in any way peculiar.) My primary questions were, What do students learn about religion in those social studies and science courses where a case might be made for the relevance of religion? To what extent is religion treated uniformly in textbooks? Is there a cumulative effect of the way religion is treated?[3]

Only the history texts dealt with religion in any significant way, and they mentioned it a good deal.[4] Nonetheless, over the past decade a half-dozen studies by individuals and organizations have concluded that the texts are highly inadequate in conveying an understanding of the place of religion in history.[5] The historian Timothy Smith has written that the thirteen high school American history texts he reviewed fell "far below the standard of American historical scholarship by ignoring or distorting the place of religion in American history. Where they do mention religious forces, the facts to which they allude are so incomplete or so warped that they deny students access to what the great majority of historical scholars think is true."[6] People for the American Way, a liberal, separationist organization established, in large part, to counter the influence of the Religious Right, was led to an unanticipated conclusion in its study of American history textbooks: "These texts simply do not treat religion as a significant element in American life—it is not portrayed as an integrated part of the American value system or as something that is important to individual Americans. . . . When religion is mentioned, it is just that—mentioned. In particular, most books give the impression that America suddenly turned into a secular state after the Civil War."[7] That the texts are inadequate is a matter of consensus. The extent and nature of their shortcomings are more controversial.

In his study of world history texts Paul Gagnon points out that the moral principles of Judaism and Christianity "lie at the heart of most subsequent world ideologies, even those determinedly anti-religious. . . . Yet the basic ideas of Judaism and Christianity are all but ignored in some of these texts and only feebly suggested in the rest."[8] In the four North Carolina world histories, all of Jewish and Christian history up to the Middle Ages is handled, on average, in six pages, while sixty pages are typically given to Greece and Rome. The texts give twice as much space to ancient Egypt as they do to ancient Israel, and three of the four give more space to Sumeria. None of the world histories provide students the Ten Commandments or mention the central claim of Christianity—that Jesus was God incarnate. (Jesus typically receives about four paragraphs, or less than half the space one text gives Eleanor of Aquitaine and another gives Joseph Stalin.) The texts typically provide a relatively liberal view of early Judaism and Christianity, emphasizing monotheism, justice, and love; they downplay or completely ignore sin, salvation, damnation, the millennium, cosmology, and faith.

The treatments of Islam and non-Western religions are marginally better in one respect. The texts give them about the same amount of space—two or three pages—given Judaism and Christianity, but as the total number of pages on Islamic, Indian, and Chinese civilizations is considerably less than that devoted to Western civilization, a somewhat higher proportion of them deal with religion; hence religion may seem to be a more important part of those civilizations.

The closer we get to the modern West, the more religion disappears, and the few references for the years after 1800 are there for their political or social significance. So, for example, the texts briefly discuss Islamic fundamentalism and the Iranian revolution, the confrontation of Hindus and Muslims in the partition of India, the creation of Israel and the wars that followed, and religious conflict in Ireland. Anti-Semitism, the Dreyfuss Affair, and the Holocaust receive several paragraphs in each of the books.

What is most obviously missing is any account of the intellectual, theological, or denominational development of religion after the Reformation. None of the texts say anything about higher criticism, the development of liberal theology, or (non-Islamic) fundamentalist responses to religious liberalism and modernity. None of them mention any post-1800 theologian or religious thinker. (A pope is mentioned here and there for political reasons.) The secularization of the modern world, one of the great themes of modern history, is ignored—though each of the books says something about the conflict of religion with Darwinism (albeit it a single sentence in two of the four books). None discuss the spiritual crisis of the modern world so much in evidence in the arts, as well as in religion (though one text does devote two paragraphs to religion as part of the modern "search for stability").

The American history texts contain just enough about Native American religions—a sentence here, a paragraph there—to mystify students completely. There will typically be several paragraphs on Spanish missions. Each of the five texts contains a section of from three to seven pages on the Puritans and Pilgrims, but this is a little misleading, for only a few paragraphs in those sections deal with anything explicitly religious, and even then it is almost always "church-state" relations that are discussed. Roger Williams, Anne Hutchinson, the Quakers, and the development of religious toleration in the eighteenth century are discussed briefly. Three of the five texts provide short accounts of the Great Awakening, and two mention Deism.

Four of the texts have sections, ranging from three paragraphs to six pages, on religion in the early nineteenth century, usually covering the Transcendentalists, the Mormons, and the revivals of the Second Great Awakening, but after the Civil War religion becomes largely invisible. None of the texts mentions the split between Protestant liberalism and fundamentalism at the beginning of the twentieth century. Only one text mentions the Social Gospel; none mentions the watershed Scopes Trial. Two of the texts relate Martin Luther King's views on nonviolence and human rights to his religious convictions, but the role of black churches in the civil rights movement is not discussed. Only two of the texts mention the rise of the Religious Right in the 1970s. No other religious topic receives more than a sentence.

One text gives more space to farming in the colonies than it does to religion; another gives more pages to cowboys and cattle drives at the end of the nineteenth century than to all of post-1800 religion. The American histories devote, on average, about 1 percent of their space to matters having anything to do with religion after 1800.[9] In his study of the American history texts, Paul Vitz correctly concluded that none of them "acknowledges, much less emphasizes, the great religious energy and creativity of the United States."[10]

More important than the particular religious topics discussed or not discussed, and the relative amount of space they receive, is the worldview within which the historian works. Obviously, historians must be selective. In spite of their length (the world histories average 785 pages, the American histories

850 pages) much must be left out. What is included and what is excluded? Political and social history receive far and away the most emphasis, while the texts make scant mention of intellectual and cultural history—of literature, science, art, education, philosophy, or religion. The world histories contain relatively more about culture generally, and religion in particular, than do the American histories, but this is largely because they treat cultures that are more distant historically and geographically; as they approach the modern West, cultural history tends to disappear there too. When religion is mentioned in any of the texts, it is almost always for its relevance to political and social events and movements. This assumption—that the history we want our children to learn is political and social, rather than cultural, intellectual, or religious—is rich with significance.

But the problem cuts deeper. Whatever stories the historian chooses to tell are open to various interpretations; they are understood differently from within different worldviews. Consider the following passage from one of the world history texts:

> Because the Egyptians feared the Hebrews, they made them slaves. The Hebrew leader Moses led the Hebrews from Egypt to Palestine. Under the rule of their early kings—Saul, David, and Solomon—the Hebrew nation prospered. . . .
>
> King Solomon died about 900 B.C. Then Palestine split into two kingdoms. The Kingdom of Israel was formed in the north. The Kingdom of Judah was formed in the south. The Kingdom of Israel lasted for 250 years. Then it was destroyed by the Assyrians. The kingdom of Judah lasted for 400 years. However, during much of its history it was part of other empires.[11]

Authors of textbooks often attempt to tiptoe gingerly around events with religious significance, leaving questions about causes and meaning aside. Still, the author of the above passage does not quite succeed: was it Moses who led the Israelites out of bondage or God? According to Scripture, "when Pharaoh let the people go, God did not guide them by the road towards the Philistines. . . . God made them go round by way of the wilderness towards the Red Sea. . . . And all the time the Lord went before them, by day a pillar of cloud to guide them on their journey, by night a pillar of fire."[12] What are the facts? For many religious conservatives it is a *fact* that God led the Israelites out of Egypt, and even on the liberal account, there is likely to be a religious meaning to the scriptural passage that is missing from the textbook account. Moreover, according to Scripture it was God who made Israel a great nation, and it was God who raised up the Assyrians and Babylonians to punish Israel for its sins. Now in these last cases the textbook author has not overtly contradicted the scriptural account; he has not said God didn't raise up the Assyrians and Babylonians. Still, he has left out what is most important to the scriptural version: the role of God in shaping history. The meaning of the scriptural story is completely lost in the textbook; it becomes, in effect, a different story. History is not, after all, a simple chronicle of events: it provides explanations of events that have a certain significance and meaning.

Clearly the author is not treating religion as people within that religious tradition would treat it. The author has chosen to tell the story from a secular rather than a religious frame of reference; he is telling us that what is important, indeed what is true, is a sequence of secular, political events with no obvious religious significance, and he makes no effort to explore the inner, religious dynamic of the scriptural account.

A few paragraphs later in the same text a student would read this statement: "The holy writings of the Hebrews included the Ten Commandments and the Old Testament."[13] Wrong. The holy writings of Christians include the Old Testament, but there is no Old Testament for ancient Hebrews (or modern Jews) because they have no New Testament. This is not just a minor matter of names, for to understand the Hebrew Scriptures as the Old Testament is to interpret it as referring prophetically to the coming of Christ.

Thus the textbook author has, within several paragraphs, managed to retell the story of the ancient Hebrews first from within the worldview of a modern, secular historian, and second, using the language of Christianity rather than Judaism. Whose story is it? From within what worldview should it be written?

Or, to bring the story a little closer to our times, we have seen that nineteenth-century schoolbooks often put Abraham Lincoln's life into the perspective of God's purposes in history. In fact, most Americans, and most of the central actors in the Civil War (certainly Lincoln and Jefferson Davis, for example) understood that war as part of the working out of God's purposes, yet none of the American histories I reviewed mentioned—much less adopted— that interpretation of events or reflected on the spiritual significance of the Civil War for the meaning of America. In its chapter on the years 1860–65 the most popular text included sections on Native Americans, women, the National Banking Act of 1863, agricultural expansion, and the growth of railroads, as well as the Civil War, but ventured not a single comment about the religious beliefs of anyone or the religious significance of the war.[14]

Everyone agrees that the texts slight religion, but the deeper questions are about causality and meaning. Textbook authors inevitably operate from within a worldview, a set of philosophical commitments which define for them what is important, what can and cannot count as a fact, what justifies claims about the meaning of events. Modern historians employ a secular, often scientific, methodology that allows no room for miracles, divine providence, or religious accounts of the meaning of historical change. It may very well be that modern, secular ways of understanding history are more reasonable than religious ways of understanding it. That is not the issue. My point is simply that religious and modern secular ways of understanding history are fundamentally different, and religious understandings of history are not found in the textbooks.

Judaism, Christianity, and Islam all understand history in terms of God's purposes. Whether or not one interprets such talk literally (as conservatives do) or mythically (as liberals do), there is an irreducible religious meaning to history that cannot be captured in fully secular language. Yet none of the books provide any sense of what that meaning might be. Indeed, none of the texts I reviewed were self-consciously reflective about the *meaning* of history at all. Paul Gagnon writes that none of the world history texts he reviewed "defines what history is, how it is written, what its strengths and weaknesses may be, how it relates to the student's life and other studies, or what connection it could have with preparing thoughtful and informed citizens."[15] Only three of the nine North Carolina texts say anything about the nature or value of history, and two of these discussions are but a single page. They include no mention of religious interpretations of history.[16]

Economics Texts

The history texts are a veritable cornucopia of information about, and sensitivity to, religion when compared with the economics texts. Of the six economics textbooks I reviewed, two do not mention religion at all.[17] According to the first of the four that do mention it, religion has often been a barrier to economic development in poor societies with traditional economies. The text cites the reluctance of Hindus to eat their sacred cows and notes the common belief in such societies that because suffering in this world is a test for admission to the life to come, we should do nothing to ameliorate the conditions of life. The total discussion is two paragraphs.[18] The second of the four includes a sentence that cites religion, along with custom, habit, and law, as a source of economic values in traditional societies and a sentence that claims that some ancient Greeks and early Christians "practiced forms of socialism."[19] The third claims that the goals and values assumed in the text are "described in economic terms because this is an economics text." It adds, "However, these goals have moral, social, and religious elements as well"—though it says nothing about any religious elements.[20] The fourth text takes a little more than a page to treat the growth in trade that followed the Crusades, the idea of a "just price" in the Middle Ages, the transition from a feudal economy to capitalism, the view of Calvinists that profit and interest need not be seen as sinful, and the connection between the Protestant Reformation and the rise of the Middle Class.[21] In the twenty-six hundred pages of these six economics texts, about a page and a half deal with religion—and they are silent after Calvin in 1550.

The books are essentially present-oriented, social-science tours of the world of economics though they typically make two historical detours: they briefly trace the rise of labor unions, and they discuss Marx and the development of communism. All but one ignore the relationship between the Reformation and the development of capitalism. There is no discussion of the many nineteenth- and twentieth-century religious conservatives who were horrified by the effects of market economies on the traditional order. None discusses (or even mentions) the Social Gospel or Christian socialism, the role of religion in various urban reform movements, the Catholic "middle way" or liberation theology (though they all discuss the Third World). Nor do any of the books discuss the modern Religious Right's defense of capitalism. None of the books makes any reference to the classic studies of the relationship of religion and economics, such as R. H. Tawny's *Religion and the Rise of Capitalism*, Max Weber's *Protestant Ethic and the Spirit of Capitalism*, Walter Rauschenbusch's *Theology for the Social Gospel*, or Michael Novak's *Spirit of Democratic Capitalism*. Nor do they mention any of the many papal encyclicals that deal with economics, the American Catholic Bishops' recent pastoral letter on the economy, or the official statements of the World Council of Churches and many of the mainline American Protestant denominations on economic issues. One of the texts has ninety-seven boxes containing primary source material from economists and social critics (ranging from Marx to Milton Friedman), but not one of the excerpted authors is a religious writer.[22] There is no reference in any of the texts to the teachings of any of the great religious figures of the past, other than Calvin, who is graced with a single sentence in one book.

It is not the omission of religious ideas and thinkers that is most important, however. The more fundamental—and controversial—aspect of the books is their more or less shared account of human nature, values, and society. Each of the texts defines the economic world in terms of the competition of self-interested individuals with unlimited wants for scarce resources—though not all of them are so exultantly forthright as the one that advises, "Make no mistake about it, competition is a contest. There are winners and there are losers. It may sound heartless, but that is the way it is. Each seller is out to make money. The task is to produce and then to sell. There is no thought given for other sellers. Human values, such as love or friendship, have nothing to do with competition. No one really cares how nice a person is, or how many children he or she has to support. The rules of the game are simple. Success is rewarded, failure is punished."[23] Human nature is understood on the "rational, economic man" model.

There are, of course, good reasons to believe that most people are self-interested much of the time and that competition is necessary for productivity and economic development. Nonetheless, much religious thought takes this to be a reductive view of human nature and society. For example, the American Catholic Bishops have recently warned against a "tragic separation" between faith and our economic life, insisting that "human dignity, realized in community with others and with the whole of God's creation, is the norm against which every social institution is measured."[24] More particularly, the justice of an economic system should be measured by its treatment of the poor and defenseless. Within the Catholic and many other religious traditions people are understood to be essentially *social* beings, with clear moral duties; the task of the economic system is not to foster competition for limited resources so much as to nurture and sustain love and justice in a public world made possible by cooperation. The idea of unlimited wants is deeply problematic, for religions typically rule some of our wants misguided or sinful and find deeply troubling an economy that thrives on feeding and nurturing indiscriminate wants. (It is sometimes even suggested that we should be satisfied with what we have.) Consumerism is likely to lead us astray: where our capital is invested, there shall our hearts be also. Indeed, some theologians would argue that neoclassical economics is at least as much at odds with the teachings of Jesus as neo-Darwinism is with the first chapter of Genesis read as a historical account of creation.

My point here is not that the bishops are right or that capitalism is not the best economic system. It is simply that religious voices have been left out of the discussion. This is somewhat ironic in that at least three of the books self-consciously acknowledge that economics is a social science and is "value-free" and has nothing to tell us about values, or what should be. This being the case, one might think economics might be open to religious sources of values, but this cannot be for, as one text puts it, "Within certain limits, facts are objective, that is, they can be measured, and their truth tested. . . . Value judgments, on the other hand, are subjective, being matters of personal preference. Value judgments cannot be tested for their truth. . . . Such preferences are based on personal likes and feelings, rather than on facts and reasons." Religion is of no special help, for whatever values religion might promote would simply be additional (subjective) preferences thrown into the hopper with other "personal likes and feelings." They have no special claim to truth or to be taken seriously—at least so far as economics is concerned: "Economics makes no judgments about the rightness of individual decisions. Economics . . . follows the idea of pluralism, respecting the worth of different values and choices."[25] This, of course, is not the understanding of values to be found within religious traditions.

Nonetheless, the texts are not devoid of values: the typical list includes economic efficiency, freedom, and growth.[26] These values are justified on one or another of three grounds: they are asserted to be national values or goals; sometimes it is suggested they are common values (hence "most people agree" that economic security is good, and "no one wants" to be poor);[27] or they are simply asserted to be the values internal to the working of a market economy. The problem is that there is never any careful or systematic attempt to justify these values by appeal to moral or religious thinking and theory. Students are left completely in the dark on how to relate value-free economic theory to philosophical or theological ethics. When, if ever, should we act altruistically? The texts sometimes suggest that "fairness" and humanitarian concerns are good, but they never provide any coherent way of thinking about such things.

The economics books convey almost exactly what Robert Bellah and his colleagues have called "utilitarian individualism." Starting from what they take to be basic human appetites and conditions of scarcity, the texts portray life, at least public, economic life, as "an effort by individuals to maximize their interests relative to these given ends." Society arises "from a contract that individuals enter into only in order to advance their self-interest," and life is a constant struggle to manipulate one's environment so as to realize one's personal good. Individuals have their being apart from communities and traditions, apart from binding obligations—and apart from any relationship to God.[28]

The economics texts give us the economic world according to modern, mainstream social science. Needless to say, it is important to understand what social science tells us about economics and human nature. But there are other ways of understanding economics and human nature that embed them in a larger cultural world of tradition, community, moral rights and obligations, and religious vocation. Arguably, an educated person should know something about this world, yet the texts are completely silent about it.

Home Economics Texts

The eight home economics texts I reviewed are interesting beasts. Each follows the same pattern, beginning with one or several chapters defining human nature, values, and decision making before moving on to discussions of dating, marriage, abortion, child rearing, the family, and what I take to be more traditional home economics fare.[29] Needless to say, religion has had a great deal to say about such things, though one would never guess it from reading these books. True, there are occasional passing references to religion as a source of values, or to clergy as possible counselors, but these suggestions are simply mentioned; they are never developed and no importance is attached to them. Seven of the eight books are devoid of any but the most passing reference to religion.[30] In two books, the only mention of religion relates to dietary laws. One book has fifty pages defining "who we are" and how we should make decisions, without a single reference to religion.

The books aim to convince students that they should think well of themselves, that it is important to have a positive self-concept, and that their greatest need is that of self-actualization. Most pay homage to Abraham Maslow and his hierarchy of needs.[31] (Needless to say, this is some distance from the more traditional religious view articulated in the Westminster Catechism: "The chief end of man is to glorify God and to enjoy Him forever.") Only one of the texts acknowledges the existence of spiritual needs; none ventures into the domain of souls or sin, or those more puritan sentiments according to which there is danger in thinking too well of ourselves. The texts that discuss abortion and premarital sex are likely to do so with only a passing reference to religion—if that. None of the books even hints that there are religious conceptions of human nature, values, or decision making that may differ in significant ways from the views presented.

Not only is religion ignored, so is morality and virtually any talk of conscience, obligation, duty, tradition, or historical community. One book that does mention conscience analyzes it in terms of Erik Berne's parent-adult-child triad. The conscience is the internalized voice of the restrictive and repressive parent, and it is the task of the adult part of our personality to judge the claims of conscience—rather than, as is more traditionally the case, the other way around. (Compare Pope John Paul II: conscience "is the witness of God himself, whose voice and judgment penetrate the depths of man's soul, calling him . . . to obedience."[32])

Typically, the books use the language of generic values—which are purely personal—instead of the language of morality. Students are told over and over again that they must *choose* their own values—and, of course, in some sense so we must in a pluralistic world. But there is no suggestion that one can choose right or wrong values (as opposed to values that don't work for us), or that they must be tested against law, or Scripture, or tradition, or community standards, or their implications for human suffering. Unfortunately, one book declares, not all students are capable of setting up a "dependable value system for themselves" and are "dependent upon family members or social institutions to guide them." But, this book counsels, "*you* should determine your values, or those things which are important to you."[33] Another book advises:

> Only you can choose the best alternative in making your own decisions. Different people will have different alternatives. There is no single best solution for everyone's problems. Each individual will have different values and set different standards about the decision alternatives he or she chooses. . . . Ask yourself what benefits or advantages will result from [your] choice. Compare the good and the bad for all the alternatives that you're considering. Then choose the alternative that does the best job for you with the fewest disadvantages.[34]

So, for example, "your friend may ask you to skip a day of school and go to the beach. Your decision would depend upon your values. How highly do you value the respect of your teachers and the trust of your parents? How highly do you value the classes you would miss? How highly do you value the companionship of your friend?"[35] What works for you? Decision making is a matter of cost-benefit analysis, of thinking through the effects of various courses of action, making sure that we act in such a way as to maximize whatever it is we have chosen to value.[36]

There is considerable potential for confusion here. Yes, values do vary from person to person and from culture to culture. But many people—including most philosophers and virtually all theologians—have held that this does not mean there is no right or wrong, no better or worse values. What does "the best job" for me may not be the right thing to do. In fact, I may not be very competent at making moral judgments so that it would be better if I relied on my family, on my church, on the law, or on tradition for guidance. Yet these books require the student, as Kenneth Strike puts it, to "construct the moral universe anew largely by consulting his or her feelings."[37]

As with the economics texts, the authors show no familiarity with moral theory or theology; they are appallingly naive in dealing with theoretical questions having to do with human nature, values, or decision making. They seem only to know the language of a fairly crude social science. When the authors wish to appeal to an authority in resolving some matter, they appeal to psychologists and social scientists, counselors and public opinion surveys.

When the books leave the realm of theory and discuss specific "value" problems such as dating or premarital sex, they are a little better, even somewhat directive. For example, the books often counsel honesty and integrity in particular situations. But often the advice goes something like this: "Most experiences in premarital sex take place in less than ideal settings. The danger of being discovered inhibits feelings of relaxation and enjoyment. The security of marriage allows freer expression of love. Thus sexual experiences between spouses are usually more satisfying."[38] Needless to say, the books never suggest that premarital sex might be sinful; indeed, moral language is rarely used. It is probably true that teenagers often react negatively to moralizing so that many efforts at moral education are counterproductive (though often that is a result of the way the moralizing is done). Still, in these books there is such an absence of moral and religious context that it is hard to see how students could acquire the sense (still shared by most people) that there are moral and religious considerations that must enter into decision making on matters of some importance.

This educational approach has, for the past several decades, gone under the name "values clarification." Students should be encouraged to think about their values, the alternatives open to the them, and the likely consequences of their acts. Then they must make a choice and accept responsibility for it. But neither the teacher nor the textbook is to be too directive; they are not to "impose" their values on their students, but only help students *clarify* the values they have or freely choose.

The books express almost perfectly what Robert Bellah and his colleagues have called "expressive individualism." The expressive dimension of our culture, according to Bellah, "exists for the liberation and fulfillment of the individual. Its genius is that it enables the individual to think of commitments—from marriage and work to political and religious involvement—as enhancements of the sense of individual well-being rather than as moral imperatives." Consequently, "the question 'is this right or wrong?' becomes 'Is this going to work for me now?' Individuals must answer in terms of their own wants. The workings of the world are best seen in terms of the costs it exacts and the satisfactions it yields."[39]

As with the economics textbooks, my point here is not that this is a *wrong* view of human nature and values, but that it is incompatible with most religious ways of thinking about these things, for in a religious world people live within webs of obligations and rights with other people—and with God. Duties outweigh self-interest, and spiritual meaning takes precedence over self-actualization (or at least redefines "self-actualization" in a way that none of these books suggests). Decision making must be constrained by conscience, and we are properly guided by religious tradition. The books give no sense that this might be the case.

Unlike the economics texts, which are at least willing to discuss Marxism and socialism, the home economics texts provide no discussion whatever of *any* rival theories, secular or religious. They take no notice of the world as viewed from outside their own ideological niche. They are extraordinarily parochial. As Strike says in his review, that students "should be taught these things as though they were obvious and without any clear indication that there are other ways of thinking is astonishing."[40]

Science Texts

For the thirty or forty years following the Scopes Trial biology texts either avoided evolution (and controversy) or provided inadequate coverage. After *Sputnik* the push for better science education required that evolution assume more prominence in the books, however, and most biology texts now give at least reasonably adequate accounts of evolution.[41] Five of the six texts approved for use in North Carolina line up clearly in the evolution column, though the sixth is quite clearly out of line.[42]

Each of the five contains substantial sections on evolution, running between twenty-one and fifty-four pages. Three have sections on the evolution of humans from the higher apes (adding a further ten to twelve pages to the coverage). One has only a brief, four-page, account of human evolution, and one of the five pretty much ignores it. Each of these five texts discusses Darwin and reviews most of the major evidence for evolution. None contains any discussion or even any reference to creationism or creation-science, and none presents any argument to show that evolution did not take place.

Several of the texts do seem to go out of their way, on occasion, to avoid using the word "evolution"; for example, two have chapter headings that euphemistically and erroneously use the term "human history" rather than "human evolution." Another text claims that evolution is (merely?) a "theory" and suggests that not all scientists accept it, though the text presents a relatively full-blooded case for evolution and no counterevidence is mentioned.[43] Nonetheless, the substance of the texts clearly, and unambiguously, supports evolution.

Each biology text is a science text pure and simple, devoid of religious references. Each text includes a brief, three-to-five page account of scientific method, but with a single exception, none makes any effort to relate scientific to religious methods of understanding nature. According to the sole exception,

> Humans have asked questions about the origins of life since the beginning of recorded history. Religious answers vary to such questions as how and when life originated on Earth. One common belief is that a Divine Being made all living things. Since such acts of creation would be supernatural events, they cannot be tested scientifically. . . . Biology deals with the *scientific* study of life. This statement means that biologists gain knowledge by observing and testing natural events under controlled conditions. Other ways of knowing about life can be equally valid. But biology deals only with scientific methods that are used to learn about life.[44]

This text contains no further references to religion. Three of the texts, however, contain the germ of an argument which might be taken as gently critical of traditional religion: they suggest that science, based on facts and logic, has rescued us from the myth, ignorance, and superstition common in the (religious) Middle Ages.[45]

The sixth text devotes three pages to evolution as part of a larger chapter dealing with mutations, adaptation, and fossils.[46] There is a one-page box on Darwin, but there is nothing like an adequate account of evolution, nor is there any hint that Darwin's theory is fundamental to biology. Nothing suggests that evolution required more than six thousand years.[47] Although all of the texts are approved for high school use, this one, unlike the others, is written at only a sixth or seventh grade level and would be part of a "general" rather than an "academic" biology course.

Whether evolution has taken place at all is crucial for many religious conservatives. Religious moderates and liberals, however, often believe that evolution is simply "God's way of doing things" or that God is immanent in nature, the "Ground of Being," or a "Force" bringing goodness out of chaos. Hence it is important to remember that the biology textbooks do not teach *generic* evolution, but a neo-Darwinian view according to which change is inescapably *purposeless*, the result of natural selection working on random genetic mutations and recombinations. Such evolution has no direction or goal. This creates at least a prima facie conflict with much liberal religion, for most liberals will want to hang on to some residue of the claim that reality is personal and purposeful. It is hard to reconcile the value-free causality and rather nasty facts of neo-Darwinian natural selection with the idea that love is the ground of our being. If it is possible to reconcile religion and modern biology, it is not altogether obvious how this should be done, though theologians have proposed various ways of dealing with the problem. But none of this is discussed. Nor are recent theological and philosophical theories of evolution, those of Teilhard de Chardin and Process Philosophy, for example.

The five physics books and the seven physical science books I reviewed contained no references to religion.[48] Only four of the books (two in physics, two in physical science) mentioned the Big Bang as an account of the origin of the universe. None suggested any theological possibilities for understanding the Big Bang, however, and none mentioned the "anthropic" principle, much discussed nowadays by scientists as well as by philosophers and theologians, according to which the expansion rate of the universe in the first few seconds after the Big Bang, the strength of the strong nuclear force, and the asymmetry of matter and anti-matter, provide evidence of design in the universe. Three of the books discussed entropy and the Second Law of Thermodynamics, but only one drew out the "cosmic" implications—albeit it with no references to religion. Ten of the twelve had opening sections on scientific method, but most were a cursory two or three pages. Several showed some philosophical sophistication regarding the nature of facts and theories, but none made any effort to relate scientific to other methods for understanding nature. The impression given, sometimes implicitly, sometimes explicitly, is that science is fully adequate to the task of making sense of the world. According to one text, "Physical science helps people understand how everything in the universe works."[49] Another claims: "Scientists seek basic truths about nature. Such truths are often called facts. . . . But scientists do more than seek facts. They use the facts to solve deeper mysteries of the universe."[50] The books are saturated with mathematics. Each of the twelve has as either its opening or second chapter a discussion of measurement in science. The message is clear: what can't be measured doesn't count.

As striking as the absence of any references to religion is the lack of any significant historical, cultural, or philosophical context for understanding science or nature.

Other Texts

Elementary School Textbooks. In the mid-1980s Paul Vitz conducted an elaborate study of elementary school social studies, history, and reading texts, using quantitative methods for measuring religious references in words and images. He found that in forty social studies books used in grades one to four totaling about ten thousand pages there was not a single "primary" textual reference to a religious activity in contemporary American life though the purpose of texts at this level is to introduce students to contemporary American life. (A "primary" reference is one that is directly about religion; a

"secondary" reference mentions religion indirectly in the discussion of something else.) Twenty-one of the books made no textual mention (primary or
secondary) of religion. In fact, the books often went to striking lengths to
avoid references to religion. In one notorious case a text explained that "Pilgrims are people who make long trips," and Vitz notes that these books commonly "treat Thanksgiving without explaining to whom the Pilgrims gave
thanks."[51]

Like the high school texts, the fifth grade American histories, and the sixth
grade world histories, phased religion out of their accounts as they approached present-day America, though the religious gaps in earlier periods
could also be striking. For example, four of the ten world history texts Vitz reviewed failed to say anything about the life or teaching of Jesus. Many failed
to mention the Protestant Reformation, and those that did mention it failed to
discuss the theological differences at issue.[52]

Contemporary readers are a world apart from those of McGuffey's day. In
670 stories from eleven series of basal readers there was not one in which "the
central motivation or major content derives from Christianity or Judaism"—
though Greek, Roman, Egyptian, Polynesian, and American Indian religions
were "an important part" of or were "emphasized quite positively" in several
stories. Thirteen stories featured magic and magicians, and "many other stories have magic as central to the plot and story resolution." By far the most
"noticeable ideological position in the readers," Vitz claims, "is a feminist
one." No story set in the present celebrates motherhood, though there are
many stories about successful women in traditionally male fields and there are
"explicitly feminist stories" about leaders of the feminist movement such as
Elizabeth Cady Stanton. Vitz's most striking claim may be that there were
"no stories that feature helping others or being concerned for others as intrinsically meaningful and valuable. . . . Over and over again the emphasis is
on individual success."[53]

College Textbooks. I know of no study of the place of religion in college
texts. What I can report is the results of a small experiment I undertook at
the University of North Carolina during the fall semester of 1990. I looked at
all the books assigned for undergraduate courses in history, religious studies,
economics, and psychology, and assigned them all to one or the other of two
categories: books written by professional scholars within the respective disciplines and "primary source" books written by outsiders. My purpose was to
discover how much exposure undergraduates had to material not written by
contemporary scholars in the subject they were studying. How likely were
they to encounter another perspective, another way of thinking, another
worldview?

In the department of Religious Studies, of 68 assigned books, 53 percent were primary source books, and 47 percent were scholarly studies. Almost all of the primary source books were written from within some religious worldview. In history, of 239 assigned books, 43 percent were primary source books, and 57 percent were scholarly studies. About a dozen of the primary source books were written by authors working within a religious worldview (e.g., Luther, Erasmus, Emerson) though most of the religious primary source material antedated the seventeenth century. In economics, all 40 books were written by contemporary economists, and as near as I could make out from reviewing tables of contents and index entries for God and religion, only one of the economics books, a history of economic theory text, mentioned religion *at all*—and then only in the context of the distant past. In psychology all but 1 of the 34 assigned books were written by psychologists.

I also looked at the three college biology textbooks used in the introductory biology course. One had a half-page box and another a two-page box dealing with creation-science. In each case the text argued that creation-science was not true science. Other than this they contained no references to God, creation, design, teleology, or religious ways of understanding nature.

It is probably fair to say that college students have the opportunity to learn a fair amount about religion in history, religious studies, and literature courses and texts, though college requirements (at least at public universities) are rarely such as to guarantee this. But they are no more likely to encounter religion in college economics, psychology, or biology texts than in their high school counterparts.

Why Is There So Little Religion in the Textbooks?

It is often argued that religion is kept out of public school textbooks because it is too controversial, and there is undoubtedly something to this. As Frances Fitzgerald explains it, the textbook industry is not large; public schools spend less than 1 percent of their budgets on textbooks. Hence publishers can't afford to have more than one or two of their texts on the market at the same time. Consequently, she claims, "all of them try to compete for the center of the market, designing their books not to please anyone in particular but to be acceptable to as many people as possible. The word "controversial" is as deeply feared by textbook publishers as it is coveted by trade book publishers."[54]

So it has always been. In an effort to appeal to as wide an audience as possible, an 1844 advertisement for *McGuffey's Eclectic Fourth Reader* announced: "No *sectarian* matter has been admitted into this work." The publisher explained: "It has been submitted to the inspection of highly intelligent clergymen and teachers of the various Protestant and Catholic denominations, and nothing has been inserted, except with their united approbation."[55]

Tony Podesta, a past president of People for the American Way, has written that the "real explanation of the inadequate coverage of religion in U.S. history texts is . . . [that] textbook publishers are still afraid of offending anyone, from moral majoritarians to civil libertarians."[56] Jeffrey Pasley has suggested that "textbook publishers aren't ideologues, but merely salesmen eager to please."[57] Herbert Adams, president and CEO of Laidlaw Brothers, has said that "people are afraid that if they allude to religion, they'll get into a controversy over separation of church and state. The assumption is if you put religion in a book, it won't sell."[58] The result, Joan Delfattore argues, is that "the textbook development process in America has less to do with educating a nation than with selling a product."[59] Thou shalt not offend that ye may profit.

In 1990 California considered adopting a new series of social studies books published by Houghton Mifflin which included a great deal more about religion than other texts—enough more so that everyone could find something objectionable. At the adoption hearings, Christian fundamentalists testified that various passages demeaned them. Atheists felt their views had not been represented. Jews argued that Judaism was treated primarily as an antecedent to Christianity. "This is not a threat," one Muslim spokesmen said, "but if our demands are not met, we will withdraw our children from school and mount lawsuits." At one point, police had to be called into the hearings to restore order. Gilbert Sewall commented in the *Social Studies Review*: "It is not hard to guess the chilling message these California carnivals are sending to other publishers."[60]

Nonetheless, the books were adopted and are now used in most California school systems; indeed, the Houghton Mifflin series was the only series adopted by the state. As much of a liability as controversy is, it need not rule a book out—at least if the people who make the decisions have the wherewithal to resist some public unhappiness. Indeed, it is clear that most textbooks contain a good deal of controversial material—it is just not controversial to the relevant textbook commissions or educational bureaucracies. Evolution has returned to most biology books although it is still controversial, and feminism and multiculturalism seem to have won the day in readers and social studies texts. That is, a (relatively) liberal educational establishment has been able to ensure that controversy will not keep their issues and themes out of texts.

Stephen Bates has shown how this works in fascinating detail. In the mid-1980s fundamentalist parents sought to have their children excused from using the Holt reading series required in the Hawkins County, Tennessee, public schools. As 2,261 pages of internal Holt files subpoenaed for the resulting court case showed, the Holt readers had come under considerable criticism from both the Left and the Right. What is striking is the extent to which the Holt editors bent over backward to respond to the concerns of the Left and their almost total resistance to the concerns of the Right. For example, they devised elaborate schemes for counting characters in stories and faces in pictures to ensure that women and minorities were adequately represented (at least 50 percent must be women), and they sometimes changed the sex of characters in stories to make their quotas; they required that women and blacks not be described or pictured in stereotypical roles; sexist language (for example, "manmade, "workmanlike," "statesman") was eliminated from the texts. In a 1981 speech Holt editor Barbara Theobald denounced conservative pressure groups as "censors" of the kind one finds in "totalitarian societies." But at the "other end of the spectrum," she went on to say, "we have other groups . . . who seek to improve our educational institutions and textbooks in a positive manner." As Bates reports it, for Theobald "critics who wanted schoolbooks to feature more women were 'positive pressure groups,' whereas those who wanted fewer women were 'censors.'"[61]

The most impressive evidence that controversy is not a sufficient explanation for the absence of religion is to be found on college campuses. Given academic freedom and insulation of faculty from public pressures, controversy can add to the value of book. But college biology, economics, and psychology texts and courses are not likely to be any more sensitive to religion than high school texts. Although there is no doubt more room in college for the idiosyncratic professor and text, texts in these subjects are as secular as are the high school texts. Controversy is not the heart of the matter.

There is another explanation for secular textbooks: they are written by secular intellectuals and published by secular publishers, both of whom are committed to spreading secular ways of understanding the world. This explanation comes in two forms. The more wild-eyed of the televangelists speak darkly of a conspiracy of secular humanists. This is nonsense. Paul Vitz, no liberal, says in his study of textbooks that "there is no evidence of any kind of conscious conspiracy operating to censor textbooks." But, Vitz goes on to say, there is "a very widespread secular and liberal mindset" that "pervades the leadership in the world of education (and textbook publishing) and a secular and liberal bias is its inevitable consequence."[62] There is something to this.

Ever since the seventeenth century scholars in virtually all fields have come more and more to reject religious ways of understanding the world for those provided by modern science and social science. In the scholarly world—the world of most textbook authors and publishers—religion is marked off from respectable pursuits by an intellectual wall of separation, and most scholars never set foot on holy ground. Indeed, secular ways of thinking are so deeply embedded in the academic disciplines that religious alternatives simply cannot be taken seriously. The argument is not that scholars are atheists (though, no doubt, intellectuals are among the least religious of modern folk); it is that the conventional wisdom of their disciplines leaves no philosophical room for religious claims and arguments. At best, most modern scholarship relegates religion to the private world of faith—and often assigns it to the realm of superstition. That is, religion is left out of the texts precisely because it is *not* controversial; it is so uncontroversial that it need not be considered.

Of course, it is not just the intellectuals among us who are secularized. As I argued in chapter 1, we all live our lives in a public world which is largely secular. In fact, we have become so secular that most of us completely fail to miss religion in the textbooks.

Over the last three hundred years, business, law, politics, psychology, medicine, and education have all been secularized. We allow students to earn high school diplomas and undergraduate, graduate, and professional degrees without taking a single course in religion or discussing religion in whatever courses are required. We assume that everything worth knowing about every field of study can be learned without learning anything about religion.

Militant secularists (or atheists) are rare creatures among textbook authors as well as within the general public, and secularization proceeds nicely without them. Capitalism and consumerism, pluralism, nationalism, individualism, science, and technology divert our attention from the life of the spirit, undercut traditional religion, refocus our interests, provide us with new ways of thinking about the world, and, in the process, secularize us. Religion occupies but a small part of our time, and it influences few of our decisions. Exorcisms are rare, and the church no longer regulates the economy. This being the case, psychologists and economists can write textbooks about our (essentially) secular world without having to say very much about religion. Religion simply has not played nearly so much of a role in our public life in the last two or three hundred years as it once did.

There are, then, three different reasons why the textbooks have become secular. First, religion *is* increasingly irrelevant in our public, secular world. Second, intellectuals do not take religion seriously; it doesn't fit into the categories of their respective disciplines. Yet, third, religion possesses considerable vitality within our culture. Many people believe it is neither irrelevant nor a superstition. Hence religion continues to be the source of much controversy and of considerable danger to publishers.

Conclusions

There have been incremental improvements in the latest editions of at least a few social studies and history textbooks—due, in part at least, to the textbook studies of the late 1980s—and the new national standards for teaching American and world history give significantly more attention to religion than do the textbooks, though they continue to slight theology and do not even raise the question of using religious categories for interpreting history. (See my discussion of the standards in the Postscript.) As far as I can tell, however, texts in disciplines other than history and social studies have shown no greater sensitivity to religion.

What continues to be missing in all the texts, however, is any sensitivity to contemporary religious ways of interpreting the subject at hand. If religion is mentioned more (here and there), the governing philosophical assumptions that shape the kinds of explanations offered in the texts remain entirely secular. It is tremendously important to keep in mind that textbooks don't just teach subjects, they initiate students into intellectual disciplines; they don't just teach facts, they teach ways of thinking about the world.

There *is* something like a coherent worldview, a loosely structured set of philosophical commitments, which underlie and give shape to the texts—at least those texts I reviewed. No doubt not every author buys into it completely, and it is not typically taught self-consciously as a worldview by the authors—in part, at least, because it is so much a part of the intellectual air we breathe daily. The philosophical commitments that define this worldview are the same commitments that support and make sense of the dominant cultural and intellectual institutions of modernity: the knowledge we acquire in the present is more valuable than the wisdom of the past; our task is to free ourselves from the dead hand of tradition and superstition; we are no longer born into communities bound together in webs of (natural) social obligations; we are individuals first and foremost; human relationships are essentially contractual; the idea of the public good is problematic and is dissolved into the relative satisfaction of individuals and interest groups; reason is "deconstructed" into its scientific or narrowly utilitarian components, and though it may be competent to tell us about the facts, it is no longer competent to render judgment concerning moral matters; values are matters of personal choice or social convention; pluralism is assumed and defended—and then often confused with relativism; nature was long ago desacralized, and there is no purpose to be discovered in its processes; science and social science provide us with our only true knowledge of the world. By implication, religion is irrelevant to understanding the world

INDOCTRINATION

It is now time to put a little punch in my argument. In this chapter I will argue that the textbooks I reviewed are not religiously neutral but are hostile to religion. Indeed, a plausible case can be made—as many religious conservatives have argued—that public schools teach the "religion of secular humanism." In the end I will not choose to put it quite this way, but I do accept much of the analysis: the underlying worldview of modern education divorces humankind from its dependence on God; it replaces religious answers to many of the ultimate questions of human existence with secular answers; and, most striking, public education conveys its secular understanding of reality essentially as a matter of faith. Indeed, I will argue that at least in its textbooks and formal curriculum students are *indoctrinated* into the modern (secular) worldview and against religion.

The chapter ends with a short discussion of New Age religion, which has, to a considerable extent, replaced secular humanism as the object of much conservative religious concern.

Neutrality

Neutrality is not a simple concept; indeed, I want to distinguish six different senses of neutrality. As we saw in discussing the Establishment Clause, the Supreme Court has paid special attention to neutrality of purpose and effect so I begin with them.[1]

Purpose Neutrality. Is it the purpose of the textbook authors, or the government agents who choose textbooks, to take sides on religiously contested matters—to advance or denigrate religion? In most cases, probably not. Religious ways of understanding most textbook subjects are not live contenders for the truth; most textbook authors and publishers simply do not take religion seriously enough to take issue with it. Nor is it likely to be the purpose of textbook adoption committees to denigrate religion through their choice of textbooks. Most likely, they simply do not consider the possible relationship of claims made in the textbooks to religion for, like most everyone, they consider religion to be unrelated to the subjects addressed in the texts.

There are exceptions. Because of the long-standing controversy over evolution and creation, for example, the authors of most biology texts and the committees that adopt them know that the texts they write and adopt make claims that are not religiously neutral. Of course, their purpose may not be to denigrate religious ways of understanding nature so much as to promote science; that is what they *intend*. But insofar as they know what they are doing, they must have as a secondary purpose the denigration of at least fundamentalist truth claims. Scientific ways of understanding nature cannot be promoted without denigrating some religious ways of understanding nature. If the former is intended, so must be the latter.

Effect Neutrality. Secular textbooks have a powerful cumulative effect: if students acquire only a secular account of nature, history, economics, psychology, and values, it is not surprising that they become inclined to think and act in secular ways. Both because they ignore religion and espouse nonreligious ways of understanding the world, textbooks exile religion to irrelevance and private idiosyncrasy. They contribute to the secularization of the world; they are not effect neutral.

"Scarcely anyone," Stephen Bates argues, "disputes that schoolbooks affect the students who read them."

"Young children assimilate the content and values of reading materials with little conscious thought," observes the Civil Rights Commission. "The words and pictures children see in school," the Association of

American Publishers says, "influence the development of the attitudes they carry into adult life." Textbooks have the capacity to "indoctrinate children in societally prescribed behaviors," according to the NEA. . . . Federal judges often believe that books change attitudes, even adults' attitudes; that's why cross-burners have been sentenced to read the civil-rights chronicle *Eyes on the Prize* and *The Diary of Anne Frank*.[2]

Hence it is not surprising that survey data show that as people become more educated they become more secular. For example, people in positions of public leadership, who are likely to be well educated, are significantly less likely to call themselves religious, less likely to attend religious services, less likely to pray, and only about half as likely to have made a personal commitment to Christ.[3]

It is also true that the more educated people are, the more likely they are to be religious liberals. The effect of a college education is not neutral among religions. College graduates, for example, are twice as likely to call themselves religious "liberals" as they are religious "conservatives." A 1981 survey showed that half of all college graduates called themselves religious liberals, but only one in seven with a grade school education did so. More than half of those with a grade school education viewed the Bible as literally true, while only a fifth of college graduates believe this. Moreover, as Robert Wuthnow notes,

> college graduates are about three times more likely than persons without college education to put the Second Commandment (loving your neighbor) ahead of the First Commandment (loving God). The better educated are also about three times as likely to think it possible to be a true Christian without believing in the divinity of Christ. . . . College graduates are about twice as likely as those without college educations to be most impressed by Jesus' compassion and forgiveness. The less educated, in comparison, are more likely to be impressed by Jesus' healings, miracles, and goodness. Those with higher levels of education are considerably more likely to attribute androgynous characteristics to God; those with lover levels of education, to emphasize the masculinity of God.[4]

Why should this be? The reason is not that religious liberalism is taught in colleges but conservatism is not. Most students do not study religion. Rather, it is that the general tenor of education discredits conservative religion more obviously than it does liberal religion (which has made its compromises with modernity).

The most important effect of a secular education is not on belief but on institutions and behavior; we are secularized in ways that go beyond church attendance and belief in God. Formal education nurtures and sustains a secular culture in which it is increasingly difficult to live religiously. Education exiles religion to irrelevance in how we understand our professions and our public life.

It is true, of course, that otherwise reasonable people can read a great deal without realizing the meaning or implications of what they are reading. A part of the privatization of religion is intellectual: we isolate our religious beliefs in the private compartments of our minds and refuse to bring them into intellectual contact with what we are taught about the world. This is an intellectual defense mechanism that enables religion to survive in the modern world. It would be extraordinary, however, if our defense of textbooks must rest on the fact that many students will not be bright enough to understand the implications of what they read.

Relevance Neutrality. It is often believed that one way of maintaining neutrality is to say nothing. If we ignore a subject, we neither advance nor denigrate it. This is nonsense. It has surely become clear over the last few decades that history and social studies texts that ignored blacks and women were not maintaining neutrality on questions of race or gender but wearing their prejudices on their sleeves. So it is with religion.

A biology text that tells the story of evolution without bringing religious points of view into the discussion is taking sides. It is, in effect, saying, You don't need to understand anything about religion to understand nature. But many religious folk disagree, for religion has made any number of claims about nature, and some of them conflict with the teachings of modern biology. To ignore religion is to privilege scientific over religious accounts of the subject. Some years ago a report of the College of Literature, Science, and the Arts at the University of Michigan stated that just as "an act of omission is often as much a crime as one of commission, so inattention to religion is as much an act against religion as some more positive deed. To use William James' terms, not to offer any courses in religion is to help it become a dead option, not to remain a live one. More than that, it is to encourage a negative resolution of the option between religion and irreligion."[5] To ignore religious points of view in any text or any course in which religiously contested questions are at issue is to denigrate those alternatives.

That ignoring religion constitutes an argument against it becomes even clearer when we consider what is ignored. Max Stackhouse once wrote: "Any transcendent reality worth attending to has implications for what we think and do on earth."[6] Any God worthy of the name must make a difference. To ignore that difference, not to consider the implications of God's existence for how we think and live, is, in effect, to deny God's existence.

Of course, to ignore religion is not always to take sides. To leave religion out of mathematics classes is not to denigrate religion because religion makes no claims that are relevant to mathematics. Religion-free math education is religiously neutral.

But contemporary religions do continue to make claims about the meaning of history, human psychology, society, justice, and nature. Moreover, what religions have to say about these subjects is not trivial but goes to the very heart of what those subjects are about. That is, from most religious perspectives religion *is* highly relevant to history, home economics, economics, and biology. In choosing not to include discussions of the religious dimension of these subjects, textbook authors exile religion to irrelevance. This is to take sides.

Philosophical Neutrality. Textbook authors inevitably operate from within a worldview, a set of philosophical and methodological commitments that define for them what can and cannot count as a fact, as a legitimate theory, as a justifiable claim about values and the meaning of events. (Those commitments also define what is sufficiently important to include in the texts.) Religion does not appear in science and social science textbooks not just because it is controversial but because within a scientific worldview religious claims cannot be taken seriously as candidates for the truth. Secular historians operate with a methodology that does not allow them to cite divine purpose in explaining historical change. Nor can biologists make such an appeal in explaining evolutionary change. Truth claims, the biologist will tell us, must be testable—meaning, of course, scientifically and not theologically testable. And so also for economists and psychologists.

Religious subjects can, of course, be considered from within a secular worldview. For example, the history texts do mention religion, even though their worldview, their framework for making sense of history, is totally secular. Home economics books occasionally mention religion. They sometimes suggest, for example, that students might seek counseling from their ministers when they have problems, but this is entirely compatible with a fully secular understanding of human psychology: you do what works for you; you do not go to ministers because they have any particular competence or because they might have access to truth. There can be religious content, even though the shaping worldview is not religious. Much of the drive for textbook reform in history has been channeled into mentioning religion more often. But this stops well short of philosophical neutrality, for it leaves in place secular ways of understanding religion.

It is tremendously important to keep in mind that the conflict at issue is not primarily between any particular claims found in the textbooks and any particular religious claims. There are many statements in the textbooks that can, individually, be reconciled with religion. The fundamental conflict occurs at the level of philosophical commitments and their resulting criteria of relevance, meaning, importance, and truth. Textbooks are not just hodgepodges of statements. They possess coherence, they make arguments, they conceptualize the world in particular ways. They have a philosophical stance. *It is at the level of worldviews, at the level of making sense of their subject, that the primary conflict with religious alternatives occurs.* Textbooks do not just teach about subjects, they teach students to think in certain ways.

The core notion of neutrality is not to take sides. But it is impossible to imagine how one can avoid taking sides in thinking about history, nature, justice, and human nature because religions have staked out positions on all of these matters. There is no neutral ground on which to stand in making judgments about content, causality, meaning, and truth. All terrain is contested ground. The natural and social sciences, various philosophies and religions, divide the world up in different and conflicting ways. Philosophical neutrality will inevitably prove to be a will-o'-the-wisp, for all authors approach their subject from within particular worldviews, with philosophical commitments that define for them what counts as important, as knowledge, as reasonable, as true. *There is no such thing as a neutral point of view.* To write a textbook is to take sides.

There is a philosophical response that might be made at this point. Some philosophers, including many postmodernists, have argued that there are different "realms of discourse" or different "language games" or different "frameworks of interpretation" that are incommensurable or incomparable and hence equally valid ways of thinking about the world. On such an account, scientific and religious ways of talking can all be "true" in the only sense of truth allowed. They are simply *different* ways of talking about the world, reflecting, perhaps, our different interests and traditions, but they are not incompatible. They do not stand in logical relationships such that the "truth" of one implies the "falsity" of the other. Hence one might teach secular ways of understanding a subject which have no implications for the "truth" of religious ways of understanding that subject.

I find it difficult to believe that a neo-Darwinian account of evolution has no logical implications for the truth of a fundamentalist (or liberal) religious account of nature. I find it difficult to believe that a neoclassical account of "rational economic man" has no implications for the truth of religious claims that people should act on the basis of love for God and humankind. The history of ideas provides considerable evidence that many of the scholars who have been most attentive to conceptual tensions in our intellectual life have not hung on to both their scientific beliefs *and* their religious beliefs but have given one or the other up, or have struggled to find ways to render them logically compatible. They have not simply concluded that religion and science are different and incommensurable ways of talking about the world.

There is another reason why this move won't work here. The move to incommensurable and equally valid worldviews itself takes sides against religion for all religions have held that there is a truth to be had about the world. (Of course, some religions, Hinduism for example, have held that there are various paths to the truth; but they have not held that *everything* goes, that *all* worldviews are equally "true.") To say there is no Truth, only different and incommensurable "truths," is to forsake religious neutrality and take sides against religion.

And then there is another problem: if all worldviews are equally "true," why do we choose to teach only secular ways of thinking?

Verdict Neutrality. None of the textbooks I read brought in a formal verdict on religion. None explicitly pronounced it (at least in any of its contemporary variations) true or false, reasonable or unreasonable.

But this doesn't take us very far. Someone may by lynched without a jury verdict. So also religious themes, events, ideas, values, and worldviews may be ignored or undermined, removed from the arena of "live" alternatives, by textbooks that refuse to take them seriously or that promote incompatible ways of thinking about their subject.

Moreover, although the books render no verdict on religion, they do render formal verdicts on competing ways of thinking about the world. They either assume the truth of, or formally endorse, neo-Darwinian evolution, humanistic psychology, social scientific theories of human nature and economic systems, and secular interpretations of history. If it turns out that these alternatives are incompatible with religion, then they are, by implication, pronouncing a verdict on religion as well.

Neutrality as Fairness. If textbook authors must stand on contested philosophical ground, then neutrality is impossible. But there is another way of conceiving neutrality. Neutrality as fairness commits an author to discussing in an open and fair way all points of view on any question that is religiously contested. Rather than offer a single (inevitably non-neutral) point of view, the author takes seriously alternative points of view, different ways of judging content, causality, meaning, importance, and truth.

None of the textbooks I reviewed took religious points of view seriously. Indeed, they revealed no significant awareness of the controversial nature of their basic philosophical commitments. No home economics book says: "Look, you students should know that a lot of people think about human nature, morality, and decision making in radically different ways from those you will find in this book." Only one of the six biology books devoted as much as a single paragraph to the relationship between scientific and religious methods for understanding nature. No economics text offered the slightest hint that there are contemporary religious ways of understanding economics which differ from (indeed, conflict with) that of the text. And though several of the history texts briefly described religious views of history in the context of past historical periods, none discussed the possibility of contemporary religious ways of interpreting history.

For a textbook to be religiously neutral in this sense at least four criteria must be satisfied. First, it must take seriously religious and nonreligious ways of understanding any question that is religiously contested. I acknowledge that there is not sufficient space in textbooks to discuss *all* secular and religious positions on every issue so if neutrality as fairness is to be a practical possibility there must be some constraints on the range of alternatives considered and the space given each one. No doubt compromises would have to be made. Which questions are of sufficient importance so that neutrality becomes obligatory, and whose criteria are used to measure importance? Which alternative positions must be considered when obviously not all can be, and whose criteria are used to decide? Inevitably textbooks will be limited to discussing *major* alternative positions on the *major* questions. There will inevitably be trade-offs between the space given to discussing any single alternative and the number of alternatives considered.

Second, each alternative must be characterized *fairly*, from "the inside," as advocates of that point of view would characterize it (whether they be religious or secular). That is, authors must avoid reductionism, reconceptualizing positions in terms of competing, privileged positions. To take a point of view seriously, to treat it fairly, is to let advocates tell their own stories and make their own cases as much as possible.

Third, sufficient space in the textbook (and time in the classroom) must be given to a position so that students can make sense of it. The one- or two-page boxed excerpts of primary source reading occasionally found in the textbooks help, but not much. The power of a position depends on seeing it in the context of supporting evidence and assumptions, and this requires a much more substantial dose of material than the few paragraphs of boxed excerpts can provide.[7]

Fourth, if we are to have neutrality and not *just* fairness, the author can't take sides. Needless to say, this is asking a lot—in fact, I will argue in chapter 7 that a robust fairness and neutrality should characterize curricula, not individual textbooks. For now my point is simply that one significant form of neutrality *is* possible in textbooks—though none of the texts I reviewed attempted to achieve any degree of fairness, much less neutrality.

Humanism

Historically, "humanism" has been a scholar's word, but in our culture wars it has become a fighting word. For many religious conservatives humanism—or *secular* humanism—is the source of all things evil, and the primary carrier of secular humanism in modern culture is public education. A 1987 survey showed that 69 percent of evangelical respondents and 92 percent of evangelical clergy believed that public schools taught the values of secular humanism; 80 percent of Catholic priests agreed.[8]

Religious Conservatives and Secular Humanism. Christopher Toumey has rightly pointed out that conservative Christians give two quite different accounts of secular humanism.[9] In the first—which Toumey calls the "negation of personal beliefs" account—secular humanism is simply the name for that list of evils (abortion, pornography, one-world government, homosexuality, etc.) to which people object; of course lists differ. In the second, more theologically sophisticated account, human autonomy becomes the defining characteristic of secular humanism—and autonomy then gives rise to the list of particular evils that beset us. So, for example, Rev. Jerry Falwell defines humanism as

> man's attempt to create a heaven on earth, exempting God and His Law. Humanists propose that man is in charge of his own destiny. Humanism exalts man's reason and intelligence. It advocates situation ethics, freedom from any restraint, and defines sin as man's maladjustment to man. It even advocates the right to commit suicide and recognizes evolution as a source of man's existence. Humanism promotes the socialization of all humanity into a world commune. Christianity is ruled out of humanism and is said to be an obstacle to human progress and a threat to its existence.[10]

Humanity has replaced God at the center of things.

In *The Battle for the Mind*, perhaps the classic religious attack on humanism, Rev. Tim LaHaye argues that "there are two basic lines of reasoning that
determine the morals, values, life-style and activities of mankind—the wisdom of man or the wisdom of God (See I Corinthians 1:17–25). Today they
take the form of atheistic humanism or Christianity. What this life is all about
is THE BATTLE FOR YOUR MIND: whether you will live your life guided by
man's wisdom (humanism) or God's wisdom (Christianity). Either one will affect the way you live and where you spend eternity."[11] LaHaye traces the
roots of humanism to St. Thomas Aquinas, who admired the pagan philosopher Aristotle far too much. As a result, Aquinas had an inadequate notion of
the Fall and human sinfulness, and he overvalued reason. In effect, he raised
"human wisdom to a level that gave it equal weight with biblical revelation,"
opening the door "for freethinking educators to gradually implant more of the
wisdom of man as they discarded the wisdom of God."[12]

Humanism embodies a litany of sins for religious conservatives, but more
important than any particular sin is the emphases it places on human autonomy and the power of reason. Humanism rejects the conviction of conservative Christianity that before Scripture each knee should bend. According to
J. I. Packer, "Anything short of unconditional submission to Scripture . . . is a
kind of impenitence; any view that subjects the written word of God to the
opinions and pronouncements of men involves unbelief and disloyalty towards
Christ."[13]

But it is not only Christian conservatives who have troubles with humanism. Irving Kristol has argued that in spite of sometimes "mindless" condem-
nations of secular humanism there really is such a thing—and its impact has
been especially devastating for Jews. What are its teachings?

> They can be summed up in one phrase: "Man makes himself." That is to
> say, the universe is bereft of transcendental meaning, it has no inherent
> teleology, and humanity has it within its power to comprehend natural
> phenomena and to control and manipulate them so as to improve the hu-
> man estate. Creativity, once a divine prerogative, becomes a distinctly
> human one. . . . Man's immortal soul has been a victim of progress, re-
> placed by the temporal "self"—which he explores in such sciences as psy-
> chology, all of which proceed without benefit of what, in traditional terms,
> was regarded as a religious dimension.[14]

Smith v. Board of School Commissioners of Mobile County. In 1987
federal judge Brevard Hand of the Southern District of Alabama fired
what may have been the loudest salvo in the war of religion versus secular
humanism when he ruled that forty-four Alabama public school textbooks

unconstitutionally promoted the "religion" of secular humanism. Hand argued that secular humanism is a "belief system" that can be extracted from the *Humanist Manifestos*, the humanistic psychology of Abraham Maslow and Carl Rogers, and the writings of admitted humanists such as John Dewey. Secular humanists, according to Hand, believe that there is no God, that mankind is the result of evolutionary forces, that we have no transcendent spiritual qualities, and that the highest goal of human action is to maximize human fulfillment.

Hand's criticism was directed primarily at American history and home economics texts. The American history textbooks he reviewed "discriminate against the very concept of religion, and theistic religions in particular, by omissions so serious that a student learning history from them would not be apprised of relevant facts about America's history. The texts reviewed are not merely bad history, but lack so many facts as to equal ideological promotion." The home economics texts teach that one "must determine right and wrong based only on his own experience, feelings and values. . . . The emphasis and overall approach implies, and would cause any reasonable, thinking student to infer, that . . . moral choices are just a matter of preference."[15] The texts claim, according to Hand, that morality originates in personal needs and choices rather than in the will of God and as such they contradict theistic religion. They teach moral relativism, a tenet of secular humanism.

Now the crucial move: secular humanism is a religion. Why? For two basic reasons. First, "whenever a belief system deals with fundamental questions of the nature of reality and man's relationship to reality, it deals with essentially religious questions. A religion need not posit a belief *in* a deity, or a belief *in* supernatural existence. A religious person adheres to some position on whether supernatural and/or transcendent reality exists at all, and if so, how, and if not, why." Secular humanism, like all religions, "defines the nature of man; sets forth a goal or purpose for individual and collective human existence; and defines the nature of the universe."[16] Humanists, like other religious believers, promulgate a moral code (personal freedom and self-fulfillment) and proselytize (through periodicals, seminars, and textbooks).

Hand's second argument is that secular humanism, like other religions, is based on faith, for "to claim that there is nothing real beyond observable data is to make an assumption based not on science, but on faith, faith that observable data is all that is real. A statement that there is no transcendent or supernatural reality is a *religious* statement. A statement that there is no scientific proof of supernatural or transcendent reality is irrelevant and nonsensical, because inquiry into the fundamental nature of man and reality itself may not be confined solely within the sphere of physical, tangible, observable science."[17]

Hand acknowledged that the mere coincidence of a textbook claim with a religious belief is not enough to make it unconstitutional: schools can teach that it is wrong to kill even though the Ten Commandments—a religious text—forbid it; similarly, various secular claims can be taught even if they overlap with secular humanism. What cannot be done is to teach some *faith-based system* to the exclusion of others. Secular humanism, as a systematic, faith-based way of thinking about reality, cannot be taught to the exclusion of theistic religion anymore than theistic religion can be taught to the exclusion of secular humanism.[18]

Contrary to most reports, the case did not represent, in Hand's view, "an attempt of narrow-minded or fanatical proreligionists to force a school system to teach only those opinions and facts they find digestible. . . . The plaintiff-witnesses did not complain of simple exposure to improper ideas, but of systematic indoctrination."[19] Though Hand ruled that the texts must be removed from the schools, his argument was that, by themselves, the texts did not provide the balance required by the First Amendment. Presumably they might be used with religious texts that balanced them.

Hand's critics were not long in responding. The consensus of virtually everyone other than religious conservatives was that his decision was unpersuasive, if not outrageous. Harvard lawyer Alan Dershowitz (who has called Hand "the Ayatollah Khomeini of the federal judiciary") wrote, in response to this ruling, that Hand "is a disgrace to the federal judiciary. He is a constitutional outlaw in robes, a Torquemada of the twentieth century. His judicial opinions deserve no respect. They are simple bigotry under cover of law."[20]

Relief was not long in coming. The Court of Appeals for the Eleventh Circuit quickly overturned Hand's decision. Writing for the court, Judge Johnson argued that what was at issue was the second prong of the Lemon Test—whether the texts have the "primary effect" of advancing or inhibiting religion. As he read them, however, the textbooks had "the primary effect of conveying information that is essentially neutral in its religious content to the school children who utilize the books; none of these books convey a message of governmental approval of secular humanism or governmental disapproval of theism." The "mere omission" of facts about religion from the history texts may be unfortunate, but it conveys no message of approval of secular humanism, and he read the home economics texts as having the "entirely appropriate secular effect" of instilling in children "such values as independent thought, tolerance of diverse views, self-respect, maturity, self-reliance and logical decision-making."[21]

Before we assess Hand's arguments and the claims of religious conservatives a little perspective should prove helpful.

The Varieties of Humanism. "Humanism" is one of those words—"religion" is another—which have meant very different things to different people. There are at least four varieties we must disentangle.

Classical Humanism. The words "humanism" and "humanities" derive from the Renaissance Latin term *humanista* or "humanist." The humanists were the teachers of the *studia humanitatis* or the humanities. *Humanitatis*, in turn, was a term Cicero coined to translate a Greek word for which there was no Latin equivalent: *paideia*. The Greek *paideia* and the Latin *humanitatis* both designated a broad, literary education—what came to be called a "classical" education. During the Renaissance a humanistic education required the study of grammar, rhetoric, history, poetry, and moral philosophy, taught by way of the Greek and Latin classics.[22]

The great Renaissance humanists valued classical thought for itself, not just for how it might be used to buttress Christian theology. They took from classical thought its emphases on civic virtue, moral wisdom, and human dignity (a theme that shines through Renaissance art). They also gave education a new importance. The Renaissance humanists, according to Alan Bullock, "saw education as the process by which man was lifted out of his natural condition to discover his *humanitatis*"—his humanity.[23] To some small extent this ideal lives on under the name "humanities."

Christian Humanism. Humanism can be either secular or religious. With the notable exception of Machiavelli, the great Renaissance humanists were Christians, and some of them—More and Colet, for example, or Erasmus and Melanchton—used humanistic scholarship to deepen their understanding of the Bible and religion. What is important to religious humanism is its stress on the freedom and dignity (rather than the predestination and sinfulness) of humanity, the power (rather than the impotence) of reason and scholarship, and the relative importance of moral action (compared with theological belief). Religious humanists held that reason and the natural tendencies of human nature would lead people toward God. Though they did not adopt the name, the Protestant liberals and Reform Jews of the nineteenth and twentieth centuries might well be called religious humanists, and in the 1960s the Second Vatican Council began to proclaim a Catholic humanism in affirming a "reverence for man," the desire for "an authentic and full humanity of every man," and the quest for a world more suited to "man's surpassing dignity." Pope Paul VI reaffirmed this humanism in his Easter encyclical *Populorum Progressio* when he characterized the church's position as a "transcendent humanism," "a complete humanism," a "true humanism," and asked for a "world where every man, no matter what his race, religion, or nationality, can live a fully human life."[24]

Capital "H" Humanism. There are card-carrying Humanists who are members of Humanist organizations, most prominently the American Humanist Association, some of whom have signed (and many of whom have endorsed) one or another of several manifestos which have acquired a degree of notoriety among religious conservatives.

The first Humanist Manifesto (1933) is, in its own terms, a religious document. Its authors note the unfortunate equation of religion with "doctrines and methods which have lost their significance and which are powerless to solve the problem of human living in the Twentieth Century." The *Manifesto* assumes a scientific view of the world and argues that religion should be understood not as a matter of belief in a supernatural God but as "those actions, purposes, and experiences which are humanly significant." Religious humanism "considers the complete realization of human personality to be the end of man's life and seeks its development and fulfillment in the here and now." Religious humanists must work for a better world for everyone, and especially for a more cooperative economic order.[25]

The second *Humanist Manifesto* (1973) and the *Secular Humanist Declaration* (1981) dropped the religious language. According to the *Declaration*, Secular Humanists favor free intellectual inquiry; support the separation of church and state; defend the ideal of political freedom; believe that morality is grounded in critical thinking rather than religion; support nonindoctrinative moral education in the schools; are religious skeptics; are concerned about anti-intellectualism in our culture; assert that science provides us with the only reliable way of learning about the world; believe that the current attack on the teaching of evolution must be combated; and assert the value of education in producing a strong and humane society. Much of this is garden-variety liberalism, though the *Declaration* does make religious skepticism a tenet of secular humanism: "Secular humanists may be agnostics, atheists, rationalists, or skeptics, but they find insufficient evidence for the claim that some divine purpose exists for the universe. They reject the idea that God has intervened miraculously in history or revealed himself to a chosen few, or that he can save or redeem sinners. They believe that men and women are free and are responsible for their own destinies and that they cannot look toward some transcendent Being for salvation." The *Declaration* is rooted both in a rejection of religion and in a deep appreciation of modern science: "The modern secular humanist outlook has led to the application of science and technology to the improvement of the human condition. This has had a positive effect on reducing poverty, suffering, and disease in various parts of the world . . . and in making the good life possible for more and more people." As important, it "has led to the emancipation of hundreds of millions of people from the exercise of blind faith and fears of superstition and has contributed to their education and the enrichment of their lives."[26]

Capital "H" Humanism is not a major movement. The major humanist organizations are small, consisting of a few thousand members.[27] Paul Kurtz, the author of the second *Manifesto* and the *Secular Humanist Declaration* has written: "The truth is that humanist associations are weak institutions. . . . They have pitifully small budgets, woefully small memberships and relatively low circulations of their publications. The average local church in almost any city has more members and resources than any of the major humanist groups."[28]

Small "h" humanism. Kurtz goes on to say, however, that these various Humanist groups "are certainly not coextensive with humanism as a movement. . . . Humanism, in this broad sense, is one of the deepest currents of thought and feeling in the world." Kurtz finds the principles of (what I am calling small "h") humanism embedded in many public institutions, the most important of which "are our schools—primary and secondary, private and public—and our colleges and universities. The latter in particular are secular institutions that keep alive the basic themes of modern humanism: the quest for truth, free inquiry, the scientific outlook, the exploration of values, and aesthetic creativity."[29] Kurtz sees the most important task of the (capital "H") Humanist movement to be shoring up (small "h") humanism among educators.

Here the story becomes a little muddy, however, for "humanism" is not often a term used by people to describe their own views; it is a name used by scholars, theologians, and ideologues for somewhat different purposes in categorizing movements in intellectual history. In Kurtz's characterization of it, (small "h") humanism names the Enlightenment tradition that takes its cues from modern science and liberalism. Such humanism has been secular both because of its commitment to modern science and because of its hostility to organized religion, which it has held responsible for endless warfare, persecution, and reactionary politics. Its goal has been in large part moral and political: to reduce human suffering and liberate humanity from oppression—especially, though not exclusively, from the oppression of the church.

But we have seen, there is a second kind of (small "h") humanism that is the heir of Renaissance classicism and has its foundation in literature and the humanities rather than in modern science. This humanism has typically been wary of, if not opposed to, the dominance of modern science in modern culture. While the humanism of the humanities has nurtured a liberal arts education, the humanism of Enlightenment science and liberalism has typically led to utilitarian and expressive education. The differences are significant.[30]

Yet there are similarities as well, which, for religious conservatives, are all-important. Neither kind of humanism takes Scripture or revelation for a starting point. Both rely on the power of human reason to discern the truth. True, the humanism of the humanities is more respectful of the past, less confident of human progress, and more sensitive to the spiritual dimension of life; still, it is, in its modern manifestations, almost entirely secular.

Do the Texts Teach Secular Humanism? Textbooks undoubtedly convey to students many of the central themes of humanism in its various guises: the centrality of science to understanding reality; the power of reason; the value of individualism, autonomy, and liberal social institutions; and the progress that has resulted in the modern era. They also convey, implicitly if not explicitly, the sense that the world can be understood in fully secular terms.

What is often missing is the moral passion of humanism (in either its small "h" or capital "H" variations). Many of the texts are overtly nonmoral or "value-free." The biology books ignore moral questions; the economics texts often acknowledge being value-free; the home economics texts work hard to replace all talk of morality with what turn out to be morally neutral "values." Indeed, the books are troubling for many *secular* critics precisely because they do not take morality seriously; because, we might say, they *are insufficiently humanistic*. A humanist, as most humanists themselves define the term, is not simply an atheist or agnostic, but someone moved by a deep concern for the moral good of humanity. We may or may not believe secular humanists to be misguided in their morality, but we should not ignore the depth of their moral concern.

Religious conservatives are likely to employ the term "secular humanism" in a somewhat different (if overlapping) way. For them it is the philosophical view that we can know the truth, and know what we should do, apart from the revelation of God. It is true, as we have seen, that nowhere in any of the books is there the slightest hint that we are dependent on God for our knowledge of history, psychology, nature, society, or morality. If secular humanism is essentially a matter of moral and epistemological autonomy, the books teach it.

In fact, the claim that texts teach secular humanism is not nearly so implausible as many liberals assume. Surely the texts orient the thinking of students in a secular, vaguely humanistic direction, regarding many of the most fundamental aspects of life—history, nature, psychology, society, justice, and morality. The philosophical assumptions that constitute the underlying worldview of the textbooks are, after all, those of modernity. No doubt there are variations of emphasis and nuance, and the subjects of the books draw on different aspects of the modern worldview. Moreover, the authors may very well not think of themselves as promoting anything so grand as a worldview. But in the end what is important is that there *is* a more or less coherent set of philosophical assumptions underlying the textbooks (and much teaching) and they are not religiously neutral.[31]

Is Secular Humanism a Religion? There is, of course, something jarring about calling *secular* humanism (or the philosophical assumptions that comprise the modern worldview) religious, for we usually associate religion with belief in God. But this need not be so. Some religions—the oldest forms of Buddhism and Confucianism, for example—are agnostic about God or the gods, and a good deal of contemporary religion places much less emphasis on belief in God than in tradition, morality, and how people live their lives.

"Religion" is as hard to define as "humanism." Such words function as what Wittgenstein called "family-resemblance" terms.[32] People within a family resemble each other in various ways: in physique, the color of eyes or hair, the shape of the nose, the size of the ears, gait, intelligence, personality, and so on. There is no single or simple characteristic which all family members must possess to be recognizably members of the family—and yet they resemble each other. So it is with religions. What we call religions all share, like members of a family, in a complicated and crisscrossing network of similarities. Our question, then, is whether secular humanism resembles the great world religions enough so that we might want to extend the use of the word "religion" to it.

For years, scholars of comparative religion and the sociology of religion have talked about "functional religions"—symbol systems or ideologies or worldviews that *function* like traditional religions even though their *content* is quite different. For example, many scholars have argued that communism functions (or functioned) as a religion. John Hick has written that "the Communist ideology constitutes a mythic framework for life, providing both a motivation for idealism and a validation of the existing social order; and the Communist Party is, sociologically, a church with its own hierarchy, its sacred scriptures, its system of dogma, including doctrines of the fall (the development of capitalism) and eschatology (the eventual classless society) and having its exegetical disputes and heresies."[33] Like the great Western religions, communism has held that there is a pattern, a purpose, an inevitability to history; it has its venerated founders, rituals, and a carefully defined ethic. Obviously, if a religion must involve belief in God or gods, then Marxism is not a religion. But I already noted that not all of the (conventionally accepted) great world religions do involve belief in God or the gods. In *The Scientific Study of Religion* the sociologist J. Milton Yinger defines religion as "a system of beliefs and practices by means of which a group of people struggles with [the] ultimate problems of human life" and he argues that communism and nationalism function as religions, as does science when it becomes a "way of life" for people rather than just a methodology.[34]

In 1961, well before the current controversy over secular humanism began, sociologist Will Herberg wrote that for some time the public schools had taught the "substitute religion of secularism," which he defined as "the theory and practice of human life conceived as self-sufficient and unrelated to God." In the universities, he added, "the new 'religion of no-religion' assumed the familiar forms of scientism, naturalism, and positivism."[35]

There is a theological variation on this argument. Martin Luther once claimed that "whatever the heart most desires is your God."[36] More recently, Paul Tillich has argued that "the object of theology is what concerns us ultimately."[37] Often we are not consciously aware of what our ultimate concerns are, and often what concerns us is not truly ultimate but is, in theological language, idolatrous. For Tillich, living in Germany in the 1920s and 1930s, nationalism was the pervasive idolatrous form of ultimate concern. Nationalists are idolaters because they direct their "ultimate" concern to something finite, something not truly ultimate. Still, it makes perfectly good sense theologically to describe them as religious because they are ultimately concerned; nationalism defines their being; it is what gives meaning to their lives.

John Dewey, working out of a secular philosophical tradition, said some not dissimilar things. Dewey distinguished between the noun "religion," which names a body of beliefs and practices, and the adjective "religious," which "denotes attitudes that may be taken toward every object and every proposed end or ideal." Religious faith, for Dewey, is grounded in "allegiance to inclusive ideal ends, which imagination presents to us and to which the human will responds as worthy of controlling our desires and choices." Indeed, any "activity pursued in behalf of an ideal end against obstacles and in spite of threats of personal loss because of conviction of its general and enduring value is religious in quality."[38]

Dewey was the major intellectual force behind the first "Humanist Manifesto," and we can see a little more clearly now how that document could be both secular and religious. The worldview behind the *Manifesto* is largely that of modern science and liberal individualism; it explicitly rejects supernaturalism. Yet Dewey and the signers were moved by a powerful ideal—to make this a better world. The power of that ideal is such that it is essentially a "religious" ideal which governs and gives meaning to their lives. Religion, the *Manifesto* says, "consists of those actions, purposes, and experiences which are humanly significant." Indeed, it continues, "The distinction between the sacred and the secular can no longer be maintained." So the *Manifesto* frames its principles in religious language.[39]

There are two quite different ways in which one might argue that secular humanism is a religion on *legal* grounds. First, we can simply quote the Supreme Court. In a famous (some would say infamous) footnote in *Torcaso* v. *Watkins* (1961) Justice Black wrote: "Among the religions in the country which do not teach what would generally be considered a belief in the existence of God are Buddhism, Taoism, Ethical Culture, Secular Humanism and others."[40] And in *Schempp* Justice Clark warned that the state may not establish a "religion of secularism" in the schools, so presumably secularism could be a religion.[41]

The more compelling argument begins with the observation that for the last fifty years, the Court has been liberalizing its conception of religion—at least for some purposes. In *United States* v. *Macintosh* (1931) Chief Justice Charles Evans Hughes took the traditional position that the "essence of religion is belief in a relation to God involving duties superior to those arising from any human relation."[42] But by 1940, Justice Frankfurter was explaining religion in terms of our "convictions about the ultimate mystery of the universe and man's relation to it,"[43] and in *McGowan* v. *Maryland* (1961), he wrote, "By its nature, religion—in the comprehensive sense in which the Constitution uses that word—is an aspect of human thought and action which profoundly relates the life of man to the world in which he lives."[44]

A case involving conscientious objector status spelled out the more liberal reading of religion in some detail. In *United States* v. *Seeger* (1965), Justice Clark noted that "over 250 sects inhabit our land. Some believe in a purely personal God, some in a supernatural deity; others think of religion as a way of life envisioning as its ultimate goal the day when all men can live together in perfect understanding and peace. There are those who think of God as the depth of our being; others, such as the Buddhists, strive for a state of lasting rest through self denial and inner purification." Religious belief cannot be limited to those who believe in God. Appealing to Paul Tillich, Bishop John A. T. Robinson, and the Second Vatican Council, Justice Clark suggested that religion is grounded in "a power or being, or upon a faith, to which all else is subordinate or upon which all else is ultimately dependent." This being the case, the test for the religious grounds of conscientious objection to war is whether an individual holds a "sincere and meaningful belief which occupies in the life of its possessor a place parallel to that filled by the God of those admittedly qualifying for the exemption."[45]

Seeger gave "secular" opponents of war the same right to conscientious objector status as traditionally "religious" individuals under the Free Exercise Clause. Profound moral beliefs can function religiously. But if the Court were to accept functional religions for Establishment Clause purposes, then, religious conservatives argue, the implications would be momentous. The state could no longer privilege secular humanism over traditional religions in public schools, for this would constitute taking sides among religions. Of course, the Court has not taken this step but has instead applied what some observers take to be a double standard, allowing functional religions at least some protection under the Free Exercise Clause but requiring a traditional definition of religion for the purposes of the Establishment Clause.[46]

Whether secular humanism or the modern worldview functions religiously is potentially important for how the Establishment Clause is applied. There is an alternative analysis, however. Even if secular humanism (and the modern worldview) are *not* (functional) religions we still have a problem, for the Supreme Court has consistently held that the Establishment Clause requires not just neutrality among religions but neutrality between religion and nonreligion. But the texts I reviewed (and the curricula in which they are typically embedded) are not religiously neutral but promote secular over religious ways of making sense of the world. Whether we read secular humanism as religion or as nonreligion, there is a neutrality problem.

Reason and Faith

Judge Hand argued that secular humanism is grounded in faith. If this is so, we have a further reason to believe that it functions religiously and presents us with a constitutional problem; moreover, it would then be wrong to convey to students the (mistaken) claim that science and social science are matters of reason, while (only) religion is a matter of faith, for they stand on the same epistemological foundations. Needless to say, there are many ways of defining reason and faith. I offer the following distinctions not as definitive, but to help us understand the problem at hand. (To simplify the discussion I will contrast the roles of reason and faith in theology with their roles in modern science rather than in humanism more generally.)

Two Concepts of Reason. For millennia, Euclid's geometry provided a clear and compelling conception of rationality. Beginning from intuitively obvious axioms, proceeding by formal rules of reasoning, we can arrive at universally valid conclusions. Of course, as it has turned out (so near as we can now tell), the world is *not* Euclidian—at least there are non-Euclidian geometries that fit the world of relativity physics better than Euclid's. The moral is that we can be rational within a system of thought, but we can also reason about that system of thought, from the outside, as it were, to learn whether it is itself reasonable given what else we know about the world.

We all live and think within traditions or worldviews that make sense of the world for us. Assuming they survive for any length of time, traditions and worldviews achieve a measure of coherence, systematically ordering our thinking. We can be rational within them, following the internal structure of rules, without ever questioning the basic assumptions; we might also ask whether the worldview itself is reasonable, all things considered. Are there alternatives which are in some way preferable? Do our basic assumptions stand up to critical inquiry? Of course, once we step outside the system, what counts as reasonable is no longer obvious. In this case the attempt to be reasonable is inevitably less a matter of being rigorously logical than of being deliberative; it requires that we be open to new patterns of meaning; and it will not yield certainty so much as insight and, perhaps, a measure of plausibility. *Rationality*, as I shall use the term, is a matter of following rules, of being logical, within a system of accepted truths; *reasonableness* requires self-critical questioning of a system's most basic assumptions and an openness to alternative ways of making sense of the world.[47]

Many religious conservatives are rationalists, for whom Scripture defines the system within which sound reasoning takes place. Conservative theologians work from the truths of Scripture (much as geometers work from axioms) applying those truths to our lives in logically rigorous ways. They are not open to reasoning *about* Scripture (any more than traditional geometers were open to reasoning about axioms). As J. I. Packer puts it, liberals make the mistake of subjecting Scripture to their own judgment, treating "the question of the truth and authority of Scripture, which God has closed, as if it were still open." The fundamental question "is not whether we should think, but how we should think; whether or not our thinking should be controlled by our faith." Faith, not reason, guarantees the truth of Scripture. Indeed, unless reason starts from the bedrock of Scripture, Packer claims, we will be "tossed about by every wind of intellectual fashion and carried to and fro by cross-currents of reaction."[48] To forsake scriptural bedrock is to drown in a sea of conceptual relativism.

In chapter 1 I suggested that religious liberals brave the cross-currents of scriptural and theological criticism, not so much to find bedrock as to improve on their old position. Liberals assume that progress is possible if we question old beliefs and values, bringing them under the scrutiny of critical thought, making them run the gauntlet of developing human experience. They find it essential to challenge—and perhaps even reconcile—religion with the spirit of the age, constantly venturing out beyond the borders of their tradition. Indeed, almost from the beginning of Christianity the Church Fathers attempted to reconcile Christian theology and Greek philosophy, and on occasion philosophy could force changes in theology. So, for example, Augustine and his medieval successors acknowledged that Scripture might need to be read metaphorically rather than literally when it conflicts with established knowledge. Needless to say, modern-day liberals are considerably more open than their medieval predecessors. Feminist theologians, for example, argue that we must hold traditional patriarchal conceptions of God and society to the test of contemporary moral experience. If liberals accept Scripture and their religious tradition as a starting point for understanding the world, they also draw on modern science, historical criticism, liberal social ideas and ideals, and the insights and wisdom of other religious traditions to revise and reform their own traditions. Scripture is not above criticism, and theology is a critical discipline. None of this is done in a neat, rigorously logical, rule-defined way, however. Instead it is a rather messy process of deliberation, argument, reflection, and practical judgment. Liberals, then, do not rest content with rationality but seek to be *reasonable* given the total context of experience. For a conservative, this opens the door wide to relativism.

Science is typically viewed as the paradigm example of the open and progressive search for truth. Yet scientific method often functions much as Scripture does within conservative religion, providing unquestioned rules by which all disputes are to be settled. Most scientists are rationalists (in my sense of the term, proceeding logically given the rules of the system), just as are most conservative theologians—it is just that the rules are different. The rules themselves (the governing presuppositions of the modern scientific worldview) are not up for debate.

The implications of this are significant, for in adopting scientific method we rule out, a priori, the relevance of religious evidence and the possibility of religious conclusions. Ian Barbour attributes to the astronomer Arthur Eddington a parable about a man who was "studying deep-sea life using a net on a three-inch mesh. After bringing up repeated samples, the man concluded that there are no deep-sea fish less than three inches in length. Our methods of fishing, Eddington suggests, determine what we can catch."[49]

Eddington's parable suggests that there is only a quantitative difference between what scientific method allows scientists to catch and what escapes their nets. The crucial distinctions are *qualitative*, however: science looks for certain *kinds* of relationships (causal rather than teleological); it requires certain *kinds* of evidence (grounded in sense perception) rather than others (grounded, say, in moral or religious experience, in revelation or Scripture); it requires the *kind* of evidence that is replicable (something often impossible to come by when religious events are at issue); and it is designed to produce the *kind* of knowledge that gives us power over the world (rather than moral direction or the spiritual meaning of things).

I will give one example. Scientific experiments *must* be replicable, the governing assumption being that reality is lawlike. But this rules miracles out of the picture a priori, for they are singular events whose explanation hinges on their making sense within a story, not on fitting under a universal law. While we might put nature on the rack to make her divulge her secrets, as Bacon once counseled, we cannot force God to replicate miracles.[50] For Western religions, reality has the structure of a story, and there are singular events—miracles, if you will—by means of which God moves the story along. Miracles fit into different patterns of intelligibility than that provided by modern science. What may be rational to believe within a religious worldview (given the unfolding story) is irrational within a scientific worldview (given universal laws of nature).

Just as Scripture always trumps science for a religious conservative, so scientific method always trumps religion in the practice of science. Just as most religious conservatives are not open to scientific evidence that falsifies the first chapter of Genesis, so most scientists are not open to religious evidence that falsifies neo-Darwinian biology. That is, the scientist and the conservative theologian are each committed to thinking critically or rationally within their respective worldviews, but neither is open to thinking critically or reasonably about their foundational assumptions, their worldview.[51]

There is, then, a surprising symmetry between modern science and conservative religion, and there is a striking asymmetry of both with liberal religion, which is, by contrast, sensitive to the insights (and falsifying evidence) of rival worldviews. In particular, liberal theology has shown a remarkable openness to the claims of modern science and social science (much too much openness for conservative theologians). Liberals are open to reforming their own traditions based on the insights they acquire outside the tradition. Few scientists, by contrast, feel any obligation to take seriously religious ideas in the practice of their science.

I hasten to add that this does not mean that the truth is to be found in liberal theology. Perhaps Scripture and faith justifiably trump science (as religious conservatives claim); perhaps if we make the effort to be reasonable, looking at what can be said for and against religious and scientific ways of understanding the world, we shall conclude that scientific method is much more reasonable than theology. This, of course, is the conclusion of not a few scientists and philosophers who have made the effort—though there is far from any consensus about such things.

There is another possibility. It may be, as many postmodernists argue, that the whole idea of a reasonable comparison of worldviews makes no sense. It may be that all worldviews are rooted in "local" traditions such that they are culturally and historically relative. Indeed, it may be that science, like various theologies and political ideologies, provides just another way of viewing the world, and though it may be possible to be rational within any of the alternatives, reasonableness must prove to be a mistaken ideal.[52]

I make no brief for postmodernism or liberal theology here. I do suggest that reason is a rather more slippery beast than is often assumed. It surely cannot be uncritically identified with science and uncritically opposed to theology.

Two Concepts of Faith. In chapter 1 I distinguished between propositional and nonpropositional accounts of Scripture. Conservatives typically believe that God revealed Himself propositionally in the words of Scripture. Liberals, by contrast, typically hold a nonpropositional view according to which we encounter God in nature, in the events of history, and in private religious experience, but these experiences are ineffable; our accounts of God must always be symbolic, and Scripture is mythological, betraying the inadequate attempts of fallible people to put their experiences and insights into language.

There are two analogous accounts of faith. On the first, faith is a matter of *belief*, of assenting to God's *propositional revelation* in Scripture. Why should a person believe in the (inerrant) truth of Scripture? Not because it is reasonable; that places too much stress on sinful, fallible people. Rather, we have faith. But what justifies faith? It is sometimes held that there is particular merit in blind faith, in simply believing, but theologically the more common claim is that faith (as belief) is a gift of divine grace. According to the *Catechism of the Catholic Church*, for example, faith is "a gift of God," an "act of the intellect assenting to the divine truth by command of the will moved by God through grace." To have faith we must have "the interior helps of the Holy Spirit, who moves the heart and converts it to God." Such faith is certain: "To be sure, revealed truths can seem obscure to the human reason and experience, but 'the certainty that the divine light gives is greater than that which the light of natural reason gives.' 'Ten thousand difficulties do not make one doubt.'"[53] In the Protestant tradition, John Calvin held that the "only true faith is that which the spirit of God seals in our hearts." Such faith "requires no reasons" but enables us to know the truths of Scripture with "utter certainty." Similarly, the contemporary evangelical theologian J. I. Packer claims that it is through the "work of the Holy Spirit, opening and enlightening the 'eyes' of the mind . . . that man 'sees' and knows the divine source and spiritual meaning of the message that confronts him."[54]

The alternative account, grounded in nonpropositional revelation, makes faith a synonym more of *trust* than of belief. According to Wolfhart Pannenberg, the faith of the ancient Israelites did not come to them "in isolation but always in the context of a history of deeds of Yahweh in which his trustworthiness and might have already been demonstrated." That is, in the "context of history," the reliability of faith is, or can be, "well-founded." Such faith "presupposes a basis: something which continually proves to be true against all doubt."[55] Faith (or trust) is more or less reasonable given what we know of the world.

In his biography of Reinhold Niebuhr, Richard Fox says that for Niebuhr, believing in God (having faith, as I am now defining it) was a matter of "perceiving an outline of meaning in the midst of a broken existence."[56] Such faith is not a matter of clear and distinct beliefs but of experiencing reality in such as a way as to find it trustworthy and supportive. For John Hick we best understand such *nonpropositional* faith as a religious perception, the apprehension "of the divine presence within the believer's human experience."[57] Maynard Adams suggests that faith is "the sense of having a place in a friendly and supportive (even if awesome) world" in which we "may live with confidence, even in the most difficult situations," trusting that things "will (or can be made to) work together for good."[58] Such faith is less a matter of believing something than of *experiencing* reality religiously.

Consider a rough analogy: musical people do not just believe something about music that tone-deaf people disbelieve; they experience a dimension of reality that tone-deaf people are deaf to.[59] To have faith is to encounter reality as meaningful and trustworthy—in spite of its mysteries and our suffering. Such faith may be more or less reasonable; it is not held blindly, nor is it accepted on authority or as a matter of divine grace. We can argue for and against the patterns of meaning we discern in the world. Of course, faith claims are not falsifiable or verifiable scientifically; such faith rises and falls with its ability to capture the moral and spiritual insights and needs of people—insights which scientific method rules out of consideration a priori.

With modernity religion became intellectually problematic. One response is to assert that we must, and can, believe in spite of the (scientific) irrationality of what we believe. It is often held that such propositional faith can be held with certainty, for God is its guarantor; this has become a common conservative religious position. The more characteristically liberal response—following Schleiermacher—is that faith is a matter of experiencing reality as supportive and trustworthy, of discerning religious meaning in the world. It takes science seriously, modifying theological claims on occasion, but holds that much of reality evades the conceptual net of science. Such nonpropositional faith may be more or less reasonable, all things considered; it will involve risks.[60]

Does science require faith? The great majority of students probably accept the teaching of science on authority, much as they would a religious catechism, as a set of beliefs to be memorized. The chemist Michael Polanyi suggests that school science provides students with only a knowledge of "established doctrine, the dead letter of science"—though he is hopeful that the university will "bring this knowledge to life by making the student realize its uncertainties and its eternally provisional nature."[61] The historian and philosopher of science Thomas Kuhn is less optimistic. Kuhn claims that the education of scientists "is a narrow and rigid education, probably more so than any other except perhaps in orthodox theology."[62] Scientists are not educated to understand the historical or philosophical issues that underlie modern science, Kuhn argues; nor are they taught about the mistakes and blind alleys of science. They are taught largely through textbooks, which present them with the "truth" rather than, as in the humanities, a variety of conflicting historical and philosophical texts that force them to think through alternative ways of understanding the world.[63]

Kuhn understates the case. Students of religion are simply not able to avoid fairly extensive exposure to science at all levels of their education. But I know of no public university that requires students who are pursuing a degree in science to take course work in religion. The education of scientists is surely more narrow (at least when it comes to religion) than that of clergy or theologians (when it comes to science).

In effect, students—indeed, most people in our culture—accept the conclusions of science as a matter of faith. They do not accept scientific claims as a matter of *blind* faith, to be sure; they accept science on the authority of their teachers and the culture more generally (just as in premodern cultures people accepted their religious views on the authority of the church and the culture more generally). Nonetheless, students are not usually provided with any critical distance on science, with alternative ways of understanding the subject matter of science. Nor, most likely, were their teachers. Religion has become so obscure in the institutional memory of science that its continued falsity or irrelevance has become a matter of faith for most scientists.

But it is arguable that even very liberally educated scientists believe and act on faith, though this is more a matter of nonpropositional than propositional faith. In practicing science they experience the world scientifically, developing a trust both in the methods of the scientific community and correlatively in the ultimate scientific intelligibility of the world (just as theologians often develop a trust in their theological tradition and discern patterns of religious intelligibility in the world). The astronomer Robert Jastrow has suggested that there "is a kind of religion in science; it is the religion of a person who believes there is order and harmony in the Universe."[64] Albert Einstein wrote: "I have never found a better expression than 'religious' for this trust in the rational nature of reality and of its peculiar accessibility to the human mind. Where this trust is lacking science degenerates into an uninspired procedure."[65] According to Michael Polanyi, "no one can become a scientist unless he presumes that the scientific doctrine and method are fundamentally sound and that their ultimate premises can be unquestioningly accepted. We have here an instance of the process described epigrammatically by the Christian Church Fathers in the words: *fides quarens intellectum*, faith in search of understanding."[66]

As a result of such faith, the sociologist Edward Shils writes, "confidence in the powers of reason and science became a tradition accepted with the same unquestioning confidence as the belief in the Judeo-Christian accounts of the origins and meaning of human existence had been earlier."[67] And most scientists cling to their faith, even though it may close them off to other patterns of intelligibility in the world.

This is not to say that modern science is, in the end, unreasonable. It is to say that most scientists, like most everyone, live and think within a tradition that makes sense of the world for them, and by virtue of their educations they are not well equipped (again like most of us) to make judgments about the reasonableness of their tradition—their faith—compared with others.[68]

Judge Hand Again. There is an underlying worldview—whether we call it secular humanism or the modern worldview—that shapes and informs most textbooks, and modern science is at its heart. Hand argues that that worldview is religious—at least that it functions religiously—in that like religions it provides answers to our most fundamental questions about reality and it is grounded in faith.

The texts I reviewed do teach students answers to many of the most fundamental questions of life: they teach them how to think about nature, history, psychology, values, and decision making. *Cumulatively*, they function much as do religions, orienting students in the world. And by not raising the question of alternative accounts of reality, the texts at least implicitly offer "ultimate" explanations.

Moreover, as I have just argued, there is a sense—or perhaps I should say two senses—in which even modern science is grounded in faith. It requires a trust that reality can be understood through the methods of science and social science. This is, no doubt, a reasoned, not a blind faith; it is supported by a rich tradition of insights, experiments, and theory. But if most everyone would agree that reality can be captured to some considerable extent in the conceptual nets of science, the adequacy of scientific method to capture all of reality is very much contested. There are no knock-down arguments to prove this; still the normal practice of science does not grant scientists the freedom to consider alternative, perhaps religious, ways of making sense of the world. Not surprisingly, scientists have often acknowledged the dimension of faith in their work.

As important, science—and social science—can be *taught* as a matter of faith, to be accepted more on the authority of teachers and texts than because students have any critical appreciation of what is at issue. If students are not allowed access to contending religious ways of thinking about their subjects they are in no position to assess the reasonableness of scientific claims when they conflict with religious claims. Indeed, students are indoctrinated.

Indoctrination

Education provides students with critical distance on what is learned, while indoctrination, like its close cousin training, does not. Animals are trained rather than educated; babies are toilet-trained (not toilet-educated); children are trained in the multiplication tables; soldiers are trained to march. In each case, learning is more a matter of drill and habit than of critical thinking. We also talk about training accountants, doctors, and lawyers, and to the extent that there is a single right way of practicing a profession, a more or less closed system within which alternative practices are systematically excluded, students in professional schools are taught uncritically; they are trained. (In fact, students in professional schools are trained in some things and educated about others.)

In matters of morality, politics, and religion we often use the word "indoctrination" rather than "training" in that *doctrines* are at issue. We use the terms religious "training" or "indoctrination" to describe the uncritical learning that is fostered when parents or churches or the state impose a single view of the world on children. Of course, moral or religious training or indoctrination may be good in certain situations; indeed, with small children there may be no alternative.

Nonetheless, public schools (at least in the higher grades) and universities are properly concerned with education, with nurturing a critical understanding of various ways of thinking about the world. In a way, "liberal education" is redundant, just as "liberal training" is an oxymoron.

Indoctrination need not be a matter of brainwashing or social conditioning. Students who have been indoctrinated may very well be rational. They may be able to reason effectively *within* the system into which they have been indoctrinated. But if they have been indoctrinated they are not likely to be *reasonable*, for they will not be able to step outside their theology or their culture or their discipline or their ideology to participate in an informed discussion of what makes their point of view reasonable all things considered. Indoctrination is the uncritical initiation of students into some particular ideology or worldview.

Indoctrination can take place when a way of thinking is ignored. Allan Bloom has rightly noted that true freedom of the mind requires "the presence of alternative thoughts. The most successful tyranny is not one that uses force to assure uniformity but the one that removes the awareness of other possibilities, that makes it seem inconceivable that other ways are viable."[69] Public education does not indoctrinate students against religion by overtly attacking it or by promoting a militant secularism. Instead, it removes the awareness of religious possibilities; it makes religious accounts of the world seem implausible, even inconceivable. It fails to provide students with the intellectual and emotional resources that would enable them to take religion seriously. This is accomplished, in large part, by textbooks that do not take religion seriously.

Of course, children can learn about religion at home, but does this make a difference? Consider a Christian academy in which students study fundamentalist theology for twelve years but never take a course in science, though scientific beliefs are occasionally mentioned, albeit briefly, in history textbooks (which are written by fundamentalist theologians). Teachers are not required to have any education in science. The first chapter of Genesis provides students with their understanding of biology, history starts with Adam and Eve in the year 4004 B.C., and morality is a simple matter of memorizing the Ten Commandments and the Beatitudes. (No secular alternatives are mentioned.) Would students be indoctrinated in such a school? Surely they *would* be indoctrinated—even if they could learn science from their parents or watch "Nova" on public TV.

That a good education in science and liberalism might be a matter of indoctrination may strike many as strange, but students can be taught to accept both science and liberalism uncritically, as a matter of faith as it were. No matter how scrupulous science is about evidence and rationality *within* its governing framework, if the philosophical assumptions that define that framework are not held up for critical scrutiny and compared with alternatives (such as those drawn from religions), students will have been indoctrinated.

To avoid indoctrination, students must learn to think reasonably about alternative worldviews, not just think rationally within a particular worldview—even if it be that of science and modernity.

It is crucial to realize that indoctrination is not the result of a particular text or a single course. Indoctrination depends on the system, on how the text is used, on what other texts and courses are provided. No matter how narrow and prejudiced a text or a course is, it can function admirably in a good education if it is used with books or supplemented by courses that introduce students to contending ways of understanding the world. Hence the most important judgment we must make is about the overall curriculum and the cumulative effect of texts.

But in making that judgment it is tremendously important to realize that many, and probably most, texts that deal with religiously contested matters are not religiously neutral. They take sides—not overtly but by what they assume and what they ignore. They make religious ways of understanding irrelevant as they initiate students into secular ways of thinking about the world.

Finally, I note that indoctrination need not be intended. There need be no conscious intention to indoctrinate students regarding religion (or science) at all. Indoctrination is the cumulative effect of many texts, lectures, and courses that convey to students only secular understandings of the world; it inhibits their ability to think reasonably about the alternatives.[70]

Conclusions

The liberal theologian Don Cupitt attributes to fundamentalism "one interesting insight. It perceives the science-based, libertarian, humanist culture of the modern era as being itself a new kind of religion." We do not see this, Cupitt suggests, "because we are immersed in it, [because] it dominates more than nine-tenths of our lives, and it is so amorphous." Indeed, so "seductive and compelling is this new faith, that it is somehow impossible to avoid adopting its language and its way of thinking." Because we are "in the midst of it" we "are largely unaware of its awesome, unstoppable, disruptive evangelistic power." In fact, it "annihilates everything that stands in its path. To appreciate this," Cupitt argues, "we have only to step outside it awhile and go to some beautiful old traditional culture in the Third World which is just beginning to feel the impact of 'Westernisation' (for that is what its evangelistic outreach is called. . . .). We will not need to stay there for long to be convinced that Westernisation is inevitable and that it will destroy everything these people now hold dear." All of us in the West, Cupitt concludes, "are the unconscious

missionaries of a devastatingly powerful new creed which threatens to destroy the older faiths by reducing them to the status of tourist attractions and
ethnic folkways."[71]

There is a point to this way of talking, and the arguments of Judge Hand
and many religious conservatives that much secular education is functionally
religious seem to me to be plausible. But if there might be some tactical punch
in arguing that secular humanism—or, as I prefer to put it, the modern worldview—functions as a religion for constitutional purposes, I think the conceptually cleaner course of action is to maintain the fairly sharp distinction conventionally drawn between secular and (more or less traditionally) religious
ways of understanding the world, and then argue that neither the purposes of
education nor the requirements of the Establishment Clause are served by an
educational system that systematically undermines religion and uncritically
promotes the secular alternatives.

Textbooks (and the curriculum) are to a very considerable extent shaped by
the philosophical assumptions and cultural agenda of modernity; as a result,
they are not religiously neutral. No doubt much secular teaching is innocuous,
and many of the facts and theories found in the texts can be (individually) reconciled with religion. The problem lies in the underlying philosophical commitments, in the ways the subject matter is conceptualized. Students are not
just taught subjects, they are taught ways of thinking—and religious ideas,
evidence, and conclusions are all but systematically excluded from consideration. Because the modern worldview is so pervasive, because it shapes so
much of the curriculum, students are given few intellectual or emotional resources for rendering religion meaningful, and it is, in effect, shunted aside as
irrelevant if not superstitious. In effect, students are virtually indoctrinated
into modern, secular ways of understanding the world.

Indoctrination must be systematic and, no doubt, religious ideas and values
do make their way into public education here and there. Students do learn a
little about religion in history and literature courses. There are elective religion courses in many universities and in a few public schools. Many schools
still have official prayers (the Constitution notwithstanding), and some teachers express their religious convictions on occasion. What is completely missing is *any* effort to *require* students to understand *live* religious ways of
understanding the world. The occasional insights into historical religion acquired here and there count for little when measured against the years of
study we require of secular history, science, and social science.

It may well be that modern science (or secular humanism) provides us with the most reasonable account of the world, all things considered. My concern is that public education makes it all but impossible for students to think reasonably about the alternatives. When matters of fundamental importance are contested in a culture, it would seem that the reasonable course of action would be to convey as deep an understanding as possible of the alternatives.

A Note on New Age Religion

Since many religious conservatives have, over the last few years, redirected their fire from secular humanism to New Age religion, a few comments about it and its influence in the classroom are in order.

According to Marilyn Ferguson, we are standing on the edge of "the most rapid cultural realignment in history." We are witnessing "the ascendance of a startling worldview that gathers into its framework breakthrough science and insights from earliest recorded thought."[72] This is the Age of Aquarius, the New Age. The New Age is more than religion. Or better, in New Age thought it is impossible to disentangle "religion" from everything else. Indeed, New Age religion draws on a rich array of intellectual and cultural movements for its nurture—humanistic and Jungian psychology, holistic healing, Eastern religion and Theosophy, new developments in physics, the environmental movement, myth and the unconscious, left-right brain research, shamanism, psychics and mystics, feminism and goddesses, astrology and channeling, reincarnation, witchcraft, and neopaganism.[73] New Age thought is nothing if it is not eclectic, and as a result, there is no consensus, no New Age catechism, no orthodoxy. In his study of the New Age movement Ted Peters suggests that "ideas and techniques just float and mix and combine. The house of the new age can be entered through any of a large number of different doors."[74]

Nonetheless there is something to be said for Jeremy Tarcher's claim that at the heart of New Age thought "is the idea that humans have many levels of consciousness and that with the exception of a limited number of spiritual geniuses throughout history, we essentially live in a walking sleep that keeps us from a well-balanced, harmonious and direct relationship with God (however you understand that concept) nature, each other, and ourselves."[75] Everything that exists is essentially connected, a *harmonious whole*. Yet we modern folk break everything apart—into mind and matter, spirit and flesh, culture and nature, male and female—trying to understand things analytically. The result is a disconnected universe of dead particles. But the world is alive. Ferguson quotes William Blake:

Awake! awake o sleeper of the land of shadows, wake! expand!
I am in you and you in me, mutual in love. . .
Fibers of love from man to man. . .
Lo! we are One.[76]

Our goal must be to awaken to the "higher self" within us, to the God within us. New Age thought offers people, in Ferguson's words, "transformative technologies," techniques "to expand the brain's sensing," to bring people "to a new awareness of vast untapped potential." When they work, she claims, "it's like adding sonar, radar, and powerful lenses to the mind." She is much influenced by recent scientific work on the brain (hence her talk of techniques and technologies, sonar, and radar) but she also wants to establish connections with ancient religion and appeals to insight, mysticism, intuition, meditation, and spiritual experience, in which "God is experienced as flow, wholeness, the infinite kaleidoscope of life and death, Ultimate Cause, the ground of being."[77] Indeed, Ted Peters characterizes New Age thought as being, ultimately, "a phenomenon of cultural synthesis that is attempting to recover a religious grounding for understanding ourselves and the cosmos that is our home."[78]

With so much emphasis on overcoming fragmentation, harmony, and the God within, it is not surprising that New Age theology tends to be feminist. God is not the Transcendent Patriarch, set off from the world, the Wholly Other. Just as nature has traditionally been understood as maternal, so the God who infuses all of nature, human nature included, is best understood as maternal, as Goddess. The New Age writer Starhawk argues that there is a growing realization "that the dead world of mechanism, the world of domination, cannot sustain our inner lives, nor our lives in community with each other, nor the life of the planet."[79] Symbolizing the divine as the Goddess points us to the immanence of the God/dess within nature and within us; it reestablishes connectedness and community in a fragmented and alienated world. As Mary Farrell Bednarowski puts it, the New Age movement aims to "resacralize the cosmos."[80]

America, as a place of new beginnings, has provided fertile ground for a variety of new religions—Transcendentalism, Christian Science, Mesmerism and Spiritualism, New Thought, Swedenborgianism, Theosophy, Cosmic Consciousness, Baha'i, Krishna Consciousness, Transcendental Meditation— which provide New Age religion with a rich ancestry. Sydney Ahlstrom has called these "harmonial" religions for they embody "forms of piety and belief in which spiritual composure, physical health, and even economic well-being are understood to flow from a person's rapport with the cosmos. Human beatitude and immortality are believed to depend to a great degree on one's being 'in tune with the infinite.'"[81]

In somewhat different, if overlapping, ways, Catherine Albanese, Phillip C. Lucas, and Michael D'Antonio have all noted that New Age religion resonates with aspects of conservative Christianity. It preaches a radical spiritual transformation of human nature and an apocalyptic vision of the world issuing in a millennial "New Age"; like much conservative religion New Age thought emphasizes spiritual healing and self-help therapies; it is democratic, resisting the authority of intellectual elites; it places great emphasis on spiritual experience, on personal connections to God, and is critical of liberal religion for its emotional vacuity.[82]

But its resonance with liberal religion is even more striking, for like much liberal theology its major project is to move beyond traditional religion and secular science to find a way of accommodating spiritual concerns and modernity. Indeed, liberal Protestantism has helped to prepare the way for New Age thought, as Catherine Albanese has noted, for liberal Protestantism "stressed the presence of God everywhere" and "underlined American optimism about human nature with its preaching of the gospel of natural goodness. With its diffusiveness and lack of strong boundaries, it had accustomed people to live comfortably without rigid organization."[83]

New Age religion differs from both liberal and conservative religion in its lack of a foundational book, a tradition, a history, a sense of spiritual *discipline*. It is dominated by its eclecticism.

The term "New Age" may already be falling out of favor with its own adherents, a victim of media caricature.[84] No doubt a fairly small percentage of Americans conceive of themselves as New Agers. But the number of people who accept at least some New Age ideas is surprisingly large. Polls have shown that one out of five Americans believe in reincarnation, a quarter accept astrology, 28 percent believe in witchcraft, 31 percent in magical powers, and 46 percent in ESP.[85] In 1987 there were twenty-five hundred New Age bookstores, and as near as I can tell, the typical commercial bookstore in a shopping mall—surely something of a barometer of public interests and values—has a collection of New Age books (spanning the last several decades) of comparable size to its collection of religion books (spanning several thousand years).

Perhaps more impressive is the extent to which New Age ideas have worked themselves into the professions and mainstream cultural politics. Michael D'Antonio has noted that during "the roughly twenty-year lifetime of the New Age, mainstream medicine has moved from an outright rejection of the body-mind connection to a cautious acceptance." Increasingly, New Age ideas play roles in psychotherapy and in business management. The language of the environmental movement is "infused with New Age concepts. Believers seek to 'heal the Earth' and develop an environmental 'consciousness.'" But "by far the most remarkable evidence of the impact of the New Age," D'Antonio notes, "can be seen in certain segments of organized Christianity. Liberal Catholics, Episcopalians, and others are cautiously embracing New Age ideas about the feminine God, healing, and the sanctity of the environment."

In light of this influence, D'Antonio argues that the New Age must be seen as part of mainstream culture; it is no longer countercultural (though he acknowledges that some New Age ideas—UFOs, channeling, and crystals, for example—"remain on the fringe").[86]

We must be a little careful here about the direction of our causal arrows, however: it may be more helpful to say that relatively independent developments in a number of fields have been incorporated by New Age thinkers into a more or less coherent worldview. Arguably, these developments are spawning the New Age movement at least as much as the New Age movement is spawning these developments. In any case, this extraordinary mix of ideas is becoming part of our culture. Most adherents of the New Age are middle class, and increasingly they are professionals. In *The Aquarian Conspiracy* Marilyn Ferguson claims that there are now "legions of conspirators"—in corporations, state and federal agencies, and all arenas of policy-making. And, she notes, they are on the faculties of universities and public schools.[87]

Many of the old complaints about secular humanism have been refashioned into a critique of New Age religion in the classroom. Indeed, in her attack on the New Age, *The Hidden Dangers of the Rainbow: The New Age Movement and Our Coming Age of Barbarism*, Constance Cumbey simply lists "humanism" and "secular humanism" as alternative names for New Age religion.[88] (By her own account, however, New Age religion includes belief in an immanent God, reincarnation, and occult powers—hardly staples of the garden-variety secular humanism we've discussed.) Similarly, in *Subtle Serpent: New Age in the Classroom*, Darylann Whitemarsh and Bill Reisman claim that the New Age is "nothing more than secular humanism"—with "a spiritual ingredient: man is God."[89]

Clearly, New Age religion is something more than—indeed, something fundamentally different from—secular humanism; if it draws on "cutting edge" science, it also employs traditional religious categories to make sense of the world—though those categories are drawn more from Eastern than Western religion. And, in fact, much of the hostility to New Age thought is directed at its specifically religious and occult manifestations—at stories of magic and witchcraft in elementary school readers and at the practice of meditation, yoga, and visualization exercises in the classroom. Of course, such practices and ideas are as out of place in the scientific world of the *Humanist Manifestos* as they are in the religious world of conservative Christianity.

Over the last few years the *Impressions* reading series for elementary schools has come under particularly intense criticism for conveying New Age ideas and values. In one lawsuit, the plaintiffs claimed they had discerned more than forty objectionable stories and activities, leading them to argue that the texts have the "real and substantial effect of affiliating the School District with Witchcraft and/or Neo-Pagan religions"—in violation of the Establishment Clause.[90] I've already noted that in his textbook study, Paul Vitz generally found "something of an emphasis on magic" in elementary school readers.[91]

Nonetheless, stories about the occult (or, as far as that goes, about mainstream religious traditions) don't constitute an Establishment Clause problem unless the religious message is taught as true or unless the message is so commonly (if implicitly) conveyed as to suggest subtly that such religious beliefs should be taken as normal and reasonable. But, as Judge Bauer noted in his review of the texts in *Fleischfresser* v. *Directors of School District 200* (1994), the primary purpose of using such stories is not to endorse any of the (few) religious ideas contained within them but to develop the imagination and creativity of students. In fact, he argued, the stories "parents contend are offensive are a relatively small minority when compared with the series as a whole," and he notes that "the series is also comprised of some stories, also in a small minority, which presumably are consistent with the parents' Catholic and Protestant beliefs, including 'The Best Christmas Pageant Ever,' 'How Six Found Christmas,' and 'The Twelve Days of Christmas.'"[92] That is, the texts explore a few New Age and traditional religious themes, but most of the stories are entirely secular. It may very well be that schools (and courts) should grant exemptions on free exercise grounds to students whose religious beliefs are burdened by reading such stories, but the fact that the state requires students to read them does not mean that it is endorsing New Age (or any) religion.

The constitutionality of the practice of visualization, yoga, and meditation is a little more difficult to determine. In 1979, the Third Circuit Court of Appeals ruled unconstitutional an elective course called "Science of Creative Intelligence—Transcendental Meditation" in several New Jersey high schools in spite of the fact that the defendants maintained that the course (and the practices taught) were entirely secular. The course involved studying the "science" of creative intelligence, the practice of transcendental meditation, and participation in a ritual "puja" (conducted off-campus on Sundays), which involved chanting and ceremonial offerings to a deified "Guru Dev."[93] Although the court's majority opinion appears to find each aspect of the course objectionable, Judge Adams's concurring opinion questions whether transcendental meditation *by itself* would be objectionable; it might be practiced, he suggests, as no more than a relaxation technique. What made it objectionable in this case was that it was embedded in the context of a course on creative intelligence that presented it as a technique for contacting the "life force" that is at the basis of all growth and progress so as to achieve "inner contentment." Scientific creative intelligence is not theistic religion, Adams acknowledged, but, he argued, it is concerned with "the same search for ultimate truth as other religions and seeks to offer a comprehensive and critically important answer to the questions and doubts that haunt modern man."[94] In offering the course, the state of New Jersey, in effect, endorsed the religious view found in the text and required the practice of that religion, thus violating the Establishment Clause.

Obviously a good deal depends on context. Meditation, visualization, and yoga can take relatively secular or relatively religious forms. The state cannot allow, much less require, religious practices even if they seem innocuous. We should keep in mind that ceremonial, nonsectarian prayers are, in one sense, relatively innocuous, but they are prohibited by the courts nonetheless. Of course there is this difference: advocates of prayer acknowledge that those prayers are religious (though they are sometimes defended on ceremonial grounds); advocates of yoga or meditation often make no such admission. Nonetheless, just as secular teaching can function religiously (as I argued regarding secular humanism), secular practices can function religiously if embedded in the context of a system of thought that makes ultimate claims (as Judge Adams argued).

It is hard to know how widespread such (possibly) religious practices are in public schools. What does seem clear is that there is little *overt* teaching of *explicitly* New Age ideas—such as belief in the God within or reincarnation—in the formal curriculum. Indeed, of sixteen doctrines of the New Age movement listed by Constance Cumbey, only one—evolution—is likely to be overtly taught, and most New Agers give a rather more spiritual meaning to evolution than do the neo-Darwinian biologists who write high school textbooks.[95]

One response is that, instead, New Age ideas are taught implicitly. If few teachers and textbooks teach the central claim of the New Age movement—the God within—by glorifying the self, teachers and textbooks set the stage for the spiritual implications that follow. The emphasis on self-esteem in public education distances students from the more traditional Christian idea that people are inherently sinful and in need of God's grace and makes more plausible the idea that we are divine. One wonders, a critic of the self-esteem movement notes, "how many young people will be led astray, led away from discipleship for Christ, which requires losing their 'selves,' because they were told 'Feel good about yourself' rather than being told that there is a criminal inside who needs to be put to death daily."[96]

Or, to take another example, there is a good deal of emphasis in public education on *globalism*, on social interdependence and the interconnectedness of all life on our planet. Eric Buehrer has called global education "the political side of the New Age coin." It is true, Buehrer acknowledges, that not all globalists promote spiritual ideas; nonetheless, for the world to enter the New Age, "it must have a planetary consciousness," and in order to acquire this, "we must begin to think globally." Moreover, globalism encourages an uncritical syncretism, producing what he calls an "ideological undertow" in which "all cultures are basically alike." It undermines belief in the superiority of Christian (and of Western and American) values.[97]

There are, of course, powerful secular reasons for advocating globalism (as Buehrer acknowledges), and, as the courts have made clear, there is no constitutional problem in teaching beliefs and values that overlap or have their source in religion (just as it is perfectly acceptable to teach that murder is wrong even though the Sixth Commandment forbids it). New Age thought is overtly spiritual; globalism isn't—at least in its typical educational incarnations. New Age religion is at least a step removed from globalism and self-esteem.

There are surely foreshadowings and anticipations of New Age ideas in textbooks and curricula, and a good deal of what is taught overlaps with New Age thought (which is, after all, deeply syncretistic). By contrast, however, the central ideas of secular humanism, or the modern worldview, are to be found *comprehensively and explicitly* in textbooks; students in history, psychology, economics, and science courses are taught precisely those modern scientific and liberal ideas that are at the heart of the modern worldview. Indeed, it is precisely because modernity (or secular humanism) is such a powerful presence in public education that many concerns about New Age religion are overstated. The *secular* thrust of modern education is so pervasive that wisps of religious ideas and values count for little by comparison.

This is not to say that there is nothing to be concerned about. Religious practices and ceremonies—New Age, Christian, or whatever—are unconstitutional in the classroom, no matter how seemingly innocuous. And, while I don't see any Establishment Clause problem with a smattering of stories about the occult in readers (any more than I would with stories about Jewish or Christian themes), I do favor an excusal policy for students who are offended by such stories. Moreover, I suspect that a lack of sophistication keeps many teachers (and textbook authors) from appreciating the extent to which they may be conveying New Age ideas and promoting New Age practices.

RELIGION AND LIBERAL EDUCATION

A few years ago, during the brouhaha over E. D. Hirsch's book *Cultural Literacy*, I tested the religious literacy of my students at the University of North Carolina at Chapel Hill. I contrived a short exam of thirty questions dealing with the Bible, Western religious history, and world religions. To pass—to be religiously literate—students had to answer 70 percent of the questions correctly. I gave the test to two classes in the philosophy of religion, and a colleague gave it to two classes in American religious history—about 150 students in all. One might have expected them to do fairly well: like most students at research universities, they were bright, and the majority of them were juniors and seniors. Most were from North Carolina, a Bible-Belt state; and because the courses were electives the students might be expected to have some special interest in, and knowledge of, religion.

No one passed the test. In fact, the average score was 28 percent. I suppose the most obvious explanation for the low scores is that I have no realistic sense of what it means to be religiously literate. Let me give a few examples and you can judge: 55 percent of the students could name the first two books of the Bible; 42 percent could provide something approximating the first of the Ten Commandments; 14 percent had some idea of what Zionism is; just under 10 percent could name the two major divisions of Islam; 2 percent could place the *Analects* in the Confucian tradition; 2 percent could identify Pope John XXIII with the reforms of Vatican II; one student had heard of the Social Gospel.

As we shall see, understanding religion involves much more than knowing a few facts. Still, the results of the survey are suggestive. The great majority of students know *very* little about religion. They learn nothing about it at school, and, increasingly, they learn nothing about it at home or in church or synagogue.[1] (Their parents may not be very literate either: according to a 1990 Gallup Poll, only half of Americans could name even *one* of the Gospels.[2])

To this point I have documented the absence of religion from public education—indeed, the hostility of public education to religion. It is now time to begin the constructive argument for incorporating the study of religion into education. I begin this chapter by saying something about the idea of a liberal education. Is religion important enough to have a place in the curriculum? How should religion fit into the curriculum? Should it be integrated into existing courses and texts when it is relevant, should there be special courses in religion—or both? How should religion be taught? What is the relevance of religion to the multicultural movement? What does it mean to *take religion seriously*? Finally, I will respond to several of the most common arguments *against* including religion in the curriculum.

The Idea of a Liberal Education

Students should learn something about religion in elementary schools and in vocational or professional education, but that is not my concern here. I shall limit my discussion to the secondary and undergraduate schooling that are at the heart of a liberal education.

We no longer live in a traditional society in which our knowledge of what is true and false, and good and evil, are inherited securely from the past. We cannot help but be aware of many different, often conflicting ways of making sense of the world. And we have come to believe—in most fields, if not always in religion—that it is through a self-conscious, critical consideration of the alternatives that we are most likely to acquire truth. We believe in the possibility of progress.

A liberal education should initiate students into a self-conscious search for better, more reasonable, more humane ways of thinking and acting; it *liberates* students from parochialism by enabling them to see and feel the world in new ways. What do they know of England, who only England know? Or, as John Stuart Mill put it, he "who knows only his own side of the case, knows little of that. His reasons may be good, and no one may have been able to refute them. But if he is equally unable to refute the reasons on the other side; if he does not so much as know what they are, he has no ground for preferring either opinion."[3] Indeed, it is only when we can feel the intellectual and emotional power of alternative cultures and traditions that we are justified in rejecting them. If they remain lifeless and uninviting this is most likely because we do not understand them, because we have not gotten inside them so that we can feel their power as their adherents do. Only if we can do this are we in a position to make judgments, to conclude, however tentatively, that some ways of thinking and living are better or worse than others.

A liberal education is *an initiation into a conversation*. The term "conversation" suggests the civility that is proper to a liberal education, but in some ways the word "argument" might be more appropriate, for conflicting claims about truth and goodness are built into a liberal education—at least to the extent that it reflects the variety of ideas and values found in our culture and our world. Of course, the argument/conversation is ongoing—it has a history—and just as one can make little sense of an everyday conversation walking into it midstream, so students can make little sense of the conversation that constitutes a liberal education without understanding something of its history. A liberal education *must be comparative and historical*.[4]

The problem with much of what passes for liberal education is that while students hear a good number of voices, each is crying in the wilderness; none converses with others. Education has become specialized at all levels, and the higher students climb educationally, the more distant they are from climbers on other peaks of learning. Efforts at communication take place at some distance, over yawning conceptual chasms; misunderstanding—and suspicion—inevitably result. Indeed, the ways in which we separate education into disciplines and courses makes the conversation all but impossible to understand, and students are left inadequately prepared to reconstruct the conversation for themselves. The curriculum should not be a set of parallel monologues but a conversation—or argument.

This being the case, it is important to recognize that to liberate, a liberal education must *require* a good deal of students and their teachers. It is incompatible with specialization, which, in and of itself, is a form of parochialism. A liberal education requires a core curriculum, not just distribution requirements, for it must make connections as well as ensure that students hear different voices; it must be interdisciplinary and structured if the conversation is to be coherent. And because a liberal education deals with matters that require some emotional and intellectual maturity—literature and politics, for example—it should continue through the greater part of one's undergraduate years. Students should not specialize too early.

There is another reason why a liberal education must be taught historically. We distort the idea of rationality if we think of individuals as "neutral" spectators or "objective" judges of alternative worldviews and cultural possibilities. We are not primarily individuals who stand at some epistemic distance from the options open to us. We are members of communities with histories; we are characters in ongoing stories. In Alisdair MacIntyre's words: "I can only answer the question 'What am I to do?' [or 'what am I to think?'] if I can answer the prior question 'Of what story or stories do I find myself a part?' We enter human society, that is, with one or more imputed characters—roles into which we have been drafted—and we have to learn what they are in order to be able to understand how others respond to us and how our responses to them are to be construed. . . . Deprive children of stories and you leave them unscripted, anxious stutterers in their actions as in their words."[5] A self exists, according to Charles Taylor, only within "webs of interlocution."[6] Or, as Maynard Adams once put it, we would not, each of us, be an I unless we were a first a we.[7] Without a cultural location we have no place to stand in our moral and intellectual deliberations.

A liberal education should place us within the various historical communities of which we are a part. We are all members of several communities—families, nations, ethnic groups, religions, civilizations—indeed, the human community. We are born with various identities, and we do not know who we are until we know something of these communities and their histories, until we see that we are part of a story or, better yet, an anthology of stories which provides us with contexts of meaning that orient us in the world.

Much of modernity—and modern education—has been rightly directed at nurturing our individuality and autonomy, at giving us some distance on our inherited identities, but there is reason to believe that we may have gone too far. All too often, for example, students arrive at college with no firm convictions, no clear identities; the more "sophisticated" of them often assume an (all too uncritical) moral relativism.[8] Richard Rorty once suggested that "you cannot liberate a tabula rasa; you cannot make a free individual out of an unsocialized child."[9] Liberal education has both a conservative and a liberating task: it should provide students a ballast of historical identities and values at the same time that it gives them an understanding of alternatives and provides critical distance on the particularities of their respective inheritances.

I add that the understanding a liberal education provides is not merely an abstract, inert knowledge of facts and theories; it should nurture passions and imagination as well as thinking. Hence it must draw on literature and the arts to inform students' feelings, articulate their hopes and fears, nurture their sense of guilt and compassion, enrich their ability to empathize with other people and other cultures, and enliven their sense of history, of being part of developing stories.

Indeed, cultures might be understood as works of art embodying ways in which people have more or less artfully created meaning in the world. Just as our imaginations and our passions are excited as we wander through an art museum, seeing the works of various artists, cultures, and periods, so a good liberal education should inform and excite our imaginations and our passions, providing us with imaginative insight into life's possibilities as painted on the backdrop of the world's cultures. Just as there is aesthetic joy to be had in art, so there is joy to be had in the cultural creations of humankind and in a liberal education that reveals them to us.

What I want most to emphasize, however, is the significance of imagination and the passions in enabling us to get at the meaning of human experience so that we can make informed, reasonable, perhaps even wise judgments about how to live our lives.

At the end of chapter 2 I suggested there are four common, if conflicting, ways of thinking about contemporary education. There are dangers, I think, in letting any one of them control the curriculum too completely. The conception of liberal education which I am advocating incorporates a good deal of the (often conservative) historical ballast of a classical or "liberal arts" education at the same time that it incorporates many of the liberating emphases of expressive education and the Cultural Left. And I would leave a little room in the curriculum for some of the more narrowly utilitarian goals of work and vocation.

The essential tension of a liberal education, properly understood, lies in its commitment to initiating students into the communities of memory which tentatively define them, and, at the same time, nurturing critical reflection by initiating them into an ongoing conversation that enables them to understand and appreciate alternative ways of living and thinking. The error of traditional education was its overemphasis on the former; the error of much modern education is its unsystematic and uncritical emphasis on the latter.

The Importance of Religion

A *liberal* education is the opposite of a *parochial* education. It cannot be specialized, or fixate on matters of narrow interest or of no great concern. The content of a liberal education should be whatever we take to be most important in life.

There is, of course, no scientific or pedagogical formula for cranking out a definitive assessment of what is important. The criteria we use to determine what is important will be moral, political, and, for many people, religious, and this being the case, we will inevitably disagree.

With limited pages in textbooks and limited hours in the school day, is religion sufficiently important to merit precious space and time, especially given the clamor of the competition for inclusion? In his review of religion in American history textbooks, Dan Fleming noted: "Almost every special interest group that reviews history textbooks concludes that its particular topic has been shortchanged in coverage, whether it be a minority group, the Holocaust, labor, business, the family, or, in this case, religion. From the perspective of each group, they may be right. The problem is, if you increase the coverage of one topic, what can be deleted to find room for the expansion? It appears this same principle applies to the coverage of religion. . . . As is usually the case, thoroughness is in the eye of the beholder."[10] Well yes, there is a practical, political problem of priorities here. But, no, thoroughness does not lie simply in the eye of the beholder. Some things *are* more important than others, and it is not at all clear that we have our priorities straight.

For example, mightn't it be as important for students to understand the break between religious liberals and fundamentalists in the first decades of the twentieth century as it is for them to understood the concurrent split between the Republican and Bull Moose parties? Mightn't it be as important to understand religious beliefs about death and the soul as it is to understand tariffs and international trade? Mightn't it be as important to understand the Five Pillars of Islam as it is to understand the geopolitical significance of the Persian Gulf? Mightn't it be as important to understand the history of Jews in America as it is to understand the history of cowboys in America? Mightn't it be even more important for students to understand the Bible than trigonometry? (The answer in every case is yes, though no one would guess this from looking at textbooks and curricula.)

How important is religion? Let me count the ways.

Religion and Culture. Until the last century or two, nothing was so influential for good and evil in human affairs as religion. When the sacred and the secular were still fused, religion pervaded all of life: the sustaining rituals of life were religious, and people's understanding of politics, war, economics, justice, literature and art, philosophy, science, psychology, history, and morality and their feelings about death and hopes for a life to come were all religiously shaped and informed. Religion simply cannot be avoided in studying history.

But it is also true that much contemporary culture is shaped, or contested, by religion. Consider, for example, the importance of the Christian Democratic political parties in post–World War II Europe, the Catholic church in Poland, Bishop Tutu in South Africa, liberation theology in the Third World, the abortion debate, and the role of the black church in the civil rights movement. There are ongoing religious wars in Northern Ireland, India, the Middle East, Sri Lanka, Indonesia, Sudan, Bosnia, Tajikistan, Armenia, and Azerbaijan. The Holocaust is still a living memory, and anti-Semitism and religious terrorism haunt the world. People continue to be persecuted because of their religions, and all too often the persecutors persecute in the name of their religions.

Or consider the fascination that religion (and its absence from the modern world) holds for many of the greatest contemporary writers: Walker Percy, John Updike, Saul Bellow, Flannery O'Connor, Graham Greene, T. S. Eliot, Alexander Solzhenitsyn, and the existentialists. Theologians continue to contest scientific accounts of nature, and a striking number of scientists (especially in physics, cosmology, and ecology) seem to be moving toward a kind of mysticism or vaguely religious view of nature. Most of the mainline Christian denominations have issued statements on justice, the economy, and war and peace.

Religion continues to influence our contemporary world—sometimes for good and sometimes, no doubt, for evil. Religious voices continue to speak out on most matters of importance, and they contest much of what is taken as the conventional wisdom that finds its way into textbooks and the curriculum. How can students make sense of our cultural conversation without understanding what they are saying?

Religious Liberty. One historical theme is of particular importance. The Williamsburg Charter, signed in 1988 by many distinguished Americans, reaffirmed the importance of the principles of religious liberty in American life. The charter's Summary of Principles begins: "The Religious Liberty clauses of the First Amendment to the Constitution are a momentous decision, the most important political decision for religious liberty and public justice in history. Two hundred years after their enactment they stand out boldly in a century made dark by state repression and sectarian conflict. Yet the ignorance and contention now surrounding the clauses are a reminder that their advocacy and defense is a task for each succeeding generation." Religious liberty is our nation's "first liberty," undergirding "all other rights and freedoms secured by the Bill of Rights." The religion clauses allow us to "live with our deepest differences," providing us with a "common vision" that embraces "a shared understanding of the place of religion in public life and of the guiding principles by which people with deep religious differences can contend robustly but civilly with each other."[11]

Religious liberty is fragile. To understand the sources, the history, the meaning, and the implications of the First Amendment and religious liberty is a matter of great importance. Yet only 71 percent of Americans know that religious liberty is guaranteed in the Constitution. Appallingly, government leaders (64 percent) and Protestant ministers (69 percent) are less aware of this than the general public.[12] What do we know of America if we do not understand the story of religious liberty?

Religious Pluralism. Religious liberty is made more important and more difficult by the growing religious pluralism of America. If the great majority of Americans—about 85 percent—are at least nominally Christian, a growing minority of Americans are not. The number of those who claim no religious affiliation has increased from about 2 percent thirty years ago to perhaps 11 percent today.[13] Jews make up about 2 percent of the population. Muslims fall somewhere between 0.5 and 2 percent of the population depending on who does the counting, and adherents of various Eastern religions, predominantly Hindus and Buddhists, make up another 1 percent.[14] In one state, Hawaii, Christianity is a minority religion and Buddhism is the majority religion.[15] Perhaps as important is the growing split between conservatives and liberals within the same religions.

The old Protestant cultural establishment was disestablished long ago. Many fear that no American *unum* can bind together the *pluribus* of contemporary culture. We see the effects of this "exploding diversity," Os Guinness argues, in our "cultural breakdown," in the "collapse of the previously accepted understandings of the relationship of religion and public life and the triggering of the culture wars." As a result, a series of bitter "contentions over religion and politics has erupted, extremes have surfaced, the resort to the law court has become almost reflexive . . . and in the ensuing din of charge and countercharge any sense of common vision for the common good has been drowned.[16]

This situation places a tremendous burden on the schools to help devise ways of enabling us to "live with our deepest differences," as the Williamsburg Charter puts it. Certainly a part of that effort must involve a better understanding of the diverse religious backgrounds of people in our culture. Of course pluralism is not without its merits, if only we would choose to exploit the richness of our diversity, learning from—and not just about—people with different ideas and values.[17]

Religion and Morality. Moral education is an unavoidable aspect of education; we educate morally whether we intend to or not. The curriculum orients students in the world; it tells them what is important. Various courses teach students what is normal and abnormal in human behavior, what actions are rational and irrational, and what causes the suffering and flourishing of humankind. A good education cannot ignore issues such as abortion, sexuality and sex roles, justice, and politics. These issues are morally and religiously loaded—and controversial.

For most of human history, morality and religion were one and the same; morality was, in some sense, God's law. Following the Enlightenment, morality began to be secularized, becoming autonomous from religion. Of course, there are many secular accounts of what morality is, and many people continue to believe that morality makes sense only on a religious understanding of the world. The result is considerable cultural confusion. Unhappily, this confusion exists at a time when many observers sense a major moral slippage in the life of our culture. Indeed, it can be argued that our confusion about what morality is contributes to our inability to act in morally responsible ways. What could be a more important topic for education than morality? And yet it is not on most educators' agendas.

The Spiritual Dimension of Religion. It should go without saying that religion is important quite apart from any political or social or moral influences it might have. It is important because it has given voice to universal spiritual questions of ultimate concern. It has structured our thinking about suffering and salvation, death and the meaning of life, guilt and forgiveness, love and community; it has spoken to our deepest hopes and fears. Whether or not we approve of the various religious answers to these existential questions, we must acknowledge the importance of the attempts and the ultimacy and the universality of the concerns. If students have no sense of the spiritual dimension of life, they are ignorant of much that has been and is central to the human condition.

Of course, we cannot understand the story of religious liberty or the impact of religion on politics without understanding something about the spiritual—the theological, the ritual, the existential—meaning of organized religions. If students do not understand something about Puritan theology (which is typically not included in the texts), how are they to understand Puritan thinking about the relationship of church and state (which is mentioned in the texts)? If students do not understand something of souls, how are they to understand the abortion debate? If students do not understand how Islam fuses the sacred and the secular, how are they to understand the politics of the Middle East?

Religion and Modernity. Finally, we can make sense of our world only if we have some sense of the underlying movement of history. The secularization of the West is one of the great themes of modern history. The philosopher William Barrett goes a little further: the "central fact of modern history in the

West . . . is unquestionably the decline of religion."[18] Of course, even if the West has become highly secular, it has not become completely secular. Conservative religion continues to resist much of modernity, and liberal religion has accommodated itself to modernity in important ways. But unless we understand the broad outlines of this story, we will not have sufficient context for making sense of modernity itself.

Whether or not any religious account of the world is true, religion *is* important because it has had, and continues to have, a powerful impact on politics, society, and culture. The story of religious liberty is basic to our understanding of America. Growing religious pluralism makes it necessary for us to understand religion if we are to understand our neighbors and have peace. It shapes our moral beliefs and actions. It has addressed those "existential" questions which are fundamental to our humanity. The most profound "culture war" of the last three hundred years has been between religious and secular ways of understanding the world. If we are to teach about what is important, we must teach students about religion.

Religion has a particularly important educational role in fulfilling both the conserving and the liberating purposes of liberal education. By virtue of its influence in history, it has shaped our ideas and ideals, our culture, and our institutions in powerful ways. We are who we are, to some considerable (if diminishing) extent because of our religious past, and education should give students some appreciation and understanding of their place in these traditions. I will argue that just as it is not the responsibility of schools to transform children into Republicans or Democrats, so it is not their responsibility to initiate students into any particular religion. This is the proper task of parents and their religious communities. But just as a student should learn a good deal about our political heritage and the political parties that are part of it, so they should learn a good deal about our religious heritage and the religions that are part of it. Education should provide the cultural and historical context that informs and, in various ways, makes sense of our religious identities. A good liberal education will not play favorites but will provide the context within which all students will come to some understanding and appreciation of their own traditions. This is as important for nonreligious students as for religious students for we all are who we are in large part because of our religious past.

As important, it is the goal of liberal education to expose students to voices that enable them to assess critically their often parochial ways of thinking. Perhaps most important, some understanding of various religious voices provides students with critical perspective on the relentlessly secular thrust of education and so much of modern culture. Historically, the great religions oriented people in the world and structured education in the process. It is still true that if we are to listen to all of the voices speaking out on justice and injustice, human suffering and flourishing, morality and politics, economics and work, love and human relationships, the search for identity and the ways we find meaning in life, many will be religious voices. I do not suggest that the best answers to the questions inevitably posed by a liberal education are religious. I only claim that if education is to be liberal, all the voices, at least all the major voices, should be heard.

The Curriculum

The curriculum provides the conceptual map by which we orient students in reality. If we are to take religion seriously, what are the implications for the curriculum?

Religion in Courses: Natural Inclusion . In any course, if there are religious influences that bear on the subject in some important way, or if there are competing religious and secular interpretations of some important issue, it is appropriate to discuss religion. Because of the secularization of modern culture the influence of religion will be much more evident in courses that are largely historical, and teachers who are historically sensitive are likely to have a much greater appreciation for the role of religion in their subjects than will colleagues in fields that are not taught historically but are governed by a more narrowly scientific worldview.

Arguably, religion should be included in the conversation whenever it has something to say about the subject at hand, whenever it "naturally" comes up. But there is a very important ambiguity hidden in the term "natural inclusion." Natural to whom? Teachers of economics, for example, are not likely to have any background in relating religion to economics, for the relationship has been nurtured almost entirely from the side of religion over the past hundred years as the discipline of economics has become a social science. Yet religion continues to exert a powerful influence on the economic world by virtue of the ways in which it has shaped, and continues to shape, our thinking about reform movements, justice, human rights, suffering, and the good life—and by the ways in which theology challenges fundamental assumptions about human nature and morality made in economics. Many Christian denominations have statements on the economy, many of which are critical in important ways of the conventional economic wisdom.[19]

The problem is that economics is not only a *subject* that might be studied in secular or religious ways, it is a *discipline*, a way of thinking about the world. The purpose of economics courses is not just to teach students about the economic world, it is to teach them to think about the economic world *like economists*. If students should learn how to think about the economic world religiously, most economists would say they should take a religion course.

Most public schools teach economics but not religion, so this solution would discriminate against religious ways of thinking about economic matters. As important, it fragments what should be taught and renders students unlikely to see the relationships between economics and religion, between religious and social scientific ways of thinking about the economic world, and hence virtually guarantees a measure of ignorance. It also allows teachers to maintain a degree of specialization that encourages them to teach illiberally. And it assumes that the secular and the sacred can be disentangled—a controversial (typically secular) assumption.

Gerald Graff has argued that although college students "are exposed to the *results* of their professors' conflicts" they are not given access to "the process of discussion and debate they need to see in order to become something more than passive spectators to their education." The established curriculum, Graff argues, is *separatist*, "with each subject and course being an island with little regular connection to other subjects and courses. It is important to bring heretofore excluded cultures into the curriculum, but unless they are put in dialogue with traditional courses, students will continue to struggle with a disconnected curriculum, and suspicion and resentment will continue to increase." Moreover, when "teachers in rival camps do not engage one another in their classrooms, all sides get comfortable preaching to the already converted."[20]

Graff is not discussing religion, but the same principle applies. Courses and textbooks that deal with religiously contested issues should at least acknowledge the existence of those religious alternatives and engage them in conversation. In the introduction to the course, or in the first chapter of the text, students should be made aware of the religiously controversial nature of the claims in the text and offered some brief account of the (major) religious alternatives. I am not proposing that we make all courses into religion courses. Economics courses and texts should be essentially (secular) economics courses and texts. But they must not contribute to the indoctrination of students; they must observe the obligation to acknowledge the controversial nature of the claims they make and say something about the existence of alternative frameworks for interpreting their subject. They must participate in the conversation that constitutes a liberal education. They cannot pretend to students that there is only a monologue when in fact there is a lively cultural conversation going on. Economists should approach their subject not just as economists but as teachers of a liberal education.

Put more generally, liberal education texts and teachers should be governed by the Principle of Philosophical Location and Weight: that is, they are obligated to locate their positions philosophically on the map of alternatives, indicating what weight their views carry in the discipline *and* in the larger culture. If students are to be educated, they must have some sense of when they are being taught what is controversial (and for whom) and when they are learning consensus views. Good teachers or texts should not convey to students a single view only when that view is controversial; nor should they simply provide an array of alternatives without giving students some sense of which are mainstream and which are marginal (and for whom).

There is a difference, in this regard, between introductory and advanced courses. A good liberal education must require students to understand the relationship of religion to the subject matter and disciplinary perspectives of their courses, but I see no reason to insist that the same battles be re-fought over and over. If students come to understand the conceptual lay of the land in a good introductory course, there is no need for continuing to provide all the alternatives in every course that follows. But the nature of a liberal education obligates faculty to make sure that all (major) contending voices are heard at the appropriate time and place. This will certainly be in introductory courses and perhaps elsewhere as well. In high school, most courses are introductory courses: they introduce a subject and a disciplinary way of thinking about the subject. In universities, students can sometimes do advanced work without having taken the introductory courses (especially in the humanities and social sciences); here the situation is more complicated.

Courses in Religion . Most advocates of the study of religion argue for natural inclusion, rather than for (new) courses that take religion as their subject. The conventional solution is "religion in courses" rather than "courses in religion." There is some tactical advantage in this approach, for courses in religion would require a good deal of consciousness raising all around. Nonetheless, this leaves us far short of the ideal.

What would we think if economics or biology were to be taught only by natural inclusion in history or literature courses by teachers who had done no course work in economics or biology? Obviously the importance and complexity of these fields warrants separate courses taught by faculty educated to teach them. So it should be with religion. Students cannot come to understand religion if they acquire only a few facts here and a snippet of insight there. If religion is to be understood it must be studied in some depth. This view is now widely accepted at the undergraduate level, and most public universities have departments of religious studies that offer a curriculum of religion courses and often an undergraduate major.

But courses in religion should not just be offered. All students should be required to take an introductory course in religion at the high school and undergraduate level. (Of course, additional elective courses should also be available.) An introductory course should be required for at least three reasons relating to the purposes of a liberal education. First, religion is a tremendously important aspect of human experience. Second, religion is too complex a subject to be handled adequately by natural inclusion (by teachers not educated to teach about it). It is at least as subtle a field as science. Time and effort are required to read religious texts and acquire some familiarity with religious traditions and subcultures. Third, because of the power of the secular disciplines in shaping the curriculum, religion must be granted at least one required course to maintain a modest measure of critical perspective on the conventional secular wisdom of most subjects so that indoctrination can be avoided.

At the public school level there are likely to be few religion courses if any, and faculty who teach them are unlikely to have had religious studies as a primary field of study. (According to a Department of Education study conducted in the early 1980s, only 640 of 15,000 public high schools offered courses in religion, and only two-tenths of 1 percent of students were enrolled.[21]) I have noted the familiar complaint that there is not time enough in the school day now for all the courses various interest groups want to have worked into the curriculum. So what is to be done? Well, let me put it this way: how can anyone believe that a college-bound student should take twelve years of mathematics and no religion rather than eleven years of mathematics and one year of religion? Why require the study of trigonometry or calculus, which the great majority of students will never use or need, and ignore religion, a matter of profound and universal significance? This would be my first answer to the inevitable question: what should be dropped to make room for the study of religion? (If anyone opts for the twelve years of math, I will take this as additional evidence for my claims about secular indoctrination.)

There is some hope from the record of universities: fifty years ago most public universities did not have courses in or departments of religious studies; now most do.

High schools and universities cannot leave this task to each other. The shortcomings of secondary education in the United States require that universities also provide a liberal education and require that specialization be held off at least until the third undergraduate year. And because religion is not likely to be taught in many high schools, universities should require, at an absolute minimum, an introductory course in religion. In any case, religion, like all subjects in the humanities, requires a good deal of emotional and intellectual maturity.[22] Correlatively, the presence of religious studies in universities does not absolve secondary schools of responsibility. In part this is because religion is central to liberal education at whatever level, but also because a majority of students will not go on to receive a liberal education in universities, either because they will pursue no higher education at all or because they will receive a narrowly technical or professional education.

What material should be included in a required religion course? It must provide students some understanding of what it means to respond religiously to the world, giving them some sense of the tension between religious and secular ways of living in and understanding the world. It should demonstrate the power of religion to shape history and contemporary culture. More particularly, it should provide students with various religious interpretations of topics in the curriculum that are religiously contested but are likely to be taught in narrowly secular ways in their other required courses: the origin of the world; the meaning of history; the nature of morality, social justice and sexuality, for example. It should explore how several different religions have answered the major moral and existential questions of life; it should be multicultural and comparative. Finally, it should use primary source readings (especially sacred texts) and imaginative literature to enable students to appreciate religions "from the inside."

I will address the constitutionality of required classes in religion in the next chapter. For now I simply note that most political objections would be defused by offering exemptions from the course for students who object to it for reasons of conscience or religious conviction.

Taking Religion Seriously

We take religion seriously when we accord it a place in the curriculum proportional to its importance in our history and culture, convey to students an "inside" understanding of religion, and contend with it in searching for the truth.

Understanding Religion from the Inside. As Ninian Smart puts it, we convey to students an inside understanding of religion when we present them with "the beliefs, symbols and activities of the other . . . from the perspective of that other. The presuppositions, feelings and attitudes of the explorer of the other's world must be bracketed out as far as possible. That is, we should not bring external judgments to bear upon the other's world."[23] It is one thing to *understand*, another to *judge*. We understand others if we are able to think and feel our way into their hearts and minds, if we are able to understand them as they understand themselves. We take religion seriously only when we try to understand it from the inside, on its own terms. At least, this must be the first move we make in any study of religion.

Much modern scholarship attempts to make sense of actions and texts and cultures using the concepts of the scholarly observer rather than those indigenous to the actor or author or culture. The working assumption is that through scientific study, scholars can put the claims of people in a context that explains them. For example, Freudians explain behavior, including religious behavior, on the basis of unconscious causes resulting from childhood experiences; behavioral psychologists explain all behavior on the basis of environmental contingencies of reinforcement; economists often explain behavior in terms of "rational" self-interest; some neurologists explain all behavior and experience (including religious experiences) in terms of brain chemistry.

Often these accounts are reductionistic, that is, the scholars who advance them hold that reality is not nearly so rich as religious believers take it to be. Religious claims are "reduced" to being about psychological or social needs, for example. As we have seen, many modern secular intellectuals are committed to eliminating supernatural or religious understandings of events and actions and texts and replacing them with secular, scientific explanations. So, for example, to tell the story of ancient Israel from David through the Babylonian captivity, as the author of one history text did, without referring to God's actions in history, is to tell a secular version of the scriptural story that drains it of all religious meaning. The textbook author does not convey the Hebrew account of history, the inside account of ancient Israel, but rather his account, the modern secular story. I have no objection to historians telling their own story, but it must be made clear that they are telling their story, not the story of the people about whom they write, and if we are to understand the ancient Hebrews, and not just modern historians, we must first hear *their* story.

One reason why we should listen to their story is that people are, to some considerable extent, just what they take themselves to be. They do what they do for reasons that make sense to them; they live within a structure of meaning that gives coherence and direction to their lives. If we miss this essential fact, if we miss their world, then we miss them. To understand people, we must hear what they say and see what they do in the context of their beliefs about the world, their philosophical assumptions, their reasoning, their motives. To understand a religion is to be able to look out on the world and on human experience and see and feel it from the viewpoint of the categories of that religion.

Smart argues that this can be done through an "informed or structured empathy." Indeed, Smart would have us pause to "celebrate" the "glory" of empathy: "To see the world through another person's eyes: is this not a noble task? For a boy to know something of what is like to be a girl, for a lover to see herself through the eyes of *her* lover, to see the problems of one's mother-in-law, to imagine what it is like to be a starving Ethiopian or a Tamil, to conceive the thought world of the ordinary Russian or Romanian or Italian."[24] Of course, it is extraordinarily difficult, for a variety of reasons, to bracket our own way of understanding the world, our own philosophical convictions, to empathize with others—particularly with others who are very different from us, others whom we may not judge highly. Indeed, it can be argued that our intellectual and cultural biases cut so deep that we are simply unable to perform such acts of empathy, and it is probably true that when the culture we try to understand is *very* different from ours, we will not likely succeed. (This is why the Dark Ages remain dark.) But it is also certain that almost always we can succeed *more or less*, and succeeding more is surely better than succeeding less.

There is an important difference between empathy and sympathy: we might say that empathy is thinking or feeling *with* someone, while sympathy is feeling *for* someone. To have empathy does not mean that one has sympathy, though empathy often leads to sympathy. Empathy is not a "sentimental" emotion; it is, or can be, a hard-headed intellectual virtue (as it should be when we try to empathize with Hitler and the Nazis in an effort to understand them). To see the world from a certain perspective is not to believe that it is a good or true perspective. The difference between empathy and sympathy is, in part, the difference between understanding and judgment.

Still, the idea of taking other people—and their ideas, their religions—seriously is, in part, a moral notion; it is, as Smart suggests, a *noble* task. It accords others a basic respect. Put in terms of the Golden Rule it would amount to something like this: I want you to take me and my ideas seriously and I don't think you can understand me without listening to what I have to say about my beliefs and actions; therefore I must (morally) take you and your ideas seriously. John Dixon has suggested that we "are not free to treat others as less than ourselves, to be explained by our wisdom. . . . We must do them the courtesy of taking them seriously. . . . To treat them otherwise is to reduce them to an it. Explanation is an act of power inflicted on an it. True interpretation is an attempt to grasp the other as 'thou.'"[25]

In the end, some people, perhaps even some cultures, do not deserve respect. But this is a judgment we must make *after* we have attempted to understand them. It is also true that in the end we may decide that one of the reductionist accounts is, in fact, true. But first things first.

Of course, it is not always easy to know who can speak for a tradition from the inside. Are there authoritative "insiders" who can define what shall count as orthodox and who else is an insider? Who defines whether the Unification church is a part of the Christian tradition? The Reverend Moon, or the Southern Baptist Convention? Do we privilege the accounts of theologians, or do we listen to the stories of women and minorities who have been largely powerless within the tradition? The uneducated may be able to speak for only a small part of a tradition, the local subculture, and be unacquainted with large stretches of it—but then theologians may speak for an understanding of the tradition held by intellectuals only. Pursuing the insider's account of a religion is not without its conceptual problems. Indeed, it is unlikely that there would ever be a single "inside" understanding of any tradition.[26]

Religious Experience. Understanding from the inside is not exclusively, perhaps not even primarily, a matter of intellect and belief. Smart has distinguished six "dimensions" of religion.

> (1) doctrines (e.g., the Trinity, the Buddhist doctrine of impermanence); (2) the sacred narratives or myths of the tradition (Christian "salvation-history," the story of the Buddha Gautama); (3) the ethical and/or legal teachings (as in the Torah, the Shari'a, the Sermon on the Mount, etc.); (4) the ritual and practical side of a religion (the Mass, daily Muslim prayer, Buddhist Prescriptions and practices of meditation); (5) the experiential and emotional side of a religion (the nature of devotion to Christ, Paul's religious conversion, the Buddha's enlightenment, and actions to attain nirvana); and (6) the social institutions in which a religion is embodied and the social relations in which it is embedded (the organization and role of the Church of Scotland, the Sangha in Sri Lanka, etc.). And as part of all this, or in addition, it is important to see something of a tradition's artifacts—the Cathedrals of medieval Christendom, the stupas and pagodas of Buddhism, and so on.[27]

Some religions emphasize some dimensions more than others. Confucianism and Judaism, for example, emphasize the ritual, social, and ethical dimensions: to belong to that religion is to belong to a community; it is not necessarily to hold certain beliefs about God or the hereafter. This is increasingly true of liberal Protestantism. Some schools of Hinduism and Buddhism are almost entirely concerned with the experiential and ritual dimensions of religion. Conservative Protestantism has often exalted doctrine, sometimes at the cost of the ritual or ethical or experiential dimensions of religion: salvation comes through belief, not through the sacraments or good works or membership in any community.

Because religion is essentially a matter of belief for many Protestants, understanding religion has often been taken to be a matter of knowing theology and doctrine. Yet there is much more to religion than belief. Schleiermacher claimed that true religion is so rare "that whoever utters anything of it, must necessarily have had it, for nowhere could he have heard it. . . . To the man who has not himself experienced it, it would only be an annoyance and a folly."[28] Wilfred Cantwell Smith has argued that an outside observer may "know *all about* a religious system, and yet may totally miss the point. The outsider may intellectually command all the details of its external facts, and yet may be . . . untouched by the heart of the matter." The fundamental problem, according to Smith, is that the observer's understanding of a religion "is by definition constituted of what can be observed. Yet the whole pith and substance of religious life lies in its relation to what cannot be observed." What the observer will miss is transcendence—the (scientifically) unobservable experience of God. Smith notes that his argument will not carry much weight with nonbelievers, "a fact that in itself illustrates the point I wish to make."[29]

Parker Palmer reminds us that the Hebrew Bible "uses the word 'know' to indicate the conjugal relation of husband and wife (as in 'Abraham knew Sarah')" and the "most common New Testament word for 'know' is also used for lovemaking." Religious understanding is, on such accounts, *personal*; when we assume instead the role of a detached, scientific observer the world can no longer speak to us; it becomes a mere object as we become "objective."[30] Reality then remains, as Martin Buber put it, a "total stranger," an "it" rather than a "thou."[31]

Theology is the attempt to systematize and render intellectually intelligible what people experience in worship, in ritual, in communal experience, in their encounters with God. But if we miss the *experience* of God, if we settle for the *beliefs* or the behavior then we have missed what is, arguably, at the heart of religion—and what we are left with may seem unintelligible. To understand much religion we must live in the community of adherents, we must participate in the ritual, we must be open to the experience of God.

This suggests a daunting task for religious education. John Wilson and Samuel Natale have argued that "'teaching religion' is not a matter merely of *instruction*: the child also requires *experience*. In trying to educate children in those areas commonly called 'musical appreciation' or 'drama,' we are not content merely to instruct them about music and drama; we also require them to take part in concerts and plays. So too with religion. Provided we keep our aims clearly in mind, there is an obvious case to be made out for giving children that experience of religion that may be gained by particular forms of worship."[32] The analogy with music is helpful. If students only read about the beliefs of musicians, or scanned sheets of musical notation, or learned acoustics, it is safe to say they would develop neither an understanding of, nor an appreciation for, music. It is only in listening to it, or better yet, in performing or composing it, that any full understanding becomes possible. Similarly, it is a commonplace that science must be practiced to be fully understood and appreciated. It is in the laboratory that one learns what science really is.

We routinely require students to practice science and music, to *experience* them, but in public education we do not allow students to participate in the practice of religion. Of course, many students will have practiced religion in their homes and churches, synagogues, or mosques, but many will not have had such experiences. And virtually all of the students who have had such experiences will be limited to one religious tradition—their own. If we truly want to understand religion, if we want to take it seriously, then we must participate in religious ritual and open our hearts to religious experience. Yet we obviously we cannot require this of students (even if the courts allowed it).

Wilson and Natale suggest that students participate in a worship service. There are two problems. First, participating in the ritual is likely to violate our sense of moral integrity for it requires the affirmation of beliefs or intentions students may not have and that may conflict with commitments they do have. Of course, schools require students to do many things that challenge deeply held convictions, from dissecting frogs to undressing in front of other people. But at some point we draw the line, believing that the value we place on moral integrity is violated. Students should not be required to participate in political rallies or affirm beliefs or attitudes they do not have. Religious commitments are often the most deeply felt of all and must be undertaken voluntarily.

Second, ritual and worship can flood the emotions, eliminate psychological distance, and subvert reason. They can overwhelm or frighten children with images of hellfire or hypnotic mantras. Of course, this is just what some religions try to do—and understanding that they do so should be part of religious education. But education requires that we keep some critical distance on our world, some ability to compare and contrast, some objectivity. Teachers must be sensitive to the emotional maturity of students.

Nonetheless, if students could be seated in a back balcony of the synagogue (or church or mosque) so that they would not have to participate in the worship (so that they would not have to respond to the liturgy or close their eyes during prayer), and if it were clearly understood that the purpose of attending the service was not to convert them but to provide them with a deeper understanding of religion, and if they were sufficiently mature, and if there were an excusal policy for students whose religious convictions prohibited even this form of education (or if the course were an elective) and if the rabbi (or leader of the service) knew and approved, this would seem to be a legitimate, indeed, valuable form of education. Students might come to feel something of the reverence, the values, the concerns and hopes which religious folk feel.

Of course, if they know nothing intellectually or doctrinally of the religion, a religious service is likely to be perceived as a jumble of sights and sounds and smells that makes little sense. The experience must be informed by at least some background understanding of what is going on. It is, in part, the theological understanding that congregants have of doctrine and myth and history and ritual which makes worship meaningful for them; it is not just the immediate experience. Observing the ritual is no substitute for the conceptual side of religion.

It is often claimed that religious experience is ineffable—that it cannot be put into language—and this is no doubt so, at least in the usual ways we think of language conveying meaning. No dictionary definitions, scientific descriptions, or philosophical accounts of religious experience will convey its meaning or power to people who have not had it. This is also the case with many other experiences: aesthetic experience, or our experience of love or guilt or despair, for example. And yet we talk about them (often at great length).

If we think of the power of language to convey meaning by way of narratives or poetry or drama we may be more generous in our assessment, however, for language has the power to recreate experiences imaginatively. If we have never been in love, we may be caught up short by the word "love," and no number of psychology texts will help. But we can come to feel something of Natasha's love for Prince Andrey in *War and Peace*; we experience it vicariously. It is often said that good art doesn't tell us things, it shows us. It makes us experience the world in a certain way.

Language can be used to minimize emotional overtones (as is the case in most textbook accounts of religion), or it can be used to draw out and play upon emotion (as is the case in literature and poetry and drama). For example, to read Chaim Potok's *The Chosen* is to (imaginatively) live inside the mind and feelings of a Jewish boy in the New York of the 1940s. The best substitute for firsthand personal religious experience is autobiographical or literary accounts of such experience. In fact, such accounts are often much richer than any observation of religious ritual and worship.

Because of the difficulty of putting religious experience into language, religion often functions symbolically; its natural language is poetry and symbol and metaphor and myth. The extent to which religious language is to be taken symbolically or literally is a major theological question, but it cannot be denied that much religious language functions very differently from scientific language, and students need to be aware of this. It requires a different sensibility. The idea that the skills of scientific critical thinking carry over to religion is extraordinarily dangerous. Religious language and experience are part and parcel of and meaningful only within a religious worldview. There is no way to translate religious language into scientific language. Arguably, once we have opted for scientific ways of understanding religion we have thrown the baby out with the bathwater.

There are, I suggest, four ways of getting *inside* religion. The first is to live a religious life, to seek God and participate in religious ritual. I have suggested that attenuated participation, something closer to observation, is a legitimate way of proceeding pedagogically. Second, through literature and poetry and drama we can imaginatively and vicariously think and feel our way into a religious frame of mind. Third, there is autobiography, apologetic literature, Scripture, and theology, which may not operate imaginatively but is written from within a religious worldview and uses religious categories and logic. It gives students a sense of what it is to think religiously. Teachers (or guest lecturers) can talk about their own religions personally, conveying an understanding of religion from the inside. Finally, third-person accounts—Jews believe x, Buddhists do y—give some sense of what religions are all about. For novices such accounts can have considerable value because they may translate (in very rough ways) the religion into more familiar concepts. Anthropological studies often provide "thick" descriptions of religious life which are helpful in conveying a sense of lived religion.

Critical Thinking and Truth

We might stop at this point with an array of religions laid out before us, each understood and appreciated to some considerable extent from the inside—a theological smorgasbord to be sampled and enjoyed. But if we stop here, we are not taking religion as seriously as we might, for every religion claims truth and goodness, though not all religions claim to possess the exclusive truth or the sole track to goodness. If we are to take religion seriously, we must take these claims seriously.

There are also pedagogical and epistemological reasons for moving on to questions of truth. After all, a fundamental purpose of education is to help students sort out the reasonable and the unreasonable, the good and the evil, the true and the false. If we fail to think critically about religion, Wilson and

Natale suggest, education is no more than "a form of window-shopping in which the child can buy whatever happens to appeal to him."[33] Indeed, as any teacher knows, the question of truth cannot be avoided, for any good student will inevitably ask of religion: "but is it true?" or "what do *you* think?"

In chapter 7 I will argue that public schooling must be religiously neutral (though the meaning of neutrality will require a good deal of spelling out). Neutrality does not require that teachers and texts forgo all critical thinking about religion, however, so I will say just a little about what it might entail when religion is at issue.

Some scholars believe that it makes no sense to talk about truth. Instead, there are simply multiple worldviews, each "true" on its own terms perhaps, but none any more true than the others in any "objective" or "absolute" sense.[34] It is not obvious that this is a coherent view (is it *true* that there is no such thing as truth?) and it surely should not be assumed; it is, after all, a minority view even among intellectuals. Surely teachers and textbooks are obligated to argue their case, considering the alternatives.

But whatever we think of the possibility of truth, if we are to take religion seriously, we must take seriously religious claims to truth *as truth is understood within various religious traditions*. We must *engage* religious accounts of the world. We cannot simply mention them, or talk "about" them, or even limit ourselves to trying to understand them empathetically. We must grapple with them; we must see what can be said for and against them. We must think critically about them. Even if we do not believe in any final "truth," we may believe that some views are more reasonable, more satisfying, or more likely to lead to the happiness of humankind than others; there is almost always some foothold for critical assessment. In any case, if my response to your claim to possess the truth is merely, "that's nice, how interesting," I haven't taken you seriously. How do we do this?

Being Open. We have already taken the first step. In attempting to understand a religion from the inside we forgo any automatic reductionism and open ourselves to religious ways of thinking and feeling. Thinking critically about a religion is not simply a matter of applying scientific method or the critical insights we bring with us to that religion. We take it seriously when we let it question us, when we open ourselves to the possibility that we misunderstand the world and are subject to enlightenment by that religion—when we are willing to be self-critical.

Critical Distance. If one kind of understanding is acquired by immersing oneself "inside" a religion, another kind of understanding is acquired by pulling back to achieve a critical distance on the religion. We can lose sight of the forest for the trees. Perhaps the most insightful book about America was written by an outside observer—Alexis de Tocqueville (though Tocqueville first made a considerable effort to understand America from the inside). If the insider's understanding of religion must be the first word, it need not be the last word.

Moreover, if we are to take religion in general seriously—and not just a particular religion—we must take the historical and comparative study of religion seriously. This requires scholarship. It requires the effort to understand a variety of cultures, historical periods, and religions, using the resulting comparative knowledge to put the claims of a particular culture or religion or epoch in perspective, noting similarities and differences, and constructing theories to account for the particularities.[35] The Protestant emphasis on belief and salvation by faith becomes particularly striking when compared with Muslim, Jewish, and Catholic emphasis on works. The transcendent God of traditional Western religion stands out in sharp relief when compared with the immanent God of Indian religion. What, if anything, is universal among religions, and how do we account for it? What is unique to some particular religion, and why is that?

Comparative Criticism. But we cannot uncritically assume the truth (or adequacy) of the modern scholar's assumptions or conclusions any more than we can those of any particular religious tradition. A truly liberal education, I have suggested, is a conversation in which the various speakers take seriously and respond to the insights of the other participants. We take a religious tradition seriously when we try it on, when we use it to make sense of its rivals—including its scholarly rivals. Correlatively, we take those rivals seriously when we use them to try to understand the religion at issue. From within Freudian theory, what sense can we make of religious experience? Correlatively, what sense, if any, does Freud make from within the vantage point of different religions? How does a Marxist understand religion? How does a Protestant fundamentalist or Catholic liberation theologian understand Marx? How does a Christian understand Islam or Judaism? How do Jews and Muslims understand Christianity?

One can do this comparative criticism without assuming any particular vantage point, neutrally as it were (a matter of neutrality as fairness). We need not start with the assumption that any particular view contains the truth; instead, we can engage each, in its turn, for what critical light it can throw on the others. We need not ask: what is true or false about Christianity? We can just ask: what did Freud (or Luther or Muhammad) think was true or false about Christianity? When we do this we are engaging our critical faculties; we are arguing.

The Appeal to Cumulative Experience. I have suggested that what counts as a fact, what counts as evidence for the facts, what counts as a good argument, what counts as rational, is largely a matter of the worldview within which one thinks and lives. We must remember the comprehensive and systematic nature of worldviews: virtually all evidence, all reasoning, all experiences, all data can be interpreted in various ways. No data are completely theory-neutral; there are never knock-down arguments or crucial experiments or unambiguous facts that point us to the truth of one rather than another worldview.

True, there are relatively uncontroversial facts on which most everyone can agree; for example, we may be able to resolve certain matters of biblical chronology through archaeological or historical research. But it is doubtful that any scientifically ascertained facts could ever verify or falsify a foundational religious claim—the claim of Jesus' resurrection, for example. What possible evidence would be sufficiently unambiguous, sufficiently closed to rival interpretations? What uncontroversial evidence is there for or against immortality or reincarnation? It is one thing to solve problems and determine what the facts are according to fairly well defined criteria *within* a worldview (be it liberal Christian, fundamentalist Christian, Buddhist, scientific, or whatever); it is another, much more difficult thing to solve problems or determine what the facts are, or what they mean, when worldviews *conflict* and we must decide which worldview, which methodology, which criteria of reason and evidence, to think or live within.

Nonetheless, to a considerable extent religious traditions and worldviews *can* be held accountable. Our worldviews do not allow us to make of the world anything that we will, and when worldviews compete some will prove inadequate while others will be more reasonable all things considered. Everyone agrees that the facts do not support the old claim that the earth is the center of the universe; biblical geocentrism is mistaken (or is myth or poetic license). Almost everyone now agrees that slavery is wrong; therefore, biblical tolerance of slavery was wrong. Feminists argue that moral experience demonstrates the shortcomings of biblical patriarchalism; hence we need to rethink the imagery we use to understand God. This, of course, is more controversial. Liberals, who are more open to new ways of thinking, are more likely to revise (or even revolutionize) their core beliefs; conservatives are more resistant—though they too are willing to revise beliefs—at least on the periphery of what they take to be central.

Worldviews are not isolated, abstract, timeless constructs. They evolve, they respond to the discovery of new "facts," they respond to the challenges of

rival interpretations of the world, they are affected by the larger social and
cultural world in which they exist. They have a history. Some die so that they
are no longer "live" alternatives. Others thrive. Why? In some very informal
and imprecise way, worldviews constantly run what William James called "the
gauntlet of confrontation with the total context of experience."[36] Some hold
up better than others. So it is with religions. (In his book *Religion and Cultural Freedom* E. M. Adams provides a rich and nuanced account of how this
should work.)

Even though there are no simple rules, no formulas by which to test the
claims of worldviews, it still makes sense to talk of testing them, of holding
them responsible to the "total context of human experience." Some will prove
more reasonable than others. Of course, when we know only one tradition
well, most all evidence can be interpreted to support it. It is only when we become familiar with other worldviews and take them seriously that we see that
human experience may support one better than the other. No simple "fact" of
history or nature will settle any of the big questions; but human experience
can cumulatively affect our reading of the plausibility of religious (and other
scientific and philosophical) claims, at least when we have alternative ways of
reading experience available to us, when we can assess the fit with various
worldviews. The trick is to recognize the subtle interplay between facts, human experience, and worldviews. Needless to say, once we decide to take the
alternatives seriously it is not so easy, on critical grounds, to decide where the
truth lies. A good deal of humility is in order.

Students must come to appreciate that at least when dealing with fundamental questions—regarding nature, psychology, justice, history, and morality, for example—they cannot uncritically assume that the truth is made
available to them, clear-cut, in any particular course. In biology classes students learn something of the views of (most) biologists; in economics classes
students learn something of the views of (most) economists. A good curriculum will provide them with various perspectives on the world, but education is
not a matter of uncritically accepting each of these accounts in turn. Rather,
students are educated when they have the ability to enter into an informed
and reasoned discussion about where the truth lies, *all things considered,
all courses considered*. Education requires that we be reasonable, not just
rational.

The logic of education—and the idea of taking religion seriously—pulls us
toward *judgment*, toward conclusions about the reasonableness of alternative
ways of understanding the world. But we can stop short. The various elements of critical thinking I have described—openness, critical distance, comparative criticism, and the appeal to cumulative experience—are all compat-

ible with what I have called neutrality as fairness. Nothing that I have described commits us to taking sides on religion. In chapter 7 I will argue that there are good reasons for maintaining neutrality and suspending judgment about the truth of contending religious and secular ways of understanding the world in public schools. In chapter 8 I will argue that academic freedom protects the right of university scholars to take sides.

Multiculturalism

Multiculturalism comes in several shapes and sizes. Some varieties fit nicely with liberal education as I understand it; others do not fit at all.

If multiculturalism is simply the movement to understand the various cultures and subcultures that make up our world (and our neighborhoods), it is good, important, and relatively uncontroversial. Indeed, it is an integral part of a liberal education.

Multiculturalism often means something stronger, however. Many multiculturalists argue that the particular interests, ideas, and values of men, of whites, of people in the West, and of elites have been uncritically taken to be canonical and normative for Americans, when in fact they are deeply controversial. One of the truly exciting and important developments of recent scholarship has been the recovery of the lost stories, ideas, and values of people who never had the power to write history and shape the canon.

For much of American history, for example, the orthodox American story began in Puritan New England—in spite of the fact that Anglican Englishmen had already settled Virginia, Catholic Spaniards had preceded them to America, and the Native Americans, with their own religious traditions, were here first. Many other religious stories—such as those of the African slaves— were submerged and even lost as Protestant Christianity shaped the institutions and historical self-consciousness of America, defining who "we" were in the nineteenth century.

In part because Protestant Christianity did so much to shape American education and culture, many educators and members of minority religious traditions have been suspicious of religious voices (and particularly conservative Protestant voices) in the curriculum. But, as we have seen, things have changed. Secular ideas and values shape the new orthodoxy, and religious voices are now lost from the conversation. It is important that students hear women's voices, the voices of ethnic and cultural minorities in America, and Third World voices; but multiculturalism should also require that they hear religious voices.

Millions of Americans continue to find the most profound sources of meaning in their lives in their religious subcultures; indeed, many people define themselves not in terms of ethnicity or nationality but of religion. Their primary identities are as Christians or Muslims, not as whites or Americans. The *Curriculum Guidelines for Multicultural Education* issued by the National Council for the Social Studies acknowledge that people's identities may stem from "gender, social class, occupation, political affiliation, or religion" (although the guidelines then ignore everything but ethnic identities).[37] Of course, ethnic and cultural identities are often closely wrapped up with religion; only in the modern West has religion been so sharply separated from the rest of culture.

A purpose of a liberal education is to move students beyond any narrow cultural orthodoxy so that they can appreciate and think critically about the diversity of stories—and the variety of religions—that go to make up the cultures of America and the world.

There are three dangers in multiculturalism. We might call the first the danger of reverse discrimination. In affirming and giving voice to previously neglected (and subjected) cultures and subcultures, multiculturalists sometimes overcompensate for past injustices, conveying to students a distorted sense of America's or the West's contributions to progress. Indeed, a good deal of multiculturalism disparages American values and Western civilization. There is something to be said for Arthur Schlesinger's observation that the "sins of the West are no worse than the sins of Asia or of the Middle East or of Africa," and there is this mitigating factor: the "crimes of the West have produced their own antidotes. They have provoked great movements to end slavery, to raise the status of women, to abolish torture, to combat racism, to defend freedom of inquiry and expression, to advance personal liberty and human rights."[38] The virtues of America and the West are considerable—as, no doubt, are its vices.

The second danger is that of transforming education into therapy. According to the 1989 New York State Task Force on Minorities, the "systematic bias toward European culture and its derivatives" of the curriculum has had "a terribly damaging effect on the psyche of young people of African, Asian, Latino, and Native American descent."[39] Because of similar concerns the National Council for the Social Studies prescribes a curriculum in which students learn "to feel positively about their identities" and "develop a high regard for their original languages and cultures." Students should learn that every ethnic group has "worth and dignity." Hence, comparative approaches to ethnic experiences must be "descriptive and analytical, not normative or judgmental" and teachers "should avoid, as much as possible, labeling any perspective 'right' or 'wrong.'"[40] This variation on the self-esteem movement in education dictates that all cultures and subcultures be respected equally.

Of course, cultures are not just different, they have *conflicting* beliefs and values, and this makes it difficult to affirm all of the alternatives. Are we to render no judgments about the relative merits of American sexual equality and the overt sexism of many Third World cultures? Can we teach students to respect fundamentalist and gay subcultures equally? Should we uncritically affirm Nazi culture and the apartheid culture of South Africa?

Robert Fullinwider argues, rightly I believe, that multiculturalists should want students "to avoid *smug, arrogant* judgments . . . [and] the *obtuseness* of those who hear and do not understand, see and do not perceive, and who, in their obtuseness, unfairly *denigrate* or *disparage* other people's accomplishments and traditions." The problem is that in response they "recommend an uncritical attitude toward cultural difference when they should be describing instead the virtues of an open mind."[41] In any case, as Charles Taylor notes, a "favorable judgment on demand is nonsense." Such a judgment would be "an act of breathtaking condescension. No one can really mean it as a genuine act of respect."[42]

Indeed, for us to impose our sense of moral equality on all cultures is to fail to take them seriously, for just as every religion claims to possess the truth, so every culture claims to embody the True and the Good. Happily, a bigoted ethnocentrism and a mindlessly nonjudgmental approach are not the only alternatives. It is possible to take other cultures seriously, grant them a place of importance in the curriculum, try to understand them from the inside, and engage them in the effort to discover more sensitive and reasonable ways of thinking and living for all involved—just as I have proposed for the study of religion.

We can get at the third danger of multiculturalism through a distinction Diane Ravitch has drawn between "pluralistic" and "particularistic" multiculturalism: "The pluralists seek a richer common culture; the particularists insist that no common culture is possible or desirable."[43] For Stanley Fish, as for many particularists on the Cultural Left, there is no such thing as common culture: "Someone who says to you 'This is *our* common ground,' is really saying, 'This is *my* common ground, the substratum of assumptions and values that produces *my* judgments.'"[44] Whose values are embodied in the canon? Those with power; the traditional elites. Education, in such an account, is a matter of political struggle. All values are *local* values, and all moral visions are *particular* moral visions. One variation on this theme is Afrocentric education, which conceptualizes all experience in African categories. As Molefi Kete Asanti puts it, if a thought or a value "cannot be found in our culture or in our history, it is dispensed with quickly" because "it is just not ours."[45] Of course, one's local culture may be liberal and its vision broad and tolerant; but there is nothing in the logic of particularism that requires this, and there is a good deal that militates against it.

Multicultural particularism is, I suggest, a tremendously dangerous notion, for it cannot make sense of the binding obligation educators have to take seriously alternative ways of thinking about the world or the common sense intuition we have that our judgments are likely to be more reasonable for having done so. Perhaps most troubling, particularism isolates us from each other, and at a time of growing ethnic, nationalistic, and religious violence in the world, this is worrisome.

Ravitch notes that one of "the primary purposes of public education has been to create a national community, a definition of citizenship and culture that is both expansive and *inclusive*."[46] As we've seen, the old common schools fell well short of inclusivity; to some considerable extent it was their purpose to teach students an all too "particularistic" version of Protestant Americanism. Given the vestiges of such education, there is, no doubt, a need for a "pluralistic" multiculturalism that requires students to learn something of the history and culture of women as well as men, of minorities as well as whites, of the Third World as well as Europe and America. And, as I have suggested, given the secular nature of the new orthodoxy, multiculturalism requires that religious voices be included in the conversation.

I would argue (as I did in chapter 3) that in spite of our deep differences, there continues to be an "overlapping moral consensus" that grounds at least a few common moral and civic virtues. Indeed, our obligation to seek peace in a multicultural society commits us to the kind of constitutional framework we have as a nation—a framework that requires us to *take each other seriously*, to treat each other with respect, to reason with each other in the public sphere and make ours a better society. If our country is to survive, we must learn to live and work together within the shared framework that our Constitution and civic institutions provide. The American project, for all its flaws—and there are many—is a good and valuable project. America was the first nation in the world to be formed not on the basis of blood or baptism but moral principle. There's a great deal to be said for this, and students should come to appreciate it.

Two final comments. Arthur Schlesinger argues that the underlying philosophy of multiculturalism is that "America is not a nation of individuals at all but a nation of groups, that ethnicity is the defining experience for most Americans." Schlesinger contrasts this with a notion he clearly favors (good liberal that he is)—that we should instead understand ourselves as a "nation composed of individuals making [our] own unhampered choices."[47]

But this is problematic as well, for we are who "we" are, in large part, because we are members of communities defined by ethnicity, class, sex, region, nation, and religion. To think of ourselves as mere individuals, rather than as members of "communities of memory" (to use Robert Bellah's fine phrase) is to have an impoverished notion of who we are. A liberal education should provide students with a deep understanding of the various communities that make claims on them and contribute to defining their identities. *And* it should provide them with the intellectual and imaginative resources to reflect on their own and other cultures, thus allowing them to be individuals, with some critical distance on those communities as well.

Finally, because multiculturalism is so deeply controversial, it should not be taught to students uncritically (in any of its guises). If we are to teach students to think critically about the world, they must have some sense of the national debate going on about multiculturalism. Students certainly should not be taught to believe uncritically the traditional accounts of Western Civilization courses *or* any of the newer multicultural responses to it. They should acquire some sense of what is at issue in the debate.

Textbooks and Primary Sources

John Stuart Mill argued that it is not enough for students to hear the arguments of adversaries from their own teachers, "presented as they state them, and accompanied by what they offer as refutations." If justice is to be done, Mill claimed, students must hear the arguments "from persons who actually believe them . . . in their most plausible and persuasive form. . . . Ninety-nine in a hundred of what are called educated men . . . have never thrown themselves into the mental position of those who think differently from them . . . and consequently they do not, in any proper sense of the word, know the doctrine which they themselves profane."[48]

Textbooks are written from a point of view, from within a worldview that defines for its author what is true, what counts as a fact, what is normal, what is reasonable, and what is good. As a result, what students encounter in a textbook is the world (or a particular subject) as it appears when strained through the author's conceptual net of interpretation. Inevitably, the emotional power and logical coherence of alternative understandings of the world are strained out of the account. Unhappily, most authors give their readers no sense of the controversial nature of their basic philosophical commitments.

If we are to take any point of view—secular or religious—seriously, we must let its advocates tell their own stories. No textbook can convey what Jeremiah or Paul or Martin Luther King, Jr., had to say as well as they themselves can. The one- or two-page excerpts of primary source readings found in many textbooks help, but not much, for the power of a position depends on seeing it in the context of supporting evidence and assumptions, and this requires a more substantial dose of material than the few excerpted paragraphs can provide. Anthologies and supplementary primary source material, including imaginative literature and art, are essential. True, primary source material is difficult and takes time to work through, particularly when it is historical or from a non-Western culture, but the effort must be made. Students should read Jewish accounts of the Holocaust, fundamentalist arguments against abortion, papal encyclicals on economic justice, and much else.

No doubt textbooks remain essential for some purposes. For younger children the coherence of a textbook (dealing with relatively uncontroversial material) may be as important as the encounter with contending points of view is for older students. It takes some intellectual and emotional maturity to work one's way through the often confusing mix of voices found in anthologies. But when textbooks do deal with controversial material, they must be written with more sophistication. They must make students aware of the philosophical baggage they carry with them and alternative ways of thinking about their subject matter. I have suggested that there should be at least an opening chapter in each text devoted to some such discussion. Still, for the purposes of liberal education—for high school and undergraduate students—anthologies and primary source material are absolutely vital.

Arguments against Religion in Education

Religion Is No Longer a Live Alternative. The reason God and religion are absent from most scholarly work—and textbooks—is that they are no longer live alternatives for most scholars, at least within the context of their disciplines. If God was a live option, religion could not be ignored with such casual impunity. Religion is close to being academically dead. Nonetheless, religion continues to play a role of some importance in people's lives and in our public life. Religion is culturally live.

The world can be understood in ways that are both academically and culturally dead. Ancient Greek science and Babylonian religion are dead everywhere, and I make no claim that we must now treat them as live alternatives and take them seriously. Our question is whether the (near) death of religion within the academic world justifies its exclusion from courses and textbooks that deal with the contemporary world. Should students be taught only what (most) scholars take to be reasonable possibilities, or should they be exposed to points of view that may not be reputable among scholars? (I take it that virtually no one objects to the study of religion in historical settings.)

First, it is important that religion is far from dead, even among intellectuals. There are first-rate scholars (including some at our best research universities) who write with great insight about the conventional wisdom of their disciplines but argue for religious alternatives to the prevailing orthodoxies, and the secular majority should feel some obligation to take them seriously in constructing curricula and writing textbooks. Of course, many of these scholars are segregated into religious institutions, partly as a matter of professional choice (this is where they feel most comfortable) and partly because the orthodox majority makes little room for them in secular universities.

It is worth noting that religion continues to be a matter of some personal, if not scholarly, importance to the majority of university faculty members. According to a 1985 Carnegie Foundation survey, 61 percent of them claimed moderate or deep religious convictions, while 32.2 percent were largely indifferent, and 6.8 percent were opposed to religion.[49] (Scholars, like all of us, have developed an extraordinary ability to segregate their personal and intellectual worlds.)

Second, the purpose of liberal education is to prepare students for living in the world, not for graduate work or professional school. Initiating students into the conventional wisdom of the respective disciplines does not, by itself, constitute an adequate education. Whatever continues to shape people's lives and thinking in some profound way, should be taken seriously in the curriculum. Religion continues to be a force of profound importance in people's lives and in our nonacademic intellectual life.

But if we take religion seriously, must we also take astrology or flat-earthers or witchcraft seriously? Of course not. I do not deny that astrology, for example, is of some importance to a fair number of people, and perhaps of considerable importance to a very small number of people, but its cultural and intellectual significance is very small when compared with religion. It has nothing of the intellectual or cultural significance that religion continues to have. We are certain to encounter problems in drawing the line between what is and is not intellectually respectable, what is and is not culturally live, what is and is not profoundly important, but on any of these counts religion is surely on the side of the line that warrants inclusion. And surely a *liberal* education requires us to be inclusive rather than exclusive.

The Fear of Controversy. Textbook publishers and school administrators often claim that religion is too controversial to include in textbooks and the curriculum, at least at the public school level. Religion *is* controversial. My argument here is that including religion in the curriculum will prove, in the end, to be less controversial than any other proposal. In a highly pluralistic culture, and in the long run, the least controversial position is the one that takes everyone's position seriously.

Alternative proposals—to ignore religion completely or to privilege one particular religion—would inevitably prove more controversial because with either of these alternatives some significant group will suffer discrimination and will object. In fact, it is the absence of religion from public schools that generates much of the existing controversy over education (such as the voucher movement). I am proposing articles of peace: taking all (major) culturally live alternatives seriously. It may be that almost everyone would prefer to have only their own view of the world taught, but this would be a recipe for conflict. Surely everyone's second choice would be to have *all* points of view taken seriously; this allows peace. It allows us to live together civilly with our deepest differences.

The conventional wisdom has been that neutrality (and peace) can be maintained by ignoring religion, but such neutrality is chimerical. Education simply cannot avoid dealing with matters that are religiously contested, and points of view that are hostile to religion pervade the curriculum now. Of course, so long as people believe that a secular education is neutral, the absence of religion may be (relatively) uncontroversial. But too many people know that secular education is not neutral.

The proposal to incorporate religion into education is not so controversial as some people fear. According to a 1986 Gallup Poll, the great majority of Americans approve of teaching about the major religions of the world (79 percent) and using the Bible in literature, history, and social studies classes (75 percent) in public schools.[50] A more thorough survey of five hundred Americans, employing hour-long interviews, found that 82 percent believed that neutral religious education should be *required* in public schools. Wilson and Natale, who conducted the survey, write:

> There is, we believe, sufficient evidence to show that the promotion of a neutral, non-indoctrinatory education in . . . religion is not only publicly acceptable but also publicly demanded, at least in the USA and the UK. That is on any account a very striking result. Before undertaking the survey, many people told us that in the USA public opinion was firmly fixed against any sort of religious education—a view made plausible by its absence in the public school system. This turns out not to be true, for a fairly simple but extremely important reason: because (to put it

bluntly) *nobody has taken the trouble to canvass opinion in sufficient depth or with sufficient conceptual sophistication.*[51]

My own experience in conducting workshops and seminars on religion and public education for wary teachers, administrators, and school board members leads me to a similar conclusion. Once there is some understanding of the First Amendment, American religious pluralism, and fairness to all points of view, virtually everyone finds it proper and important to include religion in public education.

Perhaps the most impressive evidence in this regard is furnished by a document entitled *Religion in the Public School Curriculum: Questions and Answers*, cosponsored by a group of seventeen national religious and educational organizations, including the American Jewish Congress, the Islamic Society of North America, the National Association of Evangelicals, the National Council of Churches, the AFT, the NEA, the American Association of School Administrators, and the National School Boards Associations.

Q. Why should study about religion be included in the public school curriculum?

A. Because religion plays significant roles in history and society, study about religion is essential to understanding both the nation and the world. Omission of facts about religion can give students the false impression that the religious life of humankind is insignificant or unimportant. Failure to understand even the basic symbols, practices, and concepts of the various religions makes much of history, literature, art, and contemporary life unintelligible.

Study about religion is also important if students are to value religious liberty, the first freedom guaranteed in the Bill of Rights. Moreover, knowledge of the roles of religion in the past and present promotes cross-cultural understanding essential to democracy and world peace.[52]

There is a striking consensus about the importance of religion in the public school curriculum—at least at the national level.

The Inevitability of Ignorance and Prejudice. Many secularists and members of minority religious traditions who might accept my argument in principle believe that in practice it is extremely dangerous to include religion in the curriculum, for teachers, no matter how well intentioned, will inevitably display their ignorance and prejudices in teaching about religion. In a predominantly Christian culture, alternatives to Christianity won't be treated knowledgeably or fairly.

Given the history of public schooling, such concerns are neither surprising nor unreasonable. The novelist Cynthia Ozick has written of her "childhood dread of a school-imposed Christmas" and her "undiluted memory of the shock of public punishment for refusing to sing Christian hymns at school assembly. The pain of this inescapably overt and helpless nonconformism, forced on a diffident and profoundly frightened Jewish child, has left its lifelong mark."[53] For about a century, Lance Sussman notes, "no other issue in American Jewish life has evoked as much emotion and energy at the local level as the struggle to keep religion out of the schools."[54] Some skepticism about my proposal will come naturally to members of religious minorities who have suffered deeply felt discrimination.

I am arguing, of course, for the *study* of religion, not the *practice* of any religion in schools, and in the next chapter I will make clear why I believe the study of religion should be religiously neutral (at least at the K–12 level). Teaching about religion gives no license to proselytize or indoctrinate. Indeed, a large part of my argument for teaching about religion is to *avoid* indoctrination—secular indoctrination (a concern to many members of minority religious traditions). Still, the great majority of teachers and textbook authors are not competent to teach about religions other than their own—and they may not even be particularly well informed about their own religion (if they have one). Moreover, most teachers have too little understanding of the constitutional constraints within which they must teach. Shouldn't we then stop all teaching about religion until teachers are prepared to do it right?

There are two problems with this proposal. First, because a secular curriculum is not neutral, it makes no sense to propose that we stop teaching about religion. So long as we teach views that conflict with religious views we are giving answers to religiously contested questions. We are, in effect, teaching about it; we are teaching that it is irrelevant or mistaken.

Second, teachers must deal with religion, for in parts of the curriculum— in history and literature, for example—it is unavoidable. Indeed, much proselytizing goes on now; teachers are biased now; textbooks have distorted and inadequate accounts of minority religions now. The solution, I believe, is not to leave "well" enough alone, to allow bad and biased education to continue, but to make teachers, textbook authors, and curriculum planners self-conscious about what they are doing—and improve teacher education and textbooks.

The task of improving teacher education is formidable, but the task of improving textbooks (or making anthologies of primary source material available) is less so. There are many scholars capable of writing good textbooks and editing good anthologies. Indeed, a fair amount of good material exists now; it is just not widely known. It does require some money.

Conclusions

A good liberal education should map out the cultural space in which we find ourselves. It should help us fill in our identities, locating us in the stories, the communities of memory, into which we are born. It should root us in the past.

It should also give us the resources for thinking critically about the past and the communities of which we are a part. Our world is inescapably pluralistic, and there is a great deal about which we disagree profoundly. A good liberal education will initiate students into a conversation about these matters, taking seriously the various major points of view. I agree with Gerald Graff when he argues that "the best solution to today's conflicts over culture is to teach the conflicts themselves, making them part of our object of study and using them as a new kind of organizing principle to give the curriculum the clarity and focus that almost all sides now agree it lacks. In a sense this solution constitutes a compromise, for it is one that conflicting parties can agree on."[55] If students are to be liberally educated they must understand the alternatives. They must be taught the conflicts. But we instead paper over the conflicts. No discipline feels any obligation to take points of view in other disciplines (much less the points of view of various religions) seriously, and we make little effort to make sure that the curriculum is structured in such a way that students will hear all the voices, be able to relate them coherently to each other, and recognize the conflicts. Education is a confusing babble of voices.

This being the case, I have advanced two claims. First, because religion is important, because it is complex, and because the conventional wisdom of all academic disciplines is so uncritically secular, the curriculum, at both the high school and undergraduate levels should require that students take at least one course in religion. That course must give them the intellectual and imaginative resources to take religion seriously. Religious voices must have access to the conversation. Second, introductory courses in the various disciplines should locate the conventional wisdom of those disciplines within the larger curricular conversation. Students should be provided with some philosophical perspective on the basic assumptions of each discipline and their relationship to the major alternatives—religious alternatives included. Teachers and textbooks must do what they can to make the conversation coherent.

FAIRNESS AND NEUTRALITY

In chapter 5 I argued that there is no such thing as "philosophical" neutrality. All positions on matters of any importance—the meaning of history, human nature, morality, and justice—are philosophically contested, and there is no neutral ground on which to stand in assessing the competitors. To teach one point of view to the exclusion of others is to take sides. The only attainable neutrality requires fairness—taking each of the contending alternatives seriously. Of course, one might be fair and then take sides, much as a judge might give litigants a fair hearing before passing judgment; neutrality restrains us from taking sides after we have been fair.

In chapter 6 I argued that a good liberal education will take religion seriously, giving it a place in the curriculum proportional to its importance, conveying to students an inside understanding of religion, and contending with it in searching for the truth. That is, a liberal education requires a degree of fairness to the major culturally live alternatives, religion included, but a liberal education does not in itself require neutrality. On the face of it, neutrality is an unlikely educational virtue. After all, the purpose of education is to sort out what is reasonable from what is unreasonable, what is true from what is false. The working assumption is that through critical reason, using the methods of modern scholarship, we can divide the wheat from the chaff. Education is, and should be, critical and normative, not neutral.

I will now argue, however, that there are epistemological, political, moral, and constitutional reasons for fairness *and* neutrality on religiously contested matters in public schools. I will also argue, however, that even though fairness and neutrality are, in principle, possible in textbooks and courses, in practice they simply aren't in the cards. It is the overall curriculum that can and must be both fair and neutral regarding religion; students must be required to study religion in a way that provides curricular *balance* with their secular studies. In chapter 9 I will argue that in universities academic freedom trumps neutrality (but not fairness). In this chapter I am concerned with public schools.

The Epistemological Argument

One purpose of education is to enable students to think critically about the world, to sort out good from bad arguments, truth from falsehood. If students are to understand why one theory or worldview is more reasonable than another, they must take both seriously; otherwise their critical thinking will have been thwarted and they will have no good reasons for choosing between them. If they are systematically exposed only to one theory, one method of resolving disagreements, one worldview, they will have been indoctrinated. To the extent that we teach students secular but not religious ways of thinking about the world, we hinder their ability to think critically about such disagreements. What they believe is a matter of authority and faith.

This is an epistemological argument for fairness, not neutrality. But if students should be exposed to the alternatives, it is surely also the proper purpose of teachers and textbooks to guide students' judgment, to help them sort out which ideas and values, theories and worldviews, are most reasonable. Education cannot remain neutral about where truth is most likely to be found.

There is an epistemological argument for neutrality, nonetheless. Once we recognize the nature of our epistemological situation, once we step outside of the worldview of modern science or the particular religious traditions to which we belong in order to compare them, we have to acknowledge that sorting out the true from the false, the more reasonable from the less reasonable, is difficult indeed. Ninian Smart has suggested, rightly I think, that it is in the nature of worldviews to be debatable: "How do we decide as a matter of educational policy what is right and what is wrong? *We* may think that Christianity or Scientific Humanism or a bit of both is somehow the truth: but would the Chinese or Iranian authorities concur? And how do we show them to be wrong? Why should it be that education leads to one worldview in one country and another worldview in another country?" In response, Smart recommends what he calls a "soft non-relativism." The difficulty of assessing worldviews does not require us to embrace relativism—the claim there is no truth. The difficulties of comparing worldviews should make us wary of claiming that we have the truth, however. There is, Smart writes, "neither a God-given nor a humanity-bestowed right to teach a debatable worldview as though it is not debatable, nor to neglect the deeply held beliefs and values of other people on the ground that you consider them foolish."[1] Once we decide to take the alternatives seriously, it is not easy, on critical grounds, to decide where the truth lies.

Of course, over time, some theories and worldviews are so thoroughly discredited that it no longer seems important to continue to take them seriously—and many intellectuals would place all religion in this category. But not all scholars do, and much postmodern thought is critical of the old idea that science and modernity have triumphed over other worldviews. Moreover, religion retains considerable *cultural* vitality. And, as we become more multicultural, more aware of the wealth of worldviews that continue to shape people's lives, it seems increasingly parochial and illiberal to assume that any group of intellectuals has the truth safely in hand. Yet that is the clear message of most textbooks and much teaching.

I am *not* arguing that a science text or teacher cannot say which is the better scientific theory; scientific method can often adjudicate with some precision among contending scientific theories. What counts for truth *within* science is often not debatable. What is debatable is the sufficiency of science to explain all of reality, or the extent to which it conflicts with and provides a more or less reasonable understanding of reality than contending religious accounts.

It is the curriculum, not particular texts and courses, that must be neutral. The curriculum should not be structured so that it takes sides on matter of great philosophical difficulty and ambiguity. There is not such unanimity of opinion, even educated opinion, that a winner should be declared in these ultimate matters. A degree of humility is in order.

The Political Argument

There is some irony in the extent to which we go in protecting people's right to vote, while at the same time allowing many of them no public voice in the formal, public schooling of their children (all the while we use their money to underwrite the schools). Or, to draw a different analogy, our criminal justice system guarantees people accused of crimes, no matter how heinous, no matter how convinced we might be of their guilt, competent lawyers and the opportunity to tell their stories in a court of law with a jury of their peers. Yet we make no provision for ensuring citizens the right to tell their own stories in our schools.

If an individual's or a subculture's most fundamental beliefs about the world are not given voice in the curriculum they are, in effect, disfranchised much as if they could not vote. *Public* education must take the public seriously. Yet it is clear that the religious beliefs of Americans are not given voice in public schools. They have, in effect, been educationally disfranchised.

Of course, school boards are elected so there is a measure of democratic control over education. There is no provision for minority rights, however (at least apart from the First Amendment). To some extent, at least, the stories that make it into the curriculum are those the majority chooses—though the content and philosophical assumptions of education are usually determined by intellectuals and entrenched educational bureaucracies. I take the liberal position to be inclusive and multicultural, in principle at least. Suppressed and minority voices—and in our culture that often means religious voices— should be included in the conversation.

So far we have an argument for fairness, not neutrality. If we guarantee the right to vote, we do not guarantee that anyone's candidate will win; if we guarantee someone arrested for a crime a day in court, we do not guarantee a verdict of not guilty. To grant people the right to tell their story, to be taken seriously in our system of schooling, is not to guarantee that our considered verdict will agree with them. To avoid educational disfranchisement it is only necessary that we treat them fairly.[2] We need a stronger argument for neutrality.

America is not just a welter of warring interest groups, of majority and minority ideas and ideals. We are a community bound together by a shared history, a constitutional framework of rights and responsibilities, and an overlapping consensus of moral values. It has been, quite properly, the role of the public schools—the *common* schools—to nurture this sense of community. When the political community is deeply divided on matters of great importance—as it always is—then, as a matter of sustaining community, maintaining peace among ourselves, and respecting the rights of others, it is imperative that we agree to disagree and not align public schools with any one of the contending views.

Of course, government cannot help but take sides on contested matters such as abortion, affirmative action, economic justice, and war and peace. But unless we want the content of education to change with every election, we must agree to a conception of education that we can support as a community over time. The schools must embody a consensus and not take sides on deeply contested matters. If we want the public to entrust their children to public schools, those schools should not take sides on matters about which the public disagrees deeply. And if we want citizens to be competent to make responsible decisions about governmental policies (and much else), then government should not stack the deck by structuring education to favor certain points of view. Education must be both fair *and* neutral, not taking sides on matters of profound disagreement.

Public schools, like the old common schools, should be restricted to promoting or teaching *as true* what the public holds in common. So, for example, we (Americans) are united in our belief in democracy; hence it is proper to teach students the value of democracy; teachers and textbooks need not remain neutral about its merits. We are, however, deeply divided between the Democratic and Republican parties so public education should remain neutral as to the relative virtues of each party, treating them fairly. Or, to pick another example, we all agree about the virtue of honesty so it is proper to teach students to be honest. We disagree about abortion so we should teach fairly the alternative views without taking sides. If we are to have peace, if we are to avoid bitter political fighting and the likely destruction of public schools, if we are to sustain community, then we must withhold judgment when we disagree deeply.

According to this argument, religion has no special standing but is treated just like any other deeply controversial theory or practice. Religion is profoundly controversial; to preserve peace and sustain community, public schools should not take sides on religiously contested matters.

Of course religion *does* have special standing in the United States precisely because this argument—or a variation on it—was accepted by the Framers of the Constitution: the result was the religion clauses of the First Amendment. My argument here is that even if we did not have the First Amendment there would be a strong political argument in a pluralistic culture for accepting articles of peace requiring that our educational institutions not take sides on matters of deep disagreement, religion included.

The Moral Argument

Students, like all people, should be treated with moral respect, not merely as means to the ends of adults. One way to respect people is to let them make up their own minds. Of course, young students require a good deal of guidance, and it is not easy to know when and how to relax that guidance and begin to treat students with the respect due persons able to think for themselves. Once they achieve a measure of maturity, however, students must be reasoned with; they must be exposed to alternatives. Indoctrination is as wrong for moral reasons as it is foolish for epistemological reasons.

This is an argument for fairness only. We do not necessarily mean disrespect for our students in disagreeing with them, in concluding that they are wrong about important matters. Teachers rightly feel no compunction about criticizing students' views of molecular structure or the quality of their art or their understanding of the Taft-Hartley Act. But do we want teachers to assess the religious beliefs of their students? After all, those beliefs are very personal, almost *sacred*. Might religious beliefs be special in a way that requires neutrality?

Of course, teachers and textbooks should not hold anyone's religious beliefs up to ridicule (and young students should not be discussing the truth or falsity of religious belief at all). But part of taking religion seriously is taking its claim to have the truth seriously, and we cannot do this unless we allow it to enter the rough-and-tumble of intellectual competition. To be taken seriously involves risks.

The neutrality that seems morally required here is not one that prohibits the teacher or text from taking sides but one that respects the moral integrity of students by not requiring them to agree. There should be no *official* right answer on moral, political, or religious matters of controversy and deep personal conviction. Students should not be graded on which side they take but on how well they understand the various arguments.

The Constitutional Argument

Since the Supreme Court first applied the Establishment Clause to the states in 1947, the Court has held that government must be neutral in matters of religion. Justice Fortas provided what may be the clearest and most concise statement of this principle in *Epperson* v. *Arkansas* (1968): "Government in our democracy, state and national, must be neutral in matters of religious theory, doctrine, and practice. It may not be hostile to any religion or to the advocacy of no-religion; and it may not aid, foster, or promote one religion or religious theory against another or even against the militant opposite. The First Amendment mandates governmental neutrality between religion and religion, and between religion and nonreligion."[3] Public schools are government agencies, and public school teachers are agents of the government, employed to carry out government policy—to teach the curriculum. (As we shall see in the next chapter, the situation is somewhat different for university professors.)

I have noted the dangers of a too strict separationism and the "wall of separation" metaphor that the Supreme Court has used on occasion in explicating the Establishment Clause. In fact, the Court has never held that religion and public education must be separated; its position has been that public education must be religiously neutral. It is unconstitutional to promote (or inhibit) religion in public schools; it is not unconstitutional to teach about religion neutrally.

This position was spelled out in *Abington Township* v. *Schempp* (1963) in which the Court distinguished the unconstitutional *practice* of religion in public schools—in this case, devotional Bible reading—from constitutionally appropriate teaching *about* religion. Justice Clark, writing for the majority, declared that nothing in the ruling should be taken to mean that the "study of the Bible or religion, when presented objectively as part of a secular program of education, may not be effected consistent with the First Amendment." In a concurring opinion Justice Brennan, the strictest separationist on the Court in recent decades, wrote: "The holding of the Court today plainly does not foreclose teaching *about* the Holy Scriptures or about the differences between religious sects in classes in literature or history." In another concurring opinion, Justice Goldberg added: "It seems clear to me from the opinions in the present and past cases that the Court would recognize the propriety of . . . teaching *about* religion, as distinguished from the teaching *of* religion, in the public schools."[4] No member of the Court has ever dissented from this position. It is permissible to teach about religion if done in the right way.

The key consideration in drawing this distinction was neutrality. For Clark, the Establishment Clause requires that "the Government maintain strict neutrality, neither aiding nor opposing religion." For Brennan the "State must be steadfastly neutral in all matters of faith, and neither favor nor inhibit religion." And for Goldberg the "fullest realization of true religious liberty requires that government . . . effect no favoritism among sects or between religion and nonreligion." In essence, "the attitude of government toward religion must be one of neutrality."[5]

What does it mean to teach about religion neutrally? Two things are clear. Neutrality certainly rules out the *practice* of religion: to pray or read the Bible devotionally promotes religion; so do preaching to and indoctrinating students. It is also clear that schools must be neutral not just between religions—not favoring Baptists over Episcopalians or Christians over Jews—but they must also be neutral between religion and nonreligion, not favoring religious or secular ways of thinking. But presumably students *can* be taught about religion in ways that do not indoctrinate them, that do not involve the practice of religion, and that do not take sides by privileging any particular religion or religion generally. Unfortunately (or perhaps fortunately) the Court gives us little help in sorting out what this all means. In fact, Justice Brennan wrote: "To what extent, and at what points in the curriculum religious materials should be cited, are matters which the courts ought to entrust very largely to the experienced officials who superintend our Nation's public schools. They are experts in such matters, and we are not."[6]

It is one thing to teach about religion neutrally; it is another thing to maintain neutrality by teaching about religion. The Court has given public schools permission to teach about religion, but it has never claimed that religion must be taught to restore neutrality to a curriculum that is hostile to religion. Yet this *should* be its position. In its classic formulation by Chief Justice Burger, the second prong of the Lemon Test requires that the "principal or primary effect" of a law must be one "that neither advances or inhibits religion."[7] Yet in many courses students in public schools are taught to think about the world in secular ways which conflict with religious ways of making sense of the world.

Of course it can be argued that although one effect of secular textbooks and a secular curriculum is to undermine religious beliefs and practices, this is neither their primary nor their intended effect. So, for example, it might be claimed that the primary effect of biology textbooks and the teaching of evolution is a better understanding of science and biology, not the inhibition of religious beliefs about the origins of life. The problem with this reading of primary effect is that it is not itself religiously neutral. Any fundamentalist would say that the primary effect of teaching evolution is to undermine religion. What counts as the primary effect depends on one's fundamental beliefs and values.

What seems clear beyond all doubt is that whether or not the primary effect of a particular course or the curriculum more generally is to inhibit religion, public schooling does take sides; it does encourage students to think (and feel) about the world in secular rather than religious ways. If schools are to be religiously neutral, students must be taught about the religious alternatives. As Ninian Smart puts it, "scientific humanism" is often "in living contact and conflict with traditionally religious belief-systems. Rivals should be treated together. If they are not, then we are taking steps to entrench some determinate viewpoint into our educational system, and genuine pluralism is in this way eroded."[8]

A large part of the problem is the courts' uncritical equation of secular education with religiously neutral education. For example, in *Everson* Justice

Jackson argued that public schools are organized "on the premise that secular education can be isolated from all religious teaching so that the school can inculcate all needed temporal knowledge and also maintain a strict and lofty neutrality as to religion. The assumption is that after the individual has been instructed in worldly wisdom he will be better fitted to choose his religion."[9] This last sentence would strike many religious folks as presumptuous at best. What is important for our purposes, however, is the working assumption that secular and religious views can be disentangled so that as long as the schools stick to secular education they will maintain their neutrality. This claim has been repeated over and over again in court opinions; indeed, it has become an article of the conventional wisdom.

Justice Jackson had better days. On one of them he wrote his concurring opinion in *McCollum*. His opinion there is worth quoting at some length.

> Music without sacred music, architecture minus the cathedral, or painting without the scriptural themes would be eccentric and incomplete, even from a secular point of view. . . . Even such a "science" as biology raises the issue between evolution and creation as an explanation of our presence on this planet. Certainly a course in English literature that omitted the Bible and other powerful uses of our mother tongue for religious ends would be pretty barren. And I should suppose it is a proper, if not an indispensable, part of preparation for a worldly life to know the roles that religion and religions have played in the tragic story of mankind. The fact is that, for good or for ill, nearly everything in our culture worth transmitting, everything which gives meaning to life, is saturated with religious influences, derived from paganism, Judaism, Christianity—both Catholic and Protestant—and other faiths accepted by a large part of the world's peoples. One can hardly respect a system of education that would leave the student wholly ignorant of the currents of religious thought. . . .[10]

Everything is saturated with religious influences. Education without religion would be barren. Even biology must raise the religious question of creation.

Secularity is no guarantee of neutrality; to take it to provide such a guarantee is to demonstrate an appalling naïveté, and the slightest familiarity with the history of ideas over the past several centuries should provide an antidote. Although religious liberals have managed to accommodate religion to large parts of the modern worldview, even they should find it impossible to accept as religiously neutral much of what is taught in science, economics, home economics, and history classes.

In *Schempp* Justice Clark argued that schools could not establish a "religion of secularism" that prefers "those who believe in no religion over those who do believe," and in his concurring opinion Justice Goldberg warned that an "untutored devotion to the concept of neutrality" can lead to a "pervasive devotion to the secular and a passive, or even active, hostility to the religious."[11] Arguably, something very much like this has happened. Much secular education nurtures a "passive" hostility to religion. Courts, in particular, have applied an untutored and naive notion of neutrality: they have required a smoking gun, an overt hostility, when the hostility has been philosophically more subtle. A *substantive neutrality* requires, as Douglas Laycock puts it, judgments "about the relative significance of various encouragements and discouragements to religion."[12] My argument is that public schooling clearly and forcefully discourages students from thinking about the world in religious ways.

Occasionally courts have acknowledged the conflict between secular and religious views, but they have held that since *everything* conflicts with *some* religion there would be no curriculum at all if we insisted on neutrality and banned what was not neutral; moreover, to demand that schooling not conflict with any religious view is to give religion the right of censorship, and this is to promote religion by giving it special privileges.

The solution, of course, is not to ban the material that conflicts with (some) religion, thus eviscerating the curriculum, but to restore neutrality by including religion. To require the study of religion is not to promote religion but to maintain neutrality and provide students with a truly liberal education. Neutrality makes no sense apart from fairness.

In 1954 the Supreme Court finally recognized that "separate but equal" is an incoherent notion when applied to segregated schools. Equality requires integration. Similarly, the Court must come to see that "separate but neutral" (or "secular but neutral") is equally incoherent. Neutrality *requires* the integration of religion into the curriculum.

The refusal of the courts to take secular hostility to religion seriously prompted Judge Hand and many religious conservatives to argue that secular humanism is really a religion and therefore must be treated neutrally with other (traditional) religions. We saw in chapter 5 that this is not a matter of creating a new use of the word "religion" out of whole cloth. Many scholars—and the Supreme Court itself in Free Exercise cases—have talked about secular belief systems as (functional) religions.

We have two alternatives. We might choose to characterize the philosophical position underlying so much of education as secular humanism and then call it a religion, for it does function religiously. Or we can call it philosophical naturalism, or the "modern worldview" and note that it is hostile to much religion. The point is the same, though legal strategies may dictate one approach rather than another. If we are to have neutrality among religions, or if we are to have neutrality between religion and nonreligion, then we cannot privilege the "secular" worldview.

On several occasions the Supreme Court has appealed to a principle other than the Establishment Clause which might be used to require teaching about religion—though the Court has never gone so far as to suggest this. The principle, grounded in the free speech clause of the First Amendment, is that of constitutional intolerance for constraints on the marketplace of ideas in public institutions. The most ringing statement of this idea is to be found in *West Virginia State Board of Education* v. *Barnette* (1943) in which Justice Jackson wrote: "If there is any fixed star in our constitutional constellation, it is that no official, high or petty, can prescribe what shall be orthodox in politics, nationalism, religion, or other matters of opinion or force citizens to confess by word or act their faith therein."[13] But students are taught secular "orthodoxy"—indeed, they are often forced on exams to "confess" (in a demythologized way) the truth of secular accounts of the world that may be hostile to their personal religious beliefs. In *Tinker* v. *Des Moines Independent Community School District* (1969), Justice Fortas wrote that "students may not be regarded as closed-circuit recipients of only that which the State chooses to communicate."[14] And in *Keyishian* v. *Board of Regents* (1966), Justice Brennan wrote that the First Amendment "does not tolerate laws that cast a pall of orthodoxy over the classroom. . . . The classroom is peculiarly the 'marketplace of ideas.' The Nation's future depends upon leaders trained through wide exposure to that robust exchange of ideas which discovers truth 'out of a multitude of tongues, [rather] than through any kind of authoritative selection.'"[15]

Schools are to be marketplaces of ideas. To keep religion out of the marketplace is to cast a "pall of [secular] orthodoxy" over education; it is to discriminate against certain ideas based on their content. It is to show, at best, a passive hostility to religion; it is to prefer those who believe in no religion to believers. In a concurring opinion in *Epperson*, Justice Stewart found it astounding that a state would make it "a criminal offense for a public school teacher so much as to mention the very existence of an entire system of respected human thought [evolution]. That kind of criminal law," Stewart suggested, "would clearly impinge upon the guarantees of free communication contained in the First Amendment, and made applicable to the States by the Fourteenth."[16] It is at least equally astounding that many states, in effect, keep students from any significant understanding of the varieties of Christianity, Judaism, Islam, and other respected systems of human thought.

I conclude, then, that because the Establishment Clause requires religious neutrality of public institutions, because many topics in the curriculum are religiously contested, because neutrality requires fairness when issues are contested, and because the Court has claimed that schools should be marketplaces of ideas, the study of religion is not only constitutionally permissible, *it is constitutionally required*. The courts must ensure that students are exposed to religious as well as to secular ways of understanding the world.

How schools accomplish this end is best left to educators. As Justice Brennan wrote in *Schempp*, "They are experts in such matters, and we are not."[17] The courts should not be involved in reviewing curricula or textbooks except when violations of neutrality are flagrant. Would this lead to surveillance and the excessive entanglement prohibited by the third prong of the Lemon Test? No, for the Supreme Court has already given schools permission to teach students about religion and expressed no particular concern about court surveillance of those courses in which religion is studied. All I propose is that what is now permitted become mandatory.

Excusal Policies. Although various justices have said that a good education should include the study of religion, the Supreme Court has never ruled on whether courses in religion can or should be required. In *Vaughn* v. *Reed* (1970), a federal district court upheld the constitutionality of a required Bible course for elementary school students so long as the Bible was taught "objectively, as part of a secular program of education." In fact, the Court rejected the need for an excusal policy, for "if the course is being properly taught within the constitutional limits, there is no reason for non-attendance by any student."[18] This is worrisome. Will the Protestant, the Catholic, or the Jewish Bible be used, and whose principles will be used for interpreting it? Elementary school children (and most teachers) are simply not sophisticated enough to handle such difficult and controversial literature in a religiously neutral way. (And is the study of other sacred scriptures required?)

Most important, there is something to be said for Judge Kiser's opinion in *Crockett* v. *Sorenson* (1983) that Bible courses must be optional on free exercise grounds: "It would be extremely oppressive and, more importantly, constitutionally unacceptable to require a student to enroll in a Bible teaching class when the very subject matter being taught violated his religious beliefs."[19] It is not clear whether Judge Kiser believed that a Bible (or any religion) course must be elective, or whether there simply must be an excusal policy, though the latter alternative would seem to satisfy his concern. There is a huge difference between making religion a required course and then allowing exemptions for reasons of conscience and offering elective courses in religion which only a small minority of students might take.

The Sixth Circuit Court of Appeals has dissented from this reading of the Free Exercise Clause, however. In *Mozert* v. *Hawkins County Board of Education* (1987) it denied fundamentalist children exemptions from reading elementary school readers that included stories with themes (feminism, one-world government, witchcraft, secular humanism) which, they claimed, burdened their religious liberty. The court held that as long as students were not required to affirm or act on the ideas and values in the books, they had no right to exemptions; *mere exposure* does not burden religious liberty and is not objectionable on free exercise grounds. In this view it would follow that there is no free exercise argument to be made for excusing students from merely studying religion in a required course.

I find this reading of the Free Exercise Clause troubling, however. As Judge Boggs noted in his concurring opinion, for centuries the Catholic church held that simply to read books included in the Index (mere exposure) constituted a mortal sin. Surely what counts as burdening one's religious liberty must be a matter for each religious tradition to determine; it will vary from religion to religion and can hardly be abstractly decided by a court.

Hence I am inclined to think there should be a free exercise argument for granting students exemptions from taking required religion courses (or most any course) if they object to doing so for reasons of conscience. Some students (or their parents) will feel their religious or moral values to be unduly burdened by taking such a course. Such a view would almost surely be short-sighted, for students who did not take such a course would remain unaware of the extent to which their secular education conflicts with religious understandings of the world. Nonetheless, I can well imagine people with certain religious convictions believing that exposure to religious ways of thinking other than their own will be more threatening to their religion than naive exposure to secular education.

Under the old Sherbert Test, or under the new Religious Freedom Restoration Act, courts must balance the free exercise rights of students with the interests of the state; only those state interests which are compelling and can be accomplished in no less burdensome way can override free exercise claims. Needless to say, letting students opt out of required courses could so undermine the integrity of the curriculum and create so much disruption that the state would have a compelling interest in limiting exemptions. I make the following observation.

Educators and the government now go to great effort and expense to tailor schooling to the special needs of various categories of students with no constitutional claim on public schools. For example, the National Education Association has endorsed alternative programs for "displaced students of desegregated districts; pushouts; disruptive students; disabled readers; gifted, talented, and creative students; students of low academic ability; underachievers; students socially promoted; pregnant students and teenage parents; and students who do not qualify for or have no desire to pursue a college program."[20] Federal law requires school districts to provide an expensive array of services for handicapped students, and think of the many ways in which schools accommodate the needs of basketball and football teams. Schools should be at least as responsive to the free exercise rights of students.

Relatively speaking, exemptions for religious reasons are not likely to be particularly disruptive to schools. In any case, quite apart from any legal right to such exemptions, schools should grant them as a matter of moral and religious sensitivity and political self-interest.

Teachers, Texts, and Courses

If neutrality is required, what must be neutral? I will lump the possibilities into two categories: we might require neutrality of individual texts, teachers, and courses; or we might require neutrality of curricula and schools. I begin with the first category. There are, I suggest, eight different ways in which texts, teachers, and courses might deal with religiously contested matters.

1. Religion might be *ignored*. In some texts and courses—say in arithmetic or drivers' education, where the subject matter is not religiously contested—this is not a problem. But if the claims or theories or methods of a subject are religiously contested and the text or the teacher ignores religion, then neutrality and fairness have been violated.

2. Religion (or religious views of a contested issue) might be discussed, but only *reductively*. That is, religion is interpreted in terms of some worldview hostile to religion. This might happen if Freudian categories are used to explain religion in a psychology class or text or if a historian explains why certain events happened in fully secular terms. If the text or teacher fails to provide students with the alternative religious account(s), they are neither neutral nor fair.

3. Religion might receive *bare mention*, in which case it is neither ignored nor explained reductively, but it is still not taken seriously (from the inside, as a contender for truth). The text or teacher might mention some fairly straightforward facts relating to religion (that the ancient Hebrews were monotheists or that Christian fundamentalists reject evolution, for example) but if students are given little, if any, sense of why this is the case, and the

text or the teacher uses a secular worldview to explain the subject at hand, then neutrality is violated. The bare mention of religion, the failure to take the religious worldview seriously, puts it at a disadvantage. A few religious facts are unlikely to stay afloat in a sea of secular thinking.

In these first three approaches students are not provided with the intellectual or imaginative resources necessary to make sense of religious alternatives.

4. The text or teacher might convey to students an understanding of religion(s) *from the inside*.

5. The text or teacher might consider religious ways of understanding the world as live contenders for the truth, to be argued about and critically assessed (in ways I described in chapter 6). If the text or teacher refrains from drawing conclusions, both fairness and neutrality have been achieved.

6. A teacher might offer his or her own *personal conclusion* about the truth or significance of religious claims, perhaps in response to a student's question, but not argue for it, and certainly not insist that students accept it as an official conclusion of the course. For example, a teacher might say at the beginning of the text or course: "This is my (religious) bias, or perspective, and while I shall try to be fair, you should be aware of where I am coming from in sorting out the controversial material we will be discussing."

7. The teacher or textbook author might actively *argue* for particular conclusions after all the relevant views have been taken seriously but stop short of making them the official view. In effect, the teacher's voice is added to the conversation. This is certainly more than the expression of a personal view: it is the argument of someone with some authority in the subject, citing evidence and building a coherent case. In this case neutrality is not defined by the teacher's or author's arguments or conclusions but by the structure of the complete course or text—by *its* fairness, its openness to conclusions other than the teacher's or author's, and by the weight and priority given the teacher's or author's reasoning and conclusions. In both approaches 6 and 7 the text and the course can be neutral *overall*, even if the author and teacher are not neutral at every point in the text or course.

8. The teacher or textbook author might consider all points of view fairly, argue for the truth of a particular point of view, and make that the final and *official conclusion* of the course or text. Now (verdict) neutrality is clearly dropped.

The distinction between (7) and (8) can be subtle, or it can be fairly obvious. Much depends on the way the teacher or author frames the discussion of her or his own view. Is it *one more alternative*—albeit the one the teacher thinks best—or is it *the* correct view? Is there some respect for the philosophical ambiguity inherent in dealing with alternative worldviews? Is the teacher's purpose to convince students she or he is right, or is it to put them in a position to follow reasoned argument on their own? Are students required to agree with the teacher or text on exams so their grades suffer if they do not agree?

A great deal depends on the maturity of the students. Elementary school students are not likely to be able to distinguish the teacher's personal views (6) from official course conclusions (8). If the teacher believes something, it *must* be true. At some point, perhaps in junior high or middle school education, and almost surely by high school, students are able to draw this distinction. The distinction between (7) and (8) is more difficult, however, and even if we can see the difference in principle, in practice the difference will be one of nuance and may not be obvious to any but the most sophisticated students. Still, there *is* a difference.

My suspicion is that most high school (and undergraduate) texts, teachers, and courses fail the tests of religious fairness and neutrality as clearly as did the textbooks I reviewed in chapter 5. Most are locked into some uncritical mix of the first three positions.

But to require neutrality (or even fairness) of texts, teachers, and courses may be a virtually impossible, even misguided, reform because American education is so deeply committed to conflating subjects with intellectual disciplines. In a biology text or class students are taught about organic nature as understood by biologists (rather than, say, theologians or philosophers). In these circumstances, to ask biology texts, teachers, and courses to be neutral regarding religion would be to ask that they cease to be *science* texts, teachers, and courses. Similarly, virtually no academic historians (and certainly no textbooks used in public schools) understand history in religious categories. Can we ask historians in their texts and in their classes to be neutral about religion? In effect, we would be asking them to reject or at least give no priority to the categories and worldview in terms of which their discipline is defined.

Curricular Neutrality

In the last chapter I argued that a good liberal education requires courses in religion, not just religion in courses. An implicit part of the argument was that it is impossible to take religion seriously if our treatment of religion is limited to brief (and most likely) incidental references in courses that are essentially secular. In fact, it is simply impossible, the academic disciplines being what they are, to require neutrality in most disciplines, courses, or texts. It is possible, however, to construct neutral curricula by adding courses in religion.

Are texts and teachers relieved of the obligation to be neutral in their (secular) courses if there is a religion course which maintains overall curricular neutrality? Yes, though they should be at least minimally fair. In the last chapter I argued that all introductory texts and courses that deal with religiously contested material should acknowledge, perhaps in an introductory chapter or in the opening classes, the controversial nature of the claims students are about to encounter. Students must be given some sense of the historical and philosophical context of the current state of the discipline and some sense of the culturally live alternatives to the methods and conclusions of the discipline at issue. Every introductory course should take its role in the conversation of liberal education seriously, making connections rather than offering students yet another monologue.

In a sense, the introductory philosophical chapter of a text marks a kind of epistemological bracketing: it tells students, for example, that there are many ways of understanding nature; in this text, in this course, we are going to try to get inside the thinking of modern biologists to try to understand the world as they understand it, but there are *other* ways of making sense of nature, religious ways, for example, to be found within the context of the overall curriculum. Here you will learn about nature according to secular biologists or historians. The truth of the matter, or what it is reasonable to believe all things considered, is something that can be determined *only* after all the (major) alternative ways of making sense of the world have been explored. Biology teachers and texts must be free to bring in scientific verdicts, but students must appreciate the epistemological claims which inhere in a properly constructed curriculum to the effect that those verdicts (and the methods used to arrive at them) are not to be accepted uncritically but are subject to assessment in light of what is learned elsewhere in the curriculum.

The biology text and teacher can be part of a neutral curriculum though they are not neutral. It is essential that they not say: "Here is the final truth," or "Here is what it is most reasonable to believe all things considered." The text and teacher must say: "Here is the truth as biologists understand it," or "Here is what biologists hold it is reasonable to believe." The school—by virtue of its curriculum—must not explicitly say that the truth resides in the biology text and course; nor can it say this implicitly by not providing a religion course. Students should learn about scientific ways of understanding nature, but they should learn about religious ways of understanding nature as well so that the curriculum does not uncritically convey the assumption that science is sufficient for understanding nature. Hence each individual text and course should be at least *minimally* fair (acknowledging the competition), and the overall curriculum should be *robustly* fair, requiring some significant study of religion—at least a full course, taught by teachers qualified to teach about it.

Must religion courses be religiously neutral? The Establishment Clause requires neutrality among religions, so no particular religion should be singled out as better, or as more true, than others. Required courses should be comparative, dealing with several religious traditions. This does not mean, as I have argued, that scholarly perspective and comparative criticism (looking at each of the alternatives, critically, from the viewpoint of the others) should not be allowed.

Should the text, teacher, and course be free to promote religion in general? If we are to be neutral, we treat religion the way we treat its competitors. Religion should be taught empathetically and taken seriously as a contender for the truth, just as science should be taught empathetically and taken seriously as a contender for the truth. But in neither case should students be taught that religion (much less any particular religion) or science is, finally, true if we are to be neutral.

In courses in which students have acquired some maturity (which should be all religion courses), teachers may express their own views without jeopardizing the neutrality of the course; to very mature students teachers might even argue for a point of view without abdicating neutrality, as long as they do this in a way that clearly distinguishes their position from the official (neutral) course conclusions.

Schools typically require teaching *about* religion (which is supposed to be neutral but is often reductive) at the same time they allow the teaching *of* science and social science. Students are almost always taught to accept science uncritically, apart from any critical discussion of contending alternatives; they are taught to use the concepts of science to make sense of reality. The philosopher of science Paul Feyerabend has described this asymmetry provocatively by writing that although we enjoy "a separation between state and church, there is no separation between state and science."[21] I am arguing for a parallel separation: students should be taught "about" science just as they are taught "about" religion.

Like all government institutions, public schools should be religiously neutral and the most important way to be neutral is to provide curricular neutrality. Schools should not stack the deck for or against religion in providing students with their fundamental orientation in the world. Although no public school would announce that it has taken sides on religiously contested matters, virtually all do so by virtue of curricula that ignore religion and include courses that teach students to think and feel about the world in ways that conflict with religion. Most teachers, administrators, and parents are unaware of this because they have learned from their own educations to separate their religious beliefs from virtually everything else they believe.

Arguments against Neutrality

The Appeal to Democracy. We are a religious people and this is a democracy, so why not vote? If most Americans are Christians, why not teach the truth of Christianity in our schools? Or even if we acknowledge the pluralism of America, we might ask why in a small community where everyone, or virtually everyone, is Christian (or Protestant or Baptist) neutrality must rule the school day.

But the United States is a constitutional, not a pure, democracy. Our constitution guarantees rights to people that cannot be taken away by a majority vote. We saw fit, at our founding, to remove religion from democratic politics by way of the First Amendment, and, as I have argued, there continue to be good political reasons (of civility, peace, and political enfranchisement) for refusing to submit educational policy concerning religion to a vote. Members of majority religious traditions should also keep in mind that they might become members of disestablished minorities over time or as they move from community to community.

Neutrality among Religions. Neutrality must hold among religions as well as between religion and nonreligion. This presents two potential problems. First, since *all* religions cannot be studied in-depth (given the number of pages in the text and hours in the school day), neutrality is impossible. Second, it would be foolish to attempt to be neutral between, for example, Confucianism and Christianity, spending as much time on the former as on the latter.

Obviously there are practical limitations on neutrality; texts and courses can only consider the *major* religious alternatives. But this doesn't mean that we must give up on neutrality completely. We can (and should) be more rather than less neutral.

In referring to the "major" religious alternatives, I am not making value judgments but referring to influence.[22] Inevitably, most courses and textbooks discuss the most influential ideas and institutions. Of course, what is influential depends on the course: are we talking about North Carolina history, U.S. history, or world history, for example? In discussing Christianity but not Confucianism in our study of American history we are making no value judgment about the respective merits of these religions, just as in requiring students to study American rather than Chinese history we make no value judgment about the relative merits of America and China. It is inevitable and proper that Christianity and Judaism receive much more attention in most courses because they have been much more influential in shaping the history of the West, the history of America, and contemporary American culture. Fairness and neutrality do not impose an equal time requirement.

But not all courses assume a context in which Judaism and Christianity are the most influential religions. Students should take courses in world history and cultures in which a variety of (non-Western) religions are discussed. The introductory course in religion that I would require of all students would be multicultural, giving them some sense of the variety of religious ways of understanding the world. The message cannot be that Christianity (or any religion) is the true, or most reasonable, religion.

Finally, it is wise for teachers to be familiar with local minority traditions and incorporate some discussion of them into appropriate classes.

Implicit Relativism. It can be argued that neutrality undermines the sense that there is truth, that there are more or less reasonable ways of thinking about the world. Mary Warnock has suggested that the image of teachers standing apart from the fray of warring ideas has something of the feel of "the nightmare of knitters at the guillotine."[23] Must neutrality lead students to conclude that no view is better than any other? Dennis Cuddy has expressed the concern of many religious folks well: to teach about religion neutrally is to neutralize students' religious beliefs.[24]

Efforts to be neutral often go awry for lack of sophistication. Charles Haynes has pointed out that "in an attempt to sound 'tolerant' or 'neutral,' people speak of all religions as 'all the same' underneath their differences. . . . For many religious people, however, such 'toleration' from others distorts their faith and is anything but neutral. . . . The view that all faiths are ultimately the same may be compatible with some world views, but this is itself a philosophical position."[25] Many times I have heard teachers say: "There is no right answer" or "You must decide." Sometimes they simply mean that there is no *obvious* right answer, and in some sense it is true that we must, each of us, decide. But what many students hear is that all points of view are equally good.

The teacher's (or text's) official neutrality must not blind students to the fact that disagreements among contending worldviews are disagreements about what the *truth* is. I have argued that neutrality is compatible with a good deal of hard critical thinking about alternatives. Moreover, I have argued that for students of some maturity it is possible for teachers to say what they believe and perhaps even argue for a particular conclusion while maintaining official course neutrality. Indeed, the teacher's own convictions about the truth might be called into service here for, as Haynes points out, students learn a valuable lesson when they see "that people with deep convictions are able to teach and learn about the convictions of others in ways that are fair and balanced."[26]

Perhaps the most difficult task teachers have is impressing on students the difference between relativism and neutrality. Teachers should explain the epistemological, political, moral, and constitutional reasons why they must remain neutral in discussions of religion. A careful discussion of pedagogy is itself a powerful way of educating students and making this point.

My Conception of Neutrality Is Too Weak. It might be argued that given the extent of our problem, one course in religion, together with a little cross-referencing in other courses, falls far short of producing a true neutrality between religion and nonreligion.

But not every minute of a science or social science class must be balanced by a minute of religion, for there is much that students learn in science that is not religiously contested. It is the underlying worldview, the adequacy of scientific method to capture all of reality, and the most fundamental theories that create the conflict. Perhaps most important, it is the fact that the ultimate truth and adequacy of science is conveyed uncritically that requires balancing. Certainly one good course in religion can do a great deal to raise the critical questions, offer a variety of alternative accounts, and nurture critical thinking about the shape of reality.

There are other ways of creating fairness and neutrality in the curriculum.

First, with properly certified religion teachers, schools should offer a variety of classes in religion. (See the Postscript.)

Second, even though the Supreme Court has held out-of-school religious release time to be constitutional, aggressive release-time programs of religious education are rare. Much more might be done to educate students about their own religious traditions.

Third, serious consideration should be given to what Richard Baer has called "campus schools," which consist of public "central core schools" offering most standard subjects and "independent subschools" that are "situated close to the central school, perhaps in the same building. A student might take one or two classes a day in one of the subschools and the remaining classes in the central school. This would permit Catholics, Jews, evangelical Protestants, ecology-minded humanists, and others to teach sensitive subjects from their own particular perspectives but still have their students mix with children from different backgrounds."[27] Such schools might provide some imaginative mix of public and private education.

Neutrality Isn't Religiously Neutral. Historically and philosophically, neutrality has been a liberal virtue. Certainly many religious conservatives see little good in treating the truth (as they understand it) neutrally alongside religious and secular ideas and values they take to be false. In promoting fairness and neutrality, do we in effect discriminate against conservative religion?

Yes and no. It is true that to require students to learn about secular and religious alternatives to their own religious traditions is not neutral between those very conservative parents who would indoctrinate their children and those relatively more liberal parents who believe their children should be exposed to an array of alternatives. But liberal education is, or should be, neutral between the contending ideas, values, and worldviews, held by religious and secular, conservative and liberal, parents. A truly liberal education will take conservative (as well as liberal) ideas and values seriously—and in our secular culture this is no small thing. Of course many educators want to ensure that their own conceptions of the True and the Good capture the hearts and minds of their students; this is as true of liberals as it is of conservatives. But the purpose of a liberal education cannot be to turn students into liberals; it must be to nurture an informed and reasoned conversation about the many live, contending points of view in our culture.

Is this enough to satisfy religious conservatives? Many liberals assume that everyone on the "religious right" wants schools to teach only his or her own ideas and values. Charles Haynes, who knows the practical politics of religion and public education better than anyone, has written that "while there are extreme voices in the debate, we know from experience that most teachers, parents, administrators, and school board members are committed to a principled dialogue, and to fair, open public schools. This includes the vast majority of parents often labeled as members of the 'religious right.' Sadly, a few groups on either side [of our culture wars] thrive on 'demonizing' the opposition. . . . Tactics such as these may successfully raise millions of dollars through direct mail, but they destroy the fabric of our life together as citizens." Michael Ebert of Focus on the Family, a powerful conservative group, argues that religious parents "do not ask for public schools to endorse their faith. They ask for a place at the table and a voice in the process."[28] In effect, they ask for fairness and neutrality.

No doubt other conservatives give a rather different twist to the analysis of neutrality. For them, the most neutral policy the state could adopt is not one that requires religiously neutral public schools but one that gives parents the resources to educate their children in whatever way they believe best, *whether it be religiously neutral or not*. That is, the state should treat religious and public (secular) schools neutrally; neutrality requires vouchers or some system of true educational choice. I will postpone my analysis of this position until chapter 12, where I deal with it at some length.

One final argument against neutrality is important enough to warrant extended discussion. Should academic freedom give teachers, at least in universities, the right to take sides on religiously contested questions? This is my question in the next chapter.

Conclusions

In the late 1980s the National Council for the Social Studies, the Association for Supervision and Curriculum Development, the American Association of School Administrators, and, most impressively, the seventeen major educational and religious organizations that endorsed *Religion in the Public School Curriculum: Questions and Answers* issued statements on the role of religion in public schools. All agreed on the importance of including religion in the public school curriculum and on how to do it—neutrally, in accord with the principles articulated in the 1963 *Schempp* decision. There has come to be something of a new consensus about religion in public education.

These statements are extremely important correctives, both to the previous situation in which public schools promoted religion and to the present situation in which religion has been essentially ignored. Where this new consensus falls short is in failing to acknowledge the depth of the conflict between religious and secular ways of understanding the world—and the curricular implications. As a result, the "natural inclusion" of religion in existing courses has become the conventional wisdom. If we are to take religion seriously, however, and if there is to be neutrality between religion and nonreligion, then the study of religion must be required in some depth.

I have argued on epistemological, political, moral, and constitutional grounds that neutrality is a virtue that must be respected in public schools— at least when religion is at issue. Reasonableness, political civility and inclusivity, respect for the integrity of students, and an informed understanding of the Establishment Clause all dictate a policy of fairness to, and neutrality among, those contending religious and secular ideas about which we so deeply disagree. All texts and courses that deal with religiously contested questions should be at least minimally fair, providing some kind of philosophical preface in which the controversial nature of the issues discussed is made clear. But given the extent to which secular philosophical assumptions inform the methods and conclusions of the various disciplines, the only way to achieve a robust fairness and neutrality is to require that students take at least one substantial (year-long) course in religion as part of their liberal education.

A Note on Prayer

The role of religion in the curriculum is, I believe, a much more important issue than school prayer, yet much more public attention has been focused on prayer, at least since the Supreme Court ruled school prayer unconstitutional in 1962. Indeed, hundreds of prayer amendments have been introduced into Congress since then—many of them by Senator Jesse Helms, who has said: "I think it is possible to pinpoint when the decline of this country really began. It began when Madalyn Murray O'Hair . . . conspired with Communist attorneys who came to her home to orchestrate the lawsuit that resulted in the first Supreme Court decision banning prayer."[29] No doubt many people agree with him. A hundred years after religion disappeared from textbooks and the curriculum many schools continue to practice religion. A 1985 national survey of school administrators revealed that in spite of the Supreme Court's ban on official school prayers, 14.7 percent of school districts (42.7 percent in the South) still conducted prayers.[30] I want to be clear that my arguments for studying religion do not justify the practice of religion.

In chapter 3 I noted Justice Stewart's dissent in *Schempp*, in which he argued that to disallow religious exercises in schools is to take sides against religion, forsaking neutrality. There is a superficial similarity to my argument that by ignoring religion in the curriculum the state, in effect, takes sides against it. But the two cases are significantly different. As Justice Brennan noted, the school day is limited; students have time each day and on weekends in which to participate in religious exercises. Merely by taking a limited amount of students' time the state is not demonstrating hostility to religion any more than a business demonstrates hostility to religion by failing to gather its employees together to pray at the beginning of the workday. (I trust that anyone who favors school prayer also favors official workplace prayer.) If the state controlled students' time and movements completely (as it does with prisoners), it would have to fund chaplains and places of worship to maintain neutrality.

Of course, one might respond that students can study religion at home in the evenings and on weekends, so why require it in schools? Because when textbooks and the curriculum systematically ignore religious ways of understanding religiously contested questions or, worse, teach conflicting views, they *do* take sides, demonstrating at least an implicit hostility to religion. Moreover, to take religion seriously in textbooks and the curriculum (as I have described it) is not to promote religion, but to pray *is* to promote religion. The study of religion can be conducted neutrally; to pray is to take sides.

The current controversy centers on graduation prayers. In spite of the Supreme Court's 1992 ban on graduation prayers in *Lee* v. *Weisman*, the Fifth Circuit Court of Appeals upheld their constitutionality later that same year in *Jones* v. *Clear Creek Independent School District*. The Texas school system policy that passed the appellate court's muster required that prayers be student led and student initiated by way of vote of the senior class (unlike the Rhode Island policy addressed in *Weisman* whereby school officials mandated the prayer); it also required that any prayers be nonsectarian and nonproselytizing. The Fifth Circuit Court held that such prayers are the result of (private) student choice rather than (official) government policy. Moreover, their primary purpose and effect, according to the court, are not religious but secular: to solemnize the occasion.[31]

The Supreme Court's refusal to review this ruling was widely interpreted as sanctioning at least one category of official school prayers, and school administrators across the country soon received letters from Rev. Pat Robertson's American Center for Law and Justice threatening lawsuits if they would not allow such student-initiated graduation prayers. At least six states have now passed laws allowing student-initiated prayer in schools (usually phrased in terms of "nonsectarian, nonproselytizing" prayer), and another four states and the District of Columbia have debated such laws.[32] Affiliates of the ACLU have responded in turn, threatening lawsuits if prayers are allowed.

The fact that the Supreme Court refused to review the appellate court ruling cannot be taken to mean they approved of it. The Court reviews only a tiny fraction of the cases appealed to it. Almost certainly the Court will have to consider student-initiated prayers soon, however, for lower courts disagree about their constitutionality. Federal courts in Idaho and Florida have allowed such prayers, while courts in Iowa and Virginia and the Ninth Circuit Court have found them unconstitutional. In issuing a temporary restraining order against student-initiated prayers in a New Jersey school, the Third Circuit Court of Appeals declared: "The graduation ceremony is a school sponsored event; the fact that the school board has chosen to delegate the decision regarding one segment of the ceremony to the members of the graduating class does not alter that sponsorship, does not diminish the effect of a prayer on students who do not share the same or any religious perspective, and does not serve to distinguish in any material way, the facts of this case from the facts of *Lee* v. *Weisman*.'"[33] When the Supreme Court does pass judgment, I expect it will rule that student-initiated prayer is unconstitutional, for the policy that allows the prayer grants authority to conduct a religious exercise at an official governmental ceremony.

There is another problem with school prayer. Even the most conservative members of the Court argue that to pass constitutional muster prayer must be nonsectarian; it must not take sides among religions. But, as Justice Souter argued in *Weisman*, there is no such thing as nonsectarian prayer.[34] All prayers are formulated in the language and symbols of some religion rather than others. Indeed, in some religious traditions there is no such thing as prayer (and if we believe that secular humanism is a religion must we then affirm it somehow if we are to be nonsectarian?). There is no such thing as nonsectarian religion; to pray is to take sides among religions.

Of course, there are theological reasons for opposing nonsectarian, solemnizing, prayers. Lynn Buzzard, former director of the Christian Legal Society, argues that such prayers pervert the *religious* purpose of prayer. Indeed, he notes that it "is surprising that evangelicals and fundamentalists have become so easily drafted into the school prayer campaign. Of all religious groups, they ought to recognize the deeply spiritual character of prayer and reject secular forms of pseudo-piety." "Prayer is too sacred," he concludes, "to be secularized or used as a political tool."[35] Of course, such nonsectarian prayers will not serve any great moral or religious purpose: they will not rejuvenate our civilization or lead children to salvation—and they will alienate many people.

Finally, we should remember that the Supreme Court has not removed *all* prayers from public schools. Students can pray privately before math tests or with their friends on the playground. And as I noted in chapter 3, the Supreme Court has upheld the Equal Access Act allowing (high school) student religious groups to meet before and after the school day to pray if the school has established a "limited open forum" allowing other noncurricular groups to use school facilities. Only government-sponsored prayer is unconstitutional.

ACADEMIC FREEDOM

For the better part of this century scholars in universities have claimed the academic freedom to teach and publish research bound only by the constraints of responsible scholarship as that is understood in their respective disciplines. Beginning in the 1950s the Supreme Court acknowledged that academic freedom has constitutional standing grounded in the First Amendment.

Our question now is whether university teachers are free to take sides on religiously contested questions. Or must they, like public school teachers, be neutral about religion?

I begin by saying a little about the origins and rationale of academic freedom, and then explore three possible limitations on academic freedom: overly narrow conceptions of professional competence, the Establishment Clause, and obligations of fairness. Finally, I will review the more limited conception of academic freedom typically accorded public school teachers.

Background

In spite of the arguments of John Milton, John Locke, Thomas Jefferson, and John Stuart Mill, intellectual freedom was a dubious proposition at best in American colleges in the nineteenth century. As Richard Hofstadter and Walter Metzger note, in the denominational colleges of pre–Civil War America "the problem of academic freedom as we now understand it was hardly posed, for the sponsors of such colleges, on the whole, did not intend that they should be to any significant degree intellectually free, and the men who taught in them had for the most part only the slenderest aspirations toward intellectual freedom."[1]

The emphasis on the classics, tradition, moral paternalism, and mechanical drill kept professors away from controversy and probing questions. In 1832, when a member of the Jefferson Society at the University of Virginia spoke in favor of the emancipation of slaves, "the faculty reacted by ruling that 'there should be no oration on any distracting question of state or national policy nor on any point of theological dispute.'"[2] The term "academic freedom," when it was used at all, referred to the elective system and the freedom of students, not freedom of faculty members.[3]

As we saw in chapter 2, religion had a secure place in this world. The Bible, prayer, compulsory chapel, and revivals were a fact of life in most colleges, state sponsored as well as private. Before the Civil War, nine out of ten college presidents were ministers, as were a third of the faculty.[4] Throughout much of the nineteenth century, there were more or less formal religious tests for hiring, and teachers were expected to defend religion in the classroom.[5] Colleges were far removed from the marketplace of ideas; their task was to conserve and pass on to students the old and established truths.

Only toward the end of the nineteenth century did college teachers begin to think of themselves also as researchers—that is, as "re-searchers" for *new* knowledge, largely under the influence of modern science. In this context freedom became important.[6] The example of German research universities, where thousands of Americans studied in the second half of the nineteenth century, proved crucial in enabling American scholars to formulate a doctrine of academic freedom. In Germany academic freedom had two aspects: *Lernfreiheit*, the freedom of students to choose their own (elective) course of studies, and *Lehrfreiheit*, the freedom of professors to conduct research and teach as reason led them, in an atmosphere free from constraints and censorship. A major reason academic freedom arose in Germany, rather than America, was that there legal authority in universities rested with a self-governing faculty; universities were essentially faculty associations and scholars were legally free to define their own academic freedom. In America, universities were (and are) governed by boards of trustees. In Germany faculty were management; in America they were employees.

Concerns for academic freedom began to be articulated in disputes over evolution, but by the turn of the century Darwinism was triumphant and religion had been largely exiled from the curriculum. Academic freedom came of age during the war of economic ideologies during the first decades of the twentieth century. Boards of trustees, increasingly made up of successful businessmen, tended to be conservative; their faculties, practicing the new social sciences, often challenged the economic status quo—and many teachers lost their positions as a result. (Ideologically it could work both ways: the conservative economics department of Kansas State Agricultural College was fired after the election of 1896 for not accepting the Populist position on free silver, though when the Republicans carried the next elections three years later, the new populist economists were, in turn, dismissed.[7])

Academic freedom in America received its most important definition and institutional support from the American Association of University Professors, which was formed in 1915. Its *Declaration of Principles*, adopted that year, says nothing about student freedom (*Lernfreiheit*) but draws on and expands the freedom of research and teaching (*Lehrfreiheit*) enjoyed in German universities, to include the freedom of university scholars to speak and act freely outside the classroom, in their role as citizens, without jeopardizing their standing in the university.

In all domains of knowledge, the *Principles* assert, "the first condition of progress is complete and unlimited freedom to pursue inquiry and publish its results." The Enlightenment roots of this view are evident: "Such freedom is the breath in the nostrils of all scientific activity." The university should be "an intellectual experiment station, where new ideas may germinate and where their fruit, though still distasteful to the community as a whole, may be allowed to ripen until finally, perchance, it may become a part of the accepted intellectual food of the nation or of the world." If the dangers of ecclesiastical censorship and control had declined by 1915, the dangers of political and economic control had increased. Academic freedom and the tenure system that protects such freedom are absolutely necessary if the public is to be sure that teachers and researchers are motivated by a concern for the truth and do not simply echo the opinions of "the individuals who endow or manage universities. To the degree that professional scholars, in the formation and promulgation of their opinions, are, or by the character of their tenure appear to be, subject to any motive other than their own scientific conscience and a desire for the respect of their fellow-experts, to that degree the university teaching profession is corrupted." The responsibility of the university scholar "is primarily to the public itself, and to the judgment of his own profession," not to his employer.[8]

The AAUP has since clarified and drawn out the implications of its 1915 statement, but the *Principles* continue to stand as the primary definition of academic freedom in American universities. In public schools, academic freedom is more restricted.

If scholars possess "complete and unlimited" academic freedom, as the *Principles* claim, then surely they are free to take sides on religiously contested questions.

Professional Competence

There are constraints. Teachers are not free to promote or attack religion gratuitously in ways unrelated to the courses they are teaching or to their discipline. The 1940 AAUP statement on academic freedom and tenure states that the teacher "should be careful not to introduce into his teaching controversial matter which has no relation to his subject."[9] But not all arguments for or against religion are gratuitous. The methods and conclusions of much scholarship bear on the truth or falsity of religious claims, and it would seem reasonable to point this out to students.

Academic freedom is limited to what scholars are professionally competent to claim, however. The AAUP *Principles* assert that the "liberty of the scholar within the university to set forth his conclusions, be they what they may, is conditioned by their being conclusions gained by a scholar's methods."[10] According to a 1953 resolution adopted by the AAUP, "The tests of the fitness of a college teacher should be his integrity and his *professional competence*, as demonstrated in instruction and research."[11] So, for example, a historian who taught students that the Holocaust did not happen would almost surely be incompetent, and academic freedom was never meant to defend incompetence. Similarly, a scholar's defense of, or attack on, religion must be professionally competent if it is to be protected. In this respect, academic freedom is a considerably more restrictive notion than free speech.

Who determines competence? Not trustees, legislators, or the public, but one's scholarly peers, which creates the potential for problems. The *Principles* are very clear about the dangers to academic freedom from economic and political elites and from popular opinion—from sources outside the university. But they contain no mention of dangers resulting from pressures for orthodoxy *within* the world of scholarship. Derek Bok, formerly the president of Harvard University, claims that there is general agreement that universities "should not penalize a professor or block his promotion or appointment because they disapprove of his political, economic, or moral views." Yet in practice, he continues, "it is all too easy to mask a distaste for a person's ideological beliefs by arguing that his writings are poorly reasoned or superficial."

Nonetheless, Bok is optimistic: "With sufficient effort . . . it is usually possible to separate ideological judgments from assessments of a scholar's intellectual capacity, and most universities will take the greatest pains to do so."[12]

One does not have to believe with the Cultural Left that all knowledge is political to conclude that the situation is somewhat messier than Bok suggests. As David Rabban has pointed out, it is often impossible "to separate ideological from disciplinary objections to academic work." For example, does "a liberal law professor oppose critical legal studies or the Chicago school of economics because he has political objections to radical and conservative positions, or because he finds little merit in their intellectual approaches to legal issues? Does a radical law professor favor critical and feminist legal theory over traditional doctrinal analysis for intellectual or political reasons?" There simply is no neat way to separate moral and political matters from our understanding of reason and competence.[13]

The difficult cases are not those that grow out of a department's or a discipline's "distaste" for someone's views; rather, they are the cases that grow out of basic philosophical differences regarding what counts as good scholarship, proper method, viable evidence, and being reasonable. As Metzger notes, "Academic freedom does not theoretically justify all kinds of intellectual nonconformity, but only that kind of nonconformity that proceeds according to the rules. . . . In the modern theory, though no conclusion is unchallengeable, the method for arriving at conclusions is prescribed." In this, academic freedom "makes fewer allowances for vagaries of opinion than do, say, the doctrines of Milton and Mill."[14]

There are, of course, academic orthodoxies and heresies. In the late 1940s and 1950s, it was extremely difficult for Marxist scholars to find or keep positions. For decades after World War II most American philosophy departments excluded continental European philosophy—existentialism, phenomenology, neo-Thomism, and Marxism—from their curricula. Some psychology and psychiatry departments have an orthodoxy, whether it be behaviorism, neurological psychology, Freudianism, or humanistic psychology. To teach in most women's studies programs nowadays, one must be a feminist—perhaps even a "radical" feminist. In some other departments, being a feminist can disqualify one for a position.

The conventional wisdom in much academic life is that religious questions are beyond the intellectual pale, being matters of faith and metaphysics, and as such no fit matter for a scholar to take seriously. Robert Bellah tells about an experience he had at the University of Michigan in 1986, in a symposium on values and ethics in higher education. A professor who commented on Bellah's talk unleashed a violent attack, not on what I had said so much, but on *Habits of the Heart*, because *Habits of the Heart* is a book sympathetic to religion. And we all know where religion ends—it always ends with Jerry Falwell and the destruction of free inquiry and the destruction of everything that the free university stands for.

Then he turned to me and he said, "You shouldn't be teaching at the University of California at Berkeley. You should be at Notre Dame. Or," he said, "better yet, Bob Jones University."

And then he turned to the audience and said, "The secular university, love it or leave it."

Bellah calls this "enlightenment fundamentalism" because its advocates believe "in the absolute rightness of their point of view. They don't even imagine there is an alternative. Anyone else is simply wrong, an enemy of freedom."[15]

Such confrontations are not common, in large part because something like Bellah's "enlightenment fundamentalism" does pervade much of higher education. In some fields, religious interests and beliefs are taken to indicate a quaint sentimentalism at best and a departure from rationality at worst. Even to argue that religious claims are false may be improper, for religion is not something one can argue about—or so the argument often goes. According to constitutional law scholar Michael McConnell, "It can scarcely be doubted that religious perspectives are systematically suppressed and silenced in the modern academy under the banner of 'objective' professional or disciplinary norms." Indeed, he asks, "Is there any major intellectual or ideological perspective so 'invisible' in the modern academy as the religious?"[16] Is there room in a psychology department for debates about the soul? Economics departments in public universities have made room for a few Marxists, but there are probably fewer scholars who teach economics from a Catholic perspective. And how many scientific creationists are there in biology departments?

There are, of course, reasons for this suspicion of religion. For many centuries the church denied voice to secular ideas and values. Established religion has been, historically, a great enemy of academic freedom. Hence, as George Marsden has noted, for many scholars the exclusion of religious views was "not seen as restrictions on academic freedom. Their positivist-progressive paradigm dictated that any decline in traditional religious privilege was an advance for freedom."[17] But now the academic establishment is almost entirely secular, and religious voices are rarely heard. Philosophical and theological defenses of religion cannot be competent, the implicit argument goes, given what we secular scholars mean by reason, objectivity, and good scholarship.

It is highly unlikely that one could earn a Ph.D. or acquire tenure if one is too far (or perhaps at all) outside the range of orthodox views within a department or a discipline. Raises and promotions are not likely to follow if one does not publish in the orthodox journals. That is, there are philosophical litmus tests which scholars must pass to succeed in their careers. Indeed, Richard Schmitt has suggested that "the first step toward realizing anything resembling academic freedom in America . . . is to accept the fact that academics themselves are as guilty as anyone of violating academic freedom."[18]

In 1985 the AAUP published "Some Observations on Ideology, Competence, and Faculty Selection," in which it claimed that a university is "derelict in one of its most significant responsibilities" if it rejects prospective faculty members because "of their attack on approaches or doctrines that constitute the current conventional wisdom of their disciplines." What counts as good scholarly work is determined by "deep presuppositions" that "cannot, in the nature of things, be proved right or wrong."[19] Of course, it is difficult to escape those presuppositions to weigh alternative approaches, but the very nature of the university should make it wary of any possible orthodoxy within the disciplines.

According to one postmodernist line of argument, the whole idea of professional competence makes no sense, for it presupposes that there are objective standards by which the competence of scholars can be judged. But how are those standards justified? If all knowledge is "local" knowledge (as postmodernism maintains) and relative to the ideological commitments of particular communities, then it makes no sense to talk about objectivity. In our postmodern intellectual life we have conflicting conceptions of knowledge, none more "objectively" grounded than others; there are no standards that transcend ideology. So, for example, questions about the competence of feminist scholarship within a traditional department will inevitably be matters of cultural politics rather than objective professional standards. But if judgments of professional competence cannot be made, then what is academic freedom but a pious name for politics by other means?

I am unwilling to give up on the idea of professional competence (as I am unwilling to give up on the idea of reasonableness). Everything is not a matter of politics. I offer three observations.

First, no doubt much talk of reason and objectivity *does* mask ideological disagreement, and scholars do sometimes use judgments of competence as a pretext to rule out points of view they dislike, feel uncomfortable with, or are simply unacquainted with. I suggest that the obvious philosophical difficulties

in defining objectivity and professional competence within virtually all academic disciplines should make those disciplines much more tolerant of diversity than they often are.

Indeed, I suggest that academic freedom should not merely protect dissenting voices, it should encourage them. It should nurture what Edward
LeRoy Long has called a "dynamic ethos" of freedom.[20] The threats to academic freedom are not simply external to the university; they are internal and
result from that "hardening of the categories" (as Neil Postman puts it) that
sets in when there is not enough new blood in a department or discipline.[21] Diversity must be sought out, not just protected should it happen to appear.

Second, how should professional competence be defined? I make only this
suggestion. To be hired and to be given tenure scholars should fully understand and be prepared to engage (not defend) the prevailing range of orthodox methods within their disciplines. But being able to do that, they should
have the freedom to reject those orthodoxies with the blessing of the powers
that be.

Finally, with all of its mind-numbing potential, American culture is, in the
end, much more a marketplace of serious ideas than any university. A good
newsstand will carry a variety of intellectual journals which argue in cogent
and informed ways for various ways of thinking and living that find little expression, if any, in universities. In particular, we are carrying on a lively, *reasoned*, conversation about religion in American public life that has little echo
within universities. (Perhaps the most obvious sign of the truncated nature of
intellectual life in public universities is the absence of theology from the curriculum—a matter that will concern us at some length in chapter 10.) When
an engagement with religious issues is taken to be evidence of professional incompetence then competence has been defined much too narrowly.

Of course, there must be professional standards: competence must be assessed; everything cannot pass muster. As Kenneth Strike puts it, "Educational institutions cannot be run as though they were speaker's corner at
Hyde Park." The "process of rejection is necessary to intellectual progress. If
disciplines were not able to exclude failed ideas, they would be overcome by a
cognitive Babel."[22] Our problem is not an easy one.

The Constitution

The Supreme Court began to address questions of academic freedom in the
1950s, largely as a consequence of legislative efforts to exclude communists
from the academy. In *Sweezy* v. *New Hampshire* (1957), Chief Justice Earl
Warren wrote that the "essentiality of freedom in the community of American

universities is almost self-evident." He continued: "No one should underestimate the vital role in a democracy that is played by those who guide and train
our youth. To impose any strait jacket upon the intellectual leaders in our colleges and universities would imperil the future of our nation. . . . Scholarship
cannot flourish in an atmosphere of suspicion and distrust. Teachers and students must always remain free to inquire, to study and to evaluate, to gain
new maturity and understanding; otherwise our civilization will stagnate and
die."[23] Perhaps the landmark case was *Keyishian* v. *Board of Regents* (1966),
in which, as constitutional scholar William Van Alstyne puts it, the Court
"placed the protection of academic freedom within the *core* of the first amendment."[24] Writing for the Court, Justice Brennan said:

> Our nation is deeply committed to safeguarding academic freedom, which
> is of transcendent value to all of us and not merely to the teachers con-
> cerned. That freedom is therefore a special concern of the First Amend-
> ment, which does not tolerate laws that cast a pall of orthodoxy over the
> classroom. . . . The classroom is peculiarly the "marketplace of ideas." The
> Nation's future depends upon leaders trained through wide exposure to
> that robust exchange of ideas which discovers truth "out of a multitude of
> tongues, [rather] than through any kind of authoritative selection."[25]

The Supreme Court, and not just the AAUP, underwrites academic freedom, protecting teachers from laws and government action that would limit
what teachers can say, imposing a "pall of orthodoxy" over the classroom. Perhaps unhappily, it is also true, as David Rabban has noted, that "the Supreme
Court's glorification of academic freedom as a 'special concern of the First
Amendment' has produced hyperbolic rhetoric but only scant, and often ambiguous, analytic content. The Court has never explained systematically the
theory behind its relatively recent incorporation of academic freedom into the
first amendment, a problem occasionally acknowledged by the justices themselves."[26] In particular, it has never provided an account of the relationship of
the Court's view of academic freedom to that of the AAUP.

Moreover, the courts have, over the last few decades, articulated a principle
that can be used to restrict individual academic freedom. In a concurring opinion in *Sweezy*, Justice Frankfurter noted the "'four essential freedoms' of a
university—to determine for itself on academic grounds who may teach, what
may be taught, how it shall be taught, and who may be admitted to study."[27]
The university has the right to govern itself; it possesses an "institutional"
academic freedom. The problem, Rabban notes, is the increasing amount of
litigation initiated by scholars against universities as "administrators and
trustees have invoked institutional academic freedom not as an additional

layer of protection for professors against the state, but as a bar to judicial review of claims against universities by professors alleging institutional violations of individual academic freedom."[28] Institutional academic freedom—the right of the university to govern itself—is being used to regulate and restrict the individual academic freedom of teachers.

Public school teachers do not have the right to promote or denigrate religion in the classroom; as agents of the state they are required by the Establishment Clause to remain neutral on religion. If a good deal of indirect or subtle denigration of religion is common, as we have seen, it is probably true that any public school teacher who taught in any *overt* way the truth or falsity of any central religious claims would be subject to legal action. Is the situation legally different in universities? What happens when the Establishment Clause—requiring neutrality in the classroom—butts up against academic freedom, a "core" First Amendment right? Does the Establishment Clause cast a "pall of orthodoxy" over the classroom, dictating what can and cannot be said on religiously contested questions?

There is only one federal court case—*Bishop* v. *Aronov* (1991)—in which the courts have adjudicated such a conflict. According to the court record, Phillip Bishop, an assistant professor of exercise physiology at the University of Alabama at Birmingham, "occasionally referred to his religious beliefs during instructional time, remarks which he prefaced as personal 'bias.'"[29] Some of his comments referred to his understanding of the creative force behind human physiology; at other times he talked about the importance of religious belief in helping people deal with stress.[30] He also organized an optional after-class session for students who wished to pursue "Evidences of God in Human Physiology"—though he graded exams blind so as to show no bias against students who did not participate in the session. After complaints from students, the university sent him a memorandum which affirmed its commitment to academic freedom but nonetheless required him to discontinue "the interjection of religious beliefs and/or preferences during instructional time" and ordered him not to hold optional sessions on religious matters. Such actions are impermissible at a public institution, the university argued, for in taking the side of religion Professor Bishop violated the Establishment Clause. Carl Westerfield, Bishop's supervisor, also noted that Bishop's comments "hurt the reputation" of the University of Alabama because "professional colleagues around the nation consider this the 'Bible belt'" and may think that "a lot of this type of activity goes on in the University."[31]

The District Court held that the First Amendment entitled Bishop to academic freedom unless the university had some compelling state interest in restricting it, and the court could find none. The Establishment Clause does not provide a "sufficiently compelling" reason to justify a "content-based discrimination" against certain points of view. Indeed, it would be a violation of the First Amendment "to allow presentation of one side of a debatable public question an advantage while suppressing the other," allowing speech hostile to religion but not speech in support of religion. The court also noted that students are not likely to conclude that just because Professor Bishop sided with religion, the state was sponsoring religion.[32]

The Eleventh Circuit Court of Appeals overruled the district court. Citing the Supreme Court's ruling in *Hazelwood School District* v. *Kuhlmeier* (1988), the appellate court argued that "'educators do not offend the First Amendment by exercising editorial control over the style and content of student [or professor] speech in school-sponsored expressive activities so long as their actions are reasonably related to legitimate pedagogical concerns.'" In this case the university had the authority to issue "reasonable restrictions" over Professor Bishop's in-class speech. Because "of the potential establishment conflict, even the appearance of proselytizing by a professor should be a real concern to the University." (The court did not claim that such proselytizing had in fact occurred, only that the university was properly concerned to ensure that it did not occur.) But doesn't such regulation restrict academic freedom? The court responded: "Though we are mindful of the invaluable role academic freedom plays in our public schools, particularly at the post-secondary level, we do not find support to conclude that academic freedom is an independent First Amendment right. And, in any event, we cannot supplant our discretion for that of the University. . . . In this regard, we trust that the University will serve its own interests as well as those of its professors in pursuit of academic freedom." That is, the court gave no weight to *individual* academic freedom as a "core" First Amendment right; consequently, the *institutional* right of the university to regulate itself took clear priority.[33]

The appellate court disagreed with the district court about how to apply the Establishment Clause. For the appellate court, the university's restrictions on Bishop "neither advance nor inhibit religion—to the contrary, the University has simply attempted to maintain a neutral, secular classroom." Religion is a personal matter which should not intrude on professional responsibilities: "The University asks only that [Professor Bishop] separate his personal and professional beliefs and that he not impart the former to his students during 'instructional time' or under the guise of the courses he teaches in so-called optional classes."[34]

The Supreme Court declined to hear the case, allowing the appellate ruling to stand.

This was an appallingly bad decision for at least six reasons. First, the appellate court paid no heed to the Supreme Court's admittedly vague but persistent claims about the centrality of individual academic freedom to the First Amendment. Second, the court took as its "polestar" the Supreme Court's decision in *Kuhlmeier*, a case concerned with a high school newspaper; incredibly, it argued by analogy that just as public school officials can regulate student speech in a student newspaper, so can university officials regulate the speech of scholars in the classroom. Third, it ignored the significance of the fact that the university discriminated against speech on the basis of its content. Indeed, by prohibiting religious accounts of a subject, the university was taking sides on religiously contested issues, thus ceasing to be religiously neutral. Fourth, the court uncritically adopted the naive view we have encountered over and over that secular teaching is by its nature neutral. Fifth, the court wrongly assumed that religious interpretations of the world must be personal rather than professional. The court record is not sufficiently nuanced to tell if Bishop's references to religion were merely personal and anecdotal or scholarly, but it is certainly possible for a teacher to talk about religious alternatives to evolution or religious ways of dealing with the stresses of living in scholarly ways. Finally, the court expressed the fear that by simply mentioning religion Professor Bishop may have been proselytizing. Arguably, he attempted to avoid proselytizing by forthrightly acknowledging his biases; this was at least a bow in the direction of intellectual honesty. Indeed, because he presented students with alternative ways of understanding his subject they were *less* likely to be indoctrinated. (Neither the university nor the court charged him with making his "personal" religious beliefs the official conclusions of the course.)

Should the university have any right to regulate Professor Bishop's academic freedom? Of course. Bishop must be professionally competent—and, in fact, the university acknowledged Bishop's competence as a teacher and researcher. (He was later granted tenure.) The problem was that he interjected his religious views into the classroom. But unless his references to religion were gratuitous and unrelated to his subject (which they were not), unless the references had no serious intellectual merit, unless he put undue emotional pressure on students to agree with him, unless he failed to respect the reasoned give and take of discussion, then, I suggest, his academic freedom was unjustifiably limited.

In appealing his case to the Supreme Court Bishop's attorneys argued that from

one generation to the next, the targets of academic intolerance shift. Where once persons of a vaguely left-wing ideology were drummed out of the academy on suspicion of being subversive, the right to teach from a Marxist point of view is now a commonplace. Today, the University of Alabama would never order a Marxist professor to stop interjecting his opinions in class. . . . Such an action would be instantly, and properly, condemned by the University community. Professor Bishop is not so fortunate. His intellectual viewpoint commands little support in academia and is considered a source of embarrassment by his superiors.[35]

What do I conclude? The appellate decision simply cannot be taken seriously as an analysis of the issues at hand. Because individual academic freedom is the sine que non of teaching in a university, scholars cannot be viewed as ordinary agents of the state. Of course, they cannot conduct prayers or practice their religion in a classroom, but the fact that they take positions on religiously contested questions in their role as teachers and scholars has no implications whatever for whether the state is taking sides on religion in violation of the Establishment Clause. Undergraduates (and judges) should be sufficiently mature to realize this.

It is also true that the university has a right to limit the academic freedom of its faculty members by controlling the curriculum (faculty members do not have the right to offer any course they want) and by requiring that faculty members teach within the limits of their competence. Professors are not free to attack or defend religion in gratuitous or unprofessional ways. Although courts should stay out of good-faith disputes between individual faculty members and universities over what counts as competence, judgments of competence cannot be used as a *pretext* for discriminating against unorthodox, unpopular, or constitutionally protected speech.[36]

Indoctrination and Academic Freedom

If university teachers are free to take sides on religiously contested questions, does this mean that they are free to profess *only* their own point of view?

I have argued that students possess the right not to be indoctrinated. The 1915 AAUP statement on academic freedom states that the university teacher

in giving instruction upon controversial matters, while he is under no obligation to hide his own opinion under a mountain of equivocal verbiage, should, if he is fit for his position, be a person of a fair and judicial mind; he should, in dealing with such subjects, set forth justly, without suppression or innuendo, the divergent opinions of other investigators;

he should cause his students to become familiar with the best published expressions of the great historic types of doctrine upon the questions at issue; and he should, above all, remember that his business is not to provide his students with ready-made conclusions, but to train them to think for themselves, and to provide them access to those materials which they need if they are to think intelligently.[37]

Interestingly, the AAUP's 1966 "Statement on Professional Ethics" does not explicitly require such fairness of university teachers but claims that the primary responsibility of the professor is "to state the truth as he sees it."[38] But according to the 1982 AAUP "Recommended Institutional Regulations on Academic Freedom and Tenure" a college or university "is a marketplace of ideas, and it cannot fulfill its purposes of transmitting, evaluating, and extending knowledge if it requires conformity with any orthodoxy of content and method."[39] Similarly, the 1985 "Observations on Ideology" states: "Teaching is not the serving up of a platter of truths: students must learn how to find out what is the truth; and, where ways of finding out and assessing the truth are precisely what is under debate, good teaching requires exposing students to all major alternatives. A department ought to try to insure that different currently debated and important approaches to its subject are presented to its students fairly and objectively, so that students are able to make informed choices among them."[40]

There is, of course, a powerful tension between requiring professional competence and prohibiting "orthodoxy of content and method." However difficult this might be, it is clear that a good liberal education must ensure that students take seriously the major alternative views; standards of professional competence cannot justify indoctrination. The right to academic freedom carries with it the professional obligation to treat fairly—to take seriously—the broadest possible range of contending views.

This moral obligation constrains academic freedom at two levels. The primary way in which students are initiated into the marketplace of ideas is through a core curriculum in which they are required to inspect the wares of various sellers. If students are allowed to elect a narrow range of courses (perhaps taught by "orthodox" faculty), they run the risk of having been indoctrinated rather than liberally educated. This is incompatible with the purpose of a university. If students are to be liberally educated, the faculty must construct a curriculum that requires them to take seriously the major contending voices in our culture.[41] The faculty of a university is not free as a corporate body to ignore the purposes of a liberal education.

Second, we must distinguish between those introductory-level courses which constitute the basics of an undergraduate liberal education and more advanced courses. In chapter 6 I argued that introductory courses should enable students to make connections. Students should be initiated into a coherent conversation, not just a babble of monologues. That is, in each introductory course students must be provided with some epistemological distance on their subject, some sense of what the alternatives are, some perspective on the ways in which the discipline relates to other disciplines, and some sense of the governing orthodoxy and various heresies. The purposes of education are not well served if students are simply indoctrinated into the more or less orthodox views of each discipline in turn and left to their own devices to sort it all out. Here, I resort once more to the 1915 AAUP "Principles."

> There is one case in which the academic [university] teacher is under an obligation to observe certain special restraints—namely the instruction of immature students. In many of our American colleges, and especially in the first two years of the course, the student's character is not yet fully formed, his mind is still relatively immature. . . . The teacher ought . . . to be especially on his guard against taking unfair advantage of the student's immaturity by indoctrinating him with the teacher's own opinions before the student has had an opportunity fairly to examine other opinions upon the matter of question, and before he has sufficient knowledge and ripeness in judgment to be entitled to form any definitive opinion of his own.[42]

Not only might the teacher's "own opinions" be dangerous; disciplinary orthodoxy is equally a threat. In any introductory class (when students do not yet have their bearings within the subject matter) and, more generally, so long as students are still pursuing the broad background of a liberal education, which provides them "ripeness of judgment," teachers are obligated to be fair and not force premature judgments on students.

When do students become mature? Any line will be arbitrary. Different students will achieve the requisite maturity at different times, and in any case there is no ready test for such maturity. But there are several possibilities. No doubt it would be easiest to draw the line between high school and college, though the AAUP *Principles* suggest that the line be drawn after two years of college—that is, after the bulk of a liberal education is complete. I suggest that a more reasonable line might be drawn between introductory and advanced courses. Once students have their bearings (or at least have had the opportunity to acquire their bearings), faculty are freed from obligations of fairness.

Academic Freedom in Public Schools

There are three reasons commonly given to justify significantly less academic freedom for public school teachers than university scholars.

First, the AAUP *Principles* of academic freedom were devised by, and for, scholars, and schoolteachers are not (usually) scholars. As the conventional wisdom would have it, teachers pass on acquired knowledge, while scholars discover new knowledge; the teacher is more a conveyer of established truths, while the scholar (tentatively) establishes what is to count as truth. Hence the importance of freedom for the scholar and the necessity of limits on the freedom of teachers.

Second, public school students, even high school students, are less mature than university students. As the Court noted in *Sheldon* v. *Tucker*, "A teacher works in a sensitive area on a schoolroom. There he shapes the attitudes of young minds towards the society in which they live. In this, the state has a vital concern."[43] Students may need to be buffered from the sometimes extreme and unsettling views they would encounter if teachers enjoyed full-blown academic freedom. Moreover, they might confuse the teacher's advocacy of, or hostility to, religion with the position of school and the state.

Third, while legal authority in universities rests with a board of trustees, in practice the curriculum, choice of textbooks and reading materials, and pedagogical matters are left largely to the faculty. In public schools, curriculum and textbook decisions are typically made by state legislatures, state departments of education, and local school boards. Teachers may play some advisory role, and they will have some authority to determine how to implement decisions—but that's about it. Historically, these restrictions on teachers' freedoms have been justified in part on the basis of the local community's right to shape the education of its children—though much if not most decision making now takes place at the state level and there seems to be an increasing desire for national standards. In spite of all the talk of empowering public school teachers, they possess little of the professional autonomy of university teachers.

Courts have upheld fairly extensive rights for local school boards and states to control public education and, correlatively, limit academic freedom. As Justice Fortas put it in *Epperson*: "By and large, public education in our Nation is committed to the control of state and local authorities."[44] In *Board of Education, Island Trees Union Free School District* v. *Pico* (1982), Justice Brennan held that the "Court has long recognized that local school boards have broad discretion in the management of school affairs."[45] Even more pointedly, in *Zykan* v. *Warsaw Community School Corporation* the Seventh Circuit Court of Appeals noted that the breadth of the powers of local school boards "reflects the perception that at the secondary school level the need for education guidance predominates over many of the rights and interests comprised by 'academic freedom.'"[46]

There are limits, however. The *Epperson* court would not tolerate a state law that kept students ignorant of Darwinism. "It is much too late," Justice Fortas wrote, "to argue that the State may impose upon the teachers in its schools any conditions that it chooses, however restrictive they may be of constitutional guarantees."[47] In *Pico* Justice Brennan acknowledged that the discretion of school boards "must be exercised in a manner that comports with the transcendent imperatives of the First Amendment" and he went on to quote from *Griswold* v. *Connecticut*: "The State may not, consistently with the spirit of the First Amendment, contract the spectrum of available knowledge."[48] And in *Zykan* the court held that local boards cannot impose a "pall of orthodoxy" on secondary school classroom.

The courts have supplied no unambiguous guidelines but have attempted to balance a measure of freedom with a measure of community control. As a result, it might be said that public school teachers possess a "limited" right of academic freedom. As Tyll Van Geel puts it in his study of school law, "the board retains its authority to control the basic curriculum, but at the same time the teacher is permitted, within limits, to bring to the students' attention alternative viewpoints and perspectives. This approach prohibits the board from simply requiring the teacher to read from a board-prepared script."[49]

The school must be a marketplace of ideas; it cannot impose a pall of orthodoxy on students or contract the spectrum of available knowledge. Teachers should have the freedom to introduce students to ideas that are not to be found in the official curriculum. At the same time, however, public school teachers are agents of the state, hired to teach the state's curriculum, and that curriculum must be religiously neutral. The rationale for public schooling is largely that of common schools: they are to speak for the community as governed by our constitutional arrangements. Teachers should not take sides on religiously contested questions, either promoting or denigrating religion. They, like the curriculum, should remain officially neutral. It is one thing to give students some understanding of religious or antireligious perspectives on some contested question; it is another thing to take sides.

Of course what constitutes as taking sides is not always clear. In the last chapter I argued that teachers might remain officially neutral while expressing their personal opinions on religiously contested questions. In *Moore* v. *Gaston County Board of Education* (1973) district court judge James McMillan upheld, on grounds of academic freedom in part, the right of a seventh-grade social studies teacher to express his personal views about religion (which in his case were hostile) when questioned by his students in the context of discussing a textbook chapter on the origins of the great world religions.[50] The Ninth Circuit Court was less charitable in *Peloza* v. *Capistrano Unified School District* (1994), upholding a school directive requiring a high school biology teacher to refrain from discussing his personal religious views (which were creationist) with students on school grounds at any time during the school day, even if the discussion was initiated by students, for "the likelihood of high school students equating his views with those of the school is substantial" and the school's interest in avoiding an Establishment Clause violation trumps his right to free speech.[51] No doubt teachers might pass off their personal views as official school views, but I would argue that as long as they express what is clearly a personal opinion to students who are sufficiently mature to appreciate this, the state is not implicated and there should be no Establishment Clause problem. What teachers cannot do, as agents of the state, is proselytize, teaching students the truth or falsity of religious claims.

Because of the centrality of freedom to the purpose of a university, scholars, by contrast, are not ordinary agents of the state; what they teach as true and false has no implications for state neutrality.

No doubt this is, in some ways, a too simple distinction. A strong case can be made for conceiving of public school "teachers as intellectuals" (to use Henry Giroux's phrase[52]) rather than as mere agents or "technicians" hired simply to teach the state's curriculum (the more or less de facto situation). The demands of liberal education require teachers who are at home in the world of ideas, not teachers who simply teach to a standardized test. Moreover, as public school teachers acquire graduate degrees (in their teaching fields, not in education) they acquire some competence to make independent judgments about the importance and value of ideas in their discipline. And as they teach mature students in advanced high school courses, there should naturally be more leeway for them to argue a case, to follow reason as they understand it.

Arguably, some spectrum of possibilities should be marked out: surely there is a huge difference between elementary school teachers and research scholars in regard to their needs for academic freedom; high school and junior college teachers fall betwixt and between. We need more nuanced distinctions. But barring major reforms in how we conceive of public schools, the overriding consideration when religion is at issue must continue to be the Establishment Clause and the neutrality it requires of public institutions and their agents. This must limit the academic freedom of schoolteachers in dealing with religiously contested questions. Public school teachers are agents of the state and must respect the neutrality required of state agents.

Conclusions

Public schools—which used to be called common schools—should teach as true those beliefs that we hold in common, and when our disagreements cut deep, as is the case with religion, they should remain neutral, taking each of the (major) contending positions seriously. One purpose of the Establishment Clause is to guarantee just this. As agents of the state, public school teachers should remain neutral on religiously contested questions (though this need not keep them from expressing their personal views with suitably mature students).

Higher education and modern scholarship are alike built on the modern assumption that if progress is to be possible, scholars and university teachers must be free to pursue the truth where they will. To limit free inquiry and teaching, to establish any unquestionable orthodoxy, is to risk losing the truth. Because the nature of the institution requires that they have academic freedom, scholars are not mere agents of the state. They do not speak for the state and are not bound by the Establishment Clause. They are free to take sides on religiously contested questions.

We might consider how extraordinary it would be if scholars could not take sides on religiously contested questions. Because religion makes claims on virtually all areas of human knowledge and life, to require religious neutrality in teaching and research would, in effect, neutralize all possibility of progress. Indeed, it can be argued (and I will do so in chapter 10) that universities should both allow and encourage critical thinking about theological matters.

Academic freedom must be a two-way street. If scholars are free to teach that Freud got it right in *The Future of an Illusion* and that neo-Darwinian biology gives us a complete picture of evolution, then they must also be free to teach that people have souls and that God created the world. Of course they must *argue*, not preach; they must demonstrate professional competence. To allow criticism of religious points of view, but not defenses, would not only violate academic freedom, it would violate the Establishment Clause. (And, as George Marsden has noted, if institutions of higher learning "are unwilling to include religious perspectives among those recognized, then we might suggest some minor changes in their catalogs. For instance, where they say 'this school welcomes diverse perspectives,' there should be a note that adds: 'Except, of course, religious perspectives.' Or where their catalogs or job ads talk about discrimination, they should have a sentence that reads: 'We do discriminate on the basis of religion.'"[53])

I have also argued that academic freedom does not give scholars carte blanche to teach exclusively whatever they will. In particular, they are professionally bound to construct a curriculum that does not indoctrinate students but takes seriously and treats fairly the major contending points of view. Moreover, they have some obligation actively to nurture a "dynamic ethos" of diverse points of view within the faculty.

EVOLUTION AND ECONOMICS

It might help at this point to put a little flesh on the theoretical bones of my argument by considering how religion relates to two important subjects in the curriculum: evolution and economics. I have picked my two case studies for the contrasts they provide. The controversy over teaching evolution is long-standing; it has generated a voluminous literature and a sizable docket of court cases. There has been no similar controversy over the teaching of economics.

Evolution has been a problem almost entirely for religious conservatives; most religious liberals have uncritically accepted evolution (and, more particularly, neo-Darwinism) as God's way of doing things. The religious critique of mainstream economics, on the other hand, comes primarily from the Left, though the controversy has not spilled into the classroom; many religious conservatives have uncritically accepted capitalism (and neoclassical economic theory) as God's way of doing things.

Evolution and economics are similar in that they are subjects taught from the vantage point of scientific disciplines. Hence I begin this chapter by clarifying my understanding of the relationship of science and religion. My primary purpose, however, is to discuss how religion should figure into the study of evolution and economics given the general principles for which I have argued.

Scientific Method and Religion

There are four somewhat different ways in which we might understand the relationship of religion and science. For many religious conservatives, religious claims, grounded in Scripture or tradition, always trump science. Or, put another way, if science conflicts with religion, it must be bad science; good science and (true) religion would agree. Many creation-scientists, for example, begin from the assumption that the truth is to be found in Scripture and work as scientists to find evidence and construct theories that confirm what they already know to be true. To be a member of the Creation Research Society a scientist must affirm the inspiration of the Bible, the creative acts of God during the creation week, the historicity of the Great Flood, and Jesus Christ as savior.[1]

For some liberals science and religion present partial pictures of reality that are mutually enlightening. In chapter 5 I told Arthur Eddington's parable of the fisherman who, using a net with a three-inch mesh, concluded that there were no fishes shorter than three inches in the ocean since he never caught any. The conceptual nets of science are also selective: science requires the kind of evidence provided by sense perception (rather than by religious experience, Scripture, or revelation); it assumes that reality is lawlike and that events must be replicable (and finds no room for singular events such as miracles); it requires that reality be conceptualized in terms of causes rather than purposes; it searches for ways of controlling the world (rather than for moral guidance or religious wisdom). The scientific conceptual net was designed to catch a particular kind of fish.

But if science is selective, then it might seem reasonable to conclude that it presents us with only a partial picture of reality—one that needs to be supplemented, or perhaps even corrected, by the understanding of reality that religion provides. So, for example, the biochemist Arthur Peacocke argues that science and Christianity must always "be ultimately converging" in that he understands "the scientific and theological enterprises as interacting and mutually illuminating approaches to reality."[2] We've seen that many religious liberals give science a good deal of authority in shaping what they believe theologically about reality; similarly, scientists and social scientists must pay heed to what theologians have to say about creation, souls, and morality, for example. On this account, then, science and religion cannot ignore each other, for each is privy to aspects of reality.

It is often argued that science gives us the whole picture of reality, however: if the scientific net can't catch it, it doesn't exist. Sometimes this position
is called natural*ism* or scient*ism*—the "ism" suggesting that a philosophical
claim about ultimate reality is being made. On this account religion possesses
no independent competence to make claims about nature, and science need
not take religious claims into account in constructing its picture of nature.
Science always trumps religion.

For many, the success of Darwinism provided the final and most compelling
evidence for naturalism, for Darwin explained how nature could take the
shape it has apart from any appeal to God and purpose. The Oxford zoologist
Richard Dawkins has written that "although atheism might have been *logically* tenable before Darwin, Darwin made it possible to be an intellectually
fulfilled atheist."[3] The historian of science William Provine claims that most
evolutionary biologists have been driven to atheism by their understanding of
evolution, and the few who see no conflict between their biology and religion
"are either obtuse or compartmentalized in their thinking, or are effective
atheists without realizing it."[4] Because science is competent to tell the whole
story of reality, and because that story is, after Darwin, a compelling story,
religious claims about nature have been discredited.

There is a fourth view—one that requires some compartmentalizing. In a
1984 publication entitled *Science and Creationism: A View from the National
Academy of Sciences*, Frank Press, the academy's president, wrote that a
"great many religious leaders accept evolution on scientific grounds without
relinquishing their belief in religious principles," and he went on to cite a 1981
resolution of the Council of the National Academy of Sciences according to
which "'Religion and science are *separate and mutually exclusive* realms of
human thought whose presentation in the same context leads to misunderstanding of both scientific theory and religious belief.'" Press does not say
what falls into the domain of religious thought, but whatever it is, science
need not take it seriously for science and religion are "separate and mutually
exclusive." Hence, he concludes, it is false "to think that the theory of evolution represents an irreconcilable conflict between religion and science."[5] Science is free to ignore religion, for they are, in effect, incommensurable endeavors. Many religious liberals agree.

I have three reservations about this last account, however—particularly as
it is put forward by the NAS. First, I find an official "resolution" about the relationship of science and religion curious—as if the matter could be resolved
by a vote of scientists. After all, this is a matter of considerable controversy,
among scientists as well as among theologians. Second, as it stands, it is obviously wrong. Religious creationism does conflict with at least certain impor-

tant theories in science such as evolution. For the fundamentalist, science and religion are not separate and exclusive realms; they make competing claims about the same territory. The academy must be read to say that *true* religion (or enlightened ways of thinking about religion) do not conflict with (true) science. But do we really want scientists defining what is and is not true religion? And if scientists are competent to decide between true and false religion, then can they also be right when they say that science and religion are mutually exclusive realms of human thought? If they are mutually exclusive, whence comes science's competence regarding true and false religion?[6] But third, even if Press and the NAS are right, this would not justify scientists in ignoring religion, particularly in science texts and courses, because the relationship between science and religion is controversial; the position of the NAS is far from universally accepted. If scientists and students are to make reasoned judgments about that relationship, they must be exposed to arguments—theological arguments included—for the various alternatives.

In spite of the academy's assurances, I am skeptical of the claim that science, *at least as it is typically taught*, respects the claims made within the "separate and mutually exclusive" religious realm. As Maynard Adams puts it, science "recognizes no alien territory. It claims all reality as its province."[7] Certainly many scientists would line up behind Stephen Hawking when he argues that the "eventual goal of science is to provide a single theory that describes the whole universe."[8] In spite of the reservations of some scientists, science is typically taught as *fully adequate* to explain nature. No textbook that I have seen includes a caveat to the effect that science is inadequate to explain some aspect of nature and that religion provides some crucial part of the story. More often than not, the distinction between science (which is limited) and scientism or naturalism is lost in practice. I have already cited Thomas Kuhn's claim that with the possible exception of dogmatic theology, no subject is taught more narrowly and rigidly than science.[9] (I also suggested that the situation is worse than this, for while the educations of students of theology will surely include some, and perhaps considerable, study of science, the education of most students of science will not likely include any study of religion.) In effect, most scientists proceed by faith that scientific method *is* adequate for capturing all of reality in its conceptual nets.

Scientific method rules out certain kinds of evidence in principle. So, for example, the National Academy contrasts science with creationism in which "both authority and revelation take precedence over evidence." That is, for the academy, religious authority and revelation don't constitute evidence. Of course, the conclusions of creationism cannot "be validated when subjected to test by the methods of science."[10] But if this is the case, then, as Phillip

Johnson argues, creationism is ruled "out of court . . . before any consideration of evidence." There can be "*no* scientific points in favor of creation and there never will be any as long as naturalists control the definition of science, because creationist explanations by definition violate the fundamental commitment of science to naturalism."[11] Science wins a priori.

But why limit the evidence to what is *scientifically* available? The philosopher Alvin Plantinga suggests that the religious believer, "unlike her naturalistic counterpart, is free to look at [all] the evidence for the Grand Evolutionary Scheme, and follow it where it leads, rejecting that scheme if the evidence is insufficient. She has a freedom not available to the naturalist. The latter accepts the Grand Evolutionary Scheme because from a naturalistic point of view this scheme is the only visible answer to the question what is the explanation of the presence of all these marvelously multifarious forms of life?" The religious believer, by contrast, is not limited by any "*a priori* dogmas" but is free to consider religious as well as scientific evidence for various theories.[12]

As science is typically practiced, no religious claim could ever trump or even modify a scientific claim because scientific method allows religion no epistemological room to make claims or provide evidence about nature or human nature. No doubt within the practice of science it is rational to proceed by the rules of scientific method, but why should we accept scientific method as our final authority in delineating reality? What is reasonable, all things considered? Scientific method cannot answer this question; nor do science texts or courses deal with it.

According to the first two views I have outlined (that religion always trumps science and that they are mutually illuminating and interacting), religion is relevant to the practice and conclusions of science; according to the third and fourth views (that science always trumps religion and that they are incommensurable endeavors), science can safely ignore religion. My point, however, is that the relationship of science and religion is controversial, so students should learn something about the contending alternatives as part of a liberal education. As things are now, they learn to accept uncritically the third and fourth views (which are not likely to be carefully distinguished).

Evolution

There are at least four ways of understanding the origin of human life in modern science and the major religions of the world.

First, there is the belief held by many Christians and some Jews that all plant and animal species were created, each according to its kind, at once—

perhaps six thousand years ago—by God. The ground for this claim is the first chapter of Genesis read as a historical document.

Second, there is the belief held by most biologists, geologists, and paleontologists that the various plant and animal species were not created at once, as "natural kinds," but evolved out of other species over a period of several billion years. Obviously, the first two accounts conflict.

Arguably, the modern scientific account also conflicts with a third view, a *liberal* religious view, that evolution is the working out of God's plan, that it is purposeful. As the Catholic *Catechism* puts it, "The universe was created 'in a state of journeying' toward an ultimate perfection yet to be attained, to which God has destined it. We call 'divine providence' the dispositions by which God guides his creation toward this perfection." God is absolutely sovereign over the events of the world and its history; "the solicitude of divine providence is *concrete* and *immediate*."[13]

As we have seen, a large part of what was revolutionary about the scientific revolution was its rejection of the idea that nature, like history, could be understood only in terms of God's purposes. Darwin and his successors provided a mechanism that explained evolution apart from appeal to design—natural selection working on the random mutation and recombinations of genes. Typically, biologists take this mechanism to be sufficient to explain the evolution of species. Evolution is purposeless. Neo-Darwinian biology is incompatible not only with a six-day creation but with the idea of purposeful evolution—and hence with most nonfundamentalist religion.

What if we accept the view that science contains only a part of the story? It has often been suggested, for example, that God stands behind the Big Bang. Perhaps He set the (seemingly) purposeless billiard balls of cosmic evolution on their way 15 billion years ago knowing that human beings would eventually bounce to life.

There are two problems with such a rescue mission. First, this is not the God of most religion. The God of religion is one who intervenes in history and nature, who shapes it and interacts with it, and there is no room for such an interventionist God in science.

But second, *if* God set the whole process in motion, *if* human life is the end of nature; *if* God provides the direction for evolution, *then* science leaves the most important part out of the explanation, for *ultimately* it is God's purposes that explain the course of evolution, not natural selection and genetic mutations, which are only the "secondary" causes of evolution. (This is a little like explaining how your car ended up at the airport by talking about internal combustion engines and never mentioning your intentions.) Yet biology texts give no hint that the explanations they give might be insufficient.

The fourth view is that *scientific* evidence does not support evolution but supports creation; this is the view of creation-scientists. Some advocates of this position wish to distance creation-*science* from religion; believing the term "creation" to be religiously loaded, they prefer to talk about the "abrupt appearance" of species.[14]

Finally, there are a variety of nonbiblical religious accounts, some of which make no appeal to a creator-God.

What do Americans believe? According to a 1991 Gallup Poll, 47 percent of Americans agreed with the statement that "God created man pretty much in his present form at one time within the last 10,000 years." (The poll did not distinguish between religious and scientific creationism.) Forty percent held that "man has developed over millions of years from less-advanced forms of life, but God guided the process, including man's creation." Nine percent believed in evolution but that "God had no part in the process." Four percent believed something else or claimed not to know.[15] The more educated people are, the more likely they are to believe in evolution, and, more particularly, in Godless evolution.[16] I have seen no surveys of scientists, but I suspect that virtually all of them are evolutionists (at least all those working in biology, biochemistry, paleontology, geology, and related fields), though probably some significant percentage of them believe they can reconcile neo-Darwinian evolution with religion. A recent national survey of high school biology teachers revealed that about 30 percent of them were creationists, believing that the world was created from nothing within the last ten thousand years.[17]

What are students now taught about origins? Biology is typically an elective for both high school students and undergraduates, though it is generally required for admission to a college. In the wake of the Scopes Trial, evolution was removed from high school biology textbooks, but it reemerged after *Sputnik* and nowadays students taking biology will almost surely encounter scientific accounts of evolution, as we saw in our review of biology textbooks. Most world history texts reinforce belief in evolution in their accounts of prehistory.

What do students learn of religious accounts of the origins of life? According to one national survey, "creationism" is taught in 30.3 percent of school districts along with evolution, though what is involved in such teaching was not made clear.[18] This poll did not distinguish between scientific and religious creationism. World history texts may contain a sentence or two about religious views of origins in their sections on the major religions. Some American history texts devote several paragraphs to the Scopes Trial (though none of the five most commonly used texts in North Carolina do so). Some students may read the first chapter of Genesis in a world literature class, and a few will read *Paradise Lost* or some literary account of religious origins. Undergraduates may take an elective, undergraduate religious studies course in which origins will be discussed. In sum, college-bound students will most likely be given a good introduction to scientific evolution; exposure to religious accounts will be brief and haphazard at best.

How Should Origins Be Taught? Once again, I am not concerned with determining the truth or falsity of any particular account. My question is, What should students be taught about evolution and creation when our culture is deeply divided about the truth? My answer: A good liberal education will provide students with a critically informed understanding of the contending alternatives (maintaining, at least in public schools, neutrality among them). How does this work in practice?

I begin with creation-science. Science textbooks typically limit the range of contending alternatives they take seriously to *major, live, scientific* theories. At some point, theories are falsified to the extent that scientists no longer take them to be live alternatives. Lamarkian evolution, the view that acquired characteristics could be inherited, was once a contender for the truth, but since Darwin it has been dead (though it experienced a brief ideological resurrection as Lysenkoism in the Soviet Union) so it need no longer be taken seriously. Science textbooks typically give only cursory accounts of the historical record of dead alternatives. By contrast, some contemporary evolutionists are gradualists, and others are catastrophists, and any good biology course would explain to students the differences, taking both sides seriously. Good teachers and texts would also tell students something of how the evidence stands regarding both views and which view is held in greatest favor at the current time.

Of course, to be taken seriously a theory must also be scientific, that is, verifiable or falsifiable according to scientific method, and it is here that most scientists believe creation-science comes up short. The standard argument is that "creation-science" is a misnomer, for it is thinly disguised religion. In 1982 this view received some support from the bench when District Court judge William R. Overton ruled Arkansas's Balanced Treatment Act unconstitutional, in part on the grounds that creation-science is not a true science but religion. Overton found that the "creationists' methods do not take data, weigh it against the opposing scientific data, and thereafter reach the conclusions stated. . . . Instead, they take the literal wording of the Book of Genesis and attempt to find scientific support for it."[19] That is, creation-scientists believe that when they conflict, Scripture always trumps science.[20]

Whether creation-science is science is something for (liberally educated) scientists to decide. Of course, scientists may disagree (there are at least a *few* scientists of unquestionable credentials who believe scientific creationism should be taken seriously), and ideas of what constitutes good science do change from time to time. Indeed, the historical record makes it clear that all scientists can be wrong about very basic matters. But even if creation-science *is* science, there may be no obligation to teach about it for there is no obligation to teach about scientific views held by a small minority of scientists. In science, as in any subject, it is the major alternatives that merit pages in the textbook, and creation-science is not a major alternative—at least among scientists.

Creation-science has become a view of some importance in our cultural politics, however, and this might make it important for inclusion. An introductory biology course should prepare students for understanding ways in which biological arguments play out in culture, not just in good, academic science. Of course, if some discussion of creation-science is included in a biology text it must be treated fairly and not caricatured. Does it need to be given equal time with neo-Darwinian accounts of evolution? Of course not. Here my Principle of Philosophical Location and Weight is relevant. Students should learn that creation-science is accepted by a very small minority of scientists even if a significant number of conservative religious thinkers have come to accept it. That is, they should not see the two accounts as equally viable abstract possibilities but as alternatives with differing degrees of plausibility in the scientific and conservative religious communities.

There is, then, no obligation on biology teachers and texts to treat creation-science fairly or neutrally. Most advocates of creation-science are committed to assessing it as science, not as religion. They insist that it is qualified to run the gauntlet of scientific testing, just like any scientific theory. Most scientists believe it fails and can safely be ignored.

What about *religious* accounts of origins? Unlike creation-science, religious versions of creation (fundamentalist and liberal) possess a good deal of cultural vitality and must be taken seriously as part of a liberal education. How, and where? There are three possibilities: in biology courses, in world history or literature courses, and in religious studies courses.

There are two arguments for not including religious creationism in biology courses. First, biology courses are *science* courses. Indeed, the conventional wisdom among scientists is that science has progressed in large part because it has been freed from religious ideas. Second, biology teachers are not qualified to teach about religious accounts of nature. It is precisely because religion is different from science that science teachers are not competent to teach religion. If religious accounts of creation are to be taught adequately, they must be taught by teachers competent to do so.

Still, I reject the idea that biology teachers and texts should be free to ignore religion for three reasons. First, it is one thing to teach neo-Darwinian evolution as (unchallenged) truth and another to teach it as one among several ways of thinking about origins. Scientific claims must be put into perspective if students are not to be indoctrinated. At the minimum, every biology text should begin with a chapter in which biology and scientific ways of thinking about nature and origins are put into historical and philosophical context. In particular, some account of contending religious ways of thinking about the world should be provided. Such accounts should be written in collaboration with scholars of religion. Second, to divide reality into scientific and religious domains and then assume that scientists and theologians can go their separate ways without talking to one another is to convey uncritically a contested view of the relationship of science and religion and permit an intolerable level of specialization. Perhaps the truth about nature is to be learned by meshing scientific and religious perspectives. Finally, if students are to be initiated into the conversation that constitutes a liberal education, teachers and textbook authors cannot be free to ignore other voices in the conversation; they must help students make the conversation coherent (which means *they* must understand the conversation).

If science texts and courses provide this philosophical bracketing and background, they should then be free to ignore religion and teach students about science as scientists understand it. Needless to say, this is a *minimal* rather than a *robust* fairness, for the bulk of the text will far outweigh what will inevitably be a fairly brief account of religious alternatives; moreover, it will be clear that the text implicitly if not explicitly endorses the scientific account. Hence further balancing is required. Although some consideration of religious accounts of origins might come in world history or literature classes, these accounts will likely be even more brief than what I propose for inclusion in biology texts given the amount of material that has to be covered. Moreover, they will almost certainly fall into ancient history and be viewed as museum pieces rather than as live alternatives. And if history or literature teachers are likely to have a better feel for religion than science teachers, they are still not likely to possess any great sophistication about current religious accounts of nature and creation.

Clearly, the only viable way of introducing a robust fairness is with some discussion of nature and origins in the context of a religious studies class in which primary source reading and context provides some deeper understanding of what is claimed within various religious traditions. Indeed, any time a religiously contested claim about a matter of some importance is ignored or treated unfairly elsewhere in the curriculum there is reason for including it in an introductory religious studies course.

Any student who takes biology but not religious studies will not have received a fair or liberal education. (Correlatively, any student in a religious academy who is taught religious accounts of origins but not scientific biology will not have received a fair or liberal education). Hence the need for a core curriculum that requires students to understand the major contending positions, rather then a biased set of requirements (requiring science but not religion, or religion but not science) or a hodgepodge of electives.

Is fairness required *beyond* the introductory liberal education courses in universities? No. It is impractical constantly to refight the battles of contending alternatives. More important, academic freedom kicks in. But until students are liberally educated, until they know the basic alternatives, fairness should be required. Competence to choose among contending accounts of origins is not just a matter of technical (scientific or theological) expertise and rationality. It is a matter of being reasonable all things considered; it requires some ability to see how the contending accounts fit into the context of an ongoing conversation about religious and scientific ways of thinking about the world. Once students have been liberally educated, they are, one hopes, sufficiently sophisticated so that they no longer need protection from indoctrination but are free and competent to pursue their learning as they will.

In public schools teachers and texts should teach *about* science, conveying to students what scientists take to be the truth about nature. At the same time, students should not be taught that science has the final word on nature; they must appreciate the fact that there are contending religious accounts of nature. Neutrality and a robust fairness should characterize the curriculum. In universities academic freedom allows teachers to profess whatever they take the truth to be though the overall curriculum should be robustly fair.

The Constitutional Arguments. We have seen that the Establishment Clause requires neutrality of the government and its agents. In the language of *Epperson* v. *Arkansas* (1968), the landmark case in which the Supreme Court struck down the Arkansas law that prohibited the teaching of evolution, government "may not be hostile to any religion or to the advocacy of no-religion. . . . The First Amendment mandates governmental neutrality between religion and religion, and between religion and nonreligion." Justice Fortas acknowledged that public education should be in the hands of local authorities, but, he argued, they must respect the First Amendment. In this case, according to Fortas, "there can be no doubt that Arkansas has sought to prevent its teachers from discussing the theory of evolution because it is contrary to the belief of some that the Book of Genesis must be the exclusive source of doctrine as to the origin of man." The law was not neutral: its purpose was "to blot out a particular theory because of its supposed conflict with the Biblical account, literally read."[21]

Justice Black concurred in the decision but disagreed with Fortas's reasoning. Black argued the law was unconstitutional because it was too vague to allow for due process; it failed to make clear whether it was illegal to teach *about* evolution or to *endorse* evolution so that teachers could not know when they were violating the law. The conflict between evolution and fundamentalist religious beliefs had a very different significance for Black than it did for Fortas, however. Black argued that if the theory of evolution

is considered anti-religious, as the Court indicates, how can the State be bound by the Federal Constitution to permit its teachers to advocate such an "anti-religious" doctrine to schoolchildren? The very cases cited by the Court as supporting its conclusion hold that the State must be neutral, not favoring one religious or anti-religious view over another. . . . Since there is no indication that the literal Biblical doctrine of the origin of man is included in the curriculum of Arkansas schools, does not the removal of the subject of evolution leave the State in a neutral position toward these supposedly competing religious and anti-religious doctrines?[22]

To teach (scientific) evolution and not teach religious creation puts the state in a position of hostility to religion. So spoke Justice Black, the architect of the wall of separation. No court has ever adopted his argument, however.

In 1972, a group of students in Houston, Texas, sought an injunction to bar the schools from teaching evolution, but short of that they proposed a policy of "equal time" for all theories of origins. The court was not sympathetic. In response to their first goal Judge Seals claimed that "it is not the business of government to suppress real or imagined attacks upon a particular religious doctrine." To forbid the teaching of evolution is a "totalitarian" approach, which he likened to book-burning. What then of the equal-time proposal? "If," Seals wrote, "the beliefs of fundamentalism were the sole alternative to the Darwinian theory, such a remedy might at least be feasible. But virtually every religion known to man holds its own peculiar view of human origins. Within the scientific community itself, there is much debate over the details of the theory of evolution. . . . To insist upon the presentation of all theories of human origins is . . . to prescribe a remedy that is impractical, unworkable and ineffective."[23] In other words, neutrality may be dispensed with when it is hard to come by. Of course, there is a practical problem that stems from the number of religious versions of creation; but there are not so many *types* of creation accounts. Most religious accounts would find some resonance with one or another of some three or four or five basic types. If fairness and neutrality are difficult, it would seem that we should try to approximate, not ignore them.

Seals suggested that the plaintiffs avail themselves of a provision of the Texas Education Code allowing them to be excused from instruction that offends their family's religious beliefs. We should remember, however, that the Supreme Court has insisted that violations of the Establishment Clause cannot be removed by an excusal policy; the New York Regents prayer was unconstitutional even though there was an excusal policy. The state lost its neutrality when it endorsed the prayer, when it took sides.

Strategically, the next step was to shift the argument to neutrality between evolution and creation-science. As a result, Arkansas and Louisiana passed "balanced treatment acts," which required that if "evolution-science" is taught "creation-science" must also be taught. Arkansas's version was struck down by a federal district court in 1982. I have already mentioned that according to Judge Overton, creation-science is not true science, but thinly veiled religion; as such it is "simply and purely an effort to introduce the biblical version of creation into the public school curricula."[24] The decision was not appealed.

Louisiana's Balanced Treatment Act did make it to the Supreme Court, and in *Edwards* v. *Aguillard* (1987) the Court found it unconstitutional. Writing for the Court, Justice Brennan held that the purpose of the act was to promote religion—"to restructure the science curriculum to conform with a particular religious viewpoint"—and he cited a paper trail of comments to that effect by the backers of the act in the Louisiana legislature. Supporters of the act claimed that its official (secular) purpose was academic freedom. According to the act, "Public school instruction in only evolution-science . . . violates the principle of academic freedom because it denies students a choice between scientific models and instead indoctrinates them in evolution science alone." Justice Brennan responded that in common parlance academic freedom is "the freedom of teachers to teach what they will." Before the act was passed, teachers were free to teach any scientific theory; hence the act *reduced* academic freedom by requiring them to provide a "balanced" treatment. Brennan concluded that the act had "the distinctly different purpose of discrediting 'evolution by counterbalancing its teaching at every turn with the teaching of creation science.'"[25]

In his dissenting opinion, Justice Scalia argued that because it is obvious that the academic freedom of teachers has "little scope in the structured elementary and secondary curriculums with which the act is concerned" the majority should have taken more seriously the claim that it was the freedom of *students* that was at issue: "The legislature wanted to ensure that students would be free to decide for themselves how life began, based upon a fair and balanced presentation of the scientific evidence."[26] Academic freedom for students is freedom from indoctrination. (Seven of the fifteen appellate court judges who reviewed the case agreed, holding that balanced treatment had "a credible secular purpose" of "advancing academic freedom."[27])

Justice Brennan was surely right that the act restricted the already limited academic freedom of teachers, and he may well have been right that the real motive of many members of the legislature was to promote Christian fundamentalism, not require a truly liberal education for students. But, arguably, the Louisiana law could have been directed at restoring neutrality in view of what legislators perceived to be an antireligious orthodoxy decreed by the scientific establishment. Brennan did not address Justice Scalia's concern (and the concern of the legislature) that students were being indoctrinated.

What should the courts have said? I have argued for a separationist rather than an accommodationist reading of the Establishment Clause. Government may not promote religious creationism. Instead it is obligated to be neutral—not just among religions but between religion and nonreligion.

Justice Fortas in *Epperson* and Judge Seals in *Houston Independent School District* each cited *Joseph Burstyn, Inc.* v. *Wilson*: "The state has no legitimate interest in protecting any or all religions from views distasteful to them."[29] I agree. To restrict the voices in the conversation—whether they be religious or secular scientific voices—is to forsake fairness and neutrality and risk indoctrination.

My argument is that a balanced treatment of religious and scientific accounts of nature and origins is not only permissible but is required given the neutrality mandated by the Establishment Clause. Of course, insofar as creation-science is advocated as science rather than as religion, there is no Establishment Clause case for treating it neutrally. In requiring a balanced treatment of "scientific" theories, the Louisiana legislature was misguided and heavy-handed; it does not lie within the competence of legislatures to determine what is good and what is bad science. It *is* justifiable for a legislature (or school board or court) to require students to be (fairly and neutrally) exposed to religious as well as scientific accounts of nature and origins; after all, neo-Darwinian evolution is not religiously neutral, as Justice Black argued and Justice Fortas acknowledged in *Epperson*. The best we can do when religiously contested issues are at stake is to take the various (major types of) contenders seriously—and then not take sides.

Unfortunately, legislators and educators who argue for a balanced treatment of religious alternatives are likely to be charged with promoting religion and running afoul of the first prong of the Lemon Test. Here a crucial distinction needs to be drawn. In upholding the Congressional Equal Access Act (allowing student-initiated religious clubs to use school facilities if a school has established a limited open forum) Justice O'Connor, writing for the Court, argued that "if some legislators were motivated by a conviction that religious speech in particular was valuable and worthy of protection, that alone would not invalidate the Act, because what is relevant is the legislative *purpose* of the statute, not the possible religious *motives* of the legislators who enacted the law. Because the Act on its face grants equal access to both secular and religious speech, we think it clear that the Act's purpose was not to 'endorse or disapprove of religion.'"[28] Similarly, I would argue that legislators and school boards commit no constitutional sin in requiring students to study creationism, whatever their personal motives, so long as the purpose (and effect) of the resulting laws or policies are religiously neutral. The purposes of liberal education (which include exposing students to the major voices in our cultural conversation) and the epistemological, political, and constitutional arguments I have given for fairness and neutrality provide legislators and educators with an array of fully secular reasons for requiring the study of religion whenever a major issue is religiously contested.

Economics

For the last hundred years mainstream social science has emulated the natural sciences, but the adequacy, indeed the relevance, of scientific method for understanding *human* nature has always been, and continues to be, a matter of great controversy among social scientists (as well as among scholars in the humanities). If the natural sciences have been successful in excluding the concepts of purpose, value, and meaning from their accounts of physical nature, social scientists have been much less convincing in their efforts to use scientific method, for human nature appears to many scholars to be a richer kind of reality than physical nature, requiring conceptually richer methodologies to understand it. So, for example, it is commonly held that the mind is something more than the brain, human action is something more than the behavior of physical organisms, culture is something more than the agglomerated behavior of individuals, and morality is something more than the superego, long-term self-interest, or conventions that survive the social equivalent of natural selection—though what this "more" might be is not typically explicated in theological terms. Indeed, it is widely held that an adequate understanding of persons and cultures is multidimensional, drawing on various kinds of evidence and methodologies; it is, in the terms with which I began this chapter, interactionist.

Among social scientists, economists have worked hardest to establish their discipline as a science. Given their role in making policy, it has been particularly important to economists to convince us of their ability to discover economic laws that enable them to predict and, through manipulating social variables, control behavior. By employing modern scientific (rather than older theological or newer "humanistic") conceptions of human nature and society modern neoclassical economics plays a role of some significance in sustaining a secular understanding of human nature and modern culture. To provide one particularly graphic example of how this works I will take as my text for our discussion here a widely used and much reprinted college economics textbook, *The New World of Economics* (revised edition), by Richard B. McKenzie and Gordon Tullock (1978), which spells out, in fascinating detail, this new world of economics.

McKenzie and Tullock (hereafter M&T) ground economic theory in modern science. Because so much information is available to them, social scientists must simplify the world. They do this by abstracting that information which enables them "to explain events in the real world and to make correct predictions." Given the constraints imposed by their purposes, the science of economics can tell us only what *is*, and presumably will be, the case, not what *ought to be*. The "approach of the economist is *amoral*" so that, as they say, "the services of a prostitute are treated no differently than the services of the butcher." The purpose of economics is not to tell people what they should desire; it is tell them "how institutions may be rearranged to accomplish *whatever* objective is desired."[30] Economics makes possible social technology; by discovering economic laws we can manipulate our social environment in predictable ways to generate desired outcomes.

Individuals (rather than communities or traditions) are the primary social and economic unit, and individuals are "assumed to be 'rational' in the sense that they are able to determine within limits what they want and will strive to fulfill as many of these wants as possible." People will pursue their individual self-interests. This does not mean, M&T suggest, that people are materialistic or that they lack concern for others. After all, we may *want* to help others, for such behavior "can yield as much pleasure as anything." In their sole reference to the Bible they write: "Even the Bible admonishes that 'it is better to give than to receive,' indicating that there are gains to be had for acts of charity." (That is, they gloss the admonition to act charitably in terms of the reward received for doing so.) They ask rhetorically: "Can you think of anything you or anyone else [have] done for which you or they did not expect some gain?"[31]

How do we know what to do? Because we are rational, we calculate by way of a cost-benefit analysis in which we weigh potential gains and losses to determine what action will maximally satisfy our wants, whatever they might be. For example: should someone cheat on taxes? "Her decision as to whether or not to evade the tax involves simple profit and loss accounting. If she attempts to reduce her tax by taking, let us say, an improper deduction, then she has some chance of getting away with it and some chance of being caught. If the amount she would have times the probability that she gets away with it is greater than the fine that would have to be paid if she gets caught times the likelihood of getting caught, then she should attempt to evade the tax." And what if her conscience tells her not to cheat? That is a cost that must be calculated into the equation. If she "has been ethically indoctrinated with the view that cheating is a bad thing (and it must be remembered that this is not true of everyone) then there is some positive cost." Their conclusion is that given the number of Internal Revenue Service auditors, it is probably in most people's interest to cheat. M&T add: "There may be some people who have strong moral feelings about their own payments under the income tax, but we have never run into them."[32]

I am less concerned about this rather nasty conclusion than I am about how M&T got to it. It is dictated, in part, by their commitment to be scientific. Their goal is to be able to predict and manipulate behavior. Hence they abstract from the richness of life everything that cannot be quantified. Their idea of rationality requires this quantitative reading of life as well, for costs and benefits must be commensurable. Conscience and morality carry no intrinsic, qualitatively distinctive weight, but must be weighed in the scales along with the $25 one might save by cheating on one's taxes. Note also that M&T assume that one must be "indoctrinated" to believe that cheating is wrong; it cannot be rational—at least in their sense of rational—to believe this.

To get at what is wrong with such "neoclassical" economic theory, Amitai Etzioni tells us about asking his students whether, if they needed money badly, they would consider selling one of their kidneys: "They look at me as if the old man has finally lost his senses, and I am proud of them. Their reaction," he comments, "is what we require in more areas. *We need to return to a society in which certain actions are viewed as beyond the pale,* things that upright people would not do or even consider."[33] Neoclassical economics teaches,

Etzioni argues, that people have "one overarching goal: to satisfy their own wants." It discusses "the Bible and dope as two interchangeable consumer goods, and view both children and cars as 'durable consumer goods.'" Yet all societies "set aside certain areas as 'sacred.' When people are taught to think about them in cost-benefit terms, those areas are 'secularized' and stripped of their moral standing, ultimately causing them to be treated as neoclassicists say they are."[34] This is, as E. F. Schumacher puts it, a procedure by which "the priceless is given a price."[35] (In *The Good Society*, Robert Bellah and his colleagues report a conversation with an economist at the Environmental Protection Agency who, "when asked 'What about the theory that human life is priceless?' answered, 'We have no data to support that.'"[36]) In fact, some studies claim that students act in more self-interested and less cooperative ways as a result of course work in neoclassical economics.[37]

It is open to economists (just as it is to biologists) to say that their discipline captures only part of reality. As M&T note, economics abstracts from the wealth of information it has about the world that which it needs to provide the knowledge that gives it predictive power. The problem, of course, is that economics and the market, like biology and science, tend to be imperialistic, making claims about all reality. So, for example, M&T do not limit their analysis to the economic world in any traditional sense but apply cost-benefit analysis to sexuality, the family, child rearing, the law, test taking, and other domains of private and public life. In chapter 1 I quoted Christopher Lasch, who noted that the market "does not easily coexist with institutions that operate according to principles antithetical to itself. . . . Sooner or later the market tends to absorb them all."[38] In the end, every proposition must justify itself as a business proposition.

According to the sociologist Robert Wuthnow, the American middle class has no notion of the claims that religion once made on the economic world: "Asked if their religious beliefs had influenced their choice of a career, most of the people I have interviewed in recent years—Christians and non-Christians alike—said no. Asked if they thought of their work as a calling, most said no. Asked if they understood the concept of stewardship, most said no. Asked how religion did influence their work lives or thoughts about money, most said the two were completely separate."[39] And yet, as theologian Max Stackhouse has pointed out, "It is hard to justify the view that God is one thing, mammon another, and that we can best serve them both by keeping them entirely separate. . . . Any transcendent reality worth attending to has implications for what we think and do on earth."[40]

Consider, for example, the teachings of Jesus. "If a man wants to sue you for your shirt, let him have your coat as well" (Matt. 5:40). "You cannot serve

God and money" (Matt. 6:24). "So do not be anxious about tomorrow; tomorrow will look after itself" (Matt. 6:34). "One thing you lack: go, sell everything you have, and give to the poor" (Mark 10:21). "It is easier for a camel to pass through the eye of a needle than for a rich man to enter the Kingdom of God" (Mark 10:25). "I bid you put away anxious thought about food to keep you alive and clothes to cover your body" (Luke 12:22). "Sell your possessions and give in charity. . . . For where your treasure is, there will your heart be also" (Luke 12:33–34). "So also none of you can be a disciple of mine without parting with all his possessions" (Luke 14:33). Read literally, the ethic of Jesus conflicts with neoclassical economics as blatantly as the first chapter of Genesis, read literally, does with neo-Darwinian biology. (For some reason, however, there are fewer people who take Jesus literally than Genesis.) No doubt most theologians try to reconcile Jesus' teachings with the practical realities of economic life, but I suspect that virtually all theologians reject the analysis that M&T and neoclassical economists give of human nature and rationality, morality and justice.

Let's consider a contemporary alternative. In 1986 the National Conference of Catholic Bishops issued their pastoral letter *Economic Justice for All*. This letter, they wrote, "is based on a long tradition of Catholic social thought, rooted in the Bible and developed over the past century by the popes and the Second Vatican Council in response to modern economic conditions. This tradition insists that human dignity, realized in community with others and with the whole of God's creation, is the norm against which every social institution is measured." In Scripture we learn that "the person is sacred—the clearest reflection of God among us." This being the case, "Our faith calls us to measure this economy, not only by what it produces, but also by how it touches human life." More particularly, "From the Scriptures and church teaching, we learn that the justice of a society is tested by the treatment of the poor." Because "Jesus takes the side of those most in need" we "are challenged to make a fundamental 'option for the poor'—to speak for the voiceless, to defend the defenseless, to assess lifestyles, policies, and social institutions in terms of their impact on the poor." The bishops quote Pope John XXIII, who declared that "all people have a right to life, food, clothing, shelter, rest, medical care, education, and employment." Our economic system must recognize these economic rights. The bishops then go on to argue for a set of strong social welfare programs designed to help the poor. "No one," they conclude, "may claim the name Christian and be comfortable in the face of the hunger, homelessness, insecurity, and injustice found in this country and the world."[41]

What is most important to recognize is that the sacred and the secular cannot be divorced: Christians "must avoid a tragic separation between faith and everyday life. They can neither shirk their earthly duties nor, as the Second Vatican Council declared, 'immerse [them]selves in earthly activities as if these latter were utterly foreign to religion, and religion were nothing more than the fulfillment of acts of worship and the observance of a few moral obligations.'"[42] Economic life is one arena in which we live out our faith and fulfill God's purposes in the world. And our economic thinking must recognize this.

The issue here is not free enterprise capitalism versus the welfare state or some more leftist economic theory. It is the underlying worldview, the philosophical assumptions that shape how we think about economic matters.[43]

There is no way to reconcile neoclassical economic theory and the theology of economics articulated by the bishops and by much Catholic theology of the last century. It is true, of course, that not all economic theory is either neoclassical or so overtly hostile to religion as the text on which I have focused my attention. And, of course, not all theologians would line up behind the bishops—though most mainline Protestant denominations have statements on the economy which take issue in important ways with conventional economic theory. As Karen Lebacqz puts it, mainline Protestant statements on economic matters typically "judge current reality against a biblically-inspired picture of justice" in which economics and faith cannot be separated.[44] Indeed, their beginning point is a "vision of economics in which God is at the center, not at the periphery or excluded altogether."[45]

How then should we handle the conflict of religious and secular economic ways of thinking in the curriculum?

No doubt it may be possible to devise economics courses that do not conflict with religion and hence need not discuss religion—for example, high school courses in consumer economics in which students are taught how to balance a checkbook, how the tax system works, and what the national debt is. (The three consumer economics textbooks approved for use in North Carolina all get into religiously contested questions of human nature, values, and decision making, however.)

All serious introductions to economic theory will inevitably deal with religiously contested matters where fairness is necessary. At a minimum texts should include a full chapter in which the major, *live* religious ways of thinking about the economic world are taken seriously. The discussion of religious ways of thinking cannot be purely historical, for this would bias the treatment of religion as old-fashioned superstition. That is, contemporary religious approaches to economics must be treated as important, approached from the inside, and critically engaged in the search for truth. Of course, one chapter on religious approaches to economics and ten or twenty chapters of neoclassical theory do not produce a neutral text. Ideally, discussion of religious ideas and

ideals should be woven into the text wherever contested issues are discussed—for example, in sections on the tax system, on poverty and welfare
programs, on the Third World, or in discussions of advertising (where questions of morality and human dignity are appropriately raised).

No doubt economics texts and classes should be primarily devoted to explaining the world as economists see it. But that cannot be their exclusive purpose. They must acknowledge the religiously controversial nature of their
claims, and they must locate economic theory within the context of a coherent
curricular conversation. For the overall curriculum to be fair and neutral, the
single chapters on religious ways of thinking about economics must be supplemented by at least one course at both the high school and undergraduate levels in which students are provided with a (relatively) in-depth understanding
of religion. If they have had such a course, the single chapter in the economics
texts will resonate in important ways; it will be less likely to be viewed as an
esoteric, premodern way of thinking.

What should students learn of religious ways of thinking about the economic world? They should be taught something of the scriptural and historical
roots of contemporary religious understandings of justice and morality, rationality and human nature, tradition and community, in the major religious traditions. They should know something of mainline Catholic theory since Leo
XIII, the Social Gospel movement and its legacy in contemporary liberal
Protestantism, liberation theology, and conservative Christian defenses of
free enterprise. There has been no distinctively Jewish view of economics
since the disappearance of the Bund (Jewish socialism) in the early twentieth
century.[46] It would be good, however, for students to understand something of
another major religious tradition, and because of the economic and political
importance of the Middle East and the refusal of Islam to distinguish between
the sacred and the secular, there could hardly be a better example to use.

Upper-level or advanced economics courses in universities should be free of
fairness and neutrality requirements, provided that the introductory courses
have been minimally fair and that students have received an adequate liberal
education that takes religion seriously.

Conclusions

In their concern to avoid what they take to be fundamentalist anti-intellectualism, many religious liberals gloss over the religious difficulties with neo-
Darwinian evolution, lining themselves up uncritically with modern biology.
And in their opposition to socialists and Marxists who have often been hostile
to religion, many conservatives have glossed over the religious difficulties

with capitalism and neoclassical economic theory. What is most important for my purposes is not whether evolution happened or capitalism is the best economic system; I am concerned that we recognize the philosophical assumptions about reality that underlie neo-Darwinian biology and neoclassical economics for it is here that the conflict with religious ways of understanding the world are most directly engaged.

As currently taught, economics and biology are not just *subjects*; they are *disciplines* defined by scientific and social scientific methodologies. These disciplines assume, at least in textbooks, the adequacy of their respective methods to get at what is true and important about their subjects. And they typically do so uncritically; no heed is paid to the idea that there are competing religious ways of understanding nature or the economic world that are important for students to understand.

Of course there is a wide range of issues and subjects in the sciences and the social sciences about which contemporary theologians make claims: ecology and the environment; the Big Bang and the Anthropic Principle; technology and the nature of work; politics and justice; sexuality and sex roles; abortion and euthanasia; war and peace; human nature and morality; and the meaning of history—just to name a few. If we are to take liberal education seriously, we need to be fair to the major contending voices in our cultural marketplace—religious voices included. Biology and economics courses must be minimally fair, acknowledging the controversial nature of their methodological assumptions, saying something about contending points of view. The curriculum must be robustly fair, giving religious voices some significant and sustained opportunity to make sense of the world—including nature and the world of economics—religiously.

If we are to take neutrality and the Establishment Clause seriously, public schools cannot take sides on religiously contested questions, evolution and economics included, by teaching only secular accounts of them; their curricula must be neutral, giving voice to religious alternatives, and they must not take sides on where the final truth lies.

RELIGIOUS STUDIES

Over the course of the past few decades religious studies has become an established discipline in higher education. This is not to say that universities take religion nearly as seriously as they should, however. Not all of them have departments of religious studies, and at public universities religion is never a required course of study. Moreover, there continues to be suspicion of the discipline among faculty and administrators who either misunderstand it or have reservations about the place of religion in the secular academy.

I begin this chapter by saying something about the origins and basic philosophical commitments of this relatively new discipline. I will have a good deal to say about the relationship of theology to religious studies. Indeed, I will argue that only by including theology as a legitimate subdiscipline will religious studies take religion as seriously as it should.

I conclude with a discussion of religious studies as a discipline in public schools. I have argued that if religion is to be taken seriously in the curriculum there must be required courses in religion and there must be teachers competent to teach them. Religious studies must become an established discipline in which public school teachers can be certified.

Background

In chapter 2 I charted the decline of religion in public schools and universities, arguing that by the end of the nineteenth century the religious purposes of higher education had been discredited and religion had largely disappeared from the curriculum. Some public universities had privately funded "Bible chairs" or noncredit Bible schools attached to them for a while and religious groups continued to maintain student organizations on the periphery of campuses, but over the first half of this century public higher education shifted its perspective to the disinterested secular study of religion. Many universities offered secular courses on the sociology of religion in the sociology department, the philosophy of religion in the philosophy department, and biblical literature in the English department. A movement to create secular departments of religion or religious studies began in the 1930s, gathered some momentum after World War II, and became widespread in the 1960s after the Supreme Court's 1963 ruling in *Schempp* distinguished unconstitutional religious indoctrination of the kind presumably found in divinity schools from constitutional teaching about religion. (No Supreme Court decision has ever directly addressed the constitutionality of university departments of religious studies, however.[1]) It was also in the 1960s that the name of the primary organization of scholars in the field was changed from the badly outdated National Association of Biblical Instructors to the American Academy of Religion— reflecting the much broader domain of scholarship now pursued.

Not all universities have established departments of religious studies, however, and it can be argued that many existing departments have a second-class status in their universities.[2] The American Academy of Religion's (AAR) 1992 self-study, "Religious and Theological Studies in American Higher Education," confirmed a widespread insecurity on the part of scholars who teach religious studies in state universities; many believe that their discipline is not on equal financial footing with other social science and humanities disciplines, and they fear for the survival of their departments in economically troubled times. To some extent this is because religious studies is a new discipline, but many religious studies scholars find the "vast majority" of administrators and colleagues to be "apathetic, indifferent, or hostile toward—and *ignorant* about the study of religion." In particular, religious studies is often confused with theology, and it is commonly believed that it is "restricted to a single religious tradition . . . and that it is undertaken to inculcate or deepen credence in its claims."[3]

At first, faculty in the new departments of religious studies were drawn entirely from other disciplines—from Near Eastern or Oriental studies, from history and sociology and philosophy and the ancient languages, *and* from theology—because there were no degree-granting departments of religious studies. Indeed, in 1988 only seven public universities awarded Ph.D.'s in religious studies (Florida State, North Carolina at Chapel Hill, Indiana, Iowa, California at Santa Barbara, Virginia, and Temple).[4] With this interdisciplinary background, scholars in religious studies have worried a good deal about whether religious studies is actually a *discipline* with a more or less common method or intellectual approach. Some scholars deny disciplinary status to religious studies. Walter Capps has characterized religious studies as a "subject-field" like environmental studies in which a variety of disciplines are employed to study a variety of loosely related subjects.[5] James Wiggins, the immediate past executive director of the American Academy of Religion, acknowledges that "there are in point of fact precious few agreed-upon rules of the game to which [scholars in religious studies] are willing or able to adhere."[6] I shall continue to use the term "discipline" for religious studies, acknowledging that it must, perhaps, be used somewhat loosely. In any case, there do seem to be at least a few commonly accepted "rules of the game."

What is most important is the distinction that is drawn between theology and religious studies. A theologian assumes a starting point within a tradition—a set of sacred texts, a mythos, a way of life—and then works to order and systematize it, to render it intellectually coherent and compelling. By contrast, religious studies, like all disciplines in the contemporary university, is secular. As William Scott Green puts it, "Religion is the subject we study, not the way we study it."[7] Religious studies has followed the pattern of all other disciplines in the university—albeit almost a hundred years later. "Like other fields of learning," D. G. Hart argues, it "emerged from an existing professional outlook dominated by the old-line Protestant churches." But as it became part of the university, scholars "shifted their loyalties from the church to the academy." The result was a new commitment to specialization, secular methodologies, and a "shift of cultural authority" away from theology to the social sciences.[8] The epistemological commitments of religious studies are those of modern, secular scholarship. All disciplines have shed their theological trappings in "coming of age"; religious studies is no different.

The 1992 AAR Self-Study characterizes "religious studies" as the "largely unambiguous and unproblematic" name of the "*scholarly neutral and non-advocative study of multiple religious traditions.*"[9] The study of religion in departments of religious studies is typically grounded in the secular methods of the humanities and social sciences; it begins *outside* religion. In fact, in their concern to establish their academic legitimacy, scholars in religious studies have often bent over backward to avoid even the slightest hint of theology and advocacy. Their approaches are typically descriptive and explanatory, not normative and theological.

Even in traditionally religious colleges, the conventional wisdom has become, according to Notre Dame's James Tunstead Burtchaell, that there are "two quite distinct styles of religious instruction on the campuses: disinterested, non-normative studies, conducted in a regular academic department, and ministerial studies based on an assumption of shared commitment, in marginal divinity schools." Underlying this distinction is what Burtchaell characterizes as an "inflexible understanding" to the effect that "a rigorous academy would not harbor learned discourse about religion in its central precincts unless conducted with the systematic detachment of nonbelievers."[10]

The purpose of the discipline is not to promote religion, not to teach religiously, but to employ secular methods to understand religion.

This does not mean that scholars do not appreciate the importance of taking religion seriously from the inside. A good sense of the conventional wisdom of the field can be acquired from a 1990 task force report, *Liberal Learning and the Religion Major*, of the American Academy of Religion. That Report places special emphasis on the importance of "an empathetic study of the 'other'." According to the report, the "study of religion is both empathetic and critical." But if "criticism is uninformed by an empathetic understanding of the criticized, it chiefly serves to confirm the moral or cultural superiority of the critic. For that a liberal education is scarcely needed." The report goes on to note that the people and texts studied by scholars in religious studies are not passive: they challenge our ways of thinking; they elude easy conceptualizations. "They talk back." And we have much to learn from them, for they "have wrestled with angels, they have danced over the void, they have been terrorized by demons, they have emerged from the earth and have journeyed to the spirit world, they have known powers that we can only name, they have encountered mysteries, they have confronted death. Their words are often shrewd, sometimes wise, even sublime. They challenge our own ways of life, they contradict our wisdom, they pose severe tests of self-examination. They teach us."[11]

I noted in chapter 4 that courses in religious studies are much more likely to use primary sources (often drawn from within religious traditions) than courses in the social sciences. Still, the purpose of religious studies is typically to provide students with a secular rather than a theological framework for understanding the primary source material they encounter.

That same AAR report claims that "first and foremost, studies in depth in religion are intrinsically multi-cultural, directed to more than one religious tradition." In large part, this reflects a growing sensitivity to religious pluralism and the variety of ways in which people are religious in the world. It also stems from the widespread conviction that "religion cannot be studied academically without comparative insight." According to the report, the "academic study of religion is not ethnocentric, much less Christocentric, or even theocentric. It is directed to the cultural specificities of each religious tradition under study. It brings no preconceived definition of generic 'religion' to its study, but interrogates the tradition itself to discover what is 'religious' in it, on its own terms."[12]

In part, this is meant to demonstrate the distance of religious studies from divinity schools that may teach (or indoctrinate) students in a single religion. Religion is a dimension of human existence found in many varieties in many cultures; we understand religion only when we understand religions. In fact, many scholars would argue there is no such things as *religion*—or perhaps I should say, there is no necessary or essential characteristic of religion; there are only religions, different from each other in important ways.

With the emphasis on comparative studies and the differences between religious traditions has come an openness to non-Western ways of thinking religiously, a "globalization" of religious studies, an expansion of the field of biblical studies to include the study of Sacred Scriptures more generally, and, in particular, a concern for studying neglected peoples—Third World and minority religions, oral traditions, and women's religion.[13]

Taking Religion Seriously

In his novel *Roger's Version*, John Updike has a young student confront a religion professor, saying:

> "Anyway, what you call religion around here is what other people would call sociology. That's how you teach it, right? Everything from the Gospels to *The Golden Bough*, Martin Luther to Martin Luther King, it all happened, it's historical fact, it's anthropology, it's ancient texts, it's humanly interesting, right? But that's so safe. How can you go wrong? Not even the worst atheist in the world denies that people have been religious. They built these temples, followed these taboos, created these traditions, et cetera. So what? . . .
>
> "I looked over your catalogue before I came, and studying all that stuff doesn't say *any*thing, doesn't com*mit* you to anything, except some perfectly harmless, humane cultural history. What I'm coming to talk to you about is God as a *fact*."[14]

There are no statistics about such things, but I suspect that a good deal of teaching is well-distanced from the existential concerns of students who take courses in religious studies seeking spiritual guidance. They want to know if God exists and how to live their lives, and they are taught history, anthropology, and a little poststructuralism instead. (Similarly, many students study psychology to gain perspective on their personal psychological problems only to be taught about neurology or contingencies of reinforcement.) This distancing may be particularly evident in religious studies because teachers are often concerned to avoid any hint of theology or proselytizing.

George Marsden has noted how peculiar this detachment is: imagine, for example, asking blacks and feminists to conceal their personal commitments in courses in black studies and women's studies. Marsden sees a more sinister pattern, however: while those "who oppose any visible commitment . . . hold the upper hand" in American universities, it is nevertheless his impression that "considerable numbers of instructors in religious studies programs were once traditionally religious themselves but have since lost their faith. Like most teachers, they hope that their students will come to think as they do, so that a goal of their teaching becomes, in effect, to undermine the religious faith of their students. In this pursuit they are aided by methodological secularization, which demands a detachment from all beliefs except belief in the validity of the scientific method itself." [15]

John Dixon suggests that the term "religious studies" makes *studies* rather than religion its primary focus: "The emphasis is to be on the ways of studying religion, not on religion itself." The effect of this on the purpose of teaching, he argues, is considerable: students are taught that "truth is in the systems of study" rather than in the religion that is studied (though he acknowledges that the "actual effect is far more muddled than that, simply because so much of the material we study is more powerful than the prejudices of the methods we apply to them, and many teachers are exceedingly respectful of the integrity of their subject.") Scholars study "the faith of other people but, in fidelity to the university, cannot participate in faith." As scholars, Dixon argues, "we aren't permitted to think there are divine things or sacred things. We are permitted to observe that other people think there are gods or a god, or God, or sacred things, and we can study what they do or think. We take them seriously on our terms, we cannot take them seriously on their own terms." [16] Everything sacred becomes grist for the mill of secular scholarship; as a result, students do not learn to think religiously; they learn to think in secular ways about religion.

We take religion seriously when we try to understand it from the inside (which religious studies typically does) and when we contend with it for the truth (which is less often the case). Many scholars fail to take religious people seriously enough to argue with them; they assume that the truth, as defined by secular methodologies, is more or less safely in hand so that the only people worth arguing with are other scholars. When this is the case, education becomes *primarily* a matter of exposure to the ideas of contemporary scholars rather than the people, cultures, and texts those scholars study and teach about.

Similarly, much political science assumes that the truth is to be found in the scientific method employed by political scientists rather than in the ideas and values of the politicians, voters, and political writers they study. A good deal of literary criticism takes literature only as the occasion for making its own points; to put it crudely, often what is important in a literature course is what the critic thinks, not what the novelist writes.

Arguably, what is most important in studying politics is sorting out whether Democrats or Republicans, capitalists or socialists, have the more reasonable position. To the extent that political science can enlighten us about these normative moral and political matters it is a particularly valuable part of a liberal education. What is most important about studying literature is the insight into good and evil, beauty and suffering, that novelists and poets can provide. To the extent that literary criticism can aid in this task, it is a valuable part of a liberal education. That is, the value of the second-order study of politics and literature is, to some considerable extent, parasitic upon the first-order practice of politics and literature.

So it may be with religion. The value of religious studies in a liberal education hinges on its ability to throw light on spiritual matters. Studying religion should enable students to appreciate and think more clearly about good, evil, and the spiritual domain of life. True, the "second-order" study of religion can enlighten our thinking powerfully about first-order religious claims and practices, but in the end religious studies cannot keep its distance from normative religious claims.

Walter Capps has argued that in their concern to avoid theology, scholars in religious studies assume too easily the role of outsiders. "It is altogether too simplistic," he argues, "to think of religion as being a fixed reality, out there somewhere, about which we, active knowers, wish to gain some understanding. Rather, it is a thoroughly dynamic reality that is shaped and formed as our understanding grows." Capps argues that scholars are entitled to engage in religious speculation and in so doing transform religion. Indeed, they are extremely well placed for proposing religious insights of their own. So, for example, scholars might tell us "how the religious spirit might be advanced" and "whether or not there are grounds for cooperation between the religions of the world, or even as to whether or not religion is a detriment or enhancement to the progress of civilizations."[17] But this should be done not as theologians working within a particular tradition—Capps wants to maintain the distinction between theology and religious studies—but as secular scholars who, while using the methods of the humanities and social sciences, are also free to use their own creative intelligence and religious insights to evaluate religious claims.

It is probably fair to say that some scholars and departments see it as their task to "problematize" religion, to disabuse students of their religious naïveté—perhaps even their religious beliefs (as Marsden suggests). No doubt other scholars and departments retain an old-fashioned confessional approach, seeing it as their task to nurture students' understanding of the Judeo-Christian traditions. And many scholars and departments fall betwixt and between. But the 1992 AAR self-study makes clear that the vast majority of scholars at public universities (and many at private universities) wish to draw a sharp distinction between the secular discipline of religious studies and theology and exclude theology from the university. This is especially so among faculty in universities with graduate programs, and the "younger the scholar and the more recently out of graduate school, the more evident is the antipathy to 'theology.'"[18]

Theology

Theology is often the subject of courses in religious studies, but it is typically approached descriptively or historically rather than normatively. Students are taught what theologians have said, perhaps even why they said it (in the context of social and cultural history), but all of this is different from *doing* theology, from normative reasoning about God and religion. Should religious studies include theology? Can theology be a respectable academic discipline, particularly within a state university?

My answer is yes on both counts—with qualifications. David Ray Griffin has argued that given the other "professions of belief that are regularly made as a natural part of university teaching, it would be arbitrary to exclude in principle professions of belief in the existence and causal efficacy of a being who would in our tradition most naturally be called 'God.'" No other discipline, not physics or philosophy or psychology, is required to bracket questions about the nature of ultimate reality. Why must religious studies do so? Indeed, why "should the university thereby exclude itself from the possibility of contributing to progress on one of the most important questions faced by human beings, arguably *the* most important one?"[19] William F. May has pointed out that no "faculty in philosophy would be content simply to offer courses in the history of philosophy. Philosophers would deem it important for students to study with faculty members who themselves engage in *philosophizing*, that is, who wrestle with metaphysical, ethical, and epistemological issues."[20] May suggests that students of religion should be exposed not just to scholars who study and teach about religion from the outside; they should encounter insiders, that is, theologians.

Indeed, philosophers continue to wrestle with the existence of God—at least a few still do so—arguing for or against it in books and articles and in the classroom. Although many philosophers feel this is a particularly fruitless undertaking, I know of no one who argues that it is illegitimate or inappropriate. The existence of God is, after all, one of the traditional problems of philosophy. Why then shouldn't scholars in religious studies argue for or against the existence of God and a host of other normative religious claims? Who is (or at least should be) better prepared to take on this task?

There are several reasons why scholars take theology to be inappropriate within universities.

First, theology is typically taken to be grounded in faith or revelation and immune to falsification and critical assessment—and no fit matter for a university. But, as the advocates of theology argue, many theologians *are* willing to run the gauntlet of critical assessment. In his 1992 Presidential Address to the American Academy of Religion, Robert Neville argued for including theology within religious studies—as long, that is, as it is "publicly objective," for theologians "need to make themselves vulnerable to criticism from all sides and to sustain themselves through the process of correction."[21] Gordon Kaufman defines *critical* theology as theology "that opens itself willingly to severe criticism from outside perspectives (as well as from within)" and "that is formulated through the exercise of critical judgment with respect to all pertinent evidence and arguments."[22] Critical theology may be grounded historically and, for the theologian, personally, in a particular faith community that makes claims about a historic revelation, but it takes seriously the task of reasoning about those foundational claims and is open to the possibility of falsifying evidence. In Griffin's terms, "Biblically based ideas are not assumed to be products of infallible revelation, but are treated as hypotheses to be tested" by "seeing whether they can lead to an interpretation of reality that is . . . more self-consistent, more adequate to all the relevant data of experience, and more illuminating of those data."[23] *Dogmatic* theology, by contrast, uncritically assumes certain theological claims which cannot be challenged and about which it refuses to argue—the inerrancy of Scripture, perhaps.

Some advocates of theology point to the postmodernist contention that *all* worldviews are grounded in "faith communities." Faith, Griffin argues, is "a necessary ingredient in the rational-empirical method, whatever the subject matter," modern science included; theology differs from other worldviews only "by being more self-conscious of the source of its faith-perspective."[24] George Marsden has argued that if scholars are going to operate on the postmodern assumption that all judgments are "relative to communities," we should "follow the implications of that premise as consistently as we can and not absolutize one or perhaps a few sets of opinions and exclude all others." Universities should foster a broad pluralism that allows "all sorts of Christian and other religiously based intellectual traditions back into the discussion."[25] Gordon Kaufman speaks of the "faith-orientations" of "humanism, Buddhism, secularism, Judaism, Marxism, feminism, Americanism, hedonism, and so on" and sees a major purpose of critical theology as being the second-order work of uncovering and articulating their faith commitments, developing criteria for comparing and assessing them, and proposing ways of transforming and improving them. This would be a kind of "public theology."[26]

The point is that all of us, including secular scholars in religious studies, start somewhere with our respective assumptions about truth, evidence, and reality. We cannot question everything; we are all embedded in intellectual and cultural traditions—the most rigorously skeptical scientist or philosopher as well as the most dogmatic theologian. The question is whether we live within these traditions uncritically or are open to the full range of human experience and evidence in reasoning about them, risking falsification. Scientific, philosophical, and theological claims are no different in that they can be accepted dogmatically or they can be critically assessed. The key to *reasonableness* (as I have defined it) is not some particular method—scientific method, for example—but the willingness to think critically about one's most basic assumptions in light of the full range of human experience. Science can be just as dogmatic (in uncritically excluding moral, psychic, or religious experience as knowledge-yielding, for example) as some theology is.

Of course, there is a huge political risk in admitting theology to departments of religious studies. There is a widespread—often justified—concern among scholars in religious studies that their field is viewed askance by many colleagues and administrators in large part because it is confused with theology. The secular commitments of modern intellectual life would, no doubt, make many scholars even more dubious of the discipline should theology become part of it.

The second reason for excluding theology from the university is that theologians owe allegiance to their religious traditions, and this conflicts with the academic freedom of the university. The theologian Schubert Ogden argues that if "a theologian's fidelity to, or respect for, the teaching office of the church in any way limits what he or she can teach or publish as a proper conclusion of theological inquiry, then his or her academic freedom consists in nothing but the words."[27] But there is a difference, Ogden argues, between religious witness and theology. The purpose of an appropriately critical theology is to advance reasoned reflection, even if that risks falsifying the claims of one's faith community.

Analogously, there should be no room in a university for card-carrying Marxists, who are obligated, in their research and teaching, to follow the party line. There need be no difference in principle between a theologian and a secular scholar on this score. Indeed, some academic fields are so ideologically narrow that most mainline seminaries are paradigms of openness by comparison.[28]

But, finally, wouldn't theologians inevitably indoctrinate their students? Theology, like any subject, can be taught in an open and reasoned way or as a matter of indoctrination. As we have seen, indoctrination occurs when students are not given access to contending points of view which are taken seriously (with all that that means). If theology is taught in conjunction with contending ways of understanding religion (whether in a single course or in a required curriculum), students will not be indoctrinated.

The governing assumption of so much discussion is that theology cannot contend in a reasoned way with secular points of view. This, of course, is a highly controversial claim which is denied by many theologians. Liberal theology from the beginning entered into a reasoned dialogue with modernity. To rule this dialogue out of religious studies and the university is to adopt a controversial and extraordinarily narrow view of reason.

Does this leave us in the position of welcoming critical (or liberal) theology into the university but denying a place for dogmatic (or conservative) theology? Yes and no. Griffin, Kaufman, and Ogden would not include dogmatic theology in universities for it does not respect the critical nature of university scholarship and the demands of academic freedom.[29] But Griffin notes that what is important for the purposes of education is performance not pedigree: the "relevant question" is "how the perspective is defended."[30] It is not the conservative theological conclusions which a university cannot allow, it is dogmatic claims about them—though, admittedly, the dogmatic claims are often required by the conservative conclusions. In a university, theologians cannot *simply* appeal to revelation in asserting the inerrancy of Scripture with their students; they must argue for the reasonableness of their point of view as professionally competent scholars. They cannot limit their arguments to the rationality internal to their faith community but must be willing to engage other scholars in the give and take of intellectual debate about inerrancy. I see no problem with an evangelical Christian or an orthodox Jew or a traditional Muslim teaching theology in a public university so long as they do not do it dogmatically, they are not subject to the control of religious authorities, and they are professionally competent—that is, at home in the world of contemporary scholarship.

I should add that in claiming that theology must be subject to critical review, I do not mean to hold it hostage to any narrowly scientific conception of criticism. Theological claims typically acquire their meanings by being embedded in ritual and religious practices, in dense thickets of religious symbolism, in ways of life. As Robert Neville has pointed out, critical judgment often requires participation in a "community of practice and belief. For a theological claim to be publicly vulnerable does *not* mean that it must be reduced to what is easily grasped by an external observer." Indeed, from within religious traditions can come, Neville argues, powerful critiques of Enlightenment rationalism and empiricism in religious studies.[31]

Scholars in religious studies, like their collegues in other disciplines, are entitled to academic freedom. They are not mere agents of the state, bound to maintain neutrality on religiously contested questions. They are free to argue for and against religious claims. Indeed, if a neo-Darwinian biologist can argue that evolution and ultimate reality are purposeless, surely a scholar in religious studies can argue that reality is purposeful; if a Freudian psychologist can argue that God is nothing more than the neurotic projection of our unconscious minds, surely a scholar in religious studies can argue that some religious experiences are veridical experiences of God; if a philosopher can argue that the existentialists were right and reality is absurd, surely a scholar of religious studies can argue that the religious thinkers have it right and that God gives meaning to reality. For the state or the university to prohibit normative arguments *for* religious claims, when antireligious claims are routinely made in other fields, is to take sides against religion; it is to forgo neutrality. It is also a strikingly illiberal limitation on the university as a marketplace of ideas. There should be no reason why scholars in religious studies should not be able to pursue through research and teaching the answers to the ultimate questions of human existence as much as philosophers or cosmologists or psychologists.

A department of religious studies cannot be a seminary in miniature; it cannot have as its purpose to promote any religious claims uncritically. The university, as a state institution, cannot make religion sacrosanct; it cannot take sides. But it can, and must, allow scholars in religious studies (as in all disciplines) to take sides on religiously contested questions. The fully secular purposes of such an arrangement are twofold: to enable scholars to pursue truth in all domains of life without discrimination (so long as it is done in ways that respect professional competence) and to make the university a true marketplace of ideas in which students can receive an appropriately liberal education.

Two final notes on theology. First, the borders between theology and philosophy, the humanities and the social sciences, are in practice often indistinct. Many of the great theologians of our century—Barth, Bultmann, the Niebuhrs, Tillich, Maritain, and Buber, for example—have also been great scholars in the humanities, and their insights into religion often resulted from their use of linguistic or historical or philosophical methods and resources. Some "secular" scholars in the humanities and social sciences use theological ideas in arguing for "religious" conclusions. There is a sense in which these "blurred genres" (to use Clifford Geertz's phrase) come naturally, and our insistence on dividing life into academic disciplines, indeed into secular and religious disciplines, is unnatural and unwise.

Second, the 1992 AAR self-study found that some scholars—including many scholars at Jewish universities—reject the word "theology" as a "Christian import."[32] I would simply say that whether or not we use the word "theology" there should be room for *normative* reflection on religion, whether that takes the form of arguments for or against particular religious claims.

Religious Studies and Public Schools

I have already said something about the movement to incorporate the study of religion into public education that began in the mid-1980s.[33] Several states (California, North Carolina, and Utah) now require the study of religion, and an array of national religious and educational organizations have endorsed the study of religion in the public school curriculum. But in almost every case the argument has been made, implicitly if not explicitly, for "natural inclusion"— for the study of religion within the framework of existing courses—rather than for new courses in religion. It is true that courses on world religions and The Bible as literature can be found here and there, but with so few courses in religion there has been no need to establish the discipline of religious studies in public schools, even though religious studies has gained wide acceptance in universities.

A 1989 survey conducted by Charles Kniker showed that only three states (Idaho, Tennessee, and Wisconsin) actually licensed religion teachers, and

only four others (California, Idaho, Wisconsin, and Michigan) had laws or regulations dealing with the preparation of teachers to teach about religion.[34] I
would be surprised if more than a small minority of prospective teachers in
public universities ever take a single religion course.

I suggest a number of overlapping ways of preparing teachers to teach
about religion.

First, all prospective teachers should be introduced to the major legal and
pedagogical issues relating to religion and public education in their foundation
courses in schools of education.

Many scholars are wary of education courses, but I trust it is now clear why
some formal study of education is necessary. Education is a morally and politically charged endeavor. The shape of the curriculum, the goals of teaching,
and the content of textbooks all rest on deeply controversial cultural politics.
As Henry Giroux puts it, prospective teachers "need to understand the sociology of school cultures, the meaning of the hidden curriculum, a politics of
knowledge and power, a philosophy of school/state relations, and a sociology of
teaching."[35] Being a teacher requires a good deal of sophistication about *education* as well as one's subject. This should be especially obvious when religion
is at issue. There is no way that one can study religion and then just teach it;
a whole raft of constitutional, political, moral, and epistemological considerations must be weighed in the pedagogical balance. A good teacher education
program should do this. In an ideal world, the education of religion teachers
would be a collaborative (interdisciplinary) effort of departments of religious
studies and schools of education.

As near as I can tell, most texts in the foundations of education give little
space to the role of religion in public education. Typically, they include a few
pages on vouchers and brief references to the Supreme Court decisions dealing with prayer, Bible reading, and release time. Some texts include short sections on secular humanism and censorship, but I have yet to see a foundations
text that gives any significant space to the issues that have occupied us here.

Second, every department of religious studies should offer a course called
"Introduction to Religion for Teachers," which might fulfill a humanities requirement or simply be an elective that prospective teachers might take. It
should deal with the First Amendment and our tradition of religious liberty;
religious pluralism in America; how to understand and teach about religions;
sensitivity to religious stereotypes and the likely concerns of students from
minority traditions; and the conflict between religious and secular ways of understanding the world and the implications for teaching about controversial
issues likely to arise in courses in history, literature, and science. The course

should require students to read religious texts and provide them with some insight into at least two different religions.

Third, prospective teachers in literature, social studies, and science should be encouraged to take at least one course in religious studies specifically related to their major field of teaching.

Finally, if courses in religion are to be required in public schools—that is, if religion is to be taken seriously—then teachers of such courses must be certified in religious studies, ensuring that they are qualified to teach courses in world religions, American religious history, contemporary religious issues, and religious literature (the Bible and other sacred texts). Certification should require at least a minor in religious studies.

Should public schools employ theologians? No. After all, they do not employ research biologists or economists. They employ people who teach about biology and economics. Similarly, they should employ people who teach about religion and theology. It is not the task of public school teachers (or texts) to make judgments about where the final truth lies; nor have they traditionally been given the academic freedom to do so.

Conclusions

In arguing for theology in universities I do not want to diminish the importance of the secular study of religion that now dominates the field of religious studies. We have a tremendous amount to learn about religion from scholarship undertaken from the perspectives of the humanities and social sciences, and students are not educated about religion if they do not understand something of the historical, sociological, psychological, and philosophical ways of making sense of religious traditions, ideas, and values. But there should be more to religious studies than this—at least if religion is to be taken fully seriously.

It is not enough to use primary religious sources, which are then uncritically reinterpreted in terms of some secular framework. Religious studies must make room for scholars and theologians who do normative work within religion, who contend with secular traditions from various religious points of view. Religious studies should be, along with philosophy and literature, disciplines in which students can confront head-on the major spiritual questions of human existence: the nature of life and death, guilt and obligation, hope and despair, good and evil. Our religious traditions—and second-order scholarly reflection on those traditions—should provide students with ways of reasoning about what makes life meaningful.

Perhaps no discipline has more potential for fulfilling the critical task of liberal education than religious studies, for it is our religious traditions that now provide a true adversarial culture to the dominant secular intellectual movements of the last several hundred years. If we want to provide students with critical perspective on the basic assumptions of modernity—and postmodernity—religion is the place to begin.

RELIGION AND MORAL EDUCATION

All things considered, I believe in moral progress. The modern West is a good deal more just than its predecessor civilizations. Our commitments to freedom of conscience, liberty, and democracy distinguish our civilization from all others. In our own time, our commitment to alleviating suffering through the welfare state and our efforts to end racism and sexism are particularly laudable—even if not fully successful.

Yet, in spite of such progress, it is hard to avoid believing that we are in something of a moral crisis—one that extends all too clearly to our youth culture. The statistics are familiar, so I will offer only a brief sampling. Sixty-five percent of high school students acknowledge that they would cheat on an important exam. Promiscuity is rampant, and recourse to abortion is all too common. At least once a month 44 percent of high school seniors have five or more drinks at one sitting; 22 percent of high school freshmen admit to being binge drinkers. Drugs are everywhere and polls show that crime and violence have become our nation's foremost worry. We are preoccupied with wealth and consumerism; more than a third of entering college freshmen believe that it is important to be a millionaire by the age of thirty-five. Teenagers name Eddie Murphy, Arnold Schwarzenegger, Michael Jackson, and sports stars as their heroes. According to a 1994 Gallup Poll 5 percent of American teenagers have tried to commit suicide, and 12 percent say they "have come close to trying."[1]

The causes of our crisis go well beyond television, Colombian drug lords, permissive child-rearing, and the prohibition of prayer in public schools. Our problems are, in large part, the price we pay for modernity. Indeed, much of what contributes to the success of America—our deep-felt cultural commitments to competitiveness, individualism, liberty, technology, material abundance, and a market economy—indirectly and ironically undermines the content of our character.

In our wholehearted capitulation to the values of modernity, our culture has lost the capacity to provide moral guidance. We no longer have the confidence that we can make moral sense of the world. We believe that individuals must choose their own values and chart their own course in life. As Robert Bellah and his colleagues argue in *Habits of the Heart,* our "cultural traditions define personality, achievement, and the purpose of human life in ways that leave the individual suspended in glorious, but terrifying isolation."[2] Christopher Lasch has written: "I believe that young people in our society are living in a state of almost unbearable, though mostly inarticulate, agony. They experience the world only as a source of pleasure and pain. The culture at their disposal provides so little help in ordering the world that experience comes to them in [the] form merely of direct stimulation or deprivation."[3]

It has become a part of the conventional wisdom of our time that moral education is not the job of schools and universities. In part this may reflect the view that moral education is properly a matter for home and church; in part it follows from the inertia that sets in when there is no agreement about how moral education might be done; in part it results from the concentration of our educational efforts on other things. But it is also the logical conclusion of the modern worldview.

Our topic now is the complicated and controversial relationship between morality, religion, and education. At one time there was no relationship between morality and religion for they were one and the same. The idea of morality as autonomous, as separable from religion, is a legacy of the Enlightenment. I begin this chapter with a review of religious ways of understanding morality. I will then sketch yet another episode in the story of the secularization of the modern West. With this background, I will return to education. What does morality have to do with education? A good deal, indeed. Given the deep disagreements in our culture about morality, what obligations do educators have to take the religious voices in our cultural conversation about morality seriously? What would the pedagogy of moral education look like if it were sensitive to religion? And is there any reason to suppose that a good education might make students better people?

Religious Morality

Religious people differ greatly on particular moral and political issues: they come down on different sides of the abortion debate, some are supporters of capitalism and others of socialism, some are feminists while others hold very traditional notions of sex roles. It is also true that religious folk justify their moral beliefs in different ways. Nonetheless, there are points of agreement.

First, within all major religious traditions *reality is a moral order*. The God of Judaism, Christianity, and Islam is a moral God who has created a world in which divine purposes are served and history works to bring about that which ought to be. There is an *objective* right and wrong, a way-to-be built into reality. Morality is not subjective, a matter of personal tastes or social conventions. It is our task to set ourselves right with God. Similarly, in Hinduism and Buddhism the law of Karma—of moral desert—is built into the structure of reality; what comes to be is what ought to be.

Second, if there is a good deal of disagreement about moral particulars among the religions, there is, arguably, a measure of consensus about the most basic moral principles. C. S. Lewis found eight moral laws—of beneficence, of duty to parents and children, of mercy, and so on—in most of the world's religious traditions.[4] At a still more basic level, John Hick argues, the great religious traditions are all implicitly committed to "the utterly basic principle that it is evil to cause suffering to others and good to benefit others and to alleviate or prevent their sufferings."[5] Ronald Green goes further: all the great religions are particularly "solicitous of the needs of the disadvantaged or powerless and, in different ways, all encourage active assistance to the poor."[6] We are not free to pursue our own self-interest; we must be concerned with the good of others.

Third, in large part because of our moral responsibility for each other, religions have typically emphasized community and have been wary of individualism. Certainly our moral identities—our sense of who we are—is very much determined by being part of a traditional community. Because we must act for the good of others we must act with them, in community.

Fourth, our happiness, whether in this world or in one to come, is realized in part, at least, in the fulfillment of our responsibilities to humanity and to God. As E. A. Burtt put it, "True happiness for man does not consist in finding more successful ways of fulfilling his natural desires; it consists rather in a transformation of these desires so that he becomes capable of . . . a happiness more secure and real than any pleasure arising merely from satisfying the longings that fill man's awareness before he undergoes this transformation."[7] We are not just obligated to act for the good of others, we find fulfillment, happiness, and "salvation" in so doing. True peace is to be had when we are freed from self-concern.

Finally, to think of morality as a matter of simply doing what is right and wrong is to think in highly secular terms. For religious people, morality must be understood in part, at least, in terms of sin, salvation, and one's relationship to God. It requires that we be a particular kind of person, not just that we act in particular ways. It is bound up with our understanding of history, tradition, community and, for many, the afterlife. That is, there is a continuity of "moral" and "religious" ideas and ideals which, most religious folk would argue, it is impossible fully to disentangle. What it is for something to be right or good, how we know that, and what moves us to do what we should do is wrapped up with this larger religious understanding of the world.

There are also significant differences in how morality is understood in various religious traditions. I will sketch six (sometimes overlapping) variations to be found in Western religions historically and in our day.

Morality as Divine Command. For many Jews, Christians, and Muslims, morality is a matter of law, of God's commandments. In many ways, Judaism and Islam have placed greater emphasis on keeping the law than Christianity, which has placed relatively more emphasis on doctrine and orthodox belief. Nonetheless, a legalistic understanding of morality has been common within Christianity as well, from the early church through much contemporary conservative and fundamentalist Protestantism. For the contemporary American Protestant theologian Carl F. H. Henry, for example, "Hebrew-Christian ethics centres in the divine revelation of the statutes, commandments and precepts of the Living God. Its whole orientation of the moral life may be summarized by what the Holy Lord commands and what he forbids. What accords with his edicts is right, what opposes his holy will is wicked."[8]

Why should we obey God's law? Answers differ, but the oldest and probably the most common response within this tradition is that it is a matter of reward and punishment. When God gave the Israelites the law, God told them that if they kept the law, they would prosper. And if they didn't? "Then be sure that this is what I will do: I will bring upon you sudden terror, wasting disease, recurrent fever, and plagues that dim the sight. . . . I will set my face against you, and you shall be routed by your enemies."[9] The Sermon on the Mount is punctuated by promises of heaven for those who follow Jesus, while those who do not "will have to answer for it in the fires of Hell."[10]

Morality, on this account, is God's law. It is revealed to us in Scripture; and like human law it requires the threat of punishment or the promise of reward to motivate sinful people to obey it. Many nonreligious folk take this to be the only religious view of morality. Far from it.

Natural Law. In the book of Romans, Paul wrote: "When Gentiles who do not possess the law carry out its precepts by the light of nature, then although they have no law, they are their own law, for they display the effect of the law inscribed on their hearts."[11] The Talmud quotes Rabbi Johanan, who said, "If the Torah [the law] had not been given we could have learnt modesty from the cat, honesty from the ant, chastity from the dove, and good manners from the cock who first coaxes and then mates."[12] The question is, How is it that people who have not received God's revelation know what is right—for, the texts claim, they *can* know.

According to the natural law tradition, the world and everything in it acts for the fulfillment of God's purposes. On this, as on many things, the greatest of the Christian and Jewish medieval philosophers agreed. For both Aquinas and Maimonides, all people, whether or not they have been given God's law in revelation, can know through reason what is right. Aquinas claimed, for example, that "the law of nature, as far as general first principles are concerned, is the same for all as a norm of right conduct and is equally well known to all." Moreover, we are competent not only to know God's moral law but to do what is right, "For there is in man a natural and initial inclination to good which he has in common with all substances."[13]

Natural law is, of course, at a distant remove from the modern, scientific laws of nature which describe a purpose*less* or morally neutral nature. Aquinas and Maimonides lived in a world structured by values (by the purposes of God), where nature acts to realize what is good and where reason feels the "pull" or is naturally inclined to do what is good.

Of course, we are sinful, we often fail to do what is right. Moreover, there is much about God, the world, and morality that we can*not* know. If reason can prove that God exists and that we should be honest, it will not tell us that God is a trinity or that we shouldn't eat pork. God must reveal *these* things to us; reason must be supplemented by revelation. Nature must be perfected by grace. What is important for our purposes is that the natural law tradition claims to make sense of our ability to know what is right apart from revelation, and our natural inclination to do the good, on our own, as it were. Pope John Paul's 1993 encyclical, *Veritatis Splendor*, and the church's new *Catechism* make clear that natural law theory continues to provide the basis of orthodox Catholic moral theology.[14]

Grace. For Paul, for Augustine, for Luther and Calvin, for Jonathan Edwards, for Karl Barth, and for many contemporary Christians the human will is so deeply sinful that even if we know the law and the punishment that is due us if we disobey, we cannot obey. The purpose of the law is to convince us of our sinfulness so that we might repent. This is in stark contrast to both our first two accounts of morality. Paul discerned a recalcitrant or sinful will between our knowledge of the law and our action. Hence, "when I want to do the right, only the wrong is within my reach. In my inmost self I delight in the law of God, but I perceive that there is in my bodily members a different law, fighting against the law that my reason approves and making me a prisoner under the law that is in my members, the law of sin."[15]

For the person who has been saved, who has experienced God's grace, the moral situation is not one of obeying law. Having been transformed, we do God's will joyfully, out of love for Him. To use Luther's analogy, when a man and a woman love each other, they serve each other, doing so gladly. So, Luther argues, a Christian "does everything cheerfully and freely; not that he may gather many merits and good works, but because it is a pleasure for him to please God thereby . . ."[16] Salvation is not *earned* through obeying the law; it is freely given by God. Our motive for doing what is right is not the fear of punishment or the hope of reward, but the love of God that follows our salvation, for our whole being is reoriented. Our attitude toward the law is not one of anxiety (such as that felt so deeply by Luther before his experience of grace) but one of free and spontaneous right action.[17]

Tradition. For some Jews and some Christians, morality is not so much a matter of doing God's will as it is of being a particular kind of person, and that is a result of the communities we are born into. Richard Rubenstein has remarked that the "conception of humanity in general is a meaningless and tragic abstraction." Neither Jew nor gentile, he argues, is free "to confront God's mysterious singularity as if no one had preceded him. Jew and gentile alike are thrown into historically, culturally, psychologically, and religiously defined situations which are, in a certain sense, beyond choice." So, for the Jew "no religious way exists save through the Torah as its traditions have been inherited, reflected upon, and transmitted throughout Jewish history."[18]

Similarly, the Christian theologian Stanley Hauerwas argues that "ethics always requires a qualifier—such as Jewish, Christian, Hindu, existentialist, pragmatic, utilitarian, humanist, medieval, modern." There are no universal ethics. We are born into communities that have ongoing stories; we acquire our roles and are taught "to be the kind of person appropriate to living among these people." We do not create ourselves but are created by our historical communities. Indeed, we are "rooted in sin just to the extent we think we have the inherent power to claim our life—our character—as our particular achievement." Christians, according to Hauerwas, are people of a book and must not seek "a philosophical truth separate from the book's text." Such "truth" is "inherently contingent; it can only be passed on from one generation to another by memory."[19] Christian ethics is not for everyone but only for Christians.

God as Love. For the last hundred years or so, Protestantism has been deeply divided. On the one side are the conservatives: deeply suspicious of reason; impressed by human sinfulness; convinced of the need for God's grace; dependent on revelation; and powerfully opposed to the emphasis on good works in liberal Protestant (and Catholic) thought.

For many liberals, the major theological task of our time is demythologizing Christianity, for the old God—the supernatural God "up" there in the heavens—is no longer credible given what higher criticism and modern science tells us about the world. God is not a supernatural person, and morality is not a matter of divine commands. Rather, as Bishop John A. T. Robinson puts it, the Christian affirmation is that "the final truth and reality of the world *is* love." For Robinson and many liberal Christians, God is most clearly "revealed" in the life and teachings of Jesus, who is "utterly transparent" to God, for it is "in Jesus, and Jesus alone, that there is nothing of self to be seen, but solely the ultimate, unconditional love of God." Morality is situational; it is not a matter of following divine laws but living a life of love: "Life in Christ Jesus, in the new being, in the Spirit, means having no absolutes but his love, being totally uncommitted in every other respect but totally committed in this." How do we know what to do? In part it is a matter of reflecting on the cumulative moral experience of humankind, but it is also true that love has "a built-in moral compass, enabling it to 'home' intuitively upon the deepest need of the other." To use Paul Tillich's language, "Love is the ground of our being, to which ultimately we come home."[20]

It is acting in love, in response to the needs of the other, that we do God's work: "Did not your father eat and drink and do justice and righteousness? Then it was well with him. He judged the cause of the poor and needy; then it was well. Is not this to know me? says the Lord" (Jer. 22:15).[21] Indeed, when we act morally it is, in some sense, God acting within us.[22]

Liberation Theology. Perhaps the most prominent form of liberal religious ethics nowadays is liberation theology. Liberation theology has its roots in Latin America, where it grew out of the lived experience of oppression and the poverty of peasants and priests. (It is not what Harvey Cox has called "trickle-down" theology from the seminaries.[23]) Nonetheless, it has often drawn on Marxist social science, interpreting the world in terms of oppression and class conflict. As theology, it appeals to biblical concern for liberating the oppressed and draws heavily on the Jesus of the Synoptic Gospels. As Phillip Berryman puts it: "Jesus lives poor, associates with the poor, and preaches poverty. . . . He says: 'Blessed are you poor, the reign of God is yours. . . . But woe to you rich, for your consolation is now.'"[24] Through Jesus, God has indicated his "preferential option for the poor"; he has taken sides in history. It is the mission of the church to refashion society; God is working through the church to end oppression and bring about His kingdom.

In chapter 1 I discussed Rosemary Radford Ruether's account of feminist liberation theology: beginning with the concern for justice and liberating the oppressed in Scripture, she uses the experiences of women to supplement and sometimes correct the hiatuses and patriarchal biases built into biblical morality. There are black, Native American, and other variations on these themes.

The Secularization of Morality

For some Americans, morality continues to be grounded in, and shaped by, religion. The dominant ideas and institutions of modernity have led to a divorce between morality and religion, however. Morality has, to a considerable extent, become autonomous, secularized. How this came about is a complicated story, but as I've already told much of it in chapter 1, I will provide only the briefest outline here.

Once again, the Protestant Reformation was a key event in the story. In breaking down the religiously structured civilization of medieval Catholicism, and in their emphasis on liberty of conscience and the priesthood of all believers, the Reformers nurtured individualism. As important was the practical problem of how people were to live together in peace given their newly competing notions of what is true and good. The great religious wars and persecutions of the sixteenth and seventeenth centuries made it imperative for a new formulation of morality: as religion proved divisive, a new moral and political vocabulary became necessary.

The development of capitalism, the rise of the middle class, and the growing emphasis on democracy and political rights in the seventeenth and eighteenth centuries reinforced the Reformers' turn toward individualism. We are individuals before we are members of societies, nations, or churches. We are not born into a station with its duties, but, as the social contract thinkers said, we must freely "contract" to be obligated by the laws of the state. The purpose of the state is not to make us conform to some political or religious conception of what is good; its task is to protect our *rights* to liberty and the pursuit of happiness. We are to be free to live as we choose to live. Natural rights began to crowd talk of natural law offstage as individualism replaced community in the cast of cultural characters.

This process was furthered by the scientific revolution. In the traditional (religious) view, reality is a moral order. "What is important about the scientific outlook," Anthony Arblaster has claimed, "is the stress on the moral neutrality of the world of scientific facts, as well as the concept of the person as the detached observer of those facts. For if the world of facts, the world studied by science, is devoid of (or deprived of) any moral dimension, what happens to morality? Where do values go when they are excluded from the empirical world of science? The answer of modern liberal moral theory is that they become a matter of individual choice and commitment."[25] Nature is no longer the arena of God's providence but is neutral terrain.

The concept of reason was, in turn, redefined. In the old view, for Aquinas and Maimonides, for example, reason could discern moral and religious truths, what ought to be. In the new view, reason's competence tends to be limited to the domains of mathematics and the morally neutral world of modern science. And, as David Hume argued at the height of the Enlightenment, it is impossible to move logically from (scientific) facts to morality, from "is" to "ought." Reason became narrowly technical or instrumental. It cannot tell us what we *should* desire, only how to accomplish (technically, instrumentally, scientifically) *whatever* it is that we *do* desire. Reason is, as Hume says, "the slave of the passions, and can never pretend to any other office than to serve and obey them."[26] Increasingly morality was seen less as the product of (public, universal) reason than as the (private, particular) choices of individuals.

At the same time, the powerful new cultural forces of modernity—market economies, technology, industrialism, and democracy—were undermining the cultural institutions that had supported traditional morality and religion. The extraordinary success of these modern institutions meant that happiness in this world, rather than salvation in the world to come, became the object of life for most people. Belief in progress became axiomatic.

No way of thinking about morality captured the new cultural ethos—the individualism, the this-worldly emphasis on happiness, the commitment to being scientific—so much as utilitarianism. The principle of utility is that whatever maximizes pleasure is right or, as it came more commonly to be put, that action is right that produces the greatest happiness for the greatest number of people. The task of reason is simply to calculate what will maximize utility. The truth or falsity of moral claims depends entirely on quantities of pleasure or happiness, an empirically observable phenomenon. No qualitative distinctions are allowed: there are no higher or lower pleasures, no natural virtues or unnatural vices. Only measurable distinctions (of duration or intensity) are permitted.

For most utilitarians (as for most economists) people are essentially self-interested. Hence it is necessary that the institutions of society be structured so that people acting in their own self-interest will, quite apart from their intentions, bring about the greatest amount of pleasure. Adam Smith believed a free market would do this "naturally," but many utilitarians have seen some need for social engineering. Drawing on our growing scientific knowledge of human behavior, social scientists and government officials can manipulate the relevant variables to produce wealth, progress, and happiness.

Utilitarianism reflected—indeed, still reflects—the spirit of the age. Jeremy Bentham, the first of the great utilitarian philosophers, wrote: "On most occasions of their lives men in general embrace this principle [of utility], without thinking of it." Bentham made no appeal to God or Scripture to justify his ethics, for, he wrote, religion "is a system which nobody ever thinks of recurring to at this time of day."[27] At the beginning of the nineteenth century, utilitarianism was beginning to appear self-evident to the modern mind.

While the utilitarians were calculating how to produce the greatest amount of pleasure a "romantic" reaction set in. In his "Discourse on the Arts and Sciences," Rousseau had written: "Virtue! sublime science of simple minds, are such industry and preparation needed if we are to know you? Are not your principles graven on every heart?"[28] To know what is right we need not calculate; goodness is not a matter of utility. We need only look within; we need only listen for the voice of our inner nature. In *Emile* he wrote: "Let us lay it down as an incontrovertible rule that the first impulses of nature are always right; there is no original sin in the human heart."[29]

In Rousseau and Goethe, in late eighteenth- and early nineteenth-century German philosophy, and in English romantic poetry, calculation was replaced by feeling, sophistication by simplicity, the sovereign masters of pleasure and pain by inner nature, science by art. For a while the inner voice of nature could be identified with God—at least with an immanent God—and underwrite early liberal theology. But in the long run, the individualism of modern culture undermined religious interpretations of human nature, so that what came to be expressed was the pure, subjective particularity of people. We must, as the existentialists said, define and create ourselves.

Charles Taylor has argued that within this tradition, creating a life was understood much as creating a work of art, and just as mimetic theories of art were being replaced by expressivist accounts, so individuals were not to mimic existing models for living a life, they were to create their lives. This "expressivism" in art and in life became the basis of the view that "each individual is different and original, and that this originality determines how he or she ought to live. . . . Each one of us has an original path which we ought to tread."[30] Or, as Walt Whitman put it in the middle of the nineteenth century:

> Afoot and light-hearted I take to the open road,
> Healthy, free, the world before me,
> The long brown path before me, leading wherever I choose.[31]

We fulfill ourselves when we create ourselves, when we choose our destiny.

Here we have, in brief, the three dominant conceptions of modern, secular morality. First, morality is a matter of *rights and liberties*. Much modern political thought is but a variation on the theme of liberal individualism: the ground of the state's authority is a social contract; it is the central task of the state to guarantee its citizens the freedom to live their own lives as they see fit. Second, morality is a matter of *utility*. While talk of preference-satisfaction has replaced talk of pleasure, and the calculus has gotten considerably more complicated, the value theory that continues to shape much modern economics is only a more sophisticated version of Bentham's utilitarianism. Third, morality is a matter of *self-expression*. The romantic notion of individuality, creativity, and self-actualization plays itself out in much modern psychology, particularly in the human potentials movement. Of course, much modern morality is some amorphous mix of the three.

If these are the dominant currents of modern moral thought, there are many other streams we might have navigated. In spite of the recent discrediting of communism, many intellectuals continue to be Marxists, and no observer of our world today could doubt the ability of nationalism to define the values and identities of peoples.

And then many intellectuals have sought to discredit morality altogether. This is a task that has occupied the time of not a few social scientists and philosophers. There are two primary reasons for this. First, modern science has exerted a tremendous influence on modern thought, and what the science reveals is a world of pure factuality, a world devoid of values. Moreover, social scientists have observed that morality varies from time to time and place to place. Hence morality has come to be understood as a matter of convention rather than as part of the constitution of reality. (Of course scientific method dictated this conclusion, for with its limited sense of the powers of reason, science is not competent to assess different cultures *qualitatively*, as morally better or worse; only quantitative comparisons are legitimate. Hence it made no sense to suppose that one culture, one set of values, was better than another.)

Second, many critics of society have seen conventional morality as rationalizing the vested interest of a particular class or culture—the bourgeoisie, the church, men, the First World, or whites. Although their critiques differ in important ways, Marx, Nietzsche, Freud, and the Cultural Left have all argued that morality is an ideological defense mechanism. (Ironically, their critiques are often informed with what could only be called "moral" passion, a deep-felt sense of the injustice of conventional morality.)

There have been a plethora of reductionist theories about what morality *really* is, but they all share the conviction that morality is inescapably subjective, not part of the constitution of reality.

Where does this leave us? The power of our religious past ensures that secular ways of understanding morality will often be deeply influenced by religion, and the power of modern ideas and institutions ensures that they will influence contemporary religious accounts of morality. Still, the vocabularies of secular and religious accounts of morality are strikingly different. Secular moralists talk of rights and liberties, individualism and social contracts, self-actualization and utility, pluralism and choice. In some secular accounts, reality is morally neutral, and morality is nothing more than personal choice or social convention. Religious moralists, by contrast, talk of God's law and God's grace, sin and salvation, natural law and natural reason, community and tradition, love and liberation of the oppressed. For them, reality is a moral order.

The Question of Progress

Religious ideals and values have played an important role in sustaining the moral fabric of civilization and, on occasion, in bringing about moral progress. Religious ideals powerfully influenced both the movement to abolish slavery and the American civil rights movement, for example. But because traditional religion assumed that the truth had been given in the past, and because it was so closely aligned with the established powers of the world, it often resisted those forms of social change which we now count as progress.

The Catholic theologian Hans Küng suggests that the Enlightenment played a much more powerful role than Christianity in bringing about the recognition of human rights, securing freedom of conscience, and abolishing torture and religious persecution.[32] Reinhold Niebuhr credited the Enlightenment and Marx with greater contributions to the "progressive reassessment of the problems of justice" than Christian thought.[33] Charles Taylor has pointed out that the simple emphasis of the utilitarians on pleasure and pain "made it possible for the first time to put the relief of suffering . . . at the centre of the social agenda."[34] And Robert Bellah reminds us that "eighteenth century Americans with a few notable exceptions tolerated slavery; we do not. Nineteenth-century Americans tolerated violence and discrimination against immigrants and ethnic minorities; we do not. The early twentieth century tolerated the notion that women were basically inferior to men, even while giving them the vote; we do not."[35] Who can doubt the evidence of moral progress? And who can doubt that it is inextricably tied up with the characteristically modern notions of liberty and rights, autonomy and the new emphasis on the role of social institutions in creating human happiness?

And yet, Robert Bellah notes, we have at the same time experienced a "statistically well documented . . . decline of belief in all forms of obligation: to one's occupation, one's family, and one's country." Most everyone finds intolerable levels of greed, corruption, consumerism, narcissism, and violence in modern society; indeed, simple civility is all too often wanting. Bellah argues that this strange mixture of progress and decline may be at least partially explained by reference to the way in which our thinking about freedom has changed: in the seventeenth and eighteenth centuries "freedom was part of a whole articulated framework of moral and religious values—it meant freedom to do the good and was almost equivalent to virtue," but with the spread of modernity it "came to mean freedom to pursue self-interest."[36]

In advancing freedom in the modern world we have made great and genuine progress; but our uncritical pursuit of freedom may have undermined many of the virtues we might better have kept. No doubt the utilitarian emphasis on pleasure and pain did much to liberate us from traditional religious and political orthodoxies which paid little attention to earthly suffering; but the pursuit of pleasure as a positive program for building a civilization, is, arguably, far from sufficient.[37] The relentless individualism of modernity undermines tradition and community, and self-actualization may all too easily degenerate into selfishness and narcissism.

Here we have the solution to the irony I noted at the beginning of this chapter: the modern emphasis on rights and liberty, on utility and the pursuit of happiness, generated great progress; modernity gives us intellectual ground on which to stand in criticizing traditional societies that were repressive, aristocratic, hostile to human rights, and all too oblivious to human suffering. But modernity comes at a cost, for it undermines those traditional religious values of duty, self-sacrifice, love, and community that are, arguably, essential to our moral well-being.

In *Habits of the Heart* Robert Bellah and his colleagues argue that Americans have come to share a moral vocabulary they call the "first language" of American individualism, a rough-hewn amalgam of utilitarianism and expressive individualism that has come to provide the vocabulary we most often use to talk about our lives. Yet, they argue, this language is not nearly rich enough to allow us to articulate and make sense of those moral virtues and vices that are part of our civic and religious traditions. Some of us still speak the older "second languages" of these traditions, but they are heard less and less in our public culture. If we haven't become completely preoccupied with rights and self-interest, we are in danger of this, for we are losing our ability to speak meaningfully about duty and virtue, love and community. American education contributes to this problem.[38]

Education as a Moral Enterprise

Morality is not simply a matter of rules prohibiting what is wrong. It is a matter of character and the kind of person one should be; it is a matter of ideas and ideals, of community and critical thinking. It hinges on our conceptions of what is rational and irrational, normal and abnormal, and it is invariably bound up with our judgments about what makes for a good and meaningful life. As a result, virtually all aspects of education are shot through with moral considerations.

The Everyday Ethos of Education. It is often claimed that values are caught, not taught, and there is a good deal to this, particularly for young children. They learn morality not from reflective study and critical thinking but from the ethos of their environment: from teachers who are role models for them; from school rules; from rewards and punishments; from the hopes and expectations teachers and textbooks convey to them. This is better understood as moral training or socialization than as moral education, but such training is a necessary first step toward moral education. As R. S. Peters puts it, the "palace of reason has to be entered by the courtyard of habit."[39] To a large extent, morality is acquired by way of apprenticeship. Children become honest by practicing honesty under the tutelage of honest adults, by living in an ethos in which it is modeled and rewarded. And so it is for many other values which we may not be explicitly taught—integrity, hard work, mutual respect, timeliness, compassion, sobriety, deferred gratification—but which are practiced and encouraged in schools and universities. (Of course, students can also learn religious and racial prejudice, sexual stereotyping, mindless competitiveness, and an undue reverence for athletics from their environments.)

The Ethics of Teaching and Learning. Teaching is a moral practice. One fairly commonplace view is that teachers should nurture students who are reasonable, open-minded, fair, tolerant, tentative, and capable of making up their own minds. In pursuing this ideal we initiate students into a particular culture of learning that not everyone accepts. The theologian Stanley Hauerwas argues that it cannot be the task of education to allow students to make up their own minds, for, as he puts it, "most students do not have minds worth making up." Education is not about critical judgment; it is about "the formation of virtuous people by tradition-formed communities."[40]

Many critics of education on the Cultural Left argue that most education is (at least implicitly) committed to reproduce the dominant culture and sustain the status quo by conveying it uncritically to students. The "hidden curriculum" of schooling is to keep students passive by feeding them carefully selected information, by reinforcing the idea of the teacher as an authority, by not raising critical questions, and by withholding ideas and points of view that are critical of the status quo. Conservative critics of education often argue that teachers constantly undermine cultural authority by presenting students with a dizzying array of ideas, moral dilemmas, and alternative life-styles and by asking critical questions to which they allow no final answers, in effect denying that there is any truth and putting everything up for grabs. Clearly, a teacher's ethic of teaching conveys to students an attitude toward truth and authority, right and wrong—and, no doubt, teachers can encourage a mindless orthodoxy or a mindless relativism.

John Goodlad claims that the "most significant" finding in his massive study of America's public schools is that high-track courses devote more time to critical thinking, while low-track courses emphasize rote learning; high-track courses encourage independent judgment, low-track courses passivity and authority.[41] Although Goodlad does not use this language, what is at issue is the difference between two quite different kinds of moral character.

Textbooks. We have already seen at some length the extent to which commonly used textbooks embody a worldview complete with a particular understanding of morality. Economics, home economics, and psychology texts may shy away from overt moral language, but they have morally loaded messages about the nature of values and justice, rationality and decision making, what is normal and abnormal, mature and immature.

Often, state boards of education determine the moral content of textbooks by requiring that they take certain positions on controversial issues if they are to be adopted. So, for example, California requires that textbooks emphasize the importance of globablism, environmentalism, and cultural diversity. In Texas, by contrast, textbooks "shall promote citizenship and understanding of the essentials and benefits of the free enterprise system, emphasize patriotism and respect for recognized authority, and promote respect for individual rights." Moreover, they "shall not encourage life styles deviating from generally accepted standards of society."[42] To have their textbooks adopted, publishers must show how their texts address the requirements of the state's curriculum. Sometimes they have to rewrite sections or even individual sentences to pass the ideological tests of the textbook commissions.[43]

The Curriculum. The question of a core versus an elective curriculum is part of a long-standing debate over how to define a moral person and the good life. Was President White of Cornell right in holding that agriculture is as important as culture, agronomy as the classics? Are these decisions that can legitimately be left to students who pick and choose from an elective smorgasbord of classes? Should students be free to define their own conception of the good life and then structure a curriculum that satisfies them, or does the faculty (or the state) have the right or the obligation to guide their choices by virtue of its competence and authority?

The debate over the canon and multiculturalism is over very different understandings of people's moral identities. Is the traditional curriculum (focussed essentially on Western civilization), with its canon of Great Books (written largely by white, male authors), at the heart of our understanding of who we are, or is it cultural imperialism to impose it on women or ethnic minorities? Should different groups have their own values and histories, or is there a single definable set of Western values, ideas, and history which we properly teach?

The curriculum orients students in the world. By virtue of what we include in the curriculum we inevitably convey to students an understanding of basic truths, of what is important, and of how they should structure their lives and their thinking. So, for example, the utilitarian ideal of education so evident in the reform reports of the 1980s and in the rhetoric of business and government leaders, assumes that economic, scientific, and technological thinking and values define the good life; the important subjects are the sciences, mathematics, economics, and computers. The utilitarian ideal values analytical, critical thinking. Its goal is to produce wealth and comfortable lives for our people. But, as Richard Baer has noted, "If a curriculum emphasizes math and science and other courses which will help one become economically competent in a capitalist society, the result will be far different than if it emphasizes courses which help the student learn greater respect for the delicate ecological balances of the earth, or deepen her sense of social justice, or help her learn to know more about God and the life of prayer."[44] It is crucial that we see these as matters of fundamentally different visions, embodying conflicting moral ideals, of what an educated person should be.

Overt Moral Education. Most of what we "teach" students about morality is implicit, all too little appreciated for what it is by teachers, administrators,

curriculum planners, and textbook authors. Only now do we come to overt
moral education.

It is a striking fact about modern education that virtually everyone believes
that morality is tremendously important. Yet even if every college offers
courses in ethics, they are rarely required, and public school ethics courses
don't even exist.

At the undergraduate level, ethics courses are usually taught in philosophy
departments. It is probably fair to say that the purpose of many ethics
courses is less to determine what is actually right or wrong than it is to make
students familiar with various philosophical theories about morality—though
philosophers often argue that this is the best way to begin thinking about
what is right and wrong. Many courses do deal with practical moral problems,
however—economic justice, punishment, suicide, abortion, gender and race
and bioethical issues, for example. Religious views of morality fail to make
their way into undergraduate ethics texts except historically. With the possible exception of Kierkegaard, none of the great religious writers on morality of the nineteenth and twentieth centuries—Schleiermacher, Ritschl,
Rauschenbusch, Buber, Bonhoeffer, Maritain, Tillich, or the Niebuhrs, for example—are to be found in the anthologies. In part, this is a matter of disciplinary specialization. More important is the fact that most philosophers take
God's existence to be sufficiently unlikely that they simply do not take religious ethics seriously. For many philosophers, the point of the discipline of
ethics is to construct an understanding of morality which is compatible with
modernity.

If ethics courses are nonexistent in public schools, there is a small industry
of books and "packaged" programs that prescribe how to deal with morality
or values in various courses. No doubt the most common approach over the
last few decades has been that of values clarification. "The general thrust in
this approach," according to its founders, "is toward encouraging (1) more informed choices, (2) more awareness of what it is a person prizes and cherishes,
and (3) better integration of choices and prizings into day-to-day behavior."[45]
Values clarification exercises often involve dilemmas that force students to
make choices and think critically about what they value. For example, who
among the passengers of an overcrowded lifeboat (a young couple, their child,
a doctor, an elderly individual, an athlete, and so on) would students decide to
throw overboard? The intention of such exercises is to enable students to clarify the values they already have (hence the name of the movement), not judge
certain values as better or worse than others. Hence it is important that
teachers be nonjudgmental.[46] Indeed, it should be all right for students to
refuse to participate in the exercises, for we "do not wish to imply that every-

one *should* be more thoughtful about values issues or lead a more integrated life. Rather, we recognize that there are many people who are not up to it, or who prefer not to. . . . We do not want to communicate that a person is defective because his or her life remains confused, inconsistent, or fractured." In the end, what is most important to recognize is that a child cannot have the wrong values: teachers may be authoritative only in matters "that deal with truth or falsity," but values, being the product of personal experiences, are not the kinds of things that we can get right or wrong. It is up to students "to think and decide for themselves what it is *they* want."[47]

This is, essentially, the view of values found in the home economics textbooks I reviewed, and it also provides the theory that shapes many of the drug and sex education programs and texts used in schools. It is custom-made for modern liberal institutions: education, like the state, is to provide a neutral framework within which students are free to pursue the good as they understand it.

It should not be surprising that values clarification does little to develop character or speak to the growing lack of virtue in our society—indeed, it may be counterproductive. In response, a new movement of some force—the "character education" movement—has developed over the past few years. According to Thomas Lickona, one of its leading advocates, the emphasis on moral neutrality that controlled (and paralyzed) public education for the last few decades has given way with remarkable swiftness in the 1990s: "Escalating moral problems in society—ranging from greed and dishonesty to violent crime to self-destructive behaviors such as drug abuse and suicide—are bringing about a new consensus. Now, from all across the country . . . comes a summons to the schools: Take up the role of moral teachers of our children."[48]

According to William Kilpatrick, another of its advocates, character education is based on the claim that there are character traits which all children should acquire, "that they learn these by example, and that once they know them, they need to practice them until they become second nature." It is "more like an initiation into life than a debate about life issues."[49] It provides students with a basic moral orientation in life, a set of virtues, with *character*, so that they have the grounds and the disposition to act morally when confronted with choices. Kevin Ryan and Edward Wynne put the matter provocatively in stressing "the duty of the older generation to indoctrinate the young with what they are convinced are the essential moral realities and ethical truths the young will need to live well."[50]

Advocates of character education hold that for all our pluralism, there continues to be a consensus on at least some basic moral values; indeed, they typically argue that there are *universal* values—Lickona's list includes respect, responsibility, honesty, fairness, tolerance, prudence, self-discipline, helpful-ness, compassion, cooperation, and courage.[51] It is the task of schools, through their ethos, the experiences they provide students, and the morals of the stories that are taught, to initiate students into our common morality. To confront a child only with moral dilemmas—as in values clarification exercises— "without some prior attempt at forming character is a formula for confusing him, or worse." For example, in contrast with the values clarification lifeboat exercise, William Kilpatrick notes that when students see the film *A Night to Remember* about the sinking of the *Titanic* they are not left with "much room for ethical maneuvering" for it makes clear that there are proper codes of conduct in lifeboats: the only dilemma "is the perennial one that engages each soul: conscience versus cowardice, faith versus despair."[52]

Not everyone agrees about the virtues of character education, however. Kilpatrick tells of asking parents to choose between two possible approaches to moral education for their fifth- to seventh-grade students. The first approach involves students in discussions of moral dilemmas, with no right or wrong answers allowed. Teachers must remain nonjudgmental, and students decide for themselves what is right and wrong. The second approach introduces students to notable examples of virtues—honesty, responsibility, charity, and so on—from history and literature. Teachers express their own commitment to these virtues and encourage students to practice them in their own lives. The "vast majority" of parents choose the second approach, Kilpatrick reports, but when he has repeated the experiment with teachers they "invariably" prefer the first; indeed, "many teachers say they would not use the second approach under any circumstances."[53]

There are many other values programs emphasizing self-esteem, civic education, community involvement, cooperative learning, and ethnic pride, for example. I have focused my attention on values clarification and character education because of their influence and because they embody such very different ideas of what morality and education are all about.

Character Education—The First Dimension

I suggest we think of moral education as having four different, if sometimes overlapping, dimensions: character education, liberal education, civic education, and moral philosophy.

Elmer John Thiessen reminds us that "children simply cannot decide which particular culture, language, and so on they will be initiated into." Children inevitably acquire a set of beliefs and values before they are able to think reasonably and responsibly about the world. Of course, as they mature, "they begin to ask questions, and these need to be encouraged and taken seriously. But what children want are answers, not doubts, and it is as absurd as it is cruel to treat children at this stage with a heavy dose of 'critical thinking.'"[54] Children require a measure of stability, a vantage point from which they can began to think critically about the world. The ability to make moral judgments requires maturity; it isn't present from the beginning.

Character education in schools is a crucial part of a much larger social process—the necessarily uncritical initiation of children into a moral community. This moral community is, to some considerable extent, universal. For any society to thrive—indeed, for it to survive—it must share a broad range of settled virtues: people must be relatively honest in paying their taxes; they must be able to trust each other in business contracts; they must be willing to sacrifice their own personal good in wartime; they must care for their children; they must work hard enough to keep the economy running.

Schools and universities would grind to a halt if students and teachers were not at least moderately honest; if they did not show some respect for each other; if they were not timely and responsible and sober. Indeed, there is something to be said for Nel Noddings's claim that the "primary aim of every educational institution and of every education effort must be the maintenance and enhancement of caring."[55] Caring (which in a religious context might be called love) binds us together in webs of affection and undergirds the development of other values, for honesty, responsibility, and respect are more likely to flourish in a context of mutual caring (and in our culture of hyperindividualism this is no small thing).

None of this should be controversial; here we all agree. I trust that no principal would get in trouble at a PTA meeting by announcing that in her school students are taught to be honest and responsible, to work hard and care for each other. Whatever our disagreements and however much moral decay we detect, there continues to be a broad consensus about certain values and the need for moral character in our society. Through the ethos of the school, the examples set, the rules and regulations, the stories told, the history taught, and the personal relationships formed, educators guide the moral development of students, nurturing those moral virtues and values that we agree to be essential. (I should note that there are good political reasons why a principal might not want to *announce*, ex cathedra, what values are to be taught but instead let a consensus emerge out of community discussions in which all points of view are taken seriously.)

What does religion have to do with character education? To advocate honesty and integrity, mutual respect and caring (and a host of other values), is not to take sides among religions, or between religion and nonreligion.

Character education need create no Establishment Clause problems. Moral character and these fundamental moral values are common to all religions and all secular systems of morality. On at least a few fundamentals there continues to be an "overlapping moral consensus" that unites the religious and secular moralities of our society. (I might mention that there is no constitutional counterpart to the Establishment Clause that requires *moral neutrality* of public institutions. Promoting virtue is no constitutional vice.)

Even if the promotion of consensus virtues and values passes constitutional muster, there might still be problems with *how* those values are promoted, however. Charles Haynes has rightly pointed out that "teaching core values may not be done in such a way as to suggest that religious authority is unnecessary or unimportant." Indeed, character education "can be hollow and misleading when taught within a curriculum that is silent about religion." Hence, sound character education programs "will acknowledge that many people look to religious authority and revelation for moral guidance."[56]

There is a good deal more to moral education than character education, not least because, in the end, it inevitably entangles us in teaching about religion.

Liberal Education—The Second Dimension

If there is a good deal, morally, about which we agree, there are many moral issues about which we disagree strongly, even violently: abortion, sex roles, affirmative action, the distribution of income, the welfare system, patriotism, euthanasia, and homosexuality, to name a few. How we divide up on these matters is not likely to separate people into religious and secular camps, however. Religious folk disagree among themselves about these matters, as do secular folk.[57]

We disagree not only about moral conclusions, however, but about how to justify moral judgments. Why should one be honest? What reasons are relevant in making up one's mind about abortion? Indeed, we disagree about what counts as a moral issue. Is homosexuality a moral issue or merely a matter of life-style and personal values? We disagree about what morality is and how it works.

This is important, of course, because if we are to have moral *education* and not just moral *training* (or indoctrination) in schools, students must acquire some ability to think critically about matters of morality. People disagree just as strongly about how to justify their positions on abortion as they do about whether abortion is justifiable or not.

Worldviews Again . In chapter 1 I summarized James Davison Hunter's account of our "culture wars." Hunter argues that there is a fundamental difference between how the orthodox and progressives among us deal with moral and social issues. The orthodox appeal to the universal, unchanging, revealed moral truths of a supernatural God, while progressives appeal to a developing revelation modified by the continuing moral and religious experience of humankind. In the first part of this chapter I described a variety of (conservative and liberal) religious and secular ways of understanding morality. A part of what I wanted to show is how morality is always embedded within a worldview.

Whether or not morality can be separated from religion, it cannot be separated from an understanding of the world which makes sense of that morality. If morality were free-floating, if moral rules made no intellectual contact with anything, then we would properly ask, Why be moral? Why should we pay attention to morality? But this is not the way it works. Morality is very much bound up with our identities, with our place in a community or tradition, with our understanding of nature and human nature, with our convictions about the afterlife, with our hopes and our fears, our feelings of guilt, our experiences of the sacred, our assumptions about what the mind can know, and our understanding of what makes life meaningful. We make sense of what we ought to do, of what kind of a person we should be, in light of all of these aspects of life—at least if we are at all reflective.

This is the reason why values clarification is such a parochial approach to moral education. It removes morality from the encompassing worldviews that make sense of it. It leaves students on their own when culture provides them with rich resources for dealing with moral questions.

Historically religions provided the stories, the myths, and the worldviews that made sense of our moral values and virtues. That is no longer the case so far as public education is concerned, however. The conventional wisdom now is that morality can be understood and taught without reference to religion.

But the problem is not just that religious accounts of morality are ignored, it is that they are rendered suspect at best, and matters of superstition at worst, by the secular worldview that pervades modern education. From within almost any religious worldview, conservative or liberal, people must set themselves right with God, reconciling themselves to the basic structure of reality. They are to act in love and justice and community, being particularly mindful of those less fortunate than themselves. From within the modern worldview, by contrast, we seek power to work our will on the world. Modernity emphasizes rights rather than duties, individualism rather than community, autonomy rather than authority, and happiness rather than salvation. At various places in the curriculum students are taught self-actualization and self-esteem, utility and cost-benefit analysis, but it is unlikely they will encounter God's commandments or grace, sin or self-sacrifice. Indeed, they may be taught that there are no right or wrong answers when moral judgments are the issue. These are fundamentally different moral stances. There is little in the conventional wisdom that supports or renders meaningful a religious account of morality, and there is much that undermines it.

As we have seen, liberal education has a conservative and a liberal task. It grounds students in various communities of memory, giving them some sense of the moral identities they have by virtue of inheriting roles in various historical stories. And it should make students aware of *contending* ways of thinking about the world. A liberally educated person should understand something of the most important positions on the most important moral questions of our time when this means not just the conclusions but the ways of thinking that led to those conclusions. A liberal education requires that we initiate students into our ongoing cultural conversation about how to think about what is good and true.

Moreover, the arguments I made for fairness and neutrality in chapter 7 apply with full force to moral education. We are deeply divided about how to think about and justify moral judgments; a good education should take the alternatives seriously. Students must be taught something of religious positions on controversial issues and, more important, religious ways of making sense of morality just as they are (inevitably) taught something of secular positions and ways of understanding morality. Schools cannot leave students so ignorant of religion that they are uncritically socialized or indoctrinated into secular ways of thinking about morality which marginalize or discredit religious alternatives. That is to put schools and the state in a position of hostility to religion.

In this context, it is important to emphasize once again the importance of a core curriculum—in universities as well as in public schools. The current common mix of distribution requirements and electives allows students to miss most everything of moral importance, and it fragments our cultural conversation about what makes for good and meaningful lives into incoherence.

Whose Values Do We Teach? In discussions of moral education the question is invariably asked, *Whose* values are going to be taught? We can now see that the answer is, Everyone's values. When we agree, we initiate students into our moral tradition; we teach the truth of our common morality. This is the task of character education. When we disagree, we teach students *about* everyone's values fairly (without taking sides in the case of public schools). This is a large part of the task of a liberal education. Either way we teach everyone's values.

We agree about honesty and democracy, and we should teach students the importance and the rightness of these values, doing what we can to ensure that they are properly initiated into our common moral culture. We disagree deeply about abortion and political parties and how to think about morality; here we should teach students about the alternatives as fairly as we can, taking each of the contending points of view seriously, and then not take sides.

The problem with much conservatism is that it has likened controversial moral claims to those core values about which we agree, arguing that on most all moral issues there is a single moral position which students should be taught. The problem with much liberalism is that is has likened core values to those controversial moral claims about which we disagree, arguing that all moral values must be matters of personal choice.

Pedagogy

In some cases it should be quite clear what a liberal moral education requires. In American history students should take seriously the ideas and values of the Democratic and Republican parties. In sex education or health classes students should take seriously the major positions—religious and secular, pro-life and pro-choice—regarding abortion. They should have readings written from within the contending points of view, and they should discuss what can be said for and against each view from the position of each alternative.

The moral thrust of liberal education is often far less straightforward, however. As we have seen, there is an implicit or "hidden" moral curriculum to which we must be sensitive. I suggest that we might put the moral dimension of liberal education in perspective in six ways.

Relevance. Morality is not just a matter of overt rules about what is right and wrong. Moral judgments are enmeshed in questions of what is normal and abnormal, rational and irrational, what causes suffering and what leads to human flourishing, what is important and what is trivial, what traditions we teach and which we ignore. Virtually all of education is an object lesson in morality. Education is a moral enterprise.

Importance. If morality is taken seriously by teachers and texts in all courses, students are much more likely to attribute some importance to it—at least they will be more likely to take it seriously than if it is ignored. They will see it as having various kinds of intellectual and cultural resonances with other things they take seriously. If the economics teacher or the business professor discusses moral questions, students are more likely to believe that morality is important for how they live their lives and how they do their business than if such questions are ignored.

History and Identity. A common theme among victims of the Holocaust was well expressed by a survivor of Auschwitz who testified that "the greatest fear we had, the fear of the people around me, was not just of death but that every last one of us would die and there would be no one left alive to tell what had happened to us."[58] Elie Wiesel has written of the Holocaust that "anyone who does not actively, constantly engage in remembering and in making others remember is an accomplice of the enemy."[59] To forget the suffering of people is to grant victory to their oppressors. Remembering is a moral imperative; to be ignorant of the past is to fail to take our fellow human beings seriously.

History is more than dates and battles and discoveries. It is a record of the moral and political and religious experience and experiments of humankind; it provides a richly textured account of what has caused the suffering and flourishing of people. It provides much of the background understanding of the human condition that students need to assess the alternatives open to them in the present.

But more than this, history locates students in communities of memory, giving definition to their identities. We are not individuals, pure and simple. We are members of communities with a past. To be oblivious to the moral traditions of which we are part is a little like having amnesia: if we don't know where we have been, we don't know where we are going. Indeed, we don't know who we are.

Students—like all of us—are part of a human community in which there is a measure of agreement about morality; there are universal values. But students are also American citizens and inheritors of various political traditions; they are members of ethnic groups that embody rich complexes of values; their vocational training should initiate them into roles defined, in part, by various rights and responsibilities; and they are inheritors of religious traditions—the particular traditions of their parents and the broad traditions that have influenced the moral and cultural norms of society. Ignoring traditional communities can marginalize them. To ignore black history or non-Western history is to make a moral judgment about the sense of identity we will nurture in students. So it is with religion. Do we show students how their various religious traditions fit into history, or do we marginalize those identities?

Robert Wuthnow has argued that our moral thinking "is less likely to be shaped by the abstract claims of the philosopher than by the concrete tutelage of the storyteller." When religion is excluded from history textbooks, "the coming generation of Americans is increasingly likely to regard spirituality, if they regard it at all, as a subjective element of their personal identity, rather than a link with the history of our nation."[60] Understanding history is a matter of coming to *feel* oneself to be a part of ongoing stories, of various communities. By giving students a past, by situating them in various communities of memory, a good liberal education nurtures students' moral identities and gives direction to their lives.

Imagination, Passion, and Vicarious Experience. Too often we lack the ability to see the world as others see it; we fail to feel compassion or guilt when we should; we simply have not imagined some possibility. A liberal education should stoke our imaginations and our passions. Literature does this best, for it explores the wellsprings and crannies of people's lives, motives and experiences, providing imaginatively and emotionally rich ways of seeing and feeling the world.

Tzar Alexander II had seen the squalor of the serfs in nineteenth century Russia, but not until he (and many others) read Ivan Turgenev's *Sportsman's Sketches*, which portrayed serfs as fully human beings, did the movement for their emancipation take hold.[61] At the same time, Americans were reading Harriet Beecher Stowe's *Uncle Tom's Cabin*, the book that more than any other galvanized feelings about slavery. Two hundred years ago the poet Percy Bysshe Shelley wrote: "A man, to be greatly good, must imagine intensely and comprehensively; he must put himself in the place of another and of many others; the pains and pleasures of his species must become his own. The great instrument of moral good is the imagination."[62] When we feel more intensely, when we can empathize with others, when we can identify with them, when we can imagine outcomes and possibilities, then we are more likely to act well.[63]

The power of stories should be particularly obvious when religion is at issue because for Western religions at least, reality has the structure of a story authored by God. Reality is not static, a matter of unchangeable laws, but dynamic, purposeful. We know what we are to do when we understand our role in that story.

Several years ago I heard a college student on a television talk show describe AIDS as unfair because students no longer can experiment with sex and therefore they lack the experience necessary to choose a sexual life-style. She had an extraordinarily truncated sense of experience. One observer has noted that "the meaning of experience is a poor and haggard thing if it refers only to what has happened to me. The meaning of education and of culture is that we live vicariously a thousand lives, and all that has happened to human beings, things that have been recorded not by my experience but by the experience of others, become a second life, a third, and so on."[64] Indeed, there is some advantage to acquiring experience vicariously. Ernst Cassirer has noted that if "in real life we had to endure all those emotions through which we live in Sophocles' Oedipus or Shakespeare's King Lear we should scarcely survive the shock and strain."[65] Through history and literature students can nurture their imaginations and acquire a wealth of vicarious moral experience.

Critical Thinking. If we think of being moral as a matter of being honest or kind, it is a simple matter—most of the time. But life is complicated. Even if we believe that the moral law was given once and for all in Scripture, we must still be able to apply it in our lives. It is not enough to know that we should not commit murder. Is capital punishment murder? Is killing in wartime murder? Is abortion murder? It is not enough to know that we should love. Does love require a welfare state and national health care? Does love require pacifism? Does love require or prohibit euthanasia in the case of those who are terminally ill with painful diseases?

We must make moral judgments about matters of great complexity: whom to vote for, what to do with our money, what vocation to choose, how to improve race relations in our community. It requires a great deal of background understanding of the world, particularly of what has caused the suffering and flourishing of people. Critical thinking is not just a matter of applying the rules of logic (much less scientific method). It is a matter of thinking and feeling empathetically with others, of engaging one's imagination, of having access to a wealth of facts about the possible effects of alternative actions, of discerning patterns of meaning in experience, of looking at the world from different perspectives. Of course, all of this makes critical moral thinking difficult and controversial.

Civic Education—The Third Dimension

Character education and liberal education cannot be isolated in particular courses; they should pervade the curriculum. Civic education and ethics education are naturally, though not exclusively, taught in specific courses.

Civic education goes well beyond understanding the three branches of government and the importance of voting. It involves enabling students to understand and value the way we have constituted ourselves as a nation, the framework of rights and responsibilities that defines our public life.

In chapter 3 I argued that in our inescapably pluralistic society, in which we often disagree about matters of ultimate importance (such as morality and religion), *we must agree to disagree civilly* if we are to have peace and the freedom to pursue our respective individual conceptions of the good. That is, there are powerful moral reasons for supporting democracy and a constitutional framework of human rights. The overlapping moral consensus that binds the great majority of Americans justifies, on reflection, the ideal of freedom of conscience, religious liberty and human rights, and deliberation and democracy that are necessary if we are to live together peaceably in the pluralistic conditions of modernity.

Just as politics must be grounded in morality, so civic education is a form of moral education. It is the responsibility of public institutions, including public schools, to nurture civic virtue, even though we may disagree deeply about the ultimate justification of such virtue. It is particularly important that students understand the First Amendment, for it, more than any other aspect of our Constitution, provides the ground rules that enable us to live together with our deepest differences. No doubt our convictions about such civic virtues are not quite as obvious to us as are our convictions about honesty and integrity; moreover, in the end, there will be dissenters. Still, the consensus is broad. Indeed, it is nurtured by our sense of community as Americans—a sense of community that public schools seek to instill.

Civic education is typically provided in history and civics courses—though students should also learn a good deal about our civic ground rules from student government and the ways in which schools, as public institutions, deal with conflict and decision-making.

Moral Philosophy—The Fourth Dimension

Montaigne once noted that there was never anyone, no matter how common or foolish, "who was not sure of having as much sense as necessary."[66] Indeed, all too often we presume (sometimes with disastrous consequences) to have as much *moral* sense as necessary—and we are certainly not inclined to look at the writings of philosophers and theologians for guidance. There is a good deal of anti-intellectualism regarding morality in our culture.

Still, it is striking that we require students to understand a welter of highly complicated scientific theories (investing much time and effort, and often for little purpose) but allow them to remain *completely* ignorant of even the most basic ethical theories. How many college graduates could give even a rudimentary account of utilitarianism, social contract theory, or liberation theology? How many students could write a brief summary of Kant's ethics (Kant being widely viewed as the most profound writer on morality of modern times)? Just as the practice of science requires an understanding of scientific method and theories, so, arguably, the practice of morality would benefit from a measure of familiarity with theories that guide our moral thinking.

This is particularly important as the "first-language" of American individualism crowds the older "second-languages" of our civic, moral, and religious traditions out of our public culture and the curriculum. As Elizabeth

Fox-Genovese puts it, "in the absence of knowledge of the law, substantive traditions of moral understanding, or cohesive moral communities, we are left with only our emotions as a guide to morality." Public debate and human relations become exercises "'in emoting toward one another.'"[67]

Because morality is so important, so controversial, and so complicated, high school and college students should be required to study ethics. There is room for a rich variety of courses on ethics (as any good university provides), but what I suggest is something like the nineteenth-century capstone course in moral philosophy at both the high school and college levels. I have argued that education is first and foremost a moral enterprise (at least when morality is understood in a sufficiently broad way). What could be more fitting than to help students try to make moral sense of their education and discover how, in their life's work, they might make the world a better place?

I would not have this course taught as just another specialized course in ethics (as it is typically taught in philosophy departments), however. It should be broadly interdisciplinary, drawing on the insights and theories of philosophers, of course, but also of writers in politics, history, literature, psychology, and theology. Such a course should deal with some mix of practical moral problems (race, poverty, abortion, or sexuality, for example) and those more theoretical questions that enable students to acquire perspective and think reasonably and systematically about the world and what they have learned. It should provide them with critical distance on their educations, revealing the extent to which moral judgments are caught up in competing worldviews. It would ensure that students do not escape their studies without some understanding of our ongoing cultural conversation about how to live our lives, organize society, and find meaning in the world.[68]

Can Education Make Students Moral?

There is a great deal of skepticism about the claim that education, or even studying ethics, will make students moral. There are, I think, two major reasons for this.

First, there is the commonplace view that one learns morality at one's mother's knee, and if one has not learned to be good by the age of five it is too late. (The influence of Freud no doubt reinforces this view, though Freud saw a rather greater role for fathers in the process.) No doubt our character is, to a considerable extent, formed early in life. Nonetheless, people *do* change, more or less, throughout life—and surely they have not yet ossified by the time they start elementary school. Our characters mature; we can (with some effort) break old habits and form new ones; we do change our minds about important things.

But being moral is not just the habitual response of telling the truth or turning the other cheek. It is a matter of acting intelligently in the face of human suffering and human flourishing. It requires some sense of how the world works. It requires empathy and psychological insight. It requires historical perspective. We do not learn at our mother's knee whether abortion is justifiable, how to relate to our spouses, or how to vote. We learn a good deal that is important, but not nearly enough.

The second reason for skepticism comes from the ability of educated people to be barbarians. No one has stated this matter more forcefully than George Steiner. The evil of Nazism, he reminds us, rose from within "the core of European civilization. The cry of the murdered sounded in earshot of the universities; the sadism went on a street away from the theaters and museums. In the later eighteenth century Voltaire had looked confidently to the end of torture; ideological massacre was to be a banished shadow. In our own day the high places of literacy, of philosophy, of artistic expression, became the setting for Belsen."[69] In the early decades of this century Germany was the most highly educated country in the world; indeed, it was home to the most influential Christian and Jewish thinkers of the nineteenth and early twentieth centuries.

What can I say in one or two paragraphs in response? Obviously I make no claims for the moral value of *any* system of education. Education, like science and technology, can be used for the wrong purposes. By the end of the nineteenth century German higher education had become highly technical and divorced from moral and religious matters. Nor are bad teaching and texts likely to have any favorable effect on students' morality. Authoritarian, didactic teaching and overt indoctrination will be countereffective, at least in the long run. (This was another problem with much German education.)

For education to make a difference, it must be a particular kind of education. Even then the results cannot be guaranteed. I do not claim that the best education will in and of itself make students moral. Moral development depends on much besides teaching and study—good parenting and a nurturing environment, for example. Personal problems and cultural influences can keep students from learning from even the best courses and teachers.

I do believe that students can acquire moral insight and motivation if they are caught up in a web of caring relationships, if they learn how to be empathetic, if they can imagine life's various possibilities, if they are sensitive to human suffering, if they have some sense of history, if they know how to think critically about alternative courses of action, if they feel themselves to be part of a shared culture of moral values. Education can nurture all of these qualities. Surely such an education can make us more likely to be moral than we otherwise would have been.

Conclusions

For better or worse, the moral character of students is shaped to a great extent by their families, by our culture, and by that predisposition to self-centeredness (that theologians call "original sin") that lies in the hearts of everyone. It would be naive to think that public education can solve the moral crisis in our culture. It falls well beyond the competence of schools to eliminate the violence and drugs, the narcissism and psychopathology, of children raised in dysfunctional families and a corrupt culture.

But it would be naive and irresponsible to think that public education can do nothing to ameliorate the crisis. Indeed, precisely because our basic social institutions are failing, character education—the socialization of our children in our shared virtues and values—becomes even more urgent. Schools must set moral standards, model right behavior, punish and reward students for their actions, nurture caring relationships, and develop students' moral identities by providing them with stories and histories that give direction to their lives.

But morality requires a good deal more of us than habitual honesty and uncritical compassion. If we are to make this a better world, we must have some sense of what makes for the suffering and flourishing of people; our thinking must be informed by a broad understanding of the human condition. If we are to appreciate and respond to the needs of others, we must be able to think and feel our way, empathetically, into their hearts and minds; our imaginations must be kindled. The moral potential of our character must be nurtured and guided by a good liberal education. And, at a time when our public discourse about morality and politics (and religion) has become so intellectually barren, courses in civics and ethics can do a good deal to provide students with the language, ideas, and theoretical resources to make sense of and think critically about, their personal and public lives.

Moralities require supporting worldviews, contexts of meaning that make sense of them. Arguably a part of our problem is that the modern worldview which pervades public education provides too little support for a fully adequate morality. I have noted that religious ethics makes much more of duty and self-sacrificing love, tradition and community, than does secular ethics. Moreover, religion adds, as Reinhold Niebuhr once put it, the element of depth to morality, for it "is concerned not only with immediate values and dis-values, but with the problem of good and evil, not only with immediate objectives, but with ultimate hopes." [70] Utilitarianism and humanistic psychology do little to prepare people for the tragic dimension of life, for profound suffering, alienation, or death. No doubt much of our moral progress has come about because of the modern commitment to individualism, liberty, rights, and happiness, but we may have bought this progress at a price. In our time and place, there may be a special virtue in religious ethics.

Much contemporary education is relentlessly fixated on the ideas and values that underwrite economic and technological development. Economics, science, and technology are important, of course. But in the end they are not *as* important as our personal and cultural moral development. The greatest sources of meaning in life come not from wealth or technological wizardry (though a modicum of each is good) but from altogether different domains of experience. If students are to be adequately oriented in life, they might be educated somewhat less about the material aspects of our culture and rather more about art, the life of the mind, and those forms of community which bind us together with our fellow human beings, with the past, with our posterity, and, perhaps also, with ultimate reality.

Contemporary American education betrays a want of moral seriousness. In designing the curriculum, in writing textbooks, in educating teachers, we do not keep in mind that education is first and foremost a moral enterprise. Religion must have a central role in all of this. The idea that students can be educated about how to live, what kind of a person to be, and how to act, *without* taking religion seriously is at least illiberal and quite possibly absurd. [71]

VOUCHERS

In *Edwards* v. *Aguillard,* Justice Brennan noted that "families entrust public schools with the education of their children, but condition their trust on the understanding that the classroom will not purposely be used to advance religious views that may conflict with the private beliefs of the student and his or her family. Students in such institutions are impressionable and their attendance is involuntary."[1] Many religious folks find more than a hint of hypocrisy in Brennan's statement, for public schools *are* used to advance *secular* views that conflict with the private religious beliefs of students and their families. Although the courts have outlawed even the most innocuous nonsectarian, ceremonial prayers, they allow fundamentalist children to be taught (perhaps even indoctrinated in) evolution, feminism, sex education, and a score of ideas and ideals that offend their most basic beliefs. Public schooling is not religiously neutral. Of course, parents are free to send their children to private schools if they are sufficiently wealthy. But why shouldn't we have an educational system that actually enables families to act on their rights and educate their children according to their religious beliefs and values?

How do we sort out the respective rights of parents, the state, and children? Are vouchers constitutionally permissible? What are the major religious and moral arguments for and against vouchers? On balance, are they a good idea?

Educational Choice and Vouchers

Educational choice can be more or less restricted: parents might be given their choice of public schools within a given school district or state, or their choices might be broadened to include private schools and perhaps even religious schools. In the late 1980s and early 1990s thirteen states enacted systems of educational choice, though only one of them includes private schools and it does not include religious schools. Nonetheless, as the 1992 Carnegie Foundation study of school choice notes, "the drive to include nonpublic schools in 'choice' plans has moved from the edge of the school reform debate toward center stage."[2] Vouchers (or tax deductions or tax credits) typically enter the discussion when religious schools are alternatives because the courts have taken the Establishment Clause to prohibit *direct* government funding of religious schools (as that promotes religion). Arguably, if the state funds parents (by way of vouchers, tax deductions, or credits) then if tax money ends up in religious schools it is the parents' choice, not the government's, and is constitutionally permissible.

For reasons I will discuss, most liberals are opposed to vouchers, though many have come to favor a measure of public school choice (as has President Bill Clinton)—while conservatives often argue for including private and religious schools as options (as did President George Bush). The usual battle lines have become confused, however, for there is increasing support for choice among blacks who are unhappy with public schools in the inner cities.

For the past several years Gallup Polls have shown the public to favor a voucher system that includes religious schools by about a two-to-one margin. Indeed, in 1992, 70 percent of all adults, and 78 percent of parents with school-age children, supported vouchers.[3] In one poll, 88 percent of the black respondents who were familiar with vouchers favored them.[4] It is also true, however, that a 1992 Carnegie Foundation poll of parents with children in public schools found that only 32 percent of them favored a voucher system.[5] Moreover, in the early 1990s voters in Oregon, Colorado, and California decisively defeated voucher initiatives on the ballot. Arguably, at least some support for vouchers is really a matter of frustration with public education and declines substantially when any particular voucher scheme is proposed.[6]

Most proponents of choice argue that private schools are often more effective at educating children and that breaking down the government monopoly on public education and expanding the educational market to include private schools will set up a healthy competition that will force public schools to improve. This is the argument of the most influential book on choice of the last decade—*Politics, Markets and America's Schools*, by John E. Chubb and Terry M. Moe. Our "schools' most fundamental problems," they argue, "are rooted in the institutions of democratic control by which they are governed." So long as there is political (even if democratic) control over the "supply side" of education (the kinds of schools that exist), choice (the "demand side" of education) is of little value, for choice among politically controlled public schools will never be of any great significance. Chubb and Moe cite as their "guiding principle" that "public authority must be put to use in creating a system that is almost entirely beyond the reach of public authority."[7] That is, politics must give way to markets.

Chubb and Moe all but ignore religion, revealing the extent to which the public policy discussion of choice is carried on in entirely secular terms.[8] Their book also provides evidence of the extent to which the language of markets has replaced that of morality and religion, and this is troubling for at least some advocates of vouchers. For example, according to John Coons, Chubb and Moe reduce school choice to a "tool of supply side economics" in which "the only serious aim of school reform is to maximize those outcomes that we now measure in our econometric models."[9] Test scores, courses taken, and attendance and graduation rates are the objectives of education. Stephen Arons, another supporter of vouchers, argues that Chubb and Moe may well have done "more harm than good" to the public debate about vouchers, for they further entrap us in a "narrow-minded and commoditized conception of education likely to emerge from an economic marketplace."[10] For many advocates of choice, as we shall see, the most pressing considerations are not economic and market-driven but moral and religious.

The relative *overall* educational merits of public and private schools is beyond the scope of my competence or interest here, and I will not discuss many of the arguments relevant to an informed judgment about educational choice. Instead I will limit my discussion entirely to religious and moral considerations that are relevant to any informed judgment.

The Primary Issue

The Argument for Vouchers. In *Pierce* v. *Society of the Sisters of the Holy Names of Jesus and Mary* (1925), the Supreme Court ruled unconstitutional an Oregon law requiring all students between the ages of eight and sixteen to be educated in public schools. Writing for the Court, Justice James C.

McReynolds said that the law "unreasonably interferes with the liberty of parents and guardians to direct the upbringing and education of children under their control. . . . The fundamental theory of liberty upon which all governments in this Union repose excludes any general power of the state to standardize its children by forcing them to accept instruction from public teachers only. The child is not the mere creature of the state."[11] Parents have the constitutional right to send their children to private, religious schools.

The Court also acknowledged the rights of the state to "regulate all schools, to inspect, supervise, and examine them, their teachers and pupils, to require that all children of proper age attend some school, that teachers shall be of good moral character and patriotic disposition, that certain studies plainly essential to good citizenship must be taught, and that nothing be taught which is manifestly inimical to the public welfare."[12] Hence there must be some balance between the rights of parents and the state. Still, parents do have the right to remove their children from public schools and educate them according to their own beliefs—within limits, at least.

Currently, about 12 percent of American children take advantage of this right and attend private schools; most of them—85 percent—attend religious schools.[13]

Because of America's history of anti-Catholicism, particularly in public schools, it is not surprising that Catholics developed a parochial school system—and it not surprising that many Catholics are now strong proponents of vouchers. The Catholic argument does not depend on this unhappy history, however. In its Declaration on Christian Education the Second Vatican Council argued that since parents have "conferred life on their children" they "must be acknowledged as the first and foremost educators of their children." Moreover, because the state must respect religious liberty and pluralism, it must acknowledge the rights of parents to provide a religious education for their children and ensure "that no kind of school monopoly arises." In effect, this means that the state must allocate public subsidies so that, "when selecting schools for their children, parents are genuinely free to follow their consciences." The council did acknowledge roles that the state should play beyond funding, however: it should be "vigilant" about the preparation of teachers, look after the health of students, and "promote the whole school enterprise." Moreover, the council was clear that a proper education must provide students with the skills that enable them to "become actively involved in various community organizations, be ready for dialogue with others, and be willing to act energetically on behalf of the common good."[14] The American Catholic hierarchy has long affirmed its support for vouchers and federal aid.

About 13 percent of Jewish students attend Jewish day schools.[15] Most

Orthodox children—about 80 percent—attend them, but Conservative and Reform Jews have begun to place considerable emphasis on day schools as well.[16] Although Jews have been overwhelmingly separationist, there appears to be growing support for vouchers as the relentlessly secular thrust of American culture and public education takes its toll on Jewish identity.[17] As Jerry Muller puts it: "In a society as open as that of the United States, and in a population as educated as American Jewry, Jews are fated for complete absorption into non-Jewish culture unless they are intellectually prepared to confront that culture on Jewish grounds. Such preparation is very difficult without day-school education." And the success of day schools depends "on the availability of government funding."[18]

Often, however, the argument for vouchers is not rooted in the theology or spiritual needs of any particular religious tradition but in a more universal language of moral and political rights. Until recently, Berkeley law professor John Coons has argued, it was "the practice of our schools to force dissenting and nonbelieving children of the poor to behave like Protestants. Eventually the courts said no. That particular tyranny is behind us only to be replaced by another: children of whatever belief now must study the gospel of secular neutrality." For Coons, the case for vouchers "rests upon basic beliefs about the dignity of the person, the rights of children, and the sanctity of the family."[19]

For the philosopher Richard Baer, vouchers are necessary to protect freedom of conscience: "Parents would no longer be forced to send their children to schools whose values and practices offended, even violated, their deepest religious beliefs or their deepest convictions regarding social and political values." Most Americans, Baer acknowledges, "tend to view education largely within the context of bureaucracy, efficiency, and value neutrality rather than as a deeply personal, spiritual, and religious matter, an experience that demands freedom of a radical sort." But value neutrality is impossible; all education is based on fundamental religious and philosophical commitments. Unfortunately, insofar as "the ACLU and the courts have failed to realize the inescapably religious nature of education, their activities have been largely misdirected and . . . have tended to undermine the very First Amendment freedoms they were ostensibly fighting to preserve."[20]

After conversations with dozens of parents involved in disputes over moral and religious aspects of their children's education, legal scholar Stephen Arons concluded that they "are seeking to redress an imbalance of power over their children's education." As education has been professionalized families feel they have lost custody of their children to an alien system. Parents "who want their values and concerns for their children expressed in schooling are increasingly met with a wall of professional hostility and bureaucratic lethargy."[21] Too often parents are left with an unpleasant choice between sacrificing their freedom of belief and expression to obtain a government-subsidized education or paying twice to secure their birthright under the Constitution."[22]

The argument for vouchers is not an argument for the right of parents to send their children to religious schools. They already have that right. It is that government must provide the conditions under which they can act on this right. There is an argument for economic justice implicit in any argument for vouchers. Arons has argued that even with "constitutional protections for real educational diversity . . . most families remain too poor and overworked to make use of private schools or home education. . . . We have created a system of school finance that provides free choice for the rich and compulsory socialization for everyone else."[23] Polly Williams, the black legislator who led the fight for Milwaukee's voucher experiment, has said that "unlike those whose parents can vote with their feet and enroll in good private schools, poor black children are forced to go to the school the government selects for them. That's not right."[24]

Of course, a problem with most voucher proposals is that they are not sufficiently generous to enable the truly poor to send their children to good private schools. For example, the 1993 California voucher initiative would have provided $2,600 per child in a state where the public schools received about $5,200 per child. As John Coons pointed out, the effect would be that the poor will be largely segregated in poor schools while middle-class students will attend more affluent schools. Coons argues that a voucher system must "tilt toward the poor" for the "primary object of reform is the provision of good education to those who are presently most disadvantaged."[25] For vouchers to solve the problem of economic discrimination they must be considerably more generous, or the size of the voucher must be pegged to income, or schools must be required to reserve some significant portion of places for students from poor families.

As I see it, the major argument for vouchers is that, *if adequately funded*, they would enable poor people to exercise the right to educate their children in accord with their moral and religious values. Given the hostility of public schooling to religion, this argument must be taken seriously.

The Major Arguments against Vouchers. There are two major arguments to be made against vouchers and the rights of parents: the first gives priority to the rights of children; the second gives priority to the rights of the state and society.

Bruce Ackerman acknowledges that parents have legitimate authority over young children grounded in the need for them to have a coherent environment. But from "the child's point of view" there is something "troubling" about the control parents exercise over them. The problem with public schools is "*not* that they are insufficiently responsive to parental views but that they are *already* overly concerned with reinforcing, rather than questioning, the child's primary culture." Correlatively, the problem with vouchers is that parents will refuse to spend them on anything but schooling "that strives to reinforce whatever values they have—with so much effort—imposed on their children during infancy." Advocates of vouchers seem to assume that indoctrination is all right so long as it is the parents who are doing it. For Ackerman, by contrast, education must take its cue from a proper conception of the state. The modern liberal state must be neutral, and it must provide its children with a neutral education within which they can define the good for themselves. "It is not enough," Ackerman argues, "to indoctrinate the child into the patterns of life he happens to find at hand; what is required is a cultural environment in which the child may define his own ideals with a recognition of the full range of his moral freedom."[26]

Justice Douglas took a similar position in his often-quoted dissent in *Yoder* (in which the Court upheld the right of the Amish to withdraw their children from public schools after the age of thirteen): "While the parents, absent dissent, normally speak for the entire family, the education of the child is a matter on which the child will often have decided views." For example, the child "may want to be a pianist or an astronaut or an oceanographer," and to do so "he will have to break from the Amish tradition." But if "a child is harnessed to the Amish way of life by those in authority over him and if his education is truncated, his entire life may be stunted and deformed."[27] Douglas noted that on a number of occasions the Court had ruled that children are persons within the meaning of the Bill of Rights. Children have rights over and against their parents, and it is the obligation of the state to protect those rights in its laws regarding education. Presumably the state should require a liberal education that gives students some measure of choice.

The more common argument against vouchers begins with the rights of society and the state. Albert Shanker and Bella Rosenberg argue that "about 200 years ago this nation decided that public schools were *supposed* to have a transcendent purpose. That is why America created a public school system financed out of public funds in the first place, and that is why public schools were placed under direct democratic control; not only to enable individuals to pursue their particular academic and vocational interests in education, but to pursue the public interest in education."[28]

And what is the public interest in education? What is its "transcendent" purpose? Accounts differ, but most are variations on a common theme: the maintenance of democracy and a civil society. For Keith Geiger, president of the National Education Association, "Public schools are the glue holding our pluralistic culture together. . . . They educate America's young people to be informed citizens of our democracy. No other institution is prepared to educate all students no matter what their race, religion, economic status, abilities or disabilities."[29] Richard Walzer argues that "what is crucial is the need of every child to grow up within this democratic community and take his place as a competent citizen. Hence the schools should aim at a pattern of association anticipating that of adult men and women in a democracy." Schooling "provides the common currency of political and social life."[30]

Because he favors "strong" or participatory democratic institutions, Benjamin Barber finds some value in vouchers: they mobilize parents and this is often "the first step toward civic activity in a lethargic representative system where individuals are accustomed to deferring to politicians, bureaucrats, experts, and managers." Unhappily, however, a voucher system mobilizes people "via private incentives; it speaks exclusively to their private interests as parents." Vouchers "transform what ought to be a public question ('What is a good system of public education for *our* children?') into a personal question ('What kind of school do I want for *my* children?')." Because vouchers "replace the public mechanisms for determining what is in the public interest with market mechanisms" they contribute to the atrophy of our politics; they corrupt community.[31]

It is important to remember, Amy Gutmann points out, that children are not just individuals, nor are they just members of families, they are citizens of the state. As such, the state has rights over their education as well as parents. Indeed, parents already have a good deal of control over the moral and religious education of their children: they already "command a domain other than schools in which they can—and should—seek to educate their children, to develop their moral character and teach them religious or secular standards and skills that they value." But "the same principle that requires a state to grant adults personal and political freedom also commits it to assuring children an education that makes those freedoms both possible and meaningful in the future. A state makes choice possible by teaching its future citizens respect for opposing points of view and ways of life. It makes choice meaningful by equipping children with the intellectual skills necessary to evaluate ways of life different from that of their parents." The problem with vouchers "is not that they leave too much room for parental choice but that they leave too little room for democratic deliberation."[32]

For Gutmann, as for many liberals, the distinctive virtue of public education is that it creates the conditions under which democracy can thrive. In a pluralistic culture we disagree deeply about the nature of the good life, but we can live together because we do share a commitment to democracy. Hence we must support an educational system that teaches "democratic virtue." As citizens, Gutmann argues, we have "an important and common interest in educating future citizens."[33]

I know that I have not conveyed the profound sense of unfairness felt by many religious parents. Many liberals and secular folk find the purposes, curriculum, and ethos of public schooling so congenial and the beliefs of some religious folk so bizarre that they have a hard time seeing anything justifiable in their desire for their own schools. But to be forced, for want of wealth, to send one's children to schools which, as they see it, corrupt their children and undermine their moral and religious values, is no small thing. Parents who take offense at nonsectarian, largely ceremonial graduation prayers should have some small ability to empathize with religious parents whose most basic beliefs and values are rejected over and over again in textbooks and in the curriculum.

Most opponents of vouchers are willing to tolerate private religious schools so long as they receive no tax money (at least for religious purposes). Hence it is important that their arguments not be too strong, for if religious schools are a threat to the public good—to democratic virtues, to community, to respect for pluralism—why should they be allowed at all? Walzer acknowledges that "in principle, educational goods should not be up for purchase." Nonetheless, he claims, there is no necessity of a "frontal assault" on private schools so long as private education does not bring with it "enormous social advantages" (as in England) and its "chief effect" is only "to provide ideological diversity on the margins of a predominantly public system."[34] Because they are not very influential we can ignore them.

Gutmann argues that the state should require all schools, including private religious schools, to teach such democratic values as "religious toleration, mutual respect among races, and those cognitive skills necessary for ensuring all children an adequate education." And what if, for example, fundamentalists object? They must remember, Gutmann says, that they "are not just members of a church, they are citizens of *our* society."[35] They have no choice about it—though Gutmann acknowledges that such regulations would enjoy only limited success in practice.

On the one hand, if democratic virtues and the public good are so important, it is hard to understand why voucher opponents are not in principle, at least, opponents of private and religious schooling altogether. If, on the other hand, the *right* to private schooling is sufficiently important to warrant some risk to the public good, then it is hard to know why the state should not subsidize that right, enabling poor people as well as wealthy people to act on it.

Other Issues

Pluralism. Advocates of vouchers often understand themselves to be defenders of liberty and pluralism, and they are fond of quoting John Stuart Mill. In *On Liberty* Mill wrote:

> That the whole or any large part of the education of the people should be in State hands, I go as far as any one in deprecating. . . . A general State education is a mere contrivance for moulding people to be exactly like one another: and as the mould in which it cases them is that which please the predominant power in the government, whether this be a monarch, a priesthood, an aristocracy, or the majority of the existing generation, in proportion as it is efficient and successful, it establishes a despotism over the mind. . . . An education established and controlled by the State, should only exist, if it exist at all, as one among many competing experiments.[36]

And yet, according to Stephen Arons, the state is bent on "cannibalizing" religious subcultures.[37] It harasses and persecutes religious and political minorities who attempt to develop private schools, and it suppresses dissenting beliefs and values in the public school system. John Coons argues that the curriculum in public schools that survives the lobbying of various interest groups cannot, with justice, be described as a "marketplace of ideas." This political system of "prior restraint" censors the variety of ideas about race, religion, homosexuality, immortality, abortion, and gender roles to be found in our culture. Not only do private schools, by contrast, allow parents to transmit their own ideas, beliefs, and values to their children, they give standing to those ideas in the ideological marketplace: "The school is a loudspeaker for those who freely support it with their presence and wish to cooperate in its message."[38] It powerfully reinforces cultural pluralism over and against the deadening hand of governmental standardization.

Richard Baer argues that although it is easy for us as Americans to see the evil of a government-run newspaper, we should be even more concerned about government-run schools. For, after all, "defenders of *one* system of government-financed schools are quite willing to use the coercive power of the state to maintain a system of schools that fosters *their* vision of good education and the good life." The problem is that liberals "tend to see pluralism in terms of the individual student's right to free expression and freedom to read and learn what he or she wants. But surely this is naive, for pluralism almost certainly will not survive if it is dependent on individuals making isolated value choices. If we have learned anything from sociology, it is that values are related to *communities* and that, therefore, enabling *structures* are necessary if a tradition is to survive and flourish."[39] Sanford Levinson agrees: "If one genuinely supports pluralism, diversity, and multiculturalism, then one cannot be indifferent to the fact that such a society is possible only when each group has a genuine ability to maintain itself."[40] That is, public policy must nurture communities of diverse values if pluralism is to be robust. The public schools, on the account of most advocates of vouchers, nurture conformity.

Amy Gutmann agrees that pluralism "is an important political value insofar as social diversity enriches our lives by expanding our understanding of differing ways of life." But to "reap the benefits" of pluralism "children must be exposed to ways of life different from their parents and—in the course of their exposure—must embrace certain values, such as mutual respect among persons, that make social diversity both possible and desirable. There is no reason to assume that placing educational authority exclusively in the hands of parents is the best way of achieving these ends. . . ."[41] According to Richard Walzer, voucher plans suggest a "pluralism of a peculiar sort" for they strengthen organizations of like-minded parents and promote ideological groupings rather than loyalties based on geography. As a result, for most children, "parental choice almost certainly means less diversity, less tension, less opportunity for personal change than they would find in schools to which they were politically assigned. Their schools would be more like their homes."[42] Or, as another critic put it, "The children themselves do not sample at will from the tempting feast of options the voucher system makes available; they are bound to the one dish preselected by their parents."[43]

Other opponents of vouchers argue that they might very well lead to a Balkanization of American culture. Harold Hodgkinson warns that "private school choice, through the use of vouchers, would divide our nation. . . . These choice programs would ultimately splinter students and their parents into separate schools along ethnic, financial, and ideological lines."[44] Robert Maddox, past president of Americans United for the Separation of Church and State, writes: "I cannot believe the United States will benefit if our children are segregated into sectarian and political camps for their education. The

American public school system plays a vital role in building a single nation from an amazingly diverse collection of individuals." Yet, with public funding, Maddox argues, parents would be able to send their children to schools run by "unusual or radical groups with theologies or political views that most of us find distasteful."[45] "It takes little imagination," an editorial in *Church and State* claimed, "to expect the Rev. Louis Farrakhan and the Nation of Islam to create Moslem schools. And how about the Rev. Sun Myung Moon and his Unification Church?"[46] Similarly, Bill Honig, for many years superintendent of public instruction in California, has warned that vouchers will breed "cult schools" and encourage "tribalism." "Is it good public policy," he asks, "to use public funds to support schools that teach astrology or creationism instead of science?"[47]

Two very different conceptions of pluralism are at issue here. Most opponents of vouchers argue that private religious schools would almost certainly expose students to less diversity than do public schools; moreover, students would not likely be taught the *value* of dissent, democracy, and pluralism. There is a good deal of reason for these concerns. Many advocates of vouchers would have their children indoctrinated into a single tradition in the religious schools which they would have the government indirectly fund. (Indeed, if they could marshal a political majority, more than a few of them would turn our public schools to their religious purposes as Protestants did in the nineteenth century.) Moreover, there can be no doubt but that public funds would find their way into the coffers of organizations that most Americans would find "distasteful"—though if we are committed to religious liberty and to neutrality among religions (as Maddox and *Church and State* presumably are) we should worry a little about using this argument. As has often been said, liberty and the First Amendment are of no great importance if they only protect the freedom of people to do what the majority regards as in good taste.

No doubt many religious schools would give their students unhappily illiberal educations. But this must be balanced against two other facts. First, as the advocates of vouchers argue, the public schools are not now a true "marketplace of ideas"; they are hostile to religion and those religious subcultures whose members understandably want relief from what they take to be the indoctrination of their children against their religion. Second, many advocates of vouchers do favor liberal education.

Segregation. Opponents of vouchers argue that choice will lead not just to ideological segregation but to segregation by race and class. Vouchers will almost surely be underfunded so that only middle-class people would actually be able to use them, leaving poor people, and especially blacks, to an underfunded public school system. Public schools will become the dumping ground for the disadvantaged. The situation will then be exacerbated because middle-class parents and legislators will not support the public education system if their children do not attend public schools. Honig argues that vouchers would "almost guarantee exacerbation of income and racial stratification."[48]

It has also been argued that educational choice is a smoke screen for racism. "Over the years," according to the ACLU, "'freedom of choice' in education has come to be understood by its supporters and detractors alike as essentially a code phrase for racial segregation." Former president Bush's voucher plan, for example, "would perpetuate the de facto segregation by race and class that characterizes the majority of the national public school systems . . . [and] would serve only to maintain and contain, through an institutionalized deprivation of opportunities, a permanent, disproportionately non-white class of under- and uneducated citizens."[49]

This is a real—and distressing—possibility, although there are points to be made in defense of vouchers. First, virtually all voucher advocates acknowledge laws against racial discrimination should certainly be applied to religious schools if they are to receive vouchers. Second, as George Dent has pointed out, integration led to an exodus of whites from public schools, undermining support for public education, but no one uses this as an argument for returning to segregated schools.[50] The principle is more important than the effect. Third, if vouchers are sufficiently generous and vary by income level, the likely segregation could be mitigated. If vouchers could be pegged to spending on public education, parents of children in private schools would acquire a reason to support taxes for public schools. Fourth, as the ACLU statement acknowledges, the current situation in many public schools is one of de facto segregation by race and class. Moreover, there are huge disparities in the funding of public education between poor urban systems and some affluent suburban systems. Currently, in eight states the richest school districts spend four times more per pupil than the poorest districts.[51] Finally, although there is some truth to the idea that "choice" is a code word for segregation, it is also true, I think, that (secular) liberals often fail to appreciate the depth of the *religious* reasons people have for enrolling their children in religious schools. Moreover, in some ways private schools, Catholic schools especially, have been much more successful at integrating students than have been public schools. Indeed, about three-quarters of all Protestant Christian schools are integrated.[52]

The problem of racial segregation is particularly difficult in part because of the religious arguments for vouchers. As the authors of *Society, State, and Schools* argue, religious rather than racial identity "should qualify a student for acceptance in a school," but because religious identity often correlates with race, religious schools will often be (de facto) segregated.[53] Few members of racial minorities will apply to Jewish day schools, and few whites will apply for schools sponsored by Black Muslims. Requiring racial integration (as opposed to simply forbidding discrimination) would defeat the religious argument for vouchers.

Moral Education. Many parents believe that the moral values they nurture in their children are constantly undermined by the alien values of other children in public schools and by the inability of the schools to eliminate violence, drugs, and alcohol. One parent of children in the public schools warns, "Make no mistake: it is a battlefield that our youngsters go off to every day. Dirty words are scrawled on bathroom walls. Deskmates swear. Fights break out on the playground. A few boast of real or imagined sexual exploits. Many have as their constant frame of reference those TV shows our children are not allowed to watch. And most important, God is not acknowledged as the Lord of Learning."[54]

As important, they feel their values are undermined by the neutrality (they might say hostility) of the official curriculum. Quentin Quade argues that in the moral vacuum of public education "we dare *not* call upon religiously based moral precepts to counsel against premarital sex, but we *must* provide contraceptive or abortion advice even if it serves to legitimize promiscuity among fourteen- and fifteen-year olds and tramples on the moral beliefs of countless parents. By contrast, the independent school, precisely because it does not have to represent the whole of society, and because it is less susceptible to legal manipulation, can both teach and insist on clear ethical standards that reflect the school's founding principles."[55] According to Paul Parsons, far and away the major reason for the Christian school movement is that parents believe that "public schooling does not teach values like it used to, discipline like it used to, or instill old-fashioned morality like it used to."[56]

Public schools typically fall far short of the ideal of schooling as a "moral enterprise" for which I argued in the last chapter; there is much more they could do. Nonetheless, even if schools were much better in this regard, many parents would still find them wanting, for in our increasingly pluralistic society there are many moral questions on which *public* schools must remain neutral. And, as Elmer John Thiessen argues, "Might it not be that the anomie and rootlessness so pervasive in our societies is in part related to our liberating children too soon from the present and the particular in which they are raised? Are they exposed too soon to a 'Babel of values' in our public schools?" Perhaps, he suggests, students need a greater degree of coherence and stability in their lives—even if our eventual goal for them is a measure of moral autonomy. But this, he argues, is only possible "if it occurs in the context

of a plurality of schools reflecting the plurality of traditions in our society."[57]
Some significant sense of community and shared values must nourish moral
education if it is to take hold, but as our culture continues to fragment
morally, public schools will find it harder and harder to provide this foundation of community and consensus.

Ironies

Historically, liberals have favored maximizing personal choices and letting
people define their own lives; they have been particularly solicitous of minority rights. Conservatives, by contrast, have been wary of pluralism and unre-
strained liberty in moral and social matters and have usually argued for sustaining the traditional "common" culture (which often translates into the
traditional or majority point of view). We have seen, for example, that the
common school movement in the nineteenth century was largely a conservative movement that had the purpose of leveling our differences into a common
American character (and when Oregon tried to abolish private schools in the
1920s it was for conservative, nativist reasons).[58] Nowadays, in the controversy over multiculturalism, conservatives typically defend teaching Western
civilization and traditional American values, while liberals have advocated
sensitivity to minority traditions, sometimes to the point of defending Afrocentric curricula and schools.

On vouchers, however, it is liberals who would limit personal choices and
the rights of minority communities by appealing to the need to maintain democratic virtues and a common culture. Many conservatives, meanwhile, have
joined forces with the Cultural Left, arguing for greater social choices, diversity, and a true pluralism of communities, and against any efforts to impose
whatever remains of common social values on their children.

Myron Lieberman has suggested that the voucher controversy also constitutes "an unprecedented philosophical turnabout on equality issues." The
usual liberal position on a variety of social issues has been that parties are
equal when they possess equal power to do something, while conservatives
typically hold the line at formal legal equalities. So, for example, while conservatives support equality of opportunity, liberals favor (a rough) equality of
condition. While conservatives are opposed to various kinds of legal discrimination, liberals often favor affirmative action programs that give minorities or
women access to various social goods. But in the voucher controversy, Lieberman argues, "it is the conservatives who have adopted the idea that equality
must be viewed as equal power, not merely as an equal legal right, to take an
action. Conservative support for vouchers has repeatedly emphasized the

goal of providing the poor with the effective choice now available only to the more affluent. Meanwhile, the liberals have ignored their traditional approach to equality as the equal power to do something."[59]

This irony becomes even more pointed when we note that people who are pro-choice on education are typically anti-choice on abortion; while anti-choice folks on abortion are typically pro-choice on education. Moreover, as Michael McConnell has shown, "virtually everyone who supports the funding of abortions opposes the funding of religious schools, and virtually everyone who supports the funding of religious schools opposes the funding of abortions." But liberals should favor the funding of abortions *and* religious schools to maximize effective choice, according to McConnell. To show this, he takes Justice Brennan's argument in *Harris* v. *McRae* that by funding live births but not abortions, government, in effect, denies any effective choice to poor women and, by altering the phrases in the brackets below so that they deal with education rather than abortion, transforms it into an argument for funding religious schools. (The bracketed references are to *Lemon* v. *Kurtzman*, in which the Court denied the right of the state to subsidize religious schools.)

A poor woman [with school-age children] confronts two alternatives: she may elect either to [send them to secular schools] or to [send them to religious schools]. In the abstract, of course, this choice is hers alone, and the Court rightly observes that [*Lemon*] "places no governmental obstacle in the path of a woman who chooses to [send her children to religious school]." But the reality of the situation is that [*Lemon*] has effectively removed this choice from the indigent woman's hands. By funding all of the expenses associated with [secular education] and none of the expenses incurred in [religious education], the Government literally makes an offer that the indigent woman cannot afford to refuse. . . . Many poverty-stricken women will choose to [send their children to secular schools] simply because the Government provides funds for [this], even though these same women would have chosen [religious schools] if the Government had also paid for that option, or indeed if the Government had stayed out of the picture altogether and had defrayed the costs of neither.

McConnell notes that Brennan "would reject the argument as it applies to school funding. But he has never explained why."[60] This seeming inconsistency may be even more pointed in light of Brennan's comment in *Schempp*: "In my judgment the First Amendment forbids the State to inhibit that freedom of choice [which parents have to choose between public and private religious schools] by diminishing the attractiveness of either alternative. . . . The choice between these very different forms of education is one . . . which our Constitution leaves to the individual parent. It is no proper function of the state or local government to influence or restrict that election."[61] But, of course, by providing free public education, while requiring parents to pay taxes for public schools and tuition for private education, government does diminish the attractiveness of the latter alternative. Indeed, it is good to remember that in the late 1960s and 1970s vouchers were often supported by liberals (such as Christopher Jencks and his colleagues at the Center for the Study of Public Policy) precisely because they believed vouchers would improve education for disadvantaged children.[62]

There are, of course, good liberal reasons for opposing vouchers: fear that vouchers would promote segregation, making the public schools the "dumping ground" for blacks and the poor; concern that private religious schools would indoctrinate children and would not promote democratic virtue and a respect for pluralism; and a conviction that government funding of religious schools would break down the wall of separation between church and state. These traditional liberal concerns stand in something of an unacknowledged tension, however, with the paradigm liberal values of liberty and equality, which are, arguably, enhanced by vouchers.

For free market (or libertarian) conservatives, vouchers maximize the effect of the market. There are no ironies here. But, the primary reason why religious conservatives support vouchers is, ironically, precisely the reason that one might have thought liberals should favor them: they maximize liberty and (a certain kind of) pluralism rather than enforce, through governmental institutions, established values and orthodoxies. The problem, of course, is that the public schools don't uphold traditional religious values anymore; public education is now run by secular liberal professionals. Hence liberals end up supporting the status quo, while conservatives argue for maximizing social choices even if that means the fragmentation of society.

The First Amendment Again

In chapter 3 I cited a rather confusing welter of rulings in which the Supreme Court either approved or disapproved of state aid to religious schools. To review, briefly, the Court ruled unconstitutional the use in religious schools of state funds for instruction in secular subjects; remedial or therapeutic services or counseling; instructional supplies or field trips; public school teachers who teach secular subjects on a part-time basis in religious schools; maintenance and repair of facilities; and tuition reimbursement. But the Court upheld the use of state funds for secular textbooks; bus transportation; speech, hearing, and psychological diagnostic services; standardized texts in secular subjects; and translators for deaf students. Very roughly, the Court has rejected state aid that has the purpose or primary effect of aiding or promoting the religious mission of parochial schools (in violation of either of the first two prongs of the Lemon Test) or that requires so much supervision to ensure that it is not used for religious purposes that it entangles church and state (in violation of the third prong of that test). When funding was approved it was sometimes justified on the grounds that the benefit went to students and their families rather than to the schools, but in every case it was important that the funding went to students attending public as well as religious schools—so that it was awarded neutrally—and that it served secular purposes, albeit in the context of religious schooling.

The Supreme Court first considered the principle underlying vouchers in *Committee for Public Education and Religious Liberty (PEARL)* v. *Nyquist* (1973), when it ruled that a New York law that provided partial tuition reimbursement and tax deductions for low-income parents with children in private schools (most of which were religious) violated the second prong of the Lemon Test. Writing for the Court, Justice Lewis Powell held that by "reimbursing parents for a portion of their tuition bill, the State seeks to relieve their financial burdens sufficiently to assure that they continue to have the option to send their children to religion-oriented schools. . . . The effect of the aid is unmistakably to provide desired financial support for nonpublic, sectarian institutions." Although it is laudable, Powell wrote, "to enhance the opportunities of the poor to choose between public and nonpublic education, the State has taken a step which can only be regarded as one 'advancing' religion."[63] Such aid promoted *indiscriminately* the religious as well as any secular purposes of religious schools. The fact that the tuition reimbursements and tax deductions went to parents rather than to the religious schools directly was irrelevant; the effect was still to promote religion.

But in *Mueller* v. *Allen* (1983) the Court upheld a Minnesota law that allowed parents of children in *both* public and private schools to take tax deductions for tuition, secular books, and transportation expenses. In the majority decision, Justice Rehnquist argued that it was crucial in withstanding the strictures of the Establishment Clause that the state assistance go to parents rather than directly to religious schools: "Where, as here, aid to parochial schools is available only as a result of the decision of individual parents no 'imprimatur of State approval' . . . can be deemed to have been conferred on any particular religion, or on religion generally." How did this aid differ from that in *Nyquist*? "Most importantly," Rehnquist wrote, "the deduction is available for educational expenses incurred by *all* parents," and any program "that neutrally provides state assistance to a broad spectrum of citizens is not readily subject to challenge under the Establishment Clause."[64] Presumably *Nyquist* was still good law: government cannot single out parents of children in religious schools for aid; it must be offered neutrally, to all parents. (Justice Rehnquist had dissented in *Nyquist*; but Justice Powell, who had written the *Nyquist* opinion, sided with the majority in *Mueller*.)

Mueller was decided on a five-to-four vote. Writing for the dissenters, Justice Thurgood Marshall argued that the Minnesota statute "violates the Establishment Clause for precisely the same reason as the statute struck down in *Nyquist*: it has a direct and immediate effect of advancing religion." What was crucial for the dissenting minority was not that the financial support went to parents rather than directly to religious schools; it was that it still had, in the end, the effect of aiding religion. Marshall argued that in previous cases the Court had distinguished state funds used "exclusively for secular, neutral, and nonideological purposes" in religious schools from funds used for religious or unrestricted purposes. Fire and police protection, bus transportation, and secular textbooks are constitutional forms of state aid for they support only secular purposes; but "the assistance that flows to parochial schools as a result of the tax benefit is not restricted, and cannot be restricted, to the secular functions of those schools."[65] Moreover, the neutrality of the statute is superficial: because most children in public schools have no tuition, textbook, or transportation expenses, the vast bulk of the benefit will go to parents of children in religious schools.

Then, in *Witters* v. *Services for the Blind* (1986), the Court upheld the right of students to use Washington State vocational rehabilitation funds to cover expenses at religious colleges. Only three years after *Mueller*, Justice Marshall now defended such indirect support of religion in his majority opinion: "Vocational assistance provided under the Washington program is paid directly to the student, who transmits it to the educational institution of his or her choice. Any aid provided under Washington's program that ultimately flows to religious institutions does so only as a result of the genuinely independent and private choices of aid recipients." Hence the "mere circumstance that petitioner has chosen to use neutrally available state aid to help pay for his religious education" cannot "confer any message of state endorsement of religion." Did Marshall change his mind? He does not directly address the difference between *Mueller* and *Witters*, but he does say that the Washington program "is not one of 'the ingenious plans for channeling state aid to sectarian schools' that periodically reach this Court" (as the Minnesota plan presumably was) and that no "significant portion" of state funds would flow to religious schools (again unlike in Minnesota).[66]

In concurring opinions, however, Chief Justice Burger and Justices Powell, Rehnquist, and O'Connor took the occasion to indicate the similarity of *Witters* to *Mueller*: "State programs that are wholly neutral in offering educational assistance to a class defined without reference to religion do not violate the second part of the *Lemon v. Kurtzman* test, because any aid to religion results from the private choices of individual beneficiaries."[67] There is some reason, then, to believe that the Supreme Court would uphold a properly crafted voucher plan. *Witters* was a unanimous decision.

Is this sound jurisprudence? Should vouchers be constitutionally permissible?

Legislatures need not run afoul of the first prong of the Lemon Test in enacting voucher plans that include religious schools. There are, after all, a variety of secular purposes to be served in giving parents the choice of where to school their children—increasing competition, enhancing family values, or enlarging the domain of freedom, for example.[68] Indeed, to exclude religious schools from voucher plans would be to violate neutrality by discriminating *against* religion. Moreover, as Phillip Johnson has pointed out, "the state may certainly enact legislation to further the *free exercise* of religion, which is a purpose of the First Amendment itself."[69] Indeed, precisely because public education is hostile to religion, legislators might enact voucher plans to *restore religious neutrality* to the funding of education in the spirit of the Establishment Clause.

By giving parents a voucher they might use for religious or secular schooling, the government cannot be said to be *endorsing* religion; it is the parents, not the government, who endorse religion by virtue of their private choices. (It is worth noting that the Supreme Court has upheld tax deductions for contributions made to religious organizations. It is individual citizens, not the government, who decide that their contributions will go to churches or synagogues or mosques rather than a secular charity; government simply treats religious institutions the same as other charitable organizations.)

In arguing against vouchers, Stephen Green, legal counsel for Americans United for the Separation of Church and State, acknowledges that the "funneling of aid through private individuals removes . . . the imprimatur of government approval." But, he argues, this does not settle the question of whether such aid "advances religion by subsidizing religious education and by creating incentives for children to attend sectarian schools." Because vouchers have the *effect* of aiding religion, they violate the second prong of the Lemon Test. Vouchers, he concludes, are mere "facades" for promoting religion.[70]

Green and most opponents of vouchers are no doubt correct that vouchers would encourage religion *relative to the status quo*. But the status quo is not religiously neutral. Because the state underwrites all of the costs of public education, it now actively discourages parents from sending their children to religious schools, and because public education is, as we have seen, hostile to religion, this leaves the state in the position of promoting secular over religious ways of thinking and living. The baseline for determining neutrality must be the status quo *ante*—that is, our culture apart from governmental interference. If vouchers are worth no more than the per pupil subsidy of public education there is no incentive *on balance* for attending religious schools. A properly crafted voucher plan, one that gives expression to the governmentally uninfluenced choices of parents, would surely reflect the current array of secular and religious ideas and values in our culture more neutrally than public education does.

There are, I suggest, two different ways of achieving neutrality. I described the first in chapters 6 and 7: public schools are religiously neutral if they take religious as well as secular ideas and values seriously (reflecting the range of positions to be found in our culture) and then do not take sides. It is also open to the state to maintain neutrality by leaving decisions about education up to parents; if government is to be truly neutral, it cannot subtly encourage secular or religious schooling by providing a greater per pupil subsidy for one over the other. Which kind of neutrality we adopt is properly a policy decision and is not constitutionally dictated. I should note, however, that adding a voucher alternative to public education does not solve the government's neutrality problem, for just as an excusal policy does not make school prayers constitutional, so the availability of vouchers does not restore neutrality to public schools. If there are to be public schools at all, *they* must be religiously neutral.

But what of the wall of separation? In *Everson* v. *Board of Education* Justice Black wrote that "no tax in any amount, large or small, can be levied to support any religious activities or institutions."[71] Robert Maddox, formerly the executive director of Americans United for Separation of Church and State, claims that vouchers jeopardize "the principle of church-state separation" for "Americans will effectively be forced to pay taxes to maintain private religious schools, whether they agree with the religious and political views taught in them or not. This amounts to a church tax."[72]

I have already noted that the "wall of separation" is not to be found in the Constitution but was introduced to Establishment Clause jurisprudence by Justice Black in *Everson*. It was also in *Everson* that Black first used the language of *neutrality* to interpret the Establishment Clause. I have argued that we best understand the First Amendment in terms of neutrality, not strict separation. If a voucher plan is substantively neutral between religion and nonreligion, if it doesn't put government in the position of encouraging or discouraging religion, then the Establishment Clause has been satisfied. A plan that provides the same funding for students in religious schools and secular private and public schools would neither encourage nor discourage religion relative to the governmentally uninfluenced choices of parents.

In any case, the "separation" of church and state *is* guaranteed by the fact that it is parents, individual citizens, not government, who will make the decision concerning the destination of funds. The parents stand between government and religious schools, separating them.

Finally, I am not impressed by Maddox's claim that people will be forced to pay taxes to support religious schools whether they agree with what is taught there or not. We now force citizens to pay taxes for public education *against* their deepest moral and religious convictions. Jefferson—from whom Black acquired the concept of the "wall of separation"—put the matter in a truly religion-neutral way in the "Virginia Statute of Religious Liberty": "To compel a man to furnish contributions of money for the propagation of [any] opinions which he disbelieves, is sinful and tyrannical."[73] Of course, if we are to have tax-funded education then at least some people must pay for the propagation of opinions that they disbelieve, but I see no reason why conservative religious folk should bear this burden while secular folk need not.

Vouchers are constitutionally permissible; whether they are a good idea is something else again.[74] (I should note that I have dealt only with the federal constitution. Some *state* constitutions have amendments prohibiting the use of tax money for religious schools, so that vouchers might be unconstitutional at the state level even if they are constitutional at the federal level.)

Conclusions

If vouchers are constitutionally permissible, are they a good idea? It strikes me, unlike most people who write about vouchers, that there are powerful arguments for and against them.

I am not inclined to believe that either parents or the state should have the *sole* right to determine the nature of education. Parents should have rights over the education of their children; states should have rights over the education of their citizens. The Supreme Court has said that children are not mere creatures of the state, and it has affirmed the right of parents to educate them in private schools. But it also affirmed the right of states to regulate that education—to ensure, among other things, "that certain studies plainly essential to good citizenship must be taught."[75] As Richard Baer has argued, states can "define their compelling interest in education by setting minimal requirements in reading, writing, math, American history, and civics," leaving "the choice of subject matter and standards in areas outside the state's compelling interest to the discretion of individual schools."[76] At least some of the state's purposes can be served by regulating private education as well as by operating public schools.

I would add a third interested party to our deliberations. Children inherit more than genes and citizenship; they inherit a language and a culture. Children have the right to a liberal education that initiates them into those overlapping communities of memory that constitute their cultural inheritance. The education of children should also be determined in part by educators who speak for our history and culture.

Where does this leave us? I would like to believe that the best point of compromise among the various interested parties is a system of public education that takes seriously the ideas and values of parents (reflecting the major ideas and values found in our culture), the state (as determined by democratically elected officials within the constraints of the Constitution), and educators (who are sensitive to our history and culture and responsive to the developing understanding of the world found in their respective disciplines). I also believe that public schools have a particularly important role to play in nurturing a sense of community, respect, and mutual understanding in a pluralistic and increasingly fragmented culture.

Unfortunately public education is too often illiberal education, especially when religion is at issue, and in assessing the relative merits of vouchers we must not weigh them in the balance with an ideal system of public schooling. Neither should we weigh public education as it actually is against an ideal voucher system. The great majority of voucher proposals fail to be sufficiently generous to enable poor people access to high-quality private schools or to achieve a true neutrality in funding between public and religious schools.

In his recent book on vouchers, Peter Cookson describes an emerging consensus in America that "competition and markets will save America's schools." But, Cookson argues, "history shows us that in an unregulated market, cleverness and cunning can be used to market products and services that are expensive, shoddy, and even harmful to human and intellectual health." Markets, he concludes, "make wonderful servants but terrible masters."[77] I agree, and I worry about the "commodification" of education and market solutions to problems of great cultural importance and complexity. Moreover, a host of problems could well accompany even an adequately funded plan: the chaos that would go with its implementation; the possibility that the poor and uneducated would not be able to use it to their advantage; increased segregation; the further Balkanization of our culture; and, of course, the possibility that government would, in the end, overregulate private schools so that they lose their distinctiveness.

As things stand now, however, public education is hostile to religion, and although the wealthy might obtain relief by sending their children to private schools, the poor have no recourse. This is no small thing. I hope very much that public schools begin to take religion seriously, but until that happens there is a strong case to be made for vouchers—properly conceived, of course.

CONCLUSIONS

The usually astute Michael Kinsley recently claimed to be "honestly bewildered by the frequent complaint that American culture is hostile to religion," for, he argued, "believers predominate and nonbelievers either pretend otherwise or keep quiet about it." In fact, he continues, there is a "virtual taboo" on expressions of disbelief, and from "the evidence of American public debate, you would guess that the premise of the existence of God is as undisputed as the premise of the existence of gravity."[1]

No doubt overt hostility to religion is commonly viewed as unacceptable in public, and ceremonial expressions of religion are legion. But, as Marc Stern puts it, religious pronouncements produce no "deep resonance" in our culture. Indeed, he asks, "How can religion speak to a society whose organs of communication are secular (and in which religious affairs receive relatively little coverage), a society whose values are pragmatic and short-term, where the commitment to religion is increasingly superficial, where most of the roles that religion once filled—whether setting moral standards, providing social services, or providing community—are now filled by groups and institutions in which religion doesn't play a significant role."[2]

More important, religion no longer resonates with the deepest chords of modern intellectual life, and as our culture works toward some kind of rough consistency between its governing worldview and the motivating ideas and values of people, the remnants of older religious worldviews are increasingly ineffectual and discredited. In our educational system we teach students to think about the world in totally secular ways, and, as a result, religion inevitably comes to seem irrelevant, a matter of private and irrational faith or even superstition. Public religious rhetoric, common as it is, is all but weightless among those intellectuals who define reality for the purposes of schooling. The conventional wisdom of American education is that students can learn everything they need to know about any subject in the curriculum without knowing anything about live religion.

A Summary of Sorts

I have argued that public education must take religion seriously. I have argued for this conclusion *not* on religious grounds but for a variety of secular reasons.

Whether or not one is religious, one cannot deny that religion has been, and continues to be, tremendously important in shaping people's lives.

Religion has been a force of great evil in the world. Rarely have we engaged in war and slaughter with such great gusto (and such clear consciences) as when we have killed in the name of God—an all too frequent phenomenon. It has divided us into warring camps. Religion has buried much that is healthy and good in human nature under layers of repression. It has stifled scholarship and hindered progress. It has propped up many a reactionary political regime and nurtured charlatans. It has made humankind hate this world, longing for another. For all of these reasons it is important and warrants consideration.

Religion has been a force of great good in the world. It has stood in prophetic judgment on cruelty, selfishness, and the powers of evil. It has nurtured what is good in us: it has taught us "act justly, love mercy, and walk humbly with our God." It has bound us together in community. It has inspired great art and great literature. It has nurtured moral and religious leaders of vision and courage. It has made this a more humane world and, for those who have suffered, it has given them hope of a better world to come. It has spoken to our deepest spiritual needs. For all these reasons it is important and warrants serious consideration.

Most important, religion continues to possess a good deal of vitality in our cultural marketplace, and theologians continue to contest the secular accounts of the world—of history, nature, psychology, society, and morality—that run through the curriculum. Hence, to be liberally educated students must hear the religious voices that are part of our cultural conversation; indeed, critical thinking requires the ability to be reasonable about contending points of view. But because public education typically relegates religion to the past, systematically all but excludes live religion from the curriculum, and uncritically teaches secular ways of understanding the world, it comes close to indoctrinating students.

Public institutions have a particular responsibility to take the public seriously. When our culture is deeply divided on matters of great importance—as is the case in regard to religion—then, in order to sustain social peace and community, it is imperative that we take each other seriously and not align our public institutions with any particular faction. To exclude some voices from the conversation is to disfranchise people, much as if they were not allowed to vote. Public education has, in effect, disfranchised religious folk.

Finally, the Establishment Clause requires that public education be neutral among religions and neutral between religion and nonreligion; it cannot promote secular over religious ways of understanding reality (or vice versa). If God exists, there must be implications for how we think about the world and how we live our lives; it is hard to imagine a deity who makes no difference. To ignore the implications, to teach the contending secular accounts only, is to take sides. Public education promotes a secular mentality, and it marginalizes religion in the process.

Just as racially segregated schools are inherently unequal, so an exclusively secular education is inherently not neutral. Religious and secular ways of understanding the world must be taught together; schools and universities must be religiously integrated.

I want to be clear: I am not claiming that most teachers and administrators, textbook authors and curriculum planners, are personally hostile or even indifferent to religion. If some intellectuals are, most educators are little different from the broader public in their commitments to religious beliefs and values. The hostility of public education to religion is rather a matter of the *philosophical assumptions* about the world that shape the content and curriculum of education, and, for the most part, *educators accept these assumptions uncritically*. Secular ways of thinking and living are part of the cultural air of modernity—and educators breathe that air, taking it for granted. As I argued in Chapter 1, to some considerable extent, the secularization of the world proceeds unwittingly. Modernity teaches us to compartmentalize our religious beliefs and values; religion, so the conventional wisdom has it, is a matter of private faith, and it is essentially unrelated to how the world is to be understood in our intellectual disciplines. That this is so widely and uncritically accepted is one measure of how secular our culture has become. And, as a result, it has become all but impossible to think reasonably about religion.

Ironically, over the last few decades science and modernity have come under increasing attack from postmodern intellectuals. For many of them, science and liberalism are hardly incarnations of disinterested reason, but rather messy matters of ideology and cultural politics. The lines between reason and politics, reason and faith, have become increasingly blurred for many intellectuals.

My conclusion? Because of the massive importance of religion in human affairs, because religions continue to contest secular accounts of the world, because public institutions must take seriously the full range of ideas in our marketplace of ideas, because the Establishment Clause requires neutrality between religion and nonreligion, and because the truth has become increasingly elusive even for intellectuals, religion must be taken seriously in public schools and universities.

And how are they to do this? The curriculum must provide students with the intellectual, imaginative, and emotional resources to understand religion from the "inside," empathetically, and allow religious ideas and values to contend with secular ideas and values for the informed, critical judgment of students. The liberal arts curricula of public schools and universities must be characterized by a robust fairness, taking all major, living religious and secular points of view seriously. Courses in religion should be required of students as part of a core curriculum. And if we are to have courses in religion, we must have faculty competent to teach them—that is, religious studies must become an established field in public education as it now is in higher education. In addition, all introductory liberal education courses should be at least minimally fair, making students aware of alternative religious (and secular) ways of understanding the subject at hand, pointing out connections and tensions, nurturing the curricular *conversation* that constitutes a liberal education.

In public schools it is the task of teachers to teach *about* their subjects, withholding official verdicts about the final truth when questions are religiously contested or deeply controversial. Within universities, faculty have obligations of fairness in those introductory courses that are part of a liberal education, but they also have the academic freedom to teach what they take to be the truth on religiously contested matters whether they say yea or nay to religious claims. (Of course, their judgments must be professionally competent.) Scholars in religious studies possess this same academic freedom to argue for or against various religious claims. Within upper-level graduate and professional courses fairness is no longer obligatory.

Perhaps the punch in my argument comes in the last chapter. If public schooling is as hostile to religion as I have suggested, then vouchers must be taken seriously. Too many secular liberals are insensitive to the extent to which public education violates the deep-felt moral and religious convictions of religious folk. Either we take fairness and neutrality seriously and reform public education, or we must gracefully accept the argument for vouchers.

Resolving the Dilemma, Restoring the Tensions

One or two of my conclusions may strike some as extreme (the conventional wisdom about such things being what it is), but I believe that I have charted a

middle course. I would not have religion ignored in education as some secularists advocate; nor would I have it promoted as some religious conservatives
advocate. A totally secular education—one that ignores religion—is profoundly illiberal. An education that promotes religion may or may not be
illiberal, but it will surely be deeply divisive in a pluralistic culture in which
liberty of conscience is highly valued. We will resolve the dilemma at the
heart of our culture wars when we take each other seriously.

I am arguing for *restoring the tension* between the secular and the spiritual
in education, for having public education mirror the many ways in which religion and modernity relate to each other. Students should be taught the conflicts; they should feel the pull of the contending alternatives if they are to be
liberally (and constitutionally) educated.

Many tensions have run through our deliberations—tensions between tradition and modernity, community and individualism, consensus and pluralism,
faith and reason, and religion and secularity. That these tensions exist most
everyone will agree; many would resist the idea that they are desirable, however. Yet, I suggest, these tensions are, all things considered, *good*. For it
seems to me that there is no unmistakable formula to use, no obviously objective ground on which to stand, no tension-free vantage point from which we
can discern the truth, build the good society, or devise a sound education. We
are best able to proceed when we are aware of, and sensitive to, the tensions
between religious *and* secular ways of understanding the world, when we are
aware of the claims of faith *and* of reason, when we see the value of community *and* of individualism, when we feel the pull of tradition but *also* recognize
that we live in the modern world, when we recognize the importance of pluralism *and* of a shared culture—that is, when we are aware of the tensions and
take *each* side seriously. We almost always err when we go too far in one
direction.

Our Spiritual Situation

We modern-day Americans have a spiritual problem. There is something fundamentally wrong with our culture. We who have succeeded so brilliantly in
matters of economics, science, and technology have been less successful in
matters of the heart and soul. This is evident in our manners and our morale;
in our entertainment and our politics; in our preoccupation with sex and violence; in the ways we do our jobs and in the failure of our relationships; in our
boredom and unhappiness in this, the richest of all societies.

How did this come to be? Maynard Adams has argued that our tragic flaw
"lies not in the failures of modern Western civilization but in the condition of

its success."[3] Too much we have come to define our lives in terms of the paradigm values of modernity—liberty and individualism, rights and self-fulfillment, economic success and technological progress—and we have lost our spiritual balance. We badly need to reassert the importance of duty and virtue, tradition and community, compassion and sacrifice, reverence for nature, and even, perhaps, sin and guilt.

I do not want to overstate my case. As I argued in chapter 11, significant forms of moral progress—particularly those that result from the assertion of liberty and rights—are characteristic of modernity. We do live in a world which, in very important ways, is much to be preferred to any traditional (religious) society. We have righted old wrongs. But we have also run roughshod over ways of thinking and feeling that merit renewed attention. Once again we need to *restore the tension*, taking our spiritual well-being as seriously as our search for material well-being.

Our educational system nourishes the temper of our times and in so doing exacerbates our problems. Needless to say, the reforms I have proposed are not going to rejuvenate our culture spiritually. But then that has not been my purpose. I have argued for taking religion seriously on secular (philosophical, educational, political, and constitutional) grounds. Nonetheless, by requiring students to study religion we can give them something of the intellectual and imaginative resources necessary to acquire critical distance on the relentlessly materialistic thrust of modern culture and think in a relatively informed way about our spiritual situation. Surely religion focuses on many of the right questions whatever one thinks of the answers. Our inability to see this betrays a lack of depth in our thinking about education.

Finally, a Plea for Humility

Intellectuals are almost by definition part of the avant-garde; they are up on the latest ideas. And if the truth be known, they can be trendy—and the fashions can change with mind-numbing speed. In some disciplines, schools of thought may come and go in a generation or two. In my own field, philosophy, the conceptual revolutions in this century alone have been staggering. At the beginning of the century, absolute idealism held sway in many universities. Within a few decades, logical positivism was the most powerful movement in most Anglo-American universities, though existentialism and phenomonology dominated the Continent. After World War II, ordinary language philosophy began its reign of several decades. Of course all along there were a variety of Marxists, pragmatists, process philosophers, and, in Catholic universities, neo-Thomists. As near as I can tell, levels of disagreement in most disciplines are not noticeably different. The philosopher of science W. H. Newton-Smith has claimed that even in science there is good inductive evidence for the claim that "any [scientific] theory will be discovered to be false within, say, 200 years of being propounded."[4] Indeed, the great revolutions that shake science every now and then overturn not just theories but whole conceptual systems in ways that are likely to be inconceivable for adherents of the old views.

If we take a sufficiently long view of things—long enough so that we need to resort to history rather our memories—we might be inclined to a degree of humility that escapes us when we are anchored parochially in the conventional wisdom of the here and now. It is not unreasonable to believe, with Dean Inge, that "he who marries the spirit of the age is soon a widower." It has happened before and it will happen again.

Yet I was struck in reading high school textbooks by their authors' absence of humility: students were taught unquestionable *truth*. Alternative ways of understanding the subject were seldom in evidence; historical perspective was almost always wanting. Even in the history texts little attention was paid to historical understandings of history.

Of course, humility has often been conspicuous by its absence from the virtues practiced by religious believers. Reinhold Niebuhr once wrote that

> it must be regarded as inevitable that religion, and especially a religion which apprehends the truth about man and God by faith alone should be used as the instrument of human arrogance. This is done whenever the truth which is held by faith, because it is beyond all human attainment, comes to be regarded as a secure possession.... The man who thinks it is a rather simple matter to know God's will always ends up by defining that will rather simply and excluding from the Kingdom of God everyone who does not agree with him. A study of the history of religious intolerance and tolerance is a very good antidote for this religion optimism.[5]

And so might a history of secular intolerance be a very good antidote for those "secular fundamentalists" who are convinced they have the truth. After all, the greatest sins of the twentieth century rest on the shoulders of some very secular folk.

In any case, a little humility is in order. We teachers should speak with a little less certainty about matters of profound historical, philosophical, and cross-cultural controversy. Ninian Smart is surely right in arguing that it is in the nature of worldviews to be debatable.

In our postmodern world all orthodoxies have been, or are in danger of being, deflated, modern ones no less than ancient ones—in principle at least.

The proper response would seem to be a sense of humility at our inability to capture reality in our conceptual schemes and a sense of wonder at the richness of reality that refuses to be so captured. The better part of wisdom in this situation is an openness to the broad variety of secular *and* religious ways of making sense of the world.

POSTSCRIPT: SETTING STANDARDS

In 1994 the National Council for History Standards published its standards for teaching American and world history in grades 5–12. These standards were the collaborative effort of hundreds of scholars, teachers, and representatives of professional historical organizations. Whatever their long-term influence (and they have aroused a measure of controversy), the standards do provide valuable insight into how religion currently fares in the hands of professional historians and educators. As public schools leave religion largely to historians, the standards, in effect, define what students should learn about religion as well as history.

In Chapter 4 I noted that the high school history textbooks I reviewed fell well short of existing scholarship in their treatments of religion. The national standards pay significantly more attention to religion than do the textbooks; indeed, they strike me as at least adequate in dealing with religion in the ancient and medieval worlds and in early America. As in the textbooks, in the standards religion receives decreasing emphasis with time: the standards make religion increasingly marginal to world history after 1750 and American history after 1850. No doubt there is some justification for this given the secularization of modern culture. Arguably, however, some sense of proportion is lost. So, for example, of 191 components of standards for the study of world history after 1750, only 6 deal primarily with religion (and another 4 deal with religion as one among a number of considerations); of the 256 components of standards for the study of American history after 1850, only 7 deal primarily with religion (while another 4 deal with religion as one among a number of considerations).

In post-1750 world history the components that deal primarily with religion require students to understand anti-Semitism and the status of Jews in the nineteenth century, the causes of reform and renewal in the great world religions in the nineteenth century, the Holocaust, the creation of Israel and the resulting conflict in the Middle East, the political objectives of fundamentalist movements, and how the world's major faiths have responded to recent challenges and uncertainties. In post-1850 American history students should understand the nature of anti-Catholicism and anti-Semitism at the end of the nineteenth century, the clash between tradition and modernity in the Scopes Trial and Prohibition, the place of religion in postwar American life, the Warren Court's interpretation of religious freedom, immigration and religious diversity in contemporary America, the position of major religious groups on contemporary political and social issues, and the growth of fundamentalism and the appeal of televangelists.

As do the textbooks, the standards place considerably more emphasis on political, social, and economic history than on intellectual, religious, and cultural history. To give just one example, there are fourteen American history components of standards devoted to Progressivism covering the first 30 years of this century while, as I have noted, there are only seven devoted to religion over the course of the last 150 years. Moreover, when religion is emphasized, it is largely for its social and political significance. None of the post-1750 world history and post-1850 American history components of standards deals explicitly with theology or theologians, the spiritual aspects of religion, or the intellectual viability of religion in the contemporary world—though three or four provide something of an opening for discussion of such topics. The standards do require students to understand something of the basic theology and intellectual development of religion through the early modern period, but by virtually ignoring the theological development of religion in response to the dominant ideas and institutions of modernity the standards convey the conception of religion as a "museum piece" adequately dealt with in accounts of ancient times.

In principle, at least, the standards are considerably better than the texts in avoiding "present-mindedness" (the insistence on understanding everyone on our terms), and they place a good deal of emphasis on using primary sources to get inside historical cultures. They emphasize the importance of recognizing the difference between facts and interpretations and insist that students appreciate the extent to which history is an interpretive discipline; indeed, they require students to compare narratives written by historians who give different accounts of the causes of historical events.

While the standards are sensitive to the importance of contending interpretations, they at least implicitly limit the field to the narratives of secular historians. They do not require that students be made aware of or take seriously, much less contend with, religious interpretations of history as the working out of God's purposes. This is important for it is the conceptual categories *used* by historians that subtly but substantially influence students' interpretations of history. As a result, the religious ideas and values that students encounter in the study of history will lack plausibility because the overall explanatory framework remains so relentlessly secular.

History has, of course, become a secular discipline, and I have not proposed that historians use religious categories in constructing their narratives. I have argued, however, that it is incumbent on history teachers and texts to make students aware of—and therefore able to think critically about—alternative (religious) ways of making sense of history.

Perhaps the most daunting aspect of the standards is their comprehensiveness. Both the American and world history standards run close to three hundred pages. Although the authors make clear that history requires several years of study, it is likely that even conscientious teachers and thick textbooks will fall far short of the mark. Inevitably they will be selective, and what is likely to be lost in the shuffle is what is least emphasized—cultural, intellectual, and religious history. Of course the idea of teaching a comprehensive account of human history is, however admirable, quixotic at best. Recognizing this, educators give those subjects they take to be truly important their own place in the curriculum: they do not leave science and math, economics and sex education, to historians. To some considerable extent, they do leave religion to them.

What should students learn about religion?

In elementary school reading and social studies classes students should learn that religion has been, and continues to be, an important part of culture; textbooks and stories should not convey to children the idea that they live in a world free of religion. Students should come to know something of religious pluralism and our constitutional commitment to religious liberty. They should begin to learn about the holidays, customs, basic beliefs, and histories of different religions. An elementary education should begin to develop students' religious literacy. As children grow older, they should be asked to think more critically about the differences among religions and the tensions between religious and secular ways of understanding the world, but elementary school students are not sufficiently mature intellectually or emotionally to be thrust into the unsettling world of liberal education and critical thinking. The purpose of elementary schooling is not to raise questions of truth where we disagree so much as it is to teach students the basic skills and values, the rudimentary knowledge of the world, about which we agree. Of course there is no magic time at which a liberal education should begin; rather an elementary education prepares the way and naturally expands into a liberal education through the middle years of schooling.

I have argued that all texts and courses that deal with religiously contested matters as part of a liberal education should be minimally fair and include some discussion of contending religious ways of understanding the subject at hand. But the importance and complexity of religion, as well as the epistemological, political, and constitutional considerations I have marshaled for taking religion seriously, all dictate that religion should be a required course taught by certified teachers. Religion cannot be left to history any more than science or economics can. Hence, I have argued for requiring of all high school students a single introductory religion course as the minimally adequate (politically feasible) solution to our problem. Of course, a single course is not likely to do justice to religion. I suggest that a sequence of three courses, organized along the lines indicated below, might better approximate the ideal.

World Religions. Students should acquire a much richer understanding of the theology and doctrine, rituals and religious experience, moral teachings and practices, of the great world religions than can be acquired in the crowded context of history courses. Students should read the sacred texts of several traditions, not just as literature (as they most likely would in a literature course) but for their religious meaning. It is particularly important that students read the Bible (appreciating its Jewish, Catholic, and Protestant variations); the Bible has had, after all, a far greater influence on the course of human events than any other book. Whether or not the truth was given once and for all in Scripture, historical religions change, and students should have some sense of the moral, spiritual, and theological development of the major religions traditions.

Religion and Modernity. It is, of course, particularly important that students understand the role of religion(s) in the culture wars of modern times— let us say of the last several hundred years—though this is where the story trails off in the history standards and texts. Students should acquire some sense of the causes and significance of the secularization of modern Western civilization (one of the two or three great themes of modern history). It is especially important that they develop a critical appreciation of the tensions between religion and science, the growth of religious pluralism in modern culture, and the disestablishment of religion in the modern liberal state. Students should understand the liberal and conservative responses to modernity that run through modern religions (and read primary sources drawn from both liberal and conservative traditions). They should acquire a measure of critical distance on the secular assumptions that shape the courses they take if they are to learn to think reasonably and responsibly—and avoid indoctrination.

Moral Philosophy. Finally, students should understand the implications of secular *and* religious ideas and values for contemporary moral, political, and social debates about abortion, sexuality, sex roles, justice, the sanctity of life, war and peace, and a dozen other issues (and they should read the arguments of all of the major contending parties in primary sources). It is important that they recognize that practical moral judgments are not made in a cultural vacuum; students need not construct anew the moral world for themselves. They should recognize the extent to which their identities are embedded in historical traditions and see how practical judgments are grounded in interpretations of human nature, history, and worldviews that provide rich resources for moral reflection and direction.

This three-course sequence might be correlated to good effect with existing courses in history and literature. (Of course, interdisciplinary, team-taught, courses would be the ideal.) So, for example, in their sophomore year, when high school students study world history and literature, they might also study the origins, sacred literature, and development of the major world religions. In their junior year their study of American history and literature would complement, to some considerable extent, their study of the relationships of religion to modern ideas and institutions. And in their senior year, they would take the capstone course in moral philosophy that I described more fully in Chapter 11.

In an ideal world this three-course sequence should be required of all students (with automatic exemptions for any student whose conscience would be burdened by taking it); but I suspect that a great many educators will view this modest proposal as impractical (at best). Hence, I recommend that schools consider developing it as an elective sequence that might be phased in with the availability of teachers certified in religious studies and of adequate texts and anthologies. Clearly, however, at least one course in religion, covering the central themes of the three courses I have just described, must be required of all students (again with appropriate exemptions) for the educational, philosophical, political, and constitutional reasons I have put forward.

NOTES

Introduction

1. Schumacher, *Guide for the Perplexed*, p. 1.

2. Wills, *Under God*, pp. 15–16.

3. Gallup, *Gallup Poll: Public Opinion 1990*, p. 68.

4. Gallup, *Gallup Poll: Public Opinion 1991*, p. 238.

5. *Asheville Citizen*, April 4, 1991, p. 1A. The poll was conducted by Princeton Survey Research Associates.

6. Gallup and Castelli, *People's Religion*, p. 90.

7. Küng, *Theology for the Third Millennium*, p. 7.

8. Neuhaus, *Naked Public Square*, p. 113.

9. Gibbs, "America's Holy War," p. 61.

10. Marsden, "Soul of the American University," 11. Marsden notes that although Protestantism began "at a university with a scholar's insight," Protestants today do not support "any major universities that are Protestant in any interesting sense" (ibid., pp. 10, 9).

11. Gellner, *Legitimation of Belief*, p. 195; emphasis added.

12. Cupitt, *Sea of Faith*, p. 11.

13. I take this phrase from the Williamsburg Charter; more about the charter and "living with our deepest differences" in chapter 3.

14. *Everson v. Board of Education*, 330 U.S. 1, 23–24 (1947).

15. Fielding, *Tom Jones*, p. 105 (book 3, chapter 3).

16. Swift, *Gulliver's Travels*, pp. 43–44.

17. Hick, *Death and Eternal Life*, pp. 297–98.

18. Barbour, *Myth, Models, and Paradigms*, p. 120.

19. Cassirer, *Essay on Man*, p. 25.

20. Berger and Luckmann, *Social Construction of Reality*, p. 135.

21. We learn to decode so well, as Karl Popper suggests, that "everything becomes very 'direct' or 'immediate' to us; but so it is with the man who has learned ... to read a book: it speaks to him 'directly,' 'immediately'. Nevertheless, we know that there is a complicated process of decoding going on." (*Objective Knowledge*, p. 36).

22. Gilbert, *Making of Post-Christian Britain*, p. 14.

Chapter 1

1. See Smith, *The Meaning and End of Religion*, esp. chaps. 2 and 3.

2. And the Near East was "Islamdom." See Hodgson, *Venture of Islam*, 1:3–70.

3. Hick, *Interpretation of Religion*, p. 23.

4. See Bellah, "Religious Evolution," in *Beyond Belief*, pp. 22–23.

5. Quoted in Eliade, *The Sacred and the Profane*, p. 98.

6. Lao Tzu, *Tao te Ching*, p. 70.

7. See Horton, "African Thought and Western Science."

8. Turner, *Without God, Without Creed*, pp. 3, 10.

9. Jacob, *Cultural Meaning of the Scientific Revolution*, p. 75.

10. Thomas, *Religion and the Decline of Magic*, p. 153.

11. Turner, *Without God, Without Creed*, p. 3.

12. Kolakowski, "The Man Who Made Modernity," p. 40.

13. Taylor, *Sources of the Self*, p. 218.

14. Ozment, *Age of Reform*, p. 435. Also see Thomas, *Religion and the Decline of Magic*, pp. 51–77, and Berger, *Sacred Canopy*, pp. 111–13.

15. Ozment, *Age of Reform*, p. 436.

16. Bainton, *The Reformation in the Sixteenth Century*, p. 211.

17. Luther, "Secular Authority," p. 385. Some of the "radical" reformers argued that because God's kingdom was not of this world, church and state should be separated. But this was the minority opinion. Not for several centuries would such reasoning be taken seriously.

18. Chadwick, *Secularization of the European Mind*, p. 23. Also see pp. 23–29.

19. Luther, *Commentary on St. Paul's Epistle to the Galatians*, p. 128.

20. Skinner, *Foundations of Modern Political Thought*, 1:85–86. Also see pp. 110–12.

21. Quoted in Baumer, *Religion and the Rise of Scepticism*, p. 102. Also see pp. 98–105. Lord Herbert of Cherbury wrote: "Many faiths or religions, clearly, exist or once existed in various countries and ages, and certainly there is not one of them that the lawgivers have not pronounced to be as it were divinely ordained; so that the Wayfarer finds one in Europe, another in Africa, and in Asia, still another in the very Indies.... What Wayfarer, then, born in an unfortunate land or age, shall save himself? How, especially, shall he protect himself if every man's individual dogmas about necessary and excellent truth are so proposed as to damn all the rest?" (ibid., p. 98).

22. Quoted in Berman, *All That Is Solid Melts into Air*, p. 18.

23. Ibid., p. 345. The anthropologist Robert Redfield comments: "Heterogeneity is the first characteristic of the city, ancient or modern. And with heterogeneity come doubts as to the moral order" (*The Primitive World and Its Transformations*, p. 49).

24. Berger, *Heretical Imperative*, p. 24.

25. Ibid., p. 25.

26. See McNeill, *Rise of the West*, pp. 588–89.

27. Barnes, *In the Presence of Mystery*, p. 287.

28. Luther, "Bondage of the Will," p. 170.

29. Pascal, *Pensées*, pp. 48, 88.

30. Sagan, *Broca's Brain*, pp. 290–92.

31. Protestantism, by contrast, sanctioned "an immense shrinkage in the scope of the sacred in reality." According to Peter Berger, the "Protestant believer no longer lives in a world ongoingly penetrated by sacred beings and forces. Reality is polarized between a radically transcendent divinity and a radically 'fallen' humanity that ... is devoid of sacred qualities. Between them lies an altogether 'natural' universe, God's creation to be sure, but in itself bereft of numinosity [sacred qualities].... This reality then became amenable to the systematic, rational penetration, both in thought and in

activity, which we associate with modern science and technology" (*Sacred Canopy*, pp. 111–12).

32. Barbour, *Issues in Science and Religion*, p. 17. Or, as Maynard Adams put it, within this worldview theologians and scientists alike saw nature "as a book to be read. Not only were unusual events omens that bore messages, but the regular course of things, somewhat like human behavior, embodied an inner structure of meaning" (*Religion and Cultural Freedom*, p. 97).

33. Burtt, *Metaphysical Foundations of Modern Science*, pp. 238–39.

34. Stace, "Man Against Darkness," p. 39. The phrase "myth to math" is from Cupitt, *Sea of Faith*, p. 31.

35. Told by Stace in *Religion and the Modern Mind*, p. 78. It is true that God had a role to play for Galileo and Kepler and Newton: he set the world going in the first place; he wound up the cosmic clock. God was the First Cause of the World Machine. Still, for all practical purposes in the doing of science, God and the concept of purpose were irrelevant.

36. Monod, *Chance and Necessity*, p. 138.

37. Turner, *Without God, Without Creed*, p. 152.

38. This was especially so of those social scientists who were the major theorists of primitive religion—Tyler, Frazer, Malinowski, Durkheim, Levy-Bruhl, and Freud. Implicit in their thinking, according to Evans-Pritchard, were the optimistic convictions of Enlightenment rationalism "that people are stupid and bad only because they . . . have been exploited in the name of religion by cunning and avaricious priests and the unscrupulous classes which have supported them" (*Theories of Primitive Religion*, p. 15).

39. Freud, *Future of an Illusion*, p. 63.

40. Bellah, "Between Religion and Social Science," p. 250. Bellah continues: "None of them were believers in the ordinary sense of that word. All of them believed themselves to be in possession of a truth superior to that of religion" (ibid.).

41. Robert Wuthnow presents a wealth of survey data on the religious beliefs of social scientists and scholars. See his "Science and the Sacred," pp. 187–203.

42. According to B. F. Skinner, "Autonomous man [the free and reasoning subject] serves to explain only the things we are not yet able to explain in other ways. His existence depends upon our ignorance, and he naturally loses status as we come to know more about behavior. The task of a scientific analysis is to explain how the behavior of a person as a physical system is related to the conditions under which the human species evolved and the conditions under which the individual lives" (*Beyond Freedom and Dignity* p. 12).

43. Dickens, *A Christmas Carol*, p. 115.

44. Dickens, *Hard Times*, p. 48. A century earlier David Hume wrote his celebrated conclusion to his *Enquiry Concerning Human Understanding* (1748): "When we run over libraries, persuaded of these principles, what havoc must we make? If we take in our hand any volume; of divinity or school metaphysics, for instance; let us ask, *Does it contain any abstract reasoning concerning quantity or number?* No. *Does it contain any experimental reasoning concerning matter of fact and existence?* No. Commit it then to the flames: for it can contain nothing but sophistry and illusion" (*Enquiries Concerning the Human Understanding and Concerning the Principles of Morals*, p. 165).

45. Ross, *Origins of American Social Science*, pp. xiii–xiv.

46. Quoted from Eugen Weber in McLeod, *Religion and the People of Western Europe*, p. 73.

47. See Jacob, *Cultural Meaning of the Scientific Revolution*, pp. 3, 6–7, 105, 139, 142, and passim.

48. Baumer, *Religion and the Rise of Scepticism*, pp. 67–68.

49. According to Robert Wuthnow, "A 1979 Harris survey asked 'What will make a major contribution to America's greatness in the next 25 years?' Leading the list of responses were 'scientific research' (mentioned by 89 percent of the respondents) and 'technological genius' (73 percent). In comparison, only 57 percent selected 'deep religious beliefs.' . . . Another national survey in 1979 asked people to mention two factors 'that contributed the most to U.S. influence in the world.' At the top of the list was 'our technological know-how' (46 percent); another 22 percent mentioned 'our scientific creativity'; whereas, by comparison, only 15 percent mentioned the nation's 'religious heritage'" (*Restructuring of American Religion*, pp. 286–87).

50. Barbour, *Science and Secularity*, p. 70.

51. See Thomas, *Religion and the Decline of Magic*, chap. 22.

52. Hall, *Scientific Revolution*, p. 376.

53. Adams, *Religion and Cultural Freedom*, p. 94. See also pp. 93–102, and Adams, *Philosophy and the Modern Mind*, pp. 48–53.

54. Quoted in Tawny, *Religion and the Rise of Capitalism*, p. 38.

55. Heilbroner, *Worldly Philosophers*, pp. 22–23.

56. As Max Weber once put it, "A business career was only possible for those who were lax in their ethical thinking" (*Economy and Society*, 1:587). Weber notes that in the medieval period there was a "wide chasm separating the inevitabilites of economic life from the Christian ideal." This "ethical separation kept the most devout groups and all those with the most consistently developed ethics far from the life of trade. Above all, time and again it tended to attach an ethical stigma to the business spirit, and to impede its growth" (ibid.). Also see pp. 583–91.

57. Quoted in Hirschman, *The Passions and the Interests*, pp. 58, 60; see pp. 56–66 and passim.

58. Keynes, *Essays in Persuasion*, pp. 267–69.

59. Schumpeter, *Capitalism, Socialism and Democracy*, p. 83.

60. Polanyi, *Great Transformation*, p. 76.

61. Marx and Engels, *Manifesto of the Communist Party*, p. 10.

62. Friedrich Hayek, the great apologist of free market economics, is careful to distinguish between the conservative, who is wedded to tradition and opposed to change, and the liberal advocate of a market economy, who is open to change and "feels that no respect for established values can justify the resort to privilege or monopoly or any other coercive power of the state in order to shelter . . . people against the forces of economic change" (*Constitution of Liberty*, p. 402).

63. Berger, "Capitalism and the Disorders of Modernity," p. 15.

64. Quoted in Weber, *The Protestant Ethic and the Spirit of Capitalism*, p. 175.

65. Schleiermacher, *On Religion*, p. 124. Of the English, he wrote: "All knowledge they have robbed of life and use only as dead wood to make masts and helms for their life's voyage in pursuit of gain" (ibid., p. 10).

66. Lasch, "Communitarianism or Populism?," p. 7. Similarly, Robert Bellah argues that "the greatest threat to our genuine happiness, to real community, and to the creation of a good society comes not only from a state whose power becomes too coercive (we can never underestimate that danger), but from market forces that become too coercive, invade our private and group lives, and tempt us to a shallow competitive individualism that undermines all our connections to other people. . . . Indeed, there is a market totalitarianism that parallels state totalitarianism and is a real threat to us in America today" ("Triumph of Capitalism," p. 73).

67. Kaufman, *Redeeming Politics*, p. 3.

68. Ullmann, *Medieval Political Thought*, p. 16.

69. See the Introduction to his *Redeeming Politics*, pp. 3–13.

70. McConnell, "'God Is Dead and We Have Killed Him!,'" p. 167.

71. See Rawls, *Political Liberalism*, esp. Introduction and lecture 1.

72. Quoted in Arblaster, *Rise and Decline of Western Liberalism*, p. 22.

73. Stout, *Ethics after Babel*, p. 102.

74. Arblaster, *Rise and Decline of Western Liberalism*, p. 186.

75. Quoted, ibid.

76. McConnell, "'God Is Dead and We Have Killed Him,'" p. 174.

77. Hans Küng has asked: "Was there anything that was not forbidden or condemned by the churches in the nineteenth and twentieth centuries: democracy, liberalism, socialism, freedom of opinion, freedom of the press, freedom of conscience, freedom of religion? The failure especially (but not only) of the Catholic Church to meet sociopolitical problems with more than pious intentions, almsgiving, and individual works of charity seriously discredited belief in God at an early stage" ("God," p. 54). Franklin Baumer notes that if Catholicism was the "inveterate foe" of the French Revolution, did not "the Prussian Lutheran church likewise condemn political and social democracy? Did not the Anglican bishops oppose the Reform Bill of 1832? Were not Methodist and evangelical leaders opposed to Chartism and trade unions? Did they not teach that poverty was ordained by God?" Nineteenth-century religion, he concluded, "almost invariably threw its weight on the side of political and social reaction" (*Religion and the Rise of Scepticism*, p. 141).

78. See Marty, *Modern Schism*, p. 52.

79. Ibid., p. 74. In 1843, W. F. Hook, the vicar of Leeds, wrote that in the manufacturing districts of England the church "is an object of detestation to the working classes. . . . They consider the Church to belong to the Party of their oppressors; hence they hate it, and consider any of the working-classes who is a Churchman to be a traitor to his Party" (quoted in Cupitt, *Sea of Faith*, p. 24).

80. McLeod, *Religion and the People of Western Europe*, pp. v, 5.

81. Tocqueville, *Democracy in America*, 1:325.

82. Fukuyama, "End of History?," p. 3.

83. Schlesinger, *Disuniting of America*, p. 47. According to the philosopher Ross Poole, whenever there has been a conflict between nationalism and liberalism, "it has almost always been nationalism which has been victorious." The "political weakness of liberalism in times of crisis," Poole argues, "is a reflection of its moral emptiness. Liberalism does not provide an ethic by which people might live, nor a principle of social cohesion." Modern social life "is atomistic and cuts the individual off from broader

constitutive relations" (*Morality and Modernity*, pp. 91, 105, 92). Nationalism, by contrast, provides an identity; a sense of community; a purpose and sense of obligation; even a sense of immortality. (See pp. 90–109).

84. Smart, *Religion and the Western Mind*, p. 71.

85. Ibid., p. 75.

86. Paul Johnson writes: "Clergymen were unable, and for the most part unwilling, to place Christian faith before nationality. Most took the easy way out and equated Christianity with patriotism. Christian soldiers of all denominiations were exhorted to kill each other in the name of their Saviour" (*History of Christianity*, p. 477).

87. Ibid., p. 493.

88. According to a 1981 Gallup Poll (Gallup and Castelli, *People's Religion*, p. 47).

89. Ibid., pp. 3, 37.

90. Ibid, p. 14.

91. From Hastings and Hauser, *International Index of Public Opinion, 1983–84*, reported in *Religion and Public Education* 16 (Winter 1989): 109.

92. Gallup and Castelli, *People's Religion*, pp. 31, 48.

93. Inglehardt, *Culture Shift in Advanced Industrial Society*, p. 205. As the survey data suggest, secularization has proceeded considerably further in Europe than in America. Several decades ago Martin Marty wrote that in modern Europe the "historic churches are museums, monuments or shrines. The new ones are ordinarily empty. In many nations, at least nominal establishments of religion survive with state support. But the masses of people stay away, fail to respond, and are unmoved by appeals. . . . The intellectual, literary, and artistic communities are ordinarily godless, so much so that one expresses great surprise and fascination when a man of explicit Christian faith turns up in these areas of life" (*Modern Schism*, p. 96).

94. Gallup, *Gallup Poll: Public Opinion 1991*, p. 237.

95. Cox, *Secular City*, p. 2.

96. Smith, *The Meaning and End of Religion*, pp. 113–14.

97. Chadwick, *Secularization of the European Mind*, p. 258.

98. Tolstoy, *War and Peace*, p. 1125.

99. Turner, *Without God, Without Creed*, pp. 263–64.

100. Snow, "The Two Cultures and the Scientific Revolution," p. 19.

101. Turner, *Without God, Without Creed*, p. 59.

102. Schleiermacher, *On Religion*, p. 102.

103. Otto, introduction to *On Religion*, p. xii.

104. Schleiermacher, *On Religion*, p. 36.

105. Wordsworth, from "Lines Composed a Few Miles above Tintern Abbey, on Revisiting the Banks of the Wye During a Tour." Cf. Ralph Waldo Emerson: "Crossing a bare common, in snow puddles, at twilight, under a clouded sky, without having in my thoughts any occurrence of special good fortune, I have enjoyed a perfect exhilaration. . . . Standing on the bare ground,—my head bathed by the blithe air and uplifted into infinite space,—all mean egotism vanishes. I become a transparent eyeball; I am nothing; I see all; the currents of the Universal Being circulate through me; I am part or parcel of God" ("Nature," pp. 38–39).

106. Schleiermacher, *On Religion*, p. 15.

107. Ibid., p. 101.

108. Ibid., pp. 90–91.

109. Livingston, *Modern Christian Thought*, p. 96.

110. Ibid., p. 105.

111. Dillenberger and Welch, *Protestant Christianity*, p. 175.

112. Bultmann, *New Testament and Mythology*, p. 3.

113. Rudolf Bultmann, *Kerygma und Mythos*, quoted in Berger, *Heretical·Imperative*, p. 96.

114. Ruether, *Sexism and God-Talk*, p. 19.

115. Ibid., p. 23.

116. Ibid., p. 66.

117. Robinson, *Honest to God*, pp. 125–26. "The presupposition of such literalism," according to Paul Tillich, "is that God is a being, acting in time and space, dwelling in a special place, affecting the course of events and being affected by them like any other being in the universe. . . . Faith, if it takes its symbols literally, becomes idolatrous!" (*Dynamics of Faith*, p. 52. Also see pp. 48–54).

118. John Bennett, "A Changed Liberal," quoted in Hutchison, *Modernist Impulse in American Protestantism*, p. 308.

119. Shailer Mathews, *Faith of Modernism*, quoted, ibid., p. 281.

120. Rauschenbusch, *Theology for the Social Gospel*, p. 470.

121. A warning is in order here. Theological and social liberals do not always line up together; higher criticism does not commit us to liberation theology, and members of theologically liberal churches are often social conservatives. Still, the gist of much liberalism is that if we demythologize the worldview of Christianity what remains is the moral imperative—the centrality of divine love and justice in living our lives. Liberal theologians have typically preached the Social Gospel, even if people in the pews have not always marched to the tune, though even in the heyday of the Social Gospel not all liberal theologians were supporters. See Hutchison, *Modernist Impulse in American Protestantism*, pp. 165–66.

122. Dillenberger and Welch, *Protestant Christianity*, p. 189.

123. Hutchison, *Modernist Impulse in American Protestantism*, p. 11.

124. From the 1920s to the 1950s, the towering figure in theology was Karl Barth, whose "neo-orthodoxy" took issue with much liberal theology and the agenda of modernity.

125. All quotations are from the Pittsburgh Platform, reprinted in Martin, *History of Judaism*, 2:300–301. It also rejected the idea of restoring the Jewish state and acknowledged that Judaism is not "a nation but a religious community" (ibid., p. 301). The 1937 Columbus Platform thought better of Zionism as Hitler's aims became clearer and affirmed a greater role for tradition and the Torah in Jewish life (ibid., p. 421).

126. In 1983 the organization of Reform Rabbis rejected rabbinic law which defined a Jew as someone born to a Jewish mother or a convert; a Jew might have either a Jewish father or mother, and it is now essential that the child's acceptance of Jewish identity be "established through appropriate and timely public and formal acts of identification with the Jewish faith and people" (quoted in Wertheimer, *People Divided*, p. 108).

127. According to Richard McBrien, until Vatican II, twentieth-century Catholicism "was shaped more by the Council of Trent than by any other historically tangible event or force" (*Catholicism*, p. 635).

128. Quoted in Johnson, *History of Christianity*, pp. 507–8.

129. Dolan, *American Catholic Experience*, pp. 425–26.

130. In his 1993 encyclical *Veritatis Splendor* the Pope reminded Catholic theologians that the Magisterium "has the duty to state that some trends of theological thinking and certain philosophical affirmations are incompatible with revealed truth" (p. 45).

131. In the 1920s, J. Gresham Machen, the greatest scholar among the earliest fundamentalists, wrote that "Christianity is battling against a totally diverse type of religious belief, which is only the more destructive of the Christian faith because it makes use of traditional Christian terminology. This modern non-redemptive religion is called 'modernism' or 'liberalism'" (*Christianity and Liberalism*, p. 2).

132. Carl F. H. Henry, *Evangelicals in Search of an Identity*, quoted in Anderson, "Evangelical Theology," p. 143.

133. *Chicago Statement of Biblical Inerrancy*, p. 212. The statement was drafted at a 1978 conference of evangelical professors, clergy, and laymen.

134. Schaeffer, *Escape from Reason*, pp. 89–90.

135. Packer, *"Fundamentalism" and the Word of God*, p. 92. The influential evangelical biblical scholar George Eldon Ladd agrees: "Deeds—words; God acts—God speaks; and the words explain the deeds" (*The New Testament and Criticism*, p. 27).

136. Packer. *"Fundamentalism" and the Word of God*, p. 112.

137. John 14:6 [New English Bible].

138. Indeed, surveys continue to show that most conservative Protestants believe that people are damned if they have not accepted Christ as their savior. See Hunter, *Evangelicalism*, pp. 34–40. See Demarest, *General Revelation*, pp. 259–62, for a theological defense of this position.

139. Demarest, *General Revelation*, p. 259.

140. Machen, *Christianity and Liberalism*, p. 156.

141. Another warning: theological conservatives are not always social conservatives. There is an evangelical Left, and black churches, which are typically conservative theologically, are liberal on many political issues. According to a 1980 Gallup Poll, 20 percent of evangelicals described their political position as "Left of Center" (Gallup, *Gallup Poll: Public Opinion 1980*, p. 186).

142. Gallup and Castelli, *People's Faith*, p. 16.

143. Hatch, "Evangelicalism as a Democratic Movement," p. 72.

144. Ibid., p. 78. This is changing. More and more evangelical theologians and biblical scholars are being educated at major research universities. See Noll, *Between Faith and Criticism*.

145. In my discussion of pluralism above I followed Peter Berger in arguing that pluralism promotes secularization. But Berger also argues that "just as pluralism reinforces secularization during its ascendancy, so, paradoxically, does pluralism soften any form of established or institutionalized secularity. . . . Pluralism makes any quest for certainty more difficult" ("From the Crisis of Religion to the Crisis of Secularity," pp. 19–20).

146. Carl F. H. Henry, *Confessions of a Theologian*, quoted in Anderson, "Evangelical Theology," p. 143. Also see Sweet, "The 1960s," pp. 35, 41.

147. Sweet, "The 1960s," p. 32. Similarly, Martin Marty has suggested that "in a free society where religion is escapable, it is questionable whether many would take pains to continue to belong to groups that give them few reasons for adherence. When the Mainliners [or liberals] minimized their reasons, Americans began to take their quests to other locales on the map" (*Nation of Behavers*, p. 79).

148. Sweet, "The 1960s," p. 32.

149. Hunter, *Evangelicalism*, p. 163.

150. Ibid., pp. 31, 33.

151. Ibid., p. 46. In their introduction to a collection of articles by evangelical theologians the editors write that "until relatively recently, the task of the evangelical theologian was easily defined. Theologians were to study the biblical text, crystallize doctrines from its pages, explore their relationships, sharpen their cutting edges, proclaim their truth, and confound those who disagreed or disbelieved. This set of activities was predicated on the assumption that biblical doctrine once explained was not only readily comprehensible to reasonable people, but also self-evident in its application to daily life. These assumptions, however, are now in ruins. The theological task . . . must now concern itself with understanding what that faith means in a world whose cognitive horizons are so vastly different from the biblical and whose life poses questions the biblical authors did not foresee nor answer directly" (Noll and Wells, *Christian Faith and Practice in the Modern World*, p. 11).

152. Marty, "Fundamentalism as a Social Phenomenon," p. 58.

153. Pelikan, "Fundamentalism and/or Orthodoxy?," pp. 6–9.

154. Quoted in Boston, "Marriage of Convenience," p. 10.

155. Pelikan, *Riddle of Roman Catholicism*, p. 82.

156. Quoted, ibid. According to the church's *Catechism*, "Sacred Scripture is written principally in the Church's heart rather than in documents and records, for the Church carries in her Tradition the living memorial of God's Word" (p. 32).

157. John Paul II, *Veritatis Splendor*, p. 41.

158. Pius IX, *The Syllabus of Errors*, pp. 170, 162.

159. According to Leo, "The Catholic philosopher should bear in mind that he will violate the rights both of faith and reason, if he embrace any conclusion which he understands to be contrary to revealed doctrine" (*Aeterni Patris*, p. 179).

160. From *E Supremi Apostolatus Cathedra*; quoted in Johnson, *History of Christianity*, p. 472.

161. Coleman, "Catholic Integralism as a Fundamentalism," p. 84.

162. Ibid., p. 76.

163. Wieseltier, "The Jewish Face of Fundamentalism," p. 194; emphasis added.

164. Ibid., pp. 195–96.

165. Blau, *Modern Varieties of Judaism*, p. 62.

166. Somewhat too simply, Conservative Judaism has adopted much of the theological liberalism of Reform but is committed to maintaining much of the traditional practice of Judaism with the Orthodox. As Jacob Neusner puts it, Conservative Judaism is "orthoprax" in that it is committed to the orthodox practice of Judaism but not to "orthodox" doctrine: "The way of life was congruent in most aspects with that of the

Orthodox; the world view, with that of the Reform" (*Death and Birth of Judaism*, p. 149).

167. Ibid., p. 116. Also see pp. 115–18, 125–34.

168. According to Arthur Hertzberg, this was "the first group of Jews in all of American history to come not primarily in search of bread but to find refuge for its version of Jewishness." Indeed, Hertzberg compares them to the Puritans who came to establish a "city on a hill" (*Jews in America*, pp. 356–57).

169. Wertheimer, *People Divided*, p. 135. Wertheimer notes that few Orthodox Jews in America "any longer articulate the undergirding assumption of Modern [Neo-] Orthodoxy, namely, that a synthesis of traditional and modern Western culture is not only feasible but desirable" (ibid., p. 127).

170. Unterman, *Jews*, p. 223.

171. Wertheimer, *People Divided*, pp. 52–53.

172. Wood, *American Profile*, p. 130. The survey was conducted by the National Opinion Research Center. Interestingly, the percentages of fundamentalists and liberals are increasing, while the percentage of moderates has declined since 1972.

173. Wuthnow, *Restructuring of American Religion*, p. 133.

174. Gallup, *Gallup Poll: Public Opinion 1991*, p. 239.

175. Neuhaus, *Unsecular America*, p. 121, from a 1981 Gallup Poll.

176. Roof and McKinney, *American Mainline Religion*, p. 56; according to a 1978 Gallup Poll. Here we see again something of the power of American individualism. To a considerable extent we have adopted what Roof and McKinney call "do-it-yourself religiosity." Religion is something "to be 'worked out' on one's own terms" (ibid., pp. 56, 50). In fact, 40 percent of American Protestants have changed denominations at least once. Not surprisingly, conservatives have a much greater denominational loyalty than liberals (ibid., pp. 165, 100). The result of all of this is "the peculiarly American practice of claiming a 'religious preference.' Faith comes to be expressed as an opinion or point of view, something that can be easily modified or even discarded if one so chooses. Put simply, religion becomes even more privatized, more anchored in the personal and subjective sphere, and less bound by custom or social bounds" (ibid., p. 67).

177. Hunter, *Evangelicalism*, p. 5; according to the *World Christian Encyclopedia*.

178. See Neff and Brusheber, "Remaking of English Evangelicalism," p. 28.

179. Neuhaus, *Unsecular America*, p. 121; according to a 1981 Gallup Poll.

180. Ibid., p. 120.

181. Hunter, *Culture Wars*, p. 86.

182. Ibid., p. 96.

183. Ibid., pp. 120–21.

184. Ibid., p. 123.

185. Ibid., pp. 104–5.

186. In his recent study of contemporary Judaism, Jack Wertheimer confirms Hunter's overall analysis. He notes, however, that in their self-segregation from society, ultra-orthodox Jews are much less committed to a social agenda than Christian fundamentalists (*People Divided*, pp. 181–84).

187. Harvey, *Condition of Postmodernity*, p. 44.

188. Lyotard, *Postmodern Condition*, pp. 74–75.

189. Rorty, "Pragmatism and Philosophy," p. 33.

190. Ibid., pp. 60–61.

191. Fish, *There's No Such Thing as Free Speech*, p. 56.

192. Ibid., p. 39.

193. Ibid., p. 36.

194. Michel Foucault, *Power/Knowledge*, quoted in Baynes, Bohman, and McCarthy, *After Philosophy*, pp. 96–97.

195. Quoted in Harvey, *Condition of Postmodernity*, p. 9; emphasis added.

196. Tarnas, *Passion of the Western Mind*, p. 404.

197. Griffin, *Spirituality and Society*, p. ix.

198. Tarnas, *Passion of the Western Mind*, p. 409.

199. The "metanarratives" of traditional religion are as problematic for postmodernism as are those of modern science. Nonetheless, religion may ultimately benefit from postmodernism, in part because science, its major competitor in the intellectual marketplace, has been discredited, and in part because postmodernism is more receptive than science to the many dimensions of human experience. As Tarnas puts it, "The religious sensibility itself seems to have been revitalized by the newly ambiguous intellectual circumstances of the postmodern era. Contemporary religion has been revitalized as well by its own plurality, finding new forms of expression and new sources of inspiration and illumination ranging from Eastern mysticism and psychedelic self-exploration to liberation theology and ecofeminist spirituality" (*Passion of the Western Mind*, p. 403).

Chapter 2

1. Bailyn, *Education in the Forming of American Society*, p. 28.

2. Cremin, *American Education: The Colonial Experience*, p. 207.

3. Frederick Lewis Weis, *The Colonial Clergy and the Colonial Churches of New England*, cited in Hofstadter, *Academic Freedom in the Age of the College*, p. 82.

4. Quoted in Lucas, *Our Western Educational Heritage*, pp. 476–77.

5. Ibid.

6. Quoted in Cremin, *American Education: The Colonial Experience*, p. 16.

7. Ibid., pp. 15–16.

8. Herberg, "Religion and Education in America," p. 13. Joel Spring begins his history of American education: "In the North American colonies in the seventeenth century, the primary purpose of education was to maintain Protestant religious beliefs" (*American School*, p. 1).

9. Ford, *New England Primer*, pp. 1–2.

10. All quotations are from the Ford edition of the *Primer*.

11. Quoted in Lucas, *Our Western Educational Heritage*, p. 476.

12. Quoted in Smith, *Killing the Spirit*, p. 25.

13. Cremin, *American Education: The Colonial Experience*, p. 221.

14. Quoted in Herberg, "Religion and Education in America," pp. 13–14.

15. Quoted in Rudolph, *Curriculum*, p. 17.

16. Hofstadter, *Academic Freedom in the Age of the College*, p. 116.

17. Cremin, *American Education: The Colonial Experience*, p. 102. Cremin lists the weekly schedule of classes on p. 214.

18. Rudolph, *Curriculum*, p. 31.

19. See Kimball, *Orators and Philosophers*, p. 103.

20. Cremin, *American Education: The Colonial Experience*, p. 175.

21. Commager, Introduction to *McGuffey's 6th Eclectic Reader*, p. ix.

22. Westerhoff, *McGuffey and His Readers*, pp. 103–4.

23. Lindberg, *Annotated McGuffey*.

24. Elson, *Guardians of Tradition*, pp. 17, 21, 24, 19, 18.

25. Ibid., p. 21.

26. Ibid., pp. 61, 190–91, 59–60, 194–96, 62, 204.

27. Ibid., p. 213. The Webster catechism is quoted in Spring, *American School*, p. 38.

28. Ibid., pp. 215, 252, 255, 259.

29. Ibid., pp. 338, 341; emphasis added.

30. Ibid., pp. 41, 42.

31. In his study of the McGuffey Readers, Westerhoff notes that the 1879 edition contained considerably less religious content than the 1836–37 edition, though it never disappeared; still, "none of the first edition emphasis on salvation and piety remains. In their place is a morality of industry, self-denial, sobriety, thrift, propriety, persistence, modesty, punctuality, conformity, and submission to authority" (*McGuffey and His Readers*, p. 105).

32. Elson, *Guardians of Tradition*, pp. 47, 54.

33. Fleming, "Religion in American History Textbooks," pp. 100, 88.

34. Fitzgerald, *America Revised*, pp. 75, 76. Also see Fleming, "Religion in American History Textbooks," p. 89.

35. Mann, *Twelfth Annual Report*, pp. 124–25.

36. For the arguments see Spring, *American School*, chap. 4.

37. Mann, *Twelfth Annual Report*, pp. 123, 126.

38. Ibid., pp. 125–27.

39. See Michaelsen, *Piety in the Public School*, pp. 81–82, 67, 118.

40. Glenn, *Myth of the Common School*, p. 150. Glenn writes that Mann "appears sincerely not to have recognized the extent to which his own belief in human goodness and the centrality of morality to religion constituted an alternative faith—essentially that preached Sunday by Sunday in Unitarian churches—which could not fail to conflict with orthodox beliefs, whether of Protestants or Roman Catholics" (p. 166).

41. Ibid., chap. 7.

42. Quoted, ibid., p. 230.

43. The Blaine Amendment prohibited tax support of any school or institution "under the control of any religious or anti-religious sect, organization, or denomination, or wherein the particular creed or tenets of any religious or anti-religious sect, organization, or denomination shall be taught." The proposed amendment included the qualification that it "shall not be construed to prohibit the reading of the Bible in any school or institution," thus revealing a certain Protestant bias. See Butts, *American Tradition in Religion and Education*, pp. 143, 144, 137.

44. Laycock, "Summary and Synthesis," p. 845.

45. Ahlstrom, *Religious History of the American People*, p. 555.

46. See Ahlstrom, *A Religious History of the American People*, pp. 563–65, and Spring, *American School*, pp. 101–7.

47. Michaelsen, *Piety in the Public School*, p. 122.

48. Cremin, *American Education: The National Experience*, pp. 5, 103.

49. Quoted, ibid., pp. 138, 141.

50. Quoted in Spring, *American School*, p. 39, 37.

51. "Most individuals who supported and worked for a common school system," according to Joel Spring, "believed that government should play an active role in assuring the success of the economic and social system and that this was best achieved by centralizing and standardizing governmental processes. Many who opposed the development of the common school system believed that the government that governed best governed least" (ibid., p. 107. Also see pp. 97–101.) In the national debate over the Blaine amendment, Republicans saw pluralism as a threat and favored a strong, nonsectarian public school system, while Democrats favored decentralized decision making. See Tyack and Hansot, *Managers of Virtue*, pp. 77, 81.

52. Elson, *Guardians of Tradition*, pp. 297, 282, 314.

53. Michaelsen, *Piety in the Public School*, p. 150.

54. Ibid., pp. 61, 156.

55. Quoted, ibid., p. 59.

56. Hook, *Education for Modern Man*, pp. 115–16.

57. Herberg, "Religion and Education in America," p. 32.

58. Cremin, *American Education: The Colonial Experience*, pp. 376–77.

59. See Spring, *American School*, p. 22.

60. Elson, *Guardians of Tradition*, pp. 222, 223, 228–30.

61. See Spring, *American School*, p. 208; quotes on pp. 208, 209.

62. Cremin, *Transformation of the School*, p. 85, 47–48, 79–80.

63. Tyack and Hansot, *Managers of Virtue*, pp. 106–7. See also pp. 110, 120.

64. Quoted in Fitzgerald, *America Revised*, pp. 168–69, 92–93.

65. Ibid., p. 171.

66. Rudolph, *Curriculum*, pp. 35, 50.

67. Hofstadter, *Academic Freedom in the Age of the College*, p. 185. Hofstadter attributes this to "the growth of commerce, the enlargement of the well-to-do classes, the importation of the ideas and concerns of the European Enlightenment, and the development in America of the absorbing eighteenth-century middle-class passion for pure and applied science, for practical improvements, comforts, and conveniences." He suggests that "it would be too much to claim that the colleges took the initiative in many of these developments. It is probably nearer the truth to say that the colleges followed closely but at a safe distance" (pp. 177–78).

68. Rudolph, *Curriculum*, p. 53.

69. Quoted, ibid., p. 116.

70. Quoted in Veysey, *Emergence of the American University*, p. 84.

71. Rudolph, *Curriculum*, p. 103.

72. See Veysey, *Emergence of the American University*, chap. 3.

73. Ibid., p. 142.

74. Quoted in Rudolph, *Curriculum*, pp. 102, 202.

75. According to Rudolph, by 1905 "all of the state universities in the Midwest and West had long since dropped Greek and were about to eliminate Latin" (*Curriculum*, p. 182).

76. See Kimball, *Orators and Philosophers*, chap. 2, esp. pp. 37–38.

77. Ibid., chap. 5, esp. pp. 121–22.

78. Huxley, "Science and Culture," p. 77. Huxley would not have students receive a purely scientific education, however, for "will bring about a mental twist as surely as an exclusively literary training" (ibid.).

79. Arnold, "Literature and Science," p. 423.

80. The new study of literature was, as Gerald Graff has noted, a "subversive innovation" on the traditional, often technical, philological and historical criticism that had permeated the study of the classics (*Professing Literature*, p. 4).

81. Ibid., p. 85.

82. Quoted in Veysey, *Emergence of the American University*, p. 214.

83. Quoted, ibid., p. 205.

84. Ibid.

85. Quoted, ibid., p. 34, n. 46, p. 26.

86. Quoted in Longfield, "From Evangelicalism to Liberalism," p. 46. See page 50 for similar quotations from nineteenth-century college presidents.

87. Veysey, *Emergence of the American University*, p. 48.

88. Burtchaell, "Decline and Fall of the Christian College I," p. 24.

89. Marsden, "Soul of the American University," p. 11.

90. Hart, "American Learning and the Problem of Religious Studies," p. 199.

91. Harvard separated its divinity school from the college in 1819; Yale followed in 1822.

92. Metzger, *Academic Freedom in the Age of the University*, p. 76.

93. The quotation on competitive disadvantage is from Marsden, *Soul of the American University*, p. 80. See his discussion of amateurism and expertise in "Soul of the American University," pp. 14–15, 20. He describes the purposes and effects of the Carnegie Pension Fund in *Soul of the American University*, pp. 282–83.

94. Rudolph, *Curriculum*, pp. 39, 42, 157. Also see pp. 90, 139.

95. Quoted in Marsden, "Soul of the American University," p. 9. Marsden glosses Hedge to mean "whatever Harvard does *is* Christian" (p. 17).

96. Quoted, ibid., p. 17.

97. Richard T. Ely, *Social Aspects of Christianity and Other Essays*; quoted in Longfield, "From Evangelicalism to Liberalism," p. 59.

98. Washington Gladden, *Applied Christianity: Moral Aspects of Social Questions*, quoted in Cremin, *American Education: The Metropolitan Experience*, p. 24.

99. See Marsden, "Evangelicals and the Scientific Culture," p. 40.

100. Burtchaell, "Decline and Fall of the Christian College I," p. 26.

101. Marsden, "Soul of the American University," pp. 28–29.

102. Burtchaell, "Decline and Fall of the Christian College I," p. 29. Burtchaell has argued that Catholic universities are going through a parallel secularization, one hundred years after their Protestant counterparts. See "Decline and Fall of the Christian College II."

103. See Adler, *Paideia Proposal*, and Hirsch, *Cultural Literacy*.

104. Bloom, *Closing of the American Mind*, pp. 57–58, 344.

105. Giroux, *Schooling and the Struggle for Public Life*, p. 75.

106. Adler, *Paideia Program*, pp. 213–38. Of course a fair number of books deal with religious themes even if not written by theologians.

107. Ravitch, *Troubled Crusade*, p. 235.

108. Fitzgerald, *America Revised*, p. 199.

109. Sizer, *Horace's Compromise*, pp. 111, 207.

110. Rogers, *Freedom to Learn*, p. 105.

111. National Commission on Excellence in Education, *A Nation at Risk*, p. 23.

112. Education Commission of the States, *Action for Excellence*, p. 9.

113. Gates, "The Master's Pieces," p. 94.

114. Purpel, *Moral and Spiritual Crisis in Education*, p. 20.

115. Giroux, *Schooling and the Struggle for Public Life*, p. 18.

116. Apple, *Teachers and Texts*, p. 148.

117. Giroux, *Schooling and the Struggle for Public Life*, pp. 51, 87–91, 120; also see pp. 98, 120.

118. Stone, "Modern to Postmodern," p. 60.

119. Boyer, *High School*, p. 57. Also see Goodlad, *A Place Called School*, pp. 47–49.

120. Sizer, *Horace's Compromise*, pp. 80, 83.

121. Goodlad, *A Place Called School*, p. 238.

122. Boyer, *College*, pp. 59, 84.

123. *Chronicle of Higher Education: Almanac Issue* (August 25, 1993), p. 15.

124. Boyer, *College*, pp. 83, 283.

125. See Tyack, James, and Benavot, *Law and the Shaping of Public Education*, pp. 162–68, esp. p. 164.

Chapter 3

1. Ahlstrom, *Religious History of the American People*, pp. 113–14, 119.

2. Winthrop, "Model of Christian Charity," pp. 92–93.

3. Perry, *Puritanism and Democracy*, p. 115.

4. Quoted in Reichley, *Religion in American Public Life*, p. 56.

5. See Ahlstrom, *Religious History of the American People*, pp. 334–35.

6. Cotton, *Discourse about Civil Government*, p. 8.

7. Hudson, *Religion in America*, pp. 14–15.

8. Quoted, ibid., p. 92.

9. "Memorial to the General Assembly of Virginia from Presbytery of Hanover," pp. 90–92.

10. Quoted in Perry, *Puritanism and Democracy*, p. 348.

11. *The Federalist Papers*, p. 48. Also see paper no. 51.

12. Quoted in Estep, *Revolution within the Revolution*, p. 81.

13. Quoted in Reichley, *Religion in American Public Life*, p. 66.

14. Quoted in Marty, *Pilgrims in Their Own Land*, p. 78.

15. Quoted in Reichley, *Religion in American Public Life*, p. 66.

16. Penn, *Great Case of Liberty of Conscience*, pp. 70–71.

17. Quoted in Hudson, *Religion in America*, pp. 80–81.

18. Marty, *Pilgrims in Their Own Land*, pp. 128, 109.

19. Quoted in Estep, *Revolution Within a Revolution*, pp. 114, 159, 145.

20. Ibid., pp. 178, 7.

21. Hofstadter, *America at 1750*, p. 181.

22. Ahlstrom, *Religious History of the American People*, p. 365.

23. Quoted in Hofstadter, *America at 1750*, pp. 181–82.

24. John Courtney Murray agreed that "the development of religious freedom in society bears a distinct relationship to the growth of unbelief and indifference." He also noted: "Our historical good fortune lay in the particular kind of unbelief that American society has known. It was not Continental laicism, superficially anticlerical, fundamentally antireligious, militant in its spirit, active in its purpose to destroy what it regarded as hateful. Unbelief in America has been rather easy-going, the product more of a naive materialism than of any conscious conviction. The American unbeliever is usually content to say. 'I am not personally a religious man,' and let the subject drop there" (*We Hold These Truths*, p. 58).

25. Bailyn, *New England Merchants*, pp. 106–7, 139–40. Also see Ahlstrom, *Religious History of the American People*, pp. 161–64.

26. Quoted in Cremin, *American Education: The Colonial Experience*, p. 238; also see Ahlstrom, *Religious History of the American People*, p. 164.

27. Quoted in Hudson, *Religion in America*, p. 11; Hofstadter, *America at 1750*, pp. 188–89.

28. Ahlstrom, *Religious History of the American People*, pp. 211–12.

29. "Memorial to the General Assembly of Virginia," p. 92.

30. Kant, "What Is Enlightenment?," p. 3.

31. Jefferson, *Notes on Virginia*, p. 95.

32. Madison, "Memorial and Remonstrance," p. 99.

33. Jefferson, *Notes on Virginia*, p. 95.

34. Jefferson, "Virginia Statute of Religious Liberty," p. 102.

35. Madison, "Memorial and Remonstrance," p. 97.

36. Berns, *First Amendment*, p. 2.

37. Semonche, *Religion and Constitutional Government*, p. 23. Not until 1961 did the United States Supreme Court strike down the last test oath (a Maryland law requiring state officeholders to declare their belief in God).

38. See Levy, *Establishment Clause*, pp. 75–84.

39. *Cantwell* v. *Connecticut*, 310 U.S. 296 (1940).

40. See Semonche, *Religion and Constitutional Government*, pp. 34–35.

41. *Reynolds* v. *United States*, 98 S.S. 145, 164 (1879); emphasis added. Waite was following Jefferson, who had written that it is a "fallacy" to "suffer the civil magistrate to intrude his powers into the field of opinion," for "it is time enough for the rightful purposes of civil government, for its officers to interfere when principles break out into overt acts against peace and good order" ("Virginia Statute of Religious Liberty," p. 103).

42. *Sherbert* v. *Verner*, 374 U.S. 398 (1963).

43. *Goldman* v. *Weinberger*, 475 U.S. 503, 530 (1986).

44. *Wisconsin* v. *Yoder*, 406 U.S. 205, 211, 217–18 (1972).

45. This case points to the intimate relationship of the free exercise and establishment clauses. Walter Berns has argued that the "Old Order Amish is now an Established religion of the United States (insofar as they alone are exempt from the operation of this law)" (*First Amendment*, p. 38). Anticipating this concern, Chief Justice Burger wrote: "The Court must not ignore the danger than an exception from a general obligation of citizenship on religious grounds may run afoul of the Establishment Clause, but that danger cannot be allowed to prevent any exception no matter how vital it may be to the protection of values promoted by the right of free exercise" (*Wisconsin* v. *Yoder*, 406 U.S. 205, 220–21). If any protection of free exercise rights constituted an establishment of religion, the free exercise clause would serve little purpose.

46. *Employment Division* v. *Smith*, 108 L. Ed. 2d 876, 892 (1990).

47. Ibid., p. 893. Scalia did acknowledge that the Court had upheld free exercise claims against valid general laws, but only when they piggybacked on other First Amendment protections such as speech and press, or, in the case of *Yoder*, on the Court's ruling in *Pierce* v. *Society of Sisters*, acknowledging the right of parents to determine the upbringing of their children (ibid., p. 887).

48. Ibid., pp. 893, 895, 900, 896. O'Connor concurred in the decision, however.

49. Laycock, "Summary and Synthesis," pp. 849, 856. In *Church of the Lukumi Babalu Aye, Inc.* v. *City of Hialeah* (1993), the Court struck down Hialeah city ordinances which prohibited the ritual killing and sacrifice of animals, protecting the free exercise rights of followers of the Santeria religion who practice animal sacrifice. Although the ordinance was "facially" neutral (that is, it did not name the Santeria religion) it was clear from its history that the purpose of the ordinance was to prohibit the ritual sacrifices practiced by its members, and the free exercise clause, Justice Kennedy wrote in the majority opinion, "protects against governmental hostility which is masked, as well as overt" (53 CCH S. Ct. Bull, p. B2780). The Court chose not to reconsider its position on the Sherbert Test.

50. See Durham et al., "For the Religious Freedom Restoration Act," p. 44.

51. *Everson* v. *Board of Education*, 330 U.S. 1, 15–16, 18 (1947).

52. *Engel* v. *Vitale*, 370 U.S. 421, 422, 424–25, 430 (1962).

53. Ibid., pp. 429, 431, 436.

54. *Abington Township School District* v. *Schempp*, 374 U.S. 203, 222 (1963).

55. Ibid., p. 313.

56. Ibid., p. 299.

57. Ibid., p. 225.

58. Ibid., p. 306.

59. *Lemon* v. *Kurtzman*, 403 U.S. 602, 612–14 (1971).

60. *Epperson* v. *Arkansas*, 393 U.S. 97, 108 (1968).

61. *Edwards* v. *Aguilard*, 482 U.S. 578, 591 (1987).

62. *Stone* v. *Graham*, 449 U.S. 39, 42 (1980).

63. *Wallace* v. *Jaffre*, 472 U.S. 38 (1985).

64. *Committee for Public Education and Religious Liberty* v. *Nyquist*, 413 U.S. 756, 778, 783 (1973).

65. *Aguilar* v. *Felton*, 473 U.S. 402, 414 (1985).

66. See Justice Rehnquist's dissent, ibid., pp. 102, 420–21.

67. *Mueller* v. *Allen*, 463 U.S. 388 (1983).

68. *McCollum* v. *Board of Education*, 333 U.S. 203, 210 (1948). It made no difference that it was voluntary and the teachers were supported privately.

69. *Zorach* v. *Clauson*, 343 U.S. 306, 313–14 (1952).

70. *Board of Education* v. *Mergens*, 110 S.Ct. 2356, 2371 (1990). Justice O'Connor added: "Secondary school students are mature enough and are likely to understand that a school does not endorse or support student speech that it merely permits on a nondiscriminatory basis" (ibid., p. 2372). In *Lamb's Chapel* v. *Center Moriches Union Free School District* (1993), the Court extended the logic of *Mergens*: if schools make their facilities available to public, nonstudent secular organizations for noneducational purposes, they must also make them available to religious organizations on a neutral basis.

71. *Lee* v. *Weisman*, 60 LW 4725, 4727 (1992).

72. Quoted in Savage, "Rehnquist Court," p. 8J.

73. Neuhaus, *Naked Public Square*, p. 40.

74. In the best historical study of free exercise, Michael McConnell concludes that though the evidence is ambiguous, it tends to support the view that free exercise requires exemptions from general laws (and hence does not support the current Court's reading of it). Over the course of our colonial history, McConnell shows, governments came to view exemptions as "a natural and legitimate response to the tension between law and religious convictions" ("Origins and Historical Understanding of Free Exercise," p. 1466). By 1789, virtually all states allowed religious exemptions from taking oaths (pp. 1467–68); many states allowed exemptions from military service for religious pacifists (pp. 1468–69); colonies (and later states) with religious establishments often allowed religious exemptions from taxes paid for support of establishments (pp. 1470–71); North Carolina and Maryland even exempted Quakers from the requirement of removing their hats in court (p. 1471). The general principle seems to have been that free exercise was to be allowed so long as the peace and safety of the state were not endangered—and this is, more or less, the meaning of the Sherbert Test.

75. Wacker, "Uneasy in Zion," pp. 22–23.

76. Falwell, *Listen, America!*, pp. 29, 243–44.

77. Gallup and Castelli, *People's Religion*, p. 63.

78. Curry, *First Freedoms*, pp. 219, 221.

79. See Berman, "Religion and Law," pp. 7–8.

80. Story, *Commentaries on the Constitution*, p. 91.

81. *The Church of the Holy Trinity* v. *United States*, 143 U.S. 226, 232 (1892).

82. Marty, *Pilgrims in Their Own Land*, p. 156.

83. See Albanese, *America*, pp. 290–95.

84. Bellah, "Civil Religion in America," p. 101.

85. Noll, Hatch, and Marsden, *Search for Christian America*, pp. 133–34, 130–31.

86. Winthrop, "Christian Charity," pp. 91–92; Curry, *First Freedoms*, p. 83.

87. Noll, Hatch, and Marsden, *Search for Christian America*, p. 24.

88. *Wallace* v. *Jaffree*, 472 U.S. 38, 106.

89. Quoted by Justice Rehnquist, ibid., pp. 100–101.

90. Berns, *First Amendment*, p. 9.

91. Story, *Commentaries on the Constitution*, p. 91.

92. Levy, *Establishment Clause*, pp. 99–100. In a letter of 1822 Madison warned that an "alliance or coalition between Government and Religion . . . cannot be too carefully guarded against. . . . Every new and successful example therefore of a *perfect separation* between ecclesiastic and civil matters is of importance" (ibid., p. 100).

93. Wills, *Under God*, p. 383. Thomas Curry argues, "Customs like days of prayer and thanksgiving appeared not so much matters of religion as part of the common coin of civilized living. Sabbath laws enjoyed widespread support and were so little the subject of dissent that citizens never even felt challenged to think how those laws might impose a particular religious viewpoint." America's leaders "had not come to grips with the implications their belief in the powerlessness of government in religious matters held for a society in which the values, customs, and forms of Protestant Christianity thoroughly permeated civil and political life. The contradiction between their theory and their practice became evident to Americans only later, with the advent of a more religiously pluralistic society" (*First Freedoms*, pp. 218–19).

94. "To the generation that adopted the First Amendment an establishment had also come to mean, in the main, the financial support of religion generally, by public taxation" (Levy, *Establishment Clause*, p. 9).

95. Ibid., pp. 65–66, 84.

96. Ibid., p. 83. But also see Curry, *First Freedoms*, p. 214.

97. *Lee* v. *Weisman*, 60 LW 4732.

98. *Abington School District* v. *Schempp*, 374 U.S. 203, 240.

99. *Brown* v. *Board of Education*, p. 307.

100. Mooney, *Boundaries Dimly Perceived*, p. 110.

101. Berman, "Religion and Law," p. 11.

102. *Federalist Papers*, pp. 66–67.

103. Semonche, *Religion and Constitutional Government*, p. 18.

104. McConnell, "Religious Freedom at a Crossroads," pp. 189–90.

105. As Chief Justice Burger put it, the state has not singled out religious institutions for special benefits, but granted exemptions to a broad range of "nonprofit, quasi-public corporations which include hospitals, libraries, playgrounds, scientific, professional, historical and patriotic groups." It has treated religion neutrally within a larger category of "beneficial and stabilizing influences in community life" (*Walz* v. *Tax Commission of the City of New York*, 397 U.S. 664, 673 [1970]).

106. *Lemon* v. *Kurtzman*, 403 U.S. 602, 614.

107. Laycock, "Formal, Substantive, and Disaggregated Neutrality toward Religion," pp. 1001–2.

108. Ibid., p. 1003.

109. Wills, *Under God*, p. 383.

110. Jefferson, *Notes on Virginia*, p. 95.

111. Williamsburg Charter, June 25, 1988, reprinted in *Journal of Law and Religion* 8 (1990): 9.

112. Ibid., p. 18.

113. Ibid., pp. 8, 13.

114. See Rawls, *Political Liberalism*, esp. Introduction and lectures 1 and 4. In terms of my discussion of liberalism in chapter 1, Rawls is arguing for a merely political, as opposed to a comprehensive, liberalism.

115. Guinness, *American Hour*, p. 250.

116. Murray, *We Hold These Truths*, p. 54.

117. See, for example, Rubenstein, "Church and State," pp. 179–82. Only in a society in which religion and government are separated, Rubinstein argued, "could Jews hope to attain that normalcy of life-situation which has eluded them for almost two thousand years" (ibid., pp. 180–81). Rubenstein has since become fairly critical of a strong separationism, however. See his essay, chap. 30, in Dalin, *American Jews and the Separationist Faith*, pp. 120–23.

118. Wolfson, chap. 37, in Dalin, *American Jews and the Separationist Faith*, p. 144.

119. Quoted in *Church and State* 43 (November 1990): 11.

120. Quoted in Cremin, *American Education: The National Experience*, p. 380.

121. *Democracy in America*, 1:319–20.

122. Ibid., pp. 321–22.

123. Reprinted in *Church and State* 44 (December 1991): 11.

124. Jefferson, Letter to the Danbury Baptists, pp. 75–76.

125. Quoted in Reichley, *Religion in American Public Life*, p. 67. Emphasis added.

126. Jefferson also believed that politics could corrupt religion. In the "Virginia Statute of Religious Liberty" he wrote that mixing the two "tends only to corrupt the principles of that religion it is meant to encourage, by bribing with a monopoly of worldly honours and emoluments, those who will externally profess and conform to it" ("Virginia Statute of Religious Liberty," p. 103).

127. Declaration on Religious Freedom, pp. 681, 679. Religious bodies have the right "not to be hindered in their public teaching" but they, in turn, "ought at all times to refrain from any manner of action which might seem to carry a hint of coercion or of a kind of persuasion that would be dishonorable or unworthy, especially when dealing with poor or uneducated people" (ibid., p. 682). John Courtney Murray notes that after Vatican II a "long-standing ambiguity has finally been cleared up. The Church does not deal with the secular order in terms of a double standard—freedom for the Church when Catholics are a minority, privilege for the Church and intolerance for others when Catholics are a majority" ("Religious Freedom," p. 673).

128. *McCollum v. Board of Education*, 333 U.S. 203, 232 (1948).

129. Carter, *Culture of Disbelief*, p. 123.

130. David G. Dalin traces this history in his Introduction to *American Jews and the Separationist Faith*, pp. 1–9. Dalin's anthology provides a good sampling of the rethinking of separationism among Jews.

131. Berke, chap. 4, in Dalin, *American Jews and the Separationist Faith*, pp. 23–24.

132. Wurzburger, chap. 38, ibid., p. 148.

133. Rubenstein, chap. 30, in Dalin, *American Jews and the Separationist Faith*, pp. 122–23.

134. Bellah et al., *Habits of the Heart*, p. 224. Bellah and his colleagues argue that we have been cast adrift: our "cultural traditions define personality, achievement, and the purpose of human life in ways that leave the individual suspended in glorious, but terrifying isolation" (ibid., p. 6).

135. Neuhaus, *Naked Public Square*, pp. 8–9.

136. *Everson v. Board of Education*, 330 U.S. 1, 18.

Chapter 4

1. *Guidelines for Selecting Bias-Free Textbooks and Storybooks*, p. 68.

2. Fitzgerald, *America Revised*, pp. 18, 27.

3. See Nord, "The Place of Religion in the World of Public School Textbooks."

4. The world histories are *The Pageant of World History* (Englewood Cliffs, N.J.: Prentice-Hall, 1986); *A History of the World* (Boston: Houghton Mifflin, 1988); *People and Nations* (New York: Harcourt Brace Jovanovich, 1987); and *World History: Patterns of Civilization* (Englewood Cliffs, N.J.: Prentice-Hall, 1988). The American histories are *Land of Promise: A History of the U.S.* (Glenville, Ill.: Scott, Foresman, 1987); *Triumph of the American Nation* (New York: Harcourt Brace Jovanovich, 1986); *The United States: A History of the Republic* (Englewood Cliffs, N.J.: Prentice-Hall, 1986); *United States History* (New York: Holt, Rinehart and Winston, 1988); and *Our Land, Our Time* (New York: Holt, Rinehart and Winston, 1987).

5. Vitz, *Censorship*; ASCD, *Religion in the Curriculum*; Gagnon, *Democracy's Untold Story*; People for the American Way, *Looking at History*; Haynes, "Teaching about Religious Freedom in American Secondary Schools"; and Smith, "High School History Texts Adopted for Use in the State of Alabama."

6. Smith, "High School History Texts Adopted for Use in the State of Alabama," p. 178.

7. Podesta, "The Uphill Battle for Quality Textbooks," p. 60.

8. Gagnon, *Democracy's Untold Story*, p. 59.

9. *Our Land, Our Time* is substantially better than the others in this regard: it gives about 2.5 percent of its post-1800 space to religion and often points out religious connections even when it gives little space to them. *Triumph of the American Nation* and *United States History* show the least interest in religion, giving the subject only about 0.5 percent of their post-1800 space.

10. Vitz, *Censorship*, p. 56.

11. *Pageant of World History*, p. 24.

12. Exod. 13:17–18, 21 (NEB).

13. *Pageant of World History*, p. 26.

14. *Triumph of the American Nation*.

15. Gagnon, *Democracy's Untold Story*, p. 43.

16. Three of the texts seemed to me to be somewhat better than the others: *World History: Patterns of Civilization*; *The United States: A History of the Republic*; and *Our Land, Our Time*.

17. I reviewed the six books approved for use in North Carolina schools beginning in the 1988–89 academic year. *Economics: It's Your Business* (Syracuse: New Readers Press, 1986); *Scribner Economics* (New York: Scribner Educational Publishers, 1988); *McDougal, Littell Economics* (Evanston, Ill.: McDougal, Littell, 1988); *Economics for Decision Making* (Lexington, Mass.: D. C. Heath, 1988); *Understanding Economics* (New York: Random House, 1986); and *Economics: Principles and Practices* (Columbus: Charles E. Merrill, 1988).

18. *Economics: Principles and Practices*, p. 502.

19. *McDougal, Littell Economics*, pp. 38, 78. The first sentence is repeated in the chapter summary, p. 66.

20. *Scribner Economics*, p. 39.

21. *Economics for Decision Making*, pp. 38–40.

22. *Scribner Economics*.

23. *Economics: It's Your Business*, p. 46.

24. National Conference of Catholic Bishops, *Economic Justice for All*, p. 12.

25. *Economics for Decision Making*, p. 5.

26. See, for example, *Economics: Principles and Practices*, p. 40; *Scribner Economics*, p. 39; or *Economics for Decision Making*, p. 63.

27. *Scribner Economics*, pp. 39–41.

28. Bellah, et al., *Habits of the Heart*, p. 336.

29. In North Carolina, twenty-three high school home economics textbooks in ten categories were approved for use. I reviewed all eight of the textbooks approved in the categories of teen living, adult living, and interpersonal relationships: *Family Living* (Englewood Cliffs, N.J.: Prentice-Hall, 1985); *Succeeding On Your Own: Goals—Resources—Decisions* (New York: Harcourt Brace Jovanovich, 1986); *The Business of Living* (Cincinnati: South-Western Publishing Co., 1986); *Contemporary Living* (South Holland, Ill.: Goodheart, 1987); *Married and Single Life* (Peoria, Ill.: Glencoe, 1984); *Creative Living* (Peoria, Ill.: Glencoe, 1985); *Resources for Living* (Saint Paul: EMC Publishing, 1987); and *Teen Guide* (New York: McGraw-Hill, 1985). The other categories are child development and parenting; clothing services; clothing and textiles; consumer education; cooperative home economic education; and food and nutrition.

30. *Married and Single Life* strikes me as somewhat more sensitive to religion and morality than the others; still, the differences are more a matter of degree than kind.

31. Of course, there was a (fairly liberal) religious dimenension to Maslow's thought—in his account of peak experiences, for example. There is nothing of this in these texts, however.

32. John Paul II, *Veritatis Splendor*, p. 76.

33. *Contemporary Living*, pp. 75, 62; emphasis added.

34. *The Business of Living*, p. 35.

35. *Contemporary Living*, p. 75.

36. Again, *Married and Single Life* is a little better: according to it, "basic issues of right and wrong change very little over the years" (p. 36).

37. Strike, "Review of Five Home Economics Texts," p. 52.

38. *Contemporary Living*, p. 125.

39. Bellah et al., *Habits of the Heart*, pp. 47, 129.

40. Strike, "Review of Five Home Economics Texts," p. 43.

41. See May, "Creation, Evolution, and High School Biology Texts," and Nelkin, *Creation Controversy*, chap. 2.

42. The five texts that dealt more or less fully with evolution were *Heath Biology* (Lexington, Mass.: D. C. Heath, 1985); *Macmillan Biology* (New York: Macmillan, 1985); *Modern Biology* (New York: Holt, Rinehart and Winston, 1985); *Prentice-Hall Biology* (Englewood Cliffs, N.J.: Prentice-Hall, 1986); and *Scott, Foresman Biology* (Glencoe, Ill.: Scott, Foresman, 1985). The one that is out of line is *Biology: An Everyday Experience* (Columbus: Charles E. Merrill, 1985).

43. Several of the texts seem to back off from claiming too much by using phrases such as "Many biologists believe that organisms are not the same as they were in the

past" (*Heath Biology*, p. 35) or "According to some biologists, organs such as the human appendix or the remains of hind limbs on whales provide evidence of evolution" (*Prentice-Hall Biology*, p. 205).

44. *Scott, Foresman Biology*, p. 10.

45. *Modern Biology*, p. 4; *Heath Biology*, p. 3; *Prentice-Hall Biology*, p. x.

46. *Biology: An Everyday Experience*.

47. The following passage is typical: "*Evolution* is the change that occurs in living things over time. When a group of living things has changed, we say that they have evolved. For example, all rabbits are not alike. They have evolved in different settings" (ibid., p. 501).

48. The physics texts are *Physics* (Englewood Cliffs, N.J.: Prentice-Hall, 1985); *Physics for Career Education* (Englewood Cliffs, N.J.: Prentice-Hall, 1988); *Physics: Principles and Problems* (Columbus: Merrill, 1990); *Modern Physics* (New York: Holt, Rinehart and Winston, 1990); and *Conceptual Physics* (Menlo Park, Calif.: Addison-Wesley, 1987). The physical science texts are *Physical Science* (Englewood Cliffs, N.J.: Prentice-Hall, 1991); *Physical Science* (New York: Harcourt, Brace, Jovanovitch, 1989); *Concepts and Challenges in Physical Science* (Englewood Cliffs, N.J.: Globe Books, 1989); *Introduction to Physical Science* (Menlo Park, Calif.: Addison-Wesley, 1988); *Physical Science* (Morristown, N.J.: Silver Burdett & Ginn, 1990); *Physical Science* (Glenville, Ill.: Scott, Foresman, 1990); and *Focus on Physical Science* (Columbus: Merrill, 1989).

49. *Physical Science* (Harcourt, Brace, Jovanovitch), p. 4.

50. *Physical Science* (Prentice-Hall), p. 7.

51. Vitz, *Censorship*, pp. 11–15, 18.

52. Ibid., pp. 33, 35.

53. Ibid., pp. 65, 69, 70, 73, 74, 72.

54. Fitzgerald, *America Revised*, pp. 46–47.

55. Quoted in Lucas, *Our Western Educational Heritage*, p. 494.

56. Podesta, "The Uphill Battle for Quality Textbooks," p. 62.

57. Pasley, "Not-So-Good Books," p. 21.

58. Quoted ibid.

59. Delfatorre, *What Johnny Shouldn't Read*, p. 10.

60. Sewall, "California," pp. 11, 120.

61. Bates, *Battleground*, chap. 8, and p. 225.

62. Vitz, *Censorship*, p. 1.

Chapter 5

1. In *Abington* v. *Schempp* (1963) Justice Clark proposed what were to become, with some modifications, the first two prongs of the Lemon Test: "What are the purpose and the primary effect of the enactment?" If either is the "advancement or inhibition of religion," then that action is unconstitutional (374 U.S. 203, 222). Government must "maintain strict neutrality, neither aiding nor opposing religion" (ibid., p. 225).

2. Bates, *Battleground*, p. 310.

3. See the Connecticut Mutual Surveys reported in Neuhaus, *Unsecular America*, pp. 146–48. This "education gap," as Robert Wuthnow calls it, did not appear in the

survey data until the 1960s, suggesting that religious belief can survive a secular education if it has adequate support elsewhere in the culture. My primary argument is that secular education nurtures a secular culture in which institutions and behavior are secular. See Wuthnow, *Restructuring of American Religion*, pp. 162, 170.

4. Wuthnow, *Restructuring of American Religion*, pp. 168–69.

5. Quoted in McClusky, "Development of Religious and Moral Values," pp. 228–29.

6. Stackhouse, *Public Theology and Political Economy*, p. x.

7. The boxes can open up a text by giving voice to different positions, but often the issues discussed in the boxes are not discussed in the body of the text, thus allowing the author to mention them while at the same time sidestepping serious consideration of them.

8. Hunter, *Culture Wars*, p. 203.

9. See Toumey, *God's Own Scientists*, pp. 84–88.

10. Falwell, *Listen, America!*, p. 65. Also see pp. 205–7.

11. LaHaye, *Battle for the Mind*, p. 9. LaHaye adds: "Most people today do not realize what humanism really is and how it is destroying our culture, families, country—and one day, the entire world. Most of the evils in the world today can be traced to humanism, which has taken over our government, the UN, education, TV, and most of the other influential things of life" (ibid.).

12. Ibid., p. 29. Similarly, the evangelical theologian Francis Schaeffer argued that with the "humanistic Renaissance" that followed Aquinas, "Man" began "from himself, with no knowledge except what he himself can discover and no standards outside of himself. In this view Man is the measure of all things" (*Christian Manifesto*, p. 24).

13. Packer, *"Fundamentalism" and the Word of God*, p. 21.

14. Kristol, "The Future of American Jewery," pp. 156–57.

15. *Smith* v. *Board of School Commissioners of Mobile County*, 655 F.Supp. 939, 985–86 (S.D. Ala., 1987).

16. Ibid., pp. 979–80.

17. Ibid., p. 982.

18. See ibid., p. 983. In a very thoughtful opinion in *Malnak* v. *Yogi* (1979) Judge Adams wrote that "all programs or positions that entangle the government with issues and problems that might be classified as 'ultimate concerns' do not, because of that, become 'religious' programs or positions. Only if the government favors a comprehensive belief system and advances its teachings does it establish a religion" (592 F.2d 197, 212).

19. Ibid., pp. 974–75.

20. Dershowitz, "Judge Brevard Hand," p. 9.

21. *Smith* v. *Board of School Commissioners of Mobile County* 827 F.2d 684, 690, 692 (11th Cir., 1987). The discussion of history texts is on page 693.

22. See Kristeller, *Renaissance Thought and Its Sources*, p. 22.

23. Bullock, *Humanist Tradition in the West*, p. 35.

24. Quoted in Shinn, *Man*, pp. 48, 49. Even Karl Barth, who in the first half of the twentieth century was the great force for neo-orthodox theology, talked about the "humanism of God" in a 1956 lecture. To describe God as being the "wholly other" (as Barth had done earlier) was, he now admitted, exaggerated; God did become man after all, and what "takes place in God's humanity is . . . the *affirmation* of man" ("Humanity of God," p. 60).

25. *Humanist Manifesto I*, pp. 7, 9.

26. *Secular Humanist Declaration*, pp. 5, 3.

27. In the early 1980s the American Humanist Association had thirty-five hundred members, the American Ethical Union had thirty-five hundred, and the Fellowship of Religious Humanists, three hundred. See Kurtz, *In Defense of Secular Humanism*, p. 189.

28. Ibid., p. 177.

29. Ibid., pp. 177, 187.

30. For an account of the humanism of the humanities, see Nord, "The Humanities and the Modern World."

31. If the books don't quite teach humanism, they don't quite teach secularism either. In chapter 1 I distinguished between "secularism" and "secularization." Secularism is a philosophical position defined by its hostility to religion. (Many capital "H" Humanists are also secularists.) Secularization is a process with many causes, but it was not caused, I argued, by secularism. There can be no doubt that the textbooks teach secular rather than religious ways of thinking about the world—and hence contribute to the secularization of modern culture—but they don't teach secular*ism*.

32. See Wittgenstein, *Philosophical Investigations*, p. 32e.

33. Hick, *Interpretation of Religion*, p. 22.

34. Yinger, *Scientific Study of Religion*, pp. 7, 11–12.

35. Herberg, "Religion and Education in America," p. 28.

36. Quoted in Sealy, *Religious Education*, p. 8.

37. Tillich, *Systematic Theology*, 1:12.

38. Dewey, *Common Faith*, pp. 10, 33, 24, 27.

39. *Humanisto Manifesto I*, p. 9.

40. *Torcaso* v. *Watkins*, 367 U.S. 488, 495n. (1961). In his concurring opinion in *Malnak* v. *Yogi* Judge Adams suggested that Justice Black was not declaring secular humanism as a philosophical movement to be a religion but rather secular humanism as the *belief system of a particular group*, the Fellowship of Humanity, which met regularly on Sundays and functioned much like a church and which had some years earlier sought a legal exemption under the Free Exercise Clause (*Malnak* v. *Yogi*, 592 F.2d 197, 206, 210).

41. *Abington* v. *Schempp*, 374 U.S. 203, 225.

42. *United States* v. *Macintosh*, 283 U.S. 605, 633–34 (1931).

43. *Minersville School District* v. *Gobitis*, 310 U.S. 586, 593 (1940).

44. *McGowan* v. *Maryland*, 366 U.S. 420, 461 (1961).

45. *United States* v. *Seeger* 380 U.S. 163, 174, 176 (1965).

46. See Hunter, *Culture Wars*, p. 260.

47. Though I do not agree with him about everything, I have found Stephen Toulmin's *Human Understanding: The Collective Use and Evolution of Concepts* immensely helpful in thinking about the nature of rationality; also see his *Cosmopolis: The Hidden Agenda of Modernity*, esp. pp. 198–201. My distinction is similar to that sometimes drawn between "hard" and "soft" rationalism; see, for example, Abraham, *Introduction to the Philosophy of Religion*, chaps. 9 and 10. Also see Putnam, "Two Conceptions of Rationality."

48. Packer, *"Fundamentalism" and the Word of God*, pp. 140, 143.

49. Barbour, *Religion in an Age of Science*, p. 15.

50. See Smith, *Beyond the Post-Modern Mind*, pp. 114–15.

51. Over the course of the last several decades it has become clear that science is not so rigorously "rational" (in my sense) as has often been believed. In his very influential book, *The Structure of Scientific Revolutions* (1962), Thomas Kuhn argued that there are no clear rules for choosing between competing paradigms (or research programmes or models) in science—between, for example, Ptolemaic and Copernican astronomy, or Newtonian mechanics and relativity theory. The data can be interpreted in terms of either paradigm; they are inevitably "theory-laden." Indeed, there is never any way of directly testing any specific claims, for we always bring to experiments background webs of theories and assumptions, such that modifications in one part of the web can save a hypothesis or theory elsewhere in the web. As a result, there is no crucial experiment, no algorithm, no set of rules which allows conclusive verification or falsification. In choosing between rival scientific theories or paradigms scientists must fall back on a messy, often confusing welter of criteria: simplicity and aesthetic considerations; the scope or comprehensiveness of the competing theories; their experimental accuracy; their fruitfulness in generating hypotheses; their internal consistency, and so on. In his early work, Kuhn often made paradigm change sound completely irrational, but he soon argued that he did not mean to deny "the existence of good reasons" for theory change; rather he claimed that "such reasons constitute values to be used in making choices rather than rules of choice" ("Reflections on My Critics," p. 232). One way of reading this is that revolutionary science can be (more or less) reasonable even if it is not rational.

Philosophers and theologians like Hans Küng, Ian Barbour, and Basil Mitchell have directly applied Kuhn's insights and new developments in the philosophy of science to religion to show how religion and science develop in comparable ways. (See Küng's *Theology for the Third Millennium*, Mitchell's *Justification of Religious Belief*, and Barbour's *Myths, Models, and Paradigms*, and *Religion in an Age of Science*.) They argue that religion maps onto the world much like science. There are no straightforward ways of verifying or falsifying religious claims; instead there are competing paradigms which, over time, are sorted out as more or less reasonable given the total context of human experience. Barbour concludes: "In both fields there are no proofs, but there can be good reasons for the judgments rendered by the paradigm community" (*Religion in an Age of Science*, p. 65). No doubt religion is more "subjective" than science, but, so the argument goes, the differences are those of degree, not kind.

52. So, for example, Stephen Toulmin argues that postmodernism requires the contextualization of science: "Even at the core of twentieth-century physics, idiosyncrasies of persons and cultures cannot be eliminated." "No neutral 'scratch line' exists," he argues, "from which to jump to a self-sustaining tradition-free intellectual system. All of the cultural situations from which we pursue our practical and intellectual inquiries are historically conditioned" (*Cosmopolis*, p. 179).

53. *Catechism of the Catholic Church*, pp. 41–43. The interior quotes are from Aquinas and John Henry Cardinal Newman.

54. Calvin, *Institutes of the Christian Religion*, p. 359–60; Packer, *"Fundamentalism" and the Word of God*, p. 118.

55. Pannenberg, *Faith and Reality*, pp. 66, 69.

56. Fox, *Reinhold Niebuhr*, p. 296.

57. Hick, *Faith and Knowledge*, p. 115.

58. Adams, *Religion and Cultural Freedom*, p. 3.

59. "To the person who has found God," Hick argues, "the whole of life can thus mediate the divine presence and purpose. . . . To the believer 'the heavens declare the glory of God, and the firmament showeth his handiwork' . . . ; in his neighbors he discovers fellow children of the heavenly Father; in the imperatives of morality he feels the pressure upon him of the absolute demands of God; in life's joy and happiness he discerns the bountiful goodness of the Lord, and in its frustrations and disappointments he sees, even if usually only in retrospect, God's austere but gracious discipline saving him from too complete involvement in purely earthly hopes and purposes. In both joy and sorrow, success and failure, rejoicing and mourning, he sees, however fitfully and faintly, the hand of God. . . . All of life is for him a dialogue with the divine Thou" (*Faith and Knowledge*, pp. 146–47).

60. Hans Küng argues that the "sustaining reality of God is never granted to me intuitively, unequivocally, free of doubt, securely." But, he adds, the believer, "like the lover, can be completely certain of the Other by committing himself entirely to the Other. And this certainty is stronger than all the security established by proofs" (*On Being a Christian*, p. 163).

61. Polanyi, *Science, Faith and Society*, p. 43.

62. Kuhn, *Structure of Scientific Revolutions*, p. 165.

63. The American Association for the Advancement of Science makes some effort to improve this situation by emphasizing the importance of teaching the history of science in its newly released *Benchmarks for Scientific Literacy*. See chap. 10.

64. Jastrow, *God and the Astronomers*, p. 103.

65. Quoted in Margenau and Varghese, *Cosmos, Bios, Theos*, p. 1.

66. Polanyi, *Science, Faith and Society*, p. 45.

67. Shils, *Tradition*, p. 22.

68. No doubt many scientists also hold religious beliefs, but in many cases, perhaps most, this is a matter of compartmentalizing worldviews and never seriously exploring their relationship, rather than working out a reasoned understanding of how science and religion relate. We might say that such people have a faith in the ultimate complementarity of science and religion by virtue of their trust in science and religion respectively.

69. Bloom, *Closing of the American Mind*, p. 249.

70. There are four ways in which philosophers have often parsed indoctrination. First, indoctrination must involve doctrines—hence students might be indoctrinated in religion but not in science (which has no doctrines). False. Students can be indoctrinated, for example, to believe that scientific method is adequate to resolve all problems. Second, indoctrination involves teaching methods that fail to respect evidence and reason. True, and students can be indoctrinated into believing either the claims of science or religion. Even if science is scrupulously rational and open to falsifying evidence within its everyday practice, indoctrination can occur at the level of scientific method and the basic philosophical presuppositions of science that are seldom held up for critical assessment. Third, indoctrination has the effect of producing (an unwarranted) certainty and closed minds. True, and science education can do this as effectively as

religious education. Fourth, indoctrination must be intended. False. Teachers can use unreasonable teaching methods and nurture closed minds without intending to do so (if they have an unduly truncated notion of what it means to be reasonable). For a good discussion of these four alternatives, particularly as they play out regarding religion, see Thiessen, *Teaching for Commitment*.

71. Cupitt, *Sea of Faith*, pp. 181–82.

72. Ferguson, *Aquarian Conspiracy*, p. 23.

73. For something of the range of New Age literature see Kelly, *Treasury of Light*.

74. Peters, *Cosmic Self*, p. 8. In the Introduction to her anthology of New Age literature Mary Olsen Kelly writes: "The New Age embraces all religions and spiritual disciplines. There are many paths to God, and each person has the right to find the one that is appropriate for him or her" (*Treasury of Light*, p. 21).

75. Quoted in Kelly, *Treasury of Light*, p. 22.

76. Quoted in Ferguson, *Aquarian Conspiracy*, p. 381.

77. Ferguson, *Aquarian Conspiracy*, pp. 31, 382.

78. Peters, *Cosmic Self*, p. 5.

79. Starhawk, *Dreaming the Dark*, p. xxvii.

80. See Mary Farrell Bednarowski, "The New Age Movement and Feminist Spirituality," p. 169. Ted Peters has suggested that combining "psychology with religious metaphysics is producing a new age myth that describes the human psyche as originating in some primeval unity of body and spirit, of self and world. Then, the new age myth alleges, we fell. We fell because of the process of individuation. We left the warm symbiotic unity we once knew with our mother and our environment and entered the cold cruel world of independence, the world of separate ego consciousness. Yet we long to return. We long to overcome our individuality and experience again the wholeness we have lost. Our task is to realize the oneness of self and cosmos" (*Cosmic Self*, p. 61).

81. Ahlstrom, *Religious History of the American People*, p. 1019. See Ahlstrom's chapters on American "harmonial" religion, pp. 1019–54, and Catherine Albanese's chapter on occult and metaphysical movements in *America*, pp. 163–88.

82. See Albanese, "Religion and the American Experience," Lucas, "The New Age Movement and the Pentecostal/Charismatic Revival," and D'Antonio, *Heaven on Earth*, pp. 393–96.

83. Albanese, *America*, p. 183.

84. See Lewis, "Approaches to the Study of the New Age Movement," pp. 1–2.

85. The figures on astrology and reincarnation are reported in Lewis, "Approaches to the Study of the New Age," p. 4. The percentages on witchcraft and magical powers are reported in Patterson and Kim, *The Day America Told the Truth*, p. 204. (They also report that 45 percent of Americans believe in ghosts.) The ESP percentage is from a Gallup Poll in Gallup and Castelli, *People's Religion*, p. 75.

86. D'Antonio, *Heaven on Earth*, p. 398–400.

87. Ferguson, *Aquarian Conspiracy*, p. 24.

88. Cumbey, *Hidden Dangers of the Rainbow*, p. 249.

89. Whitemarsh and Reisman, *Subtle Serpent*, p. 19. They quickly add reincarnation as a second pillar of the New Age, however. See ibid., pp. 31–40.

90. Quoted in Delfattore, *What Johnny Shouldn't Read*, p. 173.

91. Vitz, *Censorship*, p. 69.

92. *Fleischfresser* v. *Directors of School District 200*, 15 F.3d 680, 689 (1994).

93. *Malnak* v. *Yogi*, 592 F.2d 197, 198 (1979), esp. n. 2.

94. Ibid., p. 214.

95. Cumbey's other New Age doctrines are belief in a spiritual force; belief in an immanent God; belief in the divinity of man; belief in reincarnation; belief that Jesus was not the Christ; belief in avatars; belief in salvation by works rather than grace; hatred for traditional Western religion; hatred for God the Father; belief in masters and an occult hierarchy; belief in an "inner government" of the planet; and belief in the special virtue of Aryans. Two of her doctrines have some foothold in public education: belief in the perfectibility of humans and the interconnectedness of all things (*Hidden Dangers of the Rainbow*, pp. 252–54).

Cumbey's list is idiosyncratic and would be accepted by few New Agers. In his more sympathetic analysis of the New Age movement, Ted Peters describes eight key teachings. Of the eight, wholism and an emphasis on human potentiality resonate with a good deal that is taught in public schools; but the other six—monism, the higher self, reincarnation, evolutionary (spiritual) transformation, gnostic forms of knowing, and (sometimes) appeal to Jesus as a teacher of mystical truths—are unlikely to have much space in the public school curriculum (*Cosmic Self*, pp. 53–92).

96. Jay E. Adams, *Biblical View of Self-Esteem*, p. 108. Perhaps the most important point of overlap between secular humanism and New Age religion—at least for their critics—is the "glorification" of the self. Ironically, the emphasis on self-actualization and self-esteem, personal autonomy and human potential, which as symptoms of secular humanism signified humanity cut adrift from God, in the critique of New Ageism signify the deification of the individual, the God within.

97. Buehrer, *The New Age Masquerade*, pp. 29, 85–86, 46.

Chapter 6

1. Students who identified themselves as fundamentalists or evangelicals did half-again better than students who called themselves moderates or liberals and twice as well as students who claimed to be atheists or agnostics, largely because they did much better on the Bible questions. Students who had had at least three prior courses in religion did twice as well as students who had not had any, though none of them passed either, indicating, I suppose, the relatively narrow focus of those courses. See my "Religious Literacy, Textbooks, and Religious Neutrality." The statistics in that article are slightly different from those given here because it does not include the results from the fourth and final time I gave the test.

2. Gallup, *Gallup Poll: Public Opinion 1990*, p. 158.

3. Mill, *On Liberty*, p. 287.

4. It is important that the conversation not be purely adversarial, however. As Richard Bernstein puts it, the "adversarial confrontational style can be contrasted with a model of dialogical encounter. Here one begins with the assumption that the other has something to say to us and to contribute to our understanding. The initial task is to grasp the other's position in the strongest possible light. . . . There is a play, a to-and-fro movement in dialogical encounters. . . . The other is not an adversary or an opponent, but a conversational partner" (*New Constellation*, p. 337).

5. MacIntyre, *After Virtue*, p. 201.

6. Taylor, *Sources of the Self*, p. 36. Taylor also writes: "I define who I am by defining where I speak from, in the family tree, in social space, in the geography of social statuses and functions, in my intimate relations to the ones I love" (ibid., p. 35).

7. Adams, "Personhood and Human Rights," p. 40.

8. See Bloom, *Closing of the American Mind*, esp. pp. 25–26. Also see Lovin, "Confidence and Criticism," pp. 81–82.

9. Rorty, "Two Cheers for the Cultural Left," p. 237.

10. Fleming, "Religion in American History Textbooks," p. 101.

11. *Williamsburg Charter: Summary of Principles*, p. 280.

12. See Gaffney, "Religion and Public Life," p. 280.

13. The Gallup Poll put the figure at 9 percent in 1987 (Gallup and Castelli, *People's Religion*, p. 24), while the Williamsburg Charter Foundation Survey put the number at 11 percent (Hunter, "Pluralism," p. 274).

14. In the fall of 1990 incoming college freshmen identified themselves as being 79.7 percent Christian; 11.8 percent no religious affiliation; 2.2 percent Jewish; 0.4 percent Buddhist; 0.3 percent Muslim; and 5.6 percent other. (*Chronicle of Higher Education*, Jan. 30, 1990, p. A30).

15. See Hunter, "Williamsburg Charter Survey," p. 265.

16. Guinness, *American Hour*, p. 247.

17. By many measures, we are becoming more tolerant as we become more pluralistic: in 1958, 28 percent of Americans said they would not vote for a Jewish candidate for president, while now only 10 percent say this; in 1958 25 percent would not vote for a Catholic, while now only 8 percent would not. But it is also true that in 1958, 3 percent of Americans said they would not vote for a born-again Baptist for president, while the figure now is 13 percent (Gaffney, "Religion and Public Life," p. 284). We are not very tolerant of some minority groups: 88 percent of evangelicals would not vote for an atheist for president; 29 percent of Americans question whether there is a place in America for Muslims; and 65 percent agree that "it should be against the law for unusual religious cults to try to convert teenagers" (Hunter, "Williamsburg Charter Survey," pp. 264–67). And as the abortion issue is played out, a good deal of intolerance is to be found between "conservatives" and "liberals" within the same religions.

18. Barrett, *Irrational Man*, p. 24.

19. See, for example, Brown and Brown, *Cry for Justice*.

20. Graff, *Beyond the Culture Wars*, pp. 12–13.

21. Cited in Boyer, "Teaching Religion in the Public Schools and Elsewhere," pp. 517–18.

22. Mortimer Adler is surely right that "youth is an insuperable obstacle to being an educated person" (*Paideia Proposal*, p. 9).

23. Smart, *Religion and the Western Mind*, pp. 3–4. The terms "inside" and "outside" come from Collingwood, *Idea of History*, pp. 213–15. For Collingwood, the term "outside" refers to *physical* events (which may or may not have an inside). I am using the term "outside" more broadly to refer to any interpretation *imposed* (from the outside) on an event, a text, or a culture.

24. Smart, *Religion and the Western Mind*, pp. 4–5.

25. Dixon, "What Should Religion Departments Teach?," p. 368.

26. See Brown, "Thinking about the Introductory Course," and Smart, "Teaching Religion and Religions."

27. Smart, "Teaching Religion and Religions," p. 10. For a more detailed account of these dimensions of religion see Smart, *Religious Experience of Mankind*, pp. 3–23.

28. Schleiermacher, *On Religion*, p. 9.

29. Smith, *Meaning and End of Religion*, pp. 122–24. Also see Kolakowski, *Religion*, pp. 161–206.

30. Palmer, *To Know as We Are Known*, p. 58. Palmer argues that while it is true that much Christian theology emphasizes God's words, His "propositional" truth, our richest religious insights come to us in stories and in personal relationships—with other people, with nature, and with God (ibid., pp. 47–50). In Jesus, he claims, truth, is no longer abstract and propositional, but "suddenly takes on a human face and a human frame. . . . The disembodied 'word' takes on flesh and walks among us" (ibid., p. 48).

31. Buber, *I and Thou*, p. 32.

32. Wilson and Natale, *Education in Religious Understanding*, p. 45.

33. Ibid., p. 14.

34. The claim that there is no truth may mean only that traditional or conventional ways of thinking about truth are inadequate and that some more sophisticated or nuanced approach may be required. It may be, for example, that there is no way to map "true" propositions onto the structure of the world so that there is a congruence between what language says and the world as it really is. What the world "really" is may be shaped in part, at least, by language, so that the world changes with the linguistic resources of our worldview.

I have noted the common religious view that truth must be understood *personally* in a way that makes it difficult to put into propositions something that can then be assessed as "objectively" true. Robert Bellah characterizes the "objectivist fallacy" as the confusion of belief with religion, the view that religion can be captured in objectively true propositions. Religion, as he puts it, "is embodied truth, not known truth, and it has in fact been transmitted far more through narrative, image, and enactment than through definitions and logical demonstrations" ("Religion and Belief," p. 221).

35. See Wilson, *Rationality*, pp. x–xiii.

36. James, *Varieties of Religious Experience*, p. 334.

37. National Council for the Social Studies, *Curriculum Guidelines for Multicultural Education*, p. 3. The guidelines should have been labeled "multiethnic," not "multicultural."

38. Schlesinger, *Disuniting of America*, p. 127.

39. Quoted, ibid., p. 67.

40. National Council for the Social Studies, *Curriculum Guidelines for Multicultural Education*, pp. 8, 13. What the Guidelines give with one hand they take away—in part, at least—with the other, for they also claim that there is "after all, a set of overarching values that all groups within a society or nation must endorse to maintain societal cohesion. In our nation, these core values stem from our commitment to human dignity, and include justice, equality, freedom, and due process of law. Although the school should value and reflect ethnic and cultural diversity, it should not promote the practices and beliefs of any ethnic or cultural group that contradict the core democratic

values of the United States" (p. 11). That is, America's "core values" trump those of other cultures. This is especially peculiar in that America's shortcomings are emphasized over and over in the guidelines, and teachers are never once told to explore the shortcomings of other countries or ethnic communities.

41. Fullinwider, "Ethnocentrism and Education in Judgment," p. 7.

42. Taylor, "The Politics of Recognition," p. 70.

43. Ravitch, "Multiculturalism," p. 340.

44. Fish, *There's No Such Thing as Free Speech*, p. 35.

45. Asanti, *Afrocentricity*, p. 5.

46. Ravitch, "Multiculturalism," p. 352.

47. Schlesinger, *Disuniting of America*, p. 16.

48. Mill, *On Liberty*, p. 287.

49. *Chronicle of Higher Education*, Dec. 18, 1985, p. 25.

50. Gallup, *Gallup Poll: Public Opinion 1986*, p. 243.

51. Wilson and Natale, *Education in Religious Understanding*, pp. 61–62.

52. *Religion in the Public School Curriculum*, p. 308.

53. Ozick, chap. 24, in Dalin, *American Jews and the Separationist Faith*, p. 96.

54. Sussman, chap. 34, ibid., p. 136.

55. Graff, *Beyond the Culture Wars*, p. 12.

Chapter 7

1. Smart, *Religion and the Western Mind*, pp. 11, 20.

2. Of course, we are willing to disfranchise some people—felons, for example—or exclude certain political parties from our democracy; so we may decide that certain views are too dangerous to be included in the curriculum. Needless to say, such judgments are always risky.

3. *Epperson* v. *Arkansas*, 393 U.S. 97, 103–4.

4. *Abington Township* v. *Schempp*, 374 U.S. 203, 225, 300, 306.

5. Ibid., pp. 225, 299, 305–6.

6. Ibid., p. 300.

7. *Lemon* v. *Kurtzman* 403 U.S. 602, 612–13.

8. Smart, *Religion and the Western Mind*, p. 9.

9. *Everson* v. *Board of Education*, 330 U.S 1, 23–24. Jackson goes on to say: "Whether such a disjunction is possible, and if possible whether it is wise, are questions I need not try to answer" (ibid., p. 24).

10. *McCollum* v. *Board of Education*, 333 U.S. 202, 236.

11. *Abington Township* v. *Schempp*, 374 U.S. 203, 225, 306.

12. Laycock, "Formal, Substantive, and Disaggregated Neutrality toward Religion," p. 1004.

13. *West Virginia State Board of Education* v. *Barnette*, 319 U.S. 624, 642 (1943).

14. *Tinker* v. *Des Moines Independent Community School District*, 393 U.S. 503, 511 (1969).

15. *Keyishian* v. *Board of Regents*, 385 U.S. 589, 603 (1966). *Keyishian* concerned higher education, but courts have applied Brennan's argument to public schools. See,

for example, *Zykan* v. *Warsaw Community School Corporation*, 631 F.2d 1300, 1305 (7th Cir., 1980).

16. *Epperson* v. *Arkansas*, 393 U.S. 97, 116.

17. *Abington Township* v. *Schempp*, 374 U.S. 203, 300.

18. *Vaughn* v. *Reed*, 313 F. Supp. 431, 434 (W.D. Vir., 1970). Similarly, in *Wiley* v. *Franklin* a federal district court held that if Bible courses "are religious in nature, as asserted by the plaintiffs, then they must be held unconstitutional and their continuance must be enjoined, with the consequence that no free exercise issue would then exist in the lawsuits. Upon the other hand, if those courses are not religious, but rather are secular in nature, as asserted by the defendants, then the offering of the courses and the manner of their offering could not be found to interfere in an unconstitutional manner with the plaintiffs' free exercise rights" (468 F. Supp. 133, 148–49 [E.D. Tenn., 1979]).

19. *Crockett* v. *Sorenson*, 568 F. Supp. 1422, 1432 (W.D. Vir., 1983).

20. Bates, *Battleground*, p. 311.

21. Feyerabend, *Against Method*, p. 299.

22. Most "minor" religions are not unique but are variations on "major" religions, and in discussing the major themes we implicitly include the variations to some extent. So, for example, in many contexts, it is enough to talk about Protestantism, rather than discuss the (relatively) minor differences between Baptists and Methodists, though in other contexts those distinctions might loom large. Sometimes Eastern religions can be lumped together in contrast to Western religions—though sometimes they cannot.

23. Warnock, "Neutral Teacher," p. 110. Warnock argues that "unless the teacher comes out into the open, and says in what direction he believes that the evidence points he will have failed in his duty as a teacher" (p. 107).

24. Cuddy, "The Trouble with Teaching about Religion," p. 15A.

25. Haynes, *Teacher's Guide to Study about Religion*, p. 5.

26. Ibid., p. 6.

27. Baer, "'Strict Neutrality' and Our Monopoly System," p. 33.

28. Haynes, *Finding Common Ground*, p. 1.6–7; Ebert, "A Place at the Table," p. 43.

29. Quoted in Boston, "Split Decision," p. 5. Helms made his comments in Senate debate on February 3, 1994.

30. Dierenfield, "Religious Influence in American Public Schools," pp. 42–3.

31. *Jones* v. *Clear Creek Independent School District*, 977 F.2d 963 (5th Cir. 1992).

32. Boston, "The School Prayer Mess," p. 9.

33. Quoted, ibid., p. 7.

34. *Lee* v. *Weisman*, 60 LW 4733.

35. Buzzard, *Schools*, pp. 130–31.

Chapter 8

1. Hofstadter and Metzger, *Academic Freedom in the Age of the University*, p. v.

2. Hunter, *Culture Wars*, p. 213.

3. See Veysey, *Emergence of the American University*, pp. 384–85; and Metzger, *Academic Freedom in the Age of the University*, p. 123.

4. Metzger, *Academic Freedom in the Age of the University*, p. 23.

5. See Veysey, *Emergence of the American University*, pp. 45–48.

6. See Metzger, *Academic Freedom in the Age of the University*, pp. 89–92.

7. Ibid., pp. 150–51.

8. AAUP, *Declaration of Principles*, pp. 164, 167–68, 162–63.

9. AAUP, *Statement of Principles on Academic Freedom and Tenure*, pp. 35–36.

10. AAUP, *Declaration of Principles*, p. 169.

11. Quoted in Joughin, *Academic Freedom and Tenure*, p. 37, n8; emphasis added.

12. Bok, *Beyond the Ivory Tower*, pp. 23–24.

13. Rabban, "Functional Analysis of 'Individual' and 'Institutional' Academic Freedom under the First Amendment," p. 291.

14. Metzger, *Academic Freedom in the Age of the University*, p. 90.

15. Bellah, "Can You Recite Your Creed?," pp. 6–7.

16. McConnell, "Academic Freedom in Religious Colleges and Universities," p. 315.

17. Marsden, *Soul of the American University*, p. 300.

18. Schmitt, "Academic Freedom," p. 123.

19. AAUP, "Some Observations on Ideology, Competence, and Faculty Selection," pp. 1a, 2a.

20. Long, "Dynamics of Academic Freedom," p. 1.

21. Postman, *Conscientious Objections*, p. 4. Postman suggests that a university suffers from hardening of the categories "when certified scholars resolve, against all reason, to defend their customary view of knowledge from encroachment by more novel perspectives."

22. Strike, "Are Secular Ethical Languages Religiously Neutral?," p. 492.

23. *Sweezy* v. *New Hampshire*, 354 U.S. 234, 250 (1957).

24. Van Alstyne, "Academic Freedom and the First Amendment in the Supreme Court of the United States," p. 114.

25. *Keyishian* v. *Board of Regents*, 385 U.S. 589, 603 (1966).

26. Rabban, "Functional Analysis of 'Individual' and 'Institutional' Academic Freedom under the First Amendment," p. 230.

27. *Sweezy* v. *New Hampshire*, 354 U.S. 234, 263.

28. Rabban, "A Functional Analysis of 'Individual' and 'Institutional' Academic Freedom Under the First Amendment," pp. 266, 229.

29. *Bishop* v. *Aronov*, 926 F.2nd 1066, 1068 (11th Cir 1991).

30. Bishop claimed that the time he spent on religious topics never exceed 5 minutes out of 2,250 minutes of instructional time in a semester (*Petition for a Writ of Certiorari*, p. 4).

31. Ibid., p. 6.

32. *Bishop* v. *Aronov*, 732 F. Supp. 1562, 1567–68 (N.D. Ala 1990).

33. *Bishop* v. *Aronov*, 926 F.2nd 1066, 1074, 1077, 1075. The court made no reference to the concept of "institutional academic freedom," however.

34. Ibid., 1077, 1071. Also see pp. 1076–77.

35. *Petition for a Writ of Certiorari*, p. 29.

36. See David Rabban's superb discussion of these matters in "A Functional Analysis of 'Individual' and 'Institutional' Academic Freedom under the First Amendment," pp. 280–301.

37. AAUP, *Declaration of Principles*, p. 169.

38. AAUP, *Statement on Professional Ethics*, p. 88.

39. AAUP, *Recommended Institutional Regulations on Academic Freedom and Tenure*, p. 21.

40. AAUP, "Some Observations on Ideology, Competence, and Faculty Selection," p. 2a.

41. See Strike, *Liberty and Learning*, pp. 41–53.

42. AAUP, *Declaration of Principles*, p. 170.

43. *Sheldon* v. *Tucker*, 364 U.S. 479, 485 (1960).

44. *Epperson* v. *Arkansas*, 393 U.S. 97, 104 (1968).

45. *Board of Education, Island Trees Union Free School District* v. *Pico*, 457 U.S. 863 (1982). Brennan claimed, for example, that "local school boards must be permitted 'to establish and apply their curriculum in such a way as to transmit community values,' and that 'there is a legitimate and substantial community interest in promoting respect for authority and traditional values be they social, moral, or political'" (ibid., p. 864). Brennan was quoting from the petitioners' brief.

46. *Zykan* v. *Warsaw Community School Corporation*, 631 F.2d 1300, 1305 (7th Cir. 1980).

47. *Epperson* v. *Arkansas*, 393 U.S. 97, 107.

48. *Board of Education, Island Trees Union Free School District* v. *Pico*, pp. 864, 866.

49. Van Geel, *The Courts and American Education Law*, p. 222.

50. *Moore* v. *Gaston County Board of Education*, 357 F. Supp. 1037 (W.D. N.C. 1973).

51. *Peloza* v. *Capistrano Unified School District*, 37 F.3rd 517, 522 (9th Cir., 1994).

52. See Giroux, *Teachers as Intellectuals*.

53. Marsden, "Religious Professors Are the Last Taboo," p. A10.

Chapter 9

1. See Toumey, *God's Own Scientists*, p. 101.

2. Peacocke, *Intimations of Reality*, p. 51. Peacocke provides a good example of how this works out regarding evolution and religion in chapter 2 of his book. Also see *One World: The Interaction of Science and Theology*, by the physicist and Anglican priest John Polkinghorne.

3. Dawkins, *Blind Watchmaker*, p. 6.

4. Quoted in Johnson, *Darwin on Trial*, p. 125.

5. National Academy of Science, *Science and Creationism*, pp. 5–6; emphasis added.

6. See Johnson, *Darwin on Trial*, pp. 8 and 126.

7. Adams, *Religion and Cultural Freedom*, p. 34.

8. Hawking, *Brief History of Time*, p. 10. Later he adds: "Our goal is nothing less than a complete description of the universe we live in" (p. 13).

9. Kuhn, *Structure of Scientific Revolutions*, pp. 164–65.

10. National Academy of Sciences, *Science and Creationism*, p. 8.

11. Johnson, "Evolution as Dogma," p. 19.

12. Plantinga, "When Faith and Reason Clash," pp. 28–29.

13. *Catechism of the Catholic Church*, p. 80. Also see Barbour, *Religion in an Age of Science*, pp. 174–75.

14. See Wendell Bird's exhaustive treatment of this view in his two-volume *Origin of Species Revisited*.

15. Gallup, *Gallup Poll: Public Opinion 1991*, p. 231.

16. Seventy percent of college graduates believe in evolution, while only 42 percent of high school graduates and 31 percent of grade school graduates do. See Gilbert, *Compendium of American Public Opinion*, p. 314.

17. Only 25 percent of them had degrees in biology. The survey was sent to four hundred teachers chosen at random from a list of twenty thousand names supplied by the National Science Teachers Association; the researchers received two hundred responses. *Chapel Hill Newspaper*, Sept. 11, 1988, p. 5A.

18. See Dierenfield, "Religious Influence in American Public Schools," p. 44.

19. *McLean* v. *Arkansas Board of Education*, 529 F.Supp. 1255, 1269 (E.D. Ark. 1982).

20. Ronald Numbers has pointed out that in *Science and Creationism*, the National Academy of Sciences "contrasted the provisional and testable claims of scientists with the unchanging and unsubstantiated conclusions of creationists. 'Examples of events changing scientific thought are legion,' claimed the authors, apparently unmindful that the same could be said of creationist thought. In fact, creationist opinion probably changed more radically in the half-century from 1930 to 1980 than views of evolution." (*Creationists*, p. 248).

21. *Epperson* v. *Arkansas*, 393 U.S. 97, 103–4, 109 (1968).

22. Ibid., p. 113.

23. *Wright* v. *Houston Independent School District*, 366 F.Supp. 1208, 1211 (S.D. Tex. 1972).

24. *McLean* v. *Arkansas*, 529 F.Supp. 1255, 1264.

25. *Edwards* v. *Aguillard*, 482 U.S. 578, 593, 628, 586, 589 (1987).

26. Ibid., p. 637.

27. Bird, *Origin of Species Revisited*, 2:454.

28. *Board of Education* v. *Mergens*, 110 S.Ct. 2356, 2371.

29. *Joseph Burstyn, Inc.* v. *Wilson*, 343 U.S. 495, 505 (1952).

30. McKenzie and Tullock, *New World of Economics*, p. 7; emphasis added.

31. Ibid., pp. 9–11.

32. Ibid., pp. 204, 209, 206.

33. Etzioni, *Spirit of Community*, p. 24.

34. Etzioni, "The 'Me First' Model in the Social Sciences Is Too Narrow," p. A44.

35. Schumacher, *Small Is Beautiful*, p. 46.

36. Bellah et al., *Good Society*, p. 117.

37. For a summary of these studies see Frank, Gilovich, and Regan, "Does Studying Economics Inhibit Cooperation?," pp. 159–71.

38. Lasch, "Communitarianism or Populism?," p. 7.

39. Wuthnow, *Christianity in the 21st Century*, p. 200.

40. Stackhouse, *Public Theology and Political Economy*, p. x.

41. National Conference of Catholic Bishops, *Economic Justice for All*, pp. 12, ix, v, x–xi, 13.

42. Ibid., p. vii. The bishops are quoting from the *Pastoral Constitution on the Church in the Modern World.*

43. John Paul II's 1991 encyclical *Centesimus Annus* is less critical of capitalism than the bishops' pastoral letter, but the Pontiff does not retreat from what I take the key claims to be. He insists, for example, that "there can be no genuine solution of the 'social question' apart from the Gospel" (section 5). He endorses the church's "preferential option for the poor" (sections 11 and 58), and he warns against an "idolatry" of the market that fails to acknowledge that there are "collective and qualitative needs" that cannot be satisfied by the market (section 40). We must be guided, he argues, "by a comprehensive picture of the person which respects all the dimensions of his being and which subordinates his material and instinctive dimensions to his interior and spiritual ones" (section 36).

44. Lebacqz, "Protestant Statements on Economic Justice," p. 47.

45. From "Christian Faith and Economic Life," a statement of the United Church of Christ; quoted, ibid., p. 55.

46. The Bund was essentially a secular movement. The Union of American Hebrew Congregations, the American Jewish Committee, and other Jewish organizations have issued statements on economic matters, but, as David Biale has pointed out, they "do not ground [their] political recommendations in the Jewish tradition. . . . No attempt is made to ask what kind of economic system might satisfy the criteria of Jewish tradition" ("Jewish Statements on Social Justice," p. 71). Biale notes the striking difference between Jewish and Christian statements in this regard and speculates that Jewish organizations are so staunchly separationist on church-state issues that "they often bend over backward to avoid introducing traditional values or language into political [or public] discourse" (p. 76).

Chapter 10

1. See, for example, Michaelsen, "Constitutions, Courts and the Study of Religion," and Clark, "Legal Status of Religious Studies Programs in Public Higher Education."

2. Jacob Neusner claims that if we compare the status of religious studies of at first-rate universities with the status they accord traditional secular subjects "the picture becomes clear. You can have a truly great university without first-rate study of religion, but you cannot have a truly great university without distinguished study of history or economics" ("Theology and Secularism in the Trivialization and Personalization of Religion and the West," p. 32). Neusner argues that a good part of the reason is that religion is viewed by many scholars as personal, private, and peripheral and hence inappropriate for scholarly study (ibid., p. 30).

3. Hart, "Religious and Theological Studies in American Higher Education," pp. 748, 753.

4. Green, "Something Strange, Yet Nothing New," pp. 272.

5. Capps, "On Religious Studies, in Lieu of an Overview," p. 727.

6. Wiggins, "The Study of Religion in Higher Education," p. 203. Several decades ago James Gustafson suggested that "very few, if any other, fields are as preoccupied with their legitimacy and as introspective about their self-understanding as religious studies" ("Study of Religion in Colleges and Universities," p. 330). The 1992 self-study

426 Notes to Pages 306–16

made clear that this "preoccupation with self-conception" continues unabated (Hart, "Religious and Theological Studies," pp. 725–26).

7. Green, "Something Strange, Yet Nothing New," p. 274.

8. Hart, "American Learning and the Problem of Religious Studies," pp. 217–18.

9. Hart, "Religious and Theological Studies," p. 716; emphasis added.

10. Burtchaell, "Decline and Fall of the Christian College I," p. 29.

11. *Liberal Learning and the Religion Major*, pp. 13, 15.

12. Ibid., pp. 9, 10.

13. See Hart, "Religious and Theological Studies," pp. 762–78.

14. Updike, *Roger's Version*, pp. 18–19. This passage is even more pointed because the speaker is addressing a divinity school professor.

15. Marsden, "Soul of the American University," p. 36. The theologian Stanley Hauerwas has claimed that scholars in religious studies "have allowed themselves to be intimidated by the secularists. . . . They have tried to be 'more objective than thou,' and have ended up hating God more than any one else in the academy" (quoted in Winkler, "After Years in Academic Limbo, the Study of Religion Undergoes a Revival of Interest among Scholars," p. A7).

16. Dixon, "What Should Religion Departments Teach?" pp. 369, 370, 366.

17. Capps, "Religious Studies as Creative Reflection," pp. 377, 374, 378.

18. Hart, "Religious and Theological Studies," p. 732. The minority of scholars who favor a role for theology in religious studies do not oppose the secular, social scientific study of religion; that is, the antipathy is not reciprocated (p. 733). The secular study of religion is respectable to all parties.

19. Griffin, "Professing Theology in the State University," pp. 10, 12.

20. May, "Why Theology and Religious Studies Need Each Other," p. 750.

21. Neville, "Religious Studies and Theological Studies," p. 191.

22. Kaufman, "Critical Theology as a University Discipline," p. 38.

23. Griffin, "Professing Theology in the State University," p. 7.

24. Ibid., p. 8.

25. Marsden, "Soul of the American University," pp. 38–39.

26. Kaufman, "Critical Theology as a University Discipline," pp. 40–41.

27. Ogden, "Theology in the University," p. 77.

28. Ari Goldman has noted that the faculty at Harvard Divinity School was, in his study there, so concerned not to offend others that if "there was a mention in class of the divinity of Jesus, the lecturer would offer an apology to the non-Christians in the room. If there was a Christian prayer offered at a convocation, you could be sure that some Buddhist meditation would follow for balance" (*The Search for God at Harvard*, p. 43).

29. See Griffin, "Professing Theology in the State University," pp. 23–25; Kaufman, "Critical Theology as a University Discipline," p. 36; Ogden, "Theology in the University," pp. 76–77.

30. Griffin, "Professing Theology in the State University," p. 30.

31. Neville, "Religious Studies and Theological Studies," p. 197.

32. Hart, "Religious and Theological Studies," p. 743.

33. This is the second wave of interest; the first followed the *Schempp* ruling. It failed to jell, however, and not much survived the 1970s. For a good discussion of the

ups and downs of "public education religion studies" see Piediscalzi, "Back to the Future?," pp. 237–51.

34. Kniker, "Survey of State Laws and Regulations Regarding Religion and Moral Education," p. 438.

35. Giroux, *Schooling and the Struggle for Public Life*, p. 186.

Chapter 11

1. Many studies have documented the incidence of cheating among students. The statistic I quote is from a study conducted by Robert Coles reported in Amundson, *Teaching Values and Ethics*, p. 11. The statistics on drinking are from *Education Week*, Nov. 20, 1991, p. 12. The desire of college freshmen to become millionaires is reported in the *Chronicle of Higher Education*, Sept. 3, 1986, p. 110. For heroes, see Ryan and Wynne, "Curriculum as a Moral Educator," pp. 44–46. The Gallup Poll figures on suicide were reported in the *Raleigh News and Observer*, June 16, 1994, p. 6A. According to the U.S. Center for Disease Control, 2 percent of high school students (some 276,000 students) sustained medical injuries from attempting to commit suicide, and 16 percent actually devised plans to commit suicide in the year prior to the study (1991). See *Education Week*, Oct. 2, 1991, p. 28.

2. Bellah et al., *Habits of the Heart*, p. 6.

3. Lasch, "A Life of Pain in an Empty Culture," p. 7J.

4. Lewis, *Abolition of Man*, pp. 95–121.

5. Hick, *Interpretation of Religion*, p. 312.

6. Green, "Morality and Religion," p. 99.

7. Burtt, *Man Seeks the Divine*, pp. 108–9.

8. Carl F. H. Henry, *Christian Ethics and Personal Morality*, quoted in Abraham, *Introduction to the Philosophy of Religion*, p. 133. For a good historical overview see Long, *Survey of Christian Ethics*, chap. 6.

9. Lev. 26:16–17 (NEB).

10. Matt. 5:21–22 (NEB).

11. Rom. 2:14 (NEB).

12. From the *Babylonian Talmud*, Eruvin 100b; quoted in Jacobs, "The Relationship between Religion and Ethics in Jewish Thought," p. 160.

13. Aquinas, *Summa Theologica*, excerpts reprinted in *Aquinas*, p. 125, 123.

14. According to John Paul, God created man, ordering him "with wisdom and love to his final end, through the law which is inscribed in his heart [cf. Rom. 2:15], the 'natural law.' The latter 'is nothing other than the light of understanding infused in us by God, whereby we understand what must be done and what must be avoided'" (*Veritatis Splendor*, section 12; the Pope is quoting from St. Thomas; also see sections 40–43). Also see the *Catechism of the Catholic Church*, pp. 472–74.

15. Rom. 7:21–23 (NEB).

16. Martin Luther, "Treatise on Good Works," quoted in Long, *Survey of Christian Ethics*, p. 132.

17. But the law may be devalued even more within this tradition, for knowing what is right may not be a matter of knowing law at all but of being in a right relationship with God; it is a matter of knowing what God would have us do in a particular situation,

not in general as is the case with law. Ethics is, in an important sense, *situational*. For Karl Barth, for example, the "question of good and evil is never answered by man's pointing to the authoritative Word of God in terms of a set of rules" ("Gift of Freedom," p. 85). What "this means for each of us here and there, today and tomorrow, is decided by the free word of the free Lord in ever-renewed encounter between God and an individual" (ibid, p. 84). We do not learn what is right in the law given in Scripture but in our immediate relationship to God in the here and now.

18. Rubenstein, *After Auschwitz*, pp. 118, 62–63.

19. Hauerwas, *Peaceable Kingdom*, pp. 1, 21, 47, 70.

20. Robinson, *Honest to God*, pp. 49, 73–74, 114–15, 49; also see pp. 128, 119–20.

21. Jer. 22:15; quoted, ibid., p. 60. Cf. Matt. 25.

22. Richard Niebuhr has characterized the thinkers who shaped the liberal tradition—Jefferson, Kant, Schleiermacher, Ritschl, Harnack, Rauschenbusch, Shailer Mathews—as "cultural Christians" who worked to reconcile Christianity with modern culture. The terms differ, Niebuhr suggests, "but the logic is always the same: Christ is identified with what men conceive to be their finest ideals, their noblest institutions, and their best philosophy" (*Christ and Culture*, p. 103). They believe that reason "is the highroad to the knowledge of God and salvation," and their tendency "is to identify Jesus with the immanent divine spirit that works in men" (ibid., pp. 110, 114).

23. Cox, *Religion in the Secular City*, p. 136.

24. Berryman, *Liberation Theology*, pp. 54–55.

25. Arblaster, *Rise and Decline of Western Liberalism*, p. 16.

26. Hume, *Treatise of Human Nature*, pp. 469, 415. Indeed, Hume says, "'Tis not contrary to reason to prefer the destruction of the world to the scratching of my finger" (ibid., p. 416).

27. Bentham, *Principles of Morals and Legislation*, pp. 4, 21.

28. Rousseau, *Discourse on the Arts and Sciences*, p. 174.

29. From *Emile*, quoted in Taylor, *Sources of the Self*, p. 357.

30. Ibid., p. 375.

31. Whitman, "Song of the Open Road."

32. Küng, *On Being a Christian*, p. 29.

33. Niebuhr, *Interpretation of Christian Ethics*, p. 159.

34. Taylor, *Sources of the Self*, p. 331.

35. Bellah, *Broken Covenant*, p. xii.

36. Ibid., pp. x, xii.

37. See Taylor, *Sources of the Self*, pp. 321–40.

38. See *Bellah* et al., *Habits of the Heart*, p. 20. In chapter 5 of *The Good Society*, they develop their views about education.

39. Peters, *Ethics and Education*, p. 314.

40. Hauerwas, "Honor in the University," pp. 26–27.

41. Goodlad, *A Place Called School*, pp. 152–54.

42. Quoted in Delfattore, *What Johnny Shouldn't Read*, p. 139.

43. To give just two simple but telling examples. Because California has a policy against promoting junk food, publishers changed the name of Patricia Zettner's short story "A Perfect Day for Ice Cream" to "A Perfect Day" and deleted references in the story to chiliburgers and pizza in order to have their textbook accepted (ibid.,

p. 130). The Texas board required a publisher to change a sentence in an American history text so that instead of saying that New Deal programs "were generally successful in restoring the prosperity of many Americans," it said that in spite of the New Deal programs "most of the nation was still suffering from the Great Depression" (ibid, p. 149).

44. Baer, "Character Education and Public Schools," p. 77.

45. Raths, Harmin, and Simon, *Values and Teaching*, p. 5.

46. "If a child says that he likes something, it does not seem appropriate for an older person to say, 'You shouldn't like that.' Or, if another child should say 'I am interested in that,' it does not seem quite right for an older person to say to her, 'You shouldn't be interested in things like that.' If these interests have grown out of a child's experience, they are consistent with his or her life. When we ask children to deny their own lives, we are in effect asking them to be hypocrites" (ibid., p. 34).

47. Ibid., pp. 5, 34, 55.

48. Lickona, *Educating for Character*, pp. 3–4.

49. Kilpatrick, *Why Johnny Can't Tell Right from Wrong*, pp. 15, 96.

50. Ryan and Wynne, "Curriculum as a Moral Educator," p. 24.

51. See Lickona, *Educating for Character*, p. 45.

52. Kilpatrick, *Why Johnny Can't Tell Right from Wrong*, pp. 94, 139.

53. Ibid., pp. 93–94.

54. Thiessen, *Teaching for Commitment*, p. 235.

55. Noddings, *Caring*, p. 172.

56. Haynes, *Finding Common Ground*, p. 14.2.

57. Even the most necessary and consensual of our virtues—say, honesty—can become controversial in certain situations. Does honesty require us to tell people true but hurtful things? Does being peaceable require pacifism (as Quakers believe)? We agree about the value of sobriety, but does this mean that we should avoid drinking altogether?

58. Quoted in Dawidowicz, "The Holocaust as Historical Record," p. 41.

59. Wiesel, "The Holocaust as Literary Inspiration," p. 16.

60. Wuthnow, *Christianity in the 21st Century*, pp. 58, 190.

61. See Crankshaw, *Shadow of the Winter Palace*, p. 195.

62. Shelley, "Defense of Poetry," p. 625.

63. Robert Coles describes how characters in stories become part of us. He quotes one of his students who commented that this does not happen with theories and abstract ideas "because in a story—oh, like it says in the Bible, *the word becomes flesh*" (*The Call of Stories*, p. 128).

64. Quoted from an unnamed friend by Irvin Miller in an address on the humanities and business given to the fifth Kenan Convocation at the University of North Carolina at Chapel Hill, October 19–21, 1989.

65. Cassirer, *Essay on Man*, p. 149.

66. Montaigne, *Essays*, p. 218. The quotation is from his essay, "On Presumption."

67. Fox-Genovese, "Culture Wars, Shooting Wars," p. 51. The interior quotation is from James Davison Hunter, *Before the Shooting Begins: Searching for Democracy in America's Culture War*.

68. In high schools the moral capstone course would be for seniors and follow, ideally,

the year-long course on religion I proposed in chapter 6. If students already understand something of religion, they will obviously profit more from the aspects of the capstone course that deal with religious conceptions of morality.

69. Steiner, *Language and Silence*, p. ix.

70. Niebuhr, *Interpretation of Christian Ethics*, p. 15.

71. I develop some of the ideas in this chapter more fully in my essay "Teaching and Morality."

Chapter 12

1. *Edwards* v. *Aguillard*, 482 U.S. 578, 584.

2. Carnegie Foundation for the Advancement of Teaching, *School Choice*, p. 63.

3. National Catholic Educational Association, *The People's Poll on Schools and School Choice*, p. 16. The question was, "In some nations, the government allots a certain amount of money for each child for his education. The parents can then send the child to any public, parochial or private school they choose. This is called the 'voucher system.' Would you like to see such an idea adopted in this country?"

4. Reported in *Education Week*, October 7, 1992, p. 18.

5. Carnegie Foundation for the Advancement of Teaching, *School Choice*, p. 95. The question was, "Some people think that parents should be given a voucher which they could use toward enrolling their child in a private school at public expense. Do you support or oppose this idea?"

6. See Lieberman, *Privatization and Educational Choice*, pp. 348–49.

7. Chubb and Moe, *Politics, Markets and America's Schools*, p. 216, 218.

8. Chubb and Moe do mention religion once. They argue that choice should be extended to private schools and then add, parenthetically, "Our own preference would be to include religious schools as well, as long as their sectarian functions can be kept clearly separate from their educational functions" (ibid., p. 219). Presumably it is essential to be able to separate the secular and sectarian aspects of education because Chubb and Moe would have the government fund schools directly (rather than through vouchers) and for direct funding to be constitutionally possible, the secular and sectarian functions of religious schools must be clearly discernible with no funds going for religious purposes.

9. Coons, "School Choice as Simple Justice," p. 15.

10. Arons, "Out of the Fire and Into the Frying Pan," p. 48.

11. *Pierce* v. *Society of the Sisters of the Holy Names of Jesus and Mary*, 268 U.S. 510, 534–35 (1925). *Pierce* was decided by appeal to the due process clause of the Fourteenth Amendment, but in *Wisconsin* v. *Yoder* (1972) the Court reaffirmed *Pierce*, largely on free exercise grounds. Justice Burger wrote that "a state's interest in universal education, however highly we rank it, is not totally free from a balancing process when it impinges on fundamental rights and interests, such as those specifically protected by the Free Exercise Clause of the First Amendment, and the traditional interest of parents with respect to the religious upbringing of their children" (406 U.S. 205, 214).

12. *Pierce* v. *Society of the Sisters*, p. 534.

13. Carter, *Culture of Disbelief*, p. 195.

14. Declaration on Christian Education, pp. 641, 644, 639.

15. As of 1984. See Rauch, "Jewish Day School in America," p. 148.

16. Wertheimer, *People Divided*, pp. 104, 123.

17. About a quarter of the essayists in Dalin, *American Jews and the Separationist Faith*, support vouchers. See the essays by Matthew Berke, Donna Robinson Divine, Murray Friedman, Joshua O. Haberman, Jon D. Levenson, Sanford Levinson, Jerry Muller, Richard Rubinstein, and Edward S. Shapiro.

18. Muller, chap. 22, ibid., p. 91.

19. Coons, "School Choice as Simple Justice," p. 16.

20. Baer, *Censorship and the Public Schools*, pp. 24, 26. Baer believes that vouchers should be institutionalized for higher education as well; see p. 24.

21. Arons, *Compelling Belief*, p. 28.

22. Arons, "Out of the Fire and Into the Frying Pan," p. 50.

23. Arons, *Compelling Belief*, p. 211.

24. Williams, "Inner City Kids," p. 3.

25. Coons, "School Choice as Simple Justice," pp. 21, 20. Also see Coons's book with Stephen Sugarman, *Scholarships for Children*, chap. 3.

26. Ackerman, *Social Justice in the Liberal State*, pp. 160, 162, 155–56; emphasis added.

27. *Wisconsin v. Yoder*, 406 U.S. 205, 244–46.

28. Shanker and Rosenberg. "Politics, Markets, and American Schools," p. 348. Cf. Chubb and Moe, *Politics, Markets, and America's Schools*, pp. 30, 38.

29. Geiger, "Vouchers Aren't the Answer," p. 16.

30. Walzer, *Spheres of Justice*, pp. 217, 203.

31. Barber, *Strong Democracy*, pp. 295–97, 293. Nonetheless Barber concludes that given the problems of public education, some experimentation with vouchers may be called for (ibid., p. 298).

32. Gutmann, *Democratic Education*, pp. 69, 30–31, 70.

33. Ibid., p. 67; also see pp. 39, 47.

34. Walzer, *Spheres of Justice*, p. 219.

35. Gutmann, *Democratic Education*, pp. 117–18, 120.

36. Mill, *On Liberty*, pp. 351–52. Mill added that there should "be nothing to hinder 'students' from being taught religion, if their parents chose, at the same schools where they were taught other things" for "all attempts by the State to bias the conclusions of its citizens on disputed subjects, are evil" (ibid., p. 353).

37. Arons, *Compelling Belief*, p. 178. Arons's book is largely a series of horror stories about how this has happened.

38. Coons, "School Choice as Simple Justice," p. 17.

39. Baer, *Censorship and the Public Schools*, pp. 21, 31, 33.

40. Levinson, chap. 18, in Dalin, *American Jews and the Separationist Faith*, p. 75.

41. Gutmann, *Democratic Education*, p. 33.

42. Walzer, *Spheres of Justice*, pp. 218–19.

43. "Educating Our Children," p. 3.

44. Hodgkinson, "Danger Sign: Vouchers Masquerading as Choice," p. 356.

45. Maddox, "Education Choice and the First Amendment," p. 324.

46. Editorial, *Church & State* (July/August, 1990), p. 11.

47. Honig, "Why Privatizing Public Education is a Bad Idea," p. 359.

48. Ibid.

49. ACLU, "As Our Public Schools Die," p. 11.

50. Dent, "Religious Children, Secular Schools," p. 927.

51. Carnegie Foundation for the Advancement of Teaching, *School Choice*, p. 60. The eight are California, Illinois, Montana, New York, North Dakota, Texas, Utah, and Washington.

52. See Parsons, *Inside America's Christian Schools*, p. 114. Most of the integrated schools have only a token number of blacks, however. Parsons concludes: "The Christian school movement is overwhelmingly white, reflecting the structural segregation of the churches themselves. The genesis of many Christian schools also coincides with the migration of black children into previously white public schools. Yet Christian schools have started, too, in communities where no racial overtones exist. In addition, virtually every Christian school in the nation today has adopted a nondiscriminatory racial policy. . . . Clearly, the evidence suggests that the *primary* motivation for the *continued existence* of Christian schools is religious and not racial. But that is not to say that all of these schools can evade the charge of racism" (p. 126).

53. Spykman et al., *Society, State, and Schools*, p. 187.

54. Quoted in Parsons, *Inside America's Christian Schools*, p. 166.

55. Quade, "Educational Vise," p. 11.

56. Parsons, *Inside America's Christian Schools*, p. 158.

57. Thiessen, *Teaching for Commitment*, p. 274.

58. Even the Klan strongly supported the abolition of private education. See Tyack, James, and Benavot, *Law and the Shaping of Public Education*, chap. 7.

59. Lieberman, *Privatization and Educational Choice*, pp. 230–31.

60. McConnell, "The Selective Funding Problem," pp. 8–9. The quotation is from *Harris* v. *McRae*, 448 U.S. 297, 333–34.

61. *Abington Township School District* v. *Schempp*, 374 U.S. 203, 242.

62. See Jencks, "Is the Public School Obsolete?," and Jencks and Areen, "Education Vouchers."

63. *Committee for Public Education and Religious Liberty* v. *Nyquist*, 413 U.S. 756, 783, 788.

64. *Mueller* v. *Allen*, 463 U.S. 388, 399, 397.

65. Ibid., pp. 405, 406–7, 413.

66. *Witters* v. *Washington Department of Services for the Blind*, 474 US. 481, 487, 488–89.

67. From Justice Powell's concurring opinion. Ibid., pp. 490–91.

68. Coons and Sugarman have drafted model legislation which states might adopt in authorizing vouchers or educational choice. Their purpose statement reads: "The people adopt this section to improve the quality and efficiency of public and private schools, to maximize educational opportunities for all children, and to increase the authority of parents and teachers" (*Scholarships for Children*, p. 9).

69. Johnson, "School Vouchers and the United States Constitution," p. 62.

70. Green, "The Legal Argument against Private School Choice," pp. 70, 72.

71. *Everson* v. *Board of Education*, 330 U.S. 1, 16.

72. Maddox, "Education Choice and the First Amendment," p. 324.

73. Jefferson, "Virginia Statute of Religious Liberty," p. 102.

74. The Establishment Clause case for *requiring* vouchers founders on the fact that government can enforce religious neutrality in public schools rather than enact a voucher program to restore neutrality. A more plausible case can be made on free exercise grounds for requiring vouchers, not as a general system for funding education, but for parents whose religious beliefs are burdened by public schooling. After all, the state guarantees children the right to a tax-funded education; the money is already committed. It is only a question of whether parents must send their children to public schools in order to receive it. In *Sherbert* v. *Verner*, the case that gave us the Sherbert Test for adjudicating free exercise claims, the Supreme Court ruled that Seventh Day Adventists were entitled to unemployment insurance even if they declined to accept jobs that required them to work on Saturdays, for to condition their receipt of benefits on their willingness to violate their Sabbath unjustifiably burdened their religious beliefs. Arguably, government should not be able to condition the receipt of a tax-funded education on the willingness of parents to send their children to schools that burden their free exercise rights. Moreover, there are precedents for claiming that government has a special obligation to provide the funds that enable *poor* people to act on fundamental rights. In criminal law cases the government must fund attorneys for indigent defendants. It is commonly argued that poor women have the right to government-funded abortions. And, when the government has made it impossible for individuals to act on their free exercise rights—as is the case with prisoners—it is permissible, and perhaps even required, that the government fund chaplains and religious facilities for them. Arguably, by depriving poor parents of the tax money they pay to support public schools, the state contributes to their inability to act on their free exercise rights. There remains, of course, a powerful argument for accountability in the use of tax funds, but this interest might be satisfied by regulating private education to ensure that it meets certain minimal public standards.

75. *Pierce* v. *Society of Sisters*, 268 U.S. 510, 534.

76. Baer, "'Strict Neutrality' and Our Monopoly System," p. 32.

77. Cookson, *School Choice*, pp. 105, 100.

Conclusions

1. Kinsley, "TRB," p. 4.

2. Stern, chap. 33, in Dalin, *American Jews and the Separationist Faith*, pp. 133–34.

3. Adams, "Examination of the American Way of Life," p. 589.

4. Newton-Smith, *The Rationality of Science*, p. 14.

5. Niebuhr, *Reinhold Niebuhr on Politics*, pp. 128, 130.

BIBLIOGRAPHY

AAUP. *Declaration of Principles*. 1915. Reprinted in *Academic Freedom and Tenure: A Handbook of the American Association of University Professors*. Madison: University of Wisconsin Press, 1967.

———. *Recommended Institutional Regulations on Academic Freedom and Tenure*. 1982. Reprinted in *Policy Documents and Reports*. Washington, D.C.: American Association of University Professors, 1984.

———. "Some Observations on Ideology, Competence, and Faculty Selection." *Academe* 72 (January–February, 1986): 1a–2a.

———. *Statement of Principles on Academic Freedom and Tenure*. 1940. Reprinted in *Academic Freedom and Tenure: A Handbook of the American Association of University Professors*. Madison: University of Wisconsin Press, 1967.

———. *Statement on Professional Ethics*. 1966. Reprinted in *Academic Freedom and Tenure: A Handbook of the American Association of University Professors*. Madison: University of Wisconsin Press, 1967.

Abington School District v. *Schempp* 374 U.S. 203 (1963).

Abraham, William J. *An Introduction to the Philosophy of Religion*. Englewood Cliffs, N.J., 1985.

Ackerman, Bruce. *Social Justice in the Liberal State*. New Haven: Yale University Press, 1980.

ACLU. "As Our Public Schools Die, 'Parental Choice' Would Put Several Nails in the Coffin." *Civil Liberties*, Spring–Summer 1991, p. 11.

Adams, E. M. "An Examination of the American Way of Life." *The World and I*, October, 1989, pp. 589–97.

———. "Personhood and Human Rights." *Man and World* 8 (February 1975): 36–46.

———. *Philosophy and the Modern Mind*. Chapel Hill: University of North Carolina Press, 1975.

———. *Religion and Cultural Freedom*. Philadelphia: Temple University Press, 1993.

Adams, Jay E. *The Biblical View of Self-Esteem, Self-Love, Self-Image*. Eugene, Oreg.: Harvest House, 1986.

Adler, Mortimer. *The Paideia Program: An Educational Syllabus*. New York: Macmillan, 1984.

———. *The Paideia Proposal*. New York: Macmillan, 1982.

Aguilar v. *Felton*, 473 U.S. 402 (1985).

Ahlstrom, Sydney. *A Religious History of the American People*. New Haven: Yale University Press, 1972.

Albanese, Catherine L. *America: Religions and Religion*. Belmont, Calif.: Wadsworth, 1981.

———. "Religion and the American Experience: A Century After." *Church History* 57 (1988): 337–51.

American Association for the Advancement of Science. *Benchmarks for Science Literacy*. New York: Oxford University Press, 1993.

American Association of School Administrators. *Religion in the Public Schools*. Arlington, Va.: American Association of School Administrators, 1986.

Amundson, Kristen J. *Teaching Values and Ethics: Problems and Solutions*. Arlington, Va.: American Association of School Administrators, 1991.

Anderson, Ray S. "Evangelical Theology." In *The Modern Theologians*, vol. 2, edited by David F. Ford. New York: Basil Blackwell, 1989.

Apple, Michael. *Teachers and Texts: A Political Economy of Class and Gender Relations in Education*. New York: Routledge, 1988.

Aquinas, Thomas. *Summa Theologica*. Excerpts reprinted in *Aquinas: Selected Political Writings*, edited by A. P. D'Entreves. Oxford: Basil Blackwell, 1970.

Arblaster, Anthony. *The Rise and Decline of Western Liberalism*. London: Basil Blackwell, 1984.

Arnold, Matthew. "Literature and Science." In *The Portable Matthew Arnold*, edited by Lionel Trilling. New York: Penguin Books, 1980.

Arons, Stephen. *Compelling Belief: the Culture of American Schooling*. New York: McGraw-Hill, 1983.

———. "Out of the Fire and Into the Frying Pan." *First Things*, January, 1991, pp. 48–52.

Asanti, Molefi Kete. *Afrocentricity*. Trenton, N.J.: Africa World Press, 1988.

Association for Supervision and Curriculum Development. *Religion in the Curriculum*. Alexandria, Va.: Association for Supervision and Curriculum Development, 1988.

Baer, Richard. *Censorship and the Public Schools*. Milwaukee: Catholic League for Religious and Civil Rights, 1985.

———. "Character Education and Public Schools: The Question of Context." In *Content, Character and Choice in Schooling: Public Policy and Research Implications*. The proceedings of a symposium sponsored by the National Council on Education Research. Washington, D.C.: National Advisory Council on Educational Research, 1986.

———. "'Strict Neutrality' and Our Monopoly System." In *The School Choice Controversy*, edited by James W. Skillen. Grand Rapids, Mich.: Baker Books, 1993.

Bailyn, Bernard. *Education in the Forming of American Society*. New York: Norton, 1972.

———. *The New England Merchants in the Seventeenth Century*. Cambridge, Mass.: Harvard University Press, 1955.

Bainton, Roland. *The Reformation of the Sixteenth Century*. Boston: Beacon Press, 1952.

Barber, Benjamin. *Strong Democracy: Participatory Politics for a New Age*. Berkeley: University of California Press, 1984.

Barbour, Ian. *Issues in Science and Religion*. New York: Harper Torchbooks, 1971.

———. *Myth, Models, and Paradigms*. New York: Harper & Row, 1976.

———. *Religion in an Age of Science*. San Francisco: Harper & Row, 1990.

———. *Science and Secularity: The Ethics of Technology*. New York: Harper & Row, 1970.

Barnes, Michael. *In the Presence of Mystery*. Mystic, Conn.: Twenty-Third Publications, 1984.

Barrett, William. *Irrational Man: A Study in Existential Philosophy*. Garden City, N.Y.: Anchor Books, 1962.

Barth, Karl. "The Gift of Freedom." Reprinted in *The Humanity of God*, translated by John Newton Thomas. Atlanta: John Knox Press, 1960.

———. "The Humanity of God." Reprinted in *The Humanity of God*, translated by John Newton Thomas and Thomas Wieser. Atlanta: John Knox Press, 1960.

Bates, Stephen. *Battleground*. New York: Poseidon Press, 1993.

Baumer, Franklin. *Religion and the Rise of Scepticism*. New York: Harcourt, Brace & World, 1960.

Baynes, Kenneth, James Bohman, and Thomas McCarthy, eds. *After Philosophy: End or Transformation?* Cambridge, Mass.: MIT Press, 1987.

Bednarowski, Mary Farrell. "The New Age Movement and Feminist Spirituality." In *Perspectives on the New Age*, edited by James R. Lewis and J. Gordon Melton. Albany: State University of New York Press, 1992.

Bellah, Robert. "Between Religion and Social Science." In *Beyond Belief: Essays on Religion in a Post-Traditional World*. New York: Harper & Row, 1970.

———. *The Broken Covenant: American Civil Religion in Time of Trial*. New York: Seabury Press, 1975.

———. "Can You Recite Your Creed?" *Plumbline* 15 (September 1987): 4–8.

———. "Civil Religion in America." In *Secularization and the Protestant Prospect*, edited by James F. Childress and David B. Harned. Philadelphia: Westminster Press, 1970.

———. "Religion and Belief." In *Beyond Belief: Essays on Religion in a Post-Traditional World*. New York: Harper & Row, 1970.

———. "Religious Evolution." In *Beyond Belief: Essays on Religion in a Post-Traditional World*. New York: Harper & Row, 1970.

———. "The Triumph of Capitalism—or the Rise of Market Totalitarianism?" *New Oxford Review* 58 (March 1991): 8–15.

Bellah, Robert, et al. *The Good Society*. New York: Knopf, 1991.

Bellah, Robert, et al. *Habits of the Heart: Individualism and Commitment in American Life*. Berkeley: University of California Press, 1985.

Bell, Daniel. *The Cultural Contradictions of Capitalism*. New York: Basic Books, 1978.

Bentham, Jeremy. *The Principles of Morals and Legislation*. Darien, Conn.: Hafner, 1970.

Berger, Peter. "Capitalism and the Disorders of Modernity." *First Things*, January 1991, pp. 14–19.

———. "From the Crisis of Religion to the Crisis of Secularity." In *Religion and America: Spiritual Life in a Secular Age*, edited by Steven Tipton and Mary Douglas. Boston: Beacon Press, 1983.

———. *The Heretical Imperative*. New York: Anchor Books, 1980.

———. *The Sacred Canopy*. Garden City, N.Y.: Anchor Books, 1967.

Berger, Peter, and Thomas Luckmann. *The Social Construction of Reality*. Garden City, N.Y.: Anchor Books, 1967.

Berke, Matthew. Chap. 4 of *American Jews and the Separationist Faith*, edited by David G. Dalin. Washington, D.C.: Ethics and Public Policy Center, 1993.

Berman, Harold. "Religion and Law: The First Amendment In Historical Perspective." *Quarterly* 8 (Spring 1987): 6–12.

Berman, Marshall. *All That Is Solid Melts into Air: The Experience of Modernity.* New York: Simon and Schuster, 1982.

Bernstein, Richard J. *The New Constellation: The Ethical-Political Horizons of Modernity/Postmodernity.* Cambridge, Mass.: MIT Press, 1991.

Berns, Walter. *The First Amendment and the Future of American Democracy.* New York: Basic Books, 1976.

Berryman, Philip. *Liberation Theology.* New York: Pantheon Books, 1987.

Biale, David. "Jewish Statements on Social Justice." In *A Cry for Justice*, edited by Robert McAfee Brown and Sydney Thomson Brown. New York: Paulist Press, 1989.

Bird, Wendell. *The Origin of Species Revisited.* 2 vols. New York: Philosophical Library, 1987.

Bishop v. *Aronov*, 732 F. Supp. 1562 (N.D. Ala. 1990).

Bishop v. *Aronov*, 926 F.2d 1066 (11th Cir. 1991).

Blau, Joseph L. *Modern Varieties of Judaism.* New York: Columbia University Press, 1964.

Bloom, Allan. *The Closing of the American Mind.* New York: Simon and Schuster, 1987.

Board of Education v. *Mergens*, 110 S.Ct. 2356 (1990).

Board of Education, Island Trees Union Free School District v. *Pico*, 457 U.S. 863 (1982).

Bok, Derek. *Beyond the Ivory Tower: Social Responsibilities of the Modern University.* Cambridge, Mass.: Harvard University Press, 1982.

Boston, Rob. "Marriage of Conveniences." *Church and State* 47 (May 1994): 7–10.

———. "The School Prayer Mess." *Church and State* 47 (June 1994): 7–10.

———. "Split Decision." *Church and State* 47 (March 1994): 4–6.

Boyer, Ernest. *College: The Undergraduate Experience in America.* New York: Harper & Row, 1987.

———. *High School: A Report on Secondary Education in America.* New York: Harper & Row, 1983.

———. "Teaching Religion in the Public Schools and Elsewhere." *Journal of the American Academy of Religion* 60 (Fall 1992): 515–24.

Brown, Karen McCarthy. "Thinking about the Introductory Course: Some Preliminary Questions." In *Teaching the Introductory Course in Religious Studies: A Source Book*, edited by Mark Juergensmeyer. Atlanta: Scholars Press, 1991.

Brown, Robert McAfee, and Sydney Thomson Brown, eds. *A Cry for Justice: The Churches and Synagogues Speak.* New York: Paulist Press, 1989.

Brown v. *Board of Education.* Excerpts reprinted in *The American Reader*, edited by Diane Ravitch. New York: Harper Perennial, 1991.

Buber, Martin. *I and Thou.* Translated by Ronald Gregor Smith. New York: Charles Scribner's Sons, 1958.

Buehrer, Eric. *The New Age Masquerade: The Hidden Agenda in Your Child's Classroom.* Brentwood, Tenn.: Wolgemuth and Hyatt, 1990.

Bullock, Alan. *The Humanist Tradition in the West*. New York: Norton, 1985.

Bultmann, Rudolf. *New Testament and Mythology*. Translated by Schubert M. Ogden. Philadelphia: Fortress Press, 1984.

Burtchaell, James Tunstead. "The Decline and Fall of the Christian College I." *First Things*, April 1991, pp. 16–29.

———. "The Decline and Fall of the Christian College II." *First Things*, May 1991, pp. 30–38.

Burtt, E. A. *Man Seeks the Divine: A Study of the History and Comparison of Religions*. New York: Harper Colophon Books, 1970.

———. *The Metaphysical Foundations of Modern Science*. New York: Anchor Books, 1954.

Butts, R. Freeman. *The American Tradition in Religion and Education*. Boston: Beacon Press, 1950.

Buzzard, Lynn. *Schools: They Haven't Got a Prayer*. Elgin, Ill.: David C. Cook, 1982.

Calvin, John. *Institutes of the Christian Religion*. Excerpts reprinted in *John Calvin: Selections from His Writings*, edited by John Dillenberger. Missoula: Scholars Press, 1975.

Cantwell v. *Connecticut*, 310 U.S. 296 (1940).

Capps, Walter. "On Religious Studies, in Lieu of an Overview." *Journal of the American Academy of Religion* 42 (December 1974): 727–33.

———. "Religious Studies as Creative Reflection." *Soundings* 71 (Summer–Fall, 1988): 373–79.

Carnegie Foundation for the Advancement of Teaching. *School Choice*. Princeton, N.J.: Carnegie Foundation, 1992.

Carter, Stephen. *The Culture of Disbelief: How American Law and Politics Trivialize Religious Devotion*. New York: Basic Books, 1993.

Cassirer, Ernst. *An Essay on Man*. New Haven: Yale University Press, 1944.

Catechism of the Catholic Church. Mahwah, N.J.: Paulist Press, 1994.

Chadwick, Owen. *The Secularization of the European Mind in the Nineteenth Century*. Cambridge: Cambridge University Press, 1975.

Chicago Statement on Biblical Inerrancy. 1978. Reprinted in Carl F. H. Henry, *God, Revelation and Authority*, vol. 4. Waco: Word Books, 1979.

Chubb, John E., and Terry M. Moe. *Politics, Markets and America's Schools*. Washington, D.C.: Brookings Institution, 1990.

The Church of the Holy Trinity v. *United States*, 143 U.S. 226 (1892).

Church of the Lukumi Babalu Aye, Inc. v. *City of Hialeah* 53 CCH S.Ct. Bull. (1993).

Clark, W. Royce. "The Legal Status of Religious Studies Programs in Public Higher Education." In *Beyond the Classics? Essays in Religious Studies and Liberal Education*, edited by Frank E. Reynolds and Sheryl L. Burkhalter. Atlanta: Scholars Press, 1990.

Coleman, John A. "Catholic Integralism as a Fundamentalism." In *Fundamentalism in Comparative Perspective*, edited by Lawrence Kaplan. Amherst: University of Massachusetts Press, 1992.

Coles, Robert. *The Call of Stories: Teaching and the Moral Imagination*. Boston: Houghton Mifflin, 1989.

Collingwood, R. G. *The Idea of History*. New York: Oxford University Press, 1971.

Commager, Henry Steele. Introduction to *McGuffey's 6th Eclectic Reader*. New York: Signet Classic, 1962.

Committee for Public Education & Religious Liberty v. Nyquist, 413 U.S. 756 (1973).

Cookson, Peter, Jr. *School Choice: The Struggle for the Soul of American Education*. New Haven: Yale University Press, 1994.

Coons, John. "Getting Grover's Goat." *First Things*, December 1992, pp. 9–11.

———. "School Choice as Simple Justice." *First Things*, April 1992, pp. 15–22.

Coons, John, and Stephen Sugarman. *Scholarships for Children*. Berkeley: Institute of Governmental Studies Press, 1992.

Cotton, John. "The Bloudy Tenent, Washed." Excerpts reprinted in *Religion and Law in American History*, edited by John Semonche. Chapel Hill: University of North Carolina Press, 1985.

———. *A Discourse about Civil Government*. Excerpts reprinted in *Church and State in American History*, edited by John F. Wilson. Boston: D. C. Heath, 1965.

Council for Interracial Books for Children. *Guidelines for Selecting Bias-Free Textbooks and Storybooks*. New York: Council for Interracial Books for Children, n.d.

Cox, Harvey. *Religion in the Secular City*. New York: Simon and Schuster, 1984.

———. *The Secular City*. rev. ed. New York: Macmillan, 1965.

Crankshaw, Edward. *The Shadow of the Winter Palace*. New York: Penguin Books, 1978.

Cremin, Lawrence A. *American Education: The Colonial Experience*. New York: Harper Torchbooks, 1970.

———. *American Education: The Metropolitan Experience*. New York: Harper & Row, 1990.

———. *American Education: The National Experience*. New York: Harper & Row, 1980.

———. *The Transformation of the School: Progressivism in American Education, 1876–1957*. New York: Vintage Books, 1964.

Crockett v. Sorenson, 568 F. Supp. 1422 (W.D. Vir., 1983).

Cuddy, Dennis. "The Trouble with Teaching about Religion." *Raleigh News and Observer*, January 5, 1989, p. 15A.

Cumbey, Constance. *The Hidden Dangers of the Rainbow: The New Age Movement and Our Coming Age of Barbarism*. Shreveport, La.: Huntington House, 1983.

Cupitt, Don. *The Sea of Faith*. New York: Cambridge University Press, 1984.

Curry, Thomas. *The First Freedoms: Church and State in America to the Passage of the First Amendment*. New York: Oxford University Press, 1986.

Dalin, David G. Introduction to *American Jews and the Separationist Faith*, edited by David G. Dalin. Washington, D.C.: Ethics and Public Policy Center, 1993.

D'Antonio, Michael. *Heaven on Earth: Dispatches from America's Spiritual Frontier*. New York: Crown, 1992.

Dawidowicz, Lucy. "The Holocaust as Historical Record." In *Dimensions of the Holocaust*, annotated by Elliot Lefkovitz. Evanston, Ill.: Northwestern University Press, 1977.

Dawkins, Richard. *The Blind Watchmaker*. New York: Norton, 1986.

Declaration on Christian Education. In *The Documents of Vatican II*, edited by Walter M. Abbott, S.J. Chicago: Follett, 1966.

Declaration on Religious Freedom. In *The Documents of Vatican II*, edited by
Walter M. Abbott, S.J. Chicago: Follett, 1966.

Delfattore, Joan. *What Johnny Shouldn't Read: Textbook Censorship in America.*
New Haven: Yale University Press, 1992.

Demarest, William. *General Revelation.* Grand Rapids, Mich.: Zondervan, 1982.

Dent, George. "Religious Children, Secular Schools." *Southern California Law Review* 61 (May 1988): 864–941.

Dershowitz, Alan. "Judge Brevard Hand: Alabama's Ayatollah." *Church and State* 40
(April 1987): 9.

Dewey, John. *A Common Faith.* New Haven: Yale University Press, 1934.

Dickens, Charles. *A Christmas Carol.* 1843. Reprinted in *The Complete Ghost Stories
of Charles Dickens.* New York: Pocket Books, 1983.

———. *Hard Times.* 1854. Reprint, Baltimore: Penguin Books, 1969.

Dierenfield, Richard B. "Religious Influence in American Public Schools." *Religion
and Public Education* 13 (Summer 1986): 41–46.

Dillenberger, John, and Claude Welch. *Protestant Christianity: Interpreted Through
Its Development.* 2d ed. New York: Macmillan, 1988.

Dixon, John W., Jr. "What Should Religion Departments Teach?" *Theology Today* 46
(January 1990): 364–72.

Dolan, Jay. *The American Catholic Experience.* Garden City, N.Y.: Image Books, 1987.

Durham, W. Cole, Edward McGlynn Gaffney, Douglas Laycock, and Michael W. Mc-
Connell. "For the Religious Freedom Restoration Act." *First Things*, March 1992,
pp. 42–44.

Ebert, Michael. "A Place at the Table." *Educational Leadership*, December/January
1993, pp. 41–43.

"Educating Our Children: Whose Responsibility?" Unsigned article in *Philosophy
and Public Policy* 5 (Winter 1985): 1–5.

Education Commission of the States. *Action for Excellence.* Denver: Education Commission of the States, 1983.

Edwards v. Aguilard, 482 U.S. 578 (1987).

Eliade, Mircea. *The Sacred and the Profane: The Nature of Religion.* New York: Harcourt Brace Jovanovich, 1959.

Elson, Ruth Miller. *Guardians of Tradition: American Schoolbooks of the Nineteenth
Century.* Lincoln: University of Nebraska Press, 1964.

Emerson, Ralph Waldo. "Nature." Reprinted in *Ralph Waldo Emerson: Selected Essays*, edited by Larzer Ziff. New York: Penguin Books, 1982.

Employment Division v. Smith, 108 L Ed 2d 876 (1990).

Engel v. Vitale, 370 U.S. 421 (1962).

Epperson v. Arkansas, 393 U.S. 97 (1968).

Estep, William R. *Revolution within the Revolution.* Grand Rapids, Mich.: Eerdmans,
1990.

Etzioni, Amitai. "The 'Me First' Model in the Social Sciences Is Too Narrow." *Chronicle of Higher Education*, February 1, 1989, p. A44.

———. *The Spirit of Community.* New York: Crown, 1993.

Evans-Pritchard, E. E. *Theories of Primitive Religion.* Oxford: Clarendon Press,
1965.

Everson v. *Board of Education*, 330 U.S. 1 (1947).

Falwell, Jerry. *Listen, America!* Garden City, NY: Doubleday, 1980.

The Federalist Papers. New York: Bantam Books, 1982.

Ferguson, Marilyn. *The Aquarian Conspiracy: Personal and Social Transformation in Our Time*. Los Angeles: J. B. Tarcher, 1980.

Feyerabend, Paul. *Against Method*. London: Verso, 1978.

Fielding, Henry. *Tom Jones*. 1749. Reprint, New York: Signet Books, 1963.

Fish, Stanley. *There's No Such Thing as Free Speech . . . and It's a Good Thing Too*. New York: Oxford University Press, 1994.

Fitzgerald, Frances. *America Revised*. New York: Vintage Books, 1980.

Fleischfresser v. *Directors of School District 200*, 15 F.3d 680 (1994).

Fleming, Dan. "Religion in American History Textbooks: Were the 'Good Old Days' of Textbooks Really So Good?" *Religion and Public Education* 18 (1991): 79–101.

Ford, Paul Leicester. Introduction to *The New England Primer*, 1727 ed. New York: Teachers College, 1962.

Fox, Richard. *Reinhold Niebuhr: A Biography*. New York: Pantheon Books, 1985.

Fox-Genovese, Elizabeth. "Culture Wars, Shooting Wars." *First Things*, June/July 1994, pp. 49–53.

Frank, Robert H., Thomas Gilovich, and Dennis T. Regan. "Does Studying Economics Inhibit Cooperation?" *Journal of Economic Perspectives* 7 (Spring 1993): 159–71.

Freud, Sigmund. *The Future of an Illusion*. Garden City, N.Y.: Anchor Books, 1964.

Fukuyama, Francis. "The End of History?" *National Interest*, Summer 1989, pp. 3–18.

Fullinwider, Robert K. "Ethnocentrism and Education in Judgment." *Philosophy and Public Policy* 14 (Winter/Spring 1994): 6–11.

Gaffney, Edward McGlynn, Jr. "Religion and Public Life: Comments on the Williamsburg Charter Survey." *Journal of Law and Religion* 8 (1990): 279–85.

Gagnon, Paul. *Democracy's Untold Story: What the World History Textbooks Neglect*. Washington, D.C.: Education for Democracy Project, 1987.

Gallup, George, Jr., ed. *The Gallup Poll: Public Opinion 1980*. Wilmington, Del.: Scholarly Resources, 1980.

———. *The Gallup Poll: Public Opinion 1986*. Wilmington, Del.: Scholarly Resources, 1986.

———. *The Gallup Poll: Public Opinion 1990*. Wilmington, Del.: Scholarly Resources, 1990.

———. *The Gallup Poll: Public Opinion 1991*. Wilmington, Del.: Scholarly Resources, 1991.

Gallup, George, Jr., and Jim Castelli. *The People's Religion: American Faith in the 90's*. New York: Macmillan, 1989.

Gates, Henry Louis, Jr. "The Master's Pieces: On Canon Formation and the African-American Tradition." In *The Politics of Liberal Education*, edited by Darryl J. Gless and Barbara Herrnstein Smith. Durham: Duke University Press, 1992.

Geiger, Keith. "Vouchers Aren't the Answer." *Education Week*, October 13, 1993, p. 16.

Gellner, Ernest. *The Legitimation of Belief*. Cambridge: Cambridge University Press, 1979.

Gibbs, Nancy. "America's Holy War." *Time*, December 9, 1991, pp. 61–67.

Gilbert, Alan. *The Making of Post-Christian Britain: A History of the Secularization of Modern Society*. London: Longman, 1980.

Gilbert, Dennis A., ed. *Compendium of American Public Opinion*. New York: Facts on File Publications, 1988.

Giroux, Henry. *Schooling and the Struggle for Public Life*. Minneapolis: University of Minnesota Press, 1988.

———. *Teachers as Intellectuals: Toward a Critical Pedagogy of Learning*. Granby, Mass: Bergin & Garvey, 1988.

Glenn, Charles. *The Myth of the Common School*. Amherst: University of Massachusetts Press, 1987.

Goldman, Ari. *The Search for God at Harvard*. New York: Random House, 1991.

Goldman v. Weinberger, 475 U.S. 503 (1986).

Goodlad, John. *A Place Called School*. New York: McGraw-Hill, 1984.

Graff, Gerald. *Beyond the Culture Wars*. New York: Norton, 1992.

———. *Professing Literature*. Chicago: University of Chicago Press, 1987.

Green, Ronald. "Morality and Religion." In *The Encyclopedia of Religion*, vol. 10, edited by Mircea Eliade. New York: Macmillan, 1987.

Green, Steven K. "The Legal Argument against Private School Choice." *University of Cincinnati Law Review* 62 (Summer 1993): 37–73.

Green, William Scott. "Something Strange, Yet Nothing New: Religion in the Secular Curriculum." *Soundings* 71 (Summer–Fall 1988): 271–78.

Griffin, David Ray. Introduction to *Spirituality and Society*, edited by David Ray Griffin. Albany: State University of New York Press, 1988.

———. "Professing Theology in the State University." In *Theology and the University: Essays in Honor of John B. Cobb, Jr.*, edited by David Ray Griffin and Joseph C. Hough, Jr. Albany: State University of New York Press, 1991.

Guinness, Os. *The American Hour: A Time of Reckoning and the Once and Future Role of Faith*. New York: Free Press, 1993.

Gustafson, James. "The Study of Religion in Colleges and Universities: A Practical Commentary." In *The Study of Religion in Colleges and Universities*, edited by Paul Ramsey and John F. Wilson. Princeton: Princeton University Press, 1970.

Gutmann, Amy. *Democratic Education*. Princeton: Princeton University Press, 1987.

Hall, A. R. *The Scientific Revolution, 1500–1800*, 2d ed. Boston: Beacon Press, 1962.

Hart, D. G. "American Learning and the Problem of Religious Studies." In *The Secularization of the Academy*, edited by George M. Marsden and Bradley J. Longfield. New York: Oxford University Press, 1992.

Hart, Ray S. "Religious and Theological Studies in American Higher Education." *Journal of the American Academy of Religion* 59 (Winter 1991); 715–827.

Harvey, David. *The Condition of Postmodernity*. Oxford: Basil Blackwell, 1989.

Hatch, Nathan. "Evangelicalism as a Democratic Movement." In *Evangelicalism and Modern America*, edited by George Marsden. Grand Rapids, Mich.: Eerdmans, 1984.

Hauerwas, Stanley. "Honor in the University." *First Things*, February 1991, pp. 26–31.

————. *The Peaceable Kingdom: A Primer in Christian Ethics*. Notre Dame: University of Notre Dame Press, 1983.

Hawking, Stephen. *A Brief History of Time*. New York: Bantam Books, 1988.

Hayek, Friedrich. *The Constitution of Liberty*. Chicago: A Gateway Edition, 1972.

Haynes, Charles C. *Finding Common Ground: A First Amendment Guide to Religion and Public Education*. Nashville: The Freedom Forum First Amendment Center at Vanderbilt University, 1994.

————. *A Teacher's Guide to Study about Religion in Public Schools*. Boston: Houghton Mifflin, 1991.

Heilbroner, Robert. *The Worldly Philosophers*. 3d ed. New York: Simon and Schuster, 1967.

Herberg, Will. "Religion and Education in America." In *Religious Perspectives in American Culture*, edited by James Ward Smith and A. Leland Jamison. Princeton: Princeton University Press, 1961.

Hertzberg, Arthur. *The Jews in America*. New York: A Touchstone Book, 1989.

Hick, John. *Death and Eternal Life*. San Francisco: Harper & Row, 1980.

————. *Faith and Knowledge*. 2d ed. Glasgow: Fontana Books, 1966.

————. *An Interpretation of Religion*. New Haven: Yale University Press, 1989.

Hirsch, E. D. *Cultural Literacy*. Boston: Houghton Mifflin, 1987.

Hirschman, Albert O. *The Passions and the Interests: Political Arguments for Capitalism before Its Triumph*. Princeton: Princeton University Press, 1977.

Hodgkinson, Harold. "Danger Sign: Vouchers Masquerading as Choice." *Religion and Public Education* 17 (Fall 1990): 355–56.

Hodgson, Marshall G. S. *The Venture of Islam*. Vol. 1. Chicago: University of Chicago Press, 1974.

Hofstadter, Richard. *Academic Freedom in the Age of the College*. New York: Columbia University Press, 1955.

————. *America at 1750*. New York: Vintage Books, 1973.

Hofstadter, Richard, and Walter Metzger. Introduction to *Academic Freedom in the Age of the University*, by Walter Metzger. New York: Columbia University Press, 1955.

Honig, Bill. "Why Privatizing Public Education is a Bad Idea." In *Independent Schools, Independent Thinkers*, edited by Pearl Rock Kane. San Francisco: Jossey-Bass, 1992.

Hook, Sidney. *Education for Modern Man: A New Perspective*. New York: Humanities Press, 1973.

Horton, Robin. "African Thought and Western Science." In *Rationality*, edited by Bryan R. Wilson. Oxford: Basil Blackwell, 1977.

Hudson, Winthrop. *Religion in America*. 3d ed. New York: Charles Scribner's Sons, 1981.

Humanist Manifesto I. In *Humanist Manifestos: I and II*, edited by Paul Kurtz. Buffalo: Prometheus Books, 1973.

Hume, David. *Enquiries Concerning the Human Understanding and Concerning the Principles of Morals*. 1777. Reprint, edited by L. A. Selby-Bigge. Oxford: Clarendon Press, 1962.

————. *A Treatise of Human Nature*. 1738. Reprint, edited by L. A. Selby-Bigge. Oxford: Clarendon Press, 1888.

Hunter, James Davison. *Culture Wars: The Struggle to Define America*. New York: Basic Books, 1991.

————. *Evangelicalism: The Coming Generation*. Chicago: University of Chicago Press, 1987.

————. "Pluralism: Past and Present." *Journal of Law and Religion* 8 (1990): 273–77.

————. "The Williamsburg Charter Survey: Methodology and Findings." *Journal of Law and Religion* 8 (1990): 257–71.

Hutchison, William R. *The Modernist Impulse in American Protestantism*. Oxford: Oxford University Press, 1976.

Huxley, T. H. "Science and Culture." In *Cultures in Conflict: Perspective on the Snow-Leavis Controversy*, edited by David K. Cornelius and Edwin St. Vincent. Chicago: Scott, Foresman, 1964.

Inglehardt, Ronald. *Culture Shift in Advanced Industrial Society*. Princeton: Princeton University Press, 1990.

Jacob, Margaret. *The Cultural Meaning of the Scientific Revolution*. New York: Knopf, 1988.

Jacobs, Louis. "The Relationship between Religion and Ethics in Jewish Thought." In *Religion and Morality*, edited by Gene Outka and John P. Reeder, Jr. Garden City, N.Y.: Anchor Books, 1973.

James, William. *The Varieties of Religious Experience*. 1902. Reprint, New York: Collier Books, 1961.

Jastrow, Robert. *God and the Astronomers*. New York: Warner Books, 1978.

Jefferson, Thomas. Letter to the Danbury Baptists. 1802. Reprinted in *Church and State in American History*, edited by John F. Wilson. Boston: D. C. Heath, 1965.

————. *Notes on Virginia* 1781–82. Excerpts reprinted in *Religion and Constitutional Government in the United States*, edited by John Semonche. Carrboro, N.C.: Signal Books, 1986.

————. "Virginia Statute of Religious Liberty." 1786. Reprinted in *Religion and Constitutional Government in the United States*, edited by John Semonche. Carrboro, N.C.: Signal Books, 1986.

Jencks, Christopher. "Is the Public School Obsolete?" *Public Interest*, Winter 1966, pp. 18–27.

Jencks, Christopher, and Judith Areen. "Education Vouchers: A Proposal for Diversity and Choice." *Teachers College Record* 72 (February 1971): 327–36.

John Paul II. *Centesimus Annus (On the Hundredth Anniversary of Rerum Novarum)*. Vatican translation. Boston: St. Paul Books and Media, 1991.

————. *Veritatis Splendor (The Splendor of Truth)*. Vatican translation. Boston: St. Paul Books and Media, 1993.

Johnson, Paul. *A History of Christianity*. New York: Atheneum, 1976.

Johnson, Phillip E. *Darwin on Trial*. Downer's Grove, Ill.: InterVarsity Press, 1991.

————. "Evolution as Dogma: The Establishment of Naturalism." *First Things*, October 1990, pp. 15–28.

———. "School Vouchers and the United States Constitution." In *The School-Choice Controversy: What Is Constitutional?*, edited by James W. Skillen. Grand Rapids, Mich.: Baker Books, 1993.

Jones v. *Clear Creek Independent School District*, 977 F.2d 963 (5th Cir. 1992).

Joseph Burstyn, Inc. v. *Wilson*, 343 U.S. 495 (1952).

Joughin, Louis, ed. *Academic Freedom and Tenure: A Handbook of the American Association of University Professors*. Madison: University of Wisconsin Press, 1967.

Kant, Immanuel. "What Is Enlightenment?" 1784. Reprinted in *On History*, edited by Lewis White Beck. Indianapolis: Bobbs-Merrill, 1963.

Kaufman, Gordon D. "Critical Theology as a University Discipline." In *Theology and the University: Essays in Honor of John B. Cobb, Jr.*, edited by David Ray Griffin and Joseph C. Hough, Jr. Albany: State University Press of New York, 1991.

Kaufman, Peter. *Redeeming Politics*. Princeton: Princeton University Press, 1990.

Kelly, Mary Olsen, ed. *Treasury of Light: An Anthology of the Best in New Age Literature*. New York: Simon and Schuster, 1990.

Keyishian v. *Board of Regents*, 385 U.S. 589 (1966).

Keynes, John Maynard. *Essays in Persuasion*. Vol. 9 of *The Collected Writings of John Maynard Keynes*. London: Macmillan, 1972.

Kilpatrick, William. *Why Johnny Can't Tell Right from Wrong*. New York: Simon and Schuster, 1992.

Kimball, Bruce. *Orators and Philosophers: A History of the Idea of Liberal Education*. New York: Teachers College Press, 1986.

Kinsley, Michael. "TRB." *New Republic*, September 13, 1993, p. 4.

Kniker, Charles. "A Survey of State Laws and Regulations Regarding Religion and Moral Education." *Religion and Public Education* 16 (Fall 1989): 433–57.

Kolakowski, Leszek. "The Man Who Made Modernity." *New Republic*, May 6, 1991, pp. 40–41.

———. *Religion*. New York: Oxford University Press, 1982.

Kristeller, Paul Oskar. *Renaissance Thought and Its Sources*. New York: Columbia University Press, 1979.

Kristol, Irving. "The Future of American Jewery." In *American Jews and the Separationist Faith*, edited by David G. Dalin. Washington, D.C.: Ethics and Public Policy Center, 1993.

Kuhn, Thomas. "Reflections on My Critics." In *Criticism and the Growth of Knowledge*, edited by Imre Lakatos and Alan Musgrave. Cambridge: Cambridge University Press, 1970.

———. *The Structure of Scientific Revolutions*. Chicago: University of Chicago Press, 1962.

Küng, Hans. "God: The Last Taboo." In *Theology and the University*, edited by David Ray Griffin and Joseph C. Hough, Jr. Albany: State University of New York Press, 1991.

———. *On Being a Christian*. Garden City, N.Y.: Image Books, 1984.

———. *Theology for the Third Millennium*. New York: Anchor Books, 1990.

Kurtz, Paul. *In Defense of Secular Humanism*. Buffalo: Prometheus Books, 1983.

Ladd, George Eldon. *The New Testament and Criticism*. Grand Rapids, Mich.: Eerdmans, 1967.

LaHaye, Tim. *The Battle for the Mind*. Old Tappan, N.J.: Fleming H. Revell, 1980.

Lamb's Chapel v. *Center Moriches Union Free School District*, 53 CCH S.Ct. Bull. p. B2680 (1993).

Lao Tzu. *Tao te Ching*. Translated by D. C. Lau. London: Penguin Books, 1963.

Lasch, Christopher. "Communitarianism or Populism?" *New Oxford Review* 59 (May 1992): 5–12.

————. "A Life of Pain in an Empty Culture." *Raleigh News and Observer*, December 31, 1989, p. 7J.

Laycock, Douglas. "Formal, Substantive, and Disaggregated Neutrality toward Religion." *DePaul Law Review* 39 (1990): 993–1018.

————. "Summary and Synthesis: The Crisis in Religious Liberty." *George Washington Law Review* 60 (March 1992): 841–56.

Lebacqz, Karen. "Protestant Statements on Economic Justice." In *A Cry for Justice*, edited by Robert McAfee Brown and Sydney Thomson Brown. New York: Paulist Press, 1989.

Lee v. *Weisman*, 60 LW 4725 (1992).

Lemon v. *Kurtzman*, 403 U.S. 602 (1971).

Leo XIII. *Aeterni Patris*. Reprinted in *Religion from Tolstoy to Camus*, edited by Walter Kaufmann. New York: Harper Torchbooks, 1964.

Levinson, Sanford. Chap. 18 of *American Jews and the Separationist Faith*, edited by David G. Dalin. Washington, D.C.: Ethics and Public Policy Center, 1993.

Levy, Leonard. *The Establishment Clause: Religion and the First Amendment*. New York: Macmillan, 1986.

Lewis, C. S. *The Abolition of Man*. New York: Macmillan, 1965.

Lewis, James R. "Approaches to the Study of the New Age Movement." In *Perspectives on the New Age*, edited by James R. Lewis and J. Gordon Melton. Albany: State University of New York Press, 1992.

Liberal Learning and the Religion Major. A report of the American Academy of Religion Task Force on the Religion Major, 1990.

Lickona, Thomas. *Educating for Character*. New York: Bantam Books, 1991.

Lieberman, Myron. *Privatization and Educational Choice*. New York: St. Martin's Press, 1989.

Lindberg, Stanley W., ed. *The Annotated McGuffey*. New York: Van Nostrand Reinhold, 1976.

Livingston, James. *Modern Christian Thought: From the Enlightenment to Vatican II*. New York: Macmillan, 1971.

Long, Edward LeRoy, Jr. "The Dynamics of Academic Freedom." *Faculty Forum* 49 (May 1969): 1–5.

————. *A Survey of Christian Ethics*. New York: Oxford University Press, 1967.

Longfield, Bradley J. "From Evangelicalism to Liberalism: Public Midwestern Universities in Nineteenth-Century America." In *The Secularization of the American Academy*, edited by George M. Marsden and Bradley J. Longfield. New York: Oxford University Press, 1992.

Lovin, Robin W. "Confidence and Criticism: Religious Studies and the Public Purposes of Liberal Education." In *Beyond the Classics: Essays in Religious Studies
and Liberal Education*, edited by Frank E. Reynolds and Sheryl L. Burkhalter.
Atlanta: Scholars Press, 1990.

Lucas, Christopher J. *Our Western Educational Heritage.* New York: Macmillan, 1972.

Lucas, Phillip C. "The New Age Movement and the Pentecostal/Charismatic Revival:
Distinct yet Parallel Phases of a Fourth Great Awakening?" In *Perspectives on the
New Age*, edited by James R. Lewis and J. Gordon Melton. Albany: State Univer-
sity of New York Press, 1992.

Luther, Martin. *The Bondage of the Will.* 1525. Reprinted in *Martin Luther: Selections from His writings*, edited by John Dillenberger. Garden City, N.Y.: Anchor
Books, 1961.

———. *A Commentary on St. Paul's Epistle to the Galatians.* 1531. Reprinted in
Martin Luther: Selections from His Writings, edited by John Dillenberger. Garden
City, N.Y.: Anchor Books, 1961.

———. *Secular Authority: To What Extent It Should Be Obeyed.* 1523. Reprinted in
Martin Luther: Selections from His Writings, edited by John Dillenberger.
Garden City, N.Y.: Anchor Books, 1961.

Lyotard, Jean-François. *The Postmodern Condition.* 1984. Excerpts reprinted in
After Philosophy: End or Transformation, edited by Kenneth Baynes, James
Bohman, and Thomas McCarthy. Cambridge, Mass.: MIT Press, 1987.

Machen, J. Gresham. *Christianity and Liberalism.* Grand Rapids, Mich.: Eerdmans,
1985.

MacIntyre, Alisdair. *After Virtue.* Notre Dame: University of Notre Dame Press,
1981.

Maddox, Robert. "Education Choice and the First Amendment: A Separationist Perspective." *Religion and Public Education* 17 (Fall 1990): 322–25.

Madison, James. "A Memorial and Remonstrance on the Religious Rights of Man."
1789. Reprinted in *Religion and Constitutional Government in the United States*,
edited by John Semonche. Carrboro, N.C.: Signal Books, 1986.

Malnak v. Yogi, 592 F.2d 197 (1979).

Mann, Horace. *Twelfth Annual Report of the Secretary of the Board of Education of
Massachusetts, 1848.* Reprinted in *Religion and Constitutional Government in the
United States*, edited by John F. Semonche. Carrboro, N.C.: Signal Books, 1985.

Margenau, Henry, and Roy Abraham Varghese, eds. *Cosmos, Bios, Theos.* La Salle,
Ill.: Open Court, 1992.

Marsden, George. "Evangelicals and the Scientific Culture: An Overview." In *Religion
and Twentieth Century American Intellectual Life*, edited by Michael J. Lacey.
Cambridge: Cambridge University Press, 1989.

———. "Religious Professors Are the Last Taboo." *Wall Street Journal*, December 22, 1993, p. A10.

———. *The Soul of the American University.* New York: Oxford University Press,
1994.

———. "The Soul of the American University: An Historical Overview." In *The Secularization of the Academy*, edited by George M. Marsden and Bradley J. Longfield.
New York: Oxford University Press, 1992.

Martin, Bernard. *A History of Judaism*. Vol. 2. New York: Basic Books, 1974.

Marty, Martin.. "Fundamentalism as a Social Phenomenon." In *Evangelicalism and Modern America*, edited by George Marsden. Grand Rapids, Mich.: Eerdmans, 1984.

———. *The Modern Schism: Three Paths to the Secular*. New York: Harper & Row, 1969.

———. *A Nation of Behavers*. Chicago: University of Chicago Press, 1976.

———. *Pilgrims in Their Own Land*. New York: Penguin Books, 1984.

Marx, Karl, and Friedrich Engels. *Manifesto of the Communist Party*. 1848. Reprinted in *Marx and Engels: Basic Writings on Politics and Philosophy*, edited by Lewis S. Feuer. Garden City, N.Y.: Anchor Books, 1959.

May, Robert. "Creation, Evolution, and High School Biology Texts." In *Science and Creation*, edited by Ashley Montagu. New York: Oxford University Press, 1984.

May, William F. "Why Theology and Religious Studies Need Each Other." *Journal of the American Academy of Religion* 52 (December 1984): 748–57.

McBrien, Richard P. *Catholicism*. Minneapolis: Winston Press, 1981.

McClusky, Howard Y. "The Development of Religious and Moral Values." In *Liberal Learning and Religion*, edited by Amos N. Wilder. Washington, N.Y.: Kennikat Press, 1951.

McCollum v. Board of Education, 333 U.S. 203 (1948).

McConnell, Michael. "Academic Freedom in Religious Colleges and Universities." *Law and Contemporary Problems* 53 (Summer 1990): 303–24.

———. "'God Is Dead and We Have Killed Him!': Freedom of Religion in the Post-Modern Age." *Brigham Young University Law Review*, 1993, pp. 163–88.

———. "The Origins and Historical Understanding of Free Exercise of Religion." *Harvard Law Review* 103 (May 1990): 1410–1517.

———. "Religious Freedom at a Crossroads." In *The Bill of Rights in the Modern State*, edited by Geoffrey R. Stone, Richard A. Epstein, and Cass R. Sunstein. Chicago: University of Chicago Press, 1992.

———. "The Selective Funding Problem: Abortions and Religious Schools." *Harvard Law Review* 104 (1991): 989–1050.

McGowan v. Maryland, 366 U.S. 420 (1961).

McKenzie, Richard B., and Gordon Tullock. *The New World of Economics*. Rev. ed. Homewood, Ill.: Richard D. Irwin, 1978.

McLean v. Arkansas Board of Education, 529 F.Supp. 1255 (E.D. Ark. 1982).

McLeod, Hugh. *Religion and the People of Western Europe, 1789–1970*. Oxford: Oxford University Press, 1981.

McNeill, William. *The Rise of the West*. Chicago: University of Chicago Press, 1963.

"Memorial to the General Assembly of Virginia from Presbytery of Hanover." 1776. Reprinted in *Religion and Constitutional Government in the United States*, edited by John Semonche. Carrboro, N.C.: Signal Books, 1986.

Metzger, Walter P. *Academic Freedom in the Age of the University*. New York: Columbia University Press, 1955.

Michaelsen, Robert. "Constitutions, Courts and the Study of Religion." *Journal of the American Academy of Religion* 45 1977): 291–308.

———. *Piety in the Public School*. London: Macmillan, 1970.

Mill, John Stuart. *On Liberty.* 1859. Reprinted in *Essential Works of John Stuart Mill*, edited by Max Lerner. New York: Bantam Books, 1965.

Minersville School District v. *Gobitis*, 310 U.S. 586 (1940).

Mitchell, Basil. *The Justication of Religious Belief.* New York: Oxford University Press, 1981.

Monod, Jacques. *Chance and Necessity.* New York: Knopf, 1971.

Montaigne. *Essays.* Translated with an Introduction by J. M. Cohen. New York: Penguin Books, 1958.

Mooney, Christopher. *Boundaries Dimly Perceived: Law, Religion, Education, and the Common Good.* Notre Dame: University of Notre Dame Press, 1990.

Moore v. *Gaston County Board of Education*, 357 F. Supp. 1037 (W.D. N.C. 1973).

Mozert v. *Hawkins County Board of Education*, 827 F.2d 1058 (6th Cir., 1987).

Mueller v. *Allen*, 463 U.S. 388 (1983).

Muller, Jerry Z. Chap. 22 of *American Jews and the Separationist Faith*, edited by David G. Dalin. Washington, D.C.: Ethics and Public Policy Center, 1993.

Murray, John Courtney. "Religious Freedom." In *The Documents of Vatican II*, edited by Walter M. Abbott, S.J. Chicago: Follett, 1966.

———. *We Hold These Truths: Catholic Reflections on the American Proposition.* New York: Sheed and Ward, 1960.

National Academy of Sciences. *Science and Creationism: A View from the National Academy of Sciences.* Washington, D.C.: National Academy Press, 1984.

National Catholic Educational Association. *The People's Poll on Schools and School Choice: A New Gallup Survey.* Washington, D.C.: National Catholic Educational Association, 1992.

National Commission on Excellence in Education. *A Nation at Risk.* Reprinted in *The Great School Debate*, edited by Beatrice Gross and Ronald Gross. New York: Simon and Schuster, 1985.

National Conference of Catholic Bishops. *Economic Justice for All: Pastoral Letter on Catholic Social Teaching and the U.S. Economy.* Washington, D.C.: United States Catholic Conference, 1986.

National Council for the Social Studies. *Curriculum Guidelines for Multicultural Education.* Washington, D.C.: National Council for the Social Studies, 1991.

———. Including the Study about Religions in the Social Studies Curriculum: A Position Statement and Guidelines. Reprinted in *Social Education* 54 (September 1990): 310–11.

Neff, David, and George K. Brushaber. "The Remaking of English Evangelicalism." *Christianity Today*, February 5, 1990, pp. 25–36.

Nelkin, Dorothy. *The Creation Controversy: Science or Scripture in the Schools.* Boston: Beacon Press, 1982.

Neuhaus, Richard John. *The Naked Public Square: Religion and Democracy in America.* Grand Rapids, Mich.: Eerdmans, 1984.

———. ed. *Unsecular America.* Grand Rapids, Mich.: Eerdmans, 1986.

Neusner, Jacob. *Death and Birth of Judaism.* New York: Basic Books, 1987.

———. "Theology and Secularism in the Trivialization and Personalization of Religion and the West." *Religion* 18 (1988): 21–35.

Neville, Robert Cummings. "Religious Studies and Theological Studies." *Journal of the American Academy of Religion* 61 (Summer 1993): 185–200.

Newton-Smith, W. H. *The Rationality of Science*. Boston: Routledge & Kegan Paul, 1981.

Niebuhr, H. Richard. *Christ and Culture*. New York: Harper Torchbooks, 1975.

Niebuhr, Reinhold. *An Interpretation of Christian Ethics*. New York: Living Age Books, 1960.

———. *Reinhold Niebuhr on Politics*. Edited by Harry R. Davis and Robert C. Good. New York: Scribner's, 1960.

Noddings, Nel. *Caring: A Feminine Approach to Ethics and Moral Education*. Berkeley: University of California Press, 1984.

Noll, Mark. *Between Faith and Criticism: Evangelicals, Scholarship, and the Bible in America*. San Francisco: Harper and Row, 1986.

Noll, Mark, Nathan Hatch, and George Marsden. *The Search for Christian America*. Westchester, Ill.: Crossway Books, 1983.

Noll, Mark A., and David F. Wells, eds. *Christian Faith and Practice in the Modern World*. Grand Rapids, Mich.: Eerdmans, 1988.

Nord, Warren. "The Humanities and the Modern World." In *Mind, Value, and Culture: Essays in Honor of E. M. Adams*, edited by David Weissbord. Atascadero, Calif.: Ridgeview, 1989.

———. "The Place of Religion in the World of Public School Textbooks." *Educational Forum* 54 (Spring 1990): 247–79.

———. "Religious Literacy, Textbooks, and Religious Neutrality." *Religion and Public Education* 16 (Winter 1989): 111–21.

———. "Teaching and Morality: The Knowledge Most Worth Having." In *What Teachers Need to Know*, edited by David D. Dill. San Francisco: Jossey-Bass, 1990.

Numbers, Ronald. *The Creationists*. New York: Knopf, 1992.

Ogden, Schubert M. "Theology in the University: The Question of Integrity." In *Theology and the University: Essays in Honor of John B. Cobb, Jr.*, edited by David Ray Griffin and Joseph C. Hough, Jr. Albany: State University of New York Press, 1991.

Otto, Rudolf. Introduction to *On Religion*, by Friedrich Schleiermacher. New York: Harper Torchbooks, 1958.

Ozick, Cynthia. Chap. 24 in *American Jews and the Separationist Faith*, edited by David G. Dalin. Washington, D.C.: Ethics and Public Policy Center, 1993.

Ozment, Steven. *The Age of Reform, 1250–1550*. New Haven: Yale University Press, 1980.

Packer, J. I. *"Fundamentalism" and the Word of God*. Grand Rapids, Mich.: Eerdmans, 1982.

Palmer, Parker. *To Know as We Are Known: A Spirituality of Education*. San Francisco: Harper & Row, 1983.

Pannenberg, Wolfhart. *Faith and Reality*. Translated by John Maxwell. Philadelphia: Westminster Press, 1977.

Parsons, Paul. *Inside America's Christian Schools*. Macon, Ga: Mercer University Press, 1987.

Pascal, Blaise. *Pensées*. Translted by A. J. Krailsheimer. New York: Penguin Books, 1966.

Pasley, Jeffrey. "Not-So-Good Books." *New Republic*, April 27, 1987, pp. 20–22.

Patterson, James, and Peter Kim. *The Day America Told the Truth: What People Really Believe about Everything That Matters*. New York: Prentice-Hall, 1991.

Peacocke, Arthur. *Intimations of Reality: Critical Realism in Science and Religion*. Notre Dame: University of Notre Dame Press, 1984.

Pelikan, Jaroslav. "Fundamentalism and/or Orthodoxy? Toward an Understanding of the Fundamentalist Phenomenon." In *The Fundamentalist Phenomenon*, edited by Norman J. Cohen. Grand Rapids, Mich.: Eerdmans, 1990.

———. *The Riddle of Roman Catholicism*. New York: Abingdon Press, 1959.

Peloza v. Capistrano Unified School District, 37 F.3rd 517, 522 (9th Cir., 1994).

Penn, William. *The Great Case of Liberty of Conscience*. 1670. Excerpts reprinted in *The Witness of William Penn*, edited with an Introduction by Frederick B. Tolles and E. Gordon Alderfer. New York: Macmillan, 1957.

People for the American Way. *Looking at History: A Review of Major U.S. History Textbooks*. Washington, D.C.: People for the American Way, 1986.

Perry, Ralph Barton. *Puritanism and Democracy*. New York: Vanguard Press, 1944.

Peters, R. S. *Ethics and Education*. London: George Allen & Unwin, 1970.

Peters, Ted. *The Cosmic Self*. San Francisco: Harper Collins, 1991.

Piediscalzi, Nicholas. "Back to the Future?: Public Education Religion Studies and the AAR in the 1970s and 1990s—Unique Opportunities for Development." *Religion and Public Education* 18 (1991): 237–51.

Pierce v. Society of the Sisters of the Holy Names of Jesus and Mary, 268 U.S. 510 (1925).

Pius IX. *The Syllabus of Errors*. Reprinted in *Religion from Tolstoy to Camus*, edited by Walter Kaufmann. New York: Harper Torchbooks, 1964.

Plantinga, Alvin. "When Faith and Reason Clash: Evolution and the Bible." *Christian Scholar's Review* 21 (September 1991): 8–32.

Podesta, Tony. "The Uphill Battle for Quality Textbooks." *Religion and Public Education* 13 (Summer 1986): 60–62.

Polanyi, Karl. *The Great Transformation*. Boston: Beacon Press, 1957.

Polanyi, Michael. *Science, Faith and Society*. Chicago: University of Chicago Press, 1946.

Polkinghorne, John. *One World: The Interaction of Science and Theology*. Princeton: Princeton University Press, 1986.

Poole, Ross. *Morality and Modernity*. London: Routledge, 1991.

Popper, Karl. *Objective Knowledge*. Oxford: Clarendon Press, 1979.

Postman, Neil. *Conscientious Objections: Stirring up Trouble about Language, Technology, and Education*. New York: Vintage, 1992.

Purpel, David. *The Moral and Spiritual Crisis in Education*. Granby, Mass: Bergin & Garvey, 1989.

Putnam, Hillary. "Two Conceptions of Rationality." In *Reason, Truth and History*. New York: Cambridge University Press, 1981.

Quade, Quentin. "The Educational Vise." *First Things*, October 1990, pp. 10–11.

Rabban, David. "A Functional Analysis of 'Individual' and 'Institutional' Academic Freedom under the First Amendment." *Law and Contemporary Problems* 53 (Summer 1990): 229–301.

Raths, Louis E., Merrill Harmin, and Sidney B. Simon. *Values and Teaching.* 2d ed. Columbus: Charles E. Merrill, 1978.

Rauch, Eduardo. "The Jewish Day School in America." In *Religious Schooling in America,* edited by James C. Carper and Thomas C. Hunt. Birmingham, Ala.: Religious Education Press, 1984.

Rauschenbusch, Walter. *A Theology for the Social Gospel.* Excerpts reprinted in *Christian Ethics,* 2d ed., edited by Waldo Beach and H. Richard Niebuhr. New York: Wiley, 1973.

Ravitch, Diane. "Multiculturalism: E Pluribus Plures." *American Scholar,* Summer 1990, pp. 337–54.

———. *The Troubled Crusade.* New York: Basic Books, 1983.

Rawls, John. *Political Liberalism.* New York: Columbia University Press, 1993.

Redfield, Robert. *The Primitive World and Its Transformations.* Ithaca: Cornell University Press, 1953.

Reichley, A. James. *Religion in American Public Life.* Washington, D.C.: Brookings Institution, 1985.

Religion in the Public School Curriculum: Questions and Answers. Reprinted in *Social Education* 54 (September 1990): 308.

Reynolds v. *United States,* 98 U.S. 145 (1879).

Robinson, John A. T. *Honest to God.* Philadelphia: Westminster Press, 1963.

Rogers, Carl. *Freedom to Learn.* Columbus, Ohio: Charles E. Merrill, 1969.

Roof, Wade Clark, and William McKinney. *American Mainline Religion.* New Brunswick: Rutgers University Press, 1987.

Rorty, Richard. "Pragmatism and Philosophy." Reprinted in *After Philosophy: End or Transformation,* edited by Kenneth Baynes, James Bohman, and Thomas McCarthy. Cambridge, Mass.: MIT Press, 1987.

———. "Two Cheers for the Cultural Left." In *The Politics of Liberal Education,* edited by Darryl J. Gless and Barbara Herrnstein Smith. Durham: Duke University Press, 1992.

Ross, Dorothy. *The Origins of American Social Science.* New York: Cambridge University Press, 1991.

Rousseau, Jean-Jacques. *A Discourse on the Arts and Sciences.* 1750. Reprinted in *The Social Contract and Discourses,* translated by G. D. H. Cole. New York: E. P. Dutton, 1950.

Rubenstein, Richard. *After Auschwitz: Radical Theology and Contemporary Judaism.* Indianapolis: Bobbs-Merrill, 1966.

———. Chap. 30 of *American Jews and the Separationist Faith,* edited by David S. Dalin. Washington D.C.: Ethics and Public Policy Center, 1993.

———. "Church and State: The Jewish Posture." In *Church and State in American History,* edited by John F. Wilson. Boston: D. C. Heath, 1965.

Rudolph, Frederick. *Curriculum: A History of the American Undergraduate Course of Study since 1636.* San Francisco: Jossey-Bass, 1977.

Ruether, Rosemary Radford. *Disputed Questions: On Being a Christian*. Maryknoll,
    N.Y.: Orbis Books, 1989.
————. *Sexism and God-Talk: Toward a Feminist Theology*. Boston: Beacon Press,
    1983.
Russell, Bertrand. "What I Believe." Reprinted in *Bertrand Russell: Why I Am Not a
    Christian*. New York: Simon and Schuster, 1957.
Ryan, Kevin, and Edward Wynne. "Curriculum as a Moral Educator." *American
    Educator*, Spring 1993, pp. 20–24, 43–48.
Sagan, Carl. *Broca's Brain: Reflections on the Romance of Science*. New York: Ran-
    dom House, 1974.
Savage, David G. "The Rehnquist Court." *Raleigh News and Observer*, September 29,
    1992, p. 8J.
Schaeffer, Francis. *A Christian Manifesto*. Rev. ed. Westchester Ill.: Crossway Books,
    1982.
————. *Escape from Reason*. Downer's Grove, Ill.: Inter-Varsity Press, 1968.
Schleiermacher, Friedrich. *On Religion: Speeches to Its Cultured Despisers*. Trans-
    lated by John Oman. New York: Harper & Row, 1958.
Schlesinger, Arthur M., Jr. *The Disuniting of America*. New York: Norton, 1992.
Schmitt, Richard. "Academic Freedom: The Future of a Confusion." In *The Concept
    of Academic Freedom*, edited by Edmund L. Pincoffs. Austin: University of Texas
    Press, 1972.
Schumacher, E. F. *A Guide for the Perplexed*. New York: Harper Colophon, 1978.
————. *Small Is Beautiful: Economics as If People Mattered*. New York: Harper &
    Row, 1975.
Schumpeter, Joseph. *Capitalism, Socialism and Democracy*. 3d ed. New York:
    Harper Torchbooks, 1972.
Sealy, John. *Religious Education: Philosophical Perspectives*. London: George Allen
    & Unwin, 1985.
Searle, John. "The Philosophy of Language." In *Men of Ideas*, edited by Bryan Magee.
    New York: Oxford University Press, 1982.
Secular Humanist Declaration. Reprinted in *Free Inquiry* 1 (Winter 1980–81): 3–7.
Semonche, John. *Religion and Constitutional Government in the United States*.
    Carrboro, N.C.: Signal Books, 1985.
Sewall, Gilbert. "California: The Story Continues." *Social Studies Review*, Fall 1990,
    pp. 10–12.
Shanker, Albert, and Bella Rosenberg. "Politics, Markets, and American Schools: A
    Rejoinder." In *Independent Schools, Independent Thinkers*, edited by Pearl Rock
    Kane. San Francisco: Jossey-Bass, 1992.
Sheldon v. Tucker, 364 U.S. 479 (1960).
Shelley, Percy Bysshe. "A Defense of Poetry." 1821. Excerpts reprinted in *The Norton
    Anthology of English Literature*, vol. 2, 3d ed., edited by M. H. Abrams, George H.
    Ford, and David Daiches. New York: Norton, 1974.
Sherbert v. Verner, 374 U.S. 398 (1963).
Shils, Edward. *Tradition*. Chicago: University of Chicago Press, 1981.
Shinn, Roger L. *Man: The New Humanism*. Philadelphia: Westminster Press, 1968.

Sizer, Theodore. *Horace's Compromise: The Dilemma of the American High School*.
    Boston: Houghton Mifflin, 1985.

Skinner, B. F. *Beyond Freedom and Dignity*. New York: Bantam/Vintage Books, 1972.

Skinner, Quentin. *The Foundations of Modern Political Thought*. Vol. 2. Cambridge:
    Cambridge University Press, 1978.

Smart, Ninian. *Religion and the Western Mind*. New York: Macmillan, 1987.

————. *The Religious Experience of Mankind*. 2d ed. New York: Charles Scribner's
    Sons, 1976.

————. "Teaching Religion and Religions: The 'World Religions' Course." In *Teaching
    the Introductory Course in Religious Studies: A Source Book*, edited by Mark Juer-
    gensmeyer. Atlanta: Scholars Press, 1991.

Smith, Huston. *Beyond the Postmodern Mind*. New York: Crossroad, 1982.

Smith, Page. *Killing the Spirit: Higher Education in America*. New York: Viking,
    1990.

Smith, Timothy L. "High School History Texts Adopted for Use in the State of
    Alabama: The Distortion and Exclusion of Religious Data." *Religion and Public
    Education* 15 (Spring 1988): 170–90.

Smith v. Board of School Commissioners of Mobile County, 655 F.Supp. 939, (S.D.
    Ala., 1987).

Smith v. Board of School Commissioners of Mobile County, 827 F.2d 684 (11th Cir.,
    1987).

Smith, Wilfred Cantwell. *The Meaning and End of Religion*. New York: Mentor
    Books, 1964.

Snow, C. P. "The Two Cultures and the Scientific Revolution." Reprinted in *C. P.
    Snow: Public Affairs*. New York: Charles Scribner's Sons, 1971.

Spring, Joel. *The American School, 1642–1985*. New York: Longman, 1986.

Spykman, Gordon, et al. *Society, State, and Schools*. Grand Rapids, Mich.: Eerdmans,
    1981.

Stace, W. T. "Man Against Darkness." Reprinted in *The Meaning of Life*, ed. Steven
    Sanders and David R. Cheney. Englewood Cliffs, N.J.: Prentice-Hall, 1980.

————. *Religion and the Modern Mind*. Philadelphia: J. B. Lippincott, 1960.

Stackhouse, Max. *Public Theology and Political Economy*. Grand Rapids, Mich.:
    Eerdmans, 1987.

Starhawk. *Dreaming the Dark: Magic, Sex, and Politics*. Boston: Beacon Press, 1988.

Steiner, George. *Language and Silence*. New York: Atheneum, 1982.

Stern, Marc. Chap. 33 of *American Jews and the Separationist Faith*, edited by David
    G. Dalin. Washington, D.C.: Ethics and Public Policy Center, 1993.

Stone, Lynda. "Modern to Postmodern: Social Construction, Dissonance, and Educa-
    tion." *Studies in Philosophy and Education* 13 (1994): 49–63.

Stone v. Graham, 449 U.S. 39 (1980).

Story, Joseph. *Commentaries on the Constitution of the United States*. Vol 3.
    Excerpts reprinted in *Church and State in American History*, edited by John F.
    Wilson. Boston: D. C. Heath, 1965.

Stout, Jeffrey. *Ethics after Babel: The Languages of Morals and Their Discontents*.
    Boston: Beacon Press, 1988.

Strike, Kenneth. "Are Secular Ethical Languages Religiously Neutral?" *Journal of Law and Politics* 6 (Spring 1990): 469–502.

———. *Liberty and Learning.* Oxford: Martin Robertson & Company, 1982.

———. "Review of Five Home Economics Texts." Unpublished manuscript prepared as a deposition in *Smith* v. *Board of School Commissioners of Mobile County,* 655 F. Supp. 939 (S.D. Ala., 1987).

Sussman, Lance. Chap. 34 in *American Jews and the Separationist Faith,* edited by David G. Dalin. Washington, D.C.: Ethics and Public Policy Center, 1993.

Sweet, Leonard. "The 1960s: The Crises of Liberal Christianity and the Public Emergence of Evangelicalism." In *Evangelicalism and Modern America,* edited by George Marsden. Grand Rapids, Mich.: Eerdmans, 1984.

Sweezy v. *New Hampshire,* 354 U.S. 234 (1957).

Swift, Jonathan. *Gulliver's Travels.* 1726. Reprint, New York: New American Library, 1960.

Tarnas, Richard. *The Passion of the Western Mind.* New York: Harmony Books, 1991.

Tawny, R. H. *Religion and the Rise of Capitalism.* New York: Mentor Books, 1922.

Taylor, Charles. "The Politics of Recognition." In *Multiculturalism and The Politics of Recognition,* edited by Amy Gutmann. Princeton: Princeton University Press, 1992.

———. *The Sources of the Self: The Making of the Modern Identity.* Cambridge, Mass.: Harvard University Press, 1989.

Thiessen, Elmer John. *Teaching for Commitment: Liberal Education, Indoctrination, and Christian Nurture.* Montreal: McGill-Queen's University Press, 1993.

Thomas, Keith. *Religion and the Decline of Magic.* New York: Charles Scribner's Sons, 1971.

Tillich, Paul. *Dynamics of Faith.* New York: Harper Torchbooks, 1957.

———. *Systematic Theology.* Vol. 1. Chicago: University of Chicago Press, 1951.

Tinker v. *Des Moines Independent Community School District,* 393 U.S. 511 (1969).

Tocqueville, Alexis de. *Democracy in America.* 2 vols. 1835, 1840. Reprint, edited by Phillips Bradley, New York: Vintage Books, 1958.

Tolstoy, Leo. *War and Peace.* Translated by Constance Garnett. New York: Modern Library, n.d.

Torcaso v. *Watkins,* 367 U.S. 488 (1961).

Toulmin, Stephen. *Cosmopolis: The Hidden Agenda of Modernity.* New York: Free Press, 1990.

———. *Human Understanding: The Collective Use and Evolution of Concepts.* Princeton: Princeton University Press, 1971.

Toumey, Christopher P. *God's Own Scientists: Creationists in a Secular World.* New Brunswick, N.J.: Rutgers University Press, 1994.

Turner, James. *Without God, Without Creed.* Baltimore: Johns Hopkins University Press, 1985.

Tyack, David, and Elizabeth Hansot. *Managers of Virtue: Public School Leadership in America.* New York: Basic Books, 1982.

Tyack, David, Thomas James, and Aaron Benavot. *Law and the Shaping of Public Education, 1785–1954.* Madison: University of Wisconsin Press, 1987.

Ullmann, Walter. *Medieval Political Thought.* Baltimore: Penguin Books, 1970.

United States v. *Macintosh*, 283 U.S. 605 (1931).

United States v. *Seeger*, 380 U.S. 163 (1965).

Unterman, Alan. *Jews: Their Religious Beliefs and Practices.* London: Routledge, 1981.

Updike, John. *Roger's Version.* New York: Fawcett Crest, 1986.

Van Alstyne, William. "Academic Freedom and the First Amendment in the Supreme Court of the United States: An Unhurried Historical Review." *Law and Contemporary Problems* 53 (Summer 1990): 79–154.

Van Geel, Tyll. *The Courts and American Education Law.* Buffalo: Prometheus Books, 1987.

Vaughn v. *Reed*, 313 F. Supp. 431 (W.D. Vir., 1970).

Veysey, Laurence. *The Emergence of the American University.* Chicago: University of Chicago Press, 1970.

Vitz, Paul C. *Censorship: Evidence of Bias in Our Children's Textbooks.* Ann Arbor: Servant Books, 1986.

Wacker, Grant. "Uneasy in Zion: Evangelicals in Postmodern Society." In *Evangelicalism and Modern America*, edited by George Marsden. Grand Rapids, Mich.: Eerdmans, 1984.

Wallace v. *Jaffre*, 472 U.S. 38 (1985).

Walz v. *Tax Commission of the City of New York*, 397 U.S. 664 (1970).

Walzer, Michael. *Spheres of Justice.* New York: Basic Books, 1983.

Warnock, Mary. "The Neutral Teacher." In *Progress and Problems in Moral Education*, edited by Monica Taylor. Windsor, Eng.: NFER Publishing Company, 1975.

Weber, Max. *Economy and Society.* 2 vols. Berkeley: University of California Press, 1978.

———. *The Protestant Ethic and the Spirit of Capitalism.* 1904–5. Reprint, New York: Charles Scribner's Sons, 1958.

Wertheimer, Jack. *A People Divided: Judaism in Contemporary America.* New York: Basic Books, 1993.

Westerhoff, John. *McGuffey and His Readers.* Nashville: Abingdon, 1978.

West Virginia State Board of Education v. *Barnette*, 319 U.S. 624 (1943).

Whitemarsh, Darylann, and Bill Reisman. *Subtle Serpent: New Age in the Classroom.* Lafayette, La.: Huntington House, 1993.

Whitman, Walt. "Song of the Open Road." In *New Pocket Anthology of American Verse from Colonial Days to the Present*, edited by Oscar Williams. New York: Washington Square Press, 1955.

Wiesel, Elie. "The Holocaust as Literary Inspiration." In *Dimensions of the Holocaust*, annotated by Elliot Lefkovitz. Evanston, Ill.: Northwestern University Press, 1977.

Wieseltier, Leon. "The Jewish Face of Fundamentalism." In *The Fundamentalist Phenomenon: A View from Within; A Response from Without*, edited by Norman J. Cohen. Grand Rapids, Mich.: Eerdmans, 1990.

Wiggins, James. "The Study of Religion in Higher Education: An Overview." *Religion and Public Education* 18 (1991): 201–11.

Wiley v. *Franklin*, 468 F. Supp. 133, (E.D. Tenn., 1979).

Williams, Polly. "Inner City Kids: Why Choice Is Their Only Hope." *Imprimis* 21 (March 1992): 1–5.

The Williamsburg Charter: Reprinted in *The Journal of Law and Religion* 8 (1990): 5–22.

The Williamsburg Charter: Summary of Principles. Reprinted in *Social Education* 54 (September 1990): 280.

Wills, Garry. *Under God: Religion and American Politics.* New York: Simon and Schuster, 1990.

Wilson, Bryan R. Introduction to *Rationality,* edited by Bryan R. Wilson. Oxford: Basil Blackwell, 1977.

Wilson, John, and Samuel Natale. *Education in Religious Understanding: A Report from the Foundation for Education in Religion and Morality.* Lanham, Md.: University Press of America, 1987.

Winkler, Karen J. "After Years in Academic Limbo, the Study of Religion Undergoes a Revival of Interest among Scholars." *Chronicle of Higher Education,* February 3, 1988, pp. A4–A7.

Winthrop, John. "A Model of Christian Charity." 1630. Reprinted in *Puritan Political Ideas,* edited by Edmund S. Morgan. Indianapolis: Bobbs-Merrill, 1965.

Wisconsin v. *Yoder,* 406 U.S. 205 (1972).

Witters v. *Washington Department of Services for the Blind,* 474 U.S. 481 (1986).

Wittgenstein, Ludwig. *Philosophical Investigations.* 2d ed. New York: Macmillan, 1958.

Wolfson, Nicholas. Chap. 37 of *American Jews and the Separationist Faith,* edited by David G. Dalin. Washington, D.C.: Ethics and Public Policy Center, 1993.

Wood, Floris W., ed. *An American Profile—Opinions and Behavior, 1972–1989.* Detroit: Gale Research, Inc., 1990.

Wordsworth, William. "Lines Composed a Few Miles above Tintern Abbey, on Revisiting the Banks of the Wye During a Tour." In *The Poetical Works of Wordsworth,* edited by Thomas Hutchinson; revised edition edited by Ernest De Selincourt. New York: Oxford University Press, 1950.

Wright v. *Houston Independent School District,* 366 F.Supp. 1208 (S.D. Tex. 1972).

Wurzburger, Walter. Chap. 38 of *American Jews and the Separationist Faith,* edited by David G. Dalin. Washington, D.C.: Ethics and Public Policy Center, 1993.

Wuthnow, Robert. *Christianity in the 21st Century: Reflections on the Challenges Ahead.* New York: Oxford University Press, 1993.

———. *The Restructuring of American Religion.* Princeton: Princeton University Press, 1988.

———. "Science and the Sacred." In *The Sacred in a Secular Age,* edited by Phillip E. Hammond. Berkeley: University of California Press, 1985.

Yinger, J. Milton. *The Scientific Study of Religion.* New York: Macmillan, 1970.

Zorach v. *Clauson,* 343 U.S. 306 (1952).

Zykan v. *Warsaw Community School Corporation,* 631 F.2d 1300 (7th Cir. 1980).

INDEX

Abington Township School District v. *Schempp* (1963), 367; and government neutrality, 116–17, 242; and teaching about religion, 117, 242, 247, 258, 305; and Lemon Test, 117, 411 (n. 1); and "religion of secularism," 178, 245

Abortion, 240, 343, 367

Academic freedom: of university professors, 262–77, 280, 292, 315; history of, 262–64; of students, 263, 274, 295; as discussed in AAUP *Principles*, 264–65, 274–75, 276, 277; professional competence and, 265–69, 280; constitutional law and, 269–77, 294–95; of university administration, 270–71, 272, 274, 313–14; of public school teachers, 271, 277–80; and indoctrination of students, 274–76, 295; and teaching of creationism, 279, 294–95

Accommodationism, judicial: defined, 125–27; arguments against, 127–29

Ackerman, Bruce, 358

Adams, E. Maynard, xiii, 30, 184, 202, 285, 380–81, 391 (n. 32); *Religion and Cultural Freedom*, 224

Adams, Herbert, 156

Adams, John, 68, 101, 124–25

Adler, Mortimer, 87, 89, 418 (n. 22)

Afrocentric curriculum, 227, 366

Afterlife, 12, 52, 58

Aguilar v. *Felton* (1985), 118

Ahlstrom, Sydney, 73, 99, 104–5, 192

Alabama: minute of silence law, 118; "religion of secular humanism" case, 169–70

Albanese, Catherine L., 193

Alexander II (tzar of Russia), 345

American Academy of Religion (AAR),

305, 306, 311, 316; *Liberal Learning and the Religion Major*, 307–8

American Association for the Advancement of Science, 415 (n. 63)

American Association of School Administrators, 233, 258

American Association of University Professors (AAUP), 268, 270; *Declaration of Principles*, 264–65, 274–75, 276, 277

American Center for Law and Justice, 260

American Civil Liberties Union (ACLU), 260, 364

American colonies: education in, 63, 64–66; religious liberty in, 99, 104, 106, 108–9; religious intolerance in, 99–101, 105; religious diversity in, 100–101, 103–4, 125; and separation of church and state, 102–3

American Council on Education, 95

American Federation of Teachers (AFT), 233

American Humanist Association, 173

"Americanism," 63, 75, 76, 96

American Jewish Congress, 233

Amish, 112, 358, 405 (n. 45)

Analects, 199–200

Angell, William B., 84

Anglican church, 20, 100, 101

Anglican Society for the Propagation of the Gospel, 101

Annotated McGuffey, 67

"Anthropic" principle, 153, 303

Anti-Catholicism, 70, 73–74, 96, 100, 355

Anti-intellectualism, 50, 52, 76–77, 347

Anti-Semitism, 205

Apple, Michael, 93

Arblaster, Anthony, 36, 328

Aristotle, 21, 169

Index 461

Blake, William, 191–92
Blau, Joseph L., 56
Bloom, Allan, 87–89, 188; *Closing of the American Mind*, 88–89
Board of Education, Island Trees Union Free School District v. *Pico* (1982), 277, 278, 423 (n. 45)
Board of Education of the Westside Community Schools v. *Mergens* (1990), 120, 296, 406 (n. 70)
Bok, Derek, 265–66
Boston English High School, 76
Boyer, Ernest, 94, 95
Boyle, Robert, 18
Brahmanas, 17
Brennan, William J., Jr., 367; and establishment of religion, 117, 128, 352; and creation-science laws, 118, 294, 295; and religious neutrality, 130, 242; and teaching about religion, 242, 243, 246, 247; and school prayer, 259; and academic freedom, 270, 294, 295; and local control of schools, 277, 278, 423 (n. 45)
Brewer, David Josiah, 123–24
Buber, Martin, 217, 316
Buddhism, 176, 178, 206, 216, 322
Buehrer, Eric, 197
Bullock, Alan, 172
Bultmann, Rudolf, 45, 316
Burger, Warren E., 132; and free exercise rights, 112, 405 (n. 45), 430–31 (n. 11); and establishment of religion, 117; and religious neutrality, 120, 131, 243, 371, 407 (n. 105)
Burtchaell, James Tunstead, 86, 307
Burtt, E. A., 26, 322–23
Bush, George, 135, 353, 364
Buzzard, Lynn, 261

California: school textbooks, 156, 334, 428–29 (n. 43); and religious studies, 316–17; voucher referendum, 353, 357
Calvin, John, 69, 145, 183, 325
Calvinism, 20, 33, 100, 145
"Campus schools," 256
Canon of "Great Books," 87–88, 93, 335

Cantwell v. *Connecticut* (1940), 110
Capitalism: Protestant Reformation and, 31, 145; and secularization, 31–35, 297, 327; religious conservatives and, 145, 282, 302–3; Catholic bishops and, 300–301; John Paul II and, 425 (n. 43)
Capps, Walter, 306, 310–11
Carnegie Foundation, 231, 353
Carnegie Pension Fund, 85
Carter, Jimmy, 132
Carter, Stephen L.: *Culture of Disbelief*, 136
Cassirer, Ernst, 12, 345–46
Castelli, Jim, 2
Catechism of the Catholic Church, 183, 287, 324, 397 (n. 156)
Catholic humanism, 172
Catholicism. *See* Roman Catholicism
Center for the Study of Public Policy, 368
Chadwick, Owen, 21, 41
"Character education," 337–38, 339–40, 346, 350
"Chicago Statement on Biblical Inerrancy," 50
Children: rights of, and school choice, 354–55, 357–58, 359, 373–74. *See also* Students
Christian humanism, 172
Christianity: United States as Christian nation, xi, 8, 122–25, 136; of American population, 9, 206, 254; Protestant Reformation and, 17, 20, 21–22; religious wars within, 20; and Greek philosophy, 180–81; religious diversity in, 22, 23, 100–101, 103–4; and science, 26, 28, 86, 283; and politics, 35; and nationalism, 38–39, 394 (n. 86); role in American history, 99–100, 123, 225; Founding Fathers and, 107, 122–23, 124, 126–27; and separation of church and state, 134, 135–36; humanism and, 168, 169; New Age religion and, 194; and morality, 322–27. *See also* Conservatism, religious; Liberalism, religious; Protestantism; Roman Catholicism

H. Eugene and Lillian Youngs Lehman Series

Lamar Cecil, *Wilhelm II: Prince and Emperor, 1859–1900* (1989).

Carolyn Merchant, *Ecological Revolutions: Nature, Gender, and Science in New England* (1989).

Gladys Engel Lang and Kurt Lang, *Etched in Memory: The Building and Survival of Artistic Reputation* (1990).

Howard Jones, *Union in Peril: The Crisis over British Intervention in the Civil War* (1992).

Robert L. Dorman, *Revolt of the Provinces: The Regionalist Movement in America* (1993).

Peter N. Stearns, *Meaning Over Memory: Recasting the Teaching of Culture and History* (1993).

Thomas Wolfe, *The Good Child's River*, edited with an introduction by Suzanne Stutman (1994).

Warren A. Nord, *Religion and American Education: Rethinking a National Dilemma* (1995).